P9-APQ-305

# Chapters in Western Civilization

VOLUME I

# Chapters in Western Civilization

EDITED BY THE

CONTEMPORARY CIVILIZATION STAFF OF

COLUMBIA COLLEGE, COLUMBIA UNIVERSITY

VOLUME I · THIRD EDITION · 1961

NEW YORK AND LONDON

Columbia University Press

THIRD EDITION 1961

*First printing 1961*
*Second printing 1963*

LIBRARY OF CONGRESS CATALOG CARD NUMBER: 61-13862

MANUFACTURED IN THE UNITED STATES OF AMERICA

THIS VOLUME IS DEDICATED TO

JUSTUS BUCHLER AND GEORGE T. MATTHEWS

FOR THEIR YEARS OF DEVOTED SERVICE TO

GENERAL EDUCATION AND COLUMBIA COLLEGE

# PREFACE

For many years Columbia College has sought suitable background readings to be used with the documents in its source books, *Introduction to Contemporary Civilization in the West.* Only recently has it been possible to commission a group of leading scholars in America and Europe to write these special essays for use in our Contemporary Civilization course.

These essays make this edition of *Chapters in Western Civilization* almost entirely a new work, for only one chapter from earlier editions and small parts of two other chapters have been retained. Although *Chapters in Western Civilization* is used at Columbia as a supplement to source documents, it is self-sufficient and can also be used as a basic text in European history and Western Civilization courses.

In acknowledging those who have helped make this volume possible, first recognition must be given to the two generations of scholars at Columbia who have worked enthusiastically and successfully in the Contemporary Civilization courses. The names of previous editorial committees are particularly important, and they are given below. The present editorial committee also wishes to acknowledge the gracious cooperation of the contributors to this new volume.

In addition we have had encouragement and helpful interest from John G. Palfrey, Dean of Columbia College. Daniel Bell, Peter Gay, David Hicks, Steven Marcus, Sidney Morgenbesser, and Robert Webb helped the editorial committee in determining the contents of the volume or in criticizing individual manuscripts.

Professor John H. Mundy wishes to thank the Columbia University Council for Research in the Social Sciences and the American Council of Learned Societies for their aid while writing his essay. Professor Paul O. Kristeller thanks Michael Held and Professors Edward Rosen, Josef Soudek, and Charles Trinkaus for their suggestions about his essay. We are indebted to Craig B. Brush for his translations of the chapters by Henri Marrou and Fernand Braudel.

Daisy Grandison, Phyllis Holbrook, and Jane Slater cheerfully shared the burdens of typing.

A number of Columbia College and Columbia University students assisted the Committee at various stages in preparing the volume, and much is owed them for their patience and accuracy.

EDITORIAL COMMITTEE
Joseph Rothschild
David Sidorsky
Bernard Wishy, *Chairman*

*February 1961*

EDITORIAL COMMITTEE FOR THE FIRST EDITION, 1948
JOSEPH L. BLAU
JUSTUS BUCHLER, *Chairman*
GEORGE T. MATTHEWS

EDITORIAL COMMITTEE FOR THE SECOND EDITION, 1954
JOSEPH L. BLAU
RALPH H. BOWEN
PETER J. GAY
SIDNEY GELBER
GEORGE T. MATTHEWS
RICHARD M. MORSE, *Chairman*
STEPHEN W. ROUSSEAS

# CONTENTS

# Chapters in Western Civilization

VOLUME I

# I

# THE HERITAGE OF THE ANCIENT WORLD

*Henri Marrou*

At the end of the seventeenth century the French civilization that had been developing since the Renaissance became aware of its originality and worth. To be specific, on January 27, 1687, the Académie Française met to hear the folklorist Charles Perrault read "The Age of Louis the Great," a poem that he had composed to glorify the accomplishments of the French culture of his day. The thesis which he undertook to defend, and which he was to develop later in the four volumes of his *Parallel Between the Ancients and the Moderns* (1688–97), encountered very strong opposition from the great authors of French classicism. Racine, Boileau, and La Fontaine, whom he had covered with praise, would not accept being ranked above their Greek and Roman masters, whose unequaled superiority they proclaimed. Out of this incident grew the famous Battle of the Books, which soon spread from France to England and all educated Europe.

Nearly three centuries have passed since then, and the debate remains unresolved in the Western *psyché*. We still argue with each other and within ourselves about the position that classical antiquity is to occupy in our modern civilization and particularly in our educational system. Perhaps the best way to evaluate this heritage of the ancient world to Western contemporary civilization is to present a dialogue between the Classical Scholar, aware of the permanent values of this heritage, and the Modern Man, the twentieth-century man who knows how to live (and insists on living) in the present age, whose tasks and responsibilities he shoulders.

## I

The Classical Scholar speaks first and has no difficulty demonstrating the basic, most significant fact—that the Greeks and Romans of antiquity are the direct ancestors of modern man. It has been said that when we consider the entirety of the *Weltgeschichte,* the universal history of mankind, our modern Western civilization appears to be nothing more than the latest development in the evolution of classical Hellenic civilization. Although we may emphasize the shifting rhythm of periods of decline and rebirth in this evolution, it is nonetheless a continuous evolution.

No matter how original the culture of medieval Christianity may appear in contrast to antiquity, and no matter how original the modern period may seem when compared with the Middle Ages, they are the successive stages of a single homogeneous growth. Between these different periods there is no hiatus, no serious break, nor is there any radical opposition in their contents or inspiration. From the Homeric poems down to present-day poets we have one continuous tradition. However, between the Egypt of the time of the Pharaohs and Coptic-Christian Egypt and today's Moslem Arab Egypt there is no visible relation—or at least if there is any continuity, it remains indirect and partial. To grasp the contrasting continuity in Western civilization in another way, one need only withdraw a bit and observe the West from the standpoint of India and China; there we find an entirely different cultural milieu, another humanism defined by native traditions whose deep roots go back to the Rig-Veda and the Upanishads or to the classics of Confucius and Lao-tze. Our Western tree has its roots elsewhere, on the shores of the ancient Mediterranean.

Although the effects of the barbarization of various regions of the ancient Roman Empire resulting from the Germanic invasions of the fifth and sixth centuries A.D., at the beginning of the Middle Ages, may have been disastrous, they did not succeed in breaking the cultural tradition as completely as the Dorian invasion at the end of the second millenium B.C. had ruined Minoan and Mycenaean civilization in the Aegean world. We must not forget that the period of relative barbarism which characterizes the "Dark Ages" did not make its weight felt uniformly or at the same time in all the lands formerly controlled by Rome. It is also common knowledge that in eastern Europe the passage from classical antiquity to the Byzantine Middle Ages took place without any major revolution. Therefore, when Gibbon decided to write *The Decline and Fall of the Roman Empire,* he was forced to extend his history to 1453 and the fall of Constantinople, the eastern Roman capitol, to the Turks. However, we may confine ourselves to the West itself. There, ancient Roman civilization still survived in southern Gaul in the fifth century and the first half of the sixth while northern Gaul was being profoundly shaken by the Frankish conquest. And so, at the end of the sixth century, monks and bishops who came from the south of France were able to re-educate their neighbors in the north by bringing them the essentials of a classical and Christian culture which they had preserved during this time of troubles. In an even more startling manner, medieval culture had been able to begin developing in Ireland, Scotland, and Northumberland during this difficult period, for schools of the ancient tradition, and libraries, and workshops of copyists still existed in Vandal Africa, in Visigoth Spain, and especially in Ostrogoth (later, Byzantine) Italy, and they were able to furnish Celtic and Anglo-Saxon monasteries with the materials necessary to nourish their cultural renaissance.

Nothing illustrates better this continuity of tradition in the face of so many historical vicissitudes than the study of the preservation of ancient classical texts. For example, how is it possible for us to read the works of Ammianus Marcellinus, the last great Latin Historian, a contemporary and a friend of the emperor Julian the Apostate? Because of one manuscript—only one—which was carried from Italy to Great Britain by a wandering scholar, Benedict Biscop, mentioned by the Venerable Bede, who made at least six trips from England to Rome, bringing back each time a cargo of precious manuscripts. The text of Ammianus was saved from destruction a second time when a Scots scholar with his copy of it went to educate continental Europe and to carry the Gospel to the Rhineland during the time of the Danish invasion of Britain (A.D. c.800). It was preserved in Germany in the famous abbey at Lorsch until the day in the second half of the fifteenth century, when an Italian humanist discovered it and took it to Venice to be published.

To all this the Modern Man would surely reply, "Right. I willingly concede that in these ways the Greeks and the Romans are our direct ancestors, but you must agree that by this time they are very distant relatives and that with the increasing acceleration of history that we are experiencing in our day, so rich in all kinds of innovations, their heritage somehow loses its value when compared with our recent acquisitions. Take an example from politics. If you want to understand the consequences of our acts in the present world situation, an acquaintance with the Peloponnesian War has much less bearing on the matter than an exact memory of the decisions made at the conferences of Yalta, Potsdam, or Panmunjom."

*Classical Scholar:* Obviously. But a sufficiently penetrating analysis of our political situation requires the social scientist to pursue his studies still further if he is to uncover the principles of a more complete explanation. For example, since Toynbee and others, we have known that the political techniques and behavior of the Soviet Union are not explained solely by the theories of Karl Marx, but also by a more deep-rooted Russian national tradition. The Soviet rulers would like to be pure Marxists, and they think they are. But, whether they know it or not, whether they want to be Marxists or not, every day their behavior shows them up as the heirs of the Czarist monarchy and its administration. I might cite their indifference to what we Westerners call individual liberty and the inalienable rights of man, in their acceptance of the techniques of the police state, and so on. This tradition goes back far beyond the Moscow of the Czars. ("Moscow, the third Rome,—and there will not be a fourth," the orthodox theologians of the seventeenth century used to teach.) It has its source in the Byzantine Middle Ages, which, in turn, were the result of a gradual evolution of the Roman Empire during the first five centuries after Christ that concluded with the cultural separation of the two halves of the Mediterranean basin.

No one will deny that the present political map of Europe is the result of the diplomatic maneuvers that marked the end of the Second World War or that it reflects the power position of the Western and Soviet blocks. But many geographical features of today's Europe have their origins in the events of a more distant history. It has often been remarked that the dividing line between the Catholic and Protestant sections of Western Germany is substantially the same as the limit of Roman penetration into ancient Germany in the era of the emperors of the Flavian and Antonine dynasties. The regions which remained Catholic after the Reformation are the ones which had felt most profoundly the influence of Rome and had preserved its heritage.

*Modern Man:* Perhaps so. But in the search for ultimate sources there is no reason to stop at classical antiquity. Why should it be given privileged consideration? Modern man is the heir of the past of all humanity. Even the experiences of prehistoric times have played an important role in history. Very fruitful research conducted over the last twenty years in the study of agrarian economy (such as the open field system) has explained a great many aspects of the spread of population, of economic exploitation in general, and even of the landscape of our European countryside. These researches have brought to our attention the importance of the way in which our lands were cleared during the Stone Age.

Why be satisfied with considering the West, as you suggest, from the point of view of India or China? Let us go back even further and examine it from the standpoint of the most distant prehistoric times. Viewed from very far off, the totality of human history seems to us to be made up entirely of three periods whose lines of demarcation are two great technological revolutions: the Neolithic revolution (the introduction of agriculture and the breeding of stock, and with these the creation of a settled life) and the modern industrial revolution, which had its beginning in Great Britain in the second half of the eighteenth century. The discovery of metals (classical antiquity belongs to both the Bronze Age and the Iron Age) was not of comparable importance. Technologically speaking, the Greeks and the Romans were not so very much further evolved than Neolithic Man.

*Classical Scholar:* But we modern men are not Stone Age men. The ancients are our direct predecessors and are not as far from us as they might seem at first. Not only because twenty centuries are insignificant when one considers the course of mankind since its origin, but also because the presence of the ancients in the very heart of modern Western culture is much more immediate than mere considerations of chronology would lead us to suppose. And this is due to the remarkable phenomenon of renaissances, a phenomenon so characteristic of our civilization that it has been said, with some exaggeration I admit, that the West was born with its head turned backwards. Actually, that is too strong; our West is primarily a civilization of progress. But this progress has not taken the form of a uniform advance; the course of history moves, to use Vico's formula, *per corsi e per ricorsi,* with steps forward and steps backward, in an alternating rhythm.

We would be much farther away from the ancients today, and their classicism would be much more foreign to us, if Western men had not made repeated but distinctive efforts to recapture the heritage of antiquity, to rediscover whatever time had obliterated or they had forgotten. This process of willful recovery and careful imitation of the treasures of the past we call "renaissance." We must not use this word exclusively for the revival of learning in the fifteenth and sixteenth centuries; it is a more general phenomenon which has repeated itself several times.

As early as the sixth and seventh centuries, according to the region being considered, the barbarism that had resulted from the Germanic invasions and from the collapse of Roman authority, allowed our Western culture, oriented to the Atlantic and to the lands north of the Mediterranean to be born. This civilization, which began about the eighth century A.D., did not start from nothing; it was a culture which made use of the traditions and the materials preserved from the stock of classical antiquity. In the revival of these memories and in the exploitation to the utmost of the resources furnished by these materials, the outlines of what was to become medieval civilization were fixed. From antiquity the early Middle Ages took and preserved Christianity as its religion and the dominant principle of its organization, the works of the classics as its models and its source of all knowledge, and the Latin language as its cultivated tongue. To be literate was to know Latin, and this learned language was to remain the *lingua franca* of the West until the middle of the seventeenth century. To become more cultivated, more civilized, was to deepen one's awareness of the implications of Christianity, to know Latin better, to understand more thoroughly the classics, and to profit more greatly from their lessons. This characteristic manner of thinking became more accentuated as the new Western culture developed and progressed. Just as the new culture's birth is identified by a first effort at renaissance, so each one of its later advances will be accomplished by new endeavors in the same direction. In the eighth and ninth centuries there will be the Carolingian Renaissance, and later on the movement that Charles H. Haskins so accurately calls the renaissance of the twelfth century, where we find a new interest in Roman law at Bologna, a revival of encyclopedism and Platonism at Chartres, and passionate study of the classics everywhere. This rebirth of learning stretches into the middle of the thirteenth century, especially in philosophy with the rediscovery of the corpus of Aristotle's work, and continues down to the great humanist Renaissance of the fifteenth and sixteenth centuries, from which the modern world dates its inception.

In this perpetually renewed effort to revive the memory of the ancients and to move closer to their spirit by modifying somehow the normal effects of the passage of historical time, the West was not confined strictly to its own resources. The role played by the Arabs in the transmission and study of Greek texts, above all in matters of philosophy and science, is well known. Even today there are important treatises by the great physician Galen, a contemporary of the Roman emperors Marcus Aurelius and Commodus, which we must read in an Arabic translation, the original Greek having been lost.

Even more well known, and indeed more significant, are the contributions of Byzantine Hellenism to Western humanism. The loss of Greek often seems to be the most serious deficiency in the culture of the Middle Ages, and its progressive rediscovery in Florence by Petrarch, Boccaccio, and Marsilio Ficino in the fourteenth and fifteenth centuries, seems to be the most reliable criterion of the revival of learning. In Byzantium there is unquestionably a more visible and more perfect continuity between antiquity and the Middle Ages than we find in the West. We study Homer's *Iliad* in the light of the great commentary of Eustathius of Thessalonica (died c. 1194), a commentary so filled with ancient lore and so directly inspired by the great scholars of the Hellenistic era that it requires an effort on our part to remember that its author was also an archbishop and Christian theologian, a contemporary of Saint Bernard. Nonetheless, in Byzantium as in the West, the bond with the ancients was periodically reforged, and we must speak of renaissances in Byzantium, for all the characteristic phenomena can be discerned: a return to a more direct imitation of the Hellenist classics, a more complete renewal of all their values, including even the temptation to shift from Christianity toward Paganism (which also appears in our civilization from the humanism of the fifteenth and sixteenth centuries on). As early as the sixth or seventh century we see the Byzantine theologians denouncing the heresy of the *Ethnophrones* "those who think like pagans"; the temptation of paganism was not imaginary, for example, in the case of Leo the mathematician in the ninth century, or in the case of Joannes Italus and others in the eleventh century, and so on down the line to Gemistus Pletho and the Neo-Platonists of the school of Mistra.

Such an enduring influence, appearing in such varied contexts, so stubbornly asserted and then renewed, left a profound mark on the history of Western culture, which found itself more and more cast in forms inherited from the Greeks or the Romans. This is particularly true of the periods in our own culture which we call "classical," the periods which brought the growth and maturation of the national cultures of Europe: the Golden Age of Spain, the seventeenth century in France and England, and the eighteenth century in Germany. Educated in the school of antiquity, European élites quite naturally modeled their cultures on the classical patterns they had learned.

A historian of education might mention the profound influence of the ancients on the pedagogical methods of the modern world. First, of course, there is the actual presence of antiquity in the curriculum; until very recently all forms of higher education assumed, as they had in the Middle Ages and the Renaissance, a knowledge of Latin and Greek and a thorough acquaintance with the literatures of Rome and Greece. But antiquity is present in a more subtle way in the educational methods we use. Even while a child is being trained in his native language, we have recourse to the techniques of ancient education. As soon as a child learns how to read, he is made aware of the mechanics of language, and we try to instill in him a mastery of his language by teaching him grammar. But what grammar? The very one that the Greek teacher Dionysus Thrax had formulated in his school at Rhodes around 90 B.C. (parts of speech, nouns, articles, adjectives, etc.). Then, as the ancients did, we move on to the study of classical authors, particularly poets. Whereas Greek children were raised on Homer and Latin children on Virgil, the English are exposed to Shakespeare, the French to Corneille and Racine. Next our children are taught composition, which we have long considered the crowning skill, as it was for our Hellenistic and Roman forebears.

Hence this paradox: when Charles Perrault undertook to exalt the works of the French seventeenth-century classicists, these "moderns" were themselves grateful students and ardent admirers of the ancients with whom he compared them. Raised on Cicero and Virgil, they wrote tragedies that were recapitulations of Euripides and Seneca and comedies derived from Aristophanes and Terence. When Charles Perrault's own brother, the physician and architect Claude Perrault, designed the colonnade of the Louvre, which his contemporaries greeted as the masterpiece of their age, he did not create a truly "modern" architecture in an original style as do such architects of today as Frank Lloyd Wright, Le Corbusier, or Saarinen. His classicism is really a neoclassicism, inspired by two easily recognized models, the Greek row of columns, and the podium, or raised podium, of Etruscan and Roman temples.

*Modern Man:* Now there is an example fatal to the humanist's position. The colonnade of the Louvre does not seem as admirable to us as it did to its contemporaries. And sometimes we cannot help being annoyed when we are exposed to our ancestor's taste for the neoclassical style in public buildings. Europe is not the only one to have suffered in this. In America we are faced with domes and pediments and colonnades everywhere. They are almost required in any capital building, courthouse, or library—somewhat like Gothic revival in universities.

We rightly believe that the obsession for ancient models has not always been a good thing for Western culture and has hindered our originality by paralyzing our creative imagination on more than one occasion and in many ways. In art any "neo–" style is as abhorrent as any political restoration is illusory. Without the shadow of a doubt, Greek sculpture is admirable—when it comes from the chisel of a Phidias or a Praxiteles. But can anyone help suffering when confronted with the artificiality, coldness, and sterility that resulted when the Romans imitated it? Or even worse when the academic sculptors Canova or Thorvaldsen tried their hands at it? We can only conclude that they went too often to Italian museums which were filled, not with the original masterpieces (they were unknown at the beginning of the nineteenth century), but with mediocre Roman copies.

*Classical Scholar:* But your examples are misleading too. I could speak at length about the excessive exaltation of originality at any price. That is a clay idol of the romantics and can be every bit as perilous as too exact imitation. Imitation is a fundamental law of all human "creation." I must use quotation marks because to use the term "creative" precisely we may apply it only to God. God alone can create *ex nihilo,* from nothing. Man can only transform. Any "creation" of his, whether artistic or technical, necessarily comes from some earlier point of departure, some source, some base or model.

Imitation, or to be more accurate the conscious contemplation of an ancient model, has not produced only lifeless copies. It has fertilized the modern imagination as much as it has hobbled it. Still, this influence is much more felicitous when it is exercised indirectly as a catalyst. Greek tragedy is undeniably inimitable; nevertheless the close study of its great examples has engendered the creation of art forms of profound originality, such as the Florentine opera of the 1600s or the musical drama of Wagner, not to mention other works of the modern theater.

*Modern Man:* Yes, leaving aside cases of purely formal and artificial imitation, it is quite true that Western cultural history shows that the influence of antiquity has often been a good thing and that it has helped the "classical" artists of modern Europe to reach the maturity which is their great merit. But the very success of modern classicism entails an unfortunate consequence: if the presence of the ancient heritage in our contemporary culture remains substantial, it is often an indirect presence, transformed by the talent or genius of the great writers of our different national cultures. A great many considerations—the passage of history, which separates us ever more from antiquity; the existence of recent classics; the increasing demands of our own various literatures and our civilization in general—have made it inevitable that today's man become acquainted with the ancient tradition through its imitators and its heirs. I shall take examples from French culture, but Americans will have no trouble finding others applicable to their experience. A French child does not *discover* the classical *genre* of the fable at the age of eleven or thirteen, when he meets it in Phaedrus or Aesop in his Latin or Greek class. He *rediscovers* it and recognizes it from a time much earlier, in primary school, when he studied French fables, imitations of the ancients by the great classical poet La Fontaine. Similarly, many French students will know about the stormy passions of Andromache or Phaedra from the tragedies of Racine, realizing only vaguely that the plot of the first drama comes from an episode of the *Aeneid* and the plot of the second from Euripides' *Hippolytus*. One can almost say that for a Frenchman there is more maturity, more perfection—in short, more classicism—in the beautiful verses of Péguy on the *Seven Against Thebes*

> Tydée allait foncer sur la porte Prœtide.
> Mais elle n'était pas laissée à l'abandon,
> Car la Ville opposait au roi de Calydon
> L'ardent Mélanippos, indomptable Astacide.
>
> Tydeus came to swoop on the Prœtid gate.
> Yet it was not there abandoned without recourse,
> For the City set against the Calydon king
> Fiery Melanippus, doughty Astacid.

than in Aeschylus' Greek tragedy, which he has adapted. The original is undeniably an admirable work, if only for the creative effort it entailed, but its very harshness betrays a certain primitive quality, which some might even go so far as to call outdated.

Furthermore, I chose poetry as my example. But it is the most favorable one for the classicist because poetry is in some sense eternal. In all other fields the initial stage of our culture attained by antiquity has been all but abandoned, surpassed by our subsequent progress. And so, in the sciences, even if our elementary geometry remains exactly the same as it was when the Greeks taught it, our schools have every reason to prefer textbooks which make use of all the resources of scientific teaching methods and child psychology, and not a literal translation of Euclid's *Elements,* no matter how remarkable it may have been in its day or how interesting it remains as a historical document.

*Classical Scholar:* And yet—the return to original sources is still one of the fundamental laws of the progress of culture. Suppose we extend our argument beyond the framework of classical antiquity. Take the case of the Bible. The Old Testament has certainly inspired some of the most beautiful poems of our modern literatures. Setting aside the religious problem and taking into consideration only literary questions, can we say that because Byron has written "The Assyrian came down like the wolf on the fold" and Victor Hugo has written *Boaz Asleep,* we are no longer required to reread the prophet Isaiah or the Book of Ruth? In fact the exploitation of the Greco-Roman heritage has not been limited in the West simply to the various renaissance periods and to our classical ages. One may argue that the Renaissance of the fifteenth and sixteenth centuries makes its effects felt even in our times. It is like an undamped wave whose successive pulsations can be easily observed. And so in the case of the return to the classical at the end of the eighteenth century, which indicated the reaction throughout Europe against the excessive modernism of the culture of the Enlightenment, we have a very profound movement, not simply the passing fashion of a cold academic art. Western man made a remarkable and fruitful effort to rediscover antiquity, to know it better, to know it for itself, such as it had really existed. The name of Winckelmann will suffice to convey the extent of this movement. Likewise, a century later, reacting this time against the too rigid development which had led from romanticism to realism, a second neoclassicism came into being, represented in France by Louis Ménard, Leconte de Lisle, and all the Parnassian poets. It is easy to find its equivalent elsewhere: in England, for example, with Swinburne, and also in Germany and Italy.

And I am not yet finished. Although today the formation of the mind is no longer based exclusively on the study of the classics as it was in the preceding centuries, although the evolution of modern civilization has proceeded at an accelerated rate, the return to antiquity as a source of inspiration is every bit as real a fact in our culture. It is amazing to see how many of our contemporary writers turn back spontaneously to the Greek myths as if to a common patrimony. Through them, they manage to reach the deepest layers of the Western *psyché,* to speak the most thrilling and most direct language.

Look at the repertory of the French theater in the course of the last generation. Among the most acclaimed dramas, how many of them are ones that have taken up again an ancient legend! There are Giraudoux's *Amphitryon 38, Electra, Tiger at the Gates,* Cocteau's *Orpheus* and *Oedipus,* Anouilh's *Antigone,* his *Orpheus* and *Eurydice*—and even from the pen of Sartre, who would seem the least classical of our authors, we have *The Flies,* a modern version of Aeschylus' *Eumenides.*

More significant are the cases taken from political life. When André Gide published his *Return from the USSR,* in which he expressed his disenchantment with the optimistic communist dreams which had motivated his voyage to Russia, he could think of no more suitable way to summarize his opinion than to choose as his epigraph, placed on the first page of this short book, an account of the myth of Demophoön. You will say, "But Gide took his references from the distant past precisely because he was rejecting the modern adventure of Marxism." Not at all. Look at the Marxists themselves: when the Communist-sponsored University Committee for Peace undertook in 1952 to publish a propaganda sheet, it felt that the best thing to do to commend its propaganda to the French intelligentsia was to entitle the paper *Trygaeus,* borrowing the name of a character in Aristophanes' *Peace.*

These observations could be extended to cover many other domains. We have just celebrated the Olympic Games. It is well known how the Greek example directly inspired their reestablishment at the instigation of Pierre de Coubertin. Or again, one might cite the typical case of the role of classical references in the thought of Freud, the creator of a new modern mythology with its Oedipus complex, etc.

At this point, can we not easily imagine the Modern Man giving up the contest, for fear of seeming a barbarian? He would add his voice to the Classical Scholar's and help issue a joint statement expressing their agreement:

"If the ancient heritage has preserved across the generations the same exemplary value, the same role of catalyst and fructifier, this is not only because these Greeks and Romans are the direct ancestors, more or less distant, of Western man of today, but also because they are great ancestors. If their civilization is situated relatively far back in time, it still remains young and alive, and always shall—provided we have the sense not to forget it. Because it was a great, rich, and beautiful civilization, whose accomplishments in every domain it entered are marked with the same genius and the same human perfection, in the eyes of the historian or of one who regards us from the standpoint of India or China, Western man is first and foremost a Hellenic man."

## II

We now come to the consideration of this heritage of the ancient world in itself. We shall attempt to show rapidly how our modern Western world succeeded in preserving and putting to use its creative powers. There are countless aspects of our current civilization which show the traces of their classical origin.

One preliminary remark must be made. To recount everything that our Western world owes to the Christian religion does not belong to our subject, but it is still necessary to say that Christianity, too, is part of this heritage from antiquity. It is a fact of considerable historical importance that Christianity, though born in a Semitic land—but one that had already been deeply penetrated by the Hellenic influence, especially in Galilee—did not remain confined there but spread rapidly, and took its final form in the Greco-Roman cultural world. The Old Testament was brought together in the much altered form that it had received at the hands of the Alexandrian Jews when they made their Greek translation, the Septuagint. The New Testament was edited in Greek from the beginning.

In our classrooms and in our own minds we have made too sharp a separation between pagan antiquity on one side and Christian origins on the other, as if there were a water-tight wall between them. There is no lack of histories of Western philosophy which deal with Greek antiquity and thought in Volume One from the pre-Socratics to Damascius, the sixth-century A.D. contemporary of the Catholic emperor Justinian, and then in Volume Two begin all over again as far back as Saint Paul or the time of Nero to retrace their steps through the Church Fathers down to the Christian thinkers of the Middle Ages, thereby closing their eyes to a whole series of connections and reciprocal influences between the two streams of thought. At least as early as 180 A.D. there were pagan intellectuals concerned with resisting Christian propaganda, witness Celsus, Galen, and Lucian of Apamea. And from the time of Justin Martyr (A.D. c.100–c.165) and the other apologists the Christians were profoundly influenced by classical culture. And is it necessary to wait until 180? It was in vain that Saint Paul thought of himself first as an Israelite of the race of Abraham, of the tribe of Benjamin, circumcised on the eighth day, a disciple of Gamaliel, and a Pharisee in matters of the law; he could not alter the fact that he was also a citizen of the Greek city of Tarsus, "no mean city," and more than that, a Roman citizen; he could not alter the fact that he wrote in Greek, that on occasion he cited Epimenides or Menander, that his style made use of the devices of classical rhetoric. The great scholar Rudolf Bultmann has demonstrated to what an extent he uses the stylistic procedures of the "diatribe" or popular sermon of the Greek philosophers.

Wherever it put down roots, Christianity brought with it this classical influence which had so deeply permeated it that the two could not be separated. This can be seen in the Mediterranean Near East, where the spread of the Gospel promulgated the Greek language and culture. Even when it promoted to the rank of civilized languages the old national tongues of Coptic, Syriac, Armenian, and Georgian, these languages could not assume their new role without having recourse to massive borrowings from Greek vocabulary and grammar. And we find the same phenomenon in the West. If, as we have remarked, Latin became the learned language of all Western Europe, it was because, in contrast to the East, the Christian countries of the West had known only one liturgical and ecclesiastical language, Latin. And, with Latin, the entire classical culture was progressively assimilated by our barbarian ancestors.

In the course of the first centuries of its history, in the so-called period of the Church Fathers, Christianity, far from repressing the elements of classicism that it had acquired in its origins, developed these elements in spite of the concern and resistance that such a synthesis with a civilization of pagan origin had aroused more than once in the souls of the timorous.

We may conclude from this that the conversion of the West to Christianity and the long centuries during which the Christian religion dominated and inspired all of Western life contribute heavily to the fact that our modern civilization is modeled on a classical pattern. In the simple matter of the physical preservation of this precious ancient heritage, there is not one classical philologist who does not owe a great debt of gratitude to the monk or churchman, either Latin or Byzantine, who saved the Latin or Greek text on which he was working by having it recopied. We owe our text of the *Paedagogus* of Clement of Alexandria, a moralist and Christian humanist, to the archbishop and bibliophile Arethas of Caesarea in Cappadocia, who had a copy made of it in 914. (We even know the name of the scribe, the price of his work, and the cost of the paper.) And it is to this same archbishop that we owe one of our principal manuscripts of Plato.

Having completed these preliminary remarks, let us pass to the inventory itself. If there is one characteristic which seems fundamental in our modern Western civilization, it is surely its technology. Nowhere else is its originality, its power, and its capacity for progress so evident. Who before us was able to split the atom? A nice paradox! When the word came to us from the Greeks, it meant precisely the indivisible particle, but our physics continues to elaborate upon its reconstruction of the nature of the infinitely small. Who else has escaped from gravitation? To Aristotle weight seemed to be an inherent property of the various elements of matter. Who else has penetrated cosmic space, flown so high and so fast, navigated under the seas and their glacial masses? One by one before our eyes our technology has been realizing the archetypical dreams of the human spirit, the dreams most deeply rooted in our common aspirations.

But there is not one of us who does not recognize the direct connection between technological progress and scientific progress. Only with the application of the recent discoveries of Western science to technology could we initiate or maintain our industrial revolution, which constitutes the third phase of human history as it was defined earlier. All our sciences—physical, chemical, biological, or social—derive their originality and fecundity from their roots in mathematics. Each science reaches the stage of maturity at the moment when it becomes capable of introducing mathematical measurement in its domain, and all our sciences are directly dependent on the service to which they can put mathematics, and consequently on the state of its development. It is not unusual to encounter scientists in some sector of advanced physics who declare that their progress has been retarded because our mathematicians have not yet formulated the precise systems of which they are in need.

Now, no one can deny that our mathematics are Greek. As rapid and as original as their developments may have been in the modern era, they are the lineal descendants of the great creative movement that has for its landmarks the illustrious names of Pythagoras, Theatetus, Archimedes, Diophantus, and the other great mathematicians of ancient Hellas. They only continue and complete it by integrating the results of earlier discoveries.

Here, again, it is fruitful to oppose oriental civilizations to the Hellenic-modern complex that we call the West. Without denying the contributions of the Indians and the Arabs to the formation of our mathematics, particularly in the field of algebra, one must admit that each of them had begun by learning from the Greeks. The most arresting homage given to the originality and worth of Hellenic mathematics came from the Chinese, another people of very ancient and advanced civilization, proud of their accomplishments and, like the Greeks, quick to call "barbaric" anything foreign. At the end of the reign of the emperor K'ang Hsi (d. 1723), when a nationalist reaction strove to eliminate Christianity and everything the Jesuit missionaries had brought with it on the grounds that they could not be assimilated to the Chinese tradition, only one European book found grace in the eyes of the scholars and was deemed worthy of preservation in translation to enrich their classics. It was the same textbook that had been used for so long in Western schools, Euclid's *Elements of Geometry,* from the Alexandria of the third century B.C.

In addition to mathematics, modern science derives its strength and its substance from another source, the experimental method. It is tempting, but fallacious, to assign the date of its birth to a relatively recent era, the seventeenth century, the times of Francis Bacon, Galileo, and Pascal. In fact, its roots lie deep in history and extend as far back as classical Greece. In at least one science, medicine, the ancients practiced with admirable exactness the method of observation, hypothesis, and experimental verification. Nothing could be more rational, more rigorous, or more "modern" in spirit than certain treatises by Hippocrates (fifth century B.C.) and his Hellenistic followers, whose works have come down to us in the collection known as the *Corpus Hippocraticum*. And the Greek physicians of the Roman period, such as Galen (second century A.D.) or Oribasius (fourth century A.D.) worked in the same spirit. Nor must we overlook the pharmacopeia and the great name of Dioscorides (first century A.D.) whom the scholars of the Middle Ages eagerly studied. These men remain quite close in spirit to our modern medical science. Just as the development of various non-Euclidean geometries has absorbed, but not abolished, classical Greek geometry by integrating it into a more comprehensive whole, so the astonishing progress of experimental medicine has not invalidated the original worth of the teachings of Hellenic science. In 1958 an International Convention of Hippocratic Medicine was held on the Greek island of Cos, the birthplace of the founder of medicine and for a long time the seat of the most famous school of medicine. This site was chosen because there are still doctors who believe that the lesson of Hippocrates merits serious consideration and that we can draw from it a truly humanist ideal of the healing art, an art that would aim at treating the complete man and refuse to allow medicine to disintegrate into separate specializations that care for one disease or one organ and run the risk of forgetting that there is also the organic unity of the living man.

As we have seen, these two aspects of the scientific spirit are integral parts of the heritage we have received from the world of antiquity. It is not accurate to oppose "the two cultures" (as has been done, particularly in discussions about plans for educational reform), to contend that they constitute the two horns of a dilemma between which we must make a choice; on the one hand there is supposedly our modern culture, predominantly scientific and oriented toward technical efficiency, and on the other the traditional "humanistic" culture, based on the classics and concerned primarily with philological, literary, and aesthetic interests. That is not at all the case; both belong equally to our living civilization, and both are derived equally from the heritage of the ancients.

It is clear that the influence of the classics has always been particularly important in the fields which stem from what the Greeks designated by the single word *logos:* reason, thought, language.

As for language, how important it was that for more than a thousand years all the Western intelligentsia were raised on Greek and Latin! Our modern languages today bear visible traces of this past. If they have become genuinely cultured languages rather than simple peasant dialects good merely for the expression of elementary needs, they owe their polish to this prolonged influence of the classical languages.

This is obvious for modern Greek and the Romance languages (Italian, Spanish, French, etc.), for their entire history shows clearly enough how they have returned periodically to their sources for nourishment, enrichment, and instruction. But the same phenomenon can be observed taking place with the same intensity in the Germanic and Slavic languages. Upon receiving Christianity from Byzantium, Russia opened her doors to the influence of ecclesiastical Greek; hence the importance of the vocabulary of Greek origin in the Russian language. Likewise German, especially literary German, has acquired a large number of terms of Latin origin by direct borrowing or through the intermediary of the French language. The French influence on German was so pervasive that by the eighteenth century a reaction against it grew up, but even when systematically enforced, this reaction did not eliminate all the accretions from the French. In daily language, *Fernsprecher* does not seem to have supplanted *Telephon*. Furthermore, German scholarship can exploit the wealth of words furnished by these two sources, the Germanic and the classical, to establish subtle nuances between associated words, as in the case of *Geschichte* and *Historie*.

There is no need to recall the percentage of words of Greek or Latin (and French) origin in the English language of today. Once again, any reaction against their preponderance is futile. A modern English poet like Gerard Manley Hopkins in his search for greater homogeneity and expressive power might force himself to make the utmost use of the fund of Anglo-Saxon words, but English poetry will never renounce that other source of expression furnished by the polysyllables of classical origin: "The multitudinous seas incarnadine." As for the nationalist passion which inspired polemicists like the honorable clergyman who wanted "perambulator" replaced by "childwain," "emigrant" by "outganger," and "logic" by "redecraft"—their crusades are met with ridicule.

The tendency of the modern English language is irresistibly toward borrowing from Latin (or, secondarily, from Greek). As has been often stated, this proclivity is much more marked in America than in England. And it manifests itself most obviously in learning, science, and technology. Look at the complex medical vocabulary, which uses words like neurosis, cancer, and ileitis. To the degree that the English language refuses to be reduced to a basic English just good enough for a minimum of practical exchanges and wishes to remain a civilized language, recourse to Latin and Greek seems inevitable. For every formation of a Germanic type, such as "broadcasting," how many do we come across like "television" and "video"? The first is a Greco-Latin hybrid, and the second borders on slang, but even these pathological cases illustrate the tendency.

Up to this point we have mentioned only vocabulary; the classic influence on the syntax and style of modern European languages is no less strong, though at first less easily discernible. In 1954 the Danish philologist Knud Sörensen gave an interesting report on "The Latin Influence on English Syntax." He showed clearly the mechanisms which made possible the influence, the same one finds at work in all Europe: the constant study of the classics, repeated translations (from the first attempts in Old English at the time of Alfred the Great to the works of the Elizabethan and Jacobean humanists), the modeling of English grammar on Latin, and finally the indirect influence through the French language. He assembles many facts, some less important than others, but impressive on the whole. Like M. Jourdain, who spoke prose without realizing it, in many cases the English are speaking Latin without knowing it. Some of these phenomena are on the point of disappearing—for example, the attribution of gender to inanimate objects, which can only be explained as a literary personification imitating the Latin. It is Latin that explains why the sun should be masculine and moon feminine; in Old English, as in German, the genders are reversed. Similarly, under the influence of the Latin *navis,* a ship is feminine in spite of the Old English neuter *scipu.* Other constructions, however, belong to everyday language, such as the frequent use of the progressive form of the verb or the ending *-ing* in verbal nouns which goes back to Latin participial and gerund constructions. As usual it is in the learned style in the higher levels of language that these cases are the most frequent; *notwithstanding* from the French *nonobstant* goes back to the Medieval Latin form *non obstante.*

These observations could be multiplied, and analogues could be found for all the other European languages, for they developed parallel to each other, the same causes producing the same effects. The classical influence has shaped them all in similar fashion and has contributed greatly to the startling analogies that the study of linguistics has discovered in all the languages of the Western world and that have enabled Robert A. Hall to speak of a "standard average European language."

From syntax we pass imperceptibly to style, and from there to the forms of thought and mental categories. If there exists any Western uniformity in these, it must be attributed above all to the ever-present heritage of antiquity.

We must return to the important idea, many-sided but at the same time unified, that the Greeks had of *logos*. It is the winged word that establishes the reciprocal communication of minds. It is language and expression. But one must not insist too much only on the notion of a means of expression, for form and content are always inseparable. The *logos* is a word fit for describing human life precisely because it conveys content, a thought, and this thought is a rational thought: *logos* is also reason. When they became Christians the Greeks added a further and even more profound overtone to the word. The same word, *logos,* was used to translate the Hebrew *dabar* and became the uncreated Word, co-eternal with God. And so human reason becomes that most mysterious attribute of all, by which man sees himself made in the image and likeness of his Creator: its light is revealed as an effulgence of His light.

Modern Western man, so proud of his technological intelligence and his science, is first of all a rational man, and the very idea of reason, as well as the manner in which it is applied, is a heritage of classical antiquity. Our entire philosophical tradition is directly connected to the uninterrupted train of thinkers that starts with the *phusikoi* of Ionia in the sixth century B.C., Thales of Miletus, Anaximander, Anaximenes, etc. All our mathematicians follow in the traces of Pythagoras and Diophantus, often without realizing it, but in philosophy the relationship is so obvious that it is never unconscious; there is not one of our thinkers who does not feel that he is the pupil and continuer of the ancient Greek sages, and who does not take pains to relate his statement of a problem to theirs and to contrast their solutions with his. Take for example one of the most "modern" of today's philosophers, Martin Heidegger, one of the masters of existentialism; all his readers know the place which the pre-Socratics occupy in his thought and the importance he attaches to his interpretation of Anaxagoras and Heraclitus.

This is no flash-in-the-pan fashion, but a continuing feature of philosophy. The Scholastics of the thirteenth century were very up-to-date thinkers for their day, and yet the names of Aristotle and Saint Augustine were always on their lips. In the fifteenth century the humanists of Florence and Padua shook the tyranny of Aristotelian philosophy by invoking the names of Plato and Plotinus—and so forth, from century to century.

The ubiquitous presence of Greek philosophy in Western culture exercises so great an influence that we cannot confine it to technical philosophy itself. It extends to our common mentality and daily manner of thinking. There is a Western type of logical thought which is reflected in language. We spoke earlier of the parallelism of structure which gives to all the modern European languages a sort of family resemblance, no matter how diverse their origins. Robert A. Hall formulated his notion of a "standard average European language" while studying the grammar of Hungarian, a language belonging to a most unusual linguistic family, the Finno-Ugric, which one would not expect to show many similarities to Indo-European tongues. This family resemblance is most clearly evident in clause and sentence structure, i.e. in the mode of reasoning, in the logical structure of the mentality formed by a philosophic tradition of Hellenic origin.

To take an example from the simpler and more accessible world of vocabulary, words like *quality* and *quantity* belong to the everyday language of the man in the street; their application to quite various aspects of daily life seems totally natural to us. But that is because we are Western men. Actually they are Aristotelian categories and a heritage from Greek classicism. *Quality* is the Greek word *poiotês,* a creation of Plato which was a neologism in its day. The Latin word *qualitas* is Cicero's translation modeled on Plato's formation, and again was a neologism for those who first read it. Through the intermediary of the French word *qualité,* the learned borrowing *quality* came to the English language in the thirteenth century. This vital word is found in every modern Western language; the other Romance languages imitated the French (e.g., the Italian *qualità*); German, in the sixteenth century, did as the English had, and borrowed *Qualität;* and in the eleventh century Russian used Cicero's method and fabricated the word *katshestvo,* one of the ecclesiastical Slavonic inventions patterned on Byzantine Greek words.

To find all the various and hidden forms that the influence of classical philosophy has taken it would be necessary to examine systematically all the phases of our thought and life. How many remarks there would be to make concerning our moral concepts; how many of our ethical ideas come from Greece! What I am speaking about is the most deep-seated assumptions that the average man would call simple common sense. They are so firmly rooted in our moral understanding that this unconscious heritage seems to us to belong to the natural order of things. A great number of our fundamental ideas in this area are survivals of the "common ideas," *koinai ennoiai* of the Greeks: virtue, duty, good deeds, thoughtful and rational behavior, the Good, the True, justice, wisdom.

Pagan antiquity is certainly not the only source of our moral tradition, and I would not underestimate the Christian contribution to it, but a part of the Hellenic heritage can be discerned even in what Christianity has handed down to us. As we have said, from the end of the second century Christian thought had fused with classical humanism. We may go even further and say that Hellenic elements were already deeply a part of the New Testament's message and can even be discerned in the Old Testament, most obviously in the apocryphal Wisdom of Solomon.

Within the classical heritage, one must not forget the specific contribution of Rome beside Greece's. Though distinct, they are not in opposition. The prelude to Greece's universal mission was civilizing rustic Rome, and the history of civilization confirms the unity of what German scholars rightly call *die hellenistisch-römische Kultur*. Rome gave birth to law, Roman Law, which has contributed powerfully to the form and structure of our Western civilization. If our cultural history is to be measured by the rhythm of successive renaissances, the study, rediscovery, and heightened appreciation of Roman Law has always been a primary component of each of them from the adaptations in the barely stable barbarian kingdoms of the fifth century (e.g., the *lex Romana Visigothorum* promulgated by Alaric II) to the German historical school in the romantic period and Savigny around 1800.

This study was not merely the result of a disinterested academic curiosity; it led to practical applications and sustained the very life of modern and medieval European law. Every legal historian knows how many survivals of classical law persist today. Its deep and enduring influence has been both direct (Roman laws remained in effect for centuries, in southern France until the Revolution in 1789, in Germany almost down to the present) and indirect, either through the medium of Medieval Canon Law, which drew its inspiration frequently from the principles of Roman Law, or through the medium of the modern French Napoleonic Code filled with the spirit and letter of the classical heritage.

In antiquity, legal questions did not lie outside philosophy, and law and philosophy were always considered closely connected. We know that the great jurists of the Roman imperial period (second and third centuries A.D.) turned to Stoic philosophy and found in its noble moral doctrine the elements of a "natural law," the rational and ideal foundation of positive law. As in the case of philosophy, the influence of ancient law has been so penetrating that it has often gone beyond its purely technical framework to become part of our mentality, out daily language, and our deepest feelings. Our sense of justice, our confidence in the civilizing effects of institutions, the regularized proceedings of a criminal trial, our profoundly Western faith that law is the guarantee of civilization—all these, whether we realize it or not, are bonds with our distant Mediterranean origins.

Let us take a concrete example. The civilized world shuddered in horror when the barbarous forces of Stalinism and Nazism reintroduced into a troubled Europe the odious practice of collective punishment (holding responsible innocent people simply because a family tie related them to a criminal, even though they themselves had had no part in the crime). Undoubtedly the Christian heritage, and consequently the Judaic (*vide* Ezekiel, ch. xviii), had a part in this profound indignation, but so did the memory of the indignation of Tacitus when he stigmatized Tiberius' cruelty in slaughtering the children of Sejanus and our even older memory of the wise progress realized in the Athenian law of the time of Solon (sixth century B.C.).

From philosophy and law we pass quite naturally to politics, where once again we find the presence of the ancient heritage. Just listen to our speech. In English, in German, or in French, the minute we take up political matters, we catch ourselves speaking, and therefore thinking, like the classics. We say "politics" or "democracy," and they are Greek words; "republic," "(con)-federation," or "senator," and they are Latin words. And behind the word stands the thought. No reader who has given close consideration to the political works of Aristotle and Cicero will have failed to be struck by their consistently contemporary character.

And yet, what a difference there is when it comes to the practical application of these ideas. There is no real comparison between the immensity of the American nation and the little Greek city-state that Aristotle had in mind, or between one of our contemporary metropolitan cities, which assemble and control such multitudes with the help of modern technology, and the Rome which Cicero wanted to save. Leaving aside considerations of the absolute meaning of the word "democracy," its sociological content has undergone a significant change. Fifth-century Athens, whose constitution Aristotle analyzed, believed at one time that it was a radical democracy, but in fact political power was limited to a privileged aristocracy, the men who had the rights of citizenship. It has been estimated that they were 10 percent of the male population, or 5 percent of the total population. Our modern West has given all adult citizens, regardless of sex, the benefit of political equality. The word "equality" may be Latin, but we have now also imbued it with the precious Hellenic concept of *isonomia:* equal justice for all.

Nonetheless, the political thought of Aristotle or Cicero still has real value for us, for the problems these ancient theorists discussed are the problems of today. That a democracy may degenerate into an ochlocracy (mob rule), and that all personal or monarchical power tends to be corrupted into tyranny, are among the most pressing concerns of our times.

This up-to-date character of ancient political science is undeniably due to the perceptive genius of its thinkers, but if they seem to speak directly to us (more directly for example than a Chinese sage such as Confucius, who was also concerned with political considerations) it is because Aristotle's and Cicero's conceptions of politics have been handed down to us almost unchanged. Here as in the other fields already studied, we have remained classicists. We find the same mechanisms at work—a direct descent from the ancient world to the modern, with the action of renaissances compensating for the separation in time.

For example, it is easy to show that texts such as the Declaration of Independence and the Constitution of the United States contain many ideas and ways of thinking and feeling directly inspired by antiquity. The reason for this is that the founding fathers were Western men of the end of the eighteenth century, educated in the humanist tradition of the Renaissance and accustomed to thinking in terms of the ideal models of Athenian and Roman democracy.

But there is no reason to go so far back in the past. Consider the United Nations and a text as recent as its San Francisco charter; its preamble abounds in ideas and phrases echoing the classics. It opens with a long periodic statement, so complex that its structure had to be clarified by typographical devices. This preamble with its syntactical Latinisms, its participles, its long relative clauses, and its verb at the end is modeled on the classical sentence to such a degree that Professor Franz Blatt of Aarhus, Denmark, who made the observations about its Latinism, was able to translate it easily, almost word for word, into Latin: *"Nos, Nationes Gentium Unitarum, statutum et deliberatum habentes defendere posteritatem omnium saeculorum a flagello Martis, . . ."* "We, the Peoples of the United Nations, determined to save succeeding generations from the scourge of war, . . ." Such a periodic sentence can be easily translated from one European language to another precisely because it is entirely classical in inspiration and expression. We have come back to the fertile idea of a standard average European language.

We can take the analysis even further, following the lead of the French Hellenist and humanist Pierre Chantraine. Of the three words in its original title, *United Nations Organization,* the first two are direct borrowing from the Latin and the third has a more complicated history though it is composed entirely of classical elements. The word *organization* appears in every cultivated European language, of course with slight variations in spelling and pronunciation. It is made up of the suffix *-ation,* a learned borrowing from the Latin *-atio* and the verb *organiser* which makes its appearance in French in the fourteenth century, itself a composite of the suffix *-iser* inherited from the Vulgar Latin *-izare* (which had been taken from the Greek *-idzein*) and the noun *organe* "a part of the body considered for its function." *Organe* corresponds to the Latin *organum* borrowed from the Greek *organon,* which had originally meant a tool, but had later acquired the meanings "a part of the human body," "a musical instrument," or in the works of a philosopher such as Aristotle "the sum of logical processes."

In contemporary debates about education we note a remarkable persistence of ancient motifs. Our present-day discussions on the curriculum and educational reforms have led us to reconsider the place belonging to the school in the general task of education. The example of antiquity is very suggestive. Modern educators are again proposing that we put the accent on character formation rather than on didactic instruction dispensed by a teacher from behind the barrier of his desk. They insist upon the close, human bond that should be established between the master and his disciple. From another point of view, we can see interesting parallels between our clubs and youth movements and the analogous ancient institutions, the *hetaireiai* in Greece, and the *iuvenum collegia* in Rome.

Should our education be predominantly aesthetic or scientific and technical? No problem is more current. In antiquity it was already present in the form of the option between rhetoric and philosophy; on one side the beauty of the art of expression, on the other the severe discipline of rational truth. *Mutatis mutandis,* it is still the same problem, and our understanding of it draws on the arguments the Ancients had already formulated.

A more general, more profound problem of today brings to the fore another ancient question. What goal should education strive to achieve—the "whole man" or the technician? There are those concerned with the training of the technician. Others argue that there is a larger fundamental need to be fulfilled: namely, the acquisition by all men of a basic common and general culture—general in that it prevents the atrophy of the varied potentialities of the human being, and common to all men whatever the particular position they may occupy in the economy or the society, and therefore a warranty of the brotherhood and community of all.

This is a very serious issue; it involves us, like the ancients, with the ideal of civilization itself. It is a problem for today and for ever, and our debates revive issues that divided the utilitarian-minded Sophists and Rhetors from Socrates, Plato, and Isocrates (for in this matter the last two were allied against a common enemy). In later ages, the standard was to pass to Cicero, then Quintilian, and even to Galen, who kept alive the crusade of a high ideal of culture against the pragmatic physicians. The principle of general education—the Greeks called it *enkuklios paideia*—has since ancient times involved the opposition of the literary "arts" and the scientific "disciplines." In antiquity, as now, generous theories were occasionally in striking contrast to narrow, impoverished practice (as in Isocrates' treatment of mathematics).

The phrase *enkuklios paideia* and the opposition between the meaning the Greeks gave it and the connotation of the modern words formed on it ("cyclopedia," "encyclopedic") bring to mind another conflict familiar to us and the ancients—that conflict between the concerns of teachers and legislators, the first wanting a truly encyclopedic educational program, the second anxious to lighten the academic load on our children. In Greek, this is the distinction between *polumatheia* and *paideia.*

The existence of a highly advanced civilization in science, letters, and technology raises difficult problems for us reminiscent of those that faced classical antiquity in its maturity. The Alexandrians of the third century B.C. had already to ask themselves if it was possible for a fully developed civilization to retain the ideal of the universal man that had existed when their culture was younger. The Ionian natural philosophers of the sixth century B.C. and our own sixteenth-century humanists could be curious about everything and aspire to know everything. But does a moment come when the sum of knowledge of our entire civilization, which now covers a wide variety of subjects with great intensity, becomes much too complicated to be completely digested in the culture of one man? Here again, following Montaigne's lead, we hark back to the wisdom of the ancients, when we prefer a "well-made rather than a well-filled head."

Today we ask, "After the years specifically devoted to education, when the formation of the individual has been completed, what ideal of maturity should we hold before ourselves—the whole man or the insect specialized in the service of the beehive or the anthill?" We feel that this most disturbing question raises the spector of a new peril that increasingly threatens from within the very essence of our civilization—a new kind of barbarian, the "new Hun" which Herman Melville foresaw so prophetically, the atrocious Philistinism of the stultified technician in the service of a totalitarian society.

Our elders, the humanists of antiquity, knew this problem too. In the rich treasure of their medical literature exists a precious little treatise by Galen entitled *The Physician Is Also a Philosopher*—for *is,* read *may be* or *should be.* With great precision this contemporary of the Antonine emperors was already tracing the general lines of an argument that is still familiar to us moderns. He refused to confine himself to a narrow specialization and rejected as inadequate and too easy the comfortable solution of drawing a sharp line between the hours and minutes devoted to professional practice and those set aside for leisure and so-called disinterested culture. Galen affirmed that we encounter the great fundamental questions that lie in the philosopher's province when we probe more deeply into the problems implicit in the exercise of our profession. At the root of every technical skill, both Galen and the modern humanist insist, lie genuinely wider considerations which cannot be rejected by a flight from reality into some leisure activity that would ignore our fundamental engagement in humanity.

We have not said all there is to say; many aspects of the classical heritage in Western civilization could be added to the inventory: for example, urban planning. The regular, grid construction of our most modern cities is nothing more than the revival of an arrangement that was well known in Greek, Etruscan, and Roman antiquity. In the fifth century B.C. the original and innovating mind of Hippodamus of Miletus first formulated it and had the opportunity of putting it to practice in the model town of Thurium in Magna Graecia (southern Italy), the equivalent in those days of our western frontier. More recent development in city planning, such as civic centers and shopping centers, are closely related to their classical counterparts, the Greek *agora* and the Roman *forum,* once again through the now familiar processes of direct survival and revival through renaissance.

Mention must be made of a particularly pertinent aspect of the classical heritage. In a time like the present when our humane ideals are forced to undergo an ordeal under conditions that seem on the surface unfavorable to their survival and growth, an extraordinary example handed down to us from antiquity may yet have a role to play, a role quite different from the sort we have been discussing up to now. In the Hellenistic era and in the early period of the Roman Empire, ancient civilization knew a liberal age which, other things being equal, is roughly comparable to the experience of Europe in the nineteenth century and America in the twentieth. But we must not overlook the fact that this relatively free period fell between two others in which a far more restrictive spirit reigned, for it was preceded by the ancient Greek city-state and followed by the late Roman Empire. Yet even during these two periods classical humanism managed to be born, to spread, and to endure, certainly not without struggles, nor without suffering and martyrs. In the dark hours that the West undoubtedly has yet to encounter in one place or another, it will not be useless to contemplate the great examples of the ancient world, the men who were willing to suffer and in case of necessity to die for the ideal of the freedom of the mind, from Socrates to Cicero, from Justin Martyr to Saint John Chrysostom and Hypatia.

## III

The question that we must face finally is to determine what the future of this heritage will be in a civilization as active and as progressive as ours. Will it be preserved statically as a more and more distant memory which will be inevitably obliterated by the layers of dust that accumulate with the passage of generations? Or is it possible to conceive a new renaissance? Can the heritage of antiquity come to life again as it has so many times in the past, providing us with a source of inspiration and renewal of our living culture?

To the extent that the cultural heritage bequeathed to us by antiquity is composed of works of art, of concepts, and of human values of the highest order, it seems inconceivable that it should some day become outmoded and old-hat. As long as the West does not sink into a new barbarism, Homer will not cease to be what he has been for so many centuries, the poet par excellence, and the master of incomparable emotions. The young paperback book industry gave its editors many surprises, not the least of which was the fact that the *Iliad* and the *Odyssey* turned out to be best sellers. It is the glory of our civilization that passages like the death of Hector, Priam's prayer to Achilles, the meeting of Odysseus and Nausicaä, and his tales at Alcinoüs' banquet have retained for us today the same evocative power, the same profound scope, and the same deep significance that our predecessors found in them.

Homer is just one of many examples that could be cited; the same remarks could be repeated for much of the legacy of antiquity. Robert Browning, for example, suggests how much meaning "a chorus-ending from Euripides" may have for us; Charles Péguy reminds us that man may well make more and more overwhelming technological progress, but it is unimaginable that he should reach a stage where the wisdom of Plato becomes obsolete.

The existence of the ancient heritage is a source of riches and an insurance against barbarism for modern culture. Even if the arts and sciences of our civilization no longer develop in the same atmosphere of humble and ingenuous imitation of the ancients as they did in the Renaissance of the seventeenth century, a more subtle indirect influence may still make itself felt and be no less fertile for its indirection. Our architects no longer strive to construct churches and courthouses that are mere imitations of the Maison Carrée (a Roman temple in Nîmes) or the Parthenon, but I do not believe that any of them would deny the value of contemplating the Doric capitals of the Parthenon and the perfection of the irrational curves of their echinus.

The very antiquity of Greek civilization confers on it a privileged position. Because the early ancestors of the West had great minds, they could pose problems that are still our problems in a simpler and more concentrated form, or, as the chemists say, in a nascent state, which allowed them to submit these questions more easily to examination, to reduce them to relatively simple principles, in short, to explain them. We have already mentioned the case of politics; it is perhaps owing to the fact that the persistent questions of Western political life were presented to Aristotle and Cicero in the more reduced scale of the small city-state that they could formulate so precisely the outlines of their theories, while the political scientists of today are overwhelmed by the complexity of the societies and institutions of the great nations of our space age.

Similarly in the case of the problem of war, it has often been repeated that thanks to Thucydides the Peloponnesian War remains the most intelligible war of all history. However, there is a tremendous difference in the scale of these restricted conflicts between Hellenic city-states and our monstrous World Wars. It was the comparatively smaller scope of his subject which enabled Thucydides to impose upon it a strictly rational structure. And so he succeeded in analyzing this war with such intelligence that it has become a model and example for us to follow when we try to make at least partially intelligible other types of historical experience. One could cite numerous testimonies (Arnold J. Toynbee, for example, Albert Thibaudet in France, and many others) to show that the examination of Thucydides has aided our contemporaries in contemplating the limitless problems presented by their experience of the First and Second World Wars.

Such is the privilege of classical antiquity: an intelligence of extraordinary force and clarity applying itself to data sufficiently elementary to be totally exploitable. Our analysis of this intelligence in politics holds true also for other aspects of culture: for example, in music. We are likely to forget that the Greeks were a supremely musical people. Of course, compared with the mighty complexity of our great orchestral or choral works, Greek music appears to be an art of very limited means, a monody or a simple melodic line as tenuous as the song of a meadow lark. But Hellenic reason applied its marvelous analytical powers to it, and the theory of music in its formulations from Aristoxenus of Tarentum (a pupil of Aristotle in the fourth century B.C.) to Boethius (the last of the Roman philosophers in the sixth century A.D.) deserves the same praise as Thucydides' theory of war; it is the most intelligible that has ever been conceived. Twice in our history it has served as a model and point of departure for attempts to rethink the problems of music in the context of the transformations in musical practice; first at the time of the Carolingian Renaissance with Alcuin and his successors, then during the humanistic Renaissance starting from Glareanus and Zarlino and continuing to Rameau. The contemporary works of Louis Laloy, J. F. Mountford, and Ingemar Düring show that it could do us the same service and help us orient ourselves in the midst of the chaos of contemporary music.

Culture is not merely a congeries of already existing elements, riches, and positive values that can be preserved in an inanimate state; it belongs to the category of Becoming as much as to the category of Being. This means that culture, especially our modern Western culture, includes at least as many problems as answers. These problems have been raised in advance of us, but are still not solved, and we try gropingly to settle them, not without difficulty, argument, and uncertainty.

From this point of view the culture of classical antiquity seems to us to be more like an older brother than an ancestor. The questions that our civilization asks itself and debates are often to a large measure the same that the ancients asked themselves, and the clarity with which their genius illuminated them can help to light our own way in so far as our two situations are comparable.

Actually our cultural heritage must always be recreated; each age, each civilized world, and each man can and must take up again the dialogue with the past, asking his predecessors new questions, seeking examples or advice about the particular problems of his historical situation. Experience shows that the stock of the past is inexhaustible in practice because not the same aspects of human life and civilization interest every culture and stimulate it to appeal to the evidence preserved from former cultures.

If the study of the Greeks and the Romans seems to be a useless curiosity to many minds today, no more than an old-fashioned tradition that cannot be justified, it is often because we have gradually allowed our education to become rigid, routine, and quite unsuited to the times. What Greek or Latin texts have adolescents read? There is reason to fear that we have not exposed them to the ones which might have appealed to them the most directly or contributed the most constructively to their thinking about problems they face. We must revise the traditional image of the ancients that we have received, for example, by giving less place in our teaching and our reading to rhetoric and by putting more emphasis on pure poetry on the one hand and on the scientific spirit on the other. If every young Hellenist translated some proofs of Euclid he would see how modern Euclid's tone is and how rigorous his logic. The Latin encyclopedists, lesser minds without a doubt, but often unjustly scorned, also merit our attention. How many of us know that there existed in the time of the Christian emperors a real precursor of Leonardo da Vinci who anticipated many of our technical accomplishments, sometimes prophetically, sometimes fancifully? He is the anonymous author of the treatise *De Rebus Bellicis.*

The rediscovery of forgotten lessons or values does not come only as the result of our intellectual research or our free decisions; it is above all the consequence of the less premeditated evolution of history. Placed in new circumstances, we are inevitably led to ask the past different questions than the ones asked before our time; but parallels with the ancients are still striking. For example, one of the great differences that seemed to have been irreversibly established between ancient culture and our modern world lay in the fact that the former was a civilization of the *logos* relying on the primacy of the spoken word as the means of communication between men. With the triumph of Christianity, a learned religion that stressed the *graphê* or the written word of Scripture, and even more clearly with the advent of Gutenberg's movable type, we had become the "people of the book"—*ahl el ḳitâb,* as the Koran designates the Christians and the Jews. Our culture assumed the primacy of the written word in every respect. The writer has supplanted the orator, and in daily life the most humble acts of the economic or administrative world required letters, bills, and certificates. The Berbers and Arabs of

Maghreb were astounded at the consumption of printed and written material they witnessed after the installation of the French in their country during the nineteenth century. With some irony they called their colonizers *Ouled Karta,* the sons of paper.

Now suddenly the situation has been modified by the rapid development of technological innovations involving the spoken word: radio, television, the telephone, the phonograph, magnetic sound tapes and other recording processes. In one generation we have seen reborn the technical conditions of a civilization of the *logos*. It is already apparent how often we use the telephone or dictaphone when our fathers would have written a letter. To be sure, the consequences of these innovations make themselves felt only gradually, and it will probably take a long time for the mental habits acquired during centuries of a civilization based on writing to be lost or modified.

Still, many radical changes can already be observed. One can begin by noting the role played by television in American political life since the presidential election campaign of 1952. Aristotle claimed that a democratic state could not exist in a very large community. The maximum number of citizens seemed to him to be limited to several thousands, the largest number capable of hearing the voice of a leader speaking before a court or the assembled people. Now television has expanded the size of a democratic audience to the limits of a continent and will eventually extend it to the whole planet, thereby restoring to our modern masses the actual view and voice of the orator that Aristotle could only imagine with the dimensions of the Athenian *agora* or the Pnyx in mind.

The practical applications of these new techniques reach far beyond the limits of political life. Is there any need to mention the role of audio-visual devices in teaching or public communication? They are even beginning to transform the conditions of literary life. At present, the best and most effective way for a young poet to make himself known is not the publication of a printed book, but the recording on tape or discs of his own voice or an interpreter's reciting his poems. As this movement broadens, we moderns will return more and more to approximate the conditions that obtained for the exercise of the mind in classical antiquity. And the culture of tomorrow at least in that respect will perhaps be much closer to the past than today's or yesterday's have been, thus testifying to the truth of the statement of Horace that remains the motto of all true humanism: *"Multa renascentur quae iam cecidere"* (many forgotten things shall be born anew).

## *FOR ADDITIONAL READING*

*Acta Congressus Madvigiani, Hafniae MDMLIV.* 5 vols. Copenhagen, 1958. (Proceedings of the Second International Congress of Classical Studies, "The Classical Pattern of Modern Western Civilization.")

C. Bailey, ed. *The Legacy of Rome* (a collection of essays). Oxford, 1923.

F. Blatt. "Latin Influence on European Syntax," *Acta Congressus Madvigiani,* X, 33–69, 223–35.

A. Boëthius, J. Lauffray, A. Kriesis, and J. Ward Perkins. "Urbanism and Town-planning," *Acta Congressus Madvigiani,* IV.

C. M. Bowra. *The Greek Experience.* London, 1957.

I. Düring. "Impact of Greek Music on Western Civilization," *Acta Congressus Madvigiani,* I, 169–84.

C. P. Hadzits and D. M. Robinson, eds. *Our Debt to Greece and Rome* (a series of short books).

No. 35. H. O. Taylor. *Greek Biology and Medicine.*

No. 36. D. E. Smith. *Mathematics.*

No. 37. H. R. Fairclough. *Love of Nature among the Greeks and Romans.*

W. Jaeger. *Paideia, The Ideals of Greek Culture.* English ed. New York, 1939.

R. W. Livingstone, ed. *The Legacy of Greece* (a series of essays). Oxford, 1922.

J. F. Mountford. "Greek Music and its Relation to Modern Times," *Journal of Hellenic Studies,* XL (1920), 13–42.

G. Sarton. *A History of Science.* 2 vols. published. Cambridge, Mass., 1952.

K. Sörensen. "Latin Influence on English Syntax, a Survey with a Bibliography," *Acta Congressus Madvigiani,* V, 131–55.

## II

# MEDIEVAL THOUGHT: CHRISTIAN CONCEPTIONS OF LIFE

*Kenneth Scott Latourette*

The thought of Europe in the Middle Ages and indeed every phase of the life of medieval Europe bore the impress of Christianity. Because the kind of Christianity which contributed to the forming of medieval Europe was already several centuries old when what we call the Middle Ages began, to appreciate its role we must briefly review its background.

### I

At the outset Christianity was an obscure sect of Judaism. It faced the competition of scores of other religions that were seeking the allegiance of the peoples of the Roman Empire. As its name indicates, it owed its beginning to Christ, whom his adherents called the Anointed One and proclaimed as the Son of God, one in whom God had made Himself known as He had never been previously known and through whom God had acted for the eternal salvation of men.

The claim seemed preposterous at first, and Christianity appeared to have little prospect of winning against its rivals. In less than a hundred years after the crucifixion of Jesus, little groups of Christians were to be found in many of the cities of the Roman Empire, including Rome itself. Yet the emperors forbade any to become Christians and ordered their officials to exterminate what they branded as a disloyal and subversive movement. As the Christians multiplied, emperors undertook systematic measures to extirpate the Christians. The last of the general persecutions was by Diocletian, beginning in A.D. 303. In a striking reversal of fortunes it was followed in 312 by the conversion of Constantine, who had fought his way to the mastery of the Empire. At first he tolerated both Christianity and paganism, but his immediate successors put increasing restrictions on the non-Christian religions. In the latter half of the fourth century one of the family of Constantine, the Emperor Julian, attempted to restore the old faiths, but after about two years he perished in a war with the Persians, and Christianity quickly recovered from his efforts to stem its popularity. By the end of the fourth century the overwhelming majority of the population of the Roman Empire regarded themselves as Christians. By that time Christianity had began to spread beyond the borders of the Roman realms. The Armenians had made it their official religion. Christians constituted minorities in the Persian Empire, Rome's chief rival on the East, and were persecuted as supposed agents of Rome. Some of the Goths on the northern frontiers had adopted the faith.

## II

In the course of its rapid expansion Christianity developed an organization which embraced the entire Roman Empire. At the very beginning and while they were still small minorities, Christians gathered in what they called churches and spoke of all their number as being members of the Church. They called the Church the body of Christ, wherever it was found. Dissensions within the Church developed almost as soon as it was born, but Christians believed that by the express command of Christ they were to love one another. They sought to obey that injunction. Out of that dream and that purpose the Catholic Church arose. The Catholic Church had in its ample fold the majority of those who bore the Christian name. Its structure paralleled that of the Roman Empire. It was divided into provinces and dioceses. The names came from the administrative organization of the Roman Empire. In most cities the Catholic Church had as its head a bishop. Each province had an archbishop or metropolitan who lived in the chief city (or metropolis as it was called) and wielded a certain amount of authority over the bishops in the province. Each bishop headed a diocese. In several major cities there was a bishop who was called a patriarch and who had prestige and influence in a wide area and to some extent in the entire Catholic Church. The chief of the patriarchs were in Rome, Constantinople, Antioch, Jerusalem, and Alexandria.

The Church of Rome early came to have an outstanding place in the Catholic Church. Its bishop claimed preeminence over the other bishops and patriarchs. In time the title of pope was reserved for him. His authority was often challenged by other bishops and patriarchs, but during the Middle

Ages it was acknowledged by the majority of the Christians in western Europe. The Bishop of Rome, or the pope, owed his leadership in the Catholic Church to at least five factors. (1) Rome was long the capital of the Empire and for that reason the Church of Rome would naturally early be accorded a primacy by the other churches. (2) Peter, regarded as the chief of the original Twelve Apostles selected by Jesus as His intimates, was held to have suffered martyrdom in Rome. Catholics believed that Jesus had entrusted to Peter the keys to the kingdom of Heaven and had made him the foundation stone of the entire Church. They counted Peter as the first of the popes. (3) Paul, the outstanding Christian missionary in the first century, had also been in Rome and was believed to have met a martyr's death there. (4) In the controversies that threatened the unity of the Catholic Church, with one or two possible exceptions, the Church of Rome, headed by the pope, took positions to which the majority ultimately agreed. (5) The Church of Rome was fortunate in its leadership in some critical times. For example, Leo I, "the Great," who was pope from 440 to 461, had a decisive role in the Council of Chalcedon (451), which adopted a creed on the relation of the divine and human natures of Christ that remained standard in the Catholic Church. He persuaded Attila the Hun not to march on Rome and induced Genseric, the Vandal chief, to be lenient in his occupation of the city. Gregory I, also called the Great, pope from 590 to 604, promoted law and order in a time when wars and division were beginning to usher in the "dark ages" in western Europe; by his writings, Pope Gregory I helped to set a standard for the Catholic faith in the West. There were many others who, when the Roman Empire was in decay, gave distinction to the papacy and strengthened the Catholic Church.

A principal controversy which troubled the Catholic Church centered largely on the relation of the human and the divine in Jesus. Most Christians believed that Jesus was both God and man, but they were not agreed on how the two were present in Jesus. Some held that God as Father had created Jesus and so made Jesus subordinate to Him. Others said that God had always been Father, Son, and Holy Spirit. Additional issues also divided the Christians.

To settle these questions attempts were made to determine exactly what had been taught by the Apostles. As they had been intimate companions of Jesus and eye-witnesses of his deeds, death, and post-resurrection appearances, their accounts were esteemed to be authoritative. Although he had presumably not seen Jesus in the flesh, Paul was believed to have been personally commissioned by the risen Christ: what he had preached and written was regarded as equally dependable. It was contended that certain truths had been held everywhere and always by all who deserved the name of Christian. To establish the validity of what from the beginning had been authentic Christianity, four methods were employed by the Catholic Church. The first was called apostolic succession. It was maintained that before their deaths the Apostles had appointed, with the consent of the Christians in each locality, bishops who would transmit what they had taught. These bishops had, in turn, passed on that faith to their successors. The attempt was made, therefore, to determine the lists of the bishops who could be traced back to the Apostles. Such bishops were held to have the right to ordain clergy, who as their representatives and under their direction would serve the Christians in their dioceses. A second method was to determine which of the many writings that were being circulated among Christians were written by the Apostles or their immediate companions. In that fashion, as the outcome of a gradually achieved consensus, the twenty-seven books which now constitute the New Testament were listed as genuine and inspired by the Holy Spirit. They were held to be the climax of books of pre-Christian Judaism, the Old Testament, in which was believed to be recorded the course of the Divine revelation, that prepared the way for Christ and the Church. The third method was the formulation of creeds, which were succinct statements of the Christian faith. Several such creeds had been composed for particular churches, but eventually two were universally accepted in the Catholic Church. One was called the Apostles' Creed, so named because it was believed to be a brief summary of the teaching of the Apostles, and the other, somewhat longer but still brief, was the Nicene Creed.

The Nicene Creed took its name from a fourth method by which the Catholic Church sought to arrive at agreement as to what constitutes the Christian faith: ecumenical councils. An ecumenical council was a gathering in which the entire Catholic Church was represented and which, therefore, could speak officially for that Church. The first was convened by the Emperor Constantine at Nicaea in 325. It was called to settle what was known as the Arian controversy, Arius, a priest in the Church of Alexandria, had insisted that the Son had a beginning, but that God is without beginning. After vigorous debate the majority of the Council held that Christ was "true God from true God," that there never was a time when the Son did not exist, that through Him all things were made, and that "for us men and our salvation" He was made flesh, suffered, and rose again. The creed which later bore the name of Nicaea was a further elaboration of the statement adopted by that Council. A large minority continued to hold to the position associated with the name of Arius. Indeed, for some time they seemed to be in control of the Catholic Church. Led by Athanasius, Bishop of Alexandria, and supported by the pope, the Nicene party eventually won, but the Arians, although branded as heretics, persisted for several centuries, and their form of Christianity was in fact embraced by many of the Goths. At irregular intervals additional ecumenical councils were held in an effort to reach a consensus on other issues that troubled the unity of the Catholic Church. Several councils, like that of Nicaea, were followed by a permanent division of the Church and the exclusion of minorities from what the majority called the Catholic Church.

## III

Inevitably, the attempts to formulate the central beliefs of Christians made use of the philosophies from that Greco-Roman world which constituted the original environment of the Church. Some of the basic Christian convictions, however, were not found in those philosophies and were even alien to them. Indeed, so radically different was the core of the Gospel that it could not be made to fit into any existing philosophy or system without doing violence to both. As Paul discerningly said, to the Jews the cross (which was central in the Christian faith) seemed weakness and was a stumbling block, and to those Greeks who were nurtured in a rationalistic tradition the cross appeared stark foolishness and quite irrational. Yet Christian thinkers could not avoid the effort to put into systematic intellectual terms the distinctive Christian beliefs. In doing so they had to avail themselves of the terminology and the conceptions in the philosophies with which they and their contemporaries were familiar. Such writings by the more well-known thinkers were treasured by Christians and helped to shape Christian conceptions of life both during the Middle Ages and in our own day. Such names as Irenaeus, Tertullian, and Origen of the second and third centuries, and Gregory of Nyssa, of the fourth century, were long revered. Although not a profound thinker, Pope Gregory the Great also left writings that did much to give form to the faith held by the Christians of medieval Europe.

Augustine of Hippo (354–430) made an especially deep impression on the Christian thought of the Middle Ages. He was born and reared in North Africa, with a pagan father and a deeply religious Christian mother. In his teens he rejected his mother's faith. Intellectually brilliant and emotionally highly sensitive, he became a teacher, first in North Africa, then in Rome, and later in Milan. For a time he was attracted by Manichaeism, a religion that incorporated much from Christianity and from various Eastern faiths, but eventually he found it unconvincing. He next was impressed by Neoplatonism, a then popular form of Platonism, but it did not meet his deepest needs. He sought emancipation from the passions which he had attempted to satisfy by taking a concubine. He had not been able to free himself from what he regarded as his moral enslavement. Then, in Milan, he came under the spell of the preaching of a great archbishop, Ambrose, and found the release he had been seeking. He still held to much of Neoplatonism, but he now found in the doctrine of the incarnation something beyond its worship of the abstract ideal. The Word become flesh in Christ—this was not Neoplatonism, but Augustine became convinced that it was the key to the mystery of the universe and of life.

Augustine wrote prodigiously. His moving autobiography, the *Confessions,* gives insight into the personal experience which lay back of his mature Christian philosophy. He saw in himself as in those about him a basic corruption which could not be overcome by a man's own effort. He declared that only the grace of God—the love which no one deserves or can earn and which came from God into the world through Christ—could rescue a man from his otherwise hopeless condition. God in His great mercy, so Augustine maintained, had chosen (elected) some to receive that grace. If a man were of the elect, that grace would not be defeated, but, irresistible, it would win him to repentance and faith. He would, moreover, persevere in it to the end. If he was not of the elect nothing he did could save him from the condemnation that was justly visited on him because of his sins. Any attempt on his part to win the favor of God, so Augustine maintained, was tainted with the self-interest which is of the essence of sin. Nor, so Augustine said, could any one be certain in this life that he is among the elect, for any assurance that a man might cherish would breed pride, and pride would be evidence that God's grace had not yet saved him. In these convictions Augustine believed himself supported by the experience and writings of Paul.

Augustine was vigorous in his denunciation of the teachings of a contemporary, Pelagius, a British monk, who said that if a man really desired to do so, he could keep God's commandments by his own efforts. Augustine maintained, however, that through the Catholic Church God's grace was mediated to men. He advocated the baptism of infants, holding that it washed away the inheritance of original sin of Adam's rebellion against God. Baptism and the Eucharist (or the Lord's Supper, the Communion, or the Mass, to give its various designations) he believed to be necessary to salvation. Through God's grace men are enabled to do good works, so he said, and are gradually transformed. Yet baptism, taking the Communion, and good works did not assure one of election. Even with them, Augustine declared, a man might not have the gift of perseverance and so would ultimately be lost. "Grace," "election," "predestination," "irresistible grace," and "the perseverance of the saints" were terms which were features of the Christian conception of life in Europe in the Middle Ages and later.

Augustine concerned himself not only with the eternal fate of the individual. He was also deeply involved in the problems of the society in which he lived. In his day the Roman Empire was decaying. To the men of the Mediterranean world, ignorant or at best only dimly aware of the great contemporary cultures in India and China, that Empire was identical with civilization. When, in 410, as Augustine was approaching old age, Alaric and his Goths took and sacked Rome itself, terror gripped men's hearts. To them Rome was the symbol of law and order and of all that was stable in human society. Many pagans declared that its fall was due to the acceptance of Christianity and to the desertion of the gods who had made Rome great. Augustine set himself to refute that diagnosis. To answer it he formulated his understanding of history. In his *City of God* he contrasted the earthly city, represented by corrupt, pagan Rome, with the heavenly city, the city of God. He pointed out that the gods whom pagans had believed responsible for the greatness of Rome had not been able to save Troy in the Trojan War. Moreover, when cities that depended on the gods had been captured by pagans, the latter killed even those who had taken refuge in the temples, and the gods had been unable to protect their devotees. Whereas, so he said, when the Goths (barbarians though they were, but Christians) took Rome, they spared those who sought sanctuary in the churches. The heavenly city, the city of God, Augustine declared, is described in the Bible and is made up of the holy angels and those of the human race who have been saved by God's grace. Its citizens have peace of heart and peace with God. It is enjoyed in this life only by those who have faith but hereafter is to be shared eternally with God—whom the citizens of the heavenly kingdom will then see.

Augustine's writings were among the most revered by the men of the Middle Ages. Indeed, centuries later, the Emperor Charlemagne delighted in having *The City of God* read to him. Men of scholarly attainments regarded all that Augustine wrote as of major importance. He did much to shape not only the theology but also the entire outlook on life of the men of the Middle Ages, and his influence has persisted into our own times. Significantly, Augustine was far more influential in the Western, Latin-using portion of the Catholic Church than in the Eastern section, which had Greek as its major literary language. Here was one of the indications of the developing differences which, as we are to see, were to issue in the separation of the two great wings of the Catholic Church.

## IV

Long before Augustine the Catholic Church, of which he was a bishop and a loyal son, was an inclusive unity which embraced the majority of the population of the Roman Empire. It also had developed an organization and forms of worship and discipline which were to characterize it in the Middle Ages and were to do much to instill and nourish what were esteemed Christian conceptions of life. Very early a distinction was made between the clergy and the laity. The clergy—bishops, priests, deacons, etc.—had the spiritual direction of the laity. They conducted public worship and administered the sacraments.

The sacraments were a means by which grace was transmitted to the faithful. By the fourteenth century the church recognized seven sacraments: baptism, confirmation, penance, the Eucharist, extreme unction, marriage, and ordination. Baptism went back to the very beginning of the faith and was the means of admission to the Church. For centuries it was normally by immersion, and that form persisted in the Eastern wing of the Church. Preferably it was by a member of the clergy, but in emergency a layman might act. In the Western Church confirmation was administered by the bishop by the laying on of his hands, and through it the believer was supposed to receive the Holy Spirit. Penance was associated with the confession of sins and their forgiveness. In the early centuries some sins permanently excluded from the Church those of the baptized who had committed them. Other sins, although serious, if properly confessed did not prevent the restoration of the sinner to the congregation. In time even the more serious sins did not finally separate the penitent from the Church. But offenders were kept from the Communion for longer or shorter periods until declared forgiven. During the Middle Ages and later the normal form of confession was privately to a priest or bishop. After examination the clergyman could declare the sin forgiven and would prescribe some act or acts as a discipline to aid in the amendment of life. The Eucharist was the service of Holy Communion; according to the Church it was instituted by Christ at His last supper with the Apostles. It became the central act of worship of the Church and was commonly known as the Mass. By its name the Eucharist included the giving of thanks for the redemption wrought by Christ in His death. Following the example of Christ and His command, the bread and the wine were consecrated by the priest or bishop and the laity partook of them. Originally both the bread and the wine were given to the laity, but in the course of the Middle Ages, to prevent its desecration, the wine was withheld from the laity and received only by the clergy. The belief grew that by the act of consecration the bread and the wine became the body and the blood of Christ. In the thirteenth century "transubstantiation" was officially endorsed by the Church of Rome (or Western Church). This was the belief that although the bread and the wine continued to look and taste like bread and wine, by the act of consecration their "substance" had been changed, so that they had become the flesh and blood of Christ. Extreme unction was given to the dying by the priest and permitted a final confession of sins before facing God. By making marriage a sacrament administered by a priest or a bishop, it was given the blessing and placed under the control of the Church. The sanctity of the nuptial bond and of the family was thus presumably assured and safeguarded. Ordination as a priest of the Church, the last of the sacraments, could be given only by a bishop.

The search for a special discipline for those Christians desiring a form of life even more rigorous than that implied in the sacramental system gave rise to various monastic movements. Monasticism helped develop an ideal of life and institutions which were to affect profoundly the Christian conceptions of life held in Western Europe during the Middle Ages. Monasticism arose chiefly from the desire to attain perfectly the Christian life. Very early many Christians had held that because of its rejection of the flesh, celibacy was a higher way of life than the married state. Moreover, from the first, fasting was also practiced. Gradually the conviction grew in the West that deacons, priests, and bishops must be celibate. Late in the fourth century a pope had enjoined celibacy on all priests, and a council had commanded deacons, priests, and bishops to remain unmarried. Pope Leo the Great extended that rule to subdeacons. In the Eastern Catholic Church only the bishop was required to be unmarried, or if married he had to separate himself from his wife before being raised to that dignity; subdeacons, deacons, and priests might be married before but not after ordination.

Monasticism arose in the third century in Egypt. In part it was a protest against the laxity of life of the majority of Christians. As Christianity spread and won an increasing proportion of the population of the Roman Empire, the moral level of the rank and file of its adherents tended to differ but little from that of the pagans. In contrast, an increasing number of Christians believed that the command and example of Jesus called them to abstain from marriage, to renounce all private possessions, and to follow a life of prayer and of extreme physical austerity. Some followed the way of the hermit, living in complete solitude. Others, although hermits, dwelt near enough to other hermits to permit fellowship and might have over them one of their number as a director. Still others lived in a community, a monastery, for which rules were soon created. Each monastery was surrounded by a wall and had within it cells for its members, a church, a refectory, a kitchen, a storehouse for food, workshops, and an infirmary. The monastery had its regular hours for prayer, both private and collective. Some form of labor was compulsory, the study of the Bible was required, food and dress were to be simple, and no private ownership of property was permitted.

Long before the Middle Ages monasticism had become a feature of Christianity in Western Europe. It had several pioneers and developed a number of forms. After his conversion, for example, Augustine remained unmarried and, although he was not a monk, he gathered about him a number of clergy who had a common rule of life. A generation or so before Augustine, Martin, a soldier at the time of his conversion, later constrained by the Christians of Tours to become their bishop, lived as a hermit in a cell outside the city and was joined by admirers until in time a monastic community arose. A contemporary of Martin of Tours but from a very different background, Jerome, noted for his literary work and his scholarship, led an ascetic life in Rome, eventually established himself in Bethlehem, built a monastery there, and followed the routine of a monk. Ambrose of Milan encouraged monasticism. In Ireland, where Christianity spread in the fifth century, with Patrick (a contemporary of Augustine) as the most distinguished missionary, a special form of monasticism sprang up which continued for centuries and had a large share in the spread of the faith among the Anglo-Saxons in Great Britain and among the Germanic peoples on the Continent. In the fifth century Cassiodorus founded two monasteries on his estates in the south of Italy. In one of them he promoted the solitary, ascetic life and the other he made a center of learning that encouraged scholarship in other monasteries.

Benedict of Nursia (c.480–c.553) was the author of a rule which in one form or another was followed by a large proportion of the monasteries of the

Middle Ages. Indeed, Benedictine monasteries are still numerous in our own day. Benedict was a native of Nursia, a town north-east of Rome. In his youth his parents sent him to study in that city. Shocked by the vices and frivolities of the nominal Christians of the metropolis, in his late teens he became a hermit. Twelve monasteries eventually sprang up under his influence and leadership. In his forties he established a monastery on the summit of Monte Cassino, between Naples and Rome. There he devised a rule which stood the test of centuries. It envisaged a self-contained and self-supporting community governed by an abbot who was chosen by its members. The monks were to take vows of poverty, chastity, and obedience. Each hour of the day was provided for, with a service every three hours, and periods for sleep, eating, labor, supervised reading, meditation, and private prayer. In the community services the entire Psalter was recited each week, readings were selected from the Old and New Testaments, hymns were sung, prayers were said, including the Lord's Prayer, and Mass was celebrated. Dress and food were simple, fasting was practised at regular times, silence was required at meals and after the last service of the day, and joking and laughing were discouraged. Yet meals, while simple, were adequate, and extreme asceticism was frowned on. Labor might be in the fields or in the library. Benedict himself was a layman and so were many of his monks, but a place was made for priests, for they were needed to say Mass. In the darkest hours of the Middle Ages the Benedictine monasteries were havens of quiet, orderly life and centers both of worship and of learning. Pope Gregory the Great (c.540–604) became a Benedictine in his youth, founded a monastery in his ancestral mansion, and wrote a biography of Benedict. The priests who were members of a monastic community were called "regulars" because they were governed by monastic rules—*"regula."* Priests who were not in the monasteries were designated "seculars" because they lived in the world—*"seculum."*

## V

For a time it seemed that with the decay of the Roman Empire Christianity would disappear. By the end of the fifth century to be a Roman citizen was to be a Christian and, with notable exceptions, Christianity had not spread widely beyond the bounds of the Roman Empire but was identified with that realm. The threat to Christianity came from a succession of invasions from the north and the southeast. From the north issued wave after wave of barbarians. Many of the barbarians were incorporated into the Roman armies.

Others defeated the armies of Rome and carved out realms for themselves within what had been the Roman boundaries. The invasions are sometimes dated from the Battle of Adrianople in A.D. 378, when the Goths defeated a Roman army and slew the Emperor Valens. They continued to the end of the tenth century, when the Northmen, who had been ravaging much of Western Europe, were converted and their assimilation to Christian culture had made significant headway. From the southeast came the Arabs, bearers of a new religion, Islam. They subdued about half of what had been the Roman Empire—from Syria and Palestine along the southern Mediterranean and north almost to the Pyrenees. Within their realms the Christian communities shrank. Although they persisted in some areas, notably in the Iberian Peninsula, Sicily, western Asia, and Egypt, they completely disappeared in North Africa, an area which had produced such notable Christians as Augustine. If in about the year 700 a traveler from China, then the strongest, wealthiest, and most highly civilized empire on the globe, had visited the Mediterranean world, he would probably have reported that Christianity was clearly on the way to extinction.

Yet in these dark days Christianity was spreading among the northern invaders. By the year 1500, except for the Jews, all of western Europe was professedly Christian. This conversion of western Europe required hundreds of years. Before the close of the fourth century many of the Goths had accepted the faith; indeed, Alaric and the Goths who sacked Rome in 410 were already Christians. For several generations, however, most of the Christians among the Goths and Vandals were Arians, not Catholics. The Burgundians, who established themselves in Gaul early in the fifth century, were the first of the German tribes to become predominantly Catholic. Near the end of that century the Franks, ultimately dominant in Gaul, followed their king, Clovis, to the baptismal font and as Catholics. In the seventh century the Anglo-Saxons, the Germanic invaders of Great Britain, accepted the Catholic form of the faith, partly through missionaries sent from Rome, at the outset dispatched by Pope Gregory the Great, and partly through monks from Ireland. In the eighth century the Catholic Church was planted in the Rhine Valley, chiefly by missionaries from England with Boniface as their outstanding leader. In the eighth century Charlemagne forced baptism on the Saxons. The tenth century brought the beginnings of the faith among the Magyars and in Scandinavia, and in the next century most of the Magyars, Danes, Norwegians, and Swedes conformed. By the fifteenth century the Wends (Slavs) in what was later Germany, the Poles, the Czechs, the Finns, the Lithuanians, and the other non-Germanic peoples on the east and south shores of the Baltic were converted. Late in the fifteenth century—by an interesting coincidence in the year which marked the first voyage of Columbus to America—Ferdinand and Isabella, who had financed that expedition, erased the Kingdom of Granada, the last Moslem political foothold on the Iberian Peninsula. Early in the seventeenth century the Moriscos, former Moslems who had outwardly accepted the Christian faith but who were suspected of still clinging to Islam, were expelled from Spain.

As characteristics of this spread of Christianity in western Europe, we must note that over a thousand years were required to complete it—more than twice the length of time that had been sufficient to effect the nominal conversion of the peoples of the Roman Empire. The process began before the Middle Ages and was not consummated until after Europe had emerged from that era. Although we do not have exact statistics, probably western and central Europe at the height of the Middle Ages did not have as large a population as that of the Roman Empire in its most prosperous period. The population of Medieval Europe certainly did not cover a larger area than the Empire. The conversion of western and central Europe of the Middle Ages was accomplished in the main through two agencies—the monks and the princes. The monks initiated the process of conversion, usually at the outset in the face of persecution, and completed it through the instruction of the professedly Christian community. In almost every area the adoption of the faith did not pass beyond minorities until the ruler took the lead. His subjects then conformed. In several areas, as among the Saxons, the Wends, some of the Baltic peoples, and the Moslems of Spain, force was employed to bring compliance. Acceptance was by a social or political unit as a whole. For millions only a nominal Christianity ensued, with slight if any comprehension of the real meaning of the faith.

## VI

The Christianity which eventually triumphed in the West had Rome and the papacy as its center. As the Roman Empire disintegrated the existing structure of the Catholic Church fell apart. Since the Catholic Church had been in the main coterminous with the Roman realm and had modeled its organization in large part on the framework of the state, when the scaffolding collapsed the Catholic Church was not strong enough to preserve its own unity. The resulting fragments were largely identified with the racial divisions and jealousies that the Empire had brought into an uneasy cohesion. The ostensible reasons for the resulting divisions were disagreements over doctrine, but the major cause was what we would now call nationalism. Thus the majority of the Egyptians, most of the Syrians, and the Armenians rejected the formulation of the creeds by the Council of Chalcedon (451) and became respectively the Coptic, the Jacobite, and the Gregorian Church. But the basic cause of their dissent was restlessness under the domination of the Greeks who controlled the Eastern or Byzantine continuation of the Roman Empire, which had its capital in Constantinople. For several centuries the Western wing of the Catholic Church headed by the Pope and the Eastern wing with the Bishop of Constantinople, better known as the Ecumenical Patriarch, as its ranking ecclesiastic, maintained an uneasy unity. However, by about the twelfth century they had drifted apart. Repeated efforts were made to avoid division and to restore unity once division had occurred, but while minorities from the Eastern wing held to Rome, the majority resolutely kept aloof. Contributing divisive influences were differences in customs and in creed, but the chief obstacle to continuing union was the insistence of the Western wing that the Pope be acknowledged the authoritative head of the Catholic Church. Adherents of the Eastern wing claimed the title of Orthodox and insisted that they continued the faith as it had been delivered by Christ and His Apostles, uncorrupted by what they called the heresies of the other parts of the Catholic Church. The Western wing of the Catholic Church was in some respects the ecclesiastical continuation of the Latinized portion of the Roman Empire. The Bishop of Rome had the prestige of that city, augmented by the association with Peter and Paul that was discussed earlier. Latin was the official language of what was often and correctly called the Roman Catholic Church.

The Roman Catholic Church more nearly controlled the civilization of western Europe in the Middle Ages than did the "Orthodox" continuation of the Catholic Church that of eastern Europe. The Christian conception of life which came to prevail in western Europe in the Middle Ages held that the Church directed by the pope and the bishops should control every aspect of collective and individual spiritual life. In the near chaos which prevailed in much of western Europe as the Roman Empire disintegrated, the bishops and the pope felt themselves under obligation to step into the breach and assume some of the functions formerly discharged by the Roman state. Several of the barbarian kings who ruled in fragments of the former empire were at first very weak, and in many areas in the ages before medieval civilization came to its flowering the Church was the main and at times the only bulwark of law and order. The Church gradually developed what was called canon law, modeled in part on Roman law, and had courts to enforce obedience. For centuries the monasteries, later supplemented by schools around the bishops' churches (the cathedrals), were the only centers where scholarship and teaching continued. In Rome, shrunken to the dimensions of a small town living amid the ruins of former grandeur, many of the occupants of the throne of Peter before the tenth century were extremely able and high-minded. Indeed, in the multitudinous welter of warring principalities and states that succeeded the breakup of Roman imperial rule the papacy managed to prevent the Catholic Church in the West from falling apart into many weak churches, each subject to the whims of the local secular prince. Here was a growing central authority that brought a degree of unity. The papal power, beset by many problems, was reinforced by what was called the Donation of Constantine. That document, probably written in the eighth century, purported to have as its author the Emperor Constantine. It described the latter's conversion and baptism, told of the healing of his leprosy through the pope, and said that out of gratitude he was giving to the pope and his successors his palace in Rome and "the city of Rome and all the provinces, districts, and cities of Italy or of the Western regions." Throughout the Middle Ages the document was not seriously questioned. Only in the fifteenth century was it proved a forgery.

In the tenth century the papacy was captured by a succession of weak and corrupt pontiffs who owed their appointments to rival Roman families. In the eleventh century a fresh surge of life in the Church again brought to the papacy able men, who sought to use their position both to cleanse the Church of its corruption and to bring the entire life of western Europe to approximate the standards set by Christ and the Apostles. Outstanding among them were Hildebrand (c.1025–1085), who reigned as Gregory VII from 1073 to 1085, and Innocent III (c.1160–1216) who was pope from 1196 to his death. Innocent III is usually said to have brought the medieval papacy to the apex of its power. He held that as the successor of Peter, the pope had authority over all the churches, that Christ had left to Peter the governance of the entire world, and that while kings had their functions by divine commission their dignity and splendor were derived from the pontifical power, much as the moon received its light from the sun. Pope Boniface VIII, who reigned from 1294 to 1303, declared in the bull *Unam Sanctam* that "it is altogether necessary to salvation for every human creature to be subject to the Roman pontiff." Here was the effort to bring all mankind to conform to a Christian rule of life. Although Charlemagne revived the Roman Empire in the West in 800, his coronation on Christmas Day of that year was officiated over by the pope—presumably on the latter's initiative. In 962 a descendant of Charlemagne, Otto I, "the Great," became the founder of what was known as the Holy Roman Empire of the German Nation, an institution which endured to the beginning of the nineteenth century. He too was crowned by the pope. For centuries no coronation to that office was held to be valid unless made by that pontiff. In several countries bishops and archbishops sought similarly to bring those under their jurisdictions to a higher level of faith and morals.

The parish system, at the other end of the scale from the papacy, flourished in the Middle Ages as the cities that had characterized the Roman Empire dwindled or disappeared. It became a means by which the Church in a predominantly rural society could effectively reach the rank and file of its children. Also at the local level, the more pious and more devoted Christians were shepherded by the monasteries.

The monasteries chronically tended to fall away from the high ideals which had brought them into being. They were endowed by pious benefactors, but many of the monks succumbed to idle and physically comfortable living and even worse. But repeatedly through the centuries reforming movements arose with more austere standards. Among them were the Cluny monasteries, which began in the tenth century; the Cistercians, who arose in the eleventh century and who had as their most famous leader Bernard of Clairvaux (1090–1153); the Carthusians, also in the eleventh century; and the Augustinian Canons, inspired by the example of Augustine and founded by a friend of Bernard of Clairvaux. In the thirteenth century came the Friars—chief among them the Franciscans, Dominicans, Augustinians, and Carmelites—who sought by preaching, teaching, and pastoral care to take the Gospel to the masses, especially those gathered in the growing cities. Unlike the older monastic orders, which had lived behind walls and secluded from the world, they went out among the people.

The Franciscans, later to become the largest group of the Friars, were founded by Francis of Assisi (1182–1226), the son of a well-to-do merchant. After several years of youthful revelry, Francis was converted and in imitation of Christ began a life of complete poverty, service to the sick, and preaching the Gospel to the poor. A small circle of followers gathered about him. He called them the Minor or Humbler Brethren (*Ordo Fratrum Minorum*).

They went about the towns and countryside of central Italy, a joyous band, subsisting on such alms as were given them. They soon multiplied rapidly and spread to many countries. Francis remained a layman, but the order early included priests. After the death of their founder, the Franciscans suffered from divisions, largely between those who held to strict observance of poverty and those who relaxed the rule.

In Western Christianity, then, papacy, parish, and monastery were sources of an activism which endeavored to influence all aspects of the life of men and, eventually, to reach out and transform all mankind.

## VII

In contrast, the "Orthodox" branch of the Catholic Church was more passive, chiefly because it was in the Eastern continuation of the Roman Empire. The rulers of the Empire in its pagan days had controlled religion in their domains. They had the title of *Pontifex Maximus,* or chief priest of the official cults. When the Emperors became Christian and made Christianity the state religion, they insisted on continuing that function. They could not, however, be priests, so they had to grant the Church a nearer approach to independence than they had the pagan religions. Still they demanded a major voice in the affairs of the Church. Thus Constantine called the Council of Nicaea, presided at its opening sessions, and paid the travel expenses of the attending bishops. Later emperors also took vigorous initiative in the Church's administration. For example, the Council of Chalcedon was called by the Emperor Marcian. After the sixth century, however, the Roman Empire from its capital (at that time Constantinople) was unable to make its authority effective in most of what had been its Western domains. Except for its capture by the Fourth Crusade in 1204 and its occupation by the "Latins" until 1261, Constantinople remained the seat of the Eastern or Byzantine continuation of the Roman Empire until its capture by the Turks in 1453. The Turks, who were Moslems, gave the Church in their realms even less autonomy than had the Christian emperors. Because of the long Byzantine tradition of imperial religious prerogatives and the Turkish rule, the Orthodox Church was much more subservient to the state than was the Western Church. This was also true of its offshoots in Bulgaria and Russia.

The other churches in the East and in Africa had even less liberty than the Orthodox Church. From their beginnings, the Nestorians were a minority in the realms of the Zoroastrian Persian emperors and were subject to intermittent persecution. In the seventh century the Moslem Arab flood overwhelmed the Persian Empire and wiped out the Roman Empire from Syria through Egypt and North Africa. The Nestorians, Copts, Jacobites, and Armenians were henceforward on the defensive and could do no more than preserve their existence and their traditional worship.

In both the East and the West, whether active or passive, Christianity influenced profoundly the lives of the people and the history of their institutions. The achievement in the Greco-Roman world had been notable. As we have seen, from its humble and unpromising beginnings Christianity in the West had supplanted all its rivals except Judaism and had created in the Catholic Church a structure which outlived the Empire. It had stimulated the creation of strikingly new theologies and had modified morals and the ideals of marriage and the family. Eventually it made an impression on the laws. But it had created nothing which was basically novel in the patterns of government. By adopting the Stoic and Biblical theory of a just war it had, in fact, compromised the pacifism held by some of the early Christians. It had also done little or nothing to alter the economic life of the Empire.

In medieval Europe, Christianity was to place its imprint on every phase of an emerging civilization; but it is a mistake to call the civilization of medieval Europe really Christian, for in spite of the official profession of the Christian faith and the dreams of great idealists, lay and clerical, it never conformed fully to Christian standards. Much of it was palpably un-Christian and was even, in practice, diametrically opposed to Christian teachings. Yet all aspects of that civilization bore some impress of the faith. Indeed, the Christian conception of life developed in the European Middle Ages was based upon the dream of a society which in its every phase would embody Christian standards.

At the height of the Middle Ages (c.1300) the rival pagan cults had disappeared or had been driven underground. Church and state made efforts to teach all the population the rudiments of the Christian religion, especially those embodied in the Lord's Prayer and the Apostles' Creed. Much of the life of the rural and village communities centered around the parish church. In the cities church buildings multiplied. For the populace, largely illiterate, religious instruction was given through sermons, statues, stained glass windows, and plays and pageants built on Biblical and other Christian themes and stories. Reformers stressed the training of the parish clergy and urged that the rule of celibacy be enforced. Financial support for churches came through endowments and tithes. The latter were a matter of law as well as custom. The pageantry of the Church's services gave variety to what for multitudes was an otherwise drab existence. Since a large proportion of the parish clergy had only the minimum of education needed for the Mass and the other sacraments, collections of sermons prepared and circulated by diocesan and other ecclesiastical authorities aided their preaching. The coming of the itinerant Friars in the thirteenth century made for more popular preaching, some of it very informal and using the vernacular. Biblical stories and the lives of the saints became the familiar property of the rank and file. Attendance at Mass on Sundays was in principle obligatory. The breviary, an abridged compilation of prayers, Scriptural passages, and other religious literature, had a major development. Originally designed for the "regulars," it spread to the "secular" clergy for use in their collective services and their private devotions.

Yet, although the vast majority thus became nominally Christian and some acquaintance with Christian teachings and ethical standards was widespread, many things contributed to keep the religious life of medieval Europe far below the standards set forth by Christ and the New Testament writers. As in all ages, passion, self-interest, and other sins warred against the commands of Christ. Men might and did admire as saints those whose lives embodied the Christian ideal. Popular acclaim was given them, and the ecclesiastical authorities accorded them recognition by canonization, thus commending their virtues as worthy of emulation by Christians. Yet, although a few approximated to the Christian ideal and were admired, the practice of the multitudes both of high and low estate fell far below what was commended and preached. Although the worship of the old gods disappeared, many survivals of pre-Christian religious beliefs and customs persisted in what the Church labeled as superstitions. In spite of the rule of celibacy, which the reformers sought to enforce, concubinage was widespread among both the parish priests and the bishops. Pluralism flourished, and many of the clergy held two or more benefices (ecclesiastical posts) and received the stipends attached to them. Some prelates might accumulate a score or more benefices and never so much as visit the parishes, monasteries, or cathedrals to which they were assigned—instead they hired poorly paid substitutes. Great reforming popes such as Gregory VII and Innocent III endeavored to stamp out the abuses by having all disputes in the Church and all cases of violation of the Church's discipline referred to them as the court of last appeal. This entailed a largely augmented staff, the papal *curia*. In time the very effort at reform brought further corruption, for ambitious men sought the power and the emoluments of the offices thus created or augmented. Moreover, many of the bishops and abbots became in effect temporal princes. In their dioceses or the lands subject to their monasteries they had powers which in the Roman Empire at its height had been exercised by civil authorities. Some bishops served the kings as ministers of state and had little time for the performance of their religious duties. The Church became extremely wealthy —and with wealth came luxury and display for men in high clerical posts.

## VIII

Consciences sensitized by the Christian faith were far from viewing such abuses complacently. They stirred men and women to strive in various ways and through many channels to remove them and to bring western Europe to the standards of its professed faith. Some, both popes and bishops, as we have suggested, attempted to accomplish this through the existing structure of the Church. Others endeavored to attain it, as we have seen, by reformation of the monastic life, either by more stringently enforced forms of the Benedictine rule or through new ways, as in the mendicant orders. From these orders, especially the Franciscans and the Dominicans, missionaries went to eastern Europe and to Asia as far east as China to win non-Christians to the faith. Many of the popular religious movements remained within the Roman Catholic Church and received its blessing. In connection with such movements as the Franciscans, "third orders" arose. Their members continued "in the world" and held property, but were abstemious in food and drink, faithful in observing the sacraments and in private prayer, and gave themselves to unselfish service to the sick and the poor. Confraternities, made up of lay folk, bound themselves by rules under the authority of a bishop and had a variety of charitable and devotional purposes.

Other movements did not submit to the Catholic Church and were branded by it as heretical. The Catholic Church sought to extirpate them by the Inquisition and by the aid of lay princes. Such movements were found—although usually in small numbers—in every century of the Middle Ages; they became especially numerous in the twelfth through the fifteenth centuries. They sought to bring the Western Church into conformity with their conception of the high standards of the Christian life.

Early in the twelfth century, for example, Peter of Bruys, (possibly Bruis in southeastern France), endeavoured to follow what he believed to be the way of Christ. He was strictly ascetic and rejected the Eucharist, church buildings, ecclesiastical ceremonies, and prayers for the dead. He denounced the veneration of the cross, for he despised it as the instrument by which Christ had been killed. His followers rebaptized those who joined them, burned crosses, overthrew altars, and profaned churches. He himself is said to have been burned by a mob. Henry of Lausanne, who died in 1145, condemned the clergy of his day for their love of wealth and power and taught that the sacraments were valid only when administered by spiritually worthy priests. Arnold of Brescia, also of the twelfth century, was born in northern Italy, studied in Paris, was ordained a priest, and became the head of a community who lived by a rule. From his youth he sought to imitate Christ in purity of life and extreme poverty. He yearned to have the Church conform to what he believed were Christian ideals; and he urged that the clergy renounce all property and political power and condemned the bishops for their cupidity and their frequent irregularities. He was ordered by the pope to stop preaching and leave Italy. A succeeding pope forgave him; but he declared against the temporal power of the papacy and was expelled from Rome after espousing an unsuccessful attempt at a republic there. In 1155 he was hanged by the civil authorities, his body was burned, and his ashes were thrown into the Tiber.

The Waldensians far outnumbered any of the preceding movements. They took their name from Peter Waldo. A wealthy merchant of Lyons, troubled by the brevity and insecurity of life, Waldo sought the way to heaven. A theologian whom he consulted quoted the reply of Jesus to the rich young ruler who had come with the same question: "If you would be perfect, go, sell what you possess and give it to the poor, and you will have treasure in heaven, and come, follow me." In obedience to this command, Waldo settled with his creditors, provided for his wife and children, distributed the rest of his property among the poor, and begged his daily bread. Garbed as Christ and like Christ's disciples without a purse, Waldo began preaching to whoever would listen. He attracted followers who called themselves "the Poor in Spirit" or "the Poor Men of Lyons" and who imitated him in his dress and like him were itinerant preachers. They asked permission of the bishops and the pope. At first the pope looked favorably on them. However, a council turned down their request for recognition (1179). Believing that they must obey God rather than men, they continued their preaching and in 1184 the pope excommunicated them. Still they persisted: they went about two by two preaching as had the disciples at the command of Jesus, and, simply clad, barefoot or wearing sandals, subsisted on what was given them by those who heard them. They sought to conform to the New Testament and memorized large portions of it as translated into the vernaculars. They held that prayers for the dead, one of the practices of the Catholic Church, were without warrant in the Bible. They claimed that prayer need not be confined to churches; condemned prayers in Latin as untelligible to the rank and file of Christians; maintained that every lie is a deadly sin; said that oaths, even when given in court, were against the injunction of Christ; and taught that all taking of human life was also contrary to the explicit command of Christ. Their only forms of prayer were the prayer taught by Christ —the Lord's Prayer—and grace at meals. They declared that laymen and women could preach, that when necessary any layman could administer the Communion, that laymen were as competent as priests to hear confessions, that only bishops and priests who lived as the Apostles had were to be obeyed, and that when administered by immoral priests the sacraments were not valid. The Poor Men of Lyons spread rapidly and widely in Spain, Italy, Germany, France, and Bohemia. They were recruited chiefly among humble folk. Even their enemies described them as dressing and living simply, as industrious, chaste, honest, avoiding anger, temperate in eating and drinking, and refusing to accumulate wealth. Many continued to think of themselves as members of the Catholic Church. Pope Innocent III sought to counter them by encouraging *Pauperes Catholici* ("Poor Catholics") who followed, under the direction of the bishops, such of the Waldensian practices as the Catholic Church endorsed. He also gave his approval to the Franciscans as a movement which might, through preaching and the example of extreme poverty, offset the Waldensians. The Waldensians were persistently persecuted until they were reduced to remnants and sought refuge in remote valleys in the Italian Alps. In the sixteenth century they associated themselves with the Reformed wing of Protestantism, but not until well along in the nineteenth century did persecution of them cease.

The Cathari ("Pure"), also known as the Albigenses from their headquarters at Albi, in southern France, arose in the twelfth century, as the Waldensians had, and were most numerous in France, Spain, and northern Italy. They were found east of the Adriatic and in Constantinople as well. They were further removed from Catholic Christianity than were the Waldensians but similarly protested against the scandalous lives of many of the Catholic clergy. Theologically, however, they were "dualists." They held that two powers in the universe had always existed, the one good and the other evil. They believed that the world of the spirit was created by the good power and the visible, material world by the evil power. Some of them said that God had two sons—one had rebelled and the other, Christ, obeyed and became the Redeemer. They taught that two churches existed. One, that of Rome, was evil and had useless sacraments; the other, of which they were members, belonged to Jesus Christ and was good. As dualists, they regarded all flesh as evil and so attempted to avoid everything that had to do with the reproduction of animal life. Those who fully followed the Cathari way of life were called the "perfect." If unmarried they remained celibate; if married, husband and wife separated and were celibate from the time of their conversion. The "perfect" were not to eat meat or eggs or to drink milk, since these were the fruits of reproduction. Nor could they engage in war or own property. "Believers" who were not yet enrolled among the "perfect" might marry, hold property, and even outwardly continue to be members of the Catholic Church and share in its sacraments. But "believers" looked forward to joining the "perfect," although they might postpone that step until late in life or their last illness. The Cathari had no church buildings. As they maintained that Christ, being fully good, could not have had a body of flesh, they denied that He had died a real death. Accordingly they rejected the cross. They believed that they found support for their faith in the Bible, but rejected parts of the Old Testament as the work of the evil one and in the New Testament held as most important the Gospel of John.

Vigorous measures were taken to stamp out the Cathari. For a time the outstanding prince in Southern France, Count Raymond VI of Toulouse, supported the Cathari, but Pope Innocent III called for a crusade and a long war (the Albigensian Crusade) was waged against them. In 1229 Raymond promised obedience to the Catholic Church. Other measures were taken against them, such as the prohibition of the circulation of the Bible among the laity except the Psalms and some portions of the breviary.

The Inquisition was instituted to detect and condemn heretics, not only the Cathari but also the Waldensians and others who refused to submit to the Catholic Church. The ecclesiastical court tried the suspects. If it found them guilty it decreed penalties of varying degrees of severity, which were designed to reform the heretics and restore them to the faith. If the death penalty was invoked the heretic was turned over to the civil authorities for execution, usually by burning. If, even at the last moment, the condemned showed himself truly penitent he was saved from the fire.

Efforts were also made to combat heresy by preaching and orthodox instruction. Indeed, the Dominicans, whose official name was the Order of Preachers or the Preaching Brothers, were begun by Dominic in an effort to counter the heretics, especially the Cathari, by word and example. A native of Castile, in the Spanish peninsula, Dominic was distressed by the spread of the Cathari in the south of France. He took the leadership in a movement which had already been inaugurated. It sought through missionaries to win back the estranged by poverty, asceticism, love, and intellectually convincing arguments. Like the Franciscans, the Dominicans quickly spread to many parts of Europe.

In the fourteenth century John Wycliffe (c.1328–1384) gave rise to another popular movement which was also branded by the Roman Catholic Church as heretical and was persecuted. Wycliffe was a priest who first came into the public eye as the most distinguished philosopher, theologian, and teacher in the Oxford of his day. He was profoundly influenced by Augustine. In 1374 he was appointed rector of the parish of Lutterworth, and in 1376 he began a series of writings which brought him into conflict with the ecclesiastical authorities. He held that all property is a trust from God and if the trust is not fulfilled it is forfeited. He applied this to ecclesiastical holdings and declared that if an ecclesiastic habitually abused the trust, the civil authorities could confiscate his holdings. He maintained that popes might err, that the papacy was not essential to the administration of the Church, and that a worldly pope should be regarded as a heretic and removed from office. As he became even more radical, Wycliffe insisted that the true church is composed only of those elected by God and is invisible. Since it is God who elects, no visible church could admit or exclude from membership in that church. Nor could pope or bishop determine who were members of the true church. He attacked transubstantiation and said that under some circumstances a layman might administer the Eucharist. He repudiated such highly popular practices of the Catholic Church as pilgrimages, indulgences, masses for the dead, the collection of relics, and the cult of the saints. He was emphatic in saying that the Bible is the supreme authority in matters of faith, and he had it translated into the vernacular for circulation among the laity. He declared that the New Testament did not recognize any distinction between priests and bishops and that every one of the elect is a priest. He attacked the Friars. He sought to disseminate his convictions by sending out traveling preachers who, going about in simple garb without sandals or purse, taught in the vernacular the Lord's Prayer and the Ten Commandments. He wrote for them tracts, sermon outlines, and paraphrases of the Bible. Most of his preachers came from among the poor. Although the pope ordered Wycliffe's arrest and many of the higher clergy and the property owners opposed him, he had the support of a strong party at court. His followers, known as Lollards, multiplied, but they soon met severe persecution. The Council of Constance (1414–18) condemned Wycliffe and ordered his writings burned, and in 1428 by papal command his remains were dug up and burned, and the ashes were thrown into a near-by stream. Lollardy went underground and later contributed to the English Reformation.

Wycliffe's writings reached Bohemia and gave impetus to a reform movement headed by John Hus (c.1373–1415). Hus was a priest of blameless moral life and dean of the faculty of theology and rector of the University of Prague. By his preaching in Latin and in the vernacular he aroused nationalist sentiment and a campaign to free the Church from its notorious corruption. He denounced wickedness wherever it existed, from parish priest to pope, and held that Christ and not Peter was the rock on which God had founded His church. Hus had the support of a large proportion of the Bohemians, but the Archbishop of Prague excommunicated him. Trusting in letters of safe-conduct from the Holy Roman Emperor, he presented his case before the Council of Constance. In spite of the safe-conduct the Council imprisoned, tried, condemned him, degraded him from the priesthood, and turned him over to the secular arm. Still protesting his innocence, Hus was burned at the stake. His execution made Hus a national hero in Bohemia. A crusade was instituted against his followers, but in spite of it they persisted and won recognition from the Bohemian Parliament.

## IX

In government, political theory, and social action Christianity eventually made an extraordinary impression on medieval Europe. In principle, kings and princes reigned as Christians; coronations were Christian religious services. The lay ruler, so it was held, had his authority from God.

The question of the relation between the lay and the ecclesiastical power was chronic and often acute. As we have suggested, in the years when the Roman Empire was disintegrating in western Europe, to preserve law and order the Church assumed some of the functions hitherto performed by the state. However, as kings and princes began to establish states, conflict inevitably arose. Strong monarchs and sometimes weak ones resented the claims of popes and bishops, and popes and bishops resisted the attempts of monarchs to control the Church. Among the many instances were the long exile of Anselm, Archbishop of Canterbury from 1093 to 1109, in his contest with William II ("Rufus") and Henry I to achieve the independence of the Church in England, and the murder of Thomas Becket (1170), also Archbishop of Canterbury, in a similar struggle with Henry II.

The most famous of these conflicts was the prolonged one between the popes and the Holy Roman Emperors over the investiture issue. To offset the power of hereditary lay princes, in the tenth century the Holy Roman Emperor Otto I had given extensive authority to bishops and archbishops in their sees and made them political as well as ecclesiastical magnates. Since by the law of the Church they were celibate, those who wished to could not pass their offices on to their sons. To assure his authority Otto I insisted that he have the power to appoint churchmen and thus be certain of their loyalty to him. His successors claimed the same right. In fact, as a practice in the centuries before papal power and prestige reached maturity, so-called "lay investiture" was common in Europe. But the reforming popes of the eleventh and twelfth centuries insisted that by thus compromising the autonomy of the Church the Holy Roman Emperors were undermining its divinely ordained spiritual powers. In their effort to make effective the Christian conception of life they maintained that the Church, directed by the pope, be free to shape all aspects of life. The issue was complicated by the determination of the emperors to control the election of the popes and enhance their power in Italy by appointing the bishops to the sees in that country. Gregory VII in the eleventh century not only denied that the emperor had the right to appoint to ecclesiastical posts and insisted that the authority to depose and reinstate bishops belonged to the pope, but also declared that he alone could dispose of the imperial insignia, that he could depose emperors and release subjects from allegiance to unworthy princes, and that he could be judged by no one. A collision followed between Gregory VII and the Holy Roman Emperor Henry IV. For a time the pope seemed to be winning. He took advantage of unrest among the German nobility seriously to threaten the emperor's crown. To counter that step the emperor crossed the Alps in winter and for three successive days (in January, 1077) stood as a penitent outside the castle of Canossa where the pope was housed. The pope relented and freed the emperor from excommunication. The fortunes of the two men were soon reversed. The emperor had the pope formally deposed and a successor elected, and Gregory died a refugee. The successors of the two men continued the struggle. A compromise was reached through the Concordat of Worms (1122) by which the bishops and abbots of Germany were to be elected through the procedure prescribed by the law of the Church but, if he so wished, in the presence of the emperor. The emperor renounced his claim to invest the bishop or abbot with the symbols of spiritual authority—the ring and staff—but retained the power to invest the prelate with the temporal possessions of the office.

Almost as famous was the contest between Pope Alexander III, who reigned from 1159 to 1181, and the Holy Roman Emperor Frederick I ("Barbarossa" or "Redbeard"), the outstanding Western monarch of his day. At a low ebb in his fortunes Frederick knelt before Alexander (1177) and kissed his feet as part of the price of reconciliation. Innocent III not only brought much of Italy under papal domination but also caused the Holy Roman Emperor Otto IV to be expelled from the throne, wrung from the Emperor Frederick II the freedom of the Church in Germany, dominated that brilliant, skeptical, and ruthless ruler, and insisted on the papal overlordship in Sicily.

The issue of the relation of Church and state was continuously debated. One theory, centuries old, was that of "the two swords." The phrase came from the story that at the Last Supper, before going to the Garden of Gethsemane where Jesus was arrested, the disciples said: "Look, Lord, here are two swords," and He replied: "It is enough." The two swords were held to be symbols of the spiritual and the temporal power and it was declared that both had Christ's authorization. But opinions differed as to whether both were equal and, if not, which was to have first place. Strong popes maintained, as had Boniface VIII in his bull *Unam Sanctam* (1299), that spiritual power had been given priority. On the other hand, Dante Alighieri (1265–1321), who was involved in the political struggles of his day, in his treatise *On Monarchy* tried to reformulate the two swords theory and insisted that while both the papacy and the empire were from God, neither should trespass on the authority of the other. The pope, said Dante, should guide men to eternal happiness; but peace, the ideal condition for mankind, was best secured by the emperor, and the Church should not seek to control the state. In 1338 the Reichstag, claiming to speak officially for the Holy Roman Empire, declared that the emperor needed no confirmation by the pope to enter upon or continue in his office. In 1324 the *Defensor Pacis,* whose chief author, Marsilius of Padua, was an outstanding scholar and a former rector of the University of Paris, declared that power rightly belonged to the people and that the rulers of Church and state should be appointed by the people and be responsible to the people. Marsilius said that according to the New Testament, the basic authority for Christians, Peter was accorded no higher office than any other of the Apostles; that the New Testament gave no warrant for the assertion that Peter had been in Rome, that it did not authorize the possession of worldly property by the clergy, and did not empower bishop or pope to define Christian truth or to make laws. *Defensor Pacis* maintained that only the entire body of Christian believers acting through a representative body, a council, could rightly define what Christians should believe or could legislate for Christians. It went on to say that to the head of a Christian state, as a representative of the Christians, belonged the power to call councils, appoint bishops, and control the property of the Church. *Defensor Pacis* did not propose, as Dante had, a world-embracing Christian empire. Reflecting the rising power of national monarchs, it said that there should be many states, each based on the law of nature. The laws of each should be made by assemblies of all male citizens, and these assemblies should elect the chief executive, who might be either one man or a council. Marsilius declared that Christ rejected all claim to temporal power but submitted his property to the state, so that if the clergy were to follow his example they must accept complete poverty. He said that in the early Church all the bishops were equal and maintained that the early Church did not compel anyone, whether Christian or non-Christian, to observe its commands and so gave no precedent for canon law or Church courts.

Aspects of theories such as *Defensor Pacis* found expression in the conciliar movement. The Council of Constance, regarded by the Catholic Church as ecumenical, that is, representative of the entire Catholic Church, had successfully ended the Great Schism between rival popes at Rome and Avignon (in southern France). Many hoped that similar councils, meeting periodically, would effect the reforms in the Church which were palpably needed. Indeed, for a time it seemed probable that the popes would be subject to the councils. The council which gathered in Basel in 1431 insisted that its successors meet every ten years, ordered changes which had long been demanded (among them a reduction of papal taxes against which complaints were chronic), and in other ways limited the powers of the papacy. However, the council failed to accomplish its purpose and gradually faded away. Yet, taking advantage of the contest between council and pope, the king, clergy, and nobles of France through the "Pragmatic Sanction" of Bourges (1438) enacted significant limitations on the papal power in that country.

## X

The Christian conception of life made itself felt in contradictory ways in attitudes toward war. Both crusades and attempts to end civil strife were undertaken in the name of the Christian faith. The First Crusade, called by Pope Urban II in 1095, was designed to aid the Eastern emperors against the mounting pressures of the Moslem Seljuk Turks and to rescue from the Moslems the places in Palestine associated with the life of Christ and the beginnings of the Church, which had long been goals of the pilgrimages of devout Christians. The First Crusade succeeded in wresting Jerusalem, Bethlehem, and much of Palestine from Moslem hands. Future crusades were called by the popes either to protect these holdings or to regain them when they had been again lost to the Moslems. Bernard of Clairvaux, the most influential monk of the twelfth century, helped to stir up, by his preaching, the Second Crusade (1147–48) to win back Edessa—a key city for the defense of the Crusaders' kingdom which had fallen to the Moslems. To the intense grief of Bernard, it failed. A generation later (1187) at the decisive battle of Hattin, the Christian armies were all but wiped out, and soon Jerusalem and most of Palestine were lost. The Third Crusade (1189–92), called to redress that defeat, disintegrated because of the accidental drowning of its greatest soldier, Frederick Barbarossa, and the quarrels among its leaders. The Fourth Crusade (1202–4) had as its major achievement the capture and plunder of Constantinople and the setting up of a Latin empire there which lasted until the expulsion of the Westerners from that city by the Greeks in 1261. The ideal of a holy war in the form of a crusade continued for centuries in additional attempts to take the sacred places. Crusades were also invoked by the popes for other purposes, such as the eradication of the Cathari and the conversion of some of the Baltic peoples. As late as the sixteenth century popes were calling the faithful—in vain—to protect Europe against the Ottoman Turks.

Out of the crusades came new kinds of monastic orders: the Templars, who protected pilgrims to the Holy Places and fought in the defense of the Holy Land; the Hospitallers (Knights of St. John), who sought to care for sick pilgrims and to safeguard other pilgrims; the Knights of the Sword and the Teutonic Knights, German orders which were most noted for campaigns on the Baltic to bring peoples of that region into the Christian fold; and the

Order of Christ in Portugal, one of whose Grand Masters in the fifteenth century was the famous sponsor of Atlantic exploration, Prince Henry the Navigator. The members of these crusading orders were knights who took the accustomed monastic vows of poverty, chastity, and obedience.

Although during this time the Church invoked and blessed bloody wars that it believed to have Christian objectives, it also sought to mitigate the brutality of war and to restrain some of its more obviously un-Christian aspects. The Peace of God and the Truce of God were attempts by the Church to curb the chronic domestic wars that characterized the Middle Ages. Both were fruits of the tenth- and eleventh-century religious awakenings whose objectives were the reform of the Church through the improvement of monastic life, the creation of new kinds of monasteries, and the rescue of the papacy from its low ebb in the tenth century. The Peace of God, which dated from the tenth century, was a local French creation. It originally sought to exempt from attack all persons and places consecrated to the Church—clergy, monks, churches, monasteries, and virgins—and to stop fighting on Sundays. Later it was extended to all those protected by the Church, the poor, pilgrims, crusaders, and merchants on their journeys. It was supported by many bishops and synods and was a precedent for the distinction between combatants and noncombatants of modern times. To enforce it a number of dioceses associated themselves in confederations of peace. The Truce of God was initiated early in the eleventh century. It, too, began in France. Its purpose was to prevent fighting on certain specified days and seasons of the Church year. These included the days of the week from Saturday night to Monday morning and from Thursday through Saturday (the days when Christ was crucified, lay in the tomb, and ascended), Advent, and Lent. Parodoxically, both the Peace of God and the Truce of God were endorsed by the Council of Clermont (1095), at which the First Crusade was also launched.

The Church also endeavored to abolish jousts and tournaments and to have chaplains discontinue their ministrations in castles to which booty from unjust wars was carried. In the twelfth century a program was put forward for the arbitration by the pope of all disputes, for a papal ban on all wars, for the penalty of excommunication and deposition for a prince who failed to observe a decision when it had been rendered, and for armed assistance by the clergy and lay rulers for one who was attacked after he had submitted to a decision of a pope. Obviously, these projects were not fully carried out, but they were not entirely without results. So, too, chivalry, which sought to have the knights conform to certain ideals of Christian origin, while seldom completely embodied in practice was not without effect.

Beyond these attempts to limit the ferociousness and chaos of medieval society, Christian conceptions of life were influential in a wide variety of ways. The combination of the growing political power of the Church with the increasing prestige of the Word in the hearts and minds of men brought Christianity even greater influence. Paradoxically, however, the more the Church and Christians tried to change the world the more they found themselves using the very methods of the world that they had originally questioned and set out to reform. Churchmen tried to regulate (with irregular success) prices and interest in the name of brotherhood and in opposition to worldliness and materialism. Christianity had more notable influence in helping abolish or severely limiting slavery and the slave trade in the Middle Ages. Similarly, the ideal of monogamous marriage was strengthened by the Church. However, sexual irregularity among high and lowly in lay and in church societies remained a chronic problem. The cruelty and ruthlessness of medieval life, so hard on the weak, was often mitigated by the charitable work of monasteries and hospitals on behalf of the poor, the ill, the elderly, and the tired traveller. The draining of swamps, clearing of forests, and improvement of tillage were all notably advanced by the monks in the name of Christian ideals of useful, disciplinary labor. In intellectual activity, nothing so belies the notion of the "dark ages" as the architecture, art, and philosophy that were inspired by Christian faith, and almost continuously produced in various parts of Europe throughout the ten centuries after the fall of Rome.

At the close of the Middle Ages, therefore, no aspect of life in the West could be dissociated from Christianity, however much the thought of Europe was moving away from it. In theology, as in other aspects of civilization, Europe was passing out of the Middle Ages. Yet increasingly powerful Christian conceptions of life held by the men of the Middle Ages had done much to shape western Europe. They so entered into Western civilization that we cannot understand the world in which we now live without a knowledge and an appreciation of them.

## *FOR ADDITIONAL READING*

W. F. Albright. *From the Stone Age to Christianity.* Baltimore, 1940.
G. G. Coulton. *Five Centuries of Religion.* 4 vols. Cambridge, 1923–50.

C. Dawson. *Mediaeval Religion*. New York, 1934.
J. Finnegan. *Light from the Ancient Past*. Princeton, 1946.
E. Gebhart. *Mystics and Heretics in Italy*. New York, 1923.
E. Gilson. *History of Christian Philosophy in the Middle Ages*. New York, 1955.
———. *The Christian Philosophy of Saint Augustine*. New York, 1960.
———. *The Mystical Theology of Saint Bernard*. New York, 1940.
———. *The Philosophy of St. Bonaventure*. London, 1938.
W. R. Inge. *Christian Mysticism*. New York, 1923.
D. Knowles. *The Monastic Order in England*. Cambridge, 1940.
———. *The Religious Orders in England*. Cambridge, 1948.
M. L. W. Laistner. *Christianity and Pagan Culture in the Later Roman Empire*. Ithaca, N.Y., 1951.
———. *Thought and Letters in Western Europe, A.D. 500–900*. Ithaca, N.Y., 1957.
H. Marrou. *St. Augustine and His Influence Through the Ages*. New York, 1957.
S. Runciman. *Medieval Manichee*. Cambridge, 1947.
H. A. Wolfson. *The Philosophy of the Church Fathers*. Cambridge, Mass., 1956.
H. B. Workman. *John Wyclif*. 2 vols. Oxford, 1926.

# III

# THE GROWTH OF LEARNING IN THE WEST

*Marshall Clagett*

When we examine the beginnings of political theory we reach back into late Greek antiquity. Similarly, when we turn to the origins of modern science we find that we must also go back and examine Greek science and philosophy. Nor is such an examination of only academic interest, since modern science and philosophy are built largely upon that learning or at least upon that learning as it was modified by the Islamic and medieval Western schoolmen. Before examining the medieval legacy to modern science, an examination of science in antiquity is necessary.

How far back we can profitably trace the history of science depends to a great extent upon our definition of science. For the point of view of this account, we may think of science as *systematic* attempts to interpret, describe, and/or explain natural phenomena and the logical, mathematical, and physical tools necessary for those attempts. The breadth of such a definition permits us to investigate the most important roots of modern science. What is characteristic of modern science and distinguishes it from scientific endeavor in antiquity is the necessary use of careful observation and experiment as criteria for the acceptance of scientific theory. There were numerous instances in antiquity of the use of careful observation and even experimentation to confirm scientific theory, but Greek science did not consistently, exclusively, and of necessity utilize them as criteria of science.

## I

From the period of man's earliest development through the rise of civilization in the valley of the Nile and in the Land of the Two Rivers (Mesopo-

This chapter is a revision of Professor Clagett's essay in the second edition of *Chapters in Western Civilization.*

tamia) in the fourth millennium before Christ, there was a close relationship between man's technological activities and his knowledge of nature. An examination of his metallurgy reveals his rudimentary knowledge of the chemistry of metals. His tools of all kinds can be considered "the embodiment of science," for they represent "a practical application of remembered, compared, and collected experiences of the same kind as are systematized and summarized in scientific formulae, descriptions, and prescriptions" (V. G. Childe). But we are not so much interested in the scientific knowledge revealed by the arts as in the growth of systematized scientific knowledge itself. Among Egyptians and Babylonians such scientific systematization was restricted to mathematics, astronomy, and to some extent medicine and surgery. From an examination of their achievements in those fields of endeavor, we can deduce the main characteristics of Egyptian and Babylonian science: (1) This science was, above all, empirical in nature. For example, the methods of trial and error were particularly evident in the arithmetical procedures used by both the Egyptians and Babylonians. (2) The objectives of this early science were largely social. Pure science was almost indistinguishable from applied science. Thus the beginning of astronomy can be sought in the need for determining an adequate seasonal calendar, the calendar being a necessity for agricultural and governmental activities. Similarly, the early development of mathematics in Babylonia can be closely related to the evolution of procedures for the keeping of temple records, and in both Egypt and Babylonia to the necessity for field and constructional measurements. The only theoretical developments worthy of note were in Babylonian mathematics, in which algebraic solutions of quadratic equations (equations involving the square of the unknown, such as $ax^2 + bx = c$) are presented, and in Babylonian astronomy where mathematical techniques were applied to the construction of lunar tables. (3) There are some instances of the inductive organization of observed data. One of the best examples of this is a surgical treatise, called by the name of its modern owner—the Edwin Smith Papyrus. Copied in the seventeenth century B.C. from a work produced sometime during the third millennium B.C., this treatise is a systematic empirical exposition of the results of wounds to various parts of the body and is completely free of the tendencies toward magic found in other medical papyri. (4) This early science reveals an occasional example of the use of scientifically organized data for the prediction of natural phenomena. Again, the best example is the construction by the Babylonian astronomers of lunar tables to predict the first visibility of the new moon each month. Another example appears in the surgical papyrus mentioned above. There it was assumed that if certain symptoms were observed, then a given diagnosis must be made and a particular type of treatment followed. The author, then, was attempting to predict and control the course of disease on the basis of previous experience. (5) There was some use of mathematics among the Babylonians to describe and express scientific theory. Astronomers applied their knowledge of the properties of numbers to natural phenomena that seemed to take place with some regularity (as in the use of arithmetical series to describe the variations in the sun's apparent velocity). But such applications were more the exception than the rule. (6) In Babylonian and Egyptian science there were strong religious or magical elements, for the most part in the motivations of science, but also occasionally in the method of science. Hence, one important stimulus to the study of astronomy was the astrological use to which it was put, even when the actual recording of astronomical data was a straightforward empirical procedure. On the other hand, both Egyptian and Babylonian medicine had strong elements of magical procedure in the use of incantations as a part of prescribed cures. Here the procedure, rather than the motivation, was magical (and to some extent religious). Turning to Egyptian and Babylonian efforts to describe the origins and development of the universe (cosmogony and cosmology), we find both motivation and methodology pervaded by mythology and religion.

## II

It has been a constant source of wonder and admiration to historians of philosophy and science that in the sixth century B.C. there developed on the periphery of the Greek world (Ionia) a remarkable secular approach to the investigation of natural phenomena. This admiration has led to use of the expression "The Greek Miracle" to describe the seemingly sudden genesis of that approach. Close examination of the historical evidence goes far to eliminate the "miraculous" element. Yet our admiration remains. Such basic cultural developments as the discovery, in about 1200 B.C. in Asia Minor, of improved methods of reducing and working iron led to the cheapening of the production of tools and arms. This made possible the successful military and economic competition of smaller, less centrally organized states (such as the Greek city-states) with the older oriental monarchies. Similarly the invention of the alphabet in Phoenicia at about the same time and its spread at some later date to Greece worked for the broadening of the intellectual base in society. Learning was not to be the exclusive property of the priesthood.

While these and a number of other important factors operated to further the growth of Greek society in general, we must still remark on the reasons for the development of science in the Ionian Greek settlements in Asia Minor and more specifically in the Ionian city of Miletus. Miletus was situated on the coast of Asia Minor. It was a commercially important center, and secular tendencies were freer to develop there. Miletus was also well situated to benefit by contacts with the higher cultures of Egypt and Babylonia. To some extent Miletus learned directly from these states, but no doubt learned more indirectly from the Lydians and other peoples of Asia Minor who had fallen heir to the culture of the older states.

Both Greek tradition and modern scholarship unite in considering the Ionian philosophers as the immediate founders of Greek science and philosophy. From meager beginnings in the sixth century there developed in the course of the fifth and fourth centuries the full flower of Greek philosophy; and in the two succeeding centuries, the most significant developments of Greek science.

Before tracing the direction of Greek philosophy and science, it would be well to outline their characteristic elements, achievements, and methodology. Much of Greek intellectual activity inherits something of the secular tradition that we have characterized as first evident among the Ionian naturalists. One line of activity in which the secular approach bore particular results was the medicine of the Hippocratic school of Cos (fifth and fourth centuries B.C.). An important step was taken in the history of science and medicine when the unknown author of the medical treatise *The Sacred Disease* began with these words:

> I am about to discuss the disease called "sacred." It is not, in my opinion, any more divine or more sacred than any other disease, but has a natural cause, and its supposed divine origin is due to men's inexperience, and to their wonder at its peculiar character. . . . But if it is to be considered divine just because it is wonderful, there will not be one sacred disease but many, for I will show that other diseases are no less wonderful and portentous, and yet nobody considers them sacred.

Another distinctive feature of Greek scientific activity was the development of the concept of "generalized" sciences. This concept can be contrasted sharply with the empirical approach to scientific data that was evident among the Egyptians and Babylonians. The Egyptians were accustomed in their mathematical papyri to set a specific problem, like the area of a particular triangular plot of land, and to give the specific solution. The Greeks, on the other hand, generalized the empirical procedures used in the particular problems. Thus they arrived at the general solution of the area of any triangle. And this they did in a very logical fashion, starting from commonly accepted axioms and postulates. Whereas there were individual rules of geometry among the Egyptians, there was an abstract science of geometry among the Greeks. Another striking example of this generalizing feature of Greek scientific thought can be found in connection with the study of the lever. The lever and the balance as practical instruments, the one for moving heavy objects and the other for weighing materials, certainly go back to an early period in man's cultural history. Balances have been found in Egyptian archeological remains of the fourth millennium B.C., and they were used everywhere in the Near East before the Greeks had reached even the beginnings of their cultural development. Yet it was not until the fourth and third centuries B.C. that the principles of the lever and the balance were generalized by Greek scientists into the science of statics.

Closely associated with the development of the concept of generalized science was the evolution among the Greeks of a strict methodology of reasoning or logic. In this area it is hard to overestimate the importance for modern science of the achievements of the Greeks. Regardless of how much emphasis we put on the verification of scientific theory by careful observation and experiment in modern science, we would be at a complete loss to form scientific theory without the full development of logical thinking behind us. A historical examination of important scientific theories developed in the course of modern times will not only reveal that scientific theory proceeds out of observation or experiment and generates new observation and experiment, but will also show that the relationship of observation and experiment to scientific theory is expressed in terms of logical (and/or mathematical) procedures, namely, deduction and induction.

The establishment of a separate discipline of rational thinking, or logic, was an almost completely independent achievement of Greek thought. We associate that development in the fifth century with the Eleatic philosophers and Socrates, and in the fourth century with Plato and, above all, Aristotle. It is perfectly clear from the logical works of Aristotle that he understood and outlined the theory of induction, the drawing of general inferences from particular cases. Greek natural philosophers were prone, in many instances, to substitute reasoning by analogy for induction. Nor was Aristotle free from this procedure. We can also point to the use, and in one case the description, of induction in the medical works of the Hippocratic school of Cos.

The development of deductive thinking, that is, the derivation of necessary consequences from assumptions, was carried to great heights by Greek mathematicians and philosophers. Greek mathematics is a monument to Greek deductive thought.

It has been pointed out that Greek scientists often relied on careful observation and experimentation for the verification of scientific theory. From at least the fourth century B.C., the great test of Greek astronomical theory was whether it "saved the phenomena," that is to say, whether it accounted for observed data. Furthermore, we can cite the use of experimentation from the time of Pythagoras in the sixth century B.C., or, at least, of Empedocles (fifth century B.C.), to the time of the great mathematician and astronomer Ptolemy, in the second century A.D. For example, Empedocles showed the corporeal nature of air by experimentation, while Ptolemy carefully measured angles of refraction of light rays as they passed at various angles from one medium (air) into another medium (water). We should be careful to remember, however, as was pointed out before, that experimentation was not thought to be a *necessary* procedure for the uncovering of new facts or for the verification of scientific theory.

We have concerned ourselves up to this point largely with the characteristics and methodology of Greek science. Now some of the substantial achievements of that science must be noted briefly.

Critical for scientific development was the problem of the understanding and meaning of nature. The problem was given three different solutions by the Greeks—solutions that have been of fundamental importance in the history of Western thought and that still have vitality today. The first of these is usually called the physical or material view of nature. It emphasized the reality and permanence of matter and motion and, in its most mature form, the existence of the void, or empty space. This view of nature reached its highest expression in the atomic theory of Democritus, Epicurus, and Lucretius. The second solution to the problem of nature is called the formal or mathematical view. It emphasized the reality and permanence of forms, structures, relationships. The world of the senses, matter, was conceived to have a transitory nature. This view attained its best expression with Plato. The third and final view of nature, that of Aristotle, can be characterized as functional or biological. In this view of nature emphasis was laid on "becoming," on the actualizing of things that exist in potentiality. Nature in motion is conceived in its broadest aspect as any kind of change. Rejecting the adequacy of the emphasis that the materialists had placed on matter and the Platonists on form, this view pictured matter and form as inseparable, and thus as equally important for the understanding of the fundamental character of nature. Aristotle was probably led to this view by the necessity of accounting for generation (coming into being) and corruption (passing away), and also for the kind of organization that we find in living organisms.

We have already intimated that the Greeks created a secular medicine that often employed the methods of observation and experiment. This medicine was codified by Galen (second century A.D.) into a system which can be called the Hippocratic-Galenic system. In this form it served as the basis first for Arabic and later for Western medicine. In the fields of zoology and botany, the Greeks have left us an important inheritance in certain works of Aristotle and of his disciple and successor, Theophrastus. Aristotle's discussion of the growth of the embryo and of the classification of animal species have had profound influence on the course of biological studies.

Progress among the Greeks in physics was on the whole less important than in some of the other sciences. But the name of Archimedes (c.287–c.212 B.C.) is associated with this fundamental work in statics, and the study of dynamics received its most significant ancient treatment from Aristotle. We have already mentioned the importance of the Greek achievements in mathematics. Euclid's *Elements,* a summary of geometry and number theory (third century B.C.), has been one of the most influential works in the growth of Western thought. Even more brilliant were Archimedes' investigations into plane and solid geometry, which led him to anticipate the methods of integral calculus. Furthermore, it is to Greek mathematicians that we must turn to find the creation and development of the mathematics of conic sections (parabolas, hyperbolas, and ellipses).

Considering their important achievements in mathematics, it is little wonder that astronomy also had a fruitful growth among the Greeks, since one of the most important characteristics of Greek astronomy was its thoroughgoing use of mathematics. Of equal importance in their successful development of astronomy was the well-accepted notion that observed data formed the ultimate criteria for the acceptability of astronomical theory. Aristarchus of Samos held that the earth, instead of being at rest, as most Greek astronomers thought, actually possessed two motions—a daily rotation on its axis and an annual revolution about the sun. Thus, he proposed a system that Copernicus was to follow some twenty centuries later. Ptolemy (second century A.D.), on the other hand, assumed that each planet revolved in a small, independent circle (or epicycle) and that the center of this small circle in turn revolved around the earth. It was the Ptolemaic system that found the greatest favor with the Islamic and Western astronomers down to the time of Copernicus in the sixteenth century.

These characteristics, methods, and achievements of Greek science were taken up in most essential features by the Islamic and Western authors, and thus ultimately served as the point of departure and basis of modern science. Let us now examine briefly the course of the transmission of this science to the Latin West, as well as the accretions to it and the new forms that it took en route.

## III

By the sixth century A.D. the political and cultural division of the Roman Empire had reached an advanced stage. The quantity and quality of Greek learning and science salvaged in the West and passed to Western churchmen in the course of the early Middle Ages (up to A.D. 1000) was greatly inferior to that in the East. For in the East the great body of Greek learning was still actually read and commented upon in the schools of Athens, Alexandria, and various centers in the Syrian provinces.

In the West the early scholars depended mainly upon the Latin Patristic literature, upon certain pagan authors who reflected some Greek learning, and particularly upon Boethius (c.480–524). Boethius's prime objective was to make Greek learning available by translation, commentary, and independent discussion. A work on geometry that purports to be his translation of Euclid's *Elements* is probably not his, although it is unquestionably early medieval. In any case, it is an index to the knowledge of geometry in the early Middle Ages. The majestic proofs included in the work of Euclid are for the most part absent, and only the definitions, axioms, unsupported propositions, and theorems remain. What knowledge of Greek logic the scholars in the early Middle Ages had, they gained largely from the works or translations of Boethius. His stirring apology for philosophy, *On the Consolation of Philosophy,* written during his last days in prison, proved to be one of the most popular and widely translated philosophical works ever written. Some of the scanty knowledge of Plato in the early Middle Ages can be attributed to this work.

One characteristic type of work produced in the early medieval period was the encyclopedia. The most representative of the early encyclopedias was the *Etymologies* of Isidore of Seville (d. 636), which presents much information on the state of learning and science in the West in his day. Unlike many of the early church fathers Isidore rejected the idea that the study of nature leads one away from the objectives of religion, "for to know the nature of things is not the wisdom of superstition so long as they are considered with sound and sober judgement."

One other encyclopedic work of this early period worthy of more than passing notice is a treatise *On the Universe* by John Scotus Erigena (c.800–c.877). He was one of the few authors of his day to be thoroughly conversant with Greek, and, on the whole, his thought is of greater philosophic maturity than that of his contemporaries.

Returning to the eastern part of the Empire, where the main stream of Greek learning flowed, in the fifth, sixth, and seventh centuries there occurred great philosophical and scientific activity. The standard type of work became the commentary, a work in which a sentence or passage from some original work, most often Aristotle, would be stated and then followed by comments or a discussion on the part of the author. The commentary came to be the standard form of Islamic and Latin works up to early modern times. It was in the commentaries on the *Physics* of Aristotle in late antiquity and the Middle Ages that some of the ideas which were to overthrow Aristotelian physics were first advocated.

The Alexandrian school of natural philosophy (sixth century A.D.) and the medical studies there and elsewhere in the Near East that continued Hippocratic-Galenic medicine were still in progress when the Arabs in the first half of the seventh century quickly overran the whole Near Eastern area with the exception of Asia Minor. There the Greek Byzantine Empire maintained its independence. In the period just preceding and including the Arab conquests (actually, from at least the fifth century), a considerable portion of Hellenic learning was being turned into Syriac by native Christians who preferred to teach in Syriac, their own Semitic language. There were many Syriac centers of learning where Hellenism thrived. This is of great importance, for when Greek learning was first turned into Arabic it was often Syriac versions of the Greek that were translated; and even more important, the principal translators into the Arabic were *Syriac Christians*. In addition to those Greek and Syriac schools where Hellenic learning was still being taught, there were Persian centers, which must not be overlooked.

The famous city of Jundishapur was the most significant intellectual melting pot of the sixth, seventh, and eighth centuries. There, Greek pagan Neoplatonists mixed with Syriac Christians, Jews, Persians, and Indians. The medical center at Jundishapur acquired great fame.

It was, then, into countries where older Greek learning was very much alive that the Arabs burst in the seventh century. One of the most provocative facts of intellectual history is that the language of a people who were completely undeveloped from the standpoint of scientific learning became the language of science and philosophy over an area extending from Spain to the Indian border. It was a language that readily met the burden placed upon it. Little in the way of learning was accomplished under the Arabs until something over a century after their conquests—and the political and cultural center of the empire shifted to the East, where a new dynasty, the Abbasids, built a flourishing capital, Baghdad. There the flood of translation into Arabic of Greek texts, and to a lesser extent Indian learning, began and soon reached great proportions. This was a phenomenon of translating to be duplicated in the twelfth and thirteenth centuries, when that same body of Greek learning, with Arabic and Jewish additions, was turned into Latin from Arabic and Greek. Syriac Christians and pagans, Jews, and Persians took part in the translations into Arabic.

Underlying the achievements of Islamic science and philosophy were certain basic considerations. Islam was a monotheistic religion with a holy scripture of revealed truth and prescription—the Koran. It was no accident, then, that the Christian-Neoplatonic form of Greek learning that arose in late antiquity appealed to Islam as well. There was a basic similarity in climate of opinion. Hence, Greek learning gained entrance to Islam because of the garb it had assumed in late antiquity.

The dependence of Arabic science and philosophy on Greek learning must be stressed. It was almost as if the body of Greek learning was a second corpus of revealed truth. This unique position of Greek learning inspired attempts to harmonize its apparent differences and inconsistencies—for example, the Platonic and Aristotelian components—a tendency that had already begun in the Neoplatonic works of late antiquity. Because of this dependence on Greek thought, it has been customary to slight the originality of the contributions of Islam to science and philosophy. This is like a star of greater magnitude obscuring its fainter twin. It has long been admitted by even the most ardent Hellenophile that the scientists of Islam contributed to the various sciences by extending and advancing observational and experimental techniques. Even a cursory glance at Islamic astronomy, alchemy, and physics will reveal the truth of such an assertion. But the more closely scientific literature is investigated, the more we come to recognize currents of *theoretical* as well as *practical originality;* this is particularly true in discussions of physics, or where physics joins hands with philosophy.

Islamic philosophy points in at least three main directions. However, its philosophers can by no means be said to hew exclusively to one or another of these three lines of development. Many hold basic tenets associated with one type of development while at the same time revealing views that are characteristic of the other lines. The first position we can describe as fundamentalism, a complete dependence on and confidence in the Koranic picture of nature. God immediately and immanently controls everything, including, of course, His created things. The one God is everywhere immediately present. Nature or natural law as secondary cause either has no place in such a scheme or has only a minor role. Fundamentalism did not (either among the Christians or Moslems) lead to the scientific investigation of natural phenomena.

A second line of development was a philosophical fusion between Neoplatonic and Aristotelian tendencies. Most philosophers taking this line held to "the Neoplatonic chain of creation"—a series of gradated emanations from an ultimate "uncreated unity" down to terrestrial form and matter. On this Neoplatonic chain were welded many characteristic Aristotelian doctrines: his ideas relative to form and matter, his concepts of the four terrestrial elements (earth, air, fire, water), and sometimes his doctrine of the fifth celestial element, as well as his doctrines of change and movement. The immanent God of the fundamentalists is now removed as the immediate cause of material phenomena. Secondary causation then has been placed between God as ultimate cause and given phenomena. Philosophers in this group differ widely as to how close they are to either pole, the Neoplatonic or Aristotelian.

The third line of development consisted in a peculiar kind of atomism, whose most radical feature was the concept of time as discontinuous, as a series of "nows" or instantaneous moments. The apparent continuity of events, the continuous flow of time, is a product of the senses (just as the rapid passages of separate motion picture frames gives an apparent continuity to what transpires on the screen). This led to a revolutionary concept that Allah recreates the universe at every instant of time, making such changes or modifications as he wishes. Essentially nonscientific, this philosophy rejected all ordinary concepts of secondary causation, of natural law, leaving only immediate causation by God. He was considered the only agent or doer.

Passing to some of the actual scientific ideas of Islam, we can first note achievements in chemistry. In late antiquity (about the third century A.D.) a merger of several older intellectual traditions produced an alchemy whose central doctrine was that by chemical and other procedures baser metals could be transmuted into gold and silver. The alchemist Jabir (Geber) tells his readers: "The first essential in chemistry is that thou shouldst perform practical work and conduct experiments, for he who performs not practical work nor makes experiments will never attain the least degree of mastery." The practical knowledge of chemical substances and the fundamental procedures in chemistry such as distillation, sublimation, and the rest were greatly enhanced by the work of the Arabic chemists.

In mathematics the West owes to Islam the first systematization of algebra out of Greek, Indian, and probably Babylonian sources. This algebra included the numerical (algebraic) and geometrical solutions of quadratic equations. Islam is also responsible for providing the West with the so-called Arabic (actually Hindu) numerals and system of calculations, the great social significance of which would be apparent to anyone who tried bookkeeping and simple calculation with Roman numerals.

In physics, Islamic philosophers continued the criticism of Aristotle's ideas begun by commentators of late antiquity. Important work was done on theories of gravitational attraction between bodies, on the causes of motion of projectiles, and on the actual specific gravities of various metals, precious stones, and liquids. The Islamic philosophers utilized some highly accurate balances and performed optical experiments with reflected and refracted light that exerted considerable influence on Western writers down to the time of Descartes.

The Arabic efforts in astronomy again demonstrate the empirical and to some extent experimental tendency so strong in Islamic scientific activity. For the most part accepting the Ptolemaic system, they laid emphasis on larger and more accurate instruments, on the founding of observatories, on the finding of more accurate values for observational data and constants. At the same time they took up the beginnings which the Greeks and Indians had made in trigonometry (the chief mathematical tool of the astronomer) and advanced it considerably. They used all six of the basic trigonometric ratios (sine, cosine, tangent, and so on).

Even so cursory a summary of Islamic contributions to science shows something of the continuity in the growth of human knowledge based largely on the Greek corpus. Throughout this whole period, however, the high stage of culture in the Greek Byzantine Empire, with its capital at Constantinople, reflected only sporadic interest in the older Hellenic learning. Although its achievements in science (so far as we know at present) were not significant, it preserved that older body of learning. Constantinople was the principal source of Greek manuscripts for the Arabs and Latins alike.

## IV

By the twelfth century the whole body of Greco-Islamic learning was an impressive structure. And so it seemed to the Latins, who were having ever increasing contacts with Islam. One of the surging intellectual currents in the twelfth century was the almost feverish translating activity in the West. It recalls vividly to mind the similar activity which took place in Islam in the ninth and tenth centuries. In both cases a people with a meager background of philosophic and scientific knowledge were striving to make their own a great body of learning, and in both cases there was a tendency for schools to grow up around a few brilliant translators working in teams. The principal places of translation were in those areas where the Islamic and Christian civilizations overlapped, particularly in Spain and Sicily, but in addition there were some individuals in northern Italy and in Constantinople.

It is difficult to say just where the first translations from Arabic were made and by whom, but it is customary to begin the study of Latin translations from the Arabic with the activity of a curious figure, Constantine the African (latter part of the eleventh century). He may have been associated with the first important medical school in Europe, that at Salerno. It is certain that he obtained numerous medical manuscripts from the East and translated them into Latin, passing some of them off as original works of his own. These translations were used at Salerno, and while they have been described as "corrupt, confused, and full of misunderstood Arabic terms" they nevertheless provided Salerno with a literature that made it the most famous medical school in the twelfth century. It is equally difficult to trace the precise working area of the Englishman Adelard of Bath, the next most important figure in the early translating activity. We do know that he was active from 1116 to 1142 and that he translated from the Arabic some important astronomical tables and Euclid's *Elements*.

Translations from the Arabic made in Spain during the twelfth century were centered at the city of Toledo (recaptured from the Arabs in 1085).

Here the translators worked customarily in pairs, the one familiar with Latin and the other a native dragoman (from the Arabic *tarjama* "to translate") who understood Arabic. Often these translators started with the common language of Catalan and then translated from Catalan into Latin.

By far the most important translator of the Spanish school, and perhaps of the whole of Europe during the Middle Ages, was Gerard of Cremona (Italy). Anxious to read the *Almagest* of Ptolemy, he went to Toledo. There he saw the great abundance of learning in Arabic. The translation of some eighty important works is attributed to him. Among them was the *Almagest,* made in 1175, which was to dominate astronomy either directly or indirectly until the time of Copernicus, and the encyclopedic *Canon of Medicine* of Avicenna, a work which occupied a dominant position in the medical schools of the West until the sixteenth century.

Important translations were made in Italy and Sicily during the same period. These included several of the logical works of Aristotle not previously available to students in the early Middle Ages. These were of great importance to the intellectual development of western Europe, since the new logic was to be the most significant tool used by the schoolmen of the succeeding centuries. To the Sicilians we owe the first direct translations of certain of the dialogues of Plato, as well as other important scientific and philosophical works.

Special note should also be made of the progressive translation of other works of Aristotle, for these works were to occupy a unique and authoritative position in the curricula of the medieval universities. His logical works were translated by the second quarter of the twelfth century. By about 1200, translations from both the Arabic and Greek of Aristotle's *Physics, Metaphysics,* and *On the Heavens* had been made, as well as of some of his minor works. In the course of the next two generations the remainder of his works was translated into Latin, mainly from the Greek.

By the end of the thirteenth century the first great wave of translations from Arabic and Greek learning was completed. It should be understood that this activity was concerned mainly with scientific and philosophic works, while the later translations, made in the fifteenth and sixteenth centuries during the Renaissance, tended to be of literary works. Those works translated in the twelfth and thirteenth centuries formed the intellectual base for the development of philosophy and science in Western civilization.

## V

Increased Western interest in philosophic discourse and in the translations of Greco-Islamic learning manifested itself after the twelfth century in the great prominence assumed by cathedral schools, such as those at Laon, Chartres, Rheims, and Paris. The number of students attracted to these schools increased greatly. The fortune of each school tended to rise and fall as prominent dialecticians or teachers joined or left its staff. Just as the size of the student body fluctuated with the changing staff so the organization remained loose during the greater part of the century. The best-known cathedral schools were in France. Students were attracted to French schools from all parts of Europe, from England, Germany, and Italy. As one historian has said, "To Italy the papacy, to Germany the Empire, to France learning." But the schools of Italy were far from unimportant, particularly those that concentrated on medicine and law.

In the early Middle Ages the curriculum of the cathedral schools, such as it was, consisted of elementary study of the seven liberal arts: geometry, arithmetic, music, astronomy, grammar, rhetoric, and logic. By the twelfth century, a higher education was beginning to be differentiated from the seven liberal arts. Thus theology and dialectics were now distinguished; law was growing out of and much beyond rhetoric (particularly in Italy at Bologna), while medicine, which was never a part of the seven liberal arts, was taught separately.

By the third quarter of the twelfth century conditions were ripe for more formal university development; there was a renewed interest in the use of dialectics, a growing absorption of Greco-Islamic learning, greatly increased attendance at cathedral schools, a differentiation of higher education from the seven liberal arts, and an increasing spread of the corporate ideals and techniques as embodied in guilds and the like. Thus it was that in the last quarter of the twelfth century the universities of Bologna and Paris took form. The roots of other universities, such as Salerno, Oxford, Cambridge, Angers, and Padua, also can be found in the latter part of the twelfth or the early thirteenth centuries. Rome, Pisa, Avignon, Prague, Vienna, and Cracow were all founded in the fourteenth century.

The use of the term "university" (Latin, *universitas*) is somewhat misleading. During the thirteenth century it designated "an association or guild of either masters or students or both." But it was not limited to educational associations; it was often used for other associations or guilds. Thus a university did not mean, as it does today, a group of faculties or schools. Something more in line with our use of the word today was the Latin term *studium generale*. But even this expression is somewhat misleading, since the term *generale* does not refer so much to different faculties as to the fact that the *studium* was open to all comers. The *studium* referred to the institution, its place, its courses, but not at first to the organization of its personnel. By the end of the Middle Ages, however, both "university" and *studium generale* were being used much as we use the term "university" today.

We must also reorient our ideas with respect to the word "college." In its early usage it too meant a corporation or guild; thus we find it used at Bologna for an organization of the masters, as opposed to the "university" of the students. Our use of the term "college" is an outgrowth of its usage at Paris in the thirteenth century for houses or living quarters established for poor students and later for other students. Gradually additional instruction was inaugurated in the colleges or transferred from the universities to the colleges. The "college" system is still strongly evident at Oxford and Cambridge.

The guild privileges of masters and students were granted by royal or papal enactment and were often included in the foundation charter. These privileges included certain preferential legal treatment, freedom from various types of taxation, the right to retain absentee offices as sources of income, and the right of cessation of classes. This last has a modern ring. It was similar to the right of strike and was used when it was thought that the rights of the students or masters were being controverted. Other miscellaneous privileges which some universities enjoyed were freedom from military service and free entrance to certain kinds of entertainments. At the University of Turin on the Feast of the Epiphany every liquor dealer was obliged to offer a bottle of brandy and a pound of preserves.

We cannot study university organization in any detail, but even a cursory scrutiny of the universities of Bologna and Paris would show the roots of many present-day college and university institutions, particularly those of Europe. The organizations of Paris and Bologna were the two great prototypes followed by the great majority of universities throughout Europe, with numerous local variations, of course. The University of Bologna is spoken of as having a student type of organization, since the "universities" or corporations of the students exercised control. By the time of the thirteenth century the college of professors at Bologna was to a great extent at the mercy of the student organization. The professors were told how they were to lecture, at what hours, and what material had to be covered in a given time.

The organization at Paris was different from that at Bologna. Power was vested in the hands of a guild of masters, and the university was organized into faculties: theology, medicine, law, and arts. It was not long before the faculty of arts became the most important of the faculties, at least so far as university administration was concerned, and the rector of the faculty of arts became head of the university. His position was disputed at times by the chancellor of the university.

The modern system of granting degrees is also an outgrowth of the medieval university. In the early period at Paris the right to teach (the licentiate) was conferred by the chancellor of the cathedral chapter and was in fact little more than a permission to teach. But as the corporations or universities resembling guilds took form at Paris, examinations were introduced much in the same fashion as were examinations utilized by other guilds in the passage from apprenticeship through journeyman to the mastership. For a bachelor's degree, a board of examiners required the candidate to defend or "determine" a proposition or thesis. The examination could last several days. Upon its completion and after much ceremony before a large audience of friends, the student was "dragged off in the street" for the celebration. Wine and the usual celebrations followed. The next step beyond the "determination" was the licentiate, not the equivalent of the mastership, but often followed directly by it. The mastership was the admittance to the select corporation. In some cases it was not granted until two or three years after the granting of the licentiate. At the ceremony of mastership, the new master delivered his inaugural lecture or disputation in the presence of the faculty and received his magisterial biretta or cap.

The study of medieval universities has importance for a study of contemporary universities. It is also fruitful because it was in the medieval university that the Christian adaptation of Greek learning was made. As we shall see most of the intellectual activity of the high and late Middle Ages centered in the universities and the schoolmen.

## VI

As the universities expanded in the twelfth century, as Europe's trade grew and her cities began to flourish, a growing intellectual maturity also became evident. It reflected itself first in a revived interest in dialectics or logic, in heated discussions of problems which were ostensibly theological in character but which pointed to a deepening interest in philosophy. One such discussion centered in the nature of general concepts or terms which were called "universals" (for example, the expression "man" is a universal; it embraces Socrates and all other particular men). The controversy was rooted in a short passage of Porphyry's *Introduction to the Predicaments of Aristotle,* translated by Boethius:

Next concerning genera and species, the question indeed whether they have a substantial existence, or whether they consist in bare intellectual concepts only or whether, if they have a substantial existence, they are corporeal or incorporeal or whether they are separable from sensible properties of the things of the sense, or are only in those properties and subsisting about them, I shall forbear to discuss. For a question of this kind is very deep and one that requires a long investigation.

Opinions on the nature of "universals" in the eleventh and twelfth centuries ranged between poles called generally "nominalism" and "realism." The extreme nominalist (from Latin, *nomina,* "names") held universals to be mere words, while the extreme realist thought them to possess reality independent of the material particulars they embrace. Between these two poles were at least two positions of a compromise nature: moderate realism and conceptualism. The first emphasized that the similarity seen in material particulars has reality; the second, that the universal is neither a mere word on the one hand, nor an independent reality on the other, but a mental reality—a concept abstracted from particulars.

The nominalist-realist controversy had far-reaching practical consequences, because one or the other answer determined a theological position. For instance, those (nominalists) who denied the reality of universals altogether, found it difficult to explain the meaning of the universal, invisible *church,* which was something more than mere individual *churches;* or to explain how *mankind* had sinned in "Adam," and not just an *individual man.*

Of the early philosophers who engaged in the disputes on universals, we may point particularly to the brilliant Breton, Pierre Abelard (1079–1142), who assumed a middle-of-the-road conceptualism. His vigorous and active personality and intellect, his affair and marriage with Heloise, his intellectual struggle with St. Bernard—all combined to make him one of the most fascinating figures in the Middle Ages. In his work entitled *Sic et Non* (*Pro and Con*), Abelard employs a technique of collecting and collating opposite opinions on theological matters. This device was to develop into the "scholastic method" of the thirteenth century.

The philosophy and science of the thirteenth century reaped rich benefits from the earlier essay into dialectics and philosophy in the cathedral schools. The "new logic" of Aristotle gave to these disciplines a powerful tool for analysis, resolution, and synthesis. The body of Greek and Arabic learning provided basic texts on which to comment, as well as a fund of ideas to support, modify, or refute, according to the dictates of the various interests of medieval society. The universities served as the means of discussion, growth, and organization. And the new mendicant orders of monks provided personnel possessing a high ideal of learning.

By the thirteenth century an Aristotelian classification of philosophy or the sciences had been widely accepted as embracing the various fields of scientific endeavor. Philosophy was thought to be of two basic kinds, theoretical and practical. As one earlier schoolman put it, theoretical philosophy "makes us know what ought to be understood," while practical philosophy "makes us know what ought to be done." Theoretical philosophy was divided into metaphysics, mathematics, and physics. Physics as a general science dealt with matter in so far as this was subject to change. Mathematics was concerned with intelligible quantity in its abstract relationships. Metaphysics sought the reality and first principles underlying the changing material world. Practical or "active" philosophy concerned itself with responses to realities. Practical philosophy also had a threefold division: ethics, economics, and politics. Ethics concerned the correct conduct of one's private affairs; economics, correct household management; and politics, correct state management.

All of these parts of theoretical and practical philosophy were considered as "general" or "universal" sciences, and they thus had broad and basic subject matters. Included in them yet below them in the scale of knowledge were the "particular" sciences, which had limited objectives of study. Among these were optics, astronomy, the study of weights, zoology, botany, etc. It was considered that these particular sciences were, for the most part, built upon sensory data. Unfortunately, the conclusions and the results of the investigations undertaken in the particular sciences were not systematically utilized in developing the general sciences, at least not in the thirteenth century.

Standing above both theoretical and practical philosophy in the thirteenth century was theology, "queen of the sciences," which crowned the other studies and gave them their *raison d'être.*

While this medieval Aristotelian classification of knowledge was quite widely accepted in the thirteenth century, we must not think that there was but one basic philosophic system. It is sometimes customary to present the philosophy of Thomas Aquinas as being the characteristic medieval philosophy, but although his philosophy eventually gained authority there were many other vigorous currents in the thirteenth century that differed widely from it. We can point, for example, to the existence of a group of philosophers known as Averroists, who were particularly in evidence at Paris in this century. They were at least partially inspired by the Spanish Moslem, Averroës, who composed commentaries on the various works of Aristotle. (Aristotle was characteristically referred to as "the Philosopher"; Averroës, as "the Commentator.") Although the doctrine of the Averroists is not known in detail, its broad outlines are clear. They were influenced by Neoplatonic ideas in their conception of intermediary beings or intelligences between God and created things. They also put forth the principle that the world and all created things were co-eternal with God, a doctrine most distasteful to more orthodox philosophy. Furthermore, strong deterministic elements were present. The stars and heavens were thought to exercise controlling influence on events on the earth. The most controversial point in their doctrine was the belief in the basic unity of the "active intellect" in all human beings. The active intellect in each individual was believed to be an imperishable part of the single active intellect common to the whole human race. This doctrine was vigorously opposed by St. Thomas and other schoolmen, since it brought into question their emphasis on the personality of each man and since it put in jeopardy the fundamental Christian doctrine of the immortality of the individual soul. Another doctrine of the Averroists that brought upon them the censure of Thomas was the doctrine of the "two truths," which seems to suggest that "that which is true in philosophy may be false in theology and vice versa"—that what men accepted as truth by faith might not be acceptable to human reason.

Other groups and individuals created further divergent currents of thought in the thirteenth century, but we must restrict ourselves here to suggesting some of the more prominent opinions of Thomas Aquinas and those who followed him and were even, at the time, more influential than Aquinas.

Thomas Aquinas was born of mixed Italian and Norman parentage at Rocca, Italy (c.1224). He studied at the University of Naples, joined the Dominican order, and went to Paris in 1245, where he studied under the greatest Dominican teacher of his day, Albertus Magnus. After some other travels, he received the licentiate at Paris and became a master there. After a short stay at Paris, he returned to Italy and had a varied teaching career there, only to return to Paris again in 1269. He taught in Paris until 1272, completing his teaching in Italy, where he died in 1274.

It is not uncommon to find the thought of Thomas described as a Christianized Aristotelianism. Although this does not do justice to the vigor and originality of Thomas's writings, it does reflect an important element of truth. Logical tools that Aristotle forged were used with great skill and complete understanding by Thomas. So far as his scientific thought is concerned, particularly his physics, he is almost completely an Aristotelian. His psychology and theory of knowledge bear the imprint of both Plato and Aristotle. When he insists that human knowledge is rooted in sensory data and arises from abstractions made from those data, the Aristotelian strain is uppermost. This is a significant departure from the Augustinian-Platonic disposition to consider divine illumination as the starting point of knowledge and understanding.

Thomas engaged in a number of doctrinal struggles, not the least of which was his attack on the Averroistic doctrines. In his work entitled *Summa contra Gentiles* he gives the basic reason why he thinks the Averroists and others have gone astray: they have not properly interpreted the relations of faith and reason. His analysis of the legitimate scope of reason and revelation is of fundamental importance. Both reason and revelation can lead us to truth in divine matters, but certain doctrines relative to God, such as the doctrine of the Trinity (that God is "three in one"), are not subject to demonstration by human reason; or, as he put it, they "surpass the capability of human reason." These divinely revealed doctrines must be taken as true on faith alone. There are other revealed doctrines, however, which can be confirmed by the exercise of reason, for example, the basic doctrine of the existence of God. As a matter of fact, Thomas discusses five different logical proofs that can be given for the existence of God. In delineating the scope of reason and revelation, he is careful to emphasize again and again that there can be no conflict between revealed truth and truth attained by reason and that, although the way to truth may be twofold, there is only one truth. Here he is opposing the Averroistic doctrine of the "two truths." As a realist, Thomas opposed the nominalist view of the creation as a rationally unrelated collection of individual entities. Aquinas claimed that there existed an order in creation whose connections are intrinsic, ruled by law, harmonious, and rationally demonstrable. Since the entire cosmos was united by traceable emanations of God's goodness and rationality, Thomas's famous formulation followed: *"gratia non tollit naturam sed perficit"*—grace does not deny nature but brings it to perfection. Human reason and God's grace together open to man a life of wisdom and felicity. Both Thomas's benign view of human possibilities and his conviction that institutions such as the Church were logically justified and visible forms of eternal entities provoked continuous debate for centuries and, indeed, underlay in many ways the central intellectual conflicts during the Protestant Reformation.

Associated with Thomas and the schools of the thirteenth century was the technique of investigation and presentation commonly called "the scholastic method." It is an expression without explicit definition, being rather vaguely used by some authors to include any dialectical, or question and answer, approach to a philosophical question. Assuming such a definition, they find its existence in the early Middle Ages as well as in Thomas's time and later. But for the purposes of this account we shall accept its more common definition, as a logical technique developed in the universities of the high and late Middle Ages. This technique consisted in a detailed examination of all possible affirmative and negative arguments to a proposition or question, followed by a final determination of the truth or falsity of the proposition by utilizing the customary criteria: revelation, past authority, reason, and experience. In the form that this method assumed in the fourteenth and fifteenth centuries, it often led to a forbidding number of successive sets of arguments and counterarguments, so that the true opinion of the author seemed lost in a verbal forest, but on the whole it was productive of much fertile thought.

Not only did the schoolmen of the thirteenth century, and particularly Aquinas, present a systematic exposition of the general sciences or philosophy, but there also occurred a slowly growing movement toward the use of experience and experimental techniques in the particular sciences. The chief, but certainly not the only, protagonist of using experience to obtain certitude of knowledge was the Franciscan Roger Bacon. He thought that experience was of two kinds: the external experience which came through the senses, and the internal experience which arose from divine illumination. In stressing the necessity of external experience for the understanding of natural phenomena, Bacon also tells us that this external experience should be interpreted by mathematics; using mathematics in interpreting experience distinguishes the trained scientist from someone without training.

There is not much evidence that Bacon himself achieved any remarkable results by his experimentation. He and a number of other schoolmen repeated a number of the optical experiments already performed by the Islamic scientists before them. Their theories went little beyond the Islamic concepts. However, particularly significant experiments in optics were done by the Dominican Dietrich of Frieberg (before 1311), whose theory about the formation of rainbows was later adopted by Descartes. It was Dietrich, also, who remarked that in spite of previous authorities "one ought never to renounce what has been made manifest by the senses."

Considerable progress in the thirteenth century was also made in the science of statics, the study of bodies in equilibrium, and in the experimental study of magnetism. The *Letter on the Magnet* (1269) is a model of the observational and experimental technique in physics. It has no concern with supposed magical properties of magnets, but simply describes their physical properties.

The invention of the mechanical clock, increasing attention to the physical description of plants instead of simple statements of their medicinal properties, and certain practical zoological treatises reveal clearly growing concern with observation and experience. Technological and alchemical treatises also continued the trend toward experimentation started among the Islamic scholars.

In summary, the thirteenth century was a period rich in contributions to the intellectual heritage of the Middle Ages for contemporary civilization. It produced the university. It passed on a system for the classification of knowledge and for the relating of general sciences to particular sciences, a system which served as a framework within which and around which Western thought grew. It produced the great attempt at a universal system of knowledge in the works of Aquinas. Finally, it pointed to the growing importance of experientially based knowledge and to the increased use of mathematics and experimentation in scientific investigation.

## VII

In the fourteenth century the strong and complex traditions of nominalism produced, partly as a reaction to the Thomistic philosophy, a new critical philosophy by William of Occam (or Ockham), a Franciscan who taught as a bachelor at Oxford University in the first quarter of the century. This philosophy draws its name from Occam's psychology. His nominalism was more mature and complicated than the early nominalism of the eleventh and twelfth centuries. His reevaluation of the distinctions that must be made between intuitive or directly experienced knowledge and abstract or "thought about" knowledge was highly influential. All knowledge, intuitive or abstract, can be reduced to "signs," which stand for the object in question. In abstract concepts the immediate relationship with experience is missing. These concepts "apply to the object *as thought of,* not to the real object itself, for the abstract does not exist *in any way* outside of the mind." Thus universals have no reality as separate things but only as one kind of mental term or sign. Solely the "particular" or the "individual" stands as independently real. It thus seemed to follow that the claims directed to man in the name of such alleged universals as "God" and "Church" could only be made valid by faith, not by rational demonstration. Rather than weaken the authority of religion, however, Occam placed its claims on grounds beyond the challenge of human or natural reason and exalted the Divine aspects of priestly authority. Although Occam himself thus cannot be charged with skepticism, some of his successors were certainly led in that direction. If God becomes strictly an object of faith and not of demonstration, then men who demand demonstration may be hard put to maintain belief in God. Even for natural knowledge, where logic was used, Occam insisted that its categories not be multiplied beyond those absolutely essential to rational discourse; thus he delivered another kind of blow at the increasingly cumbersome logical structure of scholasticism and contributed to the growth of the notion that a scientific understanding of an event should aim for the simplest possible theoretical formulation.

The fourteenth and fifteenth centuries were a battleground for the struggle that took place between those who took up Occam's philosophy (the "moderns") and the followers of Thomas and the older scholastics (the "ancients"). The moderns became particularly noted for their attention to dialectical subtleties.

In physics the moderns at the universities of Oxford and Paris successfully challenged and overthrew some of the basic tenets in the scholastic-Aristotelian system and developed a number of striking concepts that were taken up in the sixteenth century and exerted some influence on the development of modern physics. These physical philosophers paid increasing attention to experience and appearances as criteria for physical theory. Many of the arguments they used in discussing such theories as the diurnal rotation of the earth reappear later in Copernicus's treatment. But most significant of the developments they furthered (first at Oxford) was the quantitative study of various modes of change, particularly of accelerated motion. Theirs was the first serious attempt in the history of scientific development to represent accelerated motion quantitatively. Oxford thinkers developed a theorem which was to be essential later in Galileo's analysis of the acceleration of falling bodies. This theorem was proved graphically by Nicholas Oresme at Paris with singular clarity. The fourteenth-century natural philosophers were never able, however, to describe correctly the free fall of bodies. Most of them believed that the speed of free fall increased directly as the distance of fall (rather than the time of fall) increased. Two scholars almost had the correct description within their grasp, but they did not realize it.

The explanation of the continuance of projectile motion by an impressed power, developed in late antiquity and picked up by the Arabs, in the hands of John Buridan at Paris and his successors ripened into a mature theory in the fourteenth century. Buridan designated this impressed force as an impetus, and his description resembled Descartes's and Newton's mathematical description of momentum, that is, the product of mass and velocity. At the same time Buridan declared that the impetus imparted to a projectile would last indefinitely if it were not destroyed by the resistance of the air and the gravity of the body. He applied his concept of impetus to the acceleration of falling bodies, and he explained that acceleration by the ever-increasing impetus imparted to the body by a continually acting gravity. We find in this idea at least the germ of one of the fundamental concepts of modern physics, namely, that a constantly acting force produces a uniform acceleration.

The study of dynamics accomplished at Paris and Oxford passed to the universities of central and eastern Europe, as well as to those of Italy. In Italy it competed successfully with a great variety of philosophical ideas. It unquestionably had some influence on the activities of Galileo, who with his successors evolved a powerful mathematical-experimental method and thus a new physics out of the modest beginnings made in antiquity and the Middle Ages.

## *FOR ADDITIONAL READING*


A. H. Armstrong. *An Introduction to Ancient Philosophy*. London, 1947.

C. M. Bowra. *The Greek Experience*. Cleveland, 1957.

G. B. Burch. *Early Medieval Philosophy*. New York, 1952.

M. Clagett. *Greek Science in Antiquity*. New York, 1955.

F. J. C. Copleston. *A History of Philosophy*. Vols. II and III. Westminster, Md., 1950, 1953.

F. Cornford. *Principium Sapientiae*. Cambridge, 1952.

A. C. Crombie. *Medieval and Modern Science*. 2 vols. Garden City, N.Y., 1959.

B. Farrington. *Science in Antiquity*. London, 1936.

H. Frankfort. *The Intellectual Adventure of Ancient Man*. Chicago, 1946.

E. Gilson. *History of Christian Philosophy in the Middle Ages*. New York, 1955.

E. Gilson. *Reason and Revelation in the Middle Ages.* New York, 1938.
G. Grube. *Plato's Thought.* London, 1935.
C. H. Haskins. *The Renaissance of the Twelfth Century.* New York, 1957.
———. *The Rise of Universities.* New York, 1923.
T. Heath. *A History of Greek Mathematics.* Oxford, 1921.
I. Husik. *A History of Mediaeval Jewish Philosophy.* New York, 1930.
H. D. F. Kitto. *The Greeks.* Baltimore, 1954.
A. Neugebauer. *The Exact Sciences in Antiquity.* Princeton, 1952.
H. Rashdall. *The Universities of Europe in the Middle Ages.* Oxford, 1936.
S. Sambursky. *The Physical World of the Greeks.* New York, 1959.
G. Sarton. *A History of Science.* 2 vols. Cambridge, Mass., 1952, 1959.
L. Thorndike. *Science and Thought in the Fifteenth Century.* New York, 1929.
E. Zeller. *Outline of the History of Greek Philosophy.* New York, 1955.

# IV

# EUROPEAN SOCIETY IN THE MIDDLE AGES

*John Hine Mundy*

The Middle Ages began during the fall of the Roman empire, the collapse of a cultural and economic union that had bound together the lands around the Mediterranean Sea. Historians have sought causes for this fall in every aspect of late classical life. A spiritual and social withdrawal from the ideals of Roman and Hellenic society seems to have been of prime importance. Beautiful in themselves, these ideas had become contaminated by being used, first, to justify the Greek and Roman conquests of the Near East and Africa, and then to buttress the growing despotism of the late Roman state. The principal practical aspects of this withdrawal were expressed in a gradual movement toward political separatism and an urge toward economic autarchy. This separatism was accompanied by the decline of cities, which had linked together the empire's parts, and by the rise of rural power. Furthermore, the turmoil within Mediterranean society invited intervention from the outside. From the fifth century A.D. until the tenth, successive waves of invaders from Europe and Asia precipitated or hastened the disintegration of Mediterranean unity. By the eighth century A.D., this once relatively unified cultural area had been divided between three grand linguistic, institutional, and religious groupings: the Latin west, the Greek east, and Islam in North Africa and the Near East.

The breakup of the Mediterranean world was also social and economic. This was most clearly exemplified in the West, the area most profoundly influenced by the earlier barbarian invasions (those of the Germans during the fifth and sixth centuries A.D.). There, from Roman times, state power and authority was slowly but surely decentralized, devolving upon ever more local authorities. In the language of institutional history, social command passed from emperors and kings, through kinglets and princes, to the petty seignorial dynasties of the medieval manor or to the "collective seignories" of medieval towns and even villages. The nadir—or fulfillment—of this immensely lengthy process was reached in the rural and urban seignories of eleventh- and twelfth-century France and northern Italy. Other parts of Europe underwent this devolution more slowly or only partially, but, local variations aside, generally followed the pattern of the central regions mentioned above.

Decentralization or devolution of social and political power was accompanied by a corresponding movement in economic life. Rome's relatively centralized economy was gradually undermined by the development of provincial and eventually local economic self-sufficiency or autarchy. This had the effect of replacing the classical "money economy" by a largely "domestic economy," based principally upon agriculture. The close coincidence of this economic movement with that of political and social devolution described above has unfortunately caused many modern historians to believe that "feudalism" with its decentralizing institutions is somehow necessarily bound to the dominance of agriculture in this period and to the consequent importance of land as a means of payment for service. This thesis obscures the obvious fact that agriculture is only one of many means of production and social service, although an important one. It also causes the historian to forget that income derived from all means of production and service may be granted as salary or remuneration for the exercise of office, and that this income may likewise become the possession of particular families or groups. Moreover, the same thesis has further encouraged historians to assert that the right to political and social power based upon hereditary succession typical of the "feudal age" is necessarily connected to an economy which is not a "money economy." The history of both the Middle Ages and other times, however, offers little evidence to support this proposition. Depending upon social circumstance, anything may be given "at fief," and the possession of anything may become hereditary. This includes money, that medium of commerce between the different means of production and social service. Offices with money salaries have become hereditary in past history, and there is no reason to presume that they could not again. The long history of the word "fee," in its successive translations from its primitive acceptation of "cattle" to "land" and eventually to monetary "salary," indicates that we are talking simply about modes of remuneration. Twelfth-century Italian jurists felt no confusion when they indifferently described monetary reward for service or office as either a "fief" or a "salary."

Indeed, the growth of hereditary right perhaps provides one of the best keys to understanding this problem. Because family authority is often in conflict with that of the state, the slow but sure development of hereditary succession to public office was one of the ways by which men of late antiquity and the early Middle Ages resisted the despotism of the late Roman state and its lesser successors in western Europe. It may therefore be proposed that "feudalism" was not a simple political and social result of an agrarian economy. Rather both it and the tendency toward economic autarchy were among the means whereby men sought to weaken central authority in order to gain a kind of liberty. What is important is that, in different ways, the religious or ideological man, the man of government and command, and the economic man in late antiquity all found their fulfillment in seceding from what they felt to be an externally enforced and unprofitable unity to an internally achieved and replete self-sufficiency or autarchy.

## I

Although causing immense hardships, Rome's fall was not disastrous. As with earlier empires, her collapse signaled a great cultural expansion. By the tenth century A.D., a watered-down Latin urban culture had spread beyond the empire's old frontiers into the whole of north and west Europe. The Byzantines had penetrated and begun to civilize Slavic Europe. Perhaps most impressive of all was the spread of Islam, a culture combining a Near Eastern inheritance with Rome's Hellenic one. Further, from the eighth century a rebirth of city life was apparent in both Islam and Byzantium. By the tenth century, this movement helped to stimulate a slow renewal of western Europe and its commerce on all of its coasts, particularly along the Mediterranean littoral and even, via the Slavic and Varangian routes of Russia, around the shores of the Baltic and North seas.

While earlier signs were not wanting, the West really began to stir in the tenth century, expanding continuously from that time until the early fourteenth century. Not merely stimulated from the outside by Byzantium or Islam, western Europe in the tenth and eleventh centuries created its own agencies capable of mobilizing sufficient social energy and capital first to arrest, and then to reverse, the trend toward decentralization that had marked its long history from late Roman times. The first of these agencies was the seignory which will be described at length later in this essay. The seignory provided a coercive form of organization that forced villagers and townsmen alike into communities capable of undertaking the initially hard and seemingly fruitless labor of expansion. The seignory was aided by the church, an ecumenical or universal institution. The most vigorous expression of the clergy's intervention in economic and social life was to be found among the monks. From the tenth through the eleventh century, the Cluniac discipline of the Benedictine order mobilized resources from the whole breadth of Europe to breathe new life into the older centers of western European settlement. From the end of the eleventh century a multiplicity of new orders, among them the Cistercians, carried the expansion into its greatest age, moving capital from older communities to new, and from older enterprises to new ones. The advantage of the monks in this activity was that they supplemented the intense local mobilization of the seignories with a relatively general or universal scheme of capitalization. Only by the late twelfth and early thirteenth centuries did secular groups succeed in replacing the church in this function. It was then that the merchants of Cahors and, far more important, the Lombards began their history as the undisputed masters of credit and capital in western Europe.

As is often the case, the growth of western Europe was partly at the expense of neighboring peoples. The Germans pushed beyond the Elbe river and into the Baltic coasts, dominating Slavic and Scandinavian regions. More impressive were victories over Mediterranean cultures. Byzantium was briefly conquered in the thirteenth century. From the eleventh, the West penetrated deeply into Islam. The Moors were driven from most of Spain, and, to the east, Westerners erected the short-lived Crusader states. With Mongol aid, they penetrated through the Islamic screen to Ceylon and China.

External conquest was profitable indeed; but far more consequential was Europe's internal expansion. This was partly in the lands bordering the Mediterranean Sea. River valleys like the Po and Garonne, only lightly exploited in ancient times, were cleared and settled intensively. Spain's central plateau was reduced by the plow for the first time. Most important of all was the first extensive clearing of the great northern European plain, extending from England to Russia. The growth of agriculture, also, entailed population growth. Eight million people lived within the frontiers of today's France in the ninth century; twenty million or more in the first quarter of the fourteenth. Towns grew everywhere, and, by the fourteenth century, Europe boasted cities approaching or exceeding one hundred thousand inhabitants, provisioned by and servicing a highly developed commerce.

During the later Middle Ages, however, Europe's expansion faltered. Led by the Ottoman Turks, resurgent Islam drove the European back. Economic and social crises, together with plague or sickness cycles, struck hard. Men of the fifteenth century, sometimes even later, saw half deserted cities and fields gone back to waste. The crisis had first struck Europe's urban center: the area running from the Lowlands and north France, along the Rhine and Rhone valleys, to north and central Italy. An important social aspect of this history was the fact that, in the parts of Europe mentioned above and the regions adjacent to them, population continued to grow into the early fourteenth century. At that time, economic life was characterized by a maximum utilization of the land—indeed, of all facilities whether urban or rural. In fact, wealthy though it appeared to be, Europe was clearly suffering from overpopulation. The frontier, it seemed, had been filled to overflowing. It is obvious, however, that nature seldom opposes absolute limits to man's increase: Europe was later to support greater populations than it did in the medieval age. A growing and inventive technology could surely have solved the problem of overpopulation.

Although the late Middle Ages brought some very significant inventions, they were not evident during the early part of the crisis. They appeared during it, as it were, not in time to prevent it. The organization of society seems related to this fact. During the early troubles a maximum subdivision of property together with an anticipation of high reward for services rendered seems to have been general. The results of this were not beneficial. Difficulty of mobilizing for common purposes is indicated by interminable lawsuits and by repetitive waves of revolutionary social action. For a time, farms and seignories morcellated to a point where they became too small to implement technological change on the scale needed by society. The rise of artisan guilds in the towns stimulated a revival of urban economic autarchy, thereby slowing the development of long range commerce.

While this malady spread during the fourteenth and early fifteenth centuries, its cure began to appear. If land and town had been overcrowded, they now became deserted. Protracted interregional and social warfare supplemented the effects of famine and sickness. Nature herself, hideous in the garb of plague and famine seemed determined to help man wipe the board clean and give him a new start. This enforced and brutal rationalization eventually cleared the ground and made it possible to erect large units of exploitation and capitalization. Neither the old rural seignory nor the jealously independent town was suited to hold its own in the intensely competitive and martial period of the fourteenth and fifteenth centuries. Indeed, their "reactionary" desire to do so inspired many of the wars and revolutions of the age. Reaction aside, late medieval or Renaissance man soon set to work to lay the foundations for a new and greater age. The unit of enterprise, both rural and urban, was enlarged. New and larger states appeared everywhere, mobilizing territory and social resources more efficiently than ever before. These were buttressed by elaborate corporate structures that, marked by real coercion and deep suffering, concentrated wealth and energy in a way undreamed of in the earlier medieval period. The reorganization of society conducted by the new state eventually gave Europe a new world: that of the cannon, the sailing vessel, the printing press. The use of these and other innovations, fostered and regulated by the state, made Europe's conquest of the globe possible.

## II

In the large, man's most significant accomplishment in the Middle Ages was the conquest of the northern European plain. The urban civilization that had begun in Near Eastern irrigated valleys and had spread to Mediterranean coastal savannas in antiquity took root in west and north Europe during this period. In the long run, the advantages of the northern plain over the lands of the Mediterranean were immense. Long human habitation had not deforested it. Northern soils were generally richer and boasted better mineral resources. These advantages, however, were not immediately apparent. The immense labor of clearing swamps and forests made the north's natural wealth slow to be realized. Besides, Mediterranean society possessed the initial advantage of a developed agrarian technology and urban culture, keeping the region around the inland sea ahead of the north until the dawn of modern times (c.1500).

Within the limited western or Latin cultural area, however, the balance between the north and the south was relatively equal. Indeed, as Rome fell, the center of Western might moved from Italy to the region between the Rhine and Loire valleys, a region already touched by Roman urbanism and the heart of the Frankish empire. Reasons for this shift are not hard to find. The gradual loss of the Black Sea, Egypt, Spain, and Sicily cut Italy and Provence off from grain exporting areas able to supply large cities. The Arab invasions or raids from Spain and Africa from the eighth through the tenth century weakened the towns on the French and Italian coasts. Besides, the Latin Mediterranean had little to offer the renascent Islamic and Byzantine cities. True, an exceptional province like Lombardy had timber and foodstuffs to export, but even here Byzantium controlled trade by its dominion, Venice. In general, the Frankish north enjoyed a clear advantage in this early period. Although commerce in goods was only occasional, the Franks had a resource that Mediterranean cities could not directly provide. As they conquered Europe, the Franks captured and exported slaves (Slavs) to Islam's expanding labor market. And when Frankish expansion ceased in the ninth century, Norse and Magyar raiders continued this profitable trade.

As the West revived from the tenth century and pushed back into the *Mare nostrum,* the picture changed. By the thirteenth century two industrial and commercial urban areas were clearly marked on the map of Europe. The first lay between the Loire and the Rhine rivers, with its center in Flanders. The second was the Mediterranean, extending from Catalonia through all of Italy, with its nucleus at Genoa, Milan, Florence and Venice. The southern center was mighty, boasting not only an industry equal to the northern but also the commercial advantage of being midway between Flanders and the Near East. Lombard merchant bankers invaded the north. Bologna's jurists taught the nascent legal professions beyond the Alps, and Rome became the diplomatic capital of the west. The north, however, had not been overwhelmed. French was the Crusaders' language and was spoken by Italian gentlefolk in the thirteenth century. As much as Englishmen and Germans, Italians viewed France as the home of architecture and domestic style. If Italy created medicine and law, Parisian philosophy set the tone for Italian studies. In short, the even balance between Mediterranean and northern culture that was the essence of medieval civilization had been achieved.

During the later Middle Ages, Mediterranean might relative to northern Europe continued to increase. Reacting against the north, particularly the French, the Italians developed and propagated their cultural style called the Renaissance. Iberia and Italy together opened the Atlantic and discovered the New World. Ottoman power spread throughout the Balkans, the Near East, and North Africa. The fact that France, Spain's greatest enemy, abutted not only on the northern European plain but also on the *Mare nostrum* is further evidence of this regions's grandeur. In fact, during the sixteenth century, the age of Charles V and Philip II, Mediterranean power almost seemed about to subjugate that of northern Europe. This consummation failed, however, principally because of the natural poverty of the inland sea in comparison with western and northern continental Europe. The seventeenth and eighteenth centuries were to witness the rise of North Atlantic power, and the nineteenth that of the North Sea and Baltic Europe. During these centuries, Europe conquered the world.

The attention given to the spread of urban civilization in these pages has perhaps assessed too highly the significance of the medieval town itself. Although urban life was more widespread in Europe than in antiquity, it is certain that no medieval town came near equaling the population of ancient Rome. Throughout ancient times and the Middle Ages, moreover, the Near East supported megalopolitan centers boasting a million or more inhabitants, whereas western cities rarely exceeded one hundred thousand.

Many reasons have been adduced to explain the absence of the great city in the medieval West. The history of technology has been used to elucidate this problem, and it is worth pausing to investigate a few of the arguments drawn from this history. Broadly speaking, it is true that basic techniques did not substantially advance from the late neolithic revolution that made city life possible until the eighteenth century. On the other hand, there were gradual improvements. As an example, the construction of a continental urban culture during the Middle Ages—perhaps the first in world history—required special inventions or adaptations of ancient techniques. The general use of the horse for agriculture and transport, the building of a Europe-wide network of roads and bridges, and the growth of Atlantic commerce tying south and north together are the most significant of these. Advances aside, the weakness of transportation prevented inland urbanism from producing the great city until well into modern times.

This fact, however, does not show why some medieval towns were not larger than they were. It is known, for example, that favorable geographical location can make up in some measure for technological weakness. Great cities in antiquity were often port cities or were located in rich alluvial river valleys like the Nile. The peculiarity of Western medieval urban life is that even when a town was located on an ideal site, it did not equal the ancient or medieval Near Eastern city in size. Venice was a port, yet it never equaled ancient Alexandria. The plains of the rivers that emptied into the North Sea near Flanders were as rich or richer than the Tigris-Euphrates, yet Bruges, Ghent, and Cologne together were not so grand as Baghdad.

The conviction that none of the reasons mentioned above is alone sufficient to explain this history is reinforced when the medieval age is compared with early modern times. In sixteenth-century Italy or France, towns had sometimes trebled the population reached at their medieval peaks. This change was not primarily caused by technological advance. True, maritime traffic on the

Atlantic had increased. The increased use of wagons and the start of a canal system had improved internal communications. Basic techniques, however, had not advanced much. The greatest technical achievements—gunpowder, ironwork, printing, and even the sailing ship—had only a gradual or indirect influence upon living standards. In fact, it seems likely that early modern European man lived scarcely any better than, if as well as, his forefather of the early thirteenth century.

There was, however, one change to which the inventions mentioned above give us the clue. All of them were connected with warfare and the state. It seems likely, therefore, that the growth of larger states in the later Middle Ages and the concomitant concentration of greater resources for economic endeavor were the principal conditions that made the great early modern town possible. The existence of unitary and centralizing states also explains why the Romans and Near Easterners had been able to build great cities in spite of technological poverty. The relative pettyness of the medieval town is therefore largely to be explained by the particularism or separatism that was the medieval social and political inheritance from the fall of Rome.

## III

Like most conceptions of society, that of the Middle Ages starts with a premise: God is good; nature, his creation, is good; and man, as part of it, is capable of goodness. Man's social objective, like that of his life in nature, is to accord himself with the good that is God's. This good is order, peace on earth, an imitation of heavenly bliss. On one hand, order provides a program imitating divine singularity, implying spiritual unity. On another, it proposes a hierarchy of functions, offices, or social orders aiding man to achieve the good of this life. Earthly good is threefold. It consists of health, a sufficiency of nature's products, and peace. All these are necessary in order to enable man to educate himself for the eventual attainment of heavenly bliss.

This idea had long been known to man: the particular voice that echoed into the early Middle Ages was that of late classical Platonism. Social thought, however, is not simply a record cut by philosophers or priests. In a practical sense, the late Roman codes of law adumbrated in infinite detail the harmonious ideal of a regulated social order linking man, nature, and God.

Accompanying the belief in a divinely ordained order for which all should strive was the recognition of the infinite diversity of the expression of the divine will in nature and in man's life. This perception was sometimes put in

Platonist terms: from divine unity devolved the infinitely multiplying and changing particulars of the earthly hierarchy. This view of life was sometimes accompanied by a sense of history in which the record of mankind or divine destiny was divided into successive ages, each prophesied by those who cried in the wilderness, each with its form of revelation. The divine origin and end of this scheme also justified the diversity and variety of human institutions for medieval social thinkers. Often, however, the same notion expressed an awareness that nature and humanity were but imperfect mirrors of divine essence: therefore, that man and his institutions could never wholly attain perfection. This conviction sometimes encouraged a natural feeling that something had been lost. Medieval imagination was often haunted by the image of a past and better age. There were even men who preached that community of property was the blissful condition of man before the Fall. Great churchmen shared the view that private right derived from the state's coercive power, itself necessitated only by man's natural incapacity or sinfulness.

This inspired regret was tempered, however, by the conception of rebirth and progress. Ancient philosophers and priests were ill content with the notion of progress that recommends itself to simple men, namely that each generation seems to know more than those which precede it. As in Christianity, they proposed a renascence of man, a recuperation of something lost, perhaps, but also a renovation toward the better. Theirs was a new teaching, they insisted, leading toward a new and higher fulfillment. Indeed, this idea is almost the very essence of the religious spirit in late antiquity and the Middle Ages. Sometimes, however, this stimulating dream could become a nightmare, as in the profound social disturbances that marked the ends of both of these great periods. Then enthusiasts predicted and even fought to create an earthly paradise in which to await the millennium. These convictions and actions remind us that the medieval conception of order was very broad indeed, and that it could occasionally be said to embrace the type of social action nowadays called "revolution."

The conception of the natural imperfectibility of man mentioned above, moreover, permitted or encouraged some classical and medieval men to go much further and to attack the very roots of social order. Such men simply denied the necessary connection between God (or nature) and society upon which the social disciplinarian must inevitably insist. Their wish to transcend nature and their conviction that God spoke to them mouth to mouth, were their be-all and end-all. They saw little good in man's company, in health, worldly knowledge, or service to peoples or princes. Those who die for themselves have no cause to live for others, they thought, and they seceded from the people.

Indeed, this intense individualism explains much of the early Christian passion and of religion generally. It also clearly expresses the urge that led men away from the goals of ancient society. But while this opinion was of enormous significance—even if it may have shown the only way to escape a secular despotism exploiting man's civil desire for good health and some wealth—it neither triumphed in the church generally nor won more than occasional loyalty on the part of mankind. Although regretfully, most men were willing to accept a compromise with an imperfect world, trusting that nature or God, individually through grace and collectively through increasing revelation, would show mankind the way to bliss.

It was a good thing that this was so because, in this imperfect world, Western man faced peoples who rejected his faith and refused to join his community. The sense of community then current in the West is worth investigating. The definition of the Western community derived from the marriage of Roman and Jewish law under Christianity. No longer the nation or the tribe, the community was that of all Christian men: the foreigner was the non-Christian. In ancient law, he was also the enemy, upon whom war might be waged, who might be enslaved, and from whom usury might be exacted. This rigorous national-religious conception had long since begun to weaken. Foreigners had regularly resided in the Roman empire protected by special statute, and the same was true during the Middle Ages. In the West, the Jews were the most important group of resident foreigners.

Medieval "Jewry law" developed from Roman, particularly late Roman Christian, legislation. Largely urban in the West, the Jews had been excluded from the civil community, making them a caste apart. By Charlemagne's time (800 A.D.), they came under the prince's protection in return for special service. Somewhat exempted then from local administration, the Jews naturally became the merchants *par excellence* of Frankish Europe. Since they lived under a similarly exclusive law in Islam, they served as intermediaries between two hostile societies, and, as foreigners in both, were able to handle essential trade, such as the trade in slaves.

Jewry reached its peak during the early Middle Ages. Valuable as a merchant, the Jew was not a simple serf: he was free in that his servitude was to public authority. Later on, his condition gradually declined. The Western urban revival of the late tenth and eleventh centuries eventually made his service as a merchant no longer so necessary. The rise of the Christian merchant gradually pushed him into the unpopular profession of usury. Popular pressure forced princes to abstain almost completely from granting public office to their reliable Jews. Stimulated by revived Roman law and protective papal legislation in the thirteenth century, the separation of the Jew from the rest of the population was underscored. Although it served to protect Jews, the growth of the ghetto in the centuries preceding the modern era evidenced the ever greater subjection and impoverishment of Europe's Jewry.

More significant was the conception of the foreigner who lived outside, particularly the Moslem. A certain grand consistency marks the whole medieval epoch. Christians could conquer other Christians, but they could not enslave them. As late as the sixteenth century, however, the Moor could be and regularly was enslaved. On the other hand, a gradual change of heart may be seen, necessitated in part by circumstance. Eleventh century Spanish princes sometimes titled themselves kings of the two or three religions—Jewish, Moslem, and Christian—because toleration was necessary for dominion.

More significantly, however, toleration grew because medieval men gradually began to separate ecclesiastical and civil government. Since cult and nation were one, the ancient Jewish and even the weaker Roman conception of the community and therefore of the foreigner was both civil and religious. The medieval conception was largely religious. Naturally, religion is not always tolerant. Nor was the medieval church always reticent in demanding the aid of civil society's coercive sword. But, because Christianity had risen as an enemy of the secular ideals and official cult of the Roman state, a certain tension and occasional overt hostility between the church and state characterized medieval life. Thinking men were therefore gradually led to separate the religious sphere from the civil. Because the state possessed coercion's sword, the church sought its weapon in missionary persuasion. Even advocates of forced conversion, therefore, longed for conversion by love. Medieval men eventually distinguished between the pagan's civil or natural rights and his religion, shying away from expropriation or enslavement. They liked to justify the "Roman war," the war against Islam, on the grounds that the other party had begun it by seizing Christian Jerusalem. Conquest aided the faith, they thought, only by giving unbelievers an open hearing of Christian doctrine.

Nor was this solely a religious question. The frontiers of Christendom never coincided with those of Europe's states in the Middle Ages. Warfare among

Christians was consequently common. Exceptions aside, a common faith made it impossible to strip the conquered of their natural rights. A nonreligious conception of the foreigner therefore appeared. Furthermore, as the national state began to replace the church and its faith as the focus of folk loyalty in the fourteenth and fifteenth centuries, Europe's wars began to evoke a quasi-religious passion that further served to weaken the distinction between Christian and non-Christian. True, the first formal alliance of Christian and Moslem states awaited modern times, but secular Europe's prophets in the early fourteenth century had long since enthusiastically justified pagan government even over Christians.

While this change exemplifies the potentially broader community or brotherhood of the secular age than the Christian one which preceded it, there were difficulties to be faced. Folk racism, for example, always persisted in the West: medieval literature refers to the "Jewish stench" and is rarely kind to Negroes. More broadly, sentiments of national racism had long since appeared. As Rome's conquerors, the Germans were necessarily struck by the difference of their own appearance and culture from those of their new subjects. Having subjected the latter, they naturally conceived themselves to be peculiarly free of "Roman servitude." These images never wholly disappeared, and, as the test of faith for "citizenship" began to weaken in the later Middle Ages, were reinvigorated to attack the clerical order. Clerical dominance of society, for example, was stigmatized as "Roman servitude" and contrasted with "German liberty." Such ideas were not, of course, fully developed racism. That awaited the language of natural science in the modern era.

Based partly upon the notion that the leopard cannot change its spots, racial sentiments were also part of a broader idea, that of historical or natural determinism. The effects of geography, climate, or of institutional tradition upon man were increasingly studied by medieval intellectuals from the thirteenth century onward. Classical thought was summoned to argue that particular areas were naturally endowed to produce man's leaders. Native institutions, such as the "freedom" of a particular law, began to be quasi-deified. A fantasy of "natural liberty" was adduced to show why the Germans, for example, had never been subject to Roman tyranny.

These remarks seem to betray a certain lack of sympathy. Obviously, there is a real measure of truth or usefulness in the ideas described above. Without some sense of the historical or natural determination of men's actions no "scientific" history is possible. Moreover, it is probably true that all men possess a natural impulse toward freedom, if only that there is no one who enjoys being made to do what he wants not to. But the rub is that some were thought to possess this "natural liberty" more than others either by virtue of their institutions or history or because of the ingrained traditions or blood of their people. As has been said before, these doctrines began to flourish as the nations rose against the church in the later Middle Ages. Once the church was subjected, however, the racial or historical differences between peoples were used to justify the wars between the nations themselves. Whereas then Moors and pagans had been joined to the broader brotherhood of secular men, these doctrines made it possible for all Christians to become equally foreigners to each other.

As a result, the law and practice of war began to change. Among medieval Christians, the justice of war between the brethren had been questioned and warfare itself severely regulated—sometimes, it seems, at the cost of non-Christians. With the changes outlined above, Mars was slowly unfettered. In modern times, Europe could envisage lawless war, the combat of nations, and the extirpation of whole peoples.

## IV

In the medieval West, society was generally described as being divided into three orders: *oratores, bellatores, laboratores*— "I pray for you," "I fight for you," and "I work for you" (or, in the sour joke, "I lay eggs for you."). This Platonic division first appears in literature during the age of the German invasions (fifth to sixth centuries A.D.). Its accent upon social function came from the late Roman attempt to weld mankind into different social orders performing state duty. The medieval orders, however, were but a primitivized reflection of the Roman. Although some aspects of Roman elaboration persisted into the eighth century, the distinction of civil as against military offices, of service nobility as against hereditary, had long been lost. Also, Constantine's great idea of self-perpetuating functional castes had partly failed because of the church's ideal of celibacy.

Though simplified, the late classical idea of functional social orders dominated social teaching in the Middle Ages—indeed, far longer than that. When eighteenth-century French jurists defined the body social, they still used the tripartite scheme. In fact, practical jurists employed this device only in the later Middle Ages. Before that it was largely a literary or clerical conceit, too general for the practical legislator. This fact provides a starting point for investigating each order individually. Medieval men were not so much attracted by schematic simplicity as they were by the immense diversity and change of practical life.

The history of the *laboratores* poses the problem of servitude. In ancient times, men were either slave or free. Slaves were largely procured by conquest. Our hunting forebears slew and perhaps even ate the conquered. With settled agriculture and urbanism, however, their labor became profitable. Once developed, the slave institution marked all antique society. The ancient slave was not a citizen with civil rights. He retained few of his labor's fruits, and had little control over his inheritance or posterity. Nor could he quit his master. In theory, the freeman was the reverse of all this. Because the distinction between a slave in the service of the state and a free citizen was anything but clear, however, social reality was more complex. Exercising legitimate regulatory functions, government was capable of limiting or obliterating the citizen's civil rights, his private right to his labor's fruits, his dominance of his posterity, and his wish to quit the body social. The essence of slavery must then be sought elsewhere. It may be found in the fact that private persons could own other men under public law, using their service more or less as they saw fit. Habitual in antiquity, slavery of this kind declined in medieval Christendom. Our problem is to find out why.

Because no society can live ever at war with itself, slaves were recruited outside. Under the empire, the stabilization of Rome's frontiers cut recruits. The emperors' attack upon private and family authority, moreover, lightened the slaves' lot and further depleted their numbers. As a result, slavery was weakening under the empire. It revived again during the German invasions, and, into the ninth century, western expansion was partly motivated by slave hunting. The revival of the Islamic economy, however, made it more profitable to sell the slaves than to keep them in western Europe. By the tenth century the slave institution was clearly in decline, and after that the whole nature of the problem changed radically.

As has been stated above, the primary medieval definition of the foreigner was religious. Whereas before the Roman citizen could not be enslaved, now all Christians were protected. Unattached to any particular tribe or nation, Christianity was moved to proselytize: the pagan, so to speak, was converted before he could be enslaved. By A.D. 1000, this religion had spread from the Mediterranean basin through Europe to the nearly empty steppes of Asia. The remaining populated frontier was that of Islam, and Christian power never reached the point where it could enslave more than a few Moslems. In short, until the Portuguese adventures of the later Middle Ages, the expansion of the Christian community had cut it off from new recruits.

External circumstance was aided by internal change. Liberty and servitude had come closer together in late Rome's regulatory state. Unless replaced, the peasant was bound to his land, the artisan to his lathe, the soldier to his sword, and the priest to his vocation. Service invaded liberty, and liberty became multiform. Each duty had its privilege, ample for the great or dangerous, small for the humble. In late Rome, the law for slaves or for freedmen became increasingly appropriate for describing the real condition of men still formally free. It had also long been the custom of the emperors to attribute partial public jurisdiction to local magnates over their tenants. A personal or private relationship thus tended to fuse with a public one. In short, although formal slavery was clearly weakening, all men were becoming servile in one way or other. Until the ninth century, however, this confusion or fusion had not penetrated deeply enough to eradicate the distinction between a free peasant bound by public law and a slave.

This distinction slowly vanished—a lengthy process paralleling the growth of the seignory whose lord inherited much of the authority once vested in emperors and kings. As has been noted above, state power devolved first to kinglets, then to dukes and counts, and finally, in eleventh-century France, for example, to the greater barons or seignors. To these chiefs of what were in effect petty states, public power had indeed become private right. More significantly, however, the reverse was also true: private or personal right to village service had become the true public right of the age. Unlike past landlords, the seignor did not merely seek labor to work land. Who would be a landlord when he could be a prince? He sought instead to govern the community no matter whose land its citizens worked. He protected the village church. He promoted, and profited from, common facilities such as mills and the forest. His were the village courts, and to him its inhabitants owed labor and blood for common defense.

The lord sought to reduce all inhabitants into a community whose members were equal—equal in service. The special laws that had separated villagers since the German invasions of the fifth century disappeared. There were no Franks, Lombards, or Romans any more; there were only "rustics." Freemen were depressed, deprived of access to courts beyond seignorial frontiers and of the right to leave the community. They became "villeins," citizens of a *villa* or jurisdictional area regulated by its own "public law." The slave, however, also rose to become a villein, a member of the community. The word *servus* became relatively rare in the documents, being often replaced by the anodyne term "rustic." Indeed, the rustic was rather like the citizen of a modern state. He served one state and court; he owed guard, taxes, and labor for community causes; his freedom to marry outside was limited; when permitted, his inheritance was taxed and controlled; and he could not leave the community at will.

There are, however, significant differences. Most of these derive from the fact that the seignory was a very petty state indeed. Many marks of ancient servitude characterized its "public law." The law itself was largely based upon personal bonds. The villein-citizen was his lord's "from the soles of his feet to the crown of his head." Moreover, the "state" was not an abstraction as it is today or as it had been in Rome. It was there in the village, personified by an all-too-human lord or his agent. Furthermore, the *oratores* and *bellatores* enjoyed different statutes that set them apart from the other inhabitants of the village. Even if the legal employment of the term *servus* diminished, the aristocracy still thought of villeins as unfree men, sometimes even as "stinking serfs."

Naturally, the rustics soon tried to lessen their burdens and restrictions. By the thirteenth century, they had generally succeeded. There were exceptions, however. Within each village, some families had risen more than others. Within each province, some villages had gained more liberty. The jurists of this later age were therefore again obliged to distinguish between different peasant groups. Whereas before, in the eleventh century, it had sufficed in parts of Italy and France to describe all except gentlemen as villeins, implicitly unfree, thirteenth-century jurists were forced to place the freeman peasant between the gentleman and the serf. This makes it sometimes seem that the early medieval pattern had just returned to new use. But it is important to remember that the new serf never reverted to the condition of the old slave. True, the new servitude was often labor and personal service unconnected with community citizenship. Christian could not enslave Christian, however; besides, the definition of what the community was had begun to expand with the rise of national and regional states from the twelfth century. In this larger community, the serf was almost as much a citizen as the freeman. Late medieval French jurists, therefore, rightly distinguished between the "liberate serfs" of their own land and the occasional real slaves they saw in Spain and Italy.

To say that slavery became uncommon in Europe during the Middle Ages, then, does not mean that servitude disappeared. "Liberate servitude" continued into modern times and even sometimes expanded, as on Europe's eastern frontiers. Stimulated by revived Roman law, pure slavery also persisted in Mediterranean lands—indeed, it grew as access to Islam's slave marts increased during the Renaissance. When ships reached West Africa, Portugal imported the human product so enthusiastically raised by slave-hunting tribes. Fortunately for Europe's free labor force, the labor required by the New World soon made it more profitable to ship the Negroes there.

From the history of servitude, we now turn to that of liberty. First preached in a world divided between slave and free, Christianity had no clear teaching concerning freedom in society. Naturally, certain teachers and sects enunciated the ancient principle of natural equality and urged the abolition of servitude. While valuing spiritual freedom and equality, however, the church at large did not affront society with revolutionary doctrines. Medieval clergy therefore usually counselled the slave to be subject with good grace. Besides, slavery was a natural institution to many, if not to most, Christians. It derived from capture in war, an institution itself originated by sin, man's common condition after Adam.

Like laymen, moreover, churchmen inherited the late Roman idea of social service. Performing on earth a divinely ordained duty, one prepared himself for salvation. While he sometimes enjoyed earthly privileges, the real liberty he possessed was the freedom to serve. This service ethos was important throughout the Middle Ages. Its weakness did not lie in the fact that some were obliged to do their duty and others not: however high, all were coerced by divine ordinance. It suffered, however, from another very human imperfection. The service of something lovely, as of the beloved by the lover, as of war by the naturally martial, or as of command by natural leaders—these services could ever find willing slaves. Those for whom service was agony were the drudging multitude.

Medieval man was therefore not deprived of the hope of freedom. A Christian, we know, could not enslave another. Furthermore, from antiquity on, the enfranchisement of one by another was believed virtuous as long as it did not disturb the fabric of church or society. This idea was clearly linked to the myth of spiritual progress and renewal so significant in Christian thought. Documents of manumission proclaim that Christ came to bring man freedom. Furthermore, the vision of a lost golden age aided that of progress. To the Roman jurists all men were naturally free, and most medieval charters consequently reminded emancipators that they were restoring a natural right lost through the establishment of the *ius gentium:* that is, the law founded by war and by sin.

Although often moved by these grand ideas, the rustic in the eleventh century seignory naturally sought a liberty both more specific and more attainable. He generally seems to have wanted first to fix the duties he owed his lord. That attained, he tried to reduce them. He wanted hereditary right to his land and usages. He wished to marry freely and to be able to quit the community if he chose to. In fact, the rustic's search for personal freedom eventually led him to attack the seignory, the petty state whose subject he was. Indeed, social history inevitably seems to require the language or forms of politics. What the peasant desired for himself involved the whole community, together with seignorial government.

A custom or community law, although rarely written down, began to appear from the moment of a seignory's foundation. The lord's advantage in this codification was that his rights were usually new and he liked to hear them stated; the peasant's, that his duties were clearly delimited. From this base, the peasant-citizen worked to alleviate the burden of government. The next stage was to exercise it. Full self-government was rarely attained, but sharing between lords and subjects became common in the twelfth and thirteenth centuries. Village councils elected political executives. Justice was separated into "high" and "low." Involving great civil suits and crimes, the former usually remained the lord's. Petty offenses and most civil contention fell to the villagers to settle for themselves.

Among the reasons advanced to explain the growth of peasant liberty described above is the fact that the age under discussion was blessed with a "frontier" or expanding economy. It cannot be shown, however, that economic expansion necessarily reduces servitude. Men do not always freely seek the risky labor of new enterprise nor can they undertake it without capital and direction from those who, having the power, exact their price. Histories of periods other than the Middle Ages show that growing slavery often accompanied the exploitation of new frontiers. Similarly, the first great age of medieval economic renewal in the tenth and eleventh centuries coincided with the formation of the seignory, where, while some slaves were freed, many freemen were enserfed. In fact, it seems likely that the creation of the seignory was one of the principal reasons for the reversal of the nearly millennial trend toward ever more intense localism characteristic of late antiquity and the early Middle Ages. From the moment when the seignory was established in the central regions of the Latin west, this trend was reversed, and the economy began both to expand again and to become increasingly recentralized.

Once the seignory had been built, once its coercive machinery had produced its beneficent work, and once the expansion was really under way, coercion was no longer so necessary. During the eleventh and twelfth centuries the whole social picture gradually changed. The happy potentialities of an expanding economy were evoked—primarily, it seems, by the competitive nature of devolving and decentralizing political and social authority. Complaints by those whose subjects' loyalty had been undermined by better terms offered elsewhere were legion. Competition made it necessary for the lords to lighten their peasants' burdens. Moreover, the sting was taken out of this by profit. New village court fees and taxes, however light, obviously offered the seignors more than uninhabited swamps or forests.

Toward the end of the thirteenth century, as we know, a new age began. By now mature, medieval economy and society entered an age of crisis and temporary contraction. Faced by more competitive markets, wars, and social troubles, agrarian society required larger and more efficient units of production and social mobilization. In these circumstances, the pursuit of freedom faltered. The need for solidarity reinforced the village community, sometimes by reintroducing servitude. Where labor was short and land plentiful, as in eastern Europe, a new serfdom was imposed. Generally, however, the developed West faced a different problem: the need to rationalize and develop new types of production. This required both recasting contracts between landlord and peasant to the benefit of the landlord and ejecting superfluous population from the land. Among those with traditional rights to the land were serfs. This age therefore witnessed the anomaly of serfs forced to become free at the cost of land or equipment. While serfdom generally decreased, therefore, liberty had somewhat soured: formally free, the peasant was sometimes more deprived economically than his servile forefathers.

Although often hard bound by economic need and still subject to some seignorial authority, the typical western European peasant of the year 1500 was a free man—"free, Frank, and a Roman citizen," as a French notary put it.

## V

As each European "race" or nation has thought itself peculiarly well endowed for the pursuit of liberty, so has each social group. Before and after the French Revolution, Europe's aristocracies believed that they had carried Western man's torch of freedom. A free blood ran in their veins, they asserted, and their privileges had restrained princely tyranny. As their power declined, however, liberty's history was rewritten. The town's good burghers were now thought to have been those who best expressed and even invented the urge toward freedom which first emerged in the Middle Ages and then triumphed over superstitious feudalism in the French Revolution. Neither privilege nor title was the mark of freedom's new aristocracy: the business of the merchant and the entrepreneur was what annointed them. A shriller voice was soon added. Man was impelled toward a purer freedom by the desire of the many, it was said, whose individual weakness made them exploitable but prevented them from exploiting others. A proletarian cult tinctured history with the incarnadine of 1848 and the Commune. Let us examine the application of these ideas by historians to the history of the medieval town.

In medieval cities of ancient foundation and some size, two relatively distinct groups participated in the early struggles for freedom in the eleventh century: the knights and the ordinary citizens. Knightly service to the prince was largely military and administrative. The other citizens shared these duties too, but their service was principally economic, in form of tax or labor. From the eleventh through the thirteenth century, the decline of princely power often followed a pattern. First, the knights gained a kind of liberty, obtaining hereditary right to their status and to their remuneration for service. What had once been duties now became rights, not subject to princely free will. In the second stage, the general citizenry achieved the same, though naturally in a more formally political contract.

In short, aristocratic historians were partly correct. The knights' "revolution" was often the first to show the way to freedom. More, the *mores* of the knightly aristocracy were eagerly aped by richer burghers, even in towns where few or no knights lived. These burghers were the patricians who governed most twelfth- and thirteenth-century free towns. Indeed, this argument may be pushed further. Viewing the whole, the more a medieval town boasted a knightly aristocracy, the freer it usually became from princely authority.

The bourgeois historian, however, was not short on grist for his mill either. The burgher was this story's hero, and rightly so, because he was the middle element in town life, the mean and central source of urban might. It is necessary to emphasize that all the burghers are spoken of here—landlords, entrepreneurs, men of industry, and merchants—not merchants alone. Admittedly, tenth-century German monarchs, for example, granted whole towns the "merchant franchise" or "power"—a practice that has led some historians to think that liberty derives from huckstering. But such grants developed from the ancient habit of freeing merchants (or, for that matter, the prince's Jews) from the jurisdiction of local officers in order to encourage trade. Neither the merchant nor the community was thereby free of the prince. That this privilege could become a foundation for later town liberty, however, is clear. In the circumstance of failing central power characteristic of Germany from the tenth into the thirteenth century, such an exemption had the effect of freeing a town from a local seignor who might have become powerful by placing it under the authority of a remote and increasingly powerless prince, in this case, the German king or emperor.

The burgher's greatest victories were won in southern Europe, particularly Italy. By the end of the thirteenth century, great Italian city republics recognized no effectual sovereign and ruled whole provinces. The burgher triumphed also over the nobilities in this area. The wealthy fused with the town's knightly lineages, and knighthood itself became a municipal accolade. Rural seignors were also subjected, being obliged by law to reside in town. In northern Europe, burgher gains were also considerable and sometimes equaled the Italian. In general, however, northern towns were not so independent, nor did they govern such large areas of the countryside outside their walls. Though northern patricians also boasted lineages and rural seignors maintained town houses, the fusion of knightly and burgher aristocracies was less advanced there. Towns feared the inclusion of seignors in political life and sometimes even prohibited their residence within the walls.

The humble also played a role in this history. Few town uprisings of the eleventh and twelfth centuries fail to give clear evidence of the might of the many. Early town associations proclaimed the membership and even the formal juridical equality of all inhabitants. Terms such as "citizen," "burgher," and "Good Men" do not at first distinguish the rich from the many. Town revolts, also, often show the first evidences of guilds. In spite of entrepreneurial and even aristocratic overtones, the growth of craft and trade corporations exemplified the people's growing social power. Individually weak, the many achieved some measure of real equality with the greater citizens through corporate power. The guild or corporation first sought to protect its members in their economic lives, and then, by the thirteenth century, advanced to demand and acquire a role in political life.

In sum, every urban social element had a part to play in the attainment of liberty. Leadership generally remained in the hands of the wealthier and experienced few. The impulse was given by the many. The truth of this proposition is indicated also by the obverse of the coin. The late medieval or Renaissance town witnessed the reimposition of princely government either from within its walls or from without. Either to protect their station in life or to attain it, all social groups seem to have been equally active in promoting the prince.

As though preparing for the renascence of princely power, citizen solidarity declined in the thirteenth-century town. Terms such as "citizen" and "burgher" no longer sufficed to describe a citizenry ranging from great burghers who "lived nobly" to simple workers "who had no lineage." From this initial awareness of stark social fact, a system of social orders slowly developed. Combats between the rich and the poor, neither of whom had the power to overthrow the other, made it necessary to formalize this system. By the end of the fifteenth century, whether in the Italian principate or the French national monarchy, the conflicts of the various social groups were generally arbitrated by external authority, that is, by the prince. The performance of this function required a government controlled by no particular class, empowered to intervene within the community to enforce its decisions. This resulted in the repudiation of medieval urban self-determination and the enervation of medieval government by election. As his ancient Roman predecessor, the prince favored a society divided into social and functional orders.

Putting aside resident foreigners such as Lombards and Jews, the urban social orders of late fifteenth-century France may be taken as typical. Governed by an especially severe law, the lowest group is describable as orderless. It included interstitial elements, immigrants and workers not yet incorporated in trade or craft guilds, and "ribald folk," from beggars to gilded youth. Above these were the artisans and smaller tradesmen brigaded in monopolistic corporations or guilds regulated and protected for the common good. These were summoned to advise public authority: masons, for example, being consulted about building codes. In general, however, the artisanry was or had been politically disenfranchised. Next came the merchants, organized but not quite so tightly, and consulted on more serious matters, those concerning the economy, notably coinage. Sometimes, merchants were also politically disenfranchised. On the highest level stood the burgher. Often "living nobly," he could ascend into the nobility of civil office, that of "the robe," and even that of the sword. He was a rentier or entrepreneur who worked "honorably, not with his hands." To him principally was entrusted magistracy and the professions, as of law or medicine. Experienced in political or juridical office, he sat in the third estate of provincial or national assemblies.

Privileged and wealthy though burghers were, their order had wide variations. A notary born of great lineage was often poorer than a successful tradesman, and correspondingly more critical of his times. Again, while burgher society clung to honors accorded by princes, the medieval tradition of republican government was part of its inheritance. Naturally, in having become the property of an urban aristocracy, this idea had become offensive to the many and hateful to men of new blood who, by serving the prince, tried to enter high society. On the other hand, the wheel had turned full circle. Participation in government had trained the early medieval town aristocracy to replace its princes. Together with others, patrician burghers and their jurisconsult sons were eventually to initiate again in modern times the defeat of Europe's monarchies.

To return to our thesis, if it cannot be argued that any one group in the medieval town desired or fought for liberty more than any other, it may still be believed that urban life encouraged this virtue more than rural. In fact, modern European historians have been inclined to attribute a particular propensity for freedom to the cities. Eliciting evidence from the history of the medieval town, they have argued that the townsman's urge for freedom differed not only in degree from that of the peasant but also in kind. This proposition is worth looking at more closely.

The medieval town was a center of communication—therefore, of trade in goods or ideas. As such, it was a seat of government, church or lay, hence of defense and social ideology. It was also a place for work or production. All of these characteristics were equally true of the medieval village. There are, however, differences. The town was usually larger to start with, or, because of its site, grew more rapidly than the village. Size, then, is one difference. The second was a function of the relationship of size to specialization. Although agrarian in comparison with the great city of today, the size of the medieval town prevented its inhabitants from living off the land directly, obliging them to specialize in industrial or intellectual pursuits. On the other hand, villagers usually farmed, spending less time on other activities. This difference was important for the relations between town and countryside. Although each needed the commodities produced by the other, conflicts of interest naturally arose, causing hostility and war between town and village and between heavily and lightly urbanized regions. Hostility aside, however, the medieval town was no more than a great village, distinguished only by size and necessary specialization.

This definition would have vastly surprised medieval man. The difference between townsmen and countryfolk was accentuated in his time to a degree unimagined in Rome or today. The strength of this attitude was probably due to the destruction of the unitary state in the early medieval period, during which rural seignories and urban "collective seignories" divided up a once united social fabric. This long process may also be seen in the history of juridical terms. In the early middle ages, terms were still inclusive: "city" meant both the town and the region around it; "town" (*villa*) was applied indifferently to either town or village. Later, both words evolved toward their modern significance. Juridical terms distinguishing between townsmen and countrymen were slow to gain general currency. In the sense of contrasting urban man with the "rustic," the word "burgher" began to spread through Europe only in the eleventh century.

Moreover, the aspirations of both peasants and townsmen seem to have been similar. If peasant liberation began after community unification under seignorial authority, so did that of many towns. If the village then began to seek liberty from its lord, so also did the town. As in the village, the search for personal liberty gradually became one for political rights. The famous phrase *Stadt Luft macht frei* ("City air makes free") conjures a picture of a onetime rural serf living as a free burgher protected by town law. This picture is reasonably accurate, but it is sometimes forgotten that *Stadt* meant "village" as well as "town," and that the same law was applied in many a "new village" or "new town" in the countryside. Indeed, village politics exhibit in simplified form the same wide range seen in the towns: there were village monarchies, oligarchies, democracies. As urban leagues appeared to pursue common aims, so did village confederacies. In a given province during the thirteenth century, villages varied from those almost wholly free of their lords to those almost wholly subject.

On the whole, however, the town gained more liberty faster and earlier than the village, and completed it by winning more political emancipation. Few villages maintained that their republics held of God and of no other, as did Marseille, and none conquered whole provinces as did Milan. The reason for this difference in degree is complex. In an age when all sought freedom, the town's central location made it the focus of provincial effort. Particularly in areas of ancient urbanism, the city was the traditional capital, and therefore always boasted a developed political tradition. Obviously, also, a village was too petty and powerless to live alone. Perhaps this was why hereditary seignorial government never seemed wholly unjustifiable to the rustic. Like the other relatively unspecialized activities of village life, government and defense were probably cheaper when left to the "professional tradition" of a family enjoying province-wide relationships.

It may therefore be concluded that there was no essential difference between a burgher's or a rustic's desire for liberty; there was only a difference in degree of attainment. Nor did the townsman particularly love liberty for itself. While he was surely moved by grandiloquent ideas about liberty, what he principally sought was freedom for himself. Naturally, this desire sometimes made him grant freedom to others. Only a community of more or less equally free men possesses the solidarity needed to defeat external authority. Lest his prince divide and rule, the burgher was obliged to eradicate enclaves of servitude within the walls. Also, towns often freed peasants from their seignors. This policy was largely motivated, however, by a desire to wreck the seignorial state, thereby subjecting rural folk to urban government and economic dominance. In fact, medieval urban history seems to teach that freedom is loved when solidarity is necessary to defeat a foreign or domestic enemy. Once he is exorcised, there seems to be no social reason why citizens should not own slaves or exploit disenfranchised labor. Urban customal law rarely obliged citizens to liberate their own rural serfs, and, when formal slavery grew in Renaissance Italy, most slaves served in town.

Lastly, no more than the rustic was the townsman an ever-constant lover of liberty. He at times surrendered the political rights essential to his desire for social freedom. Suffice it to observe here that townsmen were everywhere among the principal agents and inventors of the Renaissance princely state and of Europe's divine right monarchies. This should occasion no surprise. The traditional allurements of the service ethos in Western history have already been underscored. History also teaches that there were other ages than that of the late medieval and early modern period in which the cheerful performance of a bounden duty seemed more useful for society than the fulfillment of liberty, of each man's desire to live as he wishes. Moreover, experience reminds us that however high the achievement of liberty may be on a formal or political level, the individual ever lives the larger part of his social life subjected to his employers, teachers, and parents—a score of petty monarchies and oligarchies, sometimes even hereditary ones by virtue of private property! However free he may wish to be, man is ever instructed in the way of service and servitude.

## VI

The members of the second order, the *bellatores,* were principally defined by their function and wealth. Generally speaking, they were members of an aristocracy of hereditary wealth, which alone could afford to serve society as mounted soldiers. Constituting a *militia armata,* they defended society, and therefore administered or commanded it. Theirs was not an exclusive monopoly, however. The clergy exercised some civil authority, and all laymen participated both in defense and government, though principally as subordinates. The martial order was further defined by its tradition. There were Roman elements in this, particularly in regard to the conception of "honor" or office. Generally, however, as the inheritance of the German invasions (fifth to seventh centuries), the ethos of the aristocracy was essentially German or Germanized. While there were notable exceptions, its intellectual tradition was therefore nonliterate. This does not mean that it was anti-intellectual, for poetry and music flourished in medieval courts, but rather that the mechanics of literacy were considered ecclesiastical or plebeian. Lastly, its martial cult of the sword was well exemplified by the long persistence of trial by battle or duel, so consistently deprecated by the clergy, the commoners, and even by the state.

The medieval martial order, however, was not only founded on an aristocratic tradition of family wealth. It was also based on personal service pledged by one man to another by oath or contract. The growth of household clienteles, both of princes and of private notables, had long marked late Roman society. Offering both military and domestic service, these groups comprised individuals ranging in status from slaves to freemen under special contract. The clientage system was already widespread when the Germans, boasting a primitive but analogous institution of the war leader and his sworn band, entered the Mediterranean world. The German *comitatus* reinforced Roman clientage, and German primitivism formalized the already developed tendency to confuse personal relationships with the exercise of public functions. Indeed, semi-servile or free clienteles bound by oath or contract admirably suited late Roman society where, as we know, the frontier between slave and free, between public and private right, was being gradually obscured. This and like institutions provided means whereby social and military command could be entrusted to quasi-servile groups or even to servile aristocracies. Such systems emerged in late Rome and Visigothic

Spain (sixth to seventh centuries), and developed into a major political form in medieval Islam. They also deeply influenced the later medieval West: to be called a "vassal" long implied servitude. In fact, Europe's troubled history from late Rome to the eleventh century witnessed the slow imposition of personal bondage upon all Western officialdom and aristocracy.

During this period and even at its end, society was marked by a service ethos so strong as to imply general servility. Social terms were loosely used: "liege man," for example, could refer to a simple serf or a great officer. Princes and seignors entrusted administration to servile ministers, sergeants, provosts, or bailiffs, who usually owed foot or mounted service in war. Their condition was like that of the villein or early burgher: they could not marry freely, their offices and remuneration were not hereditary, and they could not quit their service. A ministerial spirit penetrated the whole of the aristocracy. The higher ministerial groups clearly overlapped the frontiers of the "free" aristocracy. Until liberated in the eleventh century, the lesser knights of Lombard towns were ministerial. Enfranchised, French provosts in the same period could become either knights or burghers. In areas of strong central authority, as the German empire, a ministerial knighthood came to constitute the backbone of the state. It is noteworthy that as this monarchy slowly disintegrated from the twelfth century forward its ministers gained freedom, fusing with burghers or rural nobility. This evolution took place earlier among Italy's lesser knights and the greater French bailiffs or provosts.

It is therefore not surprising that the martial and administrative order was much divided. The servile group alone varied from simple toll collectors to truly princely minister-knights. Among free knights, there were always at least two classes. Serving in princely retinues or possessing relatively little wealth, lesser knights were always distinguished from the greater ones who held seignories or high office. Moreover, simple knights were bound to perform their function. Privileges were lost to a youth who was not trained and dubbed in early adulthood. Even when overage, the knight who failed to perform service lost station.

On the whole, however, warlike prowess and wealth put the knightly aristocracy in the best position to resist the servitude imposed on Europe's freemen in the early Middle Ages. Unlike ministers, free knights could usually leave their lord's service. Moreover, they were the first social group other than the clergy to mitigate the semiservitude into which they had fallen. For France, evidence of this has been seen in the way the average rural or urban knight was paid for service. In the tenth century, a knight surrendered property in order to enter a lord's clientele, receiving its income back as salary. By the end of the eleventh century, a lord granted property or income in order to attract a clientele. There were further ameliorations of the knight's condition. Well into the tenth century, public office and its recompense or fees were not generally hereditary. Gradually, as a principal aspect of the decentralization and the devolution of state power, they became so. By the early twelfth century, most knight's fees had also become hereditary, except in areas with strong ministerial cadres. In a sense, this right was the basic aristocratic declaration of independence. What dukes and counts had won from the greater princes as remuneration for the exercise of particular offices as early as the ninth century, the knights later gained as recompense for the general function or service of their order.

Recent historians have noted the significance of a new conception of the family which flowered from the tenth and eleventh centuries: that is, the lineage idea. This conception reinforced the brotherhood and solidarity of the aristocratic family, thereby enabling it to better resist external authority. Since lineage implied an extended family group, it linked together the whole of the knightly order. Dealing with his lord or prince, the knight was no longer alone. Behind him stood his family, boasting relationships throughout his order, and, in the law of the time, dealing with other lineages almost as a sovereign entity.

Public authority's recognition of hereditary and lineage rights formed the base of local custom. As has been proposed above in regard to towns and villages, the establishment of a custom usually implied or resulted in a diminution of service. An example may be seen in the effect it had on warfare. By the mid-twelfth century, offensive war within Europe had been curtailed. The term of free military service had often been reduced to forty days a year. Expeditions to distant places were hedged about with restrictions. In short, aristocratic solidarity had made war largely defensive. Moreover, services gradually changed into rights. From being a bonded courtier, the knight became one whose role in judgment was his right—indeed, in matters concerning his order, his near monopoly. While princely caprice was often exercised and sometimes even justified, the main "feudal" tradition proposed that judgment be rendered by the defendant's peers.

Growing rights soon led gentlemen to think in political terms. New private law, new taxes, and warfare affected social station and were therefore matters about which knights wished to be consulted. In towns where a substantial group of knights lived, this desire, as we have seen, often abetted the development of a formal political constitution, a "collective seignory." In the countryside, political consciousness was slower to emerge. There aristocratic solidarity together with lineage *mores* sufficed to advance knightly interests by breaking up the great seignories of the twelfth century into the smaller ones of the thirteenth and fourteenth centuries. This period, however, also witnessed the beginnings of truly political organs, the regional judicial and semilegislative parliaments that, in turn, led to the Estates-General of the later Middle Ages.

In short, the *bellatores* were the first secular order to gain freedom. True, aristocracy had sunk during the early Middle Ages. But, at the very moment when the term "vassal" applied to almost every knight, its sting had been lost. Instead of implying servitude, it described a nobleman. It is therefore worth pausing to define the twelfth-century conception of nobility. Like other townsmen or villagers, knights owed service. But they were not ordinary members of the community. Like their burgher patrician imitators, they were usually the *patres* of lineage and rarely intermarried with other social groups. Their real community was their order, to which all western monarchs equally belonged. Like princes, their lineages claimed the right to make war. While bound by duty, they were free to come and go as they saw fit. Although the term itself had many other social connotations and restricted applications, the quality of freedom constituted the essence of "nobility."

During the later Middle Ages—sometimes earlier in precociously developed regions—this conception faded. As others, even peasants, gained liberty, the older accent on freedom became meaningless. Moreover, both burgher and ministerial aristocracies penetrated the order and emulated it by "living nobly." These changes could not have occurred, however, without the advent of the new state. When the passage of public authority from kings down to simple seignors was first described in this essay, the pettiness of the seignorial state was emphasized. By the time this devolutionary process had reached its full term in the thirteenth century, the economy of the West had matured, and Europe was recentralizing. In that context, the little seignory was no longer viable as a form of state, and the locus of real power began to shift upwards toward the regional or national state. Moreover, the lords were seriously hurt by the growth of peasant freedoms in areas of ancient settlement. New methods of exploitation could be and were introduced to alleviate this pressure, but these required both power and capital far exceeding the means of a petty lord. In a different way, similar problems were posed in towns where patrician elements faced the rise of the many to social and political power. Nobility, or aristocracy, was therefore profoundly threatened.

To these characteristics of thirteenth-century life must be added the immense crisis of the fourteenth and fifteenth centuries, when wars between social groups multiplied the effects of those between states. As each group pushed into the fray, it equipped itself with suitable arms. Towns created artillery. Peasants and townsfolk paraded ever more worthy footmen until the Swiss finally invented an infantry that could stand alone on the battlefield. The modern army, in which cavalry was only one arm, was built by society's estates in this age. Besides, a militia of occasional soldiers did not suffice for prolonged warfare. Professionals were needed, and, as a result, the martial order split into those who were real soldiers as against militiamen. A profession, the new chivalry was also somewhat indifferent to lineage. Arms were thought to ennoble the soldier, whatever his origins. Comic themes early appeared, such as the debate on whether the brawny peasant or the delicate gentleman is better at arms. As in arms, moreover, so in law. The old aristocracy was too unspecialized to serve all the functions of mature and complex society. As the lay assessors of the old courts were replaced by, or subordinated to, professionally trained jurists, another militia, the juridical, made its appearance. A simulacrum of nobility was accorded late medieval judges, the doctorate of laws sometimes being thought equal to knighthood. The nobility "of the robe" had been born, showing yet again that lineage was falling before professionalism.

These manifestations were justified by a grand idea. What makes a man noble? Ancient wealth or lineage? These were not the main factors, in the opinion of many. They were important, of course, because a good family tradition prejudices its heirs toward virtue. But the usual answer was that virtue was nobility's source. The reasons for this idea's popularity are many. In theory, it happens to be true. Again, most who adumbrated it were clerks or jurists, who often lacked lineage but always boasted at least a formal dedication to virtue. More consequential perhaps, the argument obviously justified the rise of new men and therefore excited the interest of the new state which used them. To the state, virtue is service to society, and society is the state.

The nobility reacted vigorously both to these ideas and to the social pressures behind them. A satirical literature of lament flourished. The professionalization of law was resisted, often with partial success, as in England. With awful results, nobles sometimes tried to monopolize the battlefield. Reaction, however, soon led to invention. From the thirteenth century, the once rare or restricted word "nobleman" won increasing use in legal documents. Nobles were no longer necessarily knights. Sons or grandsons of knights, they were called "esquires" or by other titles that once referred to the stage preparatory for knighthood. Knighthood continued, of course, but largely as a habilitating accolade for individual service, preeminently military. Having lost its old function, the nobility increasingly was no longer defined by what it did, but rather by what it did not do. Local customs often prevented nobles from entering "dishonorable" trades or mechanical arts, though liberal professions were usually open to them. But this was not unprofitable: noble service to society had been replaced by privilege.

In fact, despite losses, the new nobility showed marked ability in advancing its interests. As has been pointed out, larger units of power and production were needed during the later Middle Ages. In France, for example, the nobility was hampered initially by the fact that brothers shared inheritances, dismembering and therefore dissipating them. Gradually, however, ancient systems of single succession, notably primogeniture, were accepted in many families and regions, the inheritance itself being protected against alienation by law. Furthermore, what had once been the condition of knight's fees, namely that they could not be acquired by others than knights, was gradually extended to noble property as a whole, thereby protecting "noble land" from the economic enterprise of commoners. This jurisprudence of the thirteenth through the fifteenth centuries also produced the first systematic codification of seignorial powers and jurisdictions known in France, at the cost, it is true, of seignorial independence.

It sometimes seems strange that noble privilege grew at the same time as did renascent princely power. The prince certainly based his authority as much on other classes as on the nobility. Nor was it in his interest to encourage privileged groups whose rights impeded him. He was naturally egalitarian: all should be equal in service. On the other hand, the prince needed to reward his servants. Serviceable commoners could be ennobled, empowered to acquire "noble land" and enjoy noble exemptions. Here was an interest common to both aristocracy and prince. Both wished to accentuate the difference between noble and commoner. The further apart they were, the greater the prince's gift to his servants.

It is obvious, however, that the interests of the two also differed profoundly. To the state, service created nobility. From the thirteenth century, princes ennobled commoners. From the fourteenth, knightly orders were created to reward individual nobles and sometimes others. Nobility was gradually attached to the performance of specific civil and military offices, thereby creating nonhereditary nobility. Knighthood could be used for the same function. Grudgingly, the aristocracy acceded. The prince's monopoly of ennoblement was generally soon admitted, and he therefore became the arbiter of high society. Even when capitulating, however, the aristocracy clung to a different notion of what constituted nobility. Its nobility was that of hereditary privilege, of "gentility" or "gentle birth."

As political thinkers soon understood, this irrational principle alone could resist the potentially tyrannical nature of princely authority. Princes consequently tried to limit or abolish hereditary right, as in Austria from the thirteenth century to the eighteenth. The argument from lineage was less irrational in reality, moreover, than in theory. Traditional wealth, experience of government, and particularly devotion to martial glory made the noble very different from ordinary men. Always vain, he was often more than a little mad. But his advantage lay in the fact that, for him, to see was to command. Together with the urban patriciate, then, the noble set a limit to the power of early modern monarchs and princes. As in England, the stronger the aristocracy, the sooner the fall of the kings.

The doctrine of "gentle birth" soon produced a curious justification. European national racism has already been discussed; a similar idea could be applied within particular societies. In medieval terms, a family was a race. As an order defined by lineage, nobility became a race. Being martial, its blood was that of conquerors. In France, the Franks had conquered the Gallo-Romans, and the nobility claimed descent from them. This idea appeared during the Middle Ages but became a major theme only in the religious wars of the early modern period, when the aristocracy fought the prince. It did not become the main definition of the aristocracy, however, until noble legal privileges were abolished in the nineteenth century. Then aided by what might almost be termed the reverse of the argument, namely the abrogation of legal restrictions on other groups, such as the Jews, the conception of nobility's origin became an essential ingredient in modern racist politics.

The late Middle Ages produced a vast juristic and popular literature describing the body social and its parts or estates. In it the tripartite division of mankind into *oratores, bellatores,* and *laboratores* played a justly important part. Nobles still paid the *prix de sang* and wore the sword at their sides. Most peasants, artisans, and merchants still provided little more than labor, technical counsel, and recruits for other social orders. Moreover, while it undermined the medieval conception of social order, the professional spirit was partly a return to the ideals that had long ago led man to accept late Rome's regulatory social teaching. This was clearly exemplified in the doctrine that inspired the new chivalry of the modern soldier, namely, that arms ennoble the man. In part, also, the evolution of the new nobility fulfilled the same teaching. Though gentlemen may not have liked to hear it said, service was the sole—but sufficient!—justification for privilege in the eyes of both the prince and the humble many.

On the other hand, being too few in number and socially indiscriminate, the old orders were fast becoming inadequate. Although the most honorable, the *militia armata* of the soldiery was now only one of the militias needed by society. Those of the liberal professions, headed by the jurists, had risen to leadership and thus to privilege. Lastly, a burgher patriciate of hereditary wealth, professional status, political attainment, and lineage had emerged from the *laboratores*. Its member was no longer one who said, "I work for you," but rather, "You work for me."

## VII

Medieval men thought of themselves as Christians. Unless born foreign, as Jews, Moslems, or pagans, all men were obliged to be Christians. Toleration did not exist: from Rome's Christian empire until modern times, no Christian could quit the faith. The passion of a religious sect and the Roman idea of the citizen's state cult combined to make conversion from the faith or secession from Christendom the principal form of treason for the medieval mind.

The universality of the faith, however, did not wholly transform this social conception into a spiritual one. True, most men believed. But there were doubters. In no more than a few phrases, a thirteenth century book designed to edify monastic novices teaches us that the church's central doctrines on the usefulness of a good life for salvation and the relation of human will to God's providence were simple nonsense to some. Indeed, medieval life and letters generally show that the faith had not obviated man's natural spiritual disquiet. Moreover, laymen often expressed hostility to the clergy, and churchmen never succeeded in eradicating profound divisions about basic issues within their own order.

The churchman was convinced that his function was primarily spiritual. His was the duty of praying. In the extreme accents of the monk, his function was not even to teach, but rather to weep for the world. This image had been implanted in the church at its genesis, when a way of withdrawing from civil society had been wanted. Society's ideals were naturally those that accented—indeed, made divine—human bliss: good health, a sufficiency of wealth, and citizenship. But, for many reasons, the peoples around the Mediterranean had come to hate the state that embodied these ideals. Man refused to eat the food thrown into his cage, and, when he could, fled the company of other men. The search for freedom by fleeing society or the world was one of the principal reefs on which classical civilization was wrecked. A belief in the moral superiority of supra-mundane ends, therefore, colored ecclesiastical social attitudes throughout the Middle Ages. Honest labor excepted, worldly professions, particularly the soldier's and merchant's, were disparaged by the clergy. Those in the church who best realized true spiritual withdrawal were the hermits or monks, and it was they who constantly reinforced the clerical order's accent on celibacy, which was its most obvious social distinction from secular society.

Withdrawal, however, was itself imperfect. Monks were to weep and not to teach, said the preacher, but, in fact, they taught and copied books. Indeed, it was observed that a monastery without a library is like a camp without war munitions. What was the war that the monk was fighting? To flee man's company seems clear enough. But the Roman police had long ago learned that those who exit usually return. The world never left them quite alone, and they were obliged to reenter it to convince its inhabitants of the virtue of their solitude. Also, the monks' calling was so inebriating that they frequently wished all men to share it. Even this most ideal institution, therefore, somehow failed. Few indeed could really "be dead to the world" and yet live. Besides, except rarely, eremitical liberty did not provide a method for organizing society. From its earliest days, then, the church regretfully turned back toward the world, absorbing the social and ethical teaching of secular society. This action could be justified, moreover, because the world's work was obviously useful for the church's mission of salvation. A prelate once ruminated on how he could save his soul. By good works, he thought, by building the fabric of the church. It was in no way strange to him, nor is it to us, that he proposed to do this by increasing his revenues. His search for heaven implied remaking the earth.

For this and other reasons, the once rebellious church soon became the state's partner. This was no easy companionship: "If two men ride upon a horse, one must ride in front." In the long period from Constantine to the eleventh century, the church, though daily stronger, was decidedly the junior partner, even the handmaid, of princely authority. During the German invasions (fifth to sixth centuries A.D.), however, the clergy gained two new sources of power. They shielded the provincials from the German military, thus taking over the exercise of charitable and social functions from the failing Roman state. More significantly, since German society was nonliterate, churchmen became the transmitters of Mediterranean literary and juridical traditions.

This great inheritance necessarily involved the clergy very deeply in the world's work. When developed, charity involved services ranging from the repurchase of captives to the maintenance of hospitals for sick and aged folk. While service was often freely given, it was basically financed by the donations of the faithful. Indeed, as the system expanded by the twelfth century, old age provision could even be bought. While beneficiaries paid only a small part of what they received in return, this and similar social services posed the problem of church property. A rhythmic pattern was created that marked the whole of the Middle Ages: as clerical property accumulated "to excess," periods of forced secularization were precipitated. On one hand, then, one sees the churchman as the beneficent protector of the weak, sick and poor: the *pauper* was the Christ, and He was the church. On the other, one perceives an occasionally sordid and hostile relationship between the clerical order and lay society.

Clerical involvement in the world was not restricted to caritative functions; it was also political. As the clergy inadvertently gained a near monopoly of literacy in the early Middle Ages, they became ever more clearly demarcated as an order. Their language was slowly divorced from those of the laity, becoming the only written tongue. With literacy went learning in law, the science necessary for social and political life. As early as the seventh century Visigothic state in Spain and Charlemagne's Frankish empire (800), the formulation of law and general administrative policy was perhaps entrusted more to the clergy than to secular notables. By the tenth century, a typical tribunal comprised three groups: the lord who presided, the assessors who rendered the judgment, and the "judges" who "read the law." Except in areas of strong Romano-Byzantine culture, the judges were usually churchmen.

At first, the participation of the clergy in government was profitable to Western princes. Endued with sacral and quasi-priestly qualities, kings conceived of themselves as governing a society defended by the secular sword but organized under civil episcopal authority. As in the tenth-century German empire, the reliability of the episcopal office for the exercise of civil functions lay in the fact that it could not be transmitted hereditarily, a significant quality in an age when hereditary right to office was a primary means by which lay society diminished princely power. Moreover, it was the general custom of the Western church for the higher clergy to be appointed by princes.

This old church, where prince-bishops who governed the world rubbed uneasy shoulders with monks who had fled it or beguiled them into state service by the promise of advancement—this old church had long since begun to change. The change culminated in a gradual revolution extending from the early eleventh to the mid-twelfth century with its peak in the pontificate of Gregory VII (1073). It is important to remember that this grand event coincided with a time of economic troubles during which aristocratic freedom was generally established, the first widespread town revolts occurred, and Europe's expansion, both internal and external, went into high gear. Furthermore, the same event seems related to the change in Latin Europe's balance of power that has been discussed before in this essay. From before Charlemagne until well into the eleventh century, northern influence had dominated the Western church, even the papacy. The Gregorian revolt resisted and eventually defeated northern power. Aiding the rise of Italy's cities against the German emperors, it thereby fostered the growth of Mediterranean Latin might. After the revolutionary age, the balance between the Mediterranean and northern areas typical of the height of medieval civilization was achieved within the church during the twelfth and thirteenth centuries.

The Gregorian revolt against traditional secular authority has often been described as a response to the "corruption" of the church by lay government. This is partly true. Most clerical inventions evincing a desire to "reform" the church or to direct secular society began in areas where the state had most decentralized, and where, consequently, churchmen were exposed to the intimate tyranny of petty princelings and local politics. Institutions such as the Truce of God and movements of monastic renewal, for example, largely originated in relatively "state-less" regions such as the Lorraines, the Lowlands, south and southeast France, and Italy. In part, however, the argument is false. South French princelings and north Italian seignors were not the church's principal enemies. With such, said Urban II, one could ally against the greater foes, the heads of great states, the princes in northern Europe, particularly the German emperor. These higher princes had undoubtedly protected, even "reformed" the church in past times, but they also dominated it. What churchmen sought, therefore, was freedom for their order.

Moreover, they were certain to win their battle. However great the sword, the might of an order that monopolized letters and thus the promulgation of ideologies is evident. Besides, the sword's might was dissipated as the devolution of the state reached its fulfillment. Aristocracies in town and country everywhere sought liberty from their princes. Seeking their own freedom, churchmen voiced slogans that inadvertently meant liberty for all men: clergy and laymen worked together in order to defeat or diminish princely power.

Thus allied, the clergy won its freedom. Lay lordship over churches subsided to simple patronage. True, clerical elections were never completely freed from secular pressure, but much liberty was gained. Though limited, "benefit of clergy" was generally admitted by Europe's secular courts. Besides, even before the Gregorian age, the clergy had increasingly supplemented or replaced the secular state. An example is the Truce of God, which involved regulating society both economically and politically. Closely bound to peace at home was war abroad, culminating in Urban II's institution of the Crusade (1095). Moreover, as secular power had waned even before the Gregorian age, the clergy had increasingly turned toward Rome, once weak and far away. Its appeal had gradually transformed and reinvigorated the papacy, making Rome into Europe's ecclesiastical capital and diplomatic center.

Roman leadership, the direction of Crusades against the Moslem, and the maintenance of peace at home eventually necessitated the regulation of society at large. An example is economic controls, typified by legislation concerning just price and usury. The Christian prohibition of usury was borrowed from Jewish law amplified by late classical and by Frankish legislation. Early medieval canon law mainly regulated the economic activities of the clerical order itself. The Crusades and the inefficacy of civil or state controls changed this emphasis. Canon law now invaded the secular world, attempting to police the market place. Useful though this regulation was, clerical rigorism was undeniably excessive, in its theory, at least, if not frequently in practice. This fact seems partly due to the hostility of the clerical order toward lay professions, as that of the merchant. Perhaps, also, rigorism is the usury that the religious mind customarily exacts from the rest of mankind.

Regulating the world, churchmen looked at it with new eyes, becoming interested in its history, politics, and society. A new accent was added to the older late Roman and medieval conception of social order. The earlier sense of an overriding unity was mitigated and sometimes even destroyed by an ever more "practical" and intense study of particular worldly things and institutions. Clerical intellectuals, therefore, turned toward the ancients who provided the terms for such discussion. This marks a change. Although clerks acted as state officers before the Gregorian age, clerical thinkers were often indifferent to the specific forms of secular organization and rarely debated even the constitution of their own order. Afterward, however, an intense interest in these problems was everywhere evident. The church itself was increasingly viewed as a social entity, its constitutional form being carefully examined. Of course, it cannot be maintained that the church had become "materialized" in clerical thought nor that a kind of indifference to secular affairs had vanished from the ecclesiastical mind. To the degree that churchmen were intellectuals, they were naturally disinterested in particular secular governmental forms as long as they tended toward the good. But there is no doubt that the mystery of the church itself was being increasingly expressed in social or political terms.

## VIII

The immense success of clerical leadership paralleled the economic expansion and growth of freedom in twelfth- and thirteenth-century Europe. Even in success, however, the church came under attack. In part, this was because every revolution, such as the Gregorian, stirs vehement ideas that cannot be translated into immediate action, if indeed ever. We do not refer here to conceptions proposing clerical direction of secular society, however appealing these were to the minds of certain pontiffs. There was enough hostility between the clergy and laity to prevent these from being more than a minor theme in Western thought. Instead, the ideas popular among both clergy and laymen concerned the spiritual renewal and "reform" of the clerical order and of the Christian souls entrusted to its care. Churchmen were urged to exemplify and to teach a grander spiritual freedom.

The most active protagonist of these ideas was the monk, the "assimilated layman" of the early medieval church. If "the religious" (as monks were termed) had withdrawn from the world in antiquity, they returned to it with a vengeance in the Middle Ages, endowing both the clergy and laity with their high sense of vocation. During the Gregorian age, monastic orders pullulated, ranging from Carthusians totally withdrawn from the world to those busy teaching or even fighting, as the Templars. Around many orders devotional groups of layfolk accumulated, who, as Urban II said, were to be encouraged because they "emulated the apostles." "The religious" also summoned laymen to help "reform" and spiritualize the church, sometimes to the point, as an anti-Gregorian complained, of unleashing a war against the priesthood. Indeed, the clergy was transformed according to the monastic image in this age. The marriage of parish clergy which had persisted for so long was again strongly attacked. Clerks were to emulate the apostles, no longer exercising dominion or government. Apostolic poverty, said the hermit, alone justified their spiritual teaching.

The urge to spiritualize the clergy was dangerously rigorous. Although once embodied in an abortive convention between pope and emperor (A.D. 1111), the ideal was impossible to attain. A laity as yet illiterate needed clerical secular service and government. Besides, most clergy knew better than to surrender church property and earthly authority on the gamble that an otherworldly or spiritual mission would elicit voluntary lay support. One moderate reformer cautioned lest the removal of Christ's purple robe be so violent that his white robe of priesthood also be torn off, leaving him naked and powerless before the world. Although impossible of fulfillment, or, perhaps, just because it was impossible, the belief was clung to by enthusiasts with all the more passion. It was the root of all significant medieval dissent or heresy.

The religious ideal, moreover, contained a paradox. The desire to free themselves from the world had led churchmen to direct it, to organize all society. What this meant in terms of the involvement of the church in practical politics and the multiplication of ecclesiastical taxes and judicial machinery is obvious. At the highest level, that of the papacy, it involved nothing less than the supervision of the governments of Europe. Rome bore the brunt of this. Before the achievement of clerical supremacy, Rome had been kindly thought of: "Roman freedom" was a Gregorian catchword. Granted ever more authority by local churchmen to array them against secular power, Rome became the mistress of the church and bore the responsibility for fulfilling the reformers' hopes. Soon even moderate reformers raised their voices to criticise Roman policies. For all those who felt their own insufficiency before the difficulties or impossibility of the religious ideal, an escape had been found, the phrase to describe it being "Roman tyranny." Extreme critics, however, went further. To them, the whole church had become responsible for failure. In past ages, for example, the opponents of a particular churchman could maintain that he was evil. But, because there was a vision of Rome's remote and traditional authority, to say that the whole church was evil did not suggest itself very strongly. With Roman centralism, however, enthusiasts could condemn the clerical order *en bloc,* contrasting the heavenly with the earthly church.

Dissent gave birth to heresy, that is, to formal secession from the church. Historians have sought to find the cause of this malady in particular social classes, often uncovering evidence of heretical leanings in individual groups in given historical moments or places. When added together, however, these cases indicate that heresy was not limited to any one social group, whether high or low. It is true, though, that growing city life had much to do with the spread of heresy. But, since towns also boasted an equal growth of orthodox thought and missions, this fact merely proves that they had much to do with everything. The same is probably true of foreign influence: it reinforced both orthodoxy and heresy.

When the areas in which heresy flourished are pin-pointed, moreover, it is noticeable that there are other aspects to this history. Where the state was strong, in north France or south Italy, for example, heresy did not flourish. An absence of coercive authority was therefore important. More, heresy multiplied in the same areas of Italy, France, and the Rhineland that saw the greatest inventiveness in orthodox devotion, whether of the earlier monastic type or the later mendicant. Despite occasional illumined laymen, therefore, it seems most likely that monastic or clerical extremists gave the dissenters their ideas and even led them.

The varieties of dissent and heresy are too multiform to describe here. Suffice it to say that all shared certain common characteristics, each of which could become the distinctive mark of a particular sect. All thought of themselves as the pure Christians. They or their leaders were believed to be peculiarly illumined, a notion sometimes resulting in hero cults. All rigorously criticized the world's church, insisting, for example, that only those emulating the apostles could direct man to salvation. This view necessarily condemned the clergy of the practical church and reinvigorated the idea of a lay priesthood. A further tendency was to caricature or exaggerate church doctrines. Thus, under foreign influence, the Cathars personified the distinction between God's goodness and the world's imperfection by two warring deities coexistent from all eternity.

As heresy grew during the twelfth century, the church turned toward repression—reluctantly. Its reluctance stemmed from many sources. Coercion obliged the church to request state action, often against clerics. While not tolerant, the clergy believed in trying pursuasion first. Again, an idea of a critically minded thinker differed profoundly from a conviction vehement enough to stir a whole sect to quit the church. However dangerous his teaching, no principal intellectual was slain by ecclesiastical police for his religious teaching until the late Middle Ages. He was sometimes punished and his sect, if such existed, was extirpated, but he himself was not burned alive. The church did not pursue thought so much as it hunted secessionist groups. Moreover, such sects had to gain size and repute before clerical police grew enough to pursue them efficaciously. The institution of an inquisitorial system awaited the thirteenth century, and thereafter slowly spread throughout Europe.

Pure coercion was only part of clerical effort. Since the circumstance in which the church found itself was generally happy in the expanding age of the twelfth and thirteenth centuries, a mixture of pursuasion and coercion was the principal way heresy was controlled. Expanding priestly functions, obligatory auricular confession appeared together with a literature specializing in problems of conscience. Universities, such as the one at Paris, were created in order to produce an ever more instructed clergy. Preaching increased to educate the clergy and to reach laymen directly. Coercion's hand behind its back, the clergy first sought to teach, enriching lay religious knowledge. By the beginning of the fourteenth century, simple illiterates sometimes knew the names and principles of the greater schoolmen. More, the ecclesiastical order opened wide to welcome new devotion. After initial repression, the early thirteenth-century papacy inaugurated a drive to bring the enthusiasts in. From the *Humiliati* through the Franciscans and other mendicants, new orders devoted to pastoral work appeared, while associated lay groups proliferated apace. These not only taught religion, they also justified the repression of heresy.

Although advantageous, this expansion was dangerous. Clerical awareness of this fact was signaled in councils culminating at Vienne in 1311, where the multiplication of orders and devotional sects was halted. The problems were similar to those already described in the aftermath of the Gregorian age. These problems are partly to be explained in terms of the evolution of the monastic institution. To put it baldly, what had happened was that the hope of the monastic proselytizer had partly come true. The monk's religious idea and sense of vocation had so penetrated the consciousness of Western man that all men, both clerical and lay, had become monks in some part of their innermost being. When all men possess the spiritual fortitude or vanity of the monk, there is surely little need for the tonsured religious or their rules. The consequent decline of formal monasticism from the thirteenth century weakened an essential group that had long cushioned the often hostile relationship of the priestly order to that of the laity. The authority of the priest now directly confronted the religious passion of the layman.

Moreover, as the excitement of religious thought grew, so did the intensity of spiritual ambition. Some of the inestimably useful Franciscans, for example, so magnified the doctrine of apostolic poverty that they launched a general attack on church property—indeed, on any property at all. Moreover, Franciscan offshoots and other sects exaggerated the idea of progress that had stirred the church so deeply in times past. What had once been a hortatory conception of increasing spiritual revelation and multiplying devotional forms in a common belief turned into a specific revolutionary scheme with a rigid timetable. The progressively more perfect realizations of spiritual freedom envisaged by enthusiasts now threatened to abrogate the priestly authority of the church.

The repression of this belief, called by some the "worst heresy" the church had ever been called upon to face, was nearly impossible. To answer extremists by asserting that true progress can only be realized in the spiritual pilgrimage of the individual and that the historical church will never (in effect) change may be true, but it is self-defeating. Enthusiasts rarely enjoy self-examination; what they want is to remake others, to renew the world about them. Besides, rebels merely looked elsewhere, conjuring up what the church was supposed to have been at its beginning and proposing to cleave to that. The contrast between "Pauline liberty" and present "Roman slavery" typified all late medieval thought. Furthermore, the repression of these ideas required the aid of laymen instructed in the faith to a degree unknown ever before. Summoned by the clergy to police the ecclesiastical order and even, in effect, its ideas, laymen necessarily became more and more endowed with a sense of conscience and, worse, of competence in religious matters. This feeling is the spiritual essence of laicism or secularism.

Feeling was not enough, however; practical competence was also necessary. The clergy of the pre-Gregorian church had enjoyed a near monopoly of literacy, so extensive that the creation both of ideology and law had been inconceivable without its participation. This situation began to change during the Gregorian age. Seeking freedom from secular power, the clergy wished to, indeed, had to surrender the exercise of civil office. As an officer of civil government, as a notary or MD, a clerk was necessarily subject to civil law. Training laymen to replace them, therefore, churchmen gradually retired from these activities. In the late eleventh century, lay letters experienced their first revival since the German invasions, at first in France. Secular notarial, juristic, and medical professions developed first in Italy at the University of Bologna and the school at Salerno. Naturally, the degree of achievement must not be exaggerated. As late as the sixteenth century, particularly in north Europe, government and law were still partly handled by churchmen. However imaginative or poetic, the technical immaturity of early lay political thinkers is often apparent. Fortunately for them, however, their clerical mentors spelled out their ideas in imperishable form.

As each secular profession emerged, it began to borrow clerical sanction, even, to steal clerical robes. If priests boasted a certain "angelic character," for example, so did judges. Indeed, the legal profession conceived of itself as an order, others being described as "laymen." Jurists benefited from clerical theories developed to justify ecclesiastical regulation of the practical world. These had amplified the importance of the active as against the contemplative life, stressing parish work as against monastic seclusion. Jurists soon used these theories to sanctify their calling. To them, the judge who repressed evil and protected the peace was worthier than any other of divine approbation.

The self-exaltation of jurists was duplicated by other professions. Chivalry, for example, asserted the near equivalence of its duty to that of the priest, protesting that soldiers preserved peace, advanced and protected the faith. When the teaching of newly studied classical writing on ethics and law was added to this type of group justification, the origin of the secular idea of the priesthood of the learned and professional was clearly visible. Moreover, these secular priests already had ideas about the clerical ones. To quote one example from many, thirteenth-century French gentlemen echoed an earlier Italian jurist when they informed the clergy that laymen alone should "wage" the active life. A contemplative clergy, they asserted, should emulate the apostles, and, retiring from the world, "bring back the age of miracles of which it has so long been deprived."

## IX

These ideas bore fruit during the later Middle Ages. Then, as Boniface VIII prophetically stated, the clerical order was "besieged" by the laity, by men, that is, increasingly competent to serve their own ideological needs and ever more profoundly instructed in religion. In part, the success of this siege was made possible by the circumstances in which it took place. The difficult, often tragic condition of European man in the later Middle Ages was a primary cause—not of itself perhaps, but because the crisis began at the moment when the clerical order exercised Western leadership. To direct the world is to be responsible for it, to profit from the fulfillments it offers its inhabitants and to suffer for its failure. When an army is defeated, it is usually thought to be the general's fault. Moreover, Europe's power structure changed radically in the same age. In the past, social power had not been so much vested in kings or emperors as in the seignories of town and countryside. The Roman church's universal authority was made possible by the intense decentralization of secular patriotism or loyalty. As we have seen, however, the seignory failed, and, as the greater national or territorial states grew, Rome's power relatively declined.

As a result, secular authority invaded the church, stealing its spiritual jurisdiction by "reforming" the clergy, secularizing public charity and education, and, on the humblest level, creating lay associations to finance and even to control parish churches. Each successive crisis in church history—the Avignon papacy in the fourteenth century, the Great Schism (1378–1417), and the clerical attempt to "reform" and reunify Christendom in the fifteenth-century Conciliar Movement—was inadvertently used to amplify lay power over local and national churches. During the councils, signs of a breakdown of the ecumenical idea may be seen in papal concordats with the various "national" churches signed at the council of Constance (1418). During the council of Basel, a particular national church, the French, promulgated its own constitution (1438). By the end of the councils, the age of the concordats where church and state shared ecclesiastical government was near indeed.

Clerical loyalties were naturally divided. As sons of local or national churches, most churchmen initially welcomed a diminution of Roman authority. The rapid rise of the secular spirit, however, clearly threatened clerical liberty. Many churchmen doubted the spiritual efficacy of an ecclesiastical order subordinated to lay authority, and therefore stridently reasserted the validity of the sacerdotal order. To accomplish this, they multiplied the marks that separated it from laymen, magnifying priestly spiritual power. To counter lay ambition and princely tyranny, moreover, they eventually built an increasingly monarchical papacy and replenished or multiplied the universal orders associated with its work. A renewed and princely papacy appeared by the beginning of the sixteenth century, to be aided in its effort by new orders, such as the Jesuits.

Other churchmen sought freedom in a way that boasted equally deep roots in late medieval social and religious thought. This view accented the separation of divine from human things, proposing that the faith need not be embodied in any particular social institution. It therefore deprecated the sense of order of the medieval church, robbing it of religious sanction. Morally speaking, this disestablishment implied that earthly moral law could be administered by any human agency, clerical or not. Socially, it meant that the clergy was just another profession, higher in the object of its devotion than others but otherwise similar. The active life of the religious teacher provided the prime definition of this profession's duty. The contemplative life became the mark of all true Christians, no matter what their professions. Radicals who held these views were certain that they would find a higher spiritual liberty or fulfillment by surrendering the distinctions and juridical privileges that marked the ecclesiastical order. To gain this liberty, they were willing to play down sacerdotal mysteries, secularize monastic orders, and reject wholesale the social marks dividing lay and clerical orders, as celibacy, for example. Some revolutionaries even sought to exalt lay authority above that of the church.

In moderate form, both of these conflicting ideas permeated the minds of all late medieval churchmen, and persisted on both sides of the frontier between Catholicism and Protestantism even after the "Reformation," the moment when Europe's ecclesiastical unity was destroyed. It is evident, however, that the accent upon sacerdotal and papal authority was stronger in the Mediterranean area after this event, while secularization in its preliminary Protestant form triumphed in northern Europe. This difference reminds us of the struggle between these areas waged throughout medieval and modern history. Believing that they had just cause for grievance, Germans, Scandinavians, and Englishmen pushed to extremes. By the sixteenth century, they felt excluded from the papacy and exploited by it. Indeed, there may have been something in what they said. From the thirteenth century onward, Italy, France, and eventually Spain and south Germany had risen to prevail in the church. If Italy almost "possessed" the papacy by the early sixteenth century, the proximity to Rome of the other more or less southern regions had enabled them to elicit concordats so gratifying to national interests that northern envy was stimulated. Lest her closer neighbors demand still more, thereby obliterating ecclesiastical liberty, Rome begrudged similar concessions to northern powers. The north thereupon seceded, declaring independence of the Roman pontiff. While the pope remained the monarch of a spiritualized Roman empire, Christendom vanished and the secular political order of Europe began its history.

The failure of the clerical order was not immediately perceived. Until the end of the seventeenth century, Europe's wars and revolutions were still fought in the Saviour's name. Ethical and even scientific literature long remained "churchy" in tone and language. Admittedly, the basic separation of intellectual endeavour into religious as against secular interests had been promulgated by the late thirteenth- and early fourteenth-century schoolmen, and fifteenth-century Italy had already produced a developed tradition of secular moral thought and a secular view of man's relation to God and nature. But secular intellectualism did not dominate until the eighteenth century or even the nineteenth. Moreover, the institutionalization of religious as against secular spheres, as the nineteenth century separation and mutual toleration of church and state, has yet to be universally accepted, if it ever can be.

After the Reformation the ideas and institutions of secularism gradually matured and took hold. What had been in the Middle Ages a sometimes puerile and revolutionary laicism became a tolerant liberator. Secular thought was not attached to the authority of any one social order, as the clerical. It spoke a language transcending the struggle between Christian sects. Indifferent to the religions practiced by the world's inhabitants, it included all peoples. Indeed, in practical terms, its casual toleration of any and all religions and its conscious multiplication of philosophical systems resulted in a kind of beneficent polytheism. Moreover, the fortunate circumstances of modern Europe's immense expansion and its division into many rival states permitted the secular spirit to be profoundly tolerant for a time—even in a social sense. In this, the medieval inheritance of modern man played a very significant part. However mighty Europe's princes, however totalitarian the peoples of her nations, state policy was for long judged and limited by the heirs of ancient orders, both of the church and the aristocracy. By today, however, the weakening of ecclesiastical sanctions together with the slow dissolution of hereditary right and privilege has helped to pose the principal social problem of contemporary life: the secular tyranny of the state.

## FOR ADDITIONAL READING


M. Bloch. *Feudal Society*. London, 1960.

R. Coulborn, ed. *Feudalism in History*. Princeton, 1956.

F. L. Ganshof. *Feudalism*. London, 1952.

E. H. Kantorowicz. *The King's Two Bodies: A Study in Mediaeval Political Theology*. Princeton, 1957.

F. Kern. *Kingship and Law in the Middle Ages*. Oxford, 1948.

H. C. Lea. *A History of Sacerdotal Celibacy in the Christian Church*. 3d ed. New York, 1907.

H. S. Maine. *Ancient Law: Its Connection with the Early History of Society and its Relation to Modern Ideas*. London, 1861, 1946.

J. H. Mundy and P. Riesenberg. *The Medieval Town*. Princeton, 1958.

B. N. Nelson. *The Idea of Usury: From Tribal Brotherhood to Universal Otherhood*. Princeton, 1949.

H. Pirenne. *Belgian Democracy*. Manchester, 1915.

———. *Medieval Cities*. Princeton, 1925.

E. Rosenstock-Huessy. *The Driving Power of Western Civilization*. Boston, 1950.

G. Tellenbach. *Church, State, and Christian Society at the Time of the Investiture Contest*. Oxford, 1940.

M. Weber. *The Theory of Social and Economic Organization*. Glencoe, Illinois, 1957.

———. *Max Weber on Law in Economy and Society*. Cambridge, Mass., 1954.

A. Déléage. *La Vie rurale en Bourgogne*. 3 vols. Vol. I: Texte, Chap. X, part 8, Macon, 1941.

G. Duby. *La Société aux XIe et XIIe siècles dans la région Mâconnaise*. Paris, 1953.

F. L. Ganshof. *Etude sur le developpement des villes entre Loire et Rhin au moyen âge*. Paris-Brussels, 1943.

L. Génicot. *Les Lignes de faite du moyen âge*. 2d ed. Louvain, 1952.

P. Guilhermoz. *Essai sur l'origine de la noblesse en France au moyen âge*. Paris, 1902. Reprinted in New York, n.d.

G. de Lagarde. *La Naissance de l'esprit laïque au déclin du moyen âge*. Volume I: *Bilan du XIIIe siècle,* 3d ed. Louvain, 1956.

G. Dahm. *Untersuchungen zur Verfassungs- und Strafrechtsgeschichte der italienischen Stadt im Mittelalter*. Hamburg, 1941.

A. Dempf. *Sacrum imperium: Geschichts- und Staatsphilosophie des Mittelalters und der politischen Renaissance*. Munich and Berlin, 1929.

E. Ennen. *Frühgeschichte der europäischen Stadt*. Bonn, 1953.

# V

# THE MEDIEVAL ECONOMY

*Marshall Clagett*

There is a great deal of discussion and disagreement as to the conditions of the economy of the early Middle Ages. According to an older view, the barbarian infiltration, invasion, and occupation of the western half of the Roman Empire produced a great catastrophe in the economy of the West. One economic historian of considerable stature thus epitomizes this view: "Humanity has seldom known miseries so great as those of this period." He goes on to say that Roman institutions either passed away or were greatly modified by the Germanic invaders, that a considerable portion of the land changed hands, that workers were uprooted, that Germanic village and rural organization tended to displace the Roman villa communities. This "catastrophic" view is rarely held today. Research into the origins of medieval institutions has tended to support the opposite view that there was, on the whole, a surprising continuity of economic institutions from the late Roman Empire to early medieval kingdoms. For example, the basic rural or manorial system so characteristic of the Middle Ages owes much to the Roman organization of rural estates, and is, in fact, its direct heir. Furthermore, forms of land tenures, the cities, and certain municipal organizations and institutions continued to exist under the Merovingian and other Germanic kings in the sixth and seventh centuries. It appears to be little more than a fable that the barbarians shunned the cities and sought rural areas, as the older view taught us, for the greatest of the Roman cities continued their existence during the occupation, even if their population did fall off. Marseilles, Nîmes, Bordeaux—even Paris and Orléans—appear to have been flourishing centers and to have had merchant populations during the sixth century. On the whole, there was a sense among the Germans of falling heir to, or rather becoming a part of, the

---

This is a revision of Professor Clagett's essay in the second edition of *Chapters in Western Civilization.*

Empire; and, where able, the Germanic peoples tried to preserve important institutions and customs.

Intimately bound up with the question of the survival of Roman institutions is a second question as to whether or not the barbarian kingdoms adopted or sank into a natural or domestic economy, that is, an economy essentially closed, with local trade only, with exchange taking place by barter in kind (produce) rather than money. The answer is difficult, but it seems increasingly clear that the economic unity of the Mediterranean was preserved after the barbarian invasions and the formation of their kingdoms in the West. Some of the Western cities, particularly Marseilles, were still doing business with the wealthier and more highly cultured cities of the East (especially with Constantinople and the cities of the Syrian and Asia Minor coasts), as well as with ports in Africa, Egypt, Spain, and Italy. The foreign merchants at Marseilles are mentioned in contemporary accounts. We know of markets, cities, and towns near by which received the products funneled into Gaul by this, her greatest port. Of considerable support to the theory of economic continuity is the fact that the Merovingian kings continued the coinage of gold. Gaul naturally continued under the Franks and others to be an agricultural area as it had under the Empire. But there is rather good evidence that the agricultural society of Gaul under the Merovingians of the sixth and seventh centuries was still a part of the money economy of the Mediterranean. No doubt in many areas the villas were organized on a basis approaching self-sufficiency. One further observation should be made. Even where a local, domanial economy prevailed, little exchange was by barter. Money remained the medium of exchange. There simply was not much circulating in those areas.

## I

We have been speaking up to this point of the immediate period of transition from the late Empire, explaining the activity in Gaul under the Merovingians. A still further question is raised as we come down to the time of the Carolingian kings in the eighth and ninth centuries. Was the money economy which still existed in Merovingian Gaul transformed more completely into a self-sufficient economy, the so-called closed or domestic economy? The answer can tentatively be put in the affirmative. Key to the economic transformation, in the opinion of one historian, was the rise of Islam in the seventh century and her spreading over the eastern and southern Mediterranean world. Islam changed the Mediterranean from a Roman lake into a sea of perils, dominated by Moslem raiders. In this view, the economic unity of the Mediterranean was ruptured, and Gaul was transformed from a partially maritime land into an inland area. The Franks and other Germanic kingdoms sank into a relatively complete domestic and closed economy. Villas and manors became self-sufficient. Urban industry languished, and money exchange was reduced to a minimum. Evidence of this new state of affairs is revealed in documents that picture domestic self-sufficient estates, particularly the *Capitulare de Villis*. Additional evidence is found in the change from gold coinage to silver, the frittering away of minting rights to a rising feudality, and the drift of minor trading activity to the north. German historians, however, have adduced somewhat contradictory evidence designed to show that the economic unity of the Mediterranean was never really shattered and that Germanic kingdoms did not go completely into a domestic economy, trade and money exchange continuing throughout the Carolingian period. But even granting the existence of more trade than was formerly thought, there is no question that western Europe (with the possible exception of Italy) in the early Middle Ages (through the tenth century) was largely agricultural. Cities were small, and manorial economy did obtain over a considerable area. Trade was meager.

It was during the early Middle Ages that the essential agricultural unit, the manor, took form. Although the manor differed in detail from century to century and country to country, it was the predominant form of agricultural organization throughout the entire Middle Ages, even after the rise of trade and the decline of feudalism had amended the unfree status of many of its laborers. The manor continued in one form in France until the French Revolution and in eastern Europe down to the twentieth century.

The lord, or fiefholder, held the manor or several manors organized into a great estate. Tenants, or serfs, most often lived in villages within the confines of the manor or at least on the estate. Sometimes they were domiciled on their holdings rather than in villages. Since the manor always had some degree of self-sufficiency, the lord maintained workshops for various types of artisan work, from smithing to hewing and weaving.

Most important of the background institutions for the study of the manor was the Roman estate. Large estates existed in Gaul from Celtic through Roman times. But it is under the Empire that we see the developing features of organization and forms of tenure that point directly toward the medieval manor, for the estate, agricultural village, and bound labor all date back to late Imperial practices. Similarly, the later division between demesne (lord's) land and the tenant's land was also foreshadowed in the division that existed on the late Roman estates. Part of the land was worked directly by the owner under a manager and ordinarily by slaves who had no rights under the law.

Although the Roman estate with its slaves and tenants bound to the soil provided the basis from which the manor grew, it is important to realize that a system of private landholding was by no means foreign to the Germans, who from at least the time of Tacitus were dividing the land among the freemen according to rank and authority. So a system of large estates was probably not foreign to the Germans when they occupied the West. They readily accommodated themselves to the organization of the Roman estates while retaining and satisfying their distinctions of rank. If the free village community was characteristic of German society upon their entrance into the Empire, during the Merovingian and Carolingian periods it was rapidly transformed into the manorial village of inhabitants of varying degrees of freedom. And if the Germans had a system of working the land in common (which is doubtful), it disappeared in the period of German-Roman fusion. Possibly the only survival of such a great system was the sharing of common pasturage and woodlands.

The manorial system, then, was the outcome of the adaptation by the Germans of the late Roman estate organization to their own social institutions.

## II

We can now turn to a more detailed picture of manorial organization, recognizing at the outset that a great variety of detail will be glossed over in an effort to present a typical manorial organization. At the apex of the manorial organization was the lord, a noble, who held the manor as a fief or as part of a fief from some other noble. He was the equivalent in some respects of the old Roman master or owner (*dominus*). He was ordinarily domiciled on the manor in a castle or a château, or in the case of Church holdings, in an abbey, cathedral, or church. When the lord's holdings were vast, he perhaps did not live on the manor but was represented by a resident steward or manager. Except for the lord and his family and any knights he might have as retainers, the remaining people were servile and quasi-servile, with an occasional peasant freeman who, although a tenant of the manor, had retained his freedom.

Laboring classes on the manor can be broadly classified into domestic serfs and tenants. The domestic serfs worked in the lord's residence or in the workshops, the farm buildings, and the stables. The tenants worked the fields. In over-all charge was the seneschal or steward (other synonyms: *villicus, major, maire*), chosen ordinarily from the confidential domestic servants of the lord's castle called *ministeriales.* The office of seneschal gradually became hereditary, as the holdings of the tenants did. At times the *ministeriales* group assumed some importance when attached to the king or a great duke. In Germany they were given great favor by the emperor and became the basis of a new nobility.

In general we can divide the obligations owed by the serf to the lord into two main classes: labor services and payments (in kind or in money). So far as labor was concerned, the principal obligation of the serf was "week work," a fixed number of days each week in which he must work for the lord on his demesne land or in his farm buildings or workshops. This varied considerably from area to area, but two or three days a week can be considered an average. The amount of week work required of the individual serf was ordinarily carefully fixed by custom, custom that was often committed to writing. In addition to week work, the serf could be expected to do extra work known as "boon work"—seasonal work like plowing, sowing, reaping. Different kinds of boon work carried different obligations on the part of the lord (or occasionally the tenant) to provide food during the time of the work. As before, custom acted to standardize the amount and condition of boon work owed. Other types of forced labor, such as road building, ditch digging, and the like, were known as *corvées* (a word also used more generally for any kind of forced labor).

The types of payments owed by the serf varied greatly. They were paid in kind most often, but also in money, depending on the particular time and area under consideration. The serf paid a small annual head tax, and a *taille,* or forced exaction by the lord, the amount of which varied considerably. The serf was also obliged to pay a tithe to the Church. There were, in addition, a number of occasional customary payments as marks of servility such as *heriot,* a kind of inheritance tax, "banalities," that is, payments for the use of the lord's ovens, mills, and wine press.

We have already discussed the over-all organization of the manor, but a few further details are necessary for a clearer picture. The cultivable land of the manor was divided into demesne land (literally, land of the *dominus* or lord) and the tenant land. The lord's land could be either a separate plot of land or mixed in among the tenant holdings. The tenant land was divided into strips. The strips varied in size, but were often the amount a man could plow in one day (called variously the *acre, journée, morgen*—about 160 square rods). Strips were grouped together in "cultures" of parallel strips, and these cultures tended to follow the natural lay of the land; hence in rolling land the whole field might present a patchwork effect. The holding of the individual villein, then, was made up of a series of separate strips in different cultures. In this way, if the fertility of the land varied greatly, all would share in the good as well as the bad parts. So varied were the sizes and quality of the holdings that it seems foolhardy to venture an estimate, but most scholars suggest that the average holding was thirty acres.

As characteristic of medieval agriculture as the division of holdings was the over-all division of the fields known as the open-field system, whereby a holding of land was divided up into two, three, four, or five fields. The division into three fields was the most common. In this system, one field might be planted with wheat or rye, the second field with barley, oats, or peas, and the third field left unplanted, or lying fallow. Then the next year one of the first two fields would be left fallow, and the crops in the other two fields varied, according to the dictates of experience in the given area—one for crops of spring planting and the other for crops of autumn planting. In all of the open-field systems one of the fields was kept fallow. The three-field system was followed widely in England, northern and central France, much of Germany, and in parts of northern Europe. A two-field system was common in southern France and Alsace, while four- and five-field systems were employed in the upper Rhine valley and Westphalia. Closed fields were used in parts of western France and in Brittany.

The average return from the land in the Middle Ages was considerably smaller than at the present time. It has been estimated that the modern increase, on the average, has been ten- to twenty-fold. One historian has judged the average yield in England in the Middle Ages at from six to eight bushels of grain for each bushel sown.

The best guesses at population in the Middle Ages put some nine-tenths of the population in agricultural pursuits, and the manor formed the political and social as well as the economic unit for most of these people. Its court rendered the serf and tenant justice under the customs of the manor. Often manor and parish were one and the same, with the lord usually selecting the candidate for the parish priesthood and almost invariably investing him with the temporal things of his office.

Thus the manor, originating essentially in the late-Roman landed estate and including Germanic additions, comprised a rural, agricultural organization in which the lord maintained according to custom and tradition the division of his land into hereditary holdings with attached obligations of varying degrees of servitude. The tenants on the manor thus ranged from the free renter at the one extreme to the basest unfree serf (or, on rare occasions, to the slave) at the other extreme.

## III

The continuous historical development of European civilization is nowhere better illustrated than in the rise of a money economy dominated by a middle class of merchants and industrialists. This continuity is apparent from an initial acceleration of trade in the eleventh and twelfth centuries, through the increased use of capitalistic commercial techniques in the high and late Middle Ages, to the employment of similar techniques in the commerce and industry of modern times. The investigation of the causes for the "revival" (or acceleration) of trade in the eleventh and particularly the twelfth century is difficult and elusive, and it is almost impossible to separate cause from effect. But the following factors appear important: (1) Internal conditions in Europe seem to have undergone enough improvement at the end of the tenth and throughout the eleventh century to cause an increase in the population through a lowering of the death rate. The Northmen had been absorbed and were adding much to the organization and efficiency of Normandy in France and then of England after the Conquest. (2) With the rising population and expansionist activities of the Normans we witness a more general phenomenon, the expansion of Europe. We should not underestimate the religious motive in this expansion. Ever-increasing pilgrimages were transformed into battles for the faith, crusades. The reconquest of Spain from the Arabs was begun. The Normans moved into the Mediterranean, taking lower Italy and particularly Sicily, which had been under Islamic control. Above all, at the end of the eleventh century, Europe undertook the First Crusade, an event that proved to be of great importance in stimulating a rising trade. Everywhere the cross went, the merchant accompanied it. (3) Receiving the brunt of this expansion were the Arabs. Long torn politically, the Arabs were first to feel the recrudescence of Byzantine power under the Macedonian dynasty (867–1025). Then in the West in the eleventh and twelfth centuries, the Islamic fleets lost control of the seas, as well as their principal island possessions, before the aggressiveness of the fleets of Pisa and Genoa and later of the Normans. Of great significance, then, for revived trade was the termination of Moslem control of the western Mediterranean and particularly the Tyrrhenian Sea, which had been virtually a Moslem lake. (4) Control of the seas meant that the goods of the East that passed through Constantinople and the Arab commercial centers in the Levant would pass freely and in greater quantities to Europe. It is difficult to overestimate the importance of Eastern goods for the revival of commerce. Spices and luxury goods were not the only commodities of the Eastern trade; the cargoes included such important items as cotton, indigo, and the alum crystals used as mordants in the fixing of colors in textiles. (5) The actual revival of European trade came under the external stimulus of trade with the East. Two routes had been maintained through the period of Europe's relatively dormant and local economy in the ninth and tenth centuries. The city of Venice had looked toward Constantinople and acknowledged the eastern emperor during this period. Other cities in Italy under Byzantine control also continued to trade with that great and prosperous center, Constantinople. When the revival of trade started, Venice quickly leaped into a commanding lead in commercial activities, securing at that time a monopoly of the trade with Constantinople. Thus in the south, Venice, and soon afterwards Genoa and Pisa, became the points of external stimulus to the reviving European economy. Trade with the East also impinged on Europe in the north. The Scandinavians had established themselves in Russia in the ninth century, and in the course of the next two centuries built up an extensive overland trade with the Baltic and North Sea areas of Europe. The most important northern terminus of this trade in Europe was Flanders. Flanders had built up textile production even during the period of relatively little money economy. Her harbors faced invitingly northward for the Scandinavian traders. She began to provide the northern points of stimulus to Europe's economy, just as Venice, Genoa, and Pisa did in the south, but she was more the producer than the carrier. (6) At the same time a professional class of merchants, Europe's first middle class, began to multiply; as the revival of trade spread from the external points inland, great fairs sprang up. Urban areas revived, and the new class of inhabitants gained privileges and liberties. The great commercial cities of Europe began to take form. (7) Finally, the reviving trade and the increasing population stimulated and in turn were stimulated by an increase of agricultural production. This was manifested in the twelfth century by an extensive clearing of the land, or deforestation, and by the spread of agricultural colonization.

We have indicated that there were some trade contacts, particularly with Venice in the south and Flanders in the north, which were to prove most fruitful for the trade revival. They were by no means the only points of contact with the trade lines that radiated out from Constantinople, the great center and warehouse for all kinds of goods. Trading with Constantinople were Bulgarians, Armenians, Russians, Arabs, Italians, and many others. In addition, there are evidences of some internal trading in parts of Europe in the tenth and eleventh centuries in Rhenish cities and other German towns. For example, an eleventh-century document says of Bremen that "merchants of many lands frequented Bremen with their wares." Similarly, we read about the German city Goslar that "merchants of foreign nations brought to this place their accustomed wares." German and French merchants were also passing back and forth from the Continent to England. Numerous early medieval documents refer to foreign merchants in various parts of Europe, particularly to Syrians (early references), Jews, Anglo-Saxons, and Frisians.

Venice and, later in the eleventh century, Genoa and Pisa dominated the early stages of the revival of trade in the south. Dating back to the fifth and sixth centuries, Venice by her very position on the lagoons and marshes seemed to require trade for survival. During the lean years of the ninth and tenth centuries she maintained a flourishing trade with Constantinople. Taking wheat and wine from Italy, wood from Dalmatia, salt from the lagoons, and slaves from among the Slavic peoples on the Adriatic coast, she brought back the spices and precious stones of the East and the manufactured fabrics of Byzantium. Venice even traded freely with the Islamic peoples after the ninth century. In the beginning of the eleventh century her fleets cleared the Adriatic Sea of pirates and took many strategic points on the opposite coast. A contemporary chronicler calls her "rich in money" and "rich in men," and he adds that "no people in the world are more valorous in naval warfare, more skillful in the art of guiding ships on the sea."

By the eleventh century Venice had outdistanced her early Italian rivals, and she dominated the trade of many of the coastal and inland cities of Italy. She was also aided by a lack of scruples in regard to trade with the infidel. Her ships were occasionally at Aleppo, Damascus, Palermo, and other Arabic centers.

Although Venice had surpassed her early rivals, she now encountered new ones in the eleventh century. Her greatest competitors were the resurgent cities of Pisa and Genoa. The maritime activity of these two cities did much to break the Islamic domination of the western Mediterranean. They joined together to attack the island of Sardinia held by the Moslems (1015–16). The Pisans attacked Palermo. Both fleets raided the African coast, which was held by the Arabs, and were able to gain commercial privileges there.

The fleets of all three Italian cities grew enormously in the course of the eleventh century. The Venetian fleet in the second half of the century so surpassed that of Byzantium that the merchants of the small republic of the lagoons "obtained in 1082 from the [Byzantine] emperor Alexis Comenus . . . privileges which made them masters of import and export commerce in the whole Greek Empire."

When the Crusades came, the Italian cities were ready to exploit them. In return for bringing reinforcements to the Crusaders at Antioch in 1097, the Genoese gained the right of founding there a commercial colony or factory (*fondaco*) with special trading privileges. This was followed by many such colonies in Eastern ports and commercial cities. The Italian fleets did not at first carry great loads of troops but mainly supplies. In the Second Crusade (1147) Italian ships were used to a certain extent in troop transport, and they were used even more extensively for that purpose in the Third Crusade (from 1189). In the succeeding Crusades ships became the only vehicle of troop transport. The significance of the Crusades to the revival of trade has been succinctly stated by Henri Pirenne:

> Thus the one lasting and essential result of the crusades was to give the Italian towns, and in a less degree, those of Provence [Southern France] and Catalonia, the mastery of the Mediterranean. Though they did not succeed in wresting the holy places from Islam, and though no more than a few places on the coast of Asia Minor and in the islands remained of their early conquests, at least they enabled Western Europe not only to monopolize the whole trade from the Bosphorus and Syria to the Straits of Gibraltar, but to develop there an economic and strictly capitalistic activity which was gradually to communicate itself to all the lands north of the Alps.

From the principal points of contact with Europe, commerce spread inland. In the twelfth century cities such as Lucca began to manufacture silk and fabrics with the raw materials brought from overseas. Cities behind each of the three main Italian cities began to prosper, and soon goods from them went across the Alps into Germany and France.

The activity of the Italian cities in the south, as has been mentioned, had its counterpart on a smaller scale in the north, in the North Sea and Baltic areas, and particularly in Flanders. Stimulated by the trading activity of the

Scandinavians, the Flemish area deserves special notice because it had maintained an export industry in colored cloth during the period when most of Europe possessed a relatively domestic economy. In the twelfth century weaving spread throughout Flanders and the neighboring towns of Brabant. Unlike the Italians, the Flemish (except for certain periods) left the carrying trade to outsiders, first to the Scandinavians, then to the Germans and many others.

## IV

Regardless of the interesting variations observed in the early constitutions of medieval cities, it is universally accepted that the important stimulus to town growth was the increasing trade. To this we can add the closely related factors of population increase, increase in surplus goods resulting from the agricultural expansion, and the development of corporative ideas. But everywhere it was the new class, the middle class or third estate, that made the city.

As we examine the origins of towns, we should keep in mind above all that the growth of towns was not a local phenomenon or even a national one, but a European phenomenon. We can thus avoid the difficulties that so many historians have fallen into by stressing only local conditions in explaining the origin of a particular town and thereby missing the over-all importance of the general revival of trade.

Theories that call for the continuous development of towns from Roman municipalities must be abandoned for the most part. It is quite true that many of the newly stimulated cities grew up on sites of older Roman cities, and there undoubtedly was continuity of life in a number of Italian cities. But the significant point is that in the twelfth century the population of the older cities increased greatly under the stimulus of the revival of trade. Even more impossible as an adequate explanation of town growth was the theory that towns grew out of early "free German villages." Then, too, the fact that a number of towns grew up in the areas of the seats of bishoprics has stimulated a theory that stresses the activity of diocesan administration in the origin of towns. But here again the important point to notice is the quickening effect of commercial activities.

Although it is clear that the nuclei for different cities had been differently formed, their further growth was fostered by the changing economy of Europe. One theory of the way in which a great many of the towns originated has been rather widely accepted by historians, the so-called *faubourg* theory.

Groups of wandering merchants began to settle in fortified castles or *bourgs* in order to conduct business in safety. As the number of merchants multiplied, there was no longer room for them inside the bourgs. Consequently, they built up a new bourg in an area outside of or adjacent to the older one. These new settlements were spoken of as "outside burgs" (French, *faubourg;* Latin, *forisburgus*) or "ports." This theory has the great merit of stressing the mercantile influence on town growth. It explains the use of the terms *burger, bourgeois, poorters, portmen* for the new class of town inhabitants. These new towns soon overshadowed the original castles or bourgs beside which they had grown up, and they attracted industrial personnel as well as merchants. For example, the weavers spread everywhere among the Flemish towns. Centralizing their activity in towns, the nascent industrialists were thus able to facilitate the sale of their products among the people concentrated in or around the bourg and also to participate more directly in any export trade handled by the merchants.

A contemporary work describing the origin of Bruges has given us striking confirmation of the *faubourg* origin of a city. Initially, the author tells us, Count Baldwin had built a castle (after 962):

> After this castle was built, certain traders began to flock to the place in front of the gate to the bridge of the castle, that is, merchants, tavern keepers, then other outsiders (*hospitarii*) drifted in for the sake of food and shelter of those who might have business transactions with the count, who often came there. Houses and inns were erected for their accommodation, since there was not room for them within the château. These habitations increased so rapidly that soon a large ville came into being which is called Brugghe by the people from the word for bridge.

Regardless of particular origins, and whether or not the *faubourg* theory can be applied everywhere in Europe, the municipalities all over the Continent had certain features in common: trade, burghers, and some form of town government in which the middle class shared.

The new town governments were formed and based on freedoms and privileges frequently outlined in charters secured from a noble or the king. Different sets of privileges were obtained by different towns in the eleventh and twelfth centuries according to the sort of charter granted. Privileges can be generally classified into two groups: elementary and advanced. The elementary privileges included the personal freedom to come and go freely, to engage in trade, and to marry at will; a burgher's free tenure of land and goods with permission to alienate them as he saw fit; restrictions on the lord's powers of arbitrary taxation, his demand for military service and forced labor (*corvée*); the right to be tried in a local court; and so on. The advanced privileges were largely those of self-government: the town was given the right to choose its own magistrates; to administer its own justice; to collect tolls; to control its walls, gates, bridges, streets, and public works; and, finally, to impose taxes.

One of the privileges particularly pursued by the towns was the right to administer justice and thus to use the commercial and maritime law which had grown up outside of feudal and customary law. Maritime law had its source in old Roman sea law, modified by certain maritime codes formed in the Byzantine Empire. These latter codes were adopted by Italian cities such as Trani, Amalfi, and Venice, all of which had early commercial relations with Byzantium. From Italy the maritime codes spread to France, Spain, and northern Europe. Among the most often copied of the maritime codes was that of Oléron, a small island town off the coast of France, whose code was known as the "Rolls of Oléron." When the German and other Baltic cities came into prominence, new versions of the maritime law, such as the "Town Laws of Wisby" and the "Law of Lübeck," rivaled the older codes in popularity. Commercial law, growing up at fairs and markets and in the cities, also had its immediate origins in Europe in the commercial codes adopted in the Italian cities. Many a city had its code, called "Consuls of the Merchants." These served as models for other European codes. It has been pointed out with some justice that maritime and commercial law, which had gained considerable uniformity throughout Europe, was the first law to achieve the status of international law.

The gain of privileges and charters by the new cities was not always by peaceful means. Commune revolts in the eleventh and twelfth centuries are reported from many parts of Europe. Municipal offices thus arose in many towns throughout Italy, from which they spread to southern France. In northern France and Flanders, too, there were popular risings which brought about the organization of bourgeois governments.

Corporations or guilds of merchants were often associated with the formation of the early municipal governments. In some towns merchant guilds were organized before craft guilds (organizations of craftsmen) and were therefore more powerful, at least at an early date. Examples of the intimate connection of merchant guilds with the formation of municipal governments appear in Flanders particularly. Merchants living in the *portus* or *faubourg* joined together in guilds or "hanses," electing deans or "counts of the hanses" who acted as supervisors. By these organizations the merchants were then able to secure from the lord the desired municipal privileges.

In general, municipal privileges appear to have grown up in the eleventh century and then received confirmation by charters in the twelfth. The charter of Rouen, granting advanced privileges, served as a model for more than five hundred towns. Similar charters were granted in other parts of Europe. Although there was some hostility on the part of the nobles toward granting charters, most of them seem to have supported the movement. The grants were made less distasteful to the lords by the fact that they were often able to sell the charters. In addition, most of them recognized the benefit of having a prosperous city within their territory.

At the same time that the population was growing, that trade was beginning to accelerate, and that urban areas were taking form and gaining liberties, the agricultural basis of society was undergoing important changes. The principal changes were in two directions: (1) an increase in the amount of land in production through agricultural colonization; (2) changes in the manorial estate, including commutations of payments from kind to money, lightening of servile burdens, growing emancipation of the serfs, and formation of new lease tenures.

We can single out the remarkable work of agricultural colonization of the Cistercians, one of the new monastic orders of the twelfth century. Their activities were extensive from the forests of France, the Low Countries, and England to the forests, swamps, and frontier areas of Germany. The Cistercians were continually receiving grants of wooded or swampy land, and hence their initial labor was one of clearing and draining the lands to be cultivated. The conservation techniques used by the Cistercians in reclaiming the land were enlightened. It was their practice not to denude a forest completely but to leave some trees standing. The Cistercians were master drainers and the swampland in the Low Countries and Germany that they reclaimed is extensive. Using the services of lay brothers (*conversi*), the Cistercians laid out the reclaimed land in granges of about 500 to 700 acres. They were on occasion rented out but were ordinarily worked by the lay brothers under the direction of a monk. Sometimes outside agricultural labor was employed in place of the lay brothers. Grain farming and milling, grape culture and wine making, and stock raising were among the activities of these energetic monks.

A second type of colonization was that undertaken by the *hôtes* or "guests." They received this name from the fact that they were originally strangers or guests on the domain who had been given some vacant or waste land to cultivate. Their original status before becoming *hôtes* was usually forgotten, and they were quite often granted freedom, or relief from the manorial labor and monetary duties, or even quasi-free status. The *hôtes* were welcomed by the lord, for if he had some marsh or wasteland it could be cleared and put into useful production and he would thereby receive some rent or other dues.

The colonists tended to organize into villages that little resembled the manorial villages. These "new vills" were formed all over Europe. Much of the diked and reclaimed land in the Low Countries was given to *hôtes* for cultivation in return for simple rents. In Spain, land taken from the Moors was colonized in the same way, and the colonists were grouped into villages of the "new vill" type. These new vills often received charters that remind us of the town charters. The village charters gave to the colonists special privileges, such as freedom from some of the customary taxes, from military service, *corvées,* and other burdensome obligations.

Sometimes the work of colonization was organized and directed by clearance contractors, who were called in some areas *locatores*. The *locator* divided up the land among the immigrants or colonists. Under such an arrangement the colonist usually lived on the land rent free for a given period, so that he might get his land into cultivation before the rents started. It was not always easy for the contractor to attract colonizers to the frontier regions, particularly to Germany's dangerous northeast frontier. Part of the success in colonizing this region can be ascribed to advertising campaigns. One contemporary account tells us that Adolph of Holstein, one of the foremost German colonizers, sent messengers into "all the regions round about, even to Flanders and Holland," proclaiming "that all who were in want of land might come with their families and receive the best soil, a spacious country, rich in crops, abounding with fish and flesh and exceeding good pasture." No doubt the sight of the grim reality disappointed many a colonist, particularly if he recalled the propaganda of Adolph: "Be the first to come into this delectable land, and cultivate it, and have a share of its products."

By means of the increased agricultural colonization, a large part of the wooded and less fertile land in western Europe was put into cultivation. The amount of land in the Low Countries that was diked and reclaimed from the sea is equally impressive. Through this increase of arable land, and to a lesser extent through improved agricultural techniques, agricultural production was raised sufficiently to sustain the expanding population of the cities and to support the growing trade. The rising money economy in turn reacted on the organization of the manor. Lords required money for the purchase of luxury and other goods, and peasants were receiving money for the sale of surplus produce. The result was a pronounced trend toward the commutation of payments in kind into payments in money. In addition, the lords, in an effort to keep the peasants from running off to the cities or new colonial areas where they would be free, tended to free the serfs. A number of the charters of emancipation are perfectly frank as to the utilitarian motives inspiring them. The emancipated serf might still retain onerous *corvées* and other obligations and payments, but at least he gained freedom in several respects, including freedom before the law and before the king's courts and freedom of marriage.

As the money economy grew, the classic manor began to break up. In many cases demesne lands disintegrated from the encroachments of energetic stewards, bailiffs, or other agents; but more often the lord leased his demesne land out to tenants to raise his money income. Not only were the demesne land and woodlands altered, but there is evidence of considerable change in the size of individual holdings in the tenant lands, caused in part by the movement of the peasants to the towns.

Particularly important was the new system of lease holdings that became evident in the high and late Middle Ages. These new forms continued into modern times. By the end of the Middle Ages progress in accepting the new lease holdings was uneven in different countries. Equally uneven was the progress of emancipation. Serfdom was still present in various areas in western Europe, and there was even a strong tendency toward increased serfdom in parts of eastern Europe.

We must now return to an examination of the ever growing money economy and its manifestations in the expansion of commerce and industry.

## V

Much can be learned of the expansion of trade in the high and late Middle Ages by tracing the multiplication of commercial routes by land and sea. The early international trade between the East and the West was a Mediterranean trade joining Venice, Amalfi, Bari, and other "Byzantine" Italian cities with Constantinople. By the eleventh and twelfth centuries the Roman-Christian West was commercially tied with the Greek-Christian East on the one hand and the Mohammedan world on the other in a complex crisscross of routes.

At the same time, the North and Baltic seas were providing interconnecting trade routes between Russia, Poland, and Scandinavia, and England, France, Flanders, and Brabant. By the thirteenth century the northern German cities (later to be known as the Hanse cities or Hanseatic League) had already begun to compete for the carrying trade on those seas with the Scandinavians and others. They were beginning to assume in the north the role that the Italian cities had assumed earlier in the south. This northern area was connected with the eastern Mediterranean by an overland route through Russia.

In western Europe, the north and south met at first in the fairs of Champagne, in north central France, where goods were bought, ordered, exchanged, and where the first international money exchange on a large scale in Europe (discounting Italy) took place. The natural way from Italy to England passed through Champagne, and the traffic from the Mediterranean up the Rhone came to Champagne. It is little wonder, then, that products of all kinds and merchants of all nations met there. The fairs of Champagne were on a larger scale than most other European fairs, but there were numerous fairs of great importance during the twelfth, thirteenth, and fourteenth centuries, especially in England and Flanders.

Fairs were ordinarily established by law or charter. Such charters extended special privileges to an attending merchant. He was protected by a special peace; he was under the "safe conduct" of the territorial prince in whose land the fair was being held. In addition to exempting him from various kinds of tolls, the fair law guaranteed his freedom from prosecution for debts and crimes committed outside of the fair. Of similar importance was the suspension or modification of the prohibition of usury (lending money for gain, that is, at interest).

Fairs must be distinguished from markets. The latter were local in character and ordinarily served the needs of a small area only. They were held weekly or at other frequent intervals. The fairs, however, were seasonal in character. There were six in Champagne held consecutively during the year at four small towns.

A fixed order of sales became customary for Champagne fairs. There were eight days of preliminary activity: unpacking and setting up booths, materials, and the like. Then followed periods set apart for special commodities. For a ten- or twelve-day period cloth goods were sold. Other periods were devoted, for instance, to the sale of hides and furs, to things sold by weight and measure, and to animals. The fair was closed by a period of money transactions, when the money-changers and merchants straightened out their financial arrangements. It was during this period that the fairs contributed to the rise of credit forms and documents. This type of activity assisted in standardizing weights and measures. The administration of the fairs came into the hands of officials who were known throughout Europe by different names, which can usually be translated as "guards of the fair," and courts for administering commercial and other law were established.

The Champagne fairs were the most important link between the north and the south from the middle of the twelfth up to the early or middle part of the fourteenth century. By that time the fairs were declining for a number of reasons. Champagne, having passed to the French crown, was no longer neutral ground. France and England were beginning their devastating Hundred Years War. Expanding direct trade between nations was beginning to render trade at intermediate fairs unnecessary and to some extent obsolete. The commercial areas of towns, with their foreign settlements or colonies, were providing "permanent fairs" for the merchants. Evidence of the decline can be found in the increasing number of foreign merchants appearing in the various countries. Italians are found in Flanders and in England. Germans traveled into Italy, Flanders, England, and, in fact, throughout the Baltic area. As the result the fairs declined so markedly that the toll receipts in certain cases dropped from 8,380 pounds in 1296 to 1,152 pounds for the year 1340/41.

The decline was also hastened by use of the all-sea route through Gibraltar to the Low Countries and England. The Genoese had sailed through the Straits and into the Bay of Biscay in the last quarter of the thirteenth century, and Venice by 1317 had inaugurated her celebrated Flanders Fleet. This latter achievement had been made possible by the use of a new kind of vessel, "the great galley." Carrying a crew ranging up to 200, the great galley might be as long as 150 feet. She carried both oars and sails, the oars arranged in two or three banks. The regular service of the Flanders Fleet cut further into the volume of trade transacted at the Champagne fairs.

With the decline of the overland route through Champagne, other overland routes flourished. Above all, the Rhine became an important waterway for commercial traffic from Italy to Flanders. The principle route into Germany from Italy went to Basel, then down the Rhine, with various stops, to Utrecht. From Utrecht, routes spread out to England or to all ports on the North Sea. Other routes went from the upper Rhine west into Flanders and east to Hamburg. Eastern Germany and Austria were also connected with

Italy by a direct route across the Alps. For many of these routes, the Alpine passes continued throughout the Middle Ages to be the key, connecting the rest of Europe, particularly Germany, with Italy.

During the high and the late Middle Ages the city-states of Venice and Genoa dominated the Mediterranean, Pisa dropping by the wayside as the result of her defeats at the hands of the Genoese, who destroyed her harbor in 1290. Both Genoa and Venice held wide possessions in foreign cities, especially in the East. Other seaports on the Mediterranean coast of Italy, France, and Spain were second rate in comparison with these two giants of the sea. Florence was at first primarily an industrial city, producing silk and woolen cloths for export. Her goods were handled by Genoa, Ancona, and Venice. But from the early fifteenth century Florence gained control of Pisa and began to be important in the international carrying trade. Milan, of course, was an inland city. With an excellent location before the St. Gotthard Pass she played an important part in the European trade, but she was not engaged directly in the Eastern trade. Certain cities were important in bartering and money exchange—above all Florence and in addition Lucca, Siena, Rome, and the other great commercial cities already noted.

Of increasing importance, second only to the Italian cities in the south, were the German cities in the fourteenth and fifteenth centuries. As early as the eleventh and twelfth centuries German merchants from Cologne and other French cities were trading in London. They were very active at the Champagne fairs. As the fairs declined, they came in increasing numbers directly to Italy. Venice became a permanent mart for them. But Venice so controlled the Adriatic waters that the Germans did not venture any competition for the Eastern trade. In fact, they were strictly regulated and supervised while staying in Venice in the *Fondaco dei Tedeschi* (House of the Germans).

The most remarkable manifestation of expanding German trade was the league of cities known as the Hanseatic League. Although similar leagues preceding the Hanseatic League were not uncommon, the Hanseatic was easily the most important league of cities to have an economic basis. Its beginnings are obscure. The cities most prominent in the league—Hamburg, Stettin, Danzig, and Lübeck—were geographically situated to take advantage of the expanding commerce, but the number of member cities in the League was continually changing. The beginnings of the League in the thirteenth century are found by some historians in the attempts by German cities to secure common trading rights and privileges in foreign cities, and to make agreements to follow one maritime code, such as the "Law of Lübeck." During the fourteenth century it is clear that the Hanseatic League came into existence as a formal organization. Some seventy to eighty towns composed the membership of the League at its height. It gained trading privileges for its members in various foreign areas. Though its political ties were loose, it was able to take military action when necessary. After a decisive victory against Denmark, it gained a free hand in commercial matters in the Baltic (1370), and not long afterwards was recognized by the Holy Roman Emperor. Henceforth, the Hanseatic League became a European power to reckon with. It held its prominent position until the sixteenth century, when trade began to shift to the Atlantic and by-pass both the Baltic and Mediterranean areas.

The League had a flag and diplomatic representatives abroad, and it concluded commercial treaties with foreign powers. Representatives of the member cities met together, usually in the great guild hall at Lübeck, and passed on an extraordinary range of matters of common interest. The League was even able to obtain "factories" or *kontoren* in other cities. These were commercial colonies or settlements within the cities where the merchants could reside pretty much under their own law. The League had four important factories, in London, Bruges, Novgorod, and Bergen. The factory in London, named the Steelyard, had as many as 300 inhabitants and its own aldermen, councilors, warehouses and other buildings.

## VI

The expansion of trade which has been described to this point had its counterpart in an increase of industrial activity. The rise of urban areas was accompanied by the breakdown of manorial or domanial industry, which had not been organized for surplus production but rather for local consumption. But even during the period when the domanial economy was at its height, certain places did produce surplus goods. The looms of Flanders made cloth for trade purposes even when trade was at a low ebb elsewhere, and other domains produced for wide consumption: the brewers of St. Paul's Cathedral were producing annually about 67,800 gallons of ale even before the great urban centers had arisen.

After the passing of domanial industry, or at least after its significance dwindled, the towns became the industrial areas. In fact, the commercial and industrial economy of the high and late Middle Ages centered in the towns.

Some idea of the relative activity of different towns could be obtained if accurate figures of town sizes in the Middle Ages were available. But aside from occasional tax and census rolls, we are at a loss for a precise picture of the size of urban concentration. A moderately active commercial town might have from 8,000 to 10,000 inhabitants—in 1440 Frankfort had 8,719 and Basel about 8,000. Few towns exceeded 20,000: in the fifteenth century Strasbourg, Nuremberg, and Ulm had about this number, and the great Hanse town Lübeck had only about 25,000. Cologne also appears to have had over 20,000, perhaps 30,000. A reliable census for Ypres shows only 10,736 people in 1412. London has been estimated at about 35,000–40,000. The population of Florence has been estimated as growing from about 45,000 in 1280 to about 90,000 in 1339. Venice was probably over 100,000, and Paris in the fourteenth century certainly had gone beyond 100,000, perhaps as high as 200,000.

The industry that flourished in most municipal areas in the Middle Ages can be described as a craft or handicraft industry. The unit was the small shop or home of the master with one or two wageworkers (journeymen), and one or more apprentices. The number of crafts multiplied considerably from the eleventh to the fourteenth century as specialization increased. By the fourteenth century some 157 crafts are listed in a Parisian tax roll, and a number of towns had as many as 40 or 50 crafts.

With the rise of industrial activity, craftsmen began to organize in guilds. In many instances the craft guilds came at a later date than the merchant guilds (or guild merchants). In Flanders, particularly, the merchant guilds were formed before cities achieved municipal organization and, in fact, were instrumental in helping to secure the municipal charters. The broader merchant guilds were composed of the principal businessmen in town and were careful to control trade within the town. They particularly regulated and controlled the import of foodstuffs and other wares. Among these general regulations of the municipal governments or guild merchants were prohibitions of the practices known as forestalling (intercepting and buying goods before they reached the market), engrossing (cornering the market), and regrating (buying with the object of selling again at a profit).

Although formed later than the merchant guilds in many areas, the craft guilds spread everywhere and attained great power by the fourteenth and fifteenth centuries. The craft guild was essentially the same from country to country whether it was called the *métier* in France, the *arte* in Italy, *zunft* in Germany, *gild* in England, or any of another dozen names. Its origins are obscure, but, currently accepted theory sees the probable origin of the guild in (1) a voluntary association of craftsmen, supplemented by (2) the support and prescription of public authority. This, then, suggests that craftsmen, in imitation of merchant guilds and/or Church associations, began to form associations. To make the administration and government of the city easier, public authorities encouraged such associations. In Flanders, particularly, there is evidence that city authorities, who wished to control the pricing and quality of industrial products, encouraged and enjoined the formation of the crafts into guilds. In Flanders and elsewhere by the middle of the twelfth century, craft guilds had been organized in many of the new towns.

The basic objectives of the craft guild were the common gain of its members and the protection of the consumer—no doubt in that order, since the monopoly practice of the guilds in many cases did the consumer more harm than a few regulations with regard to the quality of the products benefited him. These two objectives—the gain of the members and the protection of the consumer—have been correlated neatly by one historian with the two major factors bringing about the organization of guilds. Voluntary association lay at the root of the guild's objective of benefiting its members, and direction and control by public authority acted to keep the public interest before the guild. As Henri Pirenne has stated, "In its essentials the medieval craft may be defined as an industrial corporation enjoying the monopoly of practising a particular profession, in accordance with regulations sanctioned by public authority."

Regulations covered every phase of the guild member's activities. Above all, they established the monopoly of the town's market for the guild members, forbidding anyone to practice the given trade in the city or any foreigner to import the same product, except under certain restrictions. Thus a rigid protective system was created against local and foreign competition. The regulations tended at first to assert the equality of the members of the guild, but in the late Middle Ages a few wealthy men began to control the guilds, just as the wealthy patricians tended to gain control of the municipal governments. In the interest of maintaining their monopoly, the guilds fixed prices, wages, and hours; set the number of workers; specified the kind of tools in the shops; and so on. It would seem, however, that the canonical doctrine of just price had some influence in restraining the guilds from setting prices which were too high.

A number of regulations served to assure the quality of the work and thus protect the consumer: the careful inspection of finished products by guild inspectors, the establishment of high standards of workmanship, the punishment of members who turned out poor products, the forbidding of night work to keep up the quality of production.

The guild was an organization of "masters," that is, skilled craftsmen. Before becoming a "master," a workman would ordinarily have been an apprentice and a journeyman. An apprentice was a young novice taken into the shop and home of the master with the aim of learning the trade. He was given board but received no salary (or only a small one) and, in fact, often paid a fee of apprenticeship to the master. The time of apprenticeship varied considerably—from two to eight years (or longer), depending on the difficulty of the profession, the supply and demand of the masters, and other factors. Often a contract (indenture) would be signed with the apprentice's parents, fixing the number of years and other conditions of apprenticeship.

Upon completion of the apprenticeship, the apprentice became a journeyman (from the French, *journée,* "day") or a "companion." Trained in the art, he was able to work as a wage earner. The only thing to distinguish him from the master was the means and opportunity to become a guild member. Quite often he traveled about to gain valuable experience in different masters' shops.

In the early stages of guild development, a journeyman would be accepted as a master without excessive requirements. But as the guilds came under the control of an increasingly patriarchal group of wealthy guildsmen, they tended to become closed corporations, and various, more difficult requirements for entrance into the mastership were established. The entrance fee was made excessive, or the candidate was required to produce an expensive "masterpiece" (hence, the origin of that word) in order to qualify. In addition, the applicant had to be of legitimate birth and free.

As the mastership became more exclusive, there was a tendency on the part of the journeyman to remain a wage earner. Much discontent developed among journeymen, who banded together and created riots and strikes. But these preliminary efforts at cooperative action scarcely resembled trade or industrial union activity today.

We have been describing the typical handicraft, small shop, industrial organization. But there also existed a more capitalistic type of organization in which employer and labor were divided. The employer gave to the worker the material to be worked into cloth, or some other product, which the employer then sold as export goods. Although both employer and worker were organized into guilds in this arrangement, the worker still occupied a dependent position. Most large export industries were organized in this manner, particularly the cloth industries. Although the members involved in these large export industries were much more numerous than in the small crafts, the workers were not concentrated in large factories but still worked in their homes or small shops, sometimes owning their own tools and sometimes renting them. Because the material was supplied or "put out" to the workers in their own shops and homes, this system has been called the "putting-out" system.

## VII

There remains only to trace some of the elements of capitalism which were developing in the high and late Middle Ages and which were to grow into the commercial capitalism of early modern times. In the high and late Middle Ages business ethics were undergoing a change toward the acceptance of the profit motive fundamental to capitalism. Earlier medieval business ethics emphasized the doctrine of "just price" and the prohibition of usury.

The doctrine of just price held that nothing should be sold for more than its real worth. The real worth was determined by the absolute cost of production plus a proper fraction of a living wage for all those who worked on the product. This doctrine was Judaic or Christian in origin rather than Roman. One Roman lawyer had held that it was all right for a man to buy cheaply and sell dearly, and for each man to try "to overreach the other"; another limited such blanket approval by saying that if, because of limiting circumstances, an article had been sold for less than one-half of its value the seller could recover. But the customary medieval doctrine opposed the Roman law in this case. Thomas Aquinas supported the doctrine of just price on the basis of the Golden Rule.

Much more controversial was the prohibition of usury. It was extremely difficult to rationalize the direct Biblical prohibition of lending money for gain. The third Lateran Council (1179) affirmed that "usurers shall not be admitted to Communion," and in 1311 Pope Clement V declared all secular legislation in favor of usury null and void. The prohibition of usury was also being enforced on occasion in secular courts even after the introduction of Roman law. But, as one writer has suggested, this prohibition had about the same success in preventing loans for interest as the Volstead Act had in stopping the sale of liquor in the United States during Prohibition.

In the face of the rising trade the jurists began to interpret usury more leniently. If the lender faced a possible loss, then interest could not be usurious—that is, risk of capital was involved, so interest was justifiable. As a matter of fact there always were numerous practical devices for hiding usury. For example, interest rates were often concealed in promissory notes: a man would promise to pay much more than he had actually borrowed, being careful to falsify upward the original amount of the loan. By the end of the Middle Ages the capitalistic spirit was definitely on the rise, and interest taking had become quite acceptable. The term "usury" was beginning to be applied, as it is today, only to loans at excessive rates of interest.

In addition to the rise of a capitalistic spirit, certain other signs of the growth of capitalism are evident in the Middle Ages. At the root of the nascent capitalism was the increasing coinage, circulation, and accumulation of money. In the early Middle Ages, Charlemagne coined the silver *denarius,* or penny. With the breakup of his empire the rights of coinage were feudalized. Manorial economy reached its height; monetary circulation was at its lowest point. But during this period some gold coinage from Byzantium was circulating in Italy. In addition, gold coins were in evidence in Moslem Spain.

With the revival of trade, monetary circulation increased, and coinage began to be standardized more and more at the fairs. At the same time, increased mining activity helped to get specie in circulation. The silver mines discovered in southern Germany were a major source. In addition, a few other new mines were opened between 900 and 1300. But there probably was not much increase in the annual production of coinage metal from about 1300 until the mid-fifteenth century.

Toward the end of the twelfth and into the thirteenth century there were numerous reforms in silver currency in Venice, in England, and particularly in France. In France two new coins which were struck just after the middle of the thirteenth century were spread all over Europe by their use at the Champagne fairs. In the thirteenth century gold currency was also revived in Europe. The gold florin of Florence (1254) was followed by the minting of similar coins in a number of other countries.

With the increase of money in circulation, some merchants or commercial capitalists began to build up large fortunes. Private capitalists and bankers, kings and the Church accumulated great amounts of capital. As the capitalistic spirit grew with these large fortunes, a number of techniques that were to become a part of commercial capitalism were also being developed. There was a growth of private loan operations by merchants who became at the same time financiers and bankers. These operations had their origins, at least in part, in the extensive money-exchanging activity that went on at the fairs. The forms of the loans were numerous and merged into forms of partnership. The straight loan with or without concealed interest was very common. Popular also was the loan in the form of a sale of a rent. In return for the loan the lender received a rent for a specified time.

There were, in addition, a number of partnership loans: a partnership for a limited time would be formed in order that the lender could legally recover his money with profit. There were numerous kinds of partnerships, of which we shall mention only one, the *commenda* or *accomendatio,* in which one partner put up the money and the other did the work (such as organizing and directing a commercial voyage), the former usually receiving three-fourths of the profit and the active partner the other fourth. The *commenda* was obviously a form of investment activity for a merchant with sufficient capital. But there were also opportunities for small investors on something like a joint-stock basis in Genoese and Hanseatic shipping enterprises. Records show shares (*loca*) being sold in ventures to as many as fifty investors, each expecting a fraction of the profit proportional to his investment.

Of considerable importance in the commercial activities of the medieval fairs and urban markets was the growth of several kinds of credit documents, such as the bill of exchange (a promise to pay at a later date in another currency for goods received and valued in a given currency) and the letter of fair (a promise to pay at the end of the fair or beginning of the next fair for goods received on account). Much of this credit activity started with the money-changers at the fairs.

It was, at least in part, out of the money-exchanging activity of the money-changers and the mercantile activity of Italian merchants that private banking arose. The enormous wealth of Florentine banking houses of the thirteenth and fourteenth centuries made them bankers to kings and popes, and these activities were duplicated on smaller scales in a number of other Italian cities. About 1400 the first deposit and public banks emerged in Italy and Spain.

Thus by the fifteenth century many of the elements of early modern capitalism were flourishing in a vigorous money economy. We have seen that during the Middle Ages this money economy created urban communities, industrial organizations within these communities, and at the same time important capitalistic commercial techniques and, furthermore, that it had transformed the servile manorial tenures into some form of free or semifree holdings.

### *FOR ADDITIONAL READING*

*Cambridge Economic History of Europe.* Vols. I, II. Cambridge, 1941, 1952.

A. Dopsch. *The Economic and Social Foundations of European Civilization.* New York, 1937.

L. Halphen. *Charlemagne et l'empire carolingien.* Paris, 1947.

R. Latouche. *Les Origines de l'économie occidentale.* Paris, 1956.

J. Lestocquoy. "The Tenth Century," *The Economic History Review,* XVII (No. 1, 1947).

S. Lopez and I. W. Raymond. *Medieval Trade in the Mediterranean World* (a collection of important documents). New York, 1955.

F. Lot. *The End of the Ancient World.* New York, 1931.

H. St. L. B. Moss. "The Economic Consequences of the Barbarian Invasions," *The Economic History Review,* VII (May, 1937).

H. Pirenne. *Medieval Cities.* Princeton, 1925.

A. Riising. "The Fate of Henri Pirenne's Theses," *Classica et Mediaevalia,* XIII (1952).

M. Rostovtzeff. "The Decay of the Ancient World and Its Economic Explanations," *The Economic History Review,* II (January, 1930).

E. Salin. *La Civilisation mérovingienne d'après les sépultures, les textes, et le laboratoire.* 2 vols. Paris, 1950, 1953.

L. White, Jr. "Technology and Invention in the Middle Ages," *Speculum,* XV (April, 1940).

# VI

# MEDIEVAL POLITICAL INSTITUTIONS

*Joseph R. Strayer*

Scholars have long argued as to what events and what dates mark the beginning of the Middle Ages. It is almost impossible to give precise solutions to these problems in fields such as economics and religion. In politics, however, there is an easy and appropriate answer. The political history of the Middle Ages begins in the fifth century A.D., when Germanic kings took over the government of the West from the Roman Empire.

## I

There was much more to the beginning of the Middle Ages than a transfer of political authority—there were profound transformations in all forms of human activity. But the political change was the most dramatic and the sharpest, and it cut deeply into the structure of society. The Roman Empire, which had embraced all civilized men in the Western world, broke up into petty kingdoms. Barbarian kings and their bands of warriors replaced the emperor and his bureaucrats as the source of authority. The complex organization of Roman government and the tax structure that had supported that government withered away. The idea of the state almost vanished; the Germans could not think in terms of a remote, impersonal authority which was to be obeyed in spite of all shifts in the personnel of the ruling group. They gave their allegiance to men and not to institutions, to the head of the family, to the chief man of the neighborhood, to the king. This simplification of the political structure and this emphasis on personal relations meant that governments did less and did what they did do less well. Life in the Late Roman Empire had not been happy but it had been more secure than it was to be under the Germanic kings.

The thinning out of political organization and the consequent decrease in security was not entirely the fault of the Germans. It is true that they had only rudimentary ideas of government and that they could not think in terms of a highly organized state. But the Germans were a minority, often a very small minority, in the kingdoms which they set up within the Empire. They were perfectly willing to let their Roman subjects preserve their old institutions for their own use if they so desired. In Italy the Ostrogoths made a real effort to preserve parts of the Roman system of government, and even in Gaul municipal governments survived for some time. But the Romans of the West were not very eager to maintain their old political structure. In the last centuries of the Empire there had been little popular participation in politics. The emperor and his agents ran the Empire; the only political responsibility of subjects was to obey. Government had been imposed from above; it had meant heavy burdens and few benefits. In order to preserve the tax structure and the economy, increasing numbers of people had been frozen in their jobs. The peasant and his heirs were responsible for tilling the same piece of land forever; the municipal official and his heirs had to collect taxes in the same district forever. There was very little loyalty to a government which imposed such obligations; this is one reason why a comparatively small number of Germans were able to occupy all the West. And there was no great desire to preserve institutions which had given physical security but which had denied both political and economic opportunity.

For these reasons the governments of western Europe in the early Middle Ages were based on Germanic kingship rather than on Roman imperial institutions. Now the Germanic king was not an administrator, not even, except in exceptional circumstances, a judge. He did have a representative function; he spoke for his people in their relations with the gods, with visiting foreigners, and with neighboring tribes. But first and foremost, he was a leader in war. He summoned the people to war, and he and his band of faithful companions were the core of the army. In time of peace he had little to do except to maintain his bodyguard by giving it food and drink and occasional presents of gold rings and other valuable objects.

The king did not have to worry about local administration. The people grouped themselves naturally and spontaneously by families and neighborhoods. The family was not the small household of the present day; it included grandparents, uncles, nephews, and remote cousins. Each member of the family was responsible for every other member; an injured man could count on his family to avenge him, just as he exposed the whole family to vengeance if he wronged someone outside the group. A man without a family to back him was helpless; he had to obtain protection by becoming a retainer or a servant of some powerful man.

Families that lived close together formed a neighborhood. Sometimes one family was so strong that its head dominated the neighborhood; sometimes there were several great families which furnished group leadership. The chief political task of the neighborhood was to hold a court to settle disputes among its members. There was nothing compulsory about the jurisdiction of such a court; if families preferred to wage a blood feud nothing could be done about it. But if they were willing to seek a peaceful settlement, then the neighborhood court offered them an honorable way of doing so.

These neighborhood courts did not try to settle a case on its merits; this would have risked involving the members in the original quarrel. They had no exalted ideas of doing justice; all that they wanted was to stop a fight. Their job was to act as referees in a complicated legal game; they declared what the rules were and saw that those rules were observed. Each party to the dispute had to state his case according to a precise formula and back up his assertion by a set oath. A slip in a single word was enough to lose a case. If both parties succeeded in saying exactly the right words at the right time, then the court set a test for one of them, usually the defendant. He might have to get a number of his kinsmen to take an oath on his behalf (compurgation) or he might have to meet a physical test (ordeal). One typical ordeal was to bind a man and throw him into a pond. If he sank he was innocent; if the pure element of water rejected him so that he floated, he was guilty. Another test was to make him carry a red-hot iron a fixed number of paces. If his hand healed quickly, he was innocent; if it became infected, he was guilty.

The Germans seldom imposed physical punishments on those found guilty by this procedure. The losing party usually paid a fine to the victor, a fine proportioned both to the nature of the offense and the rank of the injured man. Thus it cost more to cut off a forefinger than a little finger; it also cost more to injure a member of the king's bodyguard than an ordinary freeman. Payment of money was supposed to wipe out all memory of the grievance, but in actual fact resentment often lingered, and blood feuds sometimes broke out even after compensation had been paid. It was also impossible for courts to enforce their orders. A family might refuse or be unable to pay the required sum; in this case a feud was also likely to result.

## II

It is easy to see that the Germans would have trouble when they tried to govern the wide territories which they acquired after the fall of the Empire in the West. They had no administrative system, no means of delegating authority, no institutions to guarantee internal peace. They could not make good all these deficiencies, but they profited a little from the heritage of the Empire and the advice of the Church.

From the Empire they acquired the idea that a king should be more than a leader in war, that he was responsible for governing and administering his kingdom. It was difficult to reduce this theory to practice, but the kings did gradually come to feel that they were responsible at least for the administration of justice. The kings also realized that they could not hold their lands together without some representative of their power at the local level, and they began to delegate authority to counts. The count took his title from an old Roman military office, and he remained the military leader of his district. But he was more than a military leader; he collected revenues from royal estates, and he presided over the courts of his county. This was a rudimentary administrative system—the counts were neither very efficient nor very honest—but it was better than no administrative system at all.

The Church had grown up in the framework of the Roman Empire and had preserved many of its political ideas and techniques. The Church still had the idea of the state, and its own administrative system was modeled on that of the Empire. It used written law instead of relying wholly on custom, as did the Germans. In efforts to convert the Germans, the Church had to lean heavily on the kings; thus it was advantageous to the Church to build up royal power and to aid the kings with their political problems. For example, the Church encouraged the kings to reduce some of their customs to writing. Even after the Germans were nominally converted, generations of effort were required to make Christianity really take root among the people, and here again the support of the kings was essential. They were not ideal characters for this purpose—many of them were treacherous and bloodthirsty—but no one else could take their place. The kings had wider authority and on the whole were more enlightened than most of their subordinates. So a working alliance between Church and kings was established, in which the Church gave moral support and administrative assistance in return for protection and gifts of land.

This alliance was further developed when the Carolingian line of kings came to power in the Frankish realm in 751. Following Old Testament precedents, the Carolingians were anointed by the Church at the beginning of their reigns. This made them semi-sacred personages—"christs of the Lord," to use a phrase which was common in the early Middle Ages. They were chosen by God as His vicars; they were to defend both the Christian people and the Christian faith. These beliefs greatly increased the prestige of the kings; they ranked above all men, clergy and laity alike. They could intervene in any problem affecting their kingdom, even in Church affairs. The Christian community was one community, and the king was responsible for both its physical and its spiritual welfare.

Under Charles the Great, or Charlemagne (768–814), Germanic kingship, sanctified by the Church, reached the peak of its effectiveness. Charles inherited all of France, the Low Countries, and western Germany. To this he added by conquest the Lombard kingdom of Italy, the northwestern corner of Germany, which had been held by the heathen Saxons, and a strip of northeastern Spain. Charles ruled wider lands than any previous German king, and he ruled them more effectively. The counts who administered this vast territory were more obedient than they had been before or were to be later. Charles did not have an entirely free hand in selecting his counts; certain great families were so strong that they regularly obtained countships. But at least Charles was able to check the behavior of his counts regularly by teams of roving inspectors called *missi dominici*. There were usually two *missi* to a district, a count or some other great layman and a bishop or abbot. They heard complaints of subjects, saw that royal orders were carried out, and reported any serious problems to the king.

As the example of the *missi* demonstrates, Charles had full control of the Church and used churchmen freely in his government. There were always several abbots and bishops at his court who formed part of the king's advisory council. The other bishops were supposed to aid the counts in preserving public order and in defending their districts. Charles named bishops and abbots as freely as he did secular officials, and he took a leading role in church administration. When he made laws or administrative ordinances (and the fact that he could do this is one more sign of his power) they were as apt to deal with ecclesiastical as secular business. In dealing with the newly conquered Saxons, he was as insistent on wiping out relics of heathenism as in suppressing the power of the old native nobility. When he set rules about the behavior of secular officials he also regulated the conduct of priests and monks and ordered the bishops to set up schools for the education of the clergy. In Church councils, which he called, he went even further: he defined orthodox belief and actually made an addition to the Apostles' Creed.

Charles had a unique position in western Europe. There were a few other Christian kings—the rulers of the little Anglo-Saxon kingdoms and the heads of Spanish mountain principalities—but none of these men approached Charles in power and prestige. He was the real head of Latin Christendom, the defender and propagator of the faith. It seemed reasonable to many men that Charles should have a title which set him apart from other kings. Pope Leo III satisfied this desire by crowning Charlemagne emperor on Christmas day in the year 800. Just as the West had only one spiritual head, the pope, so it was to have only one temporal head, the emperor.

In spite of Charles's power and ability, this attempt to revive the Empire in the West proved a failure. Charles gained in prestige, but not in authority, and he did not try to build new institutions to correspond to his new title. Neither the Roman concept of the state nor the Roman administrative system was revived. Charlemagne remained a Germanic king ruling by Germanic methods. His power was due to his energy, his perseverance, and his ability to use the Church, not to any great improvement in political institutions. And while the idea of a revived Empire persisted for many centuries, it never created a framework for a meaningful and enduring type of political organization. The basic political institutions of medieval Europe did not grow out of the Carolingian Empire.

The Carolingian Empire was simply Germanic kingship raised to its highest degree of effectiveness. With the death of Charles the Great in 814 his system began to collapse. His Empire was simply too big for ordinary men to hold together, and it was subject to internal strains and external attacks. Divisions among heirs and civil wars split the Empire into separate kingdoms, and invasions by Northmen, Magyars, and Saracens weakened these kingdoms still further. Local lords took advantage of all these troubles to gain a large degree of independence. Before the year 900 the Carolingian Empire had ceased to have any meaning as a political unit.

## III

In the kingdom of France, one of the fragments of the Carolingian Empire, a peculiar form of political organization, which we call feudalism, developed in the ninth and tenth centuries. No contemporary could have called it feudalism, for the word was not invented until the seventeenth century. Men were not much in the habit of using abstract terms during the difficult years of the break-up of the Carolingian realm, but if they had had to pick one phrase to describe what was going on, they probably would have spoken of the growth of vassalage. The lord–vassal relationship was becoming more important than the king–subject relationship.

Both in the Late Roman Empire and under the Germanic kings there had been a class of landlords, proprietors of great estates, to whom lesser men looked for protection and economic benefits. The landlords received services of many kinds from these dependents; they might ask them to cultivate their fields, to furnish them with certain manufactured goods, or simply to run errands for them and serve as escorts on a journey. Gradually, during the eighth and ninth centuries, a special type of dependent began to appear—the vassal. A vassal's duties were primarily military; he fought under his lord's command in any conflict in which the lord was engaged.

The Carolingian kings had encouraged the growth of vassalage. They had constant wars on their frontiers, and they found that the great mass of free men, who were peasant cultivators of the soil, were not of much use in extended military operations. Vassals, on the other hand, were specialized fighting men; they were better soldiers and could afford to serve longer in the field than the ordinary free man. Thus the larger the number of vassals, the stronger the army.

Moreover, the vassal was bound to his lord by strong personal ties. He took an oath of loyalty to his lord; he performed the ceremony of homage by which he became the lord's man. This was a far closer and more binding relationship than between the king and an ordinary subject. Therefore, the kings tried to make important men their vassals, in order to benefit from this strong, personal loyalty. In the end most of the counts and great landlords became vassals of the king; they were bound to serve him in his army and be faithful to him in all his governmental activities. Thus the political structure of the Carolingian realm was reinforced by the personal ties of vassalage. A large class of fighting men were vassals of the great lords and counts, who in turn were vassals of the king.

This was the situation when the Carolingian Empire collapsed. Disintegration went farthest in France, where the invasions of the Northmen were especially ruinous and where the Carolingian kings had to fight for the throne against a rival dynasty. In these circumstances, the central government withered away. It could not defend outlying provinces; it could not preserve internal order. The counts and a few other great men simply took over the authority which was slipping from the hands of the king. They made their offices hereditary and became practically independent rulers of their districts. They defended their lands and carried on a minimal amount of governmental activity with the aid of their vassals. While they still owed nominal allegiance to the king, they gave him very little service and seldom obeyed his orders. Instead they spent most of their time trying to annex territories held by neighboring lords. When this confused scramble for power ended, most of France was divided among some twenty great lordships.

Meanwhile the vassals were becoming settled on the land. At first the lesser vassals were largely dependent on the lord for equipment, food, and clothing. They lived in his household or they garrisoned his fortresses. This was not always a very convenient arrangement for the lord, and it gave little security to the vassal. So the practice grew up of lending the vassal an estate from which he could supply himself with necessities and on which he could live. These loaned lands were first called benefices and then fiefs. (The medieval Latin word for fief was *feudum,* from which our word feudalism was eventually derived.) Although fiefs always remained technically part of the lord's holding, in practice they soon became hereditary, and the vassal and his heirs acquired stronger and stronger rights in them. In the end, the rule was established that the vassal kept his fief as long as he remained faithful to his lord and gave him a specified amount of service.

Feudalism, when it reached its full development, had three distinguishing characteristics. In the first place, the essential unit of government was small, a lordship or a county instead of a kingdom. In the second place, political power had become a private possession. Rights of government were treated exactly as rights over land; they were a source of private income. They could be divided among heirs or handed out as part of the fiefs granted to vassals. Third, only vassals and lords had political power. The peasants, who formed the great mass of the population, supported the governing class of lords and vassals by paying rents for their lands and fines for their offenses. But the peasants did not participate in government; their only function was to pay and to obey.

Feudalism does not appear, at first sight, to be a very promising form of government. It was effective for governing only small areas and it was limited by the selfishness and ignorance of the lords. It provided only the rudiments of government, some protection against outside enemies, and a crude set of courts to repress internal violence. Yet feudalism, with all these weaknesses, was a fertile source of new institutions. The more a region was feudalized, the more rapid its political development. In the end the most effective medieval governments grew out of feudalism.

This was possible because some of the seeming weaknesses of feudalism turned out to be strengths. For example, the fact that feudal lordships were limited to small areas overcame difficulties of communication and control. Capable feudal lords could make their power felt immediately; they could repress unruly subordinates before they had gained *de facto* independence. Moreover, the small political units of feudalism corresponded to the economic and social realities of the period. Each district was almost self-sufficient; the men of Normandy had few dealings with the men of Burgundy and had no concern with their welfare. The Germanic kingdoms had been too large to develop any common loyalties, but there was a real community of interests within most feudal states.

In the same way, the concentration of political power in the hands of the great landholders remedied another weakness of the Germanic kingdoms. Before feudalism, the landholding class had had considerable power without full responsibility. It could weaken royal government without having to assume the burdens of defense and administration. But now that royal government had dwindled to a shadow, the landholders had to carry the full load. If they did not defend the land and keep the peace, no one would. They still exploited their underlings, but at least they had to do something in return. And the best of them took their responsibilities seriously and were a constructive, not a destructive, force in politics.

Finally, the rudimentary nature of early feudal government gave large space for experimentation and growth. Even the feudal lords could see the inadequacies of their institutions. For purely selfish reasons, if nothing else, they wanted to improve these institutions and thereby increase their power and income. Since most of the work of feudal government was carried on in small informal meetings of the lord and his vassals, it was fairly easy to make changes and try experiments. Feudal customs had not yet been written down, so there were no rigid rules embodied in formal documents to block change. Thus an energetic lord could make innovations without much difficulty, and in regions which had able rulers feudal government steadily improved.

Feudalism spread only slowly from its original home in northern France. Southern France was feudalized only in the late twelfth, or, in some places, early thirteenth century. Italy and Spain were never completely feudalized, although some feudal institutions took root in those countries. England continued a Germanic monarchy of the old type until 1066, when it was conquered by the thoroughly feudalized Normans and became thoroughly feudalized itself. Germany also retained a government of the Carolingian type throughout the tenth and eleventh centuries. The eventual breakdown of this government was caused not by the spread of feudalism, but by a revolutionary movement headed by leaders of the Church.

## IV

To understand the significance of this revolutionary movement, we must remember that Germanic kingship, as modified by the Carolingians, depended heavily on the support of the higher clergy. Bishops and abbots were named by the king and served as his administrative agents. He used the military and financial resources of their lands as if they were his own. The king, after all, was an anointed ruler, representative of God on earth: it seemed only right that he should be able to use the Church in his task of governing and defending the Christian people entrusted to his care.

All these characteristics of Carolingian monarchy were accentuated in the German kingdom of the tenth and eleventh centuries. While Germany had suffered less from civil war and invasion than had France, it had not been untouched by the troubles of the ninth century. The dukes who governed the main regions into which Germany was divided were not yet feudal lords, but they had gained a certain degree of independence. Technically they were still public officials, removable at the will of the king. Actually they had acquired such power in their duchies that it took a major military expedition to punish them for disobedience. Only the free use of the resources of the Church made it possible for the king to keep some degree of control over the dukes.

Furthermore, the German king Otto I had once more revived the Empire in 962. His realm was not as big as that of Charles the Great, but it included the Low Countries, a large strip of eastern France, and much of Switzerland, as well as most of modern Germany. In addition, Otto had acquired the kingdom of Italy, which gave him the Po Valley, Tuscany, and rights of protection over Rome and the pope. The man who ruled over these wide territories was the most powerful monarch in Europe; it seemed reasonable to give him the title which had once been held by Charles the Great. But an emperor, even more than a king, seemed entitled to use the resources of the Church, and as a practical matter it would have been difficult to hold the scattered territories of the Empire together without the aid furnished by churchmen. In the same way, an emperor seemed to have a special right to name high Church officials, even at times the pope. During the reigns of Otto I and his immediate successors the Church was clearly under imperial control.

The Empire which Otto I had built around the core of the kingdom of Germany remained strong for a century. But during this century, a reform movement began in the Church. This movement at first aimed at nothing more than a purification of monastic life. As such, it was supported by the German kings, partly out of sincere religious conviction, partly because a reformed monastery was more efficient and hence more useful to them than one in which poor discipline allowed the monks to waste their income. But the reform of the monasteries was only the first wave of a great religious revival. Western Europe had been exposed to Christianity for centuries, but for a long time most people had been satisfied with purely formal observances. Now the religion was beginning to get under their skins; they felt acutely their personal unworthiness; they wanted to do things which would show their devotion. They were ready to take drastic steps at the orders of the Church, and in the eleventh century a new group of reformers were able to take advantage of this state of mind.

These new reformers felt strongly that the Church must free itself from all secular control in order to carry out its mission of establishing a Christian society on earth. This meant, first of all, that kings and feudal lords must renounce their custom of naming bishops and abbots and investing them with their offices. It meant that rulers must no longer use the resources of the Church to help them in the work of government. Finally, it meant that the Church was to be the supreme authority on earth in secular as well as religious affairs. God had given all power on earth to His Church; lay authority was to be exercised only under the guidance of ecclesiastical authority. The Church was to be free from lay control, but not from responsibility for the conduct of laymen. The Church was to determine the proper order of society and the proper behavior of individuals. It was to use all its spiritual weapons to enforce its demands. Kings and lords as well as private individuals were to be subject to its orders.

Some of these ideas had existed in theory before, but they had never been stated so systematically nor had there been such a concerted effort to put them into practice. Lay rulers were shocked by the revolutionary nature of the program, and some conservative churchmen were uneasy. But the reformers were led by a man of driving energy and strong conviction, the monk Hildebrand, later Pope Gregory VII (1073–85). As the power behind the papal throne, he pushed through the decree of 1059, giving the cardinals exclusive control of papal elections. As pope, he deliberately challenged the strongest representative of the old type of kingship, the emperor Henry IV (1056–1105). He forbade Henry to name and invest prelates of the Church. The decree forbidding laymen to invest clergymen with ecclesiastical offices touched off the most violent phase of the conflict; the struggle between the pope and lay rulers is thus usually called the Investiture Conflict. When Henry resisted this decree, the pope excommunicated him and stirred up a rebellion in Germany. Henry was so weakened that he had to humble himself before the pope at Canossa in 1077. Yet Gregory did not win a complete victory. His program was still being resisted when he died, and many kings continued to dominate the Church in their countries for another generation or two. The extreme Gregorian doctrine of a Church completely divorced from and yet directing lay governments was advocated by only a few of Gregory's successors and could not really be put into practice. But Gregory did succeed in depriving kings of their special position in the Church and in establishing the independence of the papacy. He did succeed in casting doubts on the theory that royal power came directly from God and in making many people believe that secular authority became legitimate only through the mediation of the Church. And in doing this he dealt the old type of kingship a blow from which it never recovered.

The struggle between the Church and secular rulers dragged on into the early years of the twelfth century. It ended in a series of compromises, which at first sight seemed to save a good part of the old royal position. Kings could still exert influence on the choice of bishops even if they could not name them directly; they could demand service for secular possessions held by bishops and abbots; they could use churchmen as advisers and administrative agents. But the essential point was lost. Kings no longer possessed an independent authority as vicars of God, which formerly had given them power over the Church. They were no longer members of both hierarchies, the secular and the ecclesiastical; they no longer had *rights* over the Church but merely *privileges* granted by the Church. They were heads of the lay part of society, but this part of society was less worthy than the ecclesiastical part and was subject to its admonitions and corrections. A king could no longer base his authority on his special position in the Church; he had to find some other foundation for his rule.

## V

The new foundation for royal government was discovered in the king's responsibility for the administration of justice. Kingship had been based on the king's position as vicar of God; it now became based on his position as supreme judge. This new emphasis derived in part from forces that had been working for a long time, in part from the new atmosphere of the twelfth century. The Church had long taught that kings were responsible for making justice prevail; most coronation oaths included a clause binding the king to do justice and maintain the rights of all his subjects. As feudalism developed it had become less a personal and more a contractual relationship. The rights and duties of lord and vassal were made more specific, and disputes between the two were to be settled by judgment of a court and not by force. Beginning in the tenth century, and growing stronger with every successive generation, was a desire for peace and order through due process of law. Finally, the twelfth century saw a great revival of legal studies. First Roman law was studied, then canon law (the law of the Church) and finally, at the end of the century, attempts were made to reduce customary law to a logical and coherent system.

The first rulers to take full advantage of the new emphasis on justice and law were the kings of England. They were already in a strong position, thanks to the peculiar history of England in the eleventh century. William the Conqueror had taken over a unified Anglo-Saxon kingdom which had not yet had time to disintegrate. Local courts in the counties and in many of the hundreds (subdivisions of counties) were still under royal control. The earls, who corresponded to the counts on the Continent, were becoming increasingly independent, but the earls were not in direct control of county government. Each county had its own administrative officer, the sheriff, who was named and could be removed by the king. The sheriffs, who ranked well below the earls, were on the whole obedient to the kings and provided them with regular revenues from each county. Thus William had more control over local government and a larger income than most of his contemporaries.

Moreover, William, in settling his conquering army on the land, had introduced a particularly rigorous type of feudalism. All the land was held as fiefs of the king; all the great men (and many lesser ones) were his vassals and owed definite and heavy services. All royal vassals were subject to the king's court and could be punished there for disobedience or misbehavior by confiscation of their fiefs. The king's court was so strong that it was very busy, and because it was busy it gradually developed a consistent and effective set of legal principles. Because the king's justice was sure and reasonably equitable, more and more people began to seek it.

The twelfth-century kings of England made their justice available to their subjects by two devices. In the first place, they sent out agents from their court who went from county to county dispensing justice in the king's name. These circuit judges began with William the Conqueror, but the first king to use them extensively was Henry I (1100–35). Under Henry II (1154–89) they became a regular part of the machinery of government. Year after year the judges went out to one part of England or another, holding courts, enforcing royal orders, and collecting information for the king.

The other device was the royal writ, an order from the king opening his court to a suitor and prescribing the procedure to be followed there. Here again, while there were earlier precedents, the great development of the writ system came in the reign of Henry II. He and his judges devised scores of writs, each of which made it easier to use the royal courts. Gradually the rule was developed that any case dealing with feudal holdings had to begin with a writ from the king, which meant that all important suits over property or rights of government were now under the king's control.

Another factor which made royal courts more popular was the increasing use of the jury. The jury was a body of neighbors sworn to give a true answer to any question put to them by a royal official. William the Conqueror had used juries to collect information for the Domesday Book, a great survey of the landholdings of his vassals. He and Henry I also used juries occasionally to settle disputes over land among the chief tenants of the crown. But, as usual, it was Henry II who made regular and habitual a procedure that had been used only sporadically by his predecessors. His writs established the jury as the regular instrument for deciding suits over feudal holdings and so made the jury an essential element in English law. Henry did not use the jury to decide criminal cases, although he did set up the grand jury to collect accusations of crime. But the jury gained such prestige in England that in the thirteenth century it was used to decide criminal cases as well as all civil suits of any importance.

The early jury was not a perfect way of settling lawsuits. The jurors were supposed to base their verdict on their own knowledge; they were not informed by witnesses. Often they must have been swayed by hearsay or local prejudice. However, most of the English population lived in small villages where everyone knew everyone's business, and local gossip can often be quite accurate. And whatever the weaknesses of the early jury were, it was still a more equitable method of trial than compurgation, ordeal, or trial by battle.

By getting all important cases into his courts, the king of England greatly increased his power over the country. There could be no doubt that he was the supreme authority and that his orders had to be obeyed. A large part of the population of England came into contact with his officials, either as parties to lawsuits or as jurors. And England was bound together more and more closely by the uniform application of a common law throughout the country.

## VI

The development of a state based on royal justice followed a somewhat different and slower course in France. There the king had no direct control over most of the country; responsibility for the administration of justice fell on the lords of the various feudal principalities. These men built up more effective systems of courts during the twelfth century. Normandy saw the most striking growth of judicial institutions, since the king of England held the duchy and applied many of the same principles there that we have already seen him introducing in England. Flanders and Champagne were not far behind Normandy in developing a centrally controlled judicial system, and other feudal principalities were also making progress. Moreover, from the end of the twelfth century on, there was a steadily increasing production of books attempting to summarize the customary law of each province. Thus France, unlike England, was building a score or more of different legal systems instead of one common law that applied to the whole country.

The king of France was able to profit from this situation in two ways. First, at the end of the twelfth century he began to increase greatly the area of France that he governed directly. A successful war with England gave him Normandy and most of northwestern France; the Crusade against the Albigensian heretics gave him most of the south, while Champagne and districts in the northeast were acquired by marriage. These annexations made the king far more powerful than all his vassals put together and thus greatly increased the respect which was paid to his orders. Moreover, in acquiring these lands the king acquired ready-made institutions. For example when he conquered Normandy he preserved Norman law and the Norman court system; the only change was in personnel. Norman courts were now held by judges sent out from Paris to see that the courts functioned in the king's interests. The same thing was done in other annexed provinces. They kept their laws and their courts, but these laws and these courts were administered by agents of the French king. Thus the king gained direct control of justice in much of France.

The other advance in the administration of justice stemmed directly from the increased power of the king of France. He had always had a court of his own, which met in royal palaces in and about Paris, but this court, down to the end of the twelfth century, had not been very busy. It had dealt mainly with cases arising in the old, small, royal domain. But during the thirteenth century this central court, now known as the Parlement, became the highest court for all France. It had direct jurisdiction over disputes between the king and his vassals. Even more important, it became a court of appeal. Protests against administrative and judicial actions of the king's agents were heard in the Parlement. Decisions of feudal courts could also be appealed to the Parlement, and anyone who sought the jurisdiction of this court was under the king's protection while his case was being heard. This was a very effective way of curbing the power of the great feudal lords. They no longer had the final word in matters affecting their subjects, since the latter could always appeal to the Parlement. Thus the king of France, through the use of appeals, achieved much the same result which the king of England achieved by direct intervention in local disputes.

This emphasis on appeals remained typical of the French judicial system. Conversely, medieval England never developed a full-fledged system of appellate jurisdiction. This was because England was a unified country with no separate codes of provincial laws. The English royal courts could hear directly all cases of any importance; local courts, even those held by the greatest English vassals, had no significant jurisdiction. This difference has persisted to the present day; appeals in England are far more unusual than they are in France or the United States.

## VII

The development of stronger judicial systems was paralleled, in both England and France, by the development of more efficient financial administrations. Here again, England took the lead. Early in the twelfth century King Henry I developed a special accounting office, the Exchequer. The Exchequer kept accurate records of all sums owed the king and saw to it that these sums were collected. It provided the king with a steady cash income, which made it much easier for him to carry out his policies. The Exchequer did not develop any new sources of income—this, as we shall see, was the task of the kings—but at least it made sure that no existing rights were lost. Every year the Exchequer prepared a Pipe Roll—a summary of income and expenditures by local agents. The first Pipe Roll comes from 1130; after 1154 there is an unbroken series of rolls for the rest of the Middle Ages. These rolls give us information about the operations of the English government such as we possess for no other country.

France was much slower in developing a centralized financial office. Responsibility for collecting the king's revenues in the twelfth century lay with local agents, the *prévôts.* These men usually simply paid the king a lump sum in return for the right of exploiting their districts, and so they did not have to render detailed accounts. Only under Philip Augustus (1180–1223) did the monarchy begin to check the financial operations of the *prévôts,* and only in 1202 do we find the first summary of royal income and expenditure. From this time on progress was rapid and by the middle of the thirteenth century France had a group of financial experts in the central government who reviewed and summarized local accounts and kept careful records.

The growth of royal judicial and financial systems forced the development of a professional administrative class. Judges and financial experts were obviously needed, and each major official had to be supported by dozens of clerks who prepared writs, summarized court decisions, kept records and wrote letters and memoranda. While bishops and barons were still consulted on great occasions, by the thirteenth century all the routine work of government in both France and England was performed by this professional class.

Although a bureaucracy was developing in both countries, it became far larger and more powerful in France. This difference, like many others, was caused by the fact that England was a unified country while France was divided into more or less autonomous provinces. In England local government could be safely left in the hands of local notables—country gentlemen in the rural areas, merchants in the towns. These men served as sheriffs and tax collectors; they held minor courts and enforced royal orders. They were loyal to the king, since there were no competing loyalties to divide their allegiance. They were not always very efficient, but the circuit judges checked on their work, and they had to send reports to the central offices of the government, so that they could not neglect their duties too seriously. And these local notables had the great merit of costing very little; they were either not paid at all, or paid only small sums for their expenses. Thus in England bureaucracy existed only in the central government; local government was in the hands of amateurs. This remained typical of England throughout the Middle Ages, and indeed throughout the sixteenth, seventeenth, and eighteenth centuries.

France had a very different problem. The country was unified only slowly by the annexation of one province after another to the crown. Each province was strongly attached to its own customs; local leaders thought primarily in terms of provincial interests and had little loyalty to the central government. They could not be trusted with local administration. The king of France had to send out agents from Paris, called *baillis* or seneschals, to govern his provinces. Each of these agents had to have a staff of financial and legal experts and a group of clerks to handle records and correspondence. All these men received their orders directly from Paris and reported back to Paris at fairly frequent intervals. Thus in France there was a local bureaucracy as well as a central bureaucracy, and the local bureaucracy increased steadily in number every generation.

Eventually, most other European countries followed the French rather than the English example. Like France, they were put together piece by piece as their rulers added new provinces to their original holdings, and, like France, they could not trust local notables with the work of local administration. So the typical European government became one in which local administration was closely supervised from the center, and in which the local administrator represented the ruler rather than the people of his district. As we shall see, this is one reason why representative institutions struck deeper roots in England than they did on the continent. In England the king had to keep the good will of local leaders who not only sat in Parliament but also controlled local administration. On the Continent local leaders had no administrative functions, and their wishes could be overridden by the local bureaucracy.

## VIII

During the twelfth and thirteenth centuries Germany and Italy felt the same forces that produced strong royal government in England and France, but the results were very different. Germany and Italy were theoretically united in the Holy Roman Empire; in fact the Empire had no effective institutions of central government. The emperors spread their power too thinly over the vast extent of the Empire; they were never able to build up a strong central court as in England or to annex provinces to a central core as in France. They had a long series of quarrels with the papacy, which feared their attempts to gain power in Italy, and papal support encouraged the German princes and the Italian cities to seek independence. As a result, the desire for law and order, which worked for the benefit of the kings of England and France, had to be expressed in the institutions of princely or city states in Germany and Italy. During the thirteenth century these districts acquired a virtual monopoly of the administration of justice and began to build up bureaucracies of their own.

These German and Italian states, however, were in a much weaker position than the kingdoms of the West. In the first place, they were relatively small; they lacked the financial and human resources which were needed to build strong governments. In the second place, there was always some doubt about the legitimacy of their claims to independent authority. The emperors made large concessions both to Italian cities and German princes during the thirteenth and fourteenth centuries, but they never abandoned all their rights. The possibility always remained that an able emperor might find a situation in which he could regain some of his lost authority. Moreover, in Italy rights of government were passing to tyrants who gained control over cities through *coups d'état,* or civil wars. Some of these tyrants tried to legalize their position by securing grants of power from the emperor, but on the whole they ruled by force and terror rather than by law. Thus while German and Italian states developed professional administrators during the later Middle Ages, their governments were still based on the personal power of individual rulers rather than on the impersonal strength of well-established institutions.

## IX

The rise of stronger and better organized states during the twelfth and thirteenth centuries led to a notable increase in the expenses of government. Salaries of bureaucrats and expenses of government offices were only a small part of this increase. The basic cause of the rise in expenses was that stronger governments could wage longer and bigger wars. Feudal vassals were of little use for a long war, because they had succeeded in limiting the amount of service they owed to a few days—usually forty—a year. Moreover, many vassals had become country gentlemen with no great skill in fighting. Vassals who could fight had to be paid, and their numbers had to be supplemented by large groups of mercenaries. All this enormously increased the costs of war.

During the thirteenth century every government in western Europe found itself short of money. The first reaction was usually to try to make money out of the feudal relationship. Vassals were asked to give cash in place of military service; they were also asked to give "aids"—contributions to the expenses of their superiors. But this attempt to balance budgets by levies on vassals failed everywhere, sooner or later. In the first place, vassals simply did not have enough money to meet all the needs of their lords. They formed only a small part of the population, and many of them had only small estates; any reasonable levy on them still left large deficits. In the second place, vassals were a privileged and articulate group. They disliked paying money to their lords; they argued that demands for money were an innovation which could be justified neither by earlier custom nor by the spirit of the feudal bond. These protests had to be taken seriously, both because vassals formed the most powerful class in every state and because kings whose position was based on the administration of justice were particularly vulnerable to charges that they were breaking the law.

The most notable protest was the one which led to the granting of Magna Carta in England. King John (1199–1216) had been engaged in a long and losing war with the king of France and had forced his vassals to make repeated contributions to his expenses. He had also punished many of them for real or supposed acts of disobedience without following due process of law. In 1215 they rebelled and forced the king to grant a charter which bound him to observe the law. They were not trying to tear down the judicial and administrative system which had grown up in England during the twelfth century, but they were determined to protect their persons and property from arbitrary acts of the king.

Magna Carta is a long document, but its essential ideas are expressed in the first few articles. The king is not to abuse the feudal relationship; he is not to use his position as feudal lord to demand unlimited sums of money. Most especially, he is not to take an aid without the consent of all his vassals. He also binds himself not to seize property or imprison men without trial, and to impose only reasonable fines on those convicted of offenses. The rules laid down in Magna Carta became a part of English law; they were confirmed by king after king throughout the rest of the Middle Ages. And they made it utterly impossible for any king after 1215 to raise significant sums of money by levies on his vassals alone.

There was nothing as decisive as Magna Carta in other countries, but the feudal nobility everywhere succeeded in avoiding heavy financial burdens. The result was that rulers had to go a step further; they had to develop general taxes on all their subjects. This was an extremely unpopular move; in most countries there had been no general taxes since the disintegration of the Roman Empire, and they were not sanctioned by law or custom. The attempt to levy general taxes introduced a new and disturbing element into thirteenth-century politics. It was responsible, at least in part, for the development of representative assemblies. It also led to a new quarrel between secular rulers and the popes, which reversed the results of the Investiture Conflict.

## X

The rapid development of new institutions of government during the twelfth and thirteenth centuries had already created some strains. Rulers who claimed to be basing their authority on respect for law found it a little difficult to justify all their innovations, many of which had no foundation in existing custom. It was generally agreed that basic principles of law were permanent and unchangeable; even new interpretations and applications of basic law should be made only after careful deliberation and consultation. No king could make law by his own will; he was supposed to act only with the advice and consent of the more important men of his realm. Thus there was already a strong tradition in favor of holding large assemblies to deal with important changes in law and institutions.

The development of taxation strengthened this tendency. Taxation, as men saw it then, was a direct invasion of the rights of everyone who was taxed. Government existed to protect individual and group rights, not to break them down. The only way in which such an action could be justified was for those affected to give their consent. But obviously not everyone could be individually consulted; some means had to be devised by which a small group or groups could speak for the whole population.

The feudal class alone could not take and probably did not want to take this responsibility. Feudal lords had little control over the towns, which were growing in population and wealth, and their control over their own subjects had been weakened by the increasing power of royal courts. Moreover, if they took responsibility for consent, they might also have to take responsibility for collection, and this they did not want. It would have been very difficult, for example, for a feudal lord to assess and collect a tax in a town. Leading townsmen knew more about the wealth of their fellows, and they were far more able to persuade them to surrender a share of it. But if townsmen were to take on this unpleasant job, their good will had to be secured. No one would make an honest effort to assess and collect a tax which had been imposed arbitrarily without prior consultation.

There was thus a growing need to involve all the propertied classes in basic decisions of government and especially in those decisions which had financial consequences. In the Mediterranean region the towns could not be ignored; they were rich, powerful, and closely associated with the nobility. Before the end of the twelfth century both the emperor and the pope had invited agents of Italian towns to at least one meeting of their courts, and town representatives had appeared in the courts of the Spanish kings. In southern France town officials attended local assemblies during the middle years of the thirteenth century. In England, where the towns were not yet very strong, the need was rather for representation of the class of lesser landholders, the men who carried most of the burden of local government. Knights were selected to represent their counties in purely judicial proceedings as early as the last decades of the twelfth century. In the 1250s (and perhaps a little earlier) these knights were called to meetings at which general policy was discussed.

This tendency to bring representatives of one or another of the propertied classes to meetings of central courts would probably have led to the development of parliamentary institutions in any case. But increasing familiarity with Roman law may have speeded up the growth of clearly defined representative assemblies. The Romans had had a procedure by which corporate bodies, such as towns, could appoint procurators who had full powers to act for them in judicial proceedings. This procedure could easily be adapted to the assemblies held by medieval governments. The chief business of every government was the administration of justice, and no one drew a very sharp line between judicial decisions and legislation. The central court declared what the law was, both in particular cases and, less frequently, as a general rule. Thus if agents of towns or landholders appeared before a central court, armed with full powers, their constituents were bound by decisions of that court, just as one is bound today by the acts of his attorney. It was necessary, of course, for the court to follow due process—to allow consultation and discussion—but once this had been done its decision was binding on all who had taken part. Thus representation according to the forms of Roman law made it much easier to use central courts to change the law or to impose taxes.

Representative assemblies developed everywhere in western Europe during the late thirteenth and fourteenth centuries. England and the Spanish kingdoms had them before 1300, France shortly after 1300, the German principalities somewhat later. They were usually divided into three Estates: one house represented the clergy, a second the nobility, and a third the commoners. But variations were possible; some countries divided peasants from townsmen, and so had four houses, while England had only two.

The usefulness and effectiveness of the central assemblies also varied widely. The body which did the most work was probably the English Parliament, which could speak with authority for the entire country. This was owing in part to the unity of the English kingdom: there were no provinces with rights of their own that could be opposed to the decisions of a central body. But it was also owing to the peculiar composition of the English Parliament. There the upper house included all the great men of the country—barons and bishops—while the lower house was made up of knights representing the counties and burgesses representing the towns. The knights, who spoke for the lesser landholders, would have been considered nobles in any other country; they were often relatives or retainers of the barons. Thus the two houses cooperated well and could speak effectively for all the people of any consequence in England. As a result, the English kings found it convenient to submit all important decisions to Parliament. They could thus gain general approval quickly and effectively and associate the leaders of the propertied classes with their policy. These were probably the reasons that led Edward I (1272–1307) to use Parliament more and more and to summon representatives of counties and boroughs to a large number of assemblies from 1295 on. Edward clearly thought of Parliament as a useful means of getting things done quickly, not as a body which limited his power. But Edward made Parliament such a regular part of his governmental machinery that his successors could not dispense with it, and some of them were less successful in controlling Parliament than Edward had been.

The Estates-General of France lie at the opposite extreme. They began relatively late (1302) and met infrequently. They had little authority on the few occasions when they did meet. This was largely because regional and local loyalties were so strong in France. Each province or group of provinces had its own assembly, and most important decisions had to be ratified by these local bodies. For example, it was very difficult for the Estates-General to impose a tax on the whole country. It was usually wiser for the king to negotiate with provincial assemblies and to strike a separate bargain with each one. This was a time-consuming operation, but it proved useful to the king in the long run. He seldom had to face united opposition; usually he could play one province off against another, or even override the protests of isolated groups.

## XI

Lay governments during the thirteenth century were doing their work with increasing effectiveness. They were keeping the peace and protecting the weak; they were replacing brute force by the judicial actions of their courts. They had not succeeded in repressing all injustice and disorder, but it was clear that they were working for the common welfare and basing their power on the rule of law. As a result there was increasing loyalty to lay governments and increased willingness to support rulers in any actions which they thought desirable.

Meanwhile, the Church was losing prestige. This was owing in part to the increasing prosperity and security of thirteenth-century Europe. A large number of men were concerned mainly with worldly matters and were less interested than before in religion. But the decline of Church leadership was also due to the political policy of thirteenth-century popes. A new German dynasty, the Hohenstaufen, held the Empire for a century (1152–1254) and tried to strengthen it by building up their power in Italy. The popes feared that this would threaten their independence, and they were especially worried after the Hohenstaufen acquired Sicily and Naples in 1194. Their hostility to Hohenstaufen policy reached its peak during the reign of the Emperor Frederick II (1212–50). They did their best to break his power in Italy by allying themselves with rebellious Italian towns, by financing attacks on the emperor, and finally by preaching crusades against him. They sought to depose Frederick and declared all members of his family unfit to rule.

This policy succeeded in its immediate objectives. The Hohenstaufen were exterminated, and the Empire was destroyed as an effective political instrument. But the popes paid a high price for this success. The collapse of the Empire allowed Italy and Germany to dissolve into a welter of petty states, which were often at war with each other and which followed no common policy. Political instability in Italy helped drive the popes from Rome in the fourteenth century. Political instability in Germany allowed the Protestant Reformation to take root in the sixteenth century. Moreover, in winning its victory the papacy had had to descend to the level of the secular states which it criticized. It had intrigued and made alliances; it had raised armies and fought wars. If it was on the same level as secular states it could not claim to be above and beyond secular politics. It lost much of the authority, much of the ability to control public opinion that had given it leadership in Europe.

Criticism of the Church, combined with increased loyalty and obedience to royal government, was especially noticeable in the kingdoms of England and France. Some of the attitudes that later made possible the concept of a sovereign national state were already appearing in these countries by the end of the thirteenth century. Thus there was clearly a feeling that France and England were self-sufficient political units, that their laws and customs were adequate to meet any situation, that no outside advice or guidance was welcome. There was also a feeling that enactments made for the common welfare overrode all other rights, whether of individual nobles or of the universal Church. Decisions of the royal governments were binding on all individuals, including the clergy, who lived within the boundaries of the kingdoms; no areas or persons were to be exempt.

These attitudes were a definite challenge to the leadership of the Church, as it had been established by Gregory VII after the struggle with the Empire in the eleventh century. The popes of the twelfth and thirteenth centuries had insisted that they were the final judges of what was right conduct, in politics as in all other activities. And they had been equally insistent that the clergy were subject to them alone, that the clergy were exempt from secular courts and from the payment of secular taxes. The new claims of the kings of France and England to the unqualified obedience of all their subjects could not be reconciled with the claims of the Church to be above and exempt from secular authority.

The issue came to a head in the pontificate of Boniface VIII (1294–1303). England and France had drifted into a war which strained the resources of both countries. In this situation both Edward I of England and Philip the Fair of France imposed heavy taxes on the clergy without obtaining the pope's consent. Boniface forbade the clergy to pay, but he soon discovered that he could not enforce his order. In both countries there were violent protests; laymen argued that the clergy should protect the common welfare along with all other subjects. Edward put the clergy outside the law by declaring that rights of clergymen would not be protected by royal courts. Philip forbade the export of money to Rome and seized the property of churchmen who were at the papal court. Hostility to the clergy reached such a height that the bishops of France and England begged the pope to rescind his ban. Slowly and grudgingly, Boniface complied. It took him over a year, but in the end he admitted that in an emergency a king could tax the clergy for the common welfare without papal consent.

This crisis was followed almost immediately by another, even more serious conflict. In 1302 Philip the Fair arrested a French bishop on a rather flimsy charge of treason. Boniface ordered the release of the prisoner and threatened to excommunicate the king and his ministers if he were not obeyed. The French government immediately took the offensive. The Estates-General were summoned for the first time, and charges against the pope were laid before them. The nobility and the commoners endorsed these charges enthusiastically; the clergy reluctantly went along with the other estates. Then Philip sent one of his ministers to Italy to arrest the pope and bring him to France for trial before a general council of the Church. The expedition was only partially successful. The pope was arrested, but was soon released by a rising of Italians in the neighborhood of the castle where he was being held. However the shock had been too much for him, and he died soon after his release.

The striking thing is not that violence was used against a pope, but that violence was successful. The popes who followed Boniface did not dare punish Philip and his agents. Instead, they granted the king repeated favors and finally declared that he had acted from worthy motives. Moreover, Philip's behavior was supported by his own people and was not seriously condemned by men living outside France. Kings who had done no worse had formerly been threatened by rebellion at home and invasion from abroad, but no one even talked of applying these sanctions against Philip. The Church had clearly lost its political leadership in Europe.

Thus the results of the Investiture Conflict were reversed; the political power gained by Gregory VII was lost by Boniface VIII. In a clear-cut conflict over basic principles, the loyalty of the people had gone to their kings rather than to the pope. The Church could still suggest and persuade, but it could no longer command. And with the Empire a shadow, and the Church weakened, political leadership passed to the heads of individual states, to the kings of the western countries, to the princes of Germany, and to the tyrants of Italy.

## XII

From a purely logical viewpoint, the way was now clear for the appearance of the sovereign state. Western Europe was divided into independent, self-sufficient political units, and within each unit a single supreme authority was emerging. Men were groping for phrases which would express the idea of sovereignty. For example, a French official about the year 1307 said that his king had "supreme jurisdiction and dominion over everything within the boundaries of the realm," that he could use all the property of the kingdom "for the common welfare and defense of his realm," that he was "emperor in his kingdom" (that is, subject to no outside authority), and that "all the people of the realm, clergy as well as laity, were ruled by his imperial power." Except for the word itself, this is as good a definition of sovereignty as we find in the works of sixteenth-century theorists.

Logic, however, did not dictate the course of political development in the fourteenth and fifteenth centuries any more than it does today. For generation after generation the people of western Europe balked at recognizing the full consequences of the situation that had been created at the end of the thirteenth century. They admitted that each state formed a separate body politic; they admitted that each inhabitant of a state was obliged to work for its welfare and make sacrifices for its defense, but they were not quite ready to admit that there was in each state one supreme authority, which could change any law and override any right. In short, while they were increasingly ready to accept the idea of external sovereignty, especially in denying the pope the right to interfere with the government of individual states, they were not yet ready to accept the idea of internal sovereignty. They believed that there were certain individual and corporate rights that could not be canceled by any one man or group of men, no matter what the source and extent of their authority.

There were both theoretical and practical reasons for this reluctance to go to a fully developed concept of sovereignty. On the theoretical side, the emphasis on law as the foundation of the state restricted the growth of the concept of sovereignty. The old belief that law was permanent and unchanging persisted, and it was not easy to change basic law, especially when the changes affected powerful social groups. Even in England, where acts of Parliament had great authority, it was argued that there was a higher law which could not be altered by statute. And everywhere there were privileges of individuals and corporate groups that went back into the period before the emergence of organized states. These privileges had been built into the basic structures of governments, and it seemed almost impossible to tamper with them without destroying the governments themselves. It was unthinkable that England could exist without a peerage, or France without separate provincial institutions. Peers and provinces were subordinate to the king, but their rights were independent of his authority. Privilege, after all, was a form of law, and a king bound by law was bound to respect the privileges that kept him from wielding sovereign power.

On the practical side, most European governments of the fourteenth and early fifteenth centuries were not very successful in inspiring loyalty or respect among their subjects. They had to face two crises—a long economic depression, which shook the structure of society and deprived rulers of adequate revenues, and a moral decline, which impaired all loyalties and standards. Governments were not responsible for the first crisis, though they showed little wisdom in coping with it. They were partially responsible for the moral decline, both because they had helped lessen the influence of the Church and because they themselves set rather poor examples of honesty and fair play. Loyalty to the state was not yet strong enough to replace loyalty to the Church as an organizing principle of society, and, while efforts were made to increase loyalty to the state during the later Middle Ages, these efforts were not immediately effective.

On the whole, most late medieval governments had only one policy—that of trying to extend their territories by making war on their neighbors. Even successful wars in the long run increased economic strains and so added to general discontent; unsuccessful wars naturally had more immediate and more serious consequences. Thus in almost every European country external wars led to internal rebellions in which the authority of central governments was weakened.

It is not surprising that the fourteenth and early fifteenth centuries saw repeated attempts to limit the power of central governments. These attempts often took the form of open rebellions, which sought either to depose the ruler or force him to promise to refrain from abuses of his authority. Every region of western Europe had at least one such rebellion in the later Middle Ages, and in most of them there was an uprising every generation or so. England probably held the record in this field; of the nine kings who reigned between 1307 and 1485 only four died in peaceable possession of the crown. Four others were deposed and a fifth was killed in battle against a successful usurper.

It is also not surprising that the fourteenth and fifteenth centuries saw a great, if temporary, increase in the use of Parliaments and assemblies of estates. No government was very strong, and all governments had to do unpopular things, such as raising taxes. Kings had to seek the good will of the propertied classes; usurpers had to legitimize their position. The best way for a government to obtain support or to strengthen its legal position was to call together representatives of the propertied classes. These assemblies could authorize taxes, enact reforms, and confirm the title of a new ruler. By giving at least the appearance of general consent they could gain some backing for weak governments or unpopular measures.

## XIII

The assembly which met most frequently, took its duties most seriously, and consolidated its position most successfully was the English Parliament. It approved all general taxes and all changes in law. In fact, by the fifteenth century the House of Commons was taking the initiative in legislation; most statutes were derived from its petitions rather than from proposals of the king or his council. Changes in government were still caused by baronial revolt or intrigue rather than by parliamentary votes, but at least Parliament was regularly asked to give the stamp of legitimacy to new governments. Parliament did not make major policy decisions, nor did it control the executive, but kings and baronial factions always sought parliamentary approval of their acts. In short, while Parliament was not yet the chief motive power in government, it had become an essential part of the machinery. It was unthinkable to do certain things without parliamentary validation and therefore even the strong kings of the sixteenth century used Parliament when they wanted to make statutes or levy taxes.

No other assembly managed to entrench itself so firmly in the processes of government during the fourteenth and fifteenth centuries. In most other countries the central assembly shared power with provincial estates, and most people were more interested in preserving provincial rights and privileges than in the affairs of the central government. Provincial assemblies could not approve general policies; they could only discuss the way in which already determined policy could be applied in their region. No province had strength enough to stand up to a determined ruler; one provincial assembly could be played off against another, and the views of a single province could often be ignored. Moreover, in both local and central assemblies on the Continent the close cooperation among propertied classes, which was so noticeable in England, was often lacking. It was not so much that the clergy and nobility fought the Third Estate as that they took little interest in parliamentary affairs. They preferred to defend their privileges in other ways and hence gave little leadership to assemblies. Thus there was little opportunity for most assemblies of estates to assume the responsibilities and gain the experience which marked the English Parliament.

The failure of assemblies to take deep root in constitutional procedures was especially marked in the case of the Church. Following the defeat of Boniface VIII, the popes had taken refuge from the turmoil of Italian politics at Avignon, on the borders of France. They stayed at Avignon for seventy years, much to the distress of those who felt that Rome was the only proper seat of the Catholic Church. Finally a pope moved back to Rome, and when he died the Roman population was so afraid of losing the papacy again that it put great pressure on the conclave that was to elect his successor. Some of the cardinals felt that this pressure had barred a free choice, especially after they had quarreled with the new pope. They returned to Avignon, elected another pope, and split the Church in half for forty years. Everyone was distressed by the Schism, and more and more people began to suggest that the way to end the breach was to call a Council representing the whole Church.

A Council was called, and it did finally succeed in reuniting the Church. But there were other problems—persistent accusations that many of the clergy were corrupt and worldly, that the Church needed to be reformed "in head and members." Here again, a good many religious leaders pinned their hopes on a Council. A Council might be able to break through the crust of traditional abuses, overcome the vested interests of papal administrative officers, and give earnest and honest men a chance to be heard. Reformers who took this point of view thought of a Council as the supreme authority in the Church, superior even to the pope.

Attempts were made to put these theories into practice at two Councils, the Council of Constance (1414–18) and the Council of Basel (1431–39). There were some initial successes, but in the end the attempt to make councils a sort of sovereign legislature of the Church failed completely. It failed because the members of the Councils did not remain united, but split into factions. Rivalries among states were one cause of disunity; secular rulers influenced the votes of prelates from their countries and were more interested in gaining privileges for themselves than in reform of the Church. There was always a pro-papal party, created partly by adroit use of papal patronage, but also by the sincere conviction of many men that the pope was the rightful ruler of the Church, "judging all and being judged by none." A divided Council was no match for the pope, with a centuries-old tradition of absolute authority behind him, and the conciliar movement did not survive the 1430s.

Papal power was fully restored, and the rare Councils which met after 1440 were completely controlled by the papacy.

## XIV

The restoration of papal authority was only the first phase of a Europe-wide reaction. By the middle years of the fifteenth century there was a strong tendency everywhere to concentrate authority in a single ruler, to repress opposition factions, and to decrease the importance of assemblies of estates. In Spain, in France, and finally in England strong kings emerged who succeeded in gaining the loyal support of most of the propertied classes. Monarchy was still based on law, but now the law was to be interpreted by and for the king, not by subjects in defense of their own particular interests. Western Europe was at last ready to accept the idea of sovereignty in all its aspects. It is no accident that the first complete definition of sovereignty, by the Frenchman Jean Bodin, came in the sixteenth century, after the fifteenth-century revival of strong monarchy.

Obviously, the disorders of the fourteenth and early fifteenth centuries had made men long for stronger governments and so had prepared the way for the monarchical revival. But kings and princes could not have taken advantage of this reaction if they had not already had institutions to exploit their advantage and a theory to justify it. The basic institutions—courts, councils, and administrative bureaus—had been created in the thirteenth century, and they went on developing during the later Middle Ages in spite of disorder and rebellion. In fact, the very difficulties that governments had faced had led them to reorganize and strengthen their administrative apparatus. There were more royal officials, more agencies of government, and more elaborate and sophisticated administrative procedures in 1450 than there had been in 1300. Once the habit of obedience had been restored, few new institutions were required. The so-called absolute kings of the sixteenth century ruled through essentially medieval institutions.

On the side of theory, an effort had been made to give the state some of the sanctity which had enveloped the Church. During the later Middle Ages, theorists began to speak of the state as a mystical body, a term which had once been reserved for the Church. This mystical body has a life and value of its own, they said; it is the duty of all its members to work for its welfare. The king, as head of the state, is both a mortal man and the incarnation of the undying principle of monarchy. As such, "the king never dies"; the rights and powers of the crown endure, whatever happens to the individual who holds the crown for the moment. The king must be obeyed, as the body obeys the head; rebellion is the worst crime because it destroys not only human bodies but the mystical body of the state created by God.

Thus the Middle Ages were marked at the end, as at the beginning, by a society in which the idea of the state existed, and in which strong monarchy was the dominant form of government. There were, however, two great differences between the political organization of the Roman Empire and that of early modern Europe. First, instead of one state there were many, each claiming sovereignty and each free to deal with others without restraint of law. The problem of interstate relations was one with which the Romans of the Empire had never had to deal, and it was to be one of the chief problems of modern European history. The other difference was that memories of restraints imposed on kingship and of the role of parliamentary assemblies could not be effaced. These memories were revived in the seventeenth and eighteenth centuries, and they helped cause the downfall of the strong monarchy which had emerged from the Middle Ages.

## *FOR ADDITIONAL READING*

G. Barraclough. *Mediaeval Germany*. Oxford, 1948.

H. Fichtenau. *The Carolingian Empire*. Oxford, 1957.

F. L. Ganshof. *Feudalism*. London, 1952.

C. H. Haskins. *Norman Institutions*. Cambridge, 1925.

G. L. Haskins. *Growth of English Representative Government*. Philadelphia, 1948.

J. E. A. Jolliffe. *The Constitutional History of Medieval England*. London, 1937.

E. H. Kantorowicz. *The King's Two Bodies: A Study in Mediaeval Political Theology*. Princeton, 1957.

F. Kern. *Kingship and Law in the Middle Ages*. Oxford, 1939.

E. J. Kitts. *In the Days of the Councils*. London, 1908.

F. Lot. *The End of the Ancient World*. London, 1931.

B. Lyon. *A Constitutional and Legal History of Medieval England*. New York, 1960.

C. H. McIlwain. "Medieval Estates," *Cambridge Medieval History*, VII, 665–715.

———. *Growth of Political Thought in the West*. New York, 1932.

W. S. McKechnie. *Magna Carta*. Glasgow, 1914.

D. Pasquet. *An Essay on the Origins of the House of Commons*. Cambridge, 1925.

C. Petit-Dutaillis. *Feudal Monarchy in France and England*. London, 1937.

C. Stephenson. *Medieval Feudalism*. Ithaca, 1942.

J. R. Strayer. "Laicization of French and English Society in the Thirteenth Century," *Speculum,* XV (1940).

J. R. Strayer and C. H. Taylor. *Studies in Early French Taxation.* Cambridge, Mass., 1939.

G. Tellenbach. *Church, State and Christian Society at the Time of the Investiture Contest.* Oxford, 1940.

W. Ullmann. *The Growth of Papal Government in the Middle Ages.* London, 1955.

# VII

# POLITICS IN THE AGE OF THE RENAISSANCE

*William J. Bouwsma*

In view of the difficulties that confronted the peoples of western Europe following the breakdown of the Roman imperial system, the Middle Ages' political achievement was impressive. The theoretical unity of Christendom gave to European society an ideal form; the practical tasks of government, notably protection against violence, were the responsibility of innumerable local powers; and in certain regions a real beginning had been made at relating fragmented local governments into larger wholes under the superior authority of kings. Nevertheless, this structure was far from perfect, even by its own standards. Neither the universal institutions headed by the pope and the emperor, nor local agencies, nor kings, could assure order; indeed, uncoordinated and competitive, they often threatened the peace by their mutual struggles. In medieval society, furthermore, certain ingredients were lacking which the modern world has come to take for granted in the tasks of government. Sovereign states based on the common loyalty of substantial numbers of subjects, powerful enough for indefinite survival, with an effective machinery for the control of a large and well-defined territory, had not yet emerged; and until the ideal unity of Christendom had given way to a system composed of such states, the peculiar problems and conventions of international relations as we know them could not develop.

In the transition from medieval to modern politics, both in their practice and their theory, the period which is often rather vaguely described as the "age of the Renaissance" has long been assigned a major part. Between the fourteenth and the seventeenth centuries the organization of society and the attitudes and ideas of Europeans about politics were transformed. The pressures of an increasingly complex world for more orderly government assisted ambitious rulers to develop more effective administration; and

Europe was increasingly articulated into self-consciously independent political units recognizing no law but the necessities of their own self-preservation, increasingly efficient in important areas of operation, and tending on the basis of greater power at home to expansion abroad.

At the same time, the accomplishments of this period should be neither exaggerated nor oversimplified. The more powerful states which had emerged by the sixteenth century were constructed on medieval foundations and utilized instruments in many cases inherited from the past. Again, development was not uniform throughout the whole of Europe. The problems of survival which had faced all of western Europe in the earlier Middle Ages had produced roughly similar solutions in many places, so that it is often possible to speak in general terms about European society. But local variations in detail were innumerable in spite of all family resemblances; and with the passage of time differences were confirmed and in some cases intensified. Some regions moved in one direction, others in another and at varying rates of speed; more than one kind of development, furthermore, was to prove significant for the political future of Europe. Finally, the advances of this period were neither uninterrupted nor securely established. Those made by one generation were often repudiated and lost, at least temporarily, by another. Indeed, by the closing decades of the sixteenth century the whole political accomplishment of the Renaissance seemed in the most serious jeopardy. No doubt every age, as it necessarily connects what precedes with what follows, is "transitional"; the age of the Renaissance was transitional in the special sense that it significantly promoted tendencies in the practice and theory of government which it did not succeed in bringing to complete triumph. Much was left for the future.

## I

Two changes in the medieval structure were evidently required before anything like the modern state could come into existence. One was largely negative: the destruction of such practical reality as still existed in the ideal unity of Christendom. For, while the universal institutions of empire and papacy could not impose any effective direction over the whole, they could nevertheless, by their grandiose claims and occasional interference, impede the development of other powerful agencies with a more practical, if geographically more limited, authority. The other necessary change was more positive: the substitution of orderly central government with effective and unambiguous sovereignty for the existing chaos of local powers, each in practice largely a law unto itself. The first change was more easily, quickly, and completely accomplished than the second.

The thirteenth-century struggle between papacy and empire had seriously weakened them both, and it had all but destroyed the latter. After the death of Emperor Frederick II in 1250, the imperial throne was vacant for more than two decades, during which local forces in Germany and Italy grew in power and assertiveness. When the office was finally filled again, its incumbents were capable of little effective action outside their family domains; continued papal interference and the jealousy of the German princes prevented the election of any but lesser families which could not seriously threaten any important interest. Two dynasties from western Germany, the Hapsburg and Luxemburg families, managed to exploit the imperial office to secure important lands in central Europe, the former in Austria, an acquisition of great importance for the future, and the latter in Bohemia; but their rivalry itself prevented the emergence of any clear imperial leadership.

The Luxemburg emperors Henry VII (1308–13) and Charles IV (1347–78) demonstrated their interest in the larger implications of the imperial office by making expeditions into Italy; and Dante's enthusiastic welcome to Henry indicated that the old universal idealism was not yet completely dead. But although both these emperors were crowned in Italy, neither was able to establish any genuine authority there. Italian towns and nobles were concerned only to exploit the prestige of a connection with the emperor to consolidate their own local authority or to extort from him the recognition of their claims as the price of support; meanwhile any real application of imperial control only aggravated the hostility of local interests. The death of Henry VII was followed by a split among the princes of Germany, who could not agree on his successor; and for the next generation Germany was torn by a struggle between rival emperors. Charles IV evidently recognized the unreality of the imperial claims; and to secure at least the future of his dynasty, he worked out an arrangement that at once stabilized the previously ambiguous imperial electoral system and subordinated the emperor to it. By the Golden Bull of 1356 the right of electing the emperor was permanently vested in seven dignitaries: the archbishops of Mainz, Trier, and Cologne, and the lay rulers of Saxony, Bohemia, Brandenburg, and the Palatinate; at the same time the claims of the papacy to any role in the election were ignored, so that the pope was henceforth excluded from German affairs.

After 1356 the advantage in Germany lay with the nobles who chose the emperor, and Italy was free of imperial interference. Not till the sixteenth century was an emperor capable of significant action in either region, and Charles V could take it only because he drew his primary resources from another and more modern kind of state.

The papacy, meanwhile, discredited by its long concentration on politics, fell increasingly under French influence, although its claims to the political as well as the spiritual direction of Christendom were unabated. When Philip IV of France (1285–1314) insisted on his right to tax the French clergy so that he could make war on England, Boniface VIII delivered a stern rebuke in the bull *Unam Sanctam* (1302). The pope insisted not only on his own exclusive right to direct the Church, but also on his authority over all rulers. "The temporal sword is in the power of Peter," he declared; it should be used on behalf of the church "by kings and captains but at the will and by the permission of the priest"; and, he went on, "if the earthly power err, it shall be judged by the spiritual power." But these strong words marked the end of an era; their impracticality was soon made clear. Philip promptly accepted the papal challenge. He accused Boniface of heresy and dispatched one of his followers, Guillaume Nogaret, to the papal residence at Anagni to seize the pope and carry him off to France for trial and deposition. Nogaret forced himself into Boniface's presence and announced his errand; and although he was expelled from the town before he could carry it out, the aged pope died a few weeks later.

Events soon showed how complete the victory of France had been. French pressures on the demoralized papal court secured the election of a new French pope, Clement V (1305–14), who took up residence at Avignon in southern France instead of at Rome and packed the college of cardinals with Frenchmen; and at Avignon the papacy remained until 1378. Thus not only had a particular power challenged the papacy and triumphed over it; for three generations it was able to influence papal policy and so to discredit further the claims of the Church to universal political authority. In this destructive way a major step had been taken toward the articulation of Europe into separate, independent, and sovereign states.

During the time when the emperors had lost any effective authority in Italy, the papacy was in France, and the Italian peninsula was thus relatively free from the guidance or interference of the Church or the empire, the two great institutions with which her medieval history had been so closely associated. And when the popes finally returned to Rome in 1378, their influence was severely limited by the Great Schism. The cardinals, divided into French and Italian factions, elected rival popes, one of whom remained in Rome, while the other returned to Avignon; and the authority of the papal office was further reduced as local powers exploited allegiance to one or the other in their own interest. By the end of the Schism in 1417 the political authority of the pope over Christendom was quite gone. Even his spiritual authority was now inadequate to mobilize Christian Europe against the Turks, who were attacking in the Balkans; repeated appeals by anxious popes for new crusades went unheeded. Indeed, in Italy itself the authority of the pope over the Papal State had been so eroded that a major share of the attention and energies of the fifteenth-century papacy had to be devoted to its recovery. In politics, therefore, the pope had been reduced to little more than just another local Italian prince, at a time when the emperor was reduced to little more than just another German territorial prince.

Obviously, however, destruction of the power of the universal agencies which had claimed to head a united Christendom did not automatically bring more effective government into existence; the immediate result, indeed, was quite the reverse. With the disappearance of the papacy and the empire as effective political forces, Europe had lost whatever possibility may once have existed to achieve general order on the basis of her spiritual community. More immediately, the consequence for Germany and Italy was evidently to stimulate anarchy. Into the vacuum created there by the decline of imperial and papal authority rushed a multitude of local powers, independent towns and princes of varying degrees of pettiness, now quite free to behave as they saw fit. Yet if this first result was politically destructive, the liberation which it accomplished had, at least in the long run and in some places, certain positive results. For each smaller political unit could now attempt to maintain order within its own territory in whatever way seemed most practical, claiming the full authority essential for the task.

The results of this attempt varied widely both in kind and in the degree of their success. In Germany and Italy, where universal authority had been most practical and where its disappearance was accordingly most felt, the new political arrangements were most local and ultimately least satisfactory; the fragmentation of these areas, together with the weakness and disorder which usually accompanied it, was to persist for many centuries. Where universal authority had been felt least, and where a larger territorial government had become already somewhat effective, notably in France and England, political organization could take place on a somewhat larger scale. The differences, however, were often as much differences in degree as in kind; and between the individual free town or the tiny principality ruled by some little German baron on the one hand, and the great kingdoms of the west on the other, were powers at every intermediate step. In all we may find similar problems: problems of unifying local and special interests into more coherent political communities, of securing respect for an independent governing authority above them all, of the maintenance of order. But, in the long run, two kinds of development proved most significant for the political evolution of Europe: that represented somewhat earlier by the city states of Italy, and that which took place in the larger territorial states gradually taking form in the west.

## II

The Italian peninsula itself provides a good example of the political diversity of Europe. In the south, Sicily and Naples had been feudalized and organized into a kingdom by their Norman rulers during the Middle Ages; they more resembled the territorial states of the west than they did the city-states of northern Italy, and their problems proceeded chiefly from the tension usual in such states between a refractory feudal nobility and the claims of the prince. The difficulties of the Papal State in central Italy were similar. Here too the feudal nobles tended, whenever surveillance was relaxed, to take matters into their own hands and ignore papal suzerainty. The special political interest of Italy lies rather in the cities of the north: Milan, Florence, Venice, and a host of lesser places. These city-states made significant, if not always successful, experiments with techniques for the maintenance of order; and above all, in certain cases, they managed to develop in some measure that sense of community, loyalty, and common purpose among citizens which is the only secure foundation of good government. Although they were unable to solve certain other problems, therefore, these states have an importance for the political history of Europe out of all proportion to their size.

In every part of Europe the fourteenth century brought serious political difficulties, and the towns of Italy passed through a severe crisis of internal disorder. Individuals, families, economic groups, and social classes engaged each other in a long struggle which dramatized the need for more effective government able somehow to subordinate competing special interests to the general welfare. Like so many other developments of the period, this struggle had its roots deep in the Middle Ages. In an earlier phase of urban history, local nobles who had settled in the towns and tried to control their governments had been largely excluded from power; their inadequacies as citizens had aroused general hostility. Within the walls of the towns they had constructed family fortresses with high towers, from which they engaged in the private wars so dear to their class; and they were frequently contemptuous of such civic duties as the payment of taxes and obedience to the laws which would reduce them to the level of other men. But by the fourteenth century their power had declined, and another element in urban society was generally dominant. This group consisted of the great merchants, bankers, and industrialists, organized in their guilds, who directed the most profitable economic enterprises of the towns; and the major struggles now took place between these men, who everywhere tended to exploit their power to their own advantage, and groups below them on the social scale. These latter included the lesser guilds of skilled artisans and small tradesmen, who resisted attempts to reduce their political rights, and an unorganized mass of men, most of them originally peasants who had been attracted into the towns by opportunities for employment and who formed a growing proletariat without any political voice. Between these groups, and also among factions within them, there was constant tension, which exploded in periodic and often bloody civil strife. Unable to solve the problem of order, therefore, many of the towns of Italy in the fourteenth century were turning in despair to despotism. The most striking example was Milan.

Milan had suffered from the same complicated struggles and disorders that plagued other towns, and her troubled merchants finally turned for protection to the Visconti, a noble family with large holdings of land outside the city. The Visconti, like a number of other ambitious Italian nobles, exploited a paper allegiance to the emperor, who was safely absent in Germany, to give a certain legal foundation to their lordship of Milan; but the true basis of their power was the support they managed to win from the commercial interest in the city through the provision, at least in the beginning, of more effective government. They maintained order, and their conquests of surrounding territories made trade routes more secure. The greatest of the Visconti was Giangaleazzo (1378–1402), who bought from the emperor the title of duke, married a daughter into the royal family of France, and came close to conquering and uniting into a single state the whole of northern Italy. Other lords of Milan also threatened to absorb even such distant and powerful neighbors as Bologna and Florence.

In Milan we may observe a development that has persuaded some historians that the tyrants of the Italian Renaissance pointed the way to modern politics by being the first rulers to conceive of the state and its government as a "work of art": that is, a product of rational planning, deliberate calculation, and the careful adaptation of means to ends. Thus, disregarding their own theoretical responsibility to the emperor, the Visconti dukes claimed an absolute power over all their subjects, nobles and townsmen alike. They replaced elected officials with men appointed by and responsible to themselves; they developed a large bureaucracy to enforce obedience; they imposed uniform laws over their entire state; they controlled taxes and expenditures; they took possession of all fortified points, dispossessing the local nobility; and they even instituted a censorship over mail and a kind of passport system to control travel. Such an accumulation of measures is indeed impressive, but it is doubtful that they really reflected a kind of blueprint for the state. As in other states, the dukes in Milan seem in fact to have improvised their policies piecemeal to meet particular problems as they arose.

Nevertheless, such government was effective, and the expansion of the Milanese state seemed to demonstrate the advantage of thorough tyranny for the mobilization and utilization of power. But, although they secured important advantages from the Visconti despotism, the citizens of Milan paid dearly by the loss of their freedom, a loss whose significance was clear to them when the government abused its powers. Giangaleazzo's predecessor, Bernabò, for example, extorted huge sums from his helpless subjects, and certain of his successors were notorious for an arbitrary ruthlessness against which there was no recourse. Such rule was merely personal, and it never succeeded in creating the modern kind of institutional state, independent of the individual ruler and able to rely for its stability on the loyalty of the subject. Selfish special interests were kept in check, to be sure, but they were subordinated to the special interest of the ruler, not to the general welfare. The memory of self-government and the resentment of suppressed special interests persisted in the Milanese state; and when the last of the Visconti died in 1447, the subjects combined in a pathetic effort to restore communal government. But the Ambrosian Republic, as it called itself, could not solve the problems such republics had failed to solve earlier; above all it could not control the restive Milanese state beyond the limits of the city. Thus by 1450 it had been overthrown by Francesco Sforza, a mercenary soldier who had served Milan in the past: and in this fashion a new despotism replaced the old. Milan therefore continued to be the outstanding representative of tyranny, with all its strengths and its weaknesses, among the Italian city-states. Her method of solving the problem of order was, however, common also among many lesser states.

The political experience of Florence is of unusual interest in view of her leadership in the literary and artistic movements of the Renaissance; some historians have in fact seen in the political atmosphere of Florence the essential condition of her cultural achievement. The Florentine solution to the problems of government reveals some similarities to that of Milan, but the differences are even more significant. Above all Florence retained her republican form of government; and because her citizens continued to participate in political affairs and to take some responsibility for the general welfare, certain Florentines developed explicit loyalties and attitudes to the state of peculiar importance for the formation of the modern political consciousness.

The disorderly Florentine nobility had been largely excluded from political life by a new constitution in 1282, which vested the government in an elected council whose members served for very short terms. Restrictions on the right to vote, however, insured control by the more substantial business interests, who tended, like others in their position, to favor policies advantageous to themselves. Thus they taxed property in the surrounding countryside but not in the city itself where their own possessions chiefly lay, while in the city taxes were levied largely on necessities, especially food, consumed by the lower classes. This system worked well enough except in times of crisis. In 1343, for example, a financial crisis combined with failure in a war to conquer the neighboring town of Lucca, and the discredited oligarchy gave way briefly to the dictatorship of a French adventurer named Walter of Brienne. Again, in 1378, the efforts of the narrow ruling group to tighten its hold over the city resulted in a popular revolution known as the Revolt of the Ciompi; but the popular classes were unable to construct a stable government, and the old ruling group eventually returned to power. In fact these brief experiments with dictatorship and revolution probably contributed indirectly to the ultimate stability of the republic. They interrupted the tendencies of the oligarchy to abuse its position, displaced groups that had long enjoyed power, and opened up opportunities for new men to rise into the ruling class. Florentines remained reasonably united in their support of the state; and their city continued to be a republic while many of the states around her were turning to tyranny.

The significance of her difference from these other states was brought home to the citizens of Florence by the pressure of Milanese expansion in the decades around 1400. Before this period thoughtful Florentines, wearied by constant disorder, had often longed, like medieval thinkers, for a strong autocratic government which could preserve the peace of the state and allow them to devote themselves to the private satisfactions of the contemplative life. Enthusiastic classicists, they had, again like their medieval predecessors, idealized the benevolent despotism of imperial Rome. Now, faced with the loss of their independence and the threat of absorption into a large despotic state, they became increasingly conscious of their heritage of republican liberty; and the humanists of Florence, led by Leonardo Bruni, began to praise the worth of liberty and the active life of civic responsibility. They found their model now in the Roman republic, in which medieval thinkers had taken little interest; and in this way they began the development of a new political ideal of peculiar importance. In addition, conscious through their awakened love for Florence of her special identity, they began to consider how she had developed in time; and from this crisis of embattled Florence there emerged the rich tradition of Florentine historical writing.

The histories composed by Bruni and his successors, in a long series of works which reached its climax with Machiavelli and Guicciardini in the sixteenth century, are important evidence of the contribution of Florence to the development of modern political attitudes. They reveal two significant characteristics hardly present before in the European mind. One was the assumption that historical development proceeds through a succession of natural causes, with the implication that these may be understood by men and to some degree controlled through intelligent and well-informed political action; and in this assumption we may find more convincing support than in the measures of despotic governments for the notion that Renaissance Italy was beginning to conceive of the state as a "work of art." But, possibly even more important, these histories also express a feeling for the particular political community as an abstract and continuing entity, independent of the particular men or governments in power, and worthy of human affection, loyalty, and active support. That the new spirit in Florence was not merely theoretical is suggested by the fact that the business oligarchy that continued to govern the republic, faced with a new crisis in 1427, enacted a new tax, whose burdens fell above all on themselves. Thus, although tyrannies such as Milan may have contributed to the techniques and the form of more effective government, the free atmosphere of republican Florence gave it something of far deeper significance: a moral and spiritual substance.

This substance was not destroyed in the concealed dictatorship exercised by the Medici in the fifteenth century; indeed, the indirection and tact of

Medici rule are themselves a tribute to the persistent vitality of the republican spirit. The old oligarchy had failed disastrously in another attempt to conquer Lucca (1429–33). Thus discredited, it was overthrown and replaced with a new government dominated by Cosimo de' Medici, a prominent banker who relied on broad popular support. Cosimo remained a private citizen and ruled Florence more like a modern big city political boss than a tyrant. The election of officials loyal to himself was assured by eliminating opponents from the lists of those eligible for office, the direction of foreign policy was in his hands, and the government managed to identify itself with the interests of the community. When Cosimo died in 1460, leadership passed to his son Piero, and in 1469 to the most spectacular of the Medici, Lorenzo, known as the Magnificent for his patronage of learning and the arts. Only in 1494, when the history of Florence merged with the larger political crisis in Italy brought on by the French invasion, were the Medici overthrown; meanwhile, through their service to the true interests of Florence, their relatively successful maintenance of internal and external security, and their respect for cherished republican forms of government, the Medici had enjoyed a degree of public confidence beyond anything achieved by the tyrants of Milan.

Politically, as geographically, Venice was somewhat detached from the rest of Italy. The islands in the Venetian lagoons had been settled by refugees from the mainland during the disorders of the early Middle Ages; and the homogeneous population of Venice, lacking the troublesome landed nobility which plagued other states, could turn whole-heartedly to commerce with the eastern Mediterranean. As elsewhere, the more powerful business interests tended to assume control and to convert a democratic into a more and more narrowly aristocratic republic. Tyranny was avoided by the imposition of such close restrictions on the *doge,* the nominal head of the state, that he was little more than a figurehead; and the stability of the Venetian government was maintained through such special agencies of control as the notorious Council of Ten, which investigated and took ruthless action against suspected enemies of the regime, and an efficient secret police. But these institutions of control, however effective, do not provide any fundamental explanation for the relative good order of Venice. Its basic cause was the sense of community among her people that proceeded from their participation together in a highly profitable trade. Thus Venice resembled Florence more than she resembled Milan.

Her political problems arose, therefore, chiefly out of her relations with other powers. One set of problems was connected with the establishment and maintenance of her commercial empire; in this respect Venice was a special case among the Italian states. The needs of trade had led her to seize a number of towns on the east coast of the Adriatic, and this chain of bases was extended to the islands of the Aegean and even to the shores of the Black Sea. Her efforts to preserve these bases resulted in a long series of delaying actions against the expanding Ottoman Turks, in which wars were frequently interrupted by long intervals of peace and friendly commercial intercourse which shocked the official conscience of Christendom. The strong position of Venice in the trade of the eastern Mediterranean was also challenged by Genoa; but a succession of wars in the later thirteenth and fourteenth centuries reached a climax in the War of Chioggia (1375–81), in which Venice finally crushed her rival; and she emerged from the conflict into her period of greatest prosperity and power in the fifteenth century. Her possession of an empire outside Italy, with all the problems and advantages this involved, always made Venice somewhat different from the other states of the peninsula, and her wealth made her an object of general envy.

Meanwhile the Venetians had begun to expand on the Italian mainland adjacent to their home lagoons. This expansion, by involving Venice in the political struggles of northern Italy, created a new set of problems for her. The motives of Venetian conquest on the mainland were twofold. She needed secure overland trade routes, and this meant that she could not countenance a strong and hostile power between herself and the passes through the Alps; in addition, she required a near-by agricultural province under her own permanent control as a source of food. In the fourteenth and early fifteenth centuries she felt compelled to conquer the territories of the tyrants of Verona and Padua, who were levying heavy duties on Venetian goods passing through their territories and occasionally cut off her food supply. But although she now had her farms and her access to the northern passes, the results were not altogether to her advantage. For Venice was henceforth far more a part of the political struggles of Italy than she had been before, with new responsibilities and new demands on her resources. Above all she found herself threatened, like Florence, by the aggressive ambitions of Visconti Milan.

## III

Milan, Florence, and Venice, each strong in its own way, were all three steadily extending their authority over their surrounding provinces; and the chaos of petty states in northern Italy was thus gradually replaced, chiefly through conquest, by a few much larger political units. In the center of the peninsula the papacy, after the Great Schism had ended, was struggling to recover control over its state. The feudal kingdom of Naples ruled the south of Italy; till 1435 its king came from the French house of Anjou, after that year from the Spanish house of Aragon. By the early fifteenth century, therefore, the political map of Italy had been considerably simplified: only five states dominated the peninsula. Their conflicting interests kept them in close contact with each other, and fifteenth century Italy therefore exhibits many of the features of a miniature international system, whose workings have long fascinated historians. Some scholars have seen in this system a significant anticipation of the modern principle of a balance of power, a persistent theme in later international relations; others have been doubtful. But there is general agreement that the Italian states first worked out the principles and the machinery of diplomatic practice which have governed international relations ever since.

The emergence of Italy as a kind of system based on the five major powers was possible only after it became clear that none of them was, in fact, strong enough to absorb the rest. Threats of some larger consolidation through conquest had come from both the south and the north. In the early fifteenth century King Ladislas of Naples, taking advantage of papal weakness during the Schism, secured a practical mastery over Rome and the papal domains and advanced on Tuscany; but the Florentines drove him back, and his death in 1414 ended the possibility of a larger state based on Naples. The ambitions of the Visconti constituted a more serious effort to construct a larger state in the north. Again and again Giangaleazzo and his successors attempted to expand; but the danger of Milanese conquest regularly forced Florence and Venice into a defensive alliance. Already in the first half of the century, therefore, the needs of self-protection were leading to the creation of a fairly clear alignment; Florence and Venice joined against Milan, and the Visconti, after Aragonese rulers replaced the Angevin dynasty, found support in Naples.

The alignment became even clearer, though on a somewhat different basis, after the middle of the century. When Francesco Sforza seized power in Milan in 1450, he was promptly embroiled with Venice, which had taken advantage of the temporary confusion in Milan to seize certain Milanese territories. At this point Cosimo de' Medici, persuaded that the growing Venetian power was beginning to pose an even greater danger than Milan to the interests of Florence, abruptly switched alliances by supporting the new dictator of Milan; and the diplomatic revolution was completed when Venice turned to Naples. General war seemed near when Pope Nicholas V intervened. After taking Constantinople in 1453, the Turks seemed about to threaten Italy; and the possibility also loomed that France might intervene in Milan on the pretext of the Visconti marriage so long before. The pope therefore managed to persuade the Italian states of the necessity for mending their differences so that they could present some common front to the outside world. The result was the Peace of Lodi (1454), by which the coup of Francesco Sforza was recognized by all, and a new balance was thus established. It managed a precarious survival for the next forty years, although imperiled again and again as one state attempted to secure some advantage over another.

The tensions, instability, and insecurity of the system may be illustrated by the famous Pazzi conspiracy and its sequel. Enmity had been growing between Florence and the papacy of Sixtus IV over certain lands coveted by them both. It reached a climax in a plot involving both Rome and certain opponents of the Medici in Florence led by the Pazzi family. In 1478 the conspirators attempted to assassinate Lorenzo and his brother Giuliano during a mass in the cathedral of Florence. Giuliano was stabbed to death, but Lorenzo escaped; and Medici partisans hanged the conspirators in the streets, among them the archbishop of the city. To revenge this "sacrilege," the pope excommunicated Lorenzo, placed Florence under an interdict, and declared war, in which he was joined by Naples. But at this juncture Lorenzo carried out a sudden diplomatic coup. He made a quick personal visit to Naples, where he persuaded King Ferrante to abandon the papal alliance and sign a treaty of friendship with Florence. The crisis was finally resolved with Lorenzo's public apology to Rome, and matters proceeded as before. But the incident demonstrates to what a degree the preservation of the Italian system was dependent on accident, and how trivial a conflict could threaten it. However much the Italian experience may suggest the later pattern of the balance of power, therefore, it is difficult to see in Italy the stable alignments based on a more serious calculation of the interests of states which were to characterize international relations in western Europe during later centuries.

Meanwhile the inability of the Italian states to achieve either unity or real solidarity was a constant invitation to the intervention of outside powers, especially France, which was interested in Italy both because of the Angevin claims to Naples and because of the old Visconti marriage. In the tendency of insecure, disgruntled, or ambitious elements in Italy to look for support outside the peninsular system lay another and ultimately a fatal weakness of the system which also suggests some need for modification of the view that Renaissance Italy offers an example of the behavior of mature, modern nation states. In the last decade of the fifteenth century Ludovico il Moro, uncle to the legitimate Sforza heir of Milan, was eager to take the place of his nephew, who, married to an Aragonese princess, was supported by Naples. To solve his problem, Ludovico, ignoring the larger interests of Italy, invited the French into the peninsula, in the expectation that they would deal with his enemies in the south. The French invasion of 1494 in fact ended the more or less independent operation of the Italian system; from this time Italy, hopelessly divided, was involved with and at the mercy of powers far larger and better organized than she. The Spanish kingdom of Aragon, which had its own interests in the south, met the French challenge; and for years Italy was a battleground for alien armies. A major chapter in the political history of Europe had come to an end, and to understand even the future development of Italy it will be necessary to consider what had been occurring elsewhere.

But if the Italian states did not entirely anticipate the later conduct of international relations by means of a balance of power, there is no doubt about the contribution of Italy to the techniques of diplomacy. The articulation of Italy into a group of self-consciously sovereign powers that ignored their theoretical unity in a larger Christian commonwealth had prepared the way for this development, since diplomacy in the modern sense can only be conducted by fully independent states. The interests of commerce and the feverish political activities of the fourteenth and fifteenth centuries had impelled the Italian states to create suitable instruments for dealing with other powers: foreign offices staffed by able men, which collected information, kept records, and carried on an extensive correspondence; and above all a system of permanent ambassadors residing in foreign capitals, commissioned to report on conditions abroad and to negotiate on behalf of the states they represented. The diplomatic machinery developed by Venice was particularly efficient, though it was by no means unique. Venetian ambassadors were carefully chosen for regular three-year terms and periodically transferred from one place to another. Their duties remarkably anticipated those of modern diplomats. They received detailed instructions on being sent abroad, they were expected to maintain a high standard of living in keeping with the dignity of the republic, they entertained and paid ceremonial visits, and they prepared elaborate dispatches and reports which are still today among the historian's richest sources of information about all aspects of European society for several centuries. In her development of standards for diplomacy and international communication in a new political world composed of sovereign states, Renaissance Italy served as a model for the rest of Europe.

For various reasons, therefore, Italy during the fourteenth and fifteenth centuries was instructive for the political future of the West. Fundamental to the developments we have been describing was the general abandonment of the principle that government should be subordinated to religious ends and should be carried on only within the larger framework of Christendom; this principle had been replaced with the assumption that government exists to promote the welfare in this world of a particular state. Although on a small scale, the states of Italy accordingly felt and behaved like fully sovereign powers. Some employed their sovereignty for the construction of a more effective machinery of government; and some developed among their citizens a sense of attachment, loyalty, and responsibility to the community that anticipates one of the more significant features of modern politics. In their relations with each other these states also expressed this new consciousness of secular identity and independence, and they created appropriate new instruments for communication between states. Yet there were also serious limitations to the Italian political achievement that prevented these states from a full and satisfactory realization of all these accomplishments. They anticipated future developments and contributed to them, but they did not succeed in the permanent construction of the modern political scene.

## IV

One set of limitations was connected with the novelty of many of the political arrangements in Renaissance Italy. The old order had at least been sanctioned by custom, by old personal loyalties, and by the traditional character of its institutions; it was ideally, however ineffectively, an order. The various states and their rulers had recognized papal or imperial, ecclesiastical or feudal superiors, and the rule of imperial, divine, or customary law; their governments were thus to a considerable degree *legitimate*. But no such legitimacy supported this new political structure; it rested only on the shifting purposes and calculations of men or groups of men, and on force. The result was a high degree of instability, rapid changes in political fortune, brutal seizures of power, conspiracies and aggressions, insecurity and disorder. The internal history of Milan and the dreary chronicle of the relations between the various states are sufficient evidence, but the changes even in Florence suggest that republics were not immune from such difficulties. However impressive the political achievement of the Italian Renaissance, we must not close our eyes to its darker side, which has left on posterity an impression of fascinated horror. For the Italians, protracted internal struggles often induced a mood of weariness and political helplessness in sharp contrast to the energetic creativity which is the best feature of the Renaissance, and this negative mood was only reinforced when Italy became a battleground for great foreign powers.

As these unhappier qualities of Italian political life contributed to division, they also point to a second set of limitations on the achievement of the Renaissance. The most advanced of the Italian states were based on cities, but in spite of their relative size these cities did not command sufficient resources for stable political power. The need for secure trade routes and a reliable source of food to supply the urban masses, even in the absence of that tendency to expansion for its own sake which has so often infected governments, required the city to control an extensive area around itself. But conquest was expensive, and furthermore it created new enemies and therefore a permanent burden of defense. Conquered territories also needed to be administered and policed, often a difficult task because of the resentment of the subject peoples. The problem of manpower complicated the situation as well. Urban populations were limited, and had in any case to devote themselves chiefly to economic enterprise. To secure and control outlying territories, therefore, the Italian states tended to rely on mercenary troops loyal not directly to the governments which employed them but to the military entrepreneurs who enlisted them, the celebrated *condottieri*. But such troops, and above all their leaders, presented a new problem of control. Lacking dedicated soldiers of their own, the towns were only too often threatened or blackmailed by their hired armies; frequently these troops proved unreliable; and occasionally an ambitious *condottiere,* like Francesco Sforza, seized power for himself. Evidently so small a state, constructed on so narrow a social base, could not finally solve the problem of order: it could not therefore provide any final model for the organization of the states of Europe.

These lessons of the Italian political experience were brilliantly spelled out in the writings of the Florentine Niccolò Machiavelli (1469–1527). Machiavelli had long practical experience with Italian affairs as a diplomat and secretary in the Florentine government during the difficult period of the early foreign expeditions into Italy, a time also when the republic was trying to reestablish its authority after the expulsion of the Medici. When the Medici were reinstated in 1512, he lost his official position; and while in retirement he set down his reflections on politics in a number of famous works, particularly *The Prince* and the *Discourses on Livy*. As the first consists of advice to a prince on how to secure absolute control over a state, and the second includes eloquent passages on the superiority of a republic to all other forms of government, historians have long discussed their relationship, their apparent inconsistency, and the extent to which each represents Machiavelli's true thought; but it may be that the contradictions between them really indicate their author's uncertainties about the proper course of action in a bewildering and disorderly world. In any case these writings are instructive at once for their diagnosis of the political troubles of Italy, for the remedies they prescribe, and for the general attitudes to politics implicit in them.

Contemplating the past disorders of Italy, her present vulnerability to foreign intervention, and perhaps most directly the recent instability of his own beloved Florence, Machiavelli saw clearly that something had gone seriously wrong. Comparison with other more successful societies, especially with the Roman republic, helped him to identify the trouble. The Italians of the Renaissance, he decided, had failed to preserve the political virtues, the leadership and civic responsibility, which the Romans had so long retained; their religious fervor, the most effective of social bonds, had declined; and they had employed unreliable mercenaries to do their fighting instead of creating loyal citizen armies. Their division, meanwhile, had opened Italy to invasion. What now could be done? Although Machiavelli considered a republic superior to all other sorts of government, experience had made him a pessimist; and he had adopted a view of history according to which the selfishness of men will regularly subvert the state, reduce it to chaos, and require strong and ruthless leadership to set it to rights again. This cycle will occur again and again, human nature being always the same; and it seemed obvious to Machiavelli that in his own time Italy was passing through the most disorderly phase of the cycle, in which the urgent need was for leadership. These views are probably the explanation for the republican author's flirtation with the idea of a tyrant; an extraordinary problem required extraordinary measures, perhaps even the most cynical and brutal actions, to restore political health. If successful at home, moreover, the prince might be able to organize a general Italian effort to expel the barbarians. In the long run, however, the prince would play his proper role in the historical cycle if, through sound laws and wise discipline, he prepared his subjects for the restoration of an effective republic, the only kind of political organization capable, Machiavelli believed, of the greatest achievements.

But implicit in these particular reflections are attitudes toward politics of even greater significance. Machiavelli obviously believed that it is useful to analyze political situations and problems, to draw lessons from historical experience, and thereby to establish the principles on which sound political calculations and decisions can be based. In his view man, by taking thought, can add a cubit to his political stature, at least in the short run; the political virtues can be encouraged through deliberate action, can control events and solve problems, and can thereby triumph over the whims of fortune. To this extent Machiavelli reflects that tendency of the Italian Renaissance to conceive of government as a series of problems in the adaptation of means to ends, as a matter of rational calculation based on a knowledge of men and of the workings of institutions; and for this reason he has been hailed as the father of modern political science. But equally important was his concern with the welfare of the state, conceived as an end in itself. The good for Machiavelli is quite simply what serves to preserve and strengthen the state, the bad is what tends to weaken and destroy the state. From this standpoint all religious and ethical standards are irrelevant to politics; and *reason of state,* a famous phrase now permanently associated with this great Florentine, is the only measure of political wisdom. His thought therefore assigns to the state a theoretical independence of all ideal considerations which parallels the tendency of the Italian states in their practical conduct to ignore their common membership in the Christian republic and pursue their separate interests. Thus if Machiavelli is a witness to the political failure of Italy, and if indeed his most radical prescriptions testify to his own sense of this failure, he also reflects the most significant achievements of Renaissance Italy, and expresses basic principles that other states were to realize more effectively and permanently.

## V

Although the territorial states to the north and west faced the same general problems of order and control we have been examining in Italy, their political development was affected by a number of significant differences.

One was simply their greater size. This meant, of course, that the difficulties of administering them were far greater; but it also meant that the potential resources of government, once these could be mobilized, were much larger. In the long run this was to prove a decisive advantage. But there was in addition an important difference in social structure, and therefore in political organization. In Italy the most significant achievements in the art of government had been the work of townsmen in regions where feudalism was relatively weak. But elsewhere, and indeed in much of Italy south of Tuscany, the feudal nobility was generally far stronger, while townsmen were relatively weak. In these regions, therefore, government could not be improved by a force largely independent of the feudal system; it had somehow to emerge out of that system itself. Governments which could be developed in this fashion, furthermore, could claim traditional sanctions and a certain legitimacy which gave them particular strength.

The construction of central governments on the basis of the feudal tie had begun, of course, well before the fourteenth century. Territorial princes, the most important of whom bore the title of king, had long tried to compel their vassals to fulfill the obligations required by the feudal connection, prominent among them the duty of giving support and advice in a council that had both administrative and judicial functions. They had started to develop their households into bureaucracies which could supervise the realm in various ways, attempted to maintain order through non-manorial courts, and even claimed some power to tax. The age of the Renaissance was to see the development, from these rudimentary beginnings, of far more effective governments, in which the feudal connection was gradually replaced by another kind of political allegiance.

The task was enormous. Princes were largely dependent on their vassals for military support, and above all they were severely limited by feudal notions about taxation. It was expected that all the routine expenses of government could be met from the income of crown lands; this was the king's "ordinary" revenue. If, in special circumstances such as war, he needed more, he could not tax his subjects until he had taken counsel with them and obtained their consent. Although the distinction between ordinary and extraordinary revenue during the Middle Ages is the origin of our principle of no taxation without representation, it was for a long time a major obstacle to better government. Lacking both an army and a secure and substantial income, kings were unable to impose any effective control over their more powerful vassals. Meanwhile the tasks of preserving order and administering justice at the local level were still largely in the hands of feudal landlords; the right to rule other men, in spite of royal claims, remained in large measure a function of social position rather than the responsibility of a truly political authority. But perhaps the most profound weakness in the whole structure lay in the merely personal character of the cement which held it together. Government depended primarily on the mutual obligations between the individual participants in the feudal contract; it had little basis in a sense of political community, given expression through the state, to which all owe loyalty, obedience, and support.

The representative assemblies of the later Middle Ages played a particularly important, if somewhat ambiguous, role in the transition from these conditions to more modern government. Since kings were not strong enough to rule alone, they began to summon bodies representing their more important subjects, either to consent to taxation or to demonstrate the unity of the realm in time of crisis. These assemblies had various names, but the English Parliament, the French Estates-General, the Cortes in the kingdoms of the Iberian peninsula, and the many similar bodies which met in other regions all served the same essential purposes. The ability of a ruler to compel attendance on the part of men who were frequently reluctant to come at his call was a mark of his strength; and when his demands were met, his power was increased. On the other hand, his need for such support was also proof of his dependence and weakness. Once an assembly had met, moreover, it often chose to criticize, interfere with, and limit his administration. Protected by the ruler's need for money, it might even demand some permanent part in his government. From one point of view, therefore, representative assemblies were a means by which selfish special interests could bring pressure to bear on the central government and so obstruct measures which might be genuinely in the common interest; the frequency with which they met is often an index to the weakness of kings. Yet, because they also brought diverse interests together and associated them at times in a common cause, representative assemblies could also help in the construction of that broader sense of political community which is the mark of the modern state. The positive role such bodies could play, as we shall see, is most clearly revealed in the history of England, though only through a long process of development.

In the fourteenth century, however, the increasing strength of representative bodies quite clearly made the development of royal government more difficult at a time when the growing need for order required greater power for the king; such assemblies have, therefore, chiefly a reactionary significance during this period. As in Italy, the fourteenth century brought a particularly serious political crisis to the states beyond the Alps, and these bodies aggravated the situation. But there were also deeper reasons for the special disorders of the age. A general contraction of the economy produced widespread discontent; pestilence decimated urban and rural populations alike; the feudal nobility, whether in desperation as their incomes declined in some regions or emboldened by greater wealth in others, were increasingly rebellious toward a central authority which threatened their political power; peasant revolts broke out in the countryside; townsmen were restive. Perhaps the major importance of this dismal interval in Western political history is that it demonstrated conclusively the need for strong royal leadership.

Of the three great powers which were to emerge on the Atlantic, England and France each acknowledged a single king, who was, however, still limited in many respects by continuing feudal restraints. Spain was still divided; Castile had expanded southward at the expense of the Moslems, while Aragon had turned to the east to construct an empire in the Mediterranean which included the Balearic Islands, Sardinia, and Corsica, and members of her dynasty ruled Naples and Sicily. But once the reconquest from Islam had been largely completed, the Spanish nobility, no longer united in a common enterprise, defied royal authority and split into factions which engaged in a long series of struggles for power in both major kingdoms. Their monarchies, caught in the complicated maneuvers of aggressive feudal nobles and an assertive Cortes, were reduced to impotence. Under these conditions the crusade was not completed, and the Moslem state of Granada held on to the extreme south of the peninsula. Neither order nor unity made further progress.

Developments in both France and England, meanwhile, were profoundly affected by their long and bitter struggle in the Hundred Years' War. The effort of the English king to obtain for himself the throne of France distracted the rulers of both states for over a century from the task of constructing more effective government, increased their reliance on the nobility, and aggravated the general disorder. Thus a period which had opened on a note of promise for both countries is most obviously remarkable for the setbacks it gave to their political evolution. Yet the effects of the war were not entirely negative. Much as the struggle with Milan was sharpening the sense of civic community in Florence at about the same time, so their struggle with each other sharpened the sense of national community in both France and

England. This feeling found expression, however, in significantly different ways. France was the victim of foreign attack, and had eventually to accept strong royal leadership to expel the invader and restore order; her monarchy was therefore finally strengthened by the ordeal. But the English king was the aggressor and needed massive support from his subjects in order to carry out his conquests. He had, therefore, to rely on parliament as never before; and that important body came increasingly to represent the realm and grew in power. For England some further experience with disorder at home was yet necessary to teach the need for effective central government and to redress the balance between crown and parliament.

France did not learn her lesson quickly or easily. When the fourteenth century opened, she had seemed well on the way to stronger central government even without any major stimulus from foreign war. The aggressive assertion by Philip the Fair of his rights over the clergy had been only one aspect of a broader effort to control his realm. During his reign royal officials had steadily extended their jurisdiction over local forces, and above all his government had attempted to tax important groups of subjects. The consequence was growing resentment; and Philip's death in 1314 was promptly followed by a brief feudal reaction in which leagues of nobles compelled his successor to make concessions. Much worse was ahead when the crown was discredited by defeat at the hands of the English; and the costs of the war in money, suffering, and disorder had led initially rather to widespread discontent than to a sense of common purpose. In 1356, during the crisis following the disaster at Poitiers, a battle in which a large number of the French nobles were killed and the king himself taken prisoner, the Estates-General convened at Paris. The direction of this body was promptly taken over by Étienne Marcel, leader of the Paris merchants; and it attempted to impose its authority over the royal government. The Great Ordinance which it forced on the *dauphin,* now ruling for his absent father, was more like a modern constitution than a feudal charter in its provision for control of the government in the future by the Estates. But the Estates-General in France still represented divided special interests rather than the common purposes of the nation, the Ordinance reflected little more than the ideas of Marcel and his class, and a falling out between him and his allies soon saved the crown from a tutelage which could not yet promise more effective government. The episode served only to reveal the precariousness of royal administration and the ability of the supreme representative body in France to interfere with the work of the king without providing a workable alternative. A similar crisis reinforced these lessons following further national disasters early in the fifteenth century. Again a meeting of the Estates-General provided the opportunity, this time for a coalition of ambitious nobles with certain groups in Paris; and once again an attempt to subordinate the crown to the Estates completely failed. Clearly only the king could govern France.

Yet even before this last episode a hopeful development was under way. Charles V (1364–80), known as the Wise, one of the few able monarchs of the fourteenth century, had begun the creation of a paid royal army to replace the unreliable feudal levies; and although he was forced, like his English contemporaries, to rely on the Estates-General for money, he managed to obtain it with a certain regularity which suggested the obligation of the realm to support the crown in a continuing crisis. This double achievement was carried significantly farther, after some interruption, during the reign of Charles VII (1422–61). At a crucial point in the struggle with the English, Joan of Arc had appeared, inspiring the French to summon up all their energies in a great national effort to expel the invader; and by 1453 the task had been accomplished. This success gave an enormous impetus to the prestige of the crown, which could address itself to the restoration of order in a desolated land now suffering from the depredations of unemployed troops. To accomplish this the king had at his disposal a royal army; and a royal edict, which evidently expressed the sentiments of the Estates-General, declared other military forces illegal. But above all, supported by a people who were united at least in looking to him to expel the English and restore order, the king was successful after 1440 in collecting taxes without summoning the Estates-General. That body ceased to be necessary to the government except under very special circumstances, and it met again only at times of particular national crisis. There were bitter protests in the name of tradition, but the realm was no longer able to present a solid front against the king; he dealt instead with smaller and less formidable groups of subjects. Thus the French crown emerged from the Hundred Years' War with both an army and large financial resources; the French king was accordingly an object of envy to his brother monarchs.

The contrast with England is of particular interest: the period of the Hundred Years' War clearly pushed the two states along quite different paths, and the general fourteenth-century reaction against royal government had an even more permanent significance in English history. Edward I (1272–1307) had brought central government to the greatest perfection it reached in the Middle Ages, imposing order on the royal administration and above all on the English legal system. But his ambitious foreign policy, which involved him in war with both France and Scotland, was expensive. Again and again he was forced to appeal to his subjects assembled in parliament for money; and although he received substantial sums, his demands caused deep resentment. Even more important, these regular appeals to parliament seemed to confirm its general right to participate in the governance of England and its particular power over the royal purse-strings. Under Edward I's less impressive successors, therefore, parliament was increasingly assertive. The heavy costs of the long war in France meant that it continued to be called together, and its financial powers were underlined again and again by repeated requests for money from the king. At the same time its organization and its procedures were clarified, and most important of all it managed to establish a certain right to make laws, although how far this extended was not clear.

Meanwhile baronial opponents of royal power used parliament in other ways to restrict the crown, much as opponents of the king were exploiting the Estates-General in France. Parliaments criticized royal policy, condemned unpopular servants of the crown to death, and even went so far as to depose kings of whom they disapproved. Thus parliaments were used to replace Edward II with Edward III in 1327, and Richard II with Henry IV in 1399. Yet, as in France, these assemblies were tending to represent not so much the community of the realm as powerful special interests which were not capable, without strong executive leadership, of providing effective government. That parliamentary government of this sort was inadequate to solve the problem of order was clearly demonstrated after the fighting had ended in France. War on the continent had long provided an outlet for their aggressiveness; and now, two years after their return from France, the nobles resumed their old military habits in a prolonged civil war for control of the crown. Because that agency was weak, England had to endure a generation of anarchy in the Wars of the Roses (1455–85) in order to be taught the same lesson Spain and France had so painfully learned. Meanwhile, however, the parliament had won a permanent and powerful place in the structure of her government.

Reaction against disorder began to gather even before 1485, the year when Henry Tudor, leader of the Lancastrian faction, defeated the Yorkists under Richard III at Bosworth Field, ending the civil wars and bringing about his own succession as Henry VII. As early as 1470 the Chief Justice of England,

Sir John Fortescue, in a book on the constitution entitled *In Praise of the Laws of England,* applauded the system of parliamentary controls over the king, which he contrasted with the absolutism of France; but at the same time he recommended a stronger monarchy. Edward IV (1461–83) contributed to this end by securing for the crown the huge estates of great nobles condemned for rebellion, thereby reducing his reliance on parliament; and Richard III was full of plans for a more centralized administration. Meanwhile the Wars of the Roses had slaughtered, impoverished, and generally weakened the feudal nobles, and a great wave of longing for order had swept over the increasingly significant middle class of England. The new king, insofar as he stood for peace and stability, could rely on substantial support.

## VI

Spain, France, and England, therefore, had all faced a strikingly similar problem of disorder at home; and the sudden improvement in the governments of all three during the later fifteenth century gives the appearance of a kind of general political revolution. Each began to move toward national greatness on the basis of better rule, and to assume the form of a more modern state. This development is associated with the reign of Louis XI in France (1461–83); with Henry VII in England (1485–1509); and in Spain with Ferdinand of Aragon (1489–1516) and Isabella of Castile (1474–1504), whose marriage prepared the way for a united Spanish kingdom in the sixteenth century. Ambitious, and also ruthless, realistic, and methodical, they addressed themselves promptly to the task of asserting royal power over their kingdoms, in each case with the substantial middle class support which had been growing during the long anarchy. Replacing feudal counselors with churchmen, lawyers, and other lesser men whose careers depended solely on pleasing the king, they devoted themselves above all to reducing the power of the nobility. The novelty introduced by these "new monarchs," as historians have called them, was, however, less a matter of institutional innovation than of the new spirit of resolution and aggressiveness with which they ruled and, above all, of a new degree of success.

The obvious similarities in the problems each of these rulers faced led to similar policies, but there were also significant national differences. In France the power of the king was still insecure because of the continued existence of great nobles who, though royal vassals, ruled large areas from which royal administration was effectively excluded. The power of the lords of Burgundy, of Orleans, or of Brittany, for example, was still so large that they could combine in rebellion and extort concessions from the crown, as Louis XI learned to his sorrow early in his reign. In the end, however, he proved more than a match for his enemies. By unscrupulous maneuvering, by intrigue, by playing off noble against noble, and by a certain amount of luck (as his foes died without heirs and their estates reverted to the crown), the king eliminated most of the great nobles one by one. His greatest success came when Charles the Bold, Duke of Burgundy, died fighting against the Swiss, whom Louis had secretly encouraged, and the king was able to seize French Burgundy. By the end of his reign only Brittany remained, and the marriage of its heiress to his son in 1491 prepared the way for its incorporation into the royal domain. Thus Louis XI established the superiority of the crown to the nobles of France.

Meanwhile he continued to develop the royal army created by his predecessors and strengthened his administration. Legal and administrative problems were increasingly dealt with by royal courts and the royal council, the king virtually ignored the pope in the governance of the Church in France, and he interfered constantly in the affairs of the towns. Such success was naturally expensive, but the true measure of his achievement is that he was able vastly to increase the tax burden of his subjects without provoking further serious rebellion; and although his heir was only a child when Louis died, the nobles were unable to organize any effective reaction, either in open rebellion or in a meeting of the Estates-General in 1484. The delegates protested bitterly and demanded an end to "illegal" taxation without consent; but their complaints were fruitless. The king was now supreme in France.

His successors Charles VIII (1483–98), Louis XII (1498–1515), Francis I (1515–47), and Henry II (1547–59) consolidated these gains. The invasion of Italy in 1494, with its long sequel of foreign wars, was, whatever else it may have been, a brutal demonstration of French power and of the success with which the monarchy had organized the state. At the same time the Italian wars gave employment to the nobility and prevented it from disturbing the peace at home. Meanwhile the machinery of central government developed apace. The numbers of royal officials rapidly increased, and everywhere an ambitious bureaucracy attacked what was left of local and aristocratic independence. Royal justice increased the tempo of its encroachments on local courts, and financial administration became more efficient and more demanding: taxes continued to rise. The nobles increasingly saw faithful service to the crown as their only road to advancement and riches; and with the Concordat of Bologna in 1516, the king acquired from the papacy recognition of his almost complete control over the appointments and the wealth of the Church in France. All of this, moreover, was accomplished by the crown alone; the Estates-General was not convened between 1484 and 1560. At the same time the theory of government, its tone set by the lawyers trained in the absolutist principles of Roman law who filled the administration, was uniformly royalist. Their view that the power of the king is derived directly from God and that his will is the basis of law went almost unchallenged.

Henry VII achieved a success in England similar insofar as it led to the restoration of order but strikingly different in its maintenance of that balance between the crown and the realm to which the English development had been pointing. By defeating several attempts by his Yorkist enemies to unseat him after 1485, Henry secured his position and proceeded to lay the foundation for over a century of Tudor rule. The immediate problem posed by the nobility he dealt with through the enforcement of statutes against the maintenance of armed bands and the development of a special court within the royal council, the Court of Star Chamber. This court ruthlessly disciplined even his most powerful subjects, who could not be prosecuted in the local courts exposed to their intimidation. As an instrument of order Star Chamber became an important agency in the central administration of the Tudor rulers. For the tasks of local administration Henry secured the alliance of the lesser gentry, who served as justices of the peace in the countryside; their authority and social prestige were strengthened, they were given a wide range of new duties under royal control, and their office became one of the most significant features of English government for centuries to come.

The king also worked out that partnership between crown and parliament which was fundamental to the success of later Tudor government. He secured from parliament an early confirmation of his right to the throne, summoned it frequently during the early and more precarious years of his reign, involved it in his measures of control, and was careful not to challenge its claims; parliament, in return, gave him its support. But as he grew more secure, he felt less need to call it into session and better able to rule alone; he could do this because he was so capable as a financial administrator that he could carry on his government without taxes voted by parliament. The same quality was also helpful to his popularity. In these various ways, therefore, the balance between crown and parliament was restored; the king became a true and effective leader.

The governments of his successors, Henry VIII (1509–47), Edward VI (1547–53), Mary (1553–58), and Elizabeth (1558–1603), generally continued along the same lines. They promoted the prosperity of England, thereby endearing themselves to their increasingly substantial middle-class subjects; and, until the closing decades of the century, they managed to avoid involvement in prolonged wars. The ruler's inner circle of advisers, known as the Privy Council, was increasingly effective as the central agency of the government; and its organization and procedures were improved, particularly under the direction of Thomas Cromwell, a secretary under Henry VIII. Unlike their French colleagues, of course, the rulers of England could not ignore the parliament; and this body was occasionally troublesome through its persistent reluctance to vote money and an incorrigible tendency to offer unsolicited advice and unwelcome criticism. But the Tudor rulers wisely avoided undermining their own popularity by any direct attack on parliamentary pretensions. For long intervals they were able to get along without summoning parliament at all; and when a session could not be avoided, its membership could be to some degree controlled through royal pressures on local elections, its deliberations could often be managed by the careful preparation of its agenda in the Privy Council, its procedures could be manipulated in the king's interest, and its members could be influenced by skillful lobbying. In this fashion the parliament was, in fact, involved in a far more effective way with the royal administration than ever before, and the partnership between crown and parliament grew even closer. The supreme example of this involvement came with the parliamentary actions, culminating with the Act of Supremacy in 1534, by which the English church was detached from Rome; the political significance of these measures is perhaps as great as their religious importance. By substituting the king for the pope as head of the church in England, this legislation gave the English king somewhat more power over the national church than that which the rulers of France and Spain already enjoyed. But because these laws were the work of parliament, they were also a tacit admission by the king of his dependence on his subjects as represented in that body. Nothing could have confirmed more effectively than its participation in so grave a matter the right of parliament to legislate for the realm.

In their separate kingdoms on the Iberian peninsula Ferdinand and Isabella were meanwhile working together to restore royal authority. They demolished the castles of rebellious lords, prosecuted them in special courts, recovered for the crown its ancient lands (which the nobility had taken over when rulers were weak), imposed royal direction on the old military orders in which the nobles were organized, and began to attach the greater lords to the royal court where they were constantly under the watchful eyes of the ruler. The medieval *Hermandad,* originally a federation of cities, was revived in a new form to preserve order in the countryside; its militia became a highly effective rural police force. The towns were themselves brought under royal control through the appointment by the king of officers known as *corregidores* to controlling positions on their councils. The Cortes, at least in Castile, met more and more infrequently; and the extent to which the Church in Spain had fallen under the control of the monarch is indicated by the fact that the Inquisition, established in 1478, was under the authority of the king rather than of churchmen either in Spain or in Rome. Its particular attention to ethnic and religious minorities served the interests of political as much as of religious unity, and the Spanish inquisitors have been compared with the English justices of the peace.

Charles V, the grandson of Ferdinand and Isabella who inherited both their kingdoms in 1516, had to deal with a major crisis when the towns of Castile, aggravated by heavy taxes, revolted in 1520. The revolt was suppressed with the help of the nobility, the authority of the king was reasserted, and the burden of taxation grew more and more heavy. The revolt is also important, however, because it ended the old alliance between town and crown. Henceforth the monarchy relied on the lesser gentry to staff its administration; and, exempt from taxation, this group faithfully promoted royal policy. In other respects, however, Charles continued the policies of his predecessors in his governance of Spain. His reign is chiefly significant for Spanish history because it involved the Spanish kingdom in action on a far broader stage. To understand what was involved we must turn now to developments in Germany.

## VII

The consolidation of more local political units into national states had not taken place in Germanic Europe, in spite of a longing for peace and order at least as great as existed elsewhere; particularism was too deeply entrenched and the central power too weak. The Hapsburg emperor Maximilian I (1486–1519) was unable to secure any general acceptance of his leadership of a united Germany; and the efforts of certain reformers to establish a closer federation of the German states on the basis of a few organs of central government were totally unsuccessful. Led by Berthold of Henneberg, archbishop of Mainz, these men in the last decade of the fifteenth century advocated the creation of a princely executive council; larger authority for the German Diet in which the various components of the empire were represented, including some power to tax; and a kind of supreme court to enforce the peace. But this scheme won the support neither of the emperor, whose leadership, however nominal this may have been, it threatened to displace with a species of constitutional government, nor of the princes whose independence would be limited by it. Germany was therefore left weak, divided, and disorderly, and like Italy an easy prey for the better organized states developing to the west. The Protestant Reformation only confirmed this situation after 1517, as it added religious to political division and increased the power of particular princes by putting at their disposal the wealth of the old church and the direction of the new Protestant state churches which replaced it. In a few German states, however, princes pursued policies like those being applied by the western monarchs; thus, although reduced from the national to the particular level, some political progress was made even in Germany.

The most notable example was the emperor himself. Unable to make headway in Germany as a whole, Maximilian turned to the consolidation of his rule over his own domains in central Europe. But, particularly through strategic marriages, he also began to assemble a quite different sort of political structure: a dynastic empire which was the most spectacular, if not the most successful or permanent, political phenomenon of the sixteenth century. The nucleus of this empire consisted of the Hapsburg holdings in central Europe, including Austria, Styria, Carinthia, Carniola, and the Tyrol; in addition, Hapsburgs were elected to the thrones of Bohemia and Hungary. Maximilian's marriage to the heiress of Charles the Bold secured for him the rich and extensive Netherlands, which the Burgundian house had obtained outside of France in its own dynastic expansion. But his master stroke was the arrangement of a marriage between his son Philip and the princess Juana, heiress to both Ferdinand and Isabella of Spain. His grandson Charles was thus not only the heir to the Spanish kingdoms with all their possessions in the Mediterranean and, as a result of the voyages of discovery, around the world, he was also due to inherit Hapsburg central Europe and the collection of provinces which made up the Low Countries. It remained only for Maximilian to arrange that his grandson should succeed him as Holy Roman Emperor of the German Nation, a feat which he accomplished in 1518 by making heavy cash payments to the electors.

Thus, while a well-organized English state watched from across the channel, two great powers, constructed on radically different lines, confronted each other on the continent and engaged in a struggle which provided an instructive test of rival modes of political organization. France was a national state. With her large and homogeneous population, her ruler's unique ability to tax his subjects, her territorial consolidation, and her centralized administration, she had, before the end of the fifteenth century, seemed far superior to any possible rival; and the other states of Europe tended to band together against her. Now she was challenged by a dynastic empire which, with its huge populations and its enormous territories, all but surrounded her. The potential resources of the Hapsburg emperor were now far superior even to those of France; and they included a strong and increasingly unified national state, the Spanish kingdom, from which he significantly derived much of his strength.

But the rest of his empire was less tightly organized, and its strength was more difficult to mobilize. Its only principle of unity was the accident of common leadership; it lacked common traditions, common institutions, a sense of common purpose. Widely separated geographically, each unit in the empire had its separate administration and carried with it special problems of order and defense which in many cases more than balanced the additional strength they brought their ruler. Thus the hereditary Hapsburg lands were entrusted to the emperor's younger brother Ferdinand; Charles had to deal individually with each of the largely autonomous provinces of the Netherlands; and his imperial office brought him duties without power. And if the personal bond which united these various territories reminds us more of the feudal tie than of any more modern principle of political unity, Charles' attitude to his own position makes him appear more like the last of the medieval emperors than a modern ruler. He accepted with high seriousness his responsibility for the peace of all Christendom, his duty to defend Christian Europe against the aggressive Moslems both in central Europe and the Mediterranean, and his obligation to protect the Church and to maintain the unity of the Catholic faith against the Protestant heretics. In short, he attempted, like his medieval predecessors, to do too much; and in spite of his excellent Spanish armies, the great treasures which flowed into Spain from her American colonies, the wealth of the Flemish towns, and all his other resources, Charles V was unable to crush France. Their long struggle was a stalemate and therefore a victory in principle for the new type of national state. Charles himself seems finally to have recognized this. In 1556, weary and discouraged, he divided his empire, abdicated, and retired to spend his last few years in a Spanish monastery. His brother Ferdinand received the imperial title along with the Hapsburg domains in central Europe; while his son Philip II (1556–98) inherited Spain, her Mediterranean and global empire, and the Netherlands. This abdication may be taken as marking the last failure of the ancient imperial ideal.

The struggle between France and the Hapsburg Empire, for which the Italian wars served as a kind of prologue, was significant in other ways. When Charles VIII of France invaded Italy in 1494, Ferdinand of Aragon, with his own dynastic interests to defend in the peninsula, had risen to the challenge; and, after moving rapidly all the way to Naples, the French army was driven out again even more rapidly by a combination of Italian and Spanish forces. But this episode was only the first round in a long conflict. Again and again the French tried to establish themselves in Italy, only to be met by new coalitions which included the Spanish king, the German emperor, and from time to time even England, though she took little active part in the fighting. To become a battleground for foreign powers was evidently a disaster for Italy, and the Italian wars finally reduced Italy to little more than a pawn in the calculations of the great powers. But for the rest of Europe these wars have often been regarded as the beginning of modern international relations. By involving all major states in a single problem, the Italian wars pointed to the construction of a genuine system, based on the principle of balance, however dimly this was yet grasped, in which other states naturally combine to check the designs of the most powerful among them. In this way the tendencies we have already observed developing in the smaller Italian system were transferred to a larger stage. At the same time the states outside Italy were exposed to Italian techniques in diplomacy, which they gradually adopted as their own.

With the creation of Charles V's huge dynastic empire, the Italian wars became genuinely European in scope; they raged now not only in Italy but also on the northern and eastern frontiers of France. Indeed, since France found allies in the Ottoman Turks and among the Protestant princes of Germany, the struggle was also extended at times to the eastern frontiers of Europe and into the heart of Germany. The wars were also extended in time; they continued, with intervals of tense peace, until 1559. It is difficult to see how these wars corresponded to the interests of the political communities engaged in them; for the most part they were merely the product of dynastic ambition, and they wasted energies and resources which might have been devoted to better purposes. Yet in the course of the struggle England, which had been inclined by her traditional enmity with France to favor Spain and the Hapsburgs, was slowly learning to remain aloof and to wait for some clear indication of where her national interest lay. Catholic France learned to abandon every consideration but the necessities of her own survival, and showed it by allying with infidels and heretics against the Catholic emperor. And although the wars came to an inconclusive end with the Peace of Cateau-Cambrésis (1559), which, if it left Spain dominant in Italy, confirmed the fact that neither side could destroy the other, they had established the basic pattern of European alignments for centuries to come.

## VIII

Thus by the middle decades of the sixteenth century, western Europe seemed well on the way to better and more stable domestic government and modern patterns of international conduct. The problem of order seemed close to solution in major states, where rulers were controlling their nobility and constructing effective instruments of central administration. If the dynastic principle persisted in some regions, in others the sense of identity with a national community was growing. In their relations with each other states were behaving more and more like independent powers on the basis of an increasingly clear sense of national interest and developing the machinery of modern diplomacy, and their behavior was beginning to reflect some dim apprehension of the idea of a balance of power.

But in fact this whole accomplishment was still tentative and insecure. Although they had made much progress, the governments of Europe had failed to solve fundamental problems; and certain of their policies were destined in the long run to cause difficulties at least as serious as those they were designed to eliminate. At the same time the belief that religious ideals rather than political interest should determine the policies of governments was reinvigorated by the Protestant and Catholic Reformations, so that it became increasingly difficult to achieve those realistic adjustments to circumstance which are possible when problems are conceived in the limited perspective of practical politics. As a result, the later decades of the sixteenth century brought a general reaction against the political achievement of the Renaissance.

Much of the difficulty arose because even the most effective states had never managed to solve a problem fundamental to all successful political action: the problem of financial support. An adequate and regular income, furthermore, was more and more essential, partly because society and its governance became increasingly complex and demanding, but above all because of the enormous expenses of warfare conducted on a larger and larger scale. The English crown had been placed in a relatively favorable position by Henry VII's economies, his rational financial administration, and his accumulation of crown lands. But the parliament was persistently reluctant to grant him additional money, holding firm to the medieval principle that ordinarily the government should be supported out of the king's private income. And as the expenses of government increased, his successors were forced to a variety of expedients which antagonized important groups of subjects or posed other dangers: forced loans from wealthy men and the raising of customs duties, which hurt trade; debasement of the coinage, which led to inflation and ultimately raised the costs of government; and above all confiscation of much of the wealth of the church. Sales of monastic lands by the crown were a major source of income for the English government through the reign of Elizabeth; but such a device for raising money was no permanent solution to the fiscal problem. At the same time it strengthened the landed interest, traditionally the greatest enemy of royal authority.

Spain and France were not much better off, and their expenses for war were much greater. The Spanish rulers enjoyed a huge special income as a result of the precious metals which poured in from the New World, but it was not nearly enough to pay for their vast responsibilities in Europe and overseas; so they were forced to turn again and again to the bankers, to whom they were ever more heavily in debt. Only in France had the tradition that the consent of the subject was necessary for any general taxation been partially subverted, and the French king steadily increased the sums he collected. But even in France the most substantial subjects—nobles, officials, clergy—were exempt from direct royal taxation; and its burdens fell almost entirely on the poorer classes, least likely to be capable of supplying the government with what it required.

Nothing so clearly indicates the limits of royal power in the sixteenth century as the fact that governments were perennially in financial trouble, unable to tap the wealth of those most able to pay, and likely to stir up a costly revolt whenever they attempted to develop an adequate income. It was, indeed, largely for financial reasons that France and Spain finally made peace in 1559; both governments were bankrupt. This inability of rulers to draw adequate support from their subjects suggests the limits to which national rulers had succeeded in identifying their policies, decisions, and actions with a national interest which was recognized as such and could therefore command support by the subject. Even Queen Elizabeth in England, the most popular ruler of the century, who more than any other monarch was able to identify her government with the realm, was limited in this way, and left her successor a considerable deficit. In fact, both sides were partly at fault. The purposes for which rulers sought money rarely corresponded to the national interest; all too often kings were concerned only with personal or dynastic aggrandizement, and their demands were naturally suspect. On the other hand, the subject was not yet prepared to recognize his duty to support the government; national societies still consisted for the most part not of genuine communities welded together by a sense of common purpose, but of congeries of special groups, which thought almost entirely in terms of special self-interest.

The failure of the crown fully to identify itself with the national interest was aggravated by another serious development later in the sixteenth century: a resurgence of aristocratic power, which was to some degree reconstituted on a new basis. For the rulers of the age seem to have forgotten much of the lesson which their predecessors had so painfully learned in the fifteenth century. As governments grew more complicated and direct royal control became increasingly difficult, kings were compelled to develop a new ruling group. And, brought up to think of themselves as royal leaders of the aristocracy which surrounded them at court rather than as bureaucrats and administrators, they chose either to rely once again on their old enemies, or to reward lesser men by converting them into a new aristocracy with vast political and economic power. Great nobles once again sat in the inner councils of kings; and, if in some cases they had lost much of their importance as neighborhood powers, they more than made up for it by winning control over central governments. Thus an aristocracy of royal courts and councils tended to replace an aristocracy of the countryside. The exploitation by this class of the financial resources of governments for its own enrichment contributed significantly, indeed, to the general fiscal problem. By identifying itself with the crown, furthermore, the social importance of the aristocracy became greater than ever, and this new importance was dramatized by a general revival of chivalric culture. In their different ways Spenserian romance in England and the adventures of Don Quixote in Spain testify to a social phenomenon with marked political overtones.

We have seen how in Spain the nobles had helped Charles V to crush the revolt of the towns; and this alliance between king and aristocracy had continued. The economic position of the nobility was protected by its exemption from taxation. If the crown retained the upper hand during the sixteenth century, it also relied heavily on the great nobles as military commanders, governors, and advisers, and on the lesser gentry for the tasks of routine administration. In the whole of the Hapsburg empire, indeed, the Christian ideals of the emperor and the wars in which they involved him received enthusiastic support from the chivalric class. At the same time the economic decadence of Spain prevented any shift in the relative strength of social groups which might have helped transfer political power to the middle class.

In England, below the surface of a royal leadership so apparently successful that historians have been accustomed to speak of a "Tudor absolutism," an even more serious development was taking place. The old English feudality, it is true, had been largely destroyed by civil wars and royal condemnations; but a much larger group of gentry, among whom great nobles were still strong, was emerging to take its place in a partnership with the crown, a partnership that imposed severe limits on the king's freedom of action. The new men who surrounded the king as officials and courtiers exploited their situation through the purchase of the lands that the crown had taken from the church, and in this way they converted themselves into a new and immensely wealthy landed aristocracy. Political power was added to economic when the Privy Council, on which these men sat and which administered the realm in the king's name, became increasingly independent of the monarch during the declining years of Henry VIII. When he died in 1547 leaving a minor heir, the boy king Edward VI, the Council was strong enough to set aside the late king's will and rule England by itself.

The success of this new ruling group in consolidating its power may be measured by the total failure of the Catholic Queen Mary to restore the confiscated lands of the Church, a project on which she had set her heart. The genius of Elizabeth somewhat restored the leadership of the ruler, but this achievement depended partly on the needs of England for a stronger monarchy in a time of renewed political crisis, partly on the queen's refusal to antagonize strong vested interests. If she insisted strongly on the royal prerogative and refused to tolerate discussion by parliament of matters traditionally belonging to the crown, such as the royal succession, the religious settlement, foreign affairs, or commercial policy, she was also prepared to give way in order to avoid any serious clash with her subjects. And in the later years of her reign, when the costs of the war with Spain required frequent recourse to parliament, that body, increasingly dominated by the gentry, became more and more assertive. By the end of the sixteenth century, therefore, the old partnership between crown and realm which had characterized the English development appeared less and less stable; and the role of the monarch in the English constitution was to be radically challenged in the next century.

In France, meanwhile, the personal authority of the king was also declining, even during the years when the monarchy seemed at the height of its power under Francis I and Henry II. A new ruling group was emerging whose interests were in important ways opposed to strong royal leadership. It was composed of two elements. One of these had evolved as a consequence of that general financial pressure from which all governments suffered: increasingly the French monarchy was meeting its immediate needs for money by selling judicial and administrative offices to ambitious men of the middle class. The possession of office conveyed a degree of aristocratic privilege and was a means of social advancement; office holders thus constituted a special class of nobles, the nobility of the robe, so called to distinguish them from the older nobility of the sword. But once an office was sold, it became private property. It could not be controlled by the king, nor could it be recovered without returning the purchase price; and money was always scarce. Thus in France the central government was gradually losing its ability to supervise even its own personnel. The venal office holders were a kind of new feudality which in the long run could seriously impede effective central government.

Even more significant for the near future was the fact that the powerful nobles, the men of the sword, whom earlier kings had so carefully excluded from positions of influence and responsibility, reappeared in the highest posts of the state, determined royal policy, and disposed of the resources of the crown for personal and family advantage. As in England at about the same time, they dominated the king's small inner council and controlled a central government vastly more powerful than the local position of a merely feudal nobility; but they also used this power to strengthen the old feudal connection. They exploited their control over the army to secure the support of lesser nobles, they dispensed court and church patronage, and they built up large personal followings. By the middle of the century, therefore, the high nobility were no longer the servants of the crown; they were its masters. Henry II had in 1547 to accept as his counselors the same men who had advised his father; the king was no longer free to choose his own closest advisers.

## IX

At the same time the new monarchies were being exposed to an increasingly serious ideological challenge. Medieval Catholicism had always emphasized the superiority of religious to secular standards and had tried to promote the unity of Christendom under religious leadership. The attitudes expressed in words by Machiavelli and in deeds by rulers had represented a repudiation of this idealism, and the secularization of politics had facilitated the development of states and made all political decisions simpler. Now, however, with the gathering of the Protestant and Catholic Reformations, devout men of various persuasions insisted that governments should follow religious principles once again, suppress heresy, and accept no political arrangements short of what might be religiously ideal. Such demands obviously enlarged the tasks of government, often in impractical ways; and in certain cases, by requiring that rulers attack important groups of subjects for religious reasons alone, they caused new disorders. The penalty of heeding them is especially clear in the early case of the emperor Charles V. Always sensitive to the ideal responsibilities implicit in his position, as we have seen, he wasted much of his strength in a futile attempt to crush Lutheranism in Germany. The Protestant princes defeated him, and he was compelled against his will to recognize their religious independence by the Peace of Augsburg (1555), which thus confirmed further the disunity of Germany.

But there was also a more specific hazard for rulers from the introduction of religious issues into politics: ideology gave a new weapon to special interests already eager to oppose royal power on more selfish grounds. This was amply demonstrated in a series of civil wars which ravaged France from 1562 to 1593 and prevented her from playing any great active role in international affairs. The return of her fighting men from the wars, an event always dangerous for domestic peace, coincided with the movement of large numbers of Frenchmen, including many nobles, into the Calvinist, or Huguenot, fold. At the same time the death of Henry II in 1559 left a minor heir as the new king of France; and with this new crisis of the monarchy, the Estates-General, which French rulers had significantly managed to get along without ever since 1485, was called into session. It met frequently during the next three decades. Presented by this unstable situation with such an opportunity for enlarging their control of the royal government, the high nobility who had for some time dominated the council of the king split into factions and engaged in a struggle which was complicated and embittered by religious passion, one side offering itself as Catholic, the other as Huguenot. This division, however, permitted the queen mother, Catherine de' Medici, to steer the crown into a position of some independence. Herself religiously indifferent, she tried with little success to keep the religious issue distinct from politics; but she was able in some measure to balance between the parties, favoring whichever side seemed least to threaten the power of the king until it grew too strong, and then shifting to the other side.

Such a policy clearly reflected that sense of the pragmatic and secular nature of politics which had been one of the most important developments of the Renaissance, but it offended religious idealism. As each side found itself in opposition to the crown, it advanced arguments fundamentally subversive of the Renaissance achievement. Certain Catholic theorists, led by members of the Society of Jesus, went far to revive medieval political theology. Their position most profoundly expressed by Cardinal Bellarmine (1542–1621), they insisted once more on the religious duties of a ruler and the right of the pope to depose a king who did not fulfill them. Calvinist theorists, too, justified resistance to rulers unfriendly to their cause. The degree to which those who rejected royal authority were sincere in their acceptance of these principles may be disputed; but it cannot be doubted that they helped reduce France to anarchy at home and impotence abroad. The nation that in important ways had seemed politically the most advanced among the powers of Europe was thus forced, in the later sixteenth century, to endure a broad reaction against strong royal government in both its conduct and its theory.

An important unit in the Spanish empire was meanwhile experiencing a similar alliance between religious conviction and interests opposed to the royal power. The Netherlands had never been pulled together into a modern state along the lines of France and Spain, although the Burgundian rulers of the fifteenth century had made an impressive attempt to develop a bureaucratic government staffed by men trained in the Roman law schools of France. The seventeen provinces of the Netherlands were united chiefly by the accident that each acknowledged the same man as its duke or count; their central government was rudimentary, and each province had its own estates and jealously guarded local liberties. Charles V had on the whole respected this state of affairs, but Philip II was resolved on modernization. His neglect of the old nobility in the governance of the Low Countries, his reliance instead on lawyers and bureaucrats, his financial demands, and his reorganization of the church of the Netherlands, previously under local control, all antagonized important special groups; and the fact that, governing from Madrid, he could hardly be considered a native son as his father had been regarded, exposed all his policies to the general resentment likely to be provoked by any foreign rule. He was also resolved to crush heresy at a time when Protestantism was growing in the Netherlands; and it was inevitable that the aggravated special interests should make common cause with the persecuted religion. The great nobles, members of the class that so regularly supplied the leaders in rebellions against kings (chief among them William, Prince of Orange) took up Calvinism. Disorders in the 1560s gradually turned to open war, which finally ended in 1648, when Spain at last acknowledged the independence of the seven northern provinces. Thus here too the monarchical principle of government was challenged in the late sixteenth century, and with a major degree of success. The seven United Provinces retained their loose federation in victory, constituting a kind of political anachronism in a world increasingly dominated by centralized monarchies; and even in Belgium, which Spain managed to retain, local interests survived in strength. It is true that the Dutch received important help from France and England at crucial moments in their long struggle; nevertheless the failure of the Spanish crown to reduce them to obedience is a significant commentary on the limits of its power.

## X

These internal difficulties had a considerable effect on international affairs. Both France and Spain were too preoccupied with domestic troubles and problems posed by rebellious subjects to continue their old rivalry as actively as before, so that the later part of the sixteenth century brought some decline in that dynastic aggressiveness which had marked its first half. But new international problems and new causes for strife among nations only replaced the old; Spain found a new enemy in England, and was involved in a conflict based now on religious difference and the clash of economic interest. Such motives for war were potentially far more dangerous to the peace of Europe than the dynastic rivalries of an earlier generation, for they involved not only rulers but the passions and desires of entire peoples.

Although she had given them little real help, England had long tended to side with the Hapsburgs against France because of her old claims on the mainland. But Queen Elizabeth's decision in favor of a moderate Protestantism placed her in opposition to Spain, the most militant of the Catholic powers. At the same time the English were beginning to cast greedy eyes at the Spanish overseas empire, the source of vast wealth. And while Spain was trying to crush the revolt of the Netherlands, the enmity of England grew increasingly clear. Elizabeth gave secret encouragement, and finally open help, to the Dutch; and English merchants ignored Spanish claims to a monopoly of trade with Spanish America while English buccaneers like Francis Drake preyed on Spanish treasure in the New World. Philip II of Spain first responded by supporting a series of plots in England to overthrow the queen; and when all else had failed, in desperation he dispatched a great naval expedition for the conquest of England. The destruction of this "Great Armada" in 1588, however dramatic it may have been and however useful in stirring the patriotism of England and her sense of community under royal leadership, was not decisive, and the struggle between England and Spain continued. But England had insured her survival as a great power, she continued to aid the Netherlands, and the resources of Spain continued to waste away. Thus large-scale international conflict went on to the end of the century and reached a new climax with the Thirty Years' War (1618–48), in which the rivalry between France and the Hapsburg powers was resumed. Whatever advantage the emergence of strong independent states may have had in the long run for orderly government at home, the disadvantages for international society were unrelieved.

Indeed, the conduct of international relations deteriorated. Following the example of Renaissance Italy, the national monarchies in the earlier part of the sixteenth century had established regular diplomatic services, in which ambassadors were learning to represent their states according to orderly procedures with dignity and good faith. But now they devoted themselves increasingly to bribery, espionage, and intrigue with malcontents in the countries to which they were assigned. Differences among nations also became less negotiable as religious passion insisted on total victory over the enemy. A few thinkers, like the Spanish Dominican Victoria (1480–1546) and the Dutch jurist Hugo Grotius (1583–1645), were already trying to construct a body of international law on rational rather than religious principles to restore mutual confidence and order among nations; but their views had no practical effect. In international as well as in internal politics, therefore, the tendency was rather to anarchy than to improved order. In this respect also the later half of the sixteenth century brought a reaction against the political achievement of the Renaissance.

But, if the problems of international relations only grew more severe, there were certain encouraging developments in domestic politics before the end of the century. As in the past, once again the experience of disorder within states was generating its own remedy. Indeed, in a world in which religious passion had been so widely injected into politics, rulers had never abandoned mere political wisdom. Even so devout a king as Philip II refused to accept the absolute priority of his loyalty to Catholicism over political convenience. For some time, until English hostility to Spain became clear, he had supported the Protestant Elizabeth as ruler in England because the other major claimant to the throne, Mary of Scotland, though a Catholic, was backed by his traditional enemy, France. In the Netherlands William of Orange adopted Calvinism rather for political reasons than from conviction: Calvinists provided his most effective support. In England the religious settlement imposed by Elizabeth was carefully designed to retain the broadest support for the government by avoiding sharp doctrinal definitions which, however satisfying to the pious, might divide her people.

It was in France, however, that the conflict between religious idealism and orderly government was most clearly recognized. As the civil wars dragged on, a growing number of Frenchmen became convinced of the futility of a struggle that was causing so much suffering and destruction and imperiled the very existence of France as a great power. Since neither side seemed to them strong enough to destroy the other, they concluded that religious unity could never be obtained by force; and they argued that France should therefore abandon so impractical an effort and concentrate on the restoration of peace and order under strong royal leadership. This position seemed a scandalous opportunism to idealists, who called its advocates *politiques,* much as we might describe a man in public life who lacked high principles as "only a politician." The accusation may not have been quite just: many of the *politiques* relied on the doctrine of divine right, and so answered one kind of religious argument which would have prolonged the civil wars with another designed to bring them to an end. They insisted that kings are chosen to rule by God Himself, that they are not responsible to any ecclesiastical authority, that they cannot be legally resisted even in the name of true religion, and that they may impose such settlements on their states as seem convenient. Two tendencies may therefore be discerned among the *politiques,* both designed to restore the authority and increase the power of kings. On the one hand they claimed religious sanctions for strong royal government; and this argument, which was peculiarly effective among so religious a generation, was destined for considerable amplification in the next century. But the religious argument was in the long run far less significant than the tendency among the *politiques* to insist that the state must attend first of all to its own self-preservation and the satisfaction of practical human needs. In this emphasis they were in fact returning to the Renaissance conception of a secular politics. Now, however, the conception was applied explicitly to the national state.

The most distinguished representative of this more modern position was Jean Bodin in his *Six Books of the Republic* (1576), a systematic treatise on government written to bolster royal authority at a time when it was challenged on all sides. The heart of Bodin's theory was his doctrine of sovereignty, by which he meant a wide authority wielded by the ruler over all his subjects, including most notably the right to make laws. Without such authority, Bodin argued, there can be no true state; and as the essential element in the very definition of a state, it requires no religious sanction. The implication was clear: a king has the right and duty to make whatever decisions may be for the advantage of his state, regardless of the pressures from religious or other special interests. With these views Bodin was evidently trying to strengthen central government and make it more effective. But in another way his work reveals an attachment to a traditional attitude that had long caused serious difficulties for rulers. Bodin also distinguished between sovereignty, which belongs to the ruler, and property, which belongs to the subject and which the ruler cannot touch without the subject's consent expressed through the estates of the realm. But the consent of the subject to taxation, as we have observed, still provided a most unreliable material base for effective government. Bodin's theory thus failed to offer any practical solution to the fiscal problem, which continued to trouble governments. His view of sovereignty nevertheless met a real need and expressed the position of a growing body of Frenchmen.

The transition in France from theory to practice came with the reign of Henry IV (1589–1610), whose claims to the throne were supported by the *politiques* both because he was the heir by legitimate succession (and would therefore rule by divine rather than human choice) and because he seemed likely to provide effective royal leadership. Since he was a Protestant, he was opposed by fervent Catholics; but he demonstrated his own flexible and *politique* attitude by his conversion to Catholicism, an action necessary to his peaceful acceptance as king by the Catholic majority of his people. He then gave practical expression to the views of the *politiques* by issuing the Edict of Nantes (1598), which gave complete freedom of belief and substantial freedom of worship to French Protestants; thus France abandoned the impractical struggle for an ideal religious unity in favor of peace.

Having made this choice, she was now able to resume the developments begun by the earlier Renaissance monarchy. Weary of war, France accepted strong royal leadership once again; and Henry IV, the most popular among the modern kings of France, managed with a new degree of success to identify the crown with the needs of the realm. His avoidance of prolonged or major wars and the policies of his able finance minister Sully improved the financial position of the government, and France began a rapid political and economic recovery which also restored her international position. Henry did not solve the fundamental problems confronting the governments of his time. The nobility was to cause further troubles in the next century; later French governments, more extravagant than Henry's, were in constant financial difficulties; and his assassination by a Catholic extremist in 1610 was a reminder that religious passion was not yet dead. The reign of Henry IV nevertheless prepared the way for the greatness of France during the next two centuries. It may therefore be taken not only as the resumption of the Renaissance achievement in politics but also as the beginning of a new chapter in European political history.

Since the beginning of the fourteenth century, the political structure of Europe had thus been remarkably changed. Christendom no longer existed as a political reality, and, as rulers, neither the pope nor the emperor counted for more than other monarchs. Both the ideal unity that their offices represented and the heterogeneous mosaic of local units that characterized feudal government had by the beginning of the seventeenth century largely given way to an agency of government intermediate between them, the dynastic or national state. States insisted, in practice and increasingly in theory, on their sovereignty and its secular purposes; and their relations with each other were tending more and more to take the form of alignments based on the balance of power. Major problems remained unsolved and much of the past still persisted, as the events of the second half of the sixteenth century amply demonstrated. But, however tentatively, the characteristic tendencies and problems of modern political history had now been revealed.

## FOR ADDITIONAL READING

J. W. Allen. *A History of Political Thought in the Sixteenth Century*. London, 1928.

H. Baron. *The Crisis of the Early Italian Renaissance*. Princeton, 1955.

K. Brandi. *The Emperor Charles V*. New York, 1939.

J. Burckhardt. *The Civilization of the Renaissance in Italy*. First published 1860.

F. Chabod. *Machiavelli and the Renaissance*. London, 1958.

R. T. Davies. *The Golden Century of Spain, 1501–1621*. London, 1937.

M. P. Gilmore. *The World of Humanism*. New York, 1952.

H. Holborn. *A History of Modern Germany*. Vol. I. New York, 1959.

J. Major. *Representative Institutions in Renaissance France, 1421–1559*. Madison, 1960.

G. Mattingly. *Renaissance Diplomacy*. Boston, 1955.

J. E. Neale. *Queen Elizabeth I*. London, 1934.

F. Schevill. *History of Florence*. New York, 1936.

# VIII

# EUROPEAN EXPANSION AND CAPITALISM: 1450–1650

*Fernand Braudel*

The period 1450–1650 in Europe was a glorious era characterized by a great economic and demographic expansion and by the victory of Europe in organizing the first world-wide economy, which, however fragile at first, proved itself capable of resisting future trials. The early history of the economic system that was later to develop into modern capitalism—the principal concern of this essay—took place before new and expanding horizons. It will be our task to retrace as clearly as possible complicated destinies, sometimes influencing each other directly, but often unfolding independently, side by side.

In surveying this terrain, which is more often familiar in its details than in its general contours, it will be useful to make clear from the first the distinction between those long-term considerations and short-term phenomena recognized by economists, which must not be confused with each other any more than scarlet fever with bubonic plague, to borrow a lively expression from Ernst Wagemann.

In history nothing is truer, and great historians have always known it: an actor, be he prince, monarch, or mere businessman, may win in the short term only to lose in the long run; ephemeral victories such as Pyrrhus' have become proverbial. The historian is not surprised if the landscape he is reconstructing inevitably changes radically when he pretends to judge it by whole centuries instead of counting time year by year and decade by decade. Here, as elsewhere, the scale that he adopts will determine everything. If one considers the two centuries that stretch from 1450 to 1650 as a single entity, as will be attempted below, a long-term history emerges, working out its effects slowly but powerfully. The details are obliterated in sketching the outlines of the major evolution.

If, on the contrary, one is interested solely in the Renaissance in the traditional and narrow meaning of the word, one must immediately focus on restricted observations, placing oneself perhaps at the side of Lorenzo the Magnificent (1448–92) during his short life spent almost entirely in Florence, a city which fully merits intense concentration. In the same way, a spotlight in the theater would bring into relief a detail, a character, a color, or a moment in the panorama of the drama.

These remarks serve to introduce a simple, if somewhat arbitrary, outline. First we shall consider the whole of this immense drama, which I have frequently designated the "long sixteenth century," for it actually spans a period of 200 years. How shall we strike a balance sheet on it? What are its general trends? What direction do they take? Subsequently, from the short-term point of view, we shall study its evolution and the different stages in the various periods comprising the whole.

There are, generally, two main streams of development which we must keep separate although at the same time relating them as much as their nature permits, for they unfold simultaneously, approach each other, and intermingle at certain common junctures. If one is to follow from its many sources the history of the birth of the modern world, in which Europe was the principal but not the sole actor, one must necessarily pass from one level to another and from one stage to another.

## I

We shall direct our attention first to the immense panorama of the "long" sixteenth century. In order to determine its watersheds and its ground swells we must orient ourselves with care and distinguish the more important formations.

Surely the first remark to be made is that the sixteenth century suddenly discovered the immense size of the world; the area in which it moved became much greater. If we were speaking of the glorious Europe of the thirteenth century, we would have to consider primarily Europe itself, its Mediterranean lands and their shores, the countries of the Near East, and the land or sea routes extending toward China and the Indian Ocean. In the sixteenth century, however, the entire world is our field, a vast stage for the drama that is to be observed. For the first time the West took into account the whole of the earth; our terrestrial sphere was united in a common adventure, however tenuous the bonds of its community life may have been. This revolutionary transformation has often been analyzed. From a world cut into sections, we enter a world forging its unity. Previously there had existed several planets; now only one remained, uniting or attempting to unite its parts. How was this change made possible? How was it accomplished? That is the first major question.

If we turn to general histories and textbooks for our answer, it will be found in the usual chapter assigned to the great maritime discoveries. Christopher Columbus (1451–1506), Vasco da Gama (1469?–1524), and Magellan (1480–1521) are perforce its heroes, with Columbus being justifiably the most famous of the three. The young historian Pierre Chaunu recently described the discovery of America as the greatest event in the history of man, to be supplanted perhaps by our imminent conquests of space. His enthusiasm is undoubtedly well founded, and if the tale of the Genoese navigator were retold, we would all thrill at it again, for, despite its brevity, it sheds a brilliant light on the whole drama of this revolutionary change. All this is true, but still heroes never stand alone; there are always other men without whom their exploits would not have been possible—and these exploits remain only the highpoints in a slowly unfolding history. The great discoveries were begun long before the voyage of 1492, and they continued beyond Magellan's circumnavigation of the world, even beyond the "long" sixteenth century. It took man centuries to discover and catalogue the geography of the prison in which he lives, whose limits he is trying today to leave behind him.

This long history entails extended study on our part. Naturally, we must begin by trying to establish the position from which, for better or worse, the development began. We must envisage both Europe and the other continents at this period, for the adventure involves all of mankind, not merely Europe. At this point a very simple, but very eloquent document comes to our help; it immediately clarifies the world situation on the eve of the upheavals resulting from the great discoveries. I am speaking of the map of the world as it appeared in roughly 1500, as reconstructed by the American anthropologist W. Gordon Hewes in *A Conspectus of the World's Cultures in 1500 A.D.,* in the University of Colorado Studies, Series in Anthropology, No. 4 (September, 1954). Let us accept his conclusions and the oversimplifications he was forced to make; in his account, the inhabited earth is divided into 76 collective units (civilizations or cultures), each one with its own boundaries and some with vast supplementary annexes overseas. In this enumeration, the European continental land mass is occupied by three civilizations: the so-called Mediterranean complex, the Western and Nordic group, and the

Eastern, which is essentially the Greek civilization. This system shows that our cartographer does not concern himself with political units, but rather with cultural entities. Otherwise, in the case of the eastern Mediterranean, he would have spoken not of Greek and Moslem civilizations, but of the Ottoman Empire, which had subjugated immense territories in the area, having established itself in Constantinople in 1453.

By "civilizations" we understand developed societies, with sizable urban centers, well-established agricultural systems, and densely settled populations (western Europe with more than 50 inhabitants per square mile, China with slightly less than 50 per square mile). "Cultures," on the other hand, are comprised of widely scattered populations often with a very elementary way of life. Nonetheless, the latter outnumber the former. According to our count, they are 59 to 17 and occupy the major part of the earth. Their people live on forage, fishing, hunting, livestock, and occasionally an intermittent form of agriculture. In comparison to them, the civilizations have been crowded into narrow territories—narrow, that is, when judged by the dimensions of the whole earth. But it is obvious that they play the important roles in human history. They have numbers on their side, and numbers always prevail. In their limited territories, from Japan to the pre-Columbian civilizations, are located the cities and the overpopulated zones containing the majority of mankind and profiting from advanced techniques and developed industries. This is as true of the twentieth century as it was of the sixteenth. Today, in 1961, of the three billion beings making up humanity, 2.1 billion live in highly populated areas (more than 475 inhabitants per square mile) which comprise but a small part of the earth's surface (4.5 million square miles out of the 60 million square miles of land above sea level). The highly populated lands of the sixteenth century probably occupied an area of very nearly the same dimensions, perhaps four million square miles.

But, whether populated or just barely settled, the entire earth was occupied by man at that time. Humanity numbered roughly 300 million in 1500 (that is to say, one-tenth of the present world population), but there was no territory that some form of humanity did not know. Let us not, then, be too quick to use the magic word "discovery." The entire world was, in a sense, "known" long before 1500. An excellent example of my point is furnished by the rapid and impressive discovery of the routes and waterways of South America made at the end of the sixteenth century and the beginning of the seventeenth by the *mamelucos,* half-breeds of Portuguese and Indian extraction from the little town of São Paulo. Actually, this was the reconnaissance by semi-Europeans of waterways, routes, and paths long familiar to the Indians; not really a discovery, it was at most a rediscovery. Shall we conclude that the word "discovery" is inaccurate? Yes and no. To be precise, it was not new lands that the European adventurer discovered or rediscovered; it was rather the unending salt-water routes—above all, those of the Atlantic Ocean, then of the Indian Ocean (which was already familiar, even well known, to Arab navigators), and lastly the seaways of the Far East, long since utilized by Chinese or Japanese junks, and the immense courses of the Pacific, the Southern Sea.

Europe won her great victory on these water routes of the world which she linked together, creating, for her profit, the unity of the maritime world.

But why Europe and not some other civilization or culture? We must not think *a priori* that the cultures were not in competition for the naval routes. We need only reflect on the astounding accomplishments in the Pacific Ocean of the Polynesian navigations in the enormous triangle formed by the Hawaiian Islands, the Easter Islands, and New Zealand. But this exception proves the rule. In reality, only two civilizations, Islam and China, could have competed for the prize that Europe was to win.

Islam was undoubtedly handicapped by its former successes. Economically speaking, it had been for centuries the dominant power of the Old World (Europe, Asia, and Africa), for it held the roads, the caravan routes, and the waterways (the Red Sea, the Persian Gulf, and the Indian Ocean) between Europe and the Far East, and it had profited largely by them. It was the unavoidable intermediary, firmly entrenched in its diverse and profitable trade. What reason could it have to expand beyond its favorable position?

As for China, it was engaged in a closed network of water routes with nearby nations, from Canton or Amoy to Indonesia and Malacca. However, from 1409 to 1424, after the victory of the national revolution of the Mings (1368), China had experienced a vigorous and extraordinary naval expansion. Fleets of large junks laden with soldiers landed in Ceylon and established there a Chinese protectorate, then continued to the Persian Gulf, the Red Sea, Aden, and the African coast. But everything came to an abrupt halt for the Mings with the necessity of turning their efforts to the north and the deserts of Mongolia, where the menacing advance of the nomads had started again. The restoration of Peking as the capital of China, accomplished at the expense of gigantic constructions (1421), was directed against these forces.

A strange episode in history, to be sure, and one that is far from clear. With a little imagination, we can conceive of Chinese junks rounding the

Cape of Good Hope. But history decreed otherwise and cannot be rewritten. The inactivity of others, then, redounded to the benefit of Europe. In addition to this, there was a whole series of pre-discoveries and exploits of undeniable merit—no need to speak here of the successes of the Vikings or the mysterious adventure of the Vivaldi brothers (1291). As early as the end of the thirteenth century, regular relations were established along purely naval routes between the north of Europe and the Mediterranean countries. The latter, which had taken the initiative, were the first to profit from the enterprise. The merchant galleys of Genoa which arrived in Bruges (Belgium) in 1295 were not the first ships to join the blue waters of the south to the gray waters of the north. But by establishing a *regular* connection between the two, they closed one age and opened another. It was the end of an era in which overland links had dominated, of which the outward and visible sign had been the fairs of Champagne with their pack horses and carts maintaining the bond between the navigation companies of the north and the south. Without eliminating the ancient commercial bonds, which continued to be important, the sea was henceforth to add to them the services of galleys and trading vessels.

This resulted in a sudden rush of vital forces to the periphery of the European continent facing the Atlantic Ocean. An all-water route between Venice, Ragusa (Yugoslavia), Genoa, Marseilles, or Barcelona at one end and the English Channel and the North Sea at the other presupposed concentrations of manpower, investment capital, and sizable monetary exchanges; it presupposed also organization, the training of sailors, the establishment of ports of call on the very long route (at Seville and especially Lisbon), and the selection and equipping of ports of arrival such as Southampton, Bruges, and London. A division of responsibilities was necessary if such exchanges were to run smoothly and to grow. A young and alert capitalism favored these commercial relations, a merchant capitalism based on the distribution of goods. It thrived on all the operations associated with shipments of wine, salt, and luxury articles such as pepper, spices, and silk which came from the south to the north in ships which returned bearing woolens, textiles, even wheat. This transformation was slow and gradual, requiring considerable time and effort; innovations were made and then became established practice. In the end, wine vintaged in Crete or Cyprus could be imported directly to England.

These commercial exchanges necessarily moved men as well as goods overseas: Italians began to arrive in all areas of the north. Similarly, cultural and technological exchanges occurred in both directions. The sturdy boats of the north served as models for the south, and at the same time Mediterranean designs found imitators in northern shipyards. The seaworthy cock-boat (from the Dutch *Kogge*), a solidly constructed ship of the north, was soon to brave the Mediterranean winter storms which had previously prevented navigation during the bad season. The caravel, a light ship with immense sails, was a daughter of the south but born from the union of northern and Mediterranean sea voyages. It was the ship that carried the oceanic discoverers Vasco da Gama and Christopher Columbus.

Undoubtedly the prevailing wind patterns, both on the Atlantic and the Pacific, helped simplify from the start the problem of navigation on the vast oceans. They form more or less perfect circuits: one wind takes you across, and another brings you back automatically. Christopher Columbus found the trade winds at the latitude of the Canary Islands, and they led him without incident to the Antilles. The northeast winds brought him back along the route of the Gulf Stream, from the tip of Florida to Newfoundland, then to the Azores and the coast of the Iberian Peninsula. Nothing could be simpler or more logical. Still, it was necessary to get the right wind at the right moment, and to do this meant crossing zones of unfavorable winds, cutting across one wind, heading up another. It all would have been impossible without the introduction of the stern-post rudder. A stern-post rudder, steered from the interior of the ship, lies along the ship's axis. Despite everything that has been written on this subject, it is an advantageous replacement for lateral rudders, particularly because it allows a ship to tack and to sail up to windward. Originating undoubtedly in the northern seas, it was widely used after the thirteenth century in all maritime traffic between northern and southern Europe. Along with the already familiar loadstone compass, it made possible the vast assemblages of ships in the fifteenth century. And these, after all, would not have been conceivable without centuries of apprenticeship on the rough and choppy seas of the north and long experience with the terrible dangers of the Atlantic.

The glory of Europe, and her great opportunity, lay in her ships and in their voyages, the thousands and thousands of wakes traced across the seven seas of the world and then disappearing as soon as they were made. Europe's ships gave birth and sustenance to her seaside cities, long established ones like Venice and Genoa and late-comers like Bruges and Lübeck. Each of them was a modern world in miniature, nourished by a monetary economy based on silver, by their local nationalism, by reasons of state, by self-interest, and by countless ferocities also.

Nevertheless, at the same time there were other cities, very great cities, in other countries; and other navies, and other ships . . . but the fact cannot be denied: it was Europe that took the prize.

The greatest loser by these discoveries was Islam, commercial Islam with her desert caravans and sea voyages between the Red Sea or the Persian Gulf and India or China. The Portuguese discoveries accomplished what neither the Crusades (ending with the recapture of Acre by Islam in 1291) nor the Spanish Reconquista (reaching its culmination with the seizure of Grenada in 1492) had been able to do. Even though in 1453 Islam had captured Constantinople, the heart of the Byzantine Empire, after having already taken possession of most of the imperial lands, the delicate network of Portuguese voyages imprisoned the Turkish giant in its immense meshes, and the net held. Christianity triumphed over Islam when it bypassed the Moslem middleman and arrived in India (1498), in Malacca (1511), in China (1517), and in Japan (1542).

Do not imagine that the distant giants of the Far East were suddenly overwhelmed, or subjugated, or even concerned by these events. The vast bulk of India and the immense body of China scarcely noticed the arrival of these newcomers, these new barbarians. Faraway Europe could bring them nothing superior to what their own civilization knew, and they were unable to take the proper measure of her achievement.

For Europe, on the contrary, this extraordinary exploit brought endless repercussions. At last pepper and the fabulous spices which the Middle Ages had coveted so much were within reach in abundance, and cheaper than they had been. And with them came other riches—silk, porcelain, lacquer from China, then Japanese copper, various drugs, pearls, precious stones. . . . But if Europe could henceforth do without the Moslem middleman, she could only obtain these goods in exchange for others, such as woolens, copper, and silver—above all, silver. And trade was not conducted on an equal footing; the European merchant was the inferior. To proud Japan, China, and India he could not seem truly a conqueror. What Europe had conquered was distance, the immense salt-water stretches, but not yet the men or the great civilizations of the Far East.

This relationship would reverse itself to the advantage of the West only at the time of the occupation of Bengal by Lord Clive in 1764, and then again more drastically in the nineteenth century with the decisive Opium War (1839–41). In the beginning Europe laid the foundations for a naval blockade of Asia, but did not complete it. Not to exaggerate matters, it would be better to say that she established herself as overseer of Asian maritime traffic

—*country trade* as the English say, or trade *d'Inde en Inde* (Indian coastal trade), as the French say, though in this case the trade extended as far as China and Japan. This was a considerable achievement, but it did not substantially affect the prosperity of the world. In any case, it bears repetition that throughout the entire period we are considering, Europe did not dominate the Far East. Although the Portuguese may have pillaged Moslem ships for a while during the times of Vasco da Gama, Alvárez Cabral, and Albuquerque, these early successes did not last long. Asia did not surrender her riches; she traded them. The West paid for them, and often paid dear. A considerable part of the riches wrested not without difficulty from America had to be diverted to the profit of the Far East.

In the fifteenth and sixteenth centuries the New World and Black Africa were two half-empty continents. Black Africa was certainly more populous than America, but, despite the beauty of Nigerian bronzes from Benin or of the gold from Bambouk or the Monomotapa, it had no civilization comparable to Aztec or Incan culture. Nonetheless, paradoxically enough, it was Black Africa which resisted European incursions, as in previous centuries it had resisted Islam's vigorous encroachments in the loop of the Niger and its insistent invasions along the coast of the Indian Ocean. Africa resisted by its very inertia, its difficult communications, its endemic diseases fatal to the white man, its passivity, and its docility in furnishing the two commodities its elementary civilization had to offer: gold dust and slaves. The slave trade, which came into existence as early as the first years of the sixteenth century, quickly became a necessity for the colonization of the New World.

Without making any defense, the New World opened itself to the white man, to a handful of soldiers with Cortés and to a handful of adventurers following Pizarro. The conquest was rapid and bloody and, from the European point of view, profitable. Neither the Aztecs nor the Incas fought back. War conducted in the European fashion—that is, mercilessly—took the great Amerindian civilizations by surprise and subjugated their beautiful but defenseless lands. More than its weapons, its horses, its dogs, or its firearms, the violence of Europe got the better of these patient peoples, who surrendered immediately to their invaders. In other areas, it is true, the conqueror achieved nothing as minute Indian populations fled wisely before him.

Furthermore, the shock of the meeting of two worlds, the eruption of new diseases, the harsh conditions of labor, the profuse growth of the flocks which the white man had brought with him from Europe and had let loose in the wilds, from where they ravaged native crops—all these help explain the dramatic collapse of the Amerindian population. There were less than 12 million people in the Americas at the beginning of the sixteenth century, and this figure was to decrease subsequently. To fill the void, Europe and Africa could provide only mediocre contingents. From 1492 to 1650 immigration may have reached as many as 150,000 white men and 200,000 or 250,000 Negroes. Obviously, these figures can scarcely be precise, but they are relatively accurate, and in any case they mark clearly enough the inadequacy of the Old World's means. But the graft of human beings from two sources—Europe and America—was slow to take hold and grow. If Europe relied on Africa in this task, it was because Europe needed docile labor. To obtain it she practically reinvented slavery. But the graft was also slow because the Indians often vanished before Europe's forces and Europe itself was insufficiently populous to have throngs of colonists available at the slightest call.

Nevertheless, there is no doubt that population expanded in Europe between 1450 and 1650, perhaps almost doubling itself. But it was a peasant population, attached to the soil, not mobile, and all the more determined to produce its daily bread as this task became more difficult and more essential with each year. Bread was the obsession and the major source of anxiety for the centuries we are considering. In order to survive, every year each man needed three and a third bushels of grain (wheat, corn, rye, or barley). In 1650 this amounted roughly to a total of 325 million bushels. Now, foreign trade in grains accounted for scarcely one or two percent of this total. This meant that in bad years the yield was often, if not always, insufficient. As the high cost of grain was accompanied by incredible rises in mortality, we can understand how this unending, dramatic interplay of forces chained the European peasantry to its daily tasks, immobilizing it and leaving the Old World's hands tied despite the immense fortune that had fallen in its lap.

## II

From 1450 to 1650 Europe was not alone in population growth. This is a second general consideration that demands our attention. It would seem that the population of the world as a whole increased, but, if research is accurate, we must concede a marked decrease in the American population. Still, this decrease remains a special case. Everywhere else, population seems to have held its own or increased. We have no data on Black Africa, but the mere existence of the slave trade permits us to assume a rise in population; slave trade is, after all, one form of emigration, strongly suggestive of a human surplus, and one that was to be tapped even more deeply in years to come.

It has not been proven, but it is quite possible, that the population of India rose. In China the official census would indicate a very slow rise from 1368 until the beginning of the seventeenth century, followed by a decline with the catastrophes that came with the capture of Peking by the Manchus in 1644 and soon decimated the population. We can say nothing about the case of Japan. As for Islam, if we accept the example of Turkey as a valid one, there are indications of growth. Turkish studies indicate a demographic increase without any lapses. Central to this growth is Istanbul, whose 700,000 inhabitants in the sixteenth century made it by far the largest European city; Paris accounted for 300,000 inhabitants at the most, Naples had 200,000, and London 100,000.

In the West, we have conclusive evidence of a strong demographic expansion, undoubtedly beginning around 1450. In Europe as a whole, it will not come to a halt or slow down until the middle of the seventeeth century. Spain and Italy, perhaps even the whole Christian world on the shores of the Mediterranean, may have known an earlier decline or let-up in growth toward the end of the sixteenth century or the beginning of the seventeenth. In any case, it is this demographic fact, occurring between these two dates, that has suggested doubling the usual limits of the sixteenth century; for in fact these 200 years represent a single stage in the biological development of Europe. We may ask: Of Europe alone or of the whole world? Despite interesting and impressive estimates by notable scholars, our data is too imperfect for us to conclude with any certainty that the demographic expansion in Europe was valid for the whole world.

Hazardous speculations have at least one advantage; they prevent us from assuming that Europe can be considered in isolation in the sixteenth century, as if her rise in population could be explained by itself, in terms of endogenous factors which could then be used, in turn, to explain in part her predominance in the world without taking into account conditions outside Europe. On the contrary, it seems that the case of Europe in this matter is one case out of many.

Nonetheless, the fact remains that during the sixteenth century Europe was in the throes of a long and powerful population expansion. We have countless indirect proofs of this and a few patent and irrefutable indications of it. Among the indirect proofs are the emigrations to the New World, slight as they are; internal population shifts with an undeniable extension of land under cultivation, both in eastern Prussia and in New Castile, where wheat and rye frequently make inroads on pasture lands during the time of Philip II; the gradual reduction of lands under forest, particularly clear during the second half of the fifteenth century; and the underlying currents of migration and colonization that have been uncovered for eastern Europe as a whole. Starting from the territory around Moscow, a perennial peasant colonization movement descended the course of the Volga, the Dnieper, and the Dniester or set out for Siberia, thereby establishing the pattern for Russian population shifts to come. To fill the void around Moscow, peasants from the Baltic lands or from Poland moved in, and when new population vacuums were created later—for example, in the seventeenth century—the Baltic lands attracted the poorer people from places as distant as Brandenburg, which had been impoverished by the unceasing ravages of local wars.

We may pause to ask if the wars of the sixteenth century, with their vast destruction of human life, do not also indicate the general growth of human population in Europe. No one can deny that the size of armies grew constantly everywhere. On October 7, 1571, at Lepanto, counting both the Christian and Turkish fleets, there were in all not far from 100,000 men—approximately the population of Elizabethan London, women and children included.

The growth of the European territorial states must also be related to this increase in humanity, for the one is unthinkable without the other. A mass of "officers" (today we would say "civil servants") reduced foreign peoples to obedience and subjected them to order and to taxation. As the economic writers of the sixteenth and seventeenth centuries so often repeat, it is the number of his subjects that determines the strength of a prince.

These are the most obvious indirect proofs. There are others that are more localized, less general, but more precise: for example, the widespread urban construction, the increase in the membership of artisan guilds, the development of the outskirts of cities, the displacement and expansion of city limits. Cities grew everywhere, and undoubtedly their position relative to the total population of Europe was on the rise. From this followed an accelerated dynamism and vigor, for cities provide the driving forces of the modern world. In Europe it was the role of the countryside to follow the lead of the cities, which had long since exploited and domesticated their hinterlands. In the sixteenth century, cottage industries, unhampered by guild regulations and unprotected by them, arose simultaneously in far-flung areas. The presence of weavers in the villages was not a new thing; the novelty lay in the fact that they were increasingly at the beck and call of the nearby city, caught up in the larger context of a capitalist economy.

Such are the significant facts at our disposal, though obviously we would prefer the simple, clear language of statistics. The scattered figures that we have been able to glean are insufficient and do not present a continuous picture. Nevertheless, they permit some interpolation and reasonable approximations. Using what seems the most reliable evaluation for only a small Europe—with Poland as its eastern frontier—the estimated population around 1300 was 55 million. By 1600 investigation leads to the figure of 73.5 million for an area of 1,514,000 square miles.

With this general trend in mind, we must introduce several complications in the situation between 1300 and 1650. In fact, Europe had experienced a catastrophic demographic reversal as a result of the Black Death. Naturally enough, the consequences of this chain reaction of epidemic mortalities were long felt. An enormous biological setback put the European economy under severe strain up to the middle of the fifteenth century, which is the low point in the curve and therefore considerably beneath the initial figure of 55 million. The resurgence of the sixteenth century (the "long" sixteenth century) must be gauged in reference to this depletion. We may thus say without fear of exaggeration that between 1450 and 1650 the population of Europe as a whole doubled in size. This expansion must be counted among the various forms of return to life and healthy exuberance characteristic of familiar major aspects of the Renaissance. Relative to our twentieth-century point of view, the population involved seems small, but to judge its importance at the time, we need only remind ourselves that it represented the approximate equivalent of the 600 to 700 million inhabitants of contemporary China. That many-faceted thing, the Renaissance, can be understood quite literally as the rebirth during two or three generations of the European population.

Demographic rise and population surplus were indeed riches for the prince and for the economies of the various nations. In today's jargon we would say that all progress and all expansion depend on the number of men —and this was all the more true in that period with its impoverished production techniques utilizing as their regular sources of energy either wood, domesticated animals (which were scarce and depended on the mediocre resources of the Old World agriculture), or the absurdly low motor power of waterwheels and windmills. Even lower in yield is human power (one thirtieth of one horsepower), but it was the only power present in quantity.

Any progress in the thirteenth century, as in the sixteenth and even in the eighteenth, was purchased at the expense of a heavy outlay of human labor made possible by an expansion in population. We must not be deceived by the ingenious hoisting mechanisms, the pumps, the tilt hammers, the blowing machines, and the shaft furnaces, all products of the genius of the fifteenth century, which are reproduced in the fine engravings of Georg Agricola's *De re metallica* (1551). At that time machines were brilliant exceptions, and even they required human labor and manipulation.

However, having affirmed the primacy of human beings and the work of their arms, let us be careful not to assume that their multiplication during the sixteenth century entailed immediate progress. We must further state that economic progress does not automatically mean social progress, although in the long run it implies a probable increase in the general standard of living. In the short run, the growing number of men in the sixteenth century may have been an obvious factor in the general economic expansion, but it did not always tend toward increased prosperity for the individual.

First of all, the moment that human beings in the labor market multiply beyond measure, their value depreciates and they enter into merciless competition with each other. In Europe all *real* wages between 1450 and 1650 were on the decrease, and this long-term decrease was to continue until the seventeenth century. Only then would a stabilization with a slight improvement be effected, but at a very low level. And so, at the same time that men multiplied, their lives became harder. Such was the price of economic progress. From the 1530s and even more so after the 1560s many men were no longer able to find work in the labor market, and wars did not absorb them all. Lucien Febvre has often spoken of the "sad men of the generation after 1560"; their unhappiness came not simply from within themselves, but also from the inhuman circumstances weighing on them. 1530 and 1560 are only approximations, but at some time in these years there was a turn for the worse in the economy and the human odyssey took a different tack. Though Ambrose Paré, a man worthy of credence, neither saw nor heard the Emperor, the story he tells about Charles V at the siege of Metz (1552) may well be the eyewitness account of a soldier; the words he reports are quite characteristic of a new age. "The Emperor asked who were the people who were dying, and if they were gentlemen and men of note. He was answered that they were all poor soldiers. Thereupon he said that there was no danger if they died, comparing them to caterpillars, locusts, and June bugs which eat the sprouts and other goods of the earth, and that if they were noble men, they would not be in his camp for six pounds a month. . . ." The words are doubtful, I repeat, but a movement did take place from an era more or less happy or tolerable to one of darker times. Germany, which was in the grip of a monopoly-minded capitalism, was hit early by a rise in prices, by the thousand upheavals of the Reformation, and by a short but deep-rooted social war (the Peasants' War in 1525). The downward turn seems to have taken place earlier there than elsewhere, but little by little the entire life of the West clouded over.

We must believe population experts when they say that if technological progress does not transform living conditions, every demographic advance, beneficial in its beginnings, soon changes into a calamity—and in the sixteenth century technological progress made few changes in the existing economic structure. There were men enough, to be sure, but they had to be fed. The labor of the newcomers was not competitive. Furthermore, new lands in a region long under cultivation, like Europe, are almost never good lands. There is a point beyond which further exploitation is strictly impossible. Historians can see, where documentation permits it, that decreasing marginal yields are clearly in evidence: such was the case of East Prussia, such was the case of Poland. The income yielded by farming was manifestly reduced.

As the century grew older, everything took on a darker cast. Gouberville writes in his diary:

> In my father's days, people had meat every day, food was abundant, everyone swilled down wine as if it had been water. But today things have changed indeed; everything is expensive. . . . The diet of the most prosperous peasants is quite inferior to that of the servants of the past.

Today's historians have been quite wrong to neglect these contemporary documents. Reading them, our eyes are filled increasingly with the sight of the poor, of beggars, of bandits and highwaymen. Across the whole of Italy we find banditry flourishing, from Sicily, which has no monopoly on it, to Milan and Venice. Everywhere its ravages made themselves felt, especially at the borders of states, where minor princes all too often received their neighbor's outlaws to make use of them, not without being paid in the same coin by their own enemies. The scourge grew continually with the increasing impoverishment of the poor.

Similarly, in Spain there was no city at the beginning of the seventeenth century which was not graced with its *gente del hampa,* or *hampones,* as they were called. These luckless creatures, painted by Murillo, Zurbaran, and Velásquez, were the *picaros* ("vagrants" in modern English). They worked little, nourished themselves on the gruel distributed by convents or poorhouses. They were not afraid of a little thievery. The days of their lives were spent begging, and they went from one city to another without changing their way of life. Among them could be found several refugees from an aristocracy which did not at times mind descending to the lower depths and which was sometimes pushed to it by the harsh reality of poverty. In each city the poor had their meeting places, their haunts, their Thieves' Market.

Occasionally they took to the road in huge bands, terrifying quiet cities which closed their doors on them. And always, at one time or another, they ended up at Seville, in the Triana quarter on the right bank of the Guadalquivir or else at the little port of Sanlúcar de Barrameda, the rendezvous of all the good-for-nothings of the peninsula and the headquarters of illicit traffic under the far from disinterested benediction of the dukes of Medina Sidonia, in whose territory the little city was situated. Prostitutes, panhandlers, police officials—all of them were in the conspiracy to fleece a *perulero* (the rich man returned from America, the analogue of nineteenth-century London's "nabob," or rich man returned from India) or to hoodwink a *Breton* (a man from the north, one of the countless sailors or merchants to pass through in time for the *Vendeja,* the market for the purchase of goods and new wines).

All these pictures, made familiar to us by the picaresque novels or Cervantes' picturesque *Rinconete y Cortadillo,* are not merely literature. They testify to a social impoverishment which all indications point to as the sad appendix of the "long" sixteenth century on the wane.

## III

Nonetheless, this social impoverishment, as we have said, coincides with a marked economic expansion. Let us distinguish between the two sides of the coin and direct our attention now exclusively to the great expansion of the small, artificial continent called Europe. We shall speak mostly of her because, in truth, we have almost no information about the others.

In the fifteenth century, and even more so in the sixteenth, Europe established herself at the center of a vast but weak world economy. Her role, which gradually became more precisely defined, was rather simple on the whole. Of all the economies, hers was the most imbued with monetary techniques utilizing both hard cash and other media of exchange: banknotes, acknowledgments of debt, certificates of loan, and bills of exchange. Even before the great discoveries this was true. In contrast, India was still at least half immersed in a primitive money economy, China three-quarters, and Africa entirely so, for it was acquainted only with the elementary moneys: shells, bars of iron or salt, and weights of gold. With the conquest by the white man, America was born more or less completely under a monetary economy, but the process was slow and imperfect. At the instigation of her masters, she was to produce and deliver large quantities of gold and later, after 1554, silver, but she did not retain much from her treasures, for Europe needed these precious metal products made available at a low price by slave labor. Europe had all the more need of them because her own mines with their poor yield were to slow down their activity, because she lacked the yellow and white metals for her own internal exchanges, and because she increasingly needed silver for export to the Levant, the Indian Ocean, and China in exchanges that seemed advantageous to her. Moreover, in fifteenth-century Europe and in the New World after 1554, because of the perfection of the process of amalgamation with mercury, silver had the advantage of being produced in industrial quantities, whereas gold remained the product of gold-washing by hand. From this fact emerge several simple consequences.

After 1550 gold became relatively rare in Europe; silver, on the other hand, was abundant, so much so that a gram of gold which in 1500 was worth (in mean figures) 10.5 grams of silver fetched 11.1 grams in 1550, 11.8 in 1600, and 14.3 in 1650. However, silver remained relatively rare in India and China. In the latter, the ratio between the two metals was still around one to six in 1600. This was another reason why the silver from the mines of New Spain (Zacatecas, San Luis, and Santa Barbara) or of Peru (Potosí) often followed the route to Asia in the form of *reales de a ocho,* pieces of eight. Other reasons, both old and new, existed, including the abiding taste for pepper, spices, silks, and, in time, porcelain. Thus, an unceasing traffic of ingots, coins, and merchandise grew up around the world. After 1565 annual voyages of the transport *Nao de China* joined Acapulco on New Spain's Pacific coast to Manila in the Philippines, a rendezvous for the junks from the southern coast of China. This trade route tied together the two ends of the string and completed the round-the-world network.

Such long-distance commerce was rendered possible only because of the prevalence of silver, the forced labor of the Indians who produced it, and the vigilant authority of the Catholic King and his representatives, only too frequently encroached upon by pirates.

Between 1600 and 1610 the American mines, suffering from numerous vicissitudes, the law of diminishing returns, and the uprisings of the Indian masses, delivered less and less silver. This catastrophe was felt all along the fragile network of the international economy, as fire races along a train of powder. The explosion began at Seville, which had monopolized relations with the New World since 1503. Other explosions followed, some sooner, some later, but everywhere. This was the aftermath of the expansion of the sixteenth century, and it brought with it a decline in prices.

Starting in 1470–75, or at the very latest 1500, prices in Europe had been pushed up by a powerful pressure, creating a continual rise on a world-wide scale that was to span a long period of time. At its shortest, in some areas it continued from 1500 to 1600; in others it lasted from 1475 to 1650.

This inflation must be understood as the hallmark of the surge in the European economy—perhaps, in the last analysis, of a far larger revival which included the distant economies that were linked to hers. To give an explanation of its causes is no easy matter. The reader must have at least a certain grasp of the general laws of political economy. However, the essential point may perhaps be reduced to the following negative assertion: one must not regard this European inflation, the sixteenth-century "revolution" in prices, as if it were determined simply by the arrival of precious metals from America. To believe this would be to confine oneself to an old explanation, the quantitative theory of money, which is certainly not totally untrue but which gives only part of the truth. First of all, prices rose before the great imports from America. And their rise was much more marked than one would expect merely from the action of the available stocks of money, such as have been estimated in very approximate figures. It seems, therefore, that other factors were at work, such as population, monetary devaluations, and the increased stimulation of economic life. In fact, we must turn the hourglass and reverse the usual order of the explanation. It is maintained that the increasing importation of wealth from America set off the surge in prices and economic life. Let us turn the explanation upside down: the economic surge created the rise in prices and provoked and stimulated the import of metals from the New World. In the jargon of the economists, we would like to say, with the usual qualifications: every economic growth creates its money, in specie, in paper currency, or later in fiduciary notes.

Whatever the case about the relation of prices to general economic conditions, world movements in prices, an admirable index of long-term economic life, are of signal import for the very structure of societies and their economic institutions. When world prices move, sooner or later deteriorations and realignments in economic structure are to be expected. Hence the interest of the dates 1600 and 1650. Roughly speaking, in 1600 the change in the curve set in for Spain, Italy, and southern France. It occurred only in 1650 in the northern lands, particularly in the Low Countries, where Amsterdam was to assert her dominance on the world scene. To explain this displacement and why the decline came early in the south and late in the north would involve us in an interesting controversy, but one which we need only mention here.

The movement in world prices is important both in itself and as a measuring rod. It is accompanied by other movements which must be considered in relation to it. We have already mentioned the arrival of precious metals and the all-over rise of European population; we could speak also of the depreciation in gold currency, the extension of world trade, the sums of money in commerce, the budgets of the various governments, the production curves of agriculture and industry. On the whole, all of these were on the rise. In the matter of trade, the correspondence between the movement in prices and in the volume of goods transported is considerable, at least for the figures we have, either concerning the Danish customs on the Öresund controlling the traffic between the Baltic and the North Sea or concerning the trade in both directions between America and Seville. The general trends in prices in Andalusia and the statistics of Seville's commerce reveal the same phases and the same fluctuations.

A demonstration of the same sort can be made for governmental budgets. We have little information about them, but enough to conclude that they too followed the rise in prices. The forces raising the cost of all goods did nothing to lessen the burden imposed by a multiplicity of taxes. Even the budget of the King of France, reduced as it was by the depredations of his bureaucrats, followed the progressively rising cost of living in spite of the continuous disorders resulting from the so-called Religious Wars between 1562 and 1598. The enormous Spanish Empire, from the time of Charles V to Philip IV (1516–1660), experienced a continual swelling of its receipts no less than its expenses between 1516 and 1660. Only prosperous states richly endowed with land, men, and monetary resources were able to survive the devilish pace of the price revolution. Old-fashioned states, cities, and seigniories went under in the time of this inflation that would not leave political leaders in peace.

As for agricultural and industrial production, we cannot be so definite, for documentation is lacking. Undoubtedly agricultural production rose and fell along with the world trends, but our evidence applies only to two restricted areas: the yields of land under grain in the *Vorwerke Domänen* of East Prussia and the acceleration or deceleration in land-reclaiming projects in the Low Countries. These figures give us preliminary indications to go by, but no more. It is nevertheless tempting to accept them as valid because the general price movements before the Industrial Revolution continued to be dominated by the price of wheat and other bread cereals.

We are equally badly informed about industrial production, having only three sets of long-term data: one concerning the production of light woolen textiles in Hondschoote, a village of coastal Flanders; another dealing with the manufacture of woolens and other textiles in Leyden; and the third on the looming of fine wool cloths in Venice. If the case of Leyden did not contradict somewhat the experience of the other two, we would not hesitate to draw firm conclusions. It is a complicated case anyway, and if we disregard it, it would seem to be true that industrial production during periods of inflation and of deflation always moved faster than prices and, it is worth noting, its rises always began a long time after price increases while its declines set in on the slightest sign of soft prices. In short, all the evidence leads to the conclusion that industrial prices and industrial volume follow patterns of behavior peculiar to themselves. But here, for lack of documents and of successful research, the problems have only been raised, not solved.

## IV

One last question remains for the historian who wishes to examine the general features of the powerful and expanding Europe of the long sixteenth century. How and why was it the cradle of what has since been baptized "capitalism"?

Since everyone defines capitalism in his own way, thereby giving rise to considerable inconvenience and misunderstanding, some historians have recently proposed to banish the word. But if we chase it out the door, we run the risk of having it return through the window. It is a complicated word and a rich source of debate—moreover, a word created for the needs of a cause when it first appeared, or at least made its presence felt, among socialists. Therefore, to use it to describe the past is to run the risk of anachronism, but the same considerations exist when the word "industry" or the expression "civil servant" is applied to the past.

To expel "capitalism" from our vocabulary would not liberate us from the quarrels which it has inherited without having created them, nor from those that it gives rise to even though they do not belong specifically to its province. So let us accept the word without enthusiasm and without any intent to mislead. It will be valuable if we use it with care.

*First Warning: Begin with businessmen.* There is no capitalism without capitalists. We know very little about the general nature of the former, and we argue about it. But we can see the latter, interrogate them, listen to them, and try to put ourselves in their place. And the historian, after all, is a past master in this art. Following our fancy's dictates, we may approach the Medicis, Francesco Datini of Prato (d. 1410), the Capponis in Florence, or Andrea Barbarigo in Venice (1418–49). Our curiosity may extend as far as visiting Jacob Fugger and his accountant Matthew Schwarz in the Fugger house in Augsburg. Or we may place ourselves at the side of Simon Ruiz (1525–96), a merchant from Medina del Campo whose correspondence of perhaps 100,000 letters has been preserved. Or, if we wish, we may go north to Antwerp to look at the papers of the house of Della Faille or of the Van Immerseels. This list is an abbreviated one, for the scholarship of historians in the last few years has opened up to us thousands of business letters of the sixteenth century. Today we have nothing less than an embarrassment of riches available in this correspondence.

Naturally we shall qualify only the richest of these merchants as capitalists. Men like Lucas Rem, an agent of the Welsers in Lisbon, whose numerous trips and rapid substantial profits we know thanks to his succinct *Tagebuch,* are merely secondary figures; if need be, we may interrogate them and then let them be. From the start we insist that a capitalist can only be a man of a certain importance, a certain stature, capable of resisting the abrupt reversals of the moment and making the necessary short-term adjustments. He has nothing in common with the myriad speculators who blaze up one day like a flare only to die out on the following day. So, from the onset, we will place ourselves on the side of the angels and consider only successful capitalists—a first precaution, perhaps a necessary one.

*Second Warning: Know all the facets of capitalists' endeavors.* Generally, big businessmen operated in more than one field at a time; they were simultaneously dealers in wool, wheat, and textiles, and occasional buyers or sellers of Flemish tapestry or diamonds and other precious stones. By turns they were borrowers or lenders, giving or receiving bills of exchange. They gladly dealt with princes, advancing them money in exchange for concessions, not infrequently buying titles of nobility from them. There was not a single real practitioner of higher finance who did not finish at least as the lord of many estates, if not the ruler of a state, as did the Medicis and Niccolo Grimaldi, one of the principal creditors of Philip II, who became prince of Salerno. There was nothing surprising in this; such multiplicity of roles was common long before the sixteenth century, and it continued to be the rule. There was no specialization at the highest level of business.

Although there was nothing new in this diversity of activities, it is perhaps worth while to distinguish two extreme cases. First there was the Florentine businessman, who worked "vertically," as we say today, concerning himself with the importing of wool, then with its weaving and the sale or export of textiles. One end of the chain would be represented, for example, by the possession of a wool wash-house in Old Castile; the other end, by piles of textiles in a store in Alexandria. These might one day be sold by an agent for hard cash or bartered for other goods, which might involve the merchant in another trade circuit dealing with the products of the East. The other extreme case is the businessman of Lisbon, strictly a merchant playing on the price fluctuations of "royal" merchandise—namely, goods of high quality and high revenue yield such as pepper, spices, or cochineal—but hardly ever taking risks in financial dealings or in letters of exchange. Between these two extremes were the intermediate cases which comprised the majority. Let us add a third figure, the great Genoese businessman who was to abandon dealing with goods little by little in order to handle money and credit exclusively. We shall soon have occasion to speak of him again.

However diverse the business activities might be, we must note that ordinarily they were conducted over long distances. German historians speak rightly of *Fernhandler* and *Fernhandel*. All the farsighted capitalists were businessmen who traded with distant places, taking advantage of the sizable differences in price levels or exchange rates. They needed reliable men, not to say accomplices, in these faraway lands, or, at the very least, trustworthy correspondents. For such purposes, relatives are irreplaceable; at home you have the father; in the field, scattered in various ports, sons or brothers or nephews, all agents, whether itinerant or fixed at one station.

Do not picture these middlemen or correspondents in terms of our present-day business arrangements: relations between the owner or head of the establishment and his agents have their corollary instead in the relationship of a lord and his vassal. Nothing shows this better than a little incident between Simon Ruiz and his agent at Seville, Geronimo de Valladolid; the lively quarrel ended with the humiliation of the latter and his pardon by the former.

This game of inside information and collaboration was very, very old, undoubtedly as old as the calling of the businessman, at least of the non-itinerant businessman who came into being in Europe during the middle of the twelfth century. And it was the same wherever we know of capitalist merchantmen. The Armenians who scattered during the seventeenth century over China, India, Persia, Turkey, Russia, Venice, Amsterdam, and even the Philippines, where their names abound in the documents, behaved this way. So did the Banians of India; the Chinese merchants, originating in Shansi province, who emerged in the salt trade of the eighteenth century especially at Yangchow, where they made their fortune; and, finally, the Italian and Dutch businessmen, whom we know rather well.

One can even go so far as to say that any capitalist initiative in this first epoch of capitalism required a diaspora of agents such as we find in the case of the Italian businessmen from the eleventh to the seventeenth centuries as they spread across Europe and the Near East, or in the case of the Dutch merchants of the first years of the seventeenth century, who turned up in France, at Frankfort, and at Leipzig. In fact, if southern Germany did not succeed in establishing firmly her supremacy in the days of the Fuggers, the Welsers, the Hochstätters, the Paumgärtners, and the Imhofs, in the century that is sometimes called the century of the Fuggers, it was because their collective fortunes lasted only through the first three or four decades of the 1500s. They scarcely had time to spread out, except in several well-established areas such as Venice or Lisbon, or time to colonize their markets and to establish a real network between them. The long and active presence of Kron, the Fugger agent in Goa in India, was only an exception, curious though it was. And so we find dispersion and merchant colonization—two very ancient traits of merchant capitalism, ones that the sixteenth century had not created.

Another unchanging trait that should cause no surprise lies in the technical and intellectual training of the businessman, his skill in disseminating information, and his concern for getting news rapidly. His technical training was in double-entry bookkeeping, which dates from the preceding century and was taught in all the Italian cities but, above all, in Venice. At 17 years of age, Jacob Fugger went to school there, and later his bookkeeper Matthew Schwarz followed his steps. A further part of the businessman's technical training was the study of the business textbooks, the most polished of which, though late, was Giovanni Domenico Peri's *Il Negociante* in the seventeenth century. In addition he acquired skill in writing short, clear, pithy letters, similar to those of the master Simon Ruiz and many others. Businessmen learned to say clearly what they had to say, then to repeat it tirelessly, making two and three copies of each letter against the eventuality of loss or delay in the mails. There was no man of affairs who did not bend to this iron discipline, regularly adding any news that might bear on business in this world below or be of particular interest to his correspondent, then almost ritually closing with the monetary exchange rates in his part of the world. All this, of course, was done in the expectation of similar favors in return.

What we have here is an eminently rationalistic pattern of behavior predicated on foresight and the calculation of profits and margins of risk. For capitalism is a psychology: earn your money, keep it, and safeguard your liquid funds. By 1450 none of this was new, but it became more clearly defined, more precise, and more prevalent. In 1638 a voyager wrote of the Banians from India, "There is no one who knows how to write or calculate better than they do."

These more vigorous if not new characteristics should not blind us to an important change in capitalism. First of all, across the entire European continent, the amount of money had risen considerably, especially hard, jingling coin. Castile, we are told, won America in the lottery. In fact, Europe and Asia profited mightily at the same time. There followed an undreamed-of bounty, uncounted fortunes, an increased rapidity of monetary circulation. To use the expression of the eighteenth-century Portuguese author Pinto, money "cascaded" faster than ever before. The Keynesian idea of investment and savings applies very well here. The former is possible only in the presence of the latter; if investments accelerate growth, savings put a brake on it. The gold and silver of the New World enabled Europe to live above its means, to invest beyond its savings. An immense spur in the flanks of the economy stimulated the exchange of goods.

But would the old familiar methods rise to the challenge of the new situation? The Fuggers could rely on them, delegating their powers to agents who were often remarkable, trustworthy men. The Welsers and, for a long while, the Affaitatis, international businessmen from Cremona, did the same. But the necessity for vast economic empires, such as the Portuguese monopoly in pepper, became more and more evident. Inevitably, the businessmen found themselves forced to enter into association with each other, to lend their services to each other, to merge local companies with branch offices of larger firms like the Affaitatis' affiliate in Lisbon. In place of the former association of patron and agent, whether a relative or not, more and more one finds the association of equal businessmen mutually rendering each other services as representatives or on a commission basis. Simon Ruiz became a broker at the end of his life, a central clearing office for thousands of letters. His relations with the Bonvisis in Lyons, with Baltazar Suarez in Florence, or with the Ximenes in Lisbon repeatedly allowed him to deduct substantial commissions and at the same time to circulate bills of exchange or merchandise to his greatest advantage. There is nothing surprising in the appearance, at the end of the sixteenth century or the beginning of the seventeenth, of the great urban guarantee banks such as the Banco di Rialto in Venice, the new Banco di San Giorgio in Genoa, the Bank of Amsterdam, and the Bank of Hamburg. Just as natural were the English companies of "merchant adventurers," which combined their stockholders' capital for trade with the Orient or with Muscovy or with the Indies, leaving far behind them the once great Dutch East India Company. All this took place on the very eve of the reversal in world price movements—i.e., on the eve of new difficulties—but at the time it looked as if a new stabilization had been found in the concentration and association of businesses.

Meanwhile a great many other changes had come to the fore, such, for example, as the vast reinvestment of capital in land. A recurring phenomenon undoubtedly in the life of businessmen ever since businessmen came into being, it was particularly widespread at this time. A kind of agricultural capitalism, if you wish, gradually developed across the face of Europe, especially around its cities. In Venice during the 1590s this reinvestment degenerated into speculation. Similarly, around Florence and around Barcelona commercial fortunes immobilized themselves, were frozen, or became dormant, but also saved themselves partially. No statistics can tell us how widespread the process was, but it was an old one already, going back to the days when Lorenzo the Magnificent in Renaissance Italy had invested largely in land at the end of his life when the economic climate seemed threatening. And, besides, land has always been the symbol and trapping of social pretensions.

The second process was the daily increasing mobilization of business fortunes and means for the benefit of governments whose appetites seemed inexhaustible. Of course, this process does not date from the beginning of the sixteenth century. The example of Jacques Coeur (c.1395–1456), enriched and then ruined by Charles VII of France, provides ample evidence of this. As it grew larger, the state had greater and greater need of businessmen. It confided to them the levying of its taxes and the disposal of its funds; they became its creditors, its profiteers, and its victims. In England, in France, in Spain—wherever evidence is available—collusion between princes and businessmen can be demonstrated. How could the latter fail to impose themselves on the former, and vice versa? Even before the reign of Louis XI (1461–83), we can already detect great French financial dynasties which were to be supplanted only by the Italians during the Italian wars (1494–1516). In Spain the Jews of the Middle Ages gave place to foreign businessmen, and in the last years of the Emperor Charles V, particularly after the bankruptcy of 1557, the reign of the Genoese financiers began. Their century was to last at least until the Spanish bankruptcy of 1627, when they in turn were to be supplanted or replaced for a short while by the Portuguese *marranos,* the baptized Jews of Lisbon, partisans of the reckless and futile policies of the Count-Duke Olivares.

The mechanisms of Genoese financial loans are well known to us today, for we have the facts and figures. We can follow in detail the clauses of the great *asientos,* or contracts, concluded by the Spanish government with individual businessmen at first and then later with groups of businessmen. In return for silver, to be collected primarily in Seville, though slowly, irregularly, and frequently late, the *asientistas* guaranteed regular payment of the troops fighting for the Catholic King in the Low Countries, and very often it was necessary to pay the soldiers in gold. The Genoese would ship the silver they received in galleys from Valencia or Barcelona to Genoa, then would trade it against bills of exchange payable in Antwerp which they had obtained in Florence or Venice or at the great fairs of Piacenza, over which they had uncontested control.

Every year these *asientos* represented extraordinary sums in gold. One can imagine how great a circulation of moneys and bills of exchange such transfers entailed. Financiers' profits were often negligible, less than 5 percent, but the amounts in question compensated for the low rate of profit.

Besides, the *hombres de negocios,* as the Spanish called them, did not put only their own money to work; they associated with themselves smaller lenders who were thus able to invest their capital. In this way all of Europe became involved in the trading. There ensued, both in Castile and outside it, an immense movement of liquid funds for the benefit of the Catholic King. The same was true of other princes, to the extent that government revenues were augmented through increased levies on local governments in France, Spain, and Italy. In short, dealings in money and interest-bearing loans tended to become generalized. Now, at that time lending money and making interest on it was a transaction still condemned by the Church except in the case of a contract directly with the King (who took the sin upon himself in a special clause of the *asiento* deeds). But to make loans in the form of bills of exchange which circulated—usually accruing profits on the way, but always with the possibility of suffering losses—was considered legitimate on the basis that the risk justified the profit. The profusion of bills of exchange toward the end of the sixteenth century was thus a mask that hid nothing, but which allowed the businessman to live on his loans without any pangs of conscience.

In short, then, a considerable part of liquid funds in Europe was mobilized by the financial demands of governments which were constantly burdened with ever increasing expenses. But was this not in fact tantamount to a considerable drain on funds available for investment in enterprises capable of stimulating the general economic activity of Europe and the world economy that gravitated around Europe?

In part, perhaps. But it is also true that liquid capital was less and less able to find constructive placement. To put one's money in industry with its feeble technology and poor returns was far from a blue-chip investment, for facing the businessman were the trade unions, such as the *Arte della lana* or the *Arte della seta* in Venice. They were considerable forces commanding respect and often acted as effective social brakes on capitalist exploitation of labor. The production of the *Arte della lana,* which had been so prosperous during the years 1600–1610 when prices were at their peak in Venice and elsewhere, declined afterward because of economic conditions and also for social reasons; like all urban unions, the *Arte* defended its entrenched interests and its wage levels only to find itself in stiff competition with the northern European industries, which worked on the cottage system outside the city walls and could be more flexible in the face of business needs because their labor made fewer demands.

But even this new and freer industry did not attract large investments of capital. Textile products were primarily in need of larger markets, and the industrial crafts needed more advanced techniques that were as yet lacking. Industrial capitalism existed only embryonically. It was not to move to full development until the eighteenth and nineteenth centuries.

Let us take stock. In these earliest eras, capitalism was largely limited to the activities of the merchant and the foreign trader. Capitalism implied diverse transactions running the gamut from the trading of merchandise to high finance, and involved the judicious use of funds, whether metallic or based on instruments of credit, notably the ubiquitous bill of exchange.

In the course of the two centuries that interest us particularly a general developing pattern of capitalism can be discerned, although the timing of its stages varied from economy to economy.

In the early half of the period, during the era of easy operation and "happy capitalism," enormous profits were realized—on the order of 100 percent in Lisbon, for example. The openly admitted interest rate was often 15 percent for loans to the state, but we would have to know how these transactions really took place to determine the actual rate, and such careful studies have not yet been made. As late as 1557, money was lent in Antwerp in crisis periods at an interest rate of 57 percent.

In the second half of our period, after the gray years between 1540 and 1560, came the arrival of precious metals from America. This was the age, not of gold, but of silver. The abundance of this precious white metal created an obvious rise in capitalist prosperity and brought with it also a decline of 15 to 10 percent in the *official* exchange rate for silver in Spain. Furthermore, prices rose although profit margins narrowed and resounding business failures multiplied. In these progressively distressing times only the large firms, the powerful business families, and the associations that knew how to make alliances like those of the great Genoese financiers could resist the general trend. We may say that it was an era of the businessman who was more interested in credit and banking than in trade. In Genoa the contrast between the *nobili vecchi* who took an immediate interest in finance and the *nobili novi* who concerned themselves with commerce and industry was clear-cut. As social vanities and aspirations became involved, unrest rent the city in 1575 and 1576 in a quarrel symptomatic of the times.

The reign of a higher capitalism bound to the state then began. It dealt with money or pseudo-moneys of paper and credit, all practices in which Genoa ruled supreme. But its life was not without trials. The very foundations of capitalism were shaken by the massive and repeated bankruptcies of the Spanish government in 1575, 1596, 1607, 1627, and 1647. Undoubtedly the big bankers parried these hard blows by effecting compromises with the bankrupt governments and recovering their losses at the expense of their clients and others. But the system itself had been struck deeply at its very roots. If we need any proof of this, it is furnished by the formation of urban guarantee banks in Naples, Florence, Venice, and even Genoa itself, or by the fortunes of Simon Ruiz, a capitalist on a modest scale, or rather a man heading a clearing house of information but still situated on the outskirts of high finance. From about 1590 on, Simon no longer managed to make a profit on the backward and forward trading of his letters of exchange. And so he again took up trading in wool, cochineal, and the like, although he had abandoned it earlier upon his entrance into finance in 1576. This return to the commerce of goods was a sign of the times in the last days of the century, and we see it taking place everywhere—in Augsburg in Germany, and in the Mediterranean where a curious trend around 1600 worked to the benefit of the big Portuguese merchants who held pepper monopolies, among others the Ximenes, who were setting up branch offices in Pisa, Florence, and Venice to the considerable displeasure of the local dealers.

In truth, this return to commerce may well indicate the end of a capitalist cycle, inaugurated by the arrival of merchandise on the docks of Lisbon upon the return of the first Portuguese fleets in the beginning of the century and terminated by financial transactions like the tremendous *asientos* of the Genoese businessmen. The Fuggers, vitally engaged in the mining enterprises of the Tyrol and of Hungary and in foreign trade at Antwerp and London, typify the first sort of capitalism. It was straightforward, and operated by taking advantage of the high profit margins on merchandise. The Genoese credit manipulators and speculators typify the second capitalism, complicated and sophisticated, if not always honest.

At the end of the cycle the sudden rise to eminence of Amsterdam represented the reestablishment of commercial capitalism in the narrow sense of the word. The second passage of the Cape of Good Hope in 1595 by the boats of the Dutchman Cornelius Houtman reopened the field for the trade of goods between Europe and the Pacific and Indian oceans. As a result of the new transports that were more effective than the Iberian ones, there came a new golden age of trade with large profit margins, all the more so because the richest of the traders formed groups and privileged associations in Holland as well as in England.

But it would have been strange if this rejuvenated capitalism in Holland had not soon aged, as its predecessor in the Mediterranean had. A complicated, speculative capitalism, unattached to commerce, made its appearance quickly, then spread, devouring everything, sweeping everything away. Just before the end of the seventeenth century, the Amsterdam Stock Exchange experienced all the sharp practices and stratagems of present-day exchanges. Joseph de la Vega exposed them in a very modern book, the *Confusion de Confusiones* (1688), in which he explained all these impostures with clarity.

Shortly afterward the capitalism of Amsterdam lost fruitful investment opportunities, as had the Mediterranean capitalism of former times, and, like it, it threw itself headlong into loans to the various princes and governments of Christendom—English trusts, loans to the French king, advances to the Danes, the Russians, even the Spanish.

However personal or tentative these views, the evolution of capitalism can perhaps be grasped better by concentrating on the opportunities offered or denied to businessmen than on the opportunities that they wished to create for themselves. In other words, the history of capitalism is the history of actual economic structures and institutions. In any case, the development in Holland, seen in retrospect, helps us to understand the evolution between 1500 and 1650 that we have just studied in its phases of youth, maturity, and perhaps old age—if one is willing to admit, as one should, that the youth of one people can exist alongside the old age of another.

## V

In examining the crises and catastrophes from 1450 to 1650 and now leaving aside long-term considerations, we shall undertake to measure the sixteenth century in less lengthy units of time and see it from the short-term point of view, as it were, dividing its acts into scenes. Although we have already indicated some of the prominent stages in its development, the difficulty is that we must examine these diverse stages in themselves and at the same time in relation to the preceding and succeeding stages. For, hand in hand, they make a continuous chain, the different links resembling each other or contrasting with each other, but always helping to lead us to and from each other.

To start, let us consider the classical Renaissance in its decline in Florence in the late fifteenth century under the patronage of Lorenzo the Magnificent. To choose this period is begging for difficulties, for nothing is simple in this epoch which has been often studied and, in fact, misrepresented by so many examinations and investigations. Art historians and those grappling with the problems of Florentine art and humanism must hesitate before forming their judgments. Forgetting for the moment the actual renown of Lorenzo (or his legend), we would like to ask if there may not have been a sort of regression from the greatness of Florence during the twenty-odd years of his patronage. And in his entourage, was there only talk, enjoyment, and criticism rather than the real creativity that we find in the days of his forebears Pietro and Cosimo? Finally, did Tuscan art then flourish elsewhere in Italy more than in Florence itself because of the voluntary emigration of the artists of the incredible city?

Having mentioned this possibility, if we turn to the material life of Florence during these late years of its splendor, other debates arise which cannot be settled, for the body of Florence has not received the attention accorded its heart and spirit. We do not have available accurate statistics or price data. We can comprehend the lives of the great men of affairs and the thirty or so *banchi grossi* whose most important and best-known depositor was the commercial establishment of the Medicis. The bank of the Medicis and its whole business structure and its foreign branches underwent successive difficulties during the end of the fifteenth century. Lorenzo was a bad businessman, and his financial manager Francesco Sassetti abandoned himself to the pleasures of living. Furthermore, there was a crisis in gold currency, and later a crisis in credit. The affiliates of the Medicis closed down, one after another, in Venice before 1470, in London in 1478, and in Bruges in the same year. Having had a narrow escape in 1488, the representatives in Lyons collapsed in 1494 in the general bankruptcy that struck the affiliates in Naples and Rome, and even the bank of Florence itself with the arrival from France of the invading Charles VIII. A decrease in silver currency in circulation there between 1473 and 1500 had the effects of an inflation in the local economy, striking down artisans and little people, and favoring the big businessman, but the latter experienced their share of dramatic difficulties with their international gold payments.

As previously remarked, there is not sufficient documentation to support any definitive judgment, but one cannot escape the impression that the debacle of the Medicis must be ascribed to a vast capitalist crisis. This dying capitalism was a complicated, aging capitalism, warped by the hazardous game of unthinkingly making loans to governments. The crisis of the Bruges affiliate in 1478 stemmed from the death of Charles the Bold (1477) and the collapse of his duchy of Burgundy as well as from the rashness and temerity of the manager Tomaso Portinari. Such an advanced capitalism as Florence's forces us to abandon the idea that the young capitalism of the first years of the sixteenth century was the first capitalism of the Western world.

As always, with the ebb and flow of great world-wide movements, questions of economic structure were involved. In 1492, when Lorenzo died as the last flames of the intellectual glory and the *joie de vivre* of Florence burned bright, Italy was a cloistered world, buried in its illusions, similar to the Europe of the years 1919–39, and no surer of its future than was Europe four and a half centuries later. The great states of the coming decades, Tudor England, Valois France, and Imperial Spain, were scarcely emerging from the economic difficulties of the violent and cheerless fifteenth century. The new political order grew nonetheless, despite the opposition of the barons in the English War of Roses, the opposition of the League of Public Welfare in France, and the opposition of the ecclesiastical and lay nobility of Spain. In contrast to these bloody struggles, the Italian disputes were mere courtly tournaments, debates between political parties for power, not unlike the bitter, petty quarrels of the French parties of the Third and Fourth Republics. To stave off dangerous upheavals, Italy practiced an intelligent politics of equilibrium, analagous to the one in Europe before the beginning of the seventeenth century. The "balance of power" between Florence, Genoa, Venice, Rome, Naples, and such states was a subtle and delicate thing to maintain, but it was maintained. The Italian economy did not drop near the subsistence level in 1494, for Italy was cultivated by its peasants right to the crest of its hilltops, as Guicciardini tells us in his famous history. Despite the inevitable economic adjustments, this Italy witnessed the maturity of the city-states that were its glory.

What even the most lucid men of that day did not foresee, what Machiavelli was to discover late in his life, was the imminent drama of the new state, a nascent giant, an ogre as yet harmless, to whom the future had been promised. The capture of Granada (1492), as well as being the result of a crusade, was the death of a state that had been too small to survive despite its riches. The lesson of the loss of Charles the Bold in 1477 is less clear but no less appropriate; the Flemish-Burgundian state was not big enough nor unified enough to resist the new day and the kingdom of France.

Perhaps it was from some obscure prescience that Venice strove from the beginning of the fifteenth century to conquer territories on the mainland at the same time as Florence sought to subjugate Tuscany, extending as far as Leghorn, Pisa, and the sea, and trying to include Siena in her grasp. In all events, this ambition for territorial aggrandisement was the prerequisite for the continued grandeur of certain of the city-states. But the fine minds of the Platonic Academy of Florence seem never to have suspected the awful fate that awaited them and became a reality with the descent of the barbarians, the arrival of the French in October, 1494.

## VI

These narrower observations on the nature of the late fifteenth century immediately make possible a clearer general perspective on the long sixteenth century. We are no longer able to see it as absolutely novel. Previous centuries had their material prosperity, their periods of expansion, their regressions, and their relatively complicated capitalist systems. Armado Sapori, who has solid arguments to support his contentions, would have us believe that the thirteenth century was the real Renaissance, or at least the first one.

The truth of the matter is that the contribution of the sixteenth century, other than its distinctly new geographical conquests, did not lie in unprecedented creations in politics or economics, even less in technological progress. Rather, the century brought increasingly intense activity, a lively exuberance exemplified in the deeds of the great states and the empires, the Spanish, the Portuguese, the Turkish, and the Empire of the Great Mogul. Still we must distinguish the stages of growth.

The first part of the sixteenth century, from 1500 to 1550, advanced at a slow, measured pace. The massive imports of precious metals from the New World to the Old (about 180 tons of gold and 16,000 tons of silver from 1503 to 1650) had not yet made themselves felt during these years. Of the two precious metals, gold was the more abundant or, if you prefer, the less rare. It was relatively cheap *in terms of silver,* and the white metal was the more sought after of the two. Until the years 1530–40 silver came primarily from the mines of central Europe, which gave predominance to the merchants of Augsburg who controlled them and created the so-called "century of the Fuggers."

After the years 1540–60 the situation reversed itself. America shipped such quantities of silver that it became widespread and depreciated in value as gold became correspondingly more rare. The European economy, which had been run on gold until this time, changed fuels and began to run on silver. Henceforth its prosperity was to be founded on the white metal. This reversal, in the middle of the sixteenth century, as analyzed in Frank Spooner's great book, unquestionably entailed considerable breaks in the daily life as well as the basic structure of Europe's economy. In Antwerp, the outlet for the production of those German mines which were to be ruined by the flood of American silver, it was the Genoese who first reversed the pattern of their financial speculations. Until then the essential thing had been to gain possession of the white metal, in which calling Augsburg and the Fuggers excelled. From then on it became necessary to hold gold in reserve for critical transactions. This was so much the case that in 1587, when it was learned that the King of Spain was making a large payment in gold, all of Europe began to worry. Did this gesture mean that the monarch intended to strike a blow at any moment, or had he momentarily lost his senses?

There is a rather amusing sidelight in this great readjustment. Before the middle of the century, shipments of specie were generally made by porters, for a trusted messenger could carry up to 5,000 crowns sewn in his garments. Subsequently such means of transport became the exception, for silver became the metal which usually circulated, and it was far more cumbersome than gold. A donkey could bear the weight of silver equivalent to about 4,000 crowns. This was the basis for the count made by the Venetian ambassador in Saragossa in May, 1585, as he watched the precious cargo pass by in the direction of Barcelona: 4,000 ducats per animal, so 80 mules meant a total of 320,000 crowns.

Pieces of eight and ingots of silver were shipped in the sleek Genoese galleys, which generally sailed in convoys that were veritable fleets of silver and which proliferated after 1579 on the Barcelona-Genoa run. From then on Spain was the great provider of silver for Europe and the world. Since silver no longer came from the depths of central Europe but from the Atlantic trade routes and then into the English Channel and North Sea, the position of Germany, and particularly of her glorious interior cities, declined. Europe was thus opened to the intrusion of the Dutch.

A final consequence of the flow of silver into Europe was inflation, just as the European economy was to experience the same much later in the case of copper and paper currencies. In the sixteenth century everything was swept along in the rising tide of silver, prices as well as wages, and the tremendous inflation of the second sixteenth century was thus set loose.

## VII

The presence of so much silver in its economy allowed Europe at first to weather a serious economic crisis that lasted more than ten years. This crisis occurred almost everywhere throughout the continent, longer in some areas, shorter in others, and varying in intensity from place to place. We can locate the storm center in the commerce of Seville; we suspect its presence in France between 1536 and 1564; it broke out in England from 1540 to 1560; and we perceive its vague outlines in Germany and Italy, even if available documents do not authorize us to draw any absolute conclusions.

In any case, nothing could be clearer than the "great recession," as Pierre Chaunu calls it, in Seville of the middle of the century. The crisis began in 1551 and disappeared in 1568, with its nadir distinctly reached in the year 1554. If we eliminate the twenty ships laden with agricultural products departing from the Canary Islands for the Americas in this difficult year, only three ships left Seville for the New World. This points up the debacle in that year of the *Carrera de Indias,* the great transatlantic trading combine, "a catastrophe unprecedented," as one historian has said, ". . . in the first years of the century; to find a comparable situation, we must wait for the catastrophes of the dark years of the 1640's and afterwards." A cessation of activity, a brutal change in the apparently rising fortunes of the trade between Seville and America, was evident at the mid-point of the century. This realignment can certainly not be explained only by the military and political events of those years or by the end of the dramatic conflicts between the Valois and the Hapsburgs, two exhausted adversaries unwilling to give up their differences and unable to decide upon a reasonable peace before early April, 1559, with the treaty of Cateau-Cambrésis.

Roughly speaking, this recession period, which extended well beyond 1559, corresponded with internal difficulties in Spain. Historians have frequently pointed out the distress of the public treasury and the many signs of disobedience to the King and even to the Church. At the same time, the rise in prices, reaching a height in Spain in the year 1552, was checked in the four years that followed. In Andalusia and New Castile this change can be observed even earlier, after 1549.

These are all indications of the crisis in Seville. Its commerce required considerable time to reestablish itself. When the city got on its feet again, conditions had changed, for on the other side of the Atlantic the first series of European conquests had come to an end. They had been prosperous, had realized unforeseen profits, and had created a wealthy conqueror class overseas which could afford the products of the distant Mediterranean, olive oil, wine, and wheat flour. The conquerors that survived had to retire, and when they wrote, they complained about the new times. Henceforth European America adapted itself increasingly to the indigenous foods, corn and cassavas. Here and there vineyards appeared in America, in New Spain, outside of Lima, even in the streets of what was to be Santiago, Chile. Henceforth, rather than agricultural supplies, it was manufactured products that the American customers wanted—especially textiles, but also knives, scissors, axes, and other cutlery. And, rather than the industrial cities of Spain such as Cordova, Toledo, Segovia, and Barcelona, it was the north of Europe that furnished these limited shipments of costly articles, which, in turn, made the volume and the value of the exports from Seville move in opposite directions: the volume decreased; the value increased. This change was evidenced by the arrivals, more frequent than in the past, of ships from the north bearing northern products. Hookers from Flanders, tiny Breton boats, and English ships were crammed side by side in such Spanish ports as Sanlucár de Barrameda, Puerto de Santa María, Cádiz, and on the banks of the Guadalquivir downstream from Seville. These boats were stocking the holds of the enormous ships of the *Carrera.*

This readjustment in Spanish trade and prices had repercussions in France which are difficult to assess precisely, but which probably appeared between, approximately, 1536 and 1564. These thirty years witnessed the passage from a difficult period to one yet more difficult. We find the effects of the Spanish crisis making themselves apparent in England from about 1540 to 1560 (and again in 1569–70). In Germany it showed up around 1530–40, a good ten years after the Peasants' War (1525), and lasted until the Peace of Augsburg in 1555. In Italy the readjustment was completed about the time of the treaty of Cateau-Cambrésis (1559).

Did all this disorder come from Spain and from the American mines? We can believe it did. When running children form a whip by holding each other's hands, the last in line is likely to be jerked and pulled in all directions if he is to follow the others. Could this be the reason why the English crisis is the gravest and the clearest of all the ensuing crises? Could this be the reason why the chronology of these crises is not the same across Europe—because primitive communications made the continent much larger and much more diverse than it is today? Whatever the case, the crisis of the middle of the sixteenth century cut the century into two parts. The silver inflation after the 1560s was preceded by dramatic years when the many-sided recession brought harsh, disconcerting events which then brought on the succeeding crisis.

In France, from about 1536 to 1564, the brilliant years of the early reign of François I degenerated into the sad years of Henry II and the more dismal years of his successors. France was excluded from the race for empire in Europe. In 1529 the treaty of Cambrai put a check on French dreams of domination. Internal dangers then threatened her peace; after 1534 Protestantism in all parts of the country was to organize itself, growing aware of its strength during these harsh years. In 1562, when the Religious Wars broke out, the economy was to pick up. The period from 1536 to 1564, then, all things being considered, brought the decline of foreign wars and the slow preparation for an internal explosion. One is tempted to conclude that war, foreign or internal, can develop only in the wake of a slackening in economic life.

In England these somber years were equally dramatic. We find the devaluation of the pound sterling, the "dumping" of textiles destined for export, and the closing of commercial routes such as those English ships took in the first sixteenth century through the Mediterranean as far as Cyprus, where they found the protection of a British consulate. English ships were not to reappear on the Mediterranean until twenty years later, in 1573. In seeking to understand this decline in England, we cannot neglect the political and religious upheavals, in part the result of the policies of England's sovereigns: Henry VIII, whose personal needs produced the Anglican Church; Edward VI with his Calvinist and pro-Calvinist advisers; Catholic Mary Tudor; and then Elizabeth I, the second Anglican sovereign. Nevertheless, in the series of sudden economic changes we must not emphasize only the political passions or calculations of despotic English rulers or cautious monarchs such as Elizabeth I, for England experienced in its own way the profound and general transformation of European life.

Neither Italy nor Germany escaped the great crisis. In Germany the crisis started with the decline of the silver mines of central Europe between 1530 and 1540. The choice of 1555, the year of the Peace of Augsburg, as the terminal date of the crisis is dictated by the attractiveness of an important date in political history. There is no guarantee that this date coincides with a change in economic realities, however. The same uncertainty applies in the case of Italy. The temptation to rely on the usual turning points in political history is great. In 1530 besieged Florence was taken by Imperial forces; in 1559 the treaty of Cateau-Cambrésis was concluded, and several years later an investment boom ensued. It is true that these Italian and German dates cannot inspire blind confidence about the exact limits of the disaster, but on the whole it can be demonstrated that the entire European continent felt for a long time the aftereffects of the check or disturbance of its economic life. It was not before the 1560s that silver could produce fresh possibilities.

We know that this age of silver was not long in duration; it lasted from 1560 to 1600 or 1620, generally speaking. In various regions the availability of the same white metal served different ends. Considerations of the moment and differing economic structures have the disconcerting habit of producing diverse outcomes from the same conditions. In France historians have shown that the series of civil wars known as Religious Wars did not prevent some business growth, the accumulation of fortunes by clever businessmen, and the development of commercial cities such as Lyons, Marseilles, and Rouen. In the Low Countries the provinces of the north revolted, Protestantism was victorious, and the economy soared in an unprecedented fashion. In Germany prosperity increased gradually and national wealth grew, only to suffer a disastrous setback in the Thirty Years' War. In Italy it was the age of the last splendors and the last illusions. In Spain it was the "Golden Age"—but so baptized by literary historians. The economic historian cannot help viewing the Spanish Golden Age as a precocious thing, but already threatened at its material foundations.

## VIII

We might call the succeeding crisis either the third stage of the sixteenth century or the first stage of the seventeenth century. The name matters less than the facts it represents, and they may be interpreted in the light of events preceding them or following them. It is a fact that the tide rising out of the sixteenth century ebbed twice, once around 1600 and then in 1650 (between 1640 and 1660, to be more accurate). Wherever we have precise data, they indicate an alternation of slack periods, revivals, and further slack periods before a debacle destined to last until the next great period of expansion in the eighteenth century. As we change from one European country to another, the crisis appears at different moments and in different forms.

The first setback, from 1600 to 1610, was especially serious in Spain, and only a little less so in Italy. The second affected primarily the countries of the north: England, the Low Countries, and the Baltic. France seems to have been involved in both developments. After a period of reduced activity between 1590 and 1600 which did not bring the economy to a halt, France experienced a weak growth in strength during the first decades of the seventeenth century. Perhaps there were rather clear-cut differences in the evolutions of northern and southern France, but it would require more exact studies to prove this conclusively.

The one certain established fact of the time is the fundamental diversity of Europe, which cannot be considered a single economy, but rather a complex of economies held together loosely by bonds of commerce, by instruments of credit, and by exchanges of precious metals.

What was true of Europe was true of the New World. There can be no doubt that the expansion at the end of the sixteenth century can be traced to the reduced production of American silver mines and the subsequent decline in shipments of silver to Europe dating, according to experts, either from 1601 or from 1610. This decrease in the yield of the American mines is to be ascribed to the law of diminishing returns and to the decline of the Indian population of the New World, which became increasingly serious in the seventeenth century.

It would be wrong to conclude that the situation in the seventeenth century was any less complicated in the Americas than in Europe. The economic reversal there also came in successive waves: in New Spain around 1600, in Peru around 1620, in Brazil, which had been maintained by the special prosperity of the sugar industry, around 1640 or 1650. After the middle of the seventeenth century it is only a slight exaggeration to say that the Americas continued as if they had been abandoned by Europe and left to a new autonomous destiny, semi-European, semi-indigenous. Germán Arciniegas has most aptly named the following century the "American Middle Ages."

Nonetheless, it is impossible not to notice that these economic ground waves in Europe produced tremors in the New World. In fact, in the sixteenth and seventeenth centuries, major economic adjustments are simultaneous around the entire world, and the European situation had repercussions on the whole planet, even in faraway India, China, and Japan. In the Far East it seems that there were also dislocations and deteriorations in economic exchanges. For example, in India, despite our lack of precise dates, we can discern in the seventeenth century a slow deterioration in the superficial monetary economy whose meshes had stretched as far as Bengal. In Japan and China we have much more definite indications of economic difficulties. About 1640 Japan closed her doors to all European trade but continued to carry on a limited commerce with the Dutch. China under the imperial rule of the Mings underwent its final catastrophe in 1644, the year of the unresisted but disastrous occupation of Peking by the Manchus. Even if the Manchus had been made partly Chinese by long contact with Ming civilization, they and their Mongol allies were in many respects still barbarians, as the Mongolians had been in the thirteenth century. The subjection of China to her new rulers took place slowly and not without harsh and bloody struggles. Canton was not to fall before 1650. Amoy, where an

English factory had functioned for a short while, fell in 1681, and Formosa in 1683. Only then could the *pax sinica* spread its blessings everywhere and permit a real recovery to take place.

The coincidence of these dates raises a question about the world economy. Was there a world-wide development in two stages during the seventeenth century in which one part went under before the other in the course of these difficult years? The first segment of the whole would be comprised of Seville, the Americas, and the Mediterranean, and the second would consist of Amsterdam, the Baltic, the North Sea, the English Channel, a part of the Atlantic, the Indian Ocean, China, and Japan. There is no need to say that this is merely a hypothesis. But it is the most interesting point in a recent book by Pierre Chaunu, *The Philippines and the Iberian Pacific in the Sixteenth and Seventeenth Centuries* (Paris, 1960). This little book attempts to place the Pacific archipelago in its proper economic context. Might the Philippines be the key to the question we have raised, the link uniting the two large economic blocks of West and East? The author's intentions run parallel to ours, for the Philippines seem to him to be a principal link in the first world economy in history.

In 1565 the group of islands was reached by the Spaniard Legazpi, who had sailed from Acapulco, Mexico, and named the archipelago after Philip II. From that moment a regular maritime connection was maintained between New Spain and Manila. Each year a large ship made its way slowly from America to the Philippines and regularly met Chinese junks, which traded the gold, silk, and porcelain of China for pieces of eight and ingots of silver. The documents which permit us to measure the traffic between Acapulco and Manila have survived, a fortunate find such as historians seldom make.

The commercial activity of the Philippines scarcely came into its own until 1580, when the union of the crowns of Spain and Portugal put an end to competition between the two countries in the Far East, or at least reduced it considerably. Because of their late start, the Philippines cannot provide us with unassailable evidence for the entire second part of the sixteenth century; their testimony, on the other hand, is complete for the seventeenth century. The calculations of Chaunu distinguish three recession periods in the Philippines: 1611–15, 1616–20, 1631–35. Of these, the second seems the most decisive to him. And after 1640 there is no longer "a single index whose movement does not betray a catastrophic . . . decline."

Obviously, these prudently formulated figures do not allow any hard and fast conclusions. But, in any case, it seems that the islands did not follow the rapid decline of Seville, as we would expect. The net result of an examination of the case of the Philippines reveals a world-wide economic structure—incomplete, of course, for the world did not have the means to unite itself rigidly, but in places still solid enough to resist and even to survive the recession of the seventeenth century.

It is true that the bonds established in the optimistic commercial expansion of the sixteenth century were fated to be loosened, but they were not broken. It is also true that the establishment of these bonds had cost dearly: Chaunu estimates that the presence of Spain in the Philippines cost the Spanish King 15 to 20 percent of the total wealth he received from America. If we add to this the annual flight of precious metals to ports of the eastern Mediterranean and the drain on silver made by voyages around the Cape of Good Hope, we can only conclude that Europe paid a high price for the new economic unity of the world. Still, there were compensations which are difficult to calculate. In any case, there can be no doubt that during the first decades of the seventeenth century the effort to keep the world unified at any cost extended the economy as far as was possible at that time. A period of slackness followed, a period short of silver and accompanied by many financial credit stratagems and ruthless wars. These were characterized by a harsh discrimination between the victors and the vanquished natives rather than by the peaceful hegemony on the part of the whites that had been known during the periods of the sixteenth-century expansion. But this loosening of commercial bonds did not mean the complete abandonment of the world economy. The great world-wide adventure of Europe was not over; it was only suspended, awaiting the illustrious achievements of the eighteenth century.

## IX

We would like to review rapidly the conclusions of this essay. We took as a standpoint the growing unity of a world economy. We examined it as it came into being and then as arrested or suspended, or at least delayed, before it took hold vigorously a second time and produced the modern world.

First we must emphasize once again the fragility of this first unity of the world. One ship or one hundred ships cannot profoundly change the history of vast continents; they may open new horizons, of course, but that is not the same thing, especially in the short run. Furthermore, Europe exhausted her strength organizing, maintaining, and reestablishing the unending naval expeditions which lasted months and even years, frequently failed, resulted in numerous shipwrecks, and meant great losses of men and capital. Relatively speaking, they required as vast a mobilization of forces as the interplanetary missiles of today do. Moreover, in addition to the limitations imposed by the long distances and the rude technology of the times, rivalries between men and groups of men raised further obstacles. There was not one capitalism, but several European capitalisms, each with its zone and its circuits. Likewise, on a world-wide scale, one capitalism existed beside another, "rubbing elbows" perhaps, but never really coming in close touch with each other. The Italians gave a place to Jewish merchants from Portugal who were often masters of the trade from Alexandria or Cairo. Or they dealt with the Armenians, whose dealings in turn extended as far as the territory of the Banians from India. And if Italians traded with Moorish merchants or the Chinese, they did not enter those domains directly. We are concerned with regional capitalisms which penetrated each other very little. And each one was incapable of encircling the world singly.

All these obstacles added up to a definite limitation on the world economy, which remained delicate both in its over-all structure and in its imperfect parts. The reader must imagine a world far different from today's, inhabited by men whose economic problems were basically the same as ours, but whose solutions and whose resources could not equal ours. Each time the economy progressed, it was at an expense in human effort and human means which rapidly encountered insurmountable barriers. Then the momentum that had been built up came to a sudden halt and what had been a successful forward movement was undone and transformed into a regression. The retreat of the seventeenth century is one of these debacles of early capitalism. But the eighteenth century after 1750 was to embrace everything in its grasp and was not to be followed by a powerful check such as those of 1650–1750 and 1350–1450. This was because it lived to see an abrupt break-through in the conditions that had up to then severely handicapped human effort, for it witnessed the rapid developments of the industrial revolution which is still with us today.

It is perhaps difficult for students to imagine the immense importance of this break-through. In 1959, a Belgian economist, Fernand Baud'huin, heard a lecture by M. Medi, the president of Euratom, in which he predicted the miracles to come, such as artificial suns that would eliminate the night, the services of an inexhaustible source of energy at man's disposal to satisfy his needs and his whims. Envisioning a repetition of the revolution accomplished only yesterday by the steam engine, Baud'huin wrote, "If, in 1750, at the dawn of the industrial revolution the President of 'Eursteam' had announced the transformations he visualized, he would have stupefied his listeners. Instead of manual labor or animal power, in place of power from windmills or water mills, he would have spoken of 'fire machines' capable of producing energy in unlimited quantities. He would have said that sailboats were going to be replaced by steamboats, that even public works would no longer be able to use any but the most specialized labor force, replacing ditch-diggers. He would probably have produced the same impression as M. Medi when he announced discoveries destined to revolutionize the world and its products."

This comparison is not fanciful; it has the real value of reminding us that the first capitalism never really had available the resources and possibilities of harnessed energy and that we must judge the value of its achievements in the light of this essential limitation, for it provides us with the reasons for its successes and its failures.

## *FOR ADDITIONAL READING*

F. Braudel and F. Spooner. *The History of Prices, 1450–1750,* to be published in the forthcoming volume of *The Cambridge Economic History of Europe* (edited by E. Rich and C. Wilson).

A. Christensen. *Dutch Trade to the Baltic about 1600*. Copenhagen, 1941.

M. Dobb. *Studies in the Development of Capitalism*. London, 1947.

F. J. Fisher. "Commercial Trends and Policies in the Sixteenth Century," *Economic History Review,* 1940.

K. Glamann. *Dutch-Asiatic Trade 1620–1740*. Copenhagen, 1958.

E. J. Hamilton. *American Treasure and the Price Revolution in Spain, 1501-1650*. Cambridge, Mass., 1934.

F. C. Lane. *Venetian Ships and Shipbuilders of the Renaissance*. Baltimore, 1934.

K. M. Panikkar. *Asia and Western Dominance*. London, 1953.

R. de Roover. *The Medici Bank*. New York, 1948.

R. H. Tawney. *Religion and the Rise of Capitalism*. London, 1926.

A. P. Usher. *The Early History of Deposit Banking in Europe*. Cambridge, Mass., 1943.

M. Weber. *General Economic History*. Translated by F. H. Knight. New York, 1927.

C. Bauer. *Unternehmung und Unternehmungsformen im Spätmittelalter und in der beginnenden Neuzeit*. Jena, 1936.

L. Beutin. *Einführung in die Wirtschaftsgeschichte.* Cologne, 1958.

F. Braudel. *La Méditerranée et le monde méditerranéen à l'époque de Philippe II.* Paris, 1949.

R. Carande. *Carlos V y sus banqueros.* 2 vols. Madrid, 1941–49.

H. Hauser. *La modernité du XVIe siècle.* Paris, 1930.

G. Imbert. *Des mouvements de longue durée Kondratieff.* Aix-en-Provence, 1960.

A. and E. Kulischer. *Kriegs- und Wanderzüge; Weltgeschichte als Völkerbewegung.* Berlin, 1932.

J. M. Kulischer. *Allgemeine Wirtschaftsgeschichte des Mittelalters und Neuzeit.* Munich, 1928–29.

G. Luzzatto. *Storia economica.* Part I. Padua, 1932.

W. Sombart. *Der moderne Kapitalismus.* Munich, 1928.

F. Spooner. *L'économie mondiale et les frappes monétaires en France 1493–1680.* Paris, 1956.

# IX

# THE MORAL THOUGHT OF RENAISSANCE HUMANISM

*Paul Oskar Kristeller*

Moral Philosophy!

In the Western tradition that began with classical antiquity and continued through the Middle Ages down to modern times, the period commonly called the Renaissance occupies a place of its own and has its own peculiar characteristics. Historians have tried for a long time, and in various ways, to describe the civilization of the Renaissance. As a result, there has been so much controversy and difference of views that the so-called problem of the Renaissance has become the subject of an entire literature.

The traditional view of the Renaissance was formulated exactly 100 years ago by Jacob Burckhardt. In a most perceptive synthesis which focused on Italy in the fifteenth and early sixteenth century, he described the achievement of the period in the arts, literature, and scholarship, and stressed such general characteristics as individualism, the revival of antiquity, and the discovery of the world and of man. This picture was expanded and popularized by J. A. Symonds and others, among them those who stressed the pagan tendencies of the period more than Burckhardt had ever done. Other historians engaged in the task of analyzing the Renaissance as a broader European phenomenon, especially during the sixteenth century, and of exploring both the Italian influences and the national characteristics which the period assumed in each of the major European countries.

Burckhardt's views were challenged and criticized in a number of ways. Historians of the Middle Ages discovered that this period, especially in its later phases, had its own impressive achievements as a civilization, and was very far from a "dark age" that needed to make room for a period of "rebirth." In many instances, phenomena considered peculiar to the Renaissance were found to have had their counterparts or precedents in the Middle Ages. Historians of French literature, followed by those of other literatures, tended to minimize the Italian influences and to stress the independent contributions, during and before the Renaissance, of the other countries. Johan Huizinga, in his *Waning of the Middle Ages,* emphasized the thoroughly medieval features of so late a time as the fifteenth century, and his contribution is especially impressive since he focused on the Low Countries, an area that was at that time the chief artistic and economic center of Europe outside of Italy. While many historians, albeit with different evaluations, agreed that the Protestant and Catholic reformations of the sixteenth century put a sudden end to the secular and pagan culture radiating from Italy during the fifteenth century, others stressed the thoroughly religious character of the Renaissance in the northern countries, or even in Italy. One scholar, Giuseppe Toffanin, went so far as to suggest that Renaissance humanism was basically a Catholic reaction against the heretical tendencies inherent in the thought of the later Middle Ages. Continuity with the Middle Ages was the watchword of many historians who studied the economic and scientific development of the period —aspects that had been neglected by Burckhardt but have been particularly important in recent historical scholarship. Other historians speak of an actual economic and scientific decline during the fifteenth century, but this view is by no means shared by all specialists on the subject. These controversies are the more confusing since they affect even the chronological limits of the Renaissance period, whose beginning and end are subject to considerable fluctuation, depending on the persons or regions, developments or cultural aspects, on which the historian focuses his attention.

In the face of so much disagreement, one may only suggest that we apply the term Renaissance, which has by now become conventional, to the period in European history that goes at least from the middle of the fourteenth century to the beginning of the seventeenth. If we attach no value judgment to the term Renaissance, we shall not be surprised if we discover in the period many shortcomings as well as many achievements. If we grant that the Renaissance was a period of transition, we shall not be surprised to find in it many medieval as well as modern traits, and also some that are peculiar only to the Renaissance. There is no need to emphasize one of these aspects over the others for we can accept continuity as basic to history, while also realizing that historical continuity involves change as well as stability, and that a gradual change taking place over a period of several centuries is bound to be not only cumulative, but also to become considerable in the end. Each European country, we can also agree, made its own contribution to the civilization of the Renaissance, and did so in part by drawing upon its native medieval traditions, but Italy, both by the excellence of her own contributions and by the influence she exercised upon all other countries, occupied a position of cultural predominance that she never possessed before or after.

If the claim made by some older historians that the Renaissance was a period of revival after many dark centuries must now be subjected to severe qualification, the fact remains that writers of the period thought of their age as one that witnessed the rebirth of arts, letters, and learning after a long decay. Finally, in a complex, but articulated, civilization each area of culture may have its own distinct line of development. We have no reason to assume that the Renaissance, or any other period, must show the same characteristics, the same "style," the same rate of development or regional diffusion in art and literature, in politics, economy, or religion, in philosophy, or in the sciences. The perception of such a common style may be the ultimate aim of the historian of a period, but he cannot take it for granted at the start. Many of the controversies about the Renaissance are due to the tendency of historians to focus exclusively on one aspect of the culture of the period to make one-sided generalizations on the basis of their favorite subject matter, and to ignore the other relevant aspects of the era. To approach a more objective view of the Renaissance, it seems preferable to respect the independence of the various fields of human endeavor, without denying or neglecting their mutual relations.

## I

Within the broader outlines of Renaissance civilization, humanism may be considered as one of the more important, but limited, aspects or movements. The interpretation of Renaissance humanism, like that of the Renaissance itself, has been subject to a great deal of controversy and disagreement among recent historians. Moreover, humanism is even more difficult to define than is the Renaissance, since it is not enough to indicate its chronological limits. We must also try to describe its intellectual content and the range of its activities. This task is further complicated since the word *humanism* has come to stand for any kind of emphasis on human values. Quite naturally, when we hear Renaissance humanism mentioned, we think of an emphasis on human values that was supposedly current in the Renaissance period, or even was characteristic of that period. Humanism in this sense may certainly be found in the Renaissance, yet it was not as widespread as is often assumed. When historians speak of Renaissance humanism, they use the word in a sense that is different from our contemporary meaning. They are referring to a broad class of Renaissance intellectuals who are traditionally called humanists and who were active as teachers and secretaries, writers, scholars and thinkers; who exercised a wide and deep influence on all aspects of Renaissance civilization; and who left to posterity, along with the record of their lives and activities, vast writings that may be roughly classified as literature, historical and philological scholarship, and moral thought, but which often deal with such diverse subjects as philosophy and the sciences, literary and art criticism, education, government, and religion. The revival of antiquity generally associated with the Renaissance period, the thoroughgoing classicism that we notice in all its literary and artistic manifestations, is surely the direct or indirect effect of Renaissance humanism. When Georg Voigt, in 1859, described the earlier phases of Italian humanism, he emphasized its contributions to classical scholarship. Burckhardt and Symonds, without neglecting the impact of the humanists on Renaissance thought and literature, gave due importance to their work as historians and classical scholars. In later German scholarship this emphasis continued and was facilitated by the nineteenth-century use of the word *humanism,* then almost exclusively associated with the humanistic disciplines, that is, history and philology, and with the humanistic schools in which these disciplines were cultivated. On the other hand, because humanism seemed to predominate in Italian literature and civilization during the fifteenth century but to lose some of its importance during the sixteenth, Italian scholars tended to use "humanism" as a name for a period—mainly the fifteenth century—a period which scholars in other countries have called the early Renaissance. Recently, the tendency has been to shift emphasis from the scholarly and literary achievements of the humanists and to define the movement in terms of certain ideas or ideals. This tendency may be due to a declining respect for scholarship as such, and to the feeling that Renaissance humanism must be identified with a set of well-defined ideas if it is to be acceptable to contemporary opinion. The modern undertones of the word may also have played their part in the process. Konrad Burdach assigned to humanism a religious origin and considered its secular orientation a later development. Giuseppe Toffanin believed that Renaissance humanism was a Catholic reaction against certain heretical tendencies inherent in medieval thought. Douglas Bush, thinking of northern rather than Italian humanists, identifies the core of Renaissance humanism as Christian humanism, which shares with Thomas Aquinas the concern for harmony between ancient reason and

Christian faith. On the other hand, Hans Baron placed in the center of his interpretation the civic humanism of fifteenth-century Florence, which was primarily concerned with the training of responsible citizens leading active lives in a republican community. Finally, Eugenio Garin, in a number of well-informed and influential studies, used the term humanism as a common denominator for what was best in the philosophical thought of the Renaissance, stressing its preoccupation with the human and moral problems of the layman and its contrast with the theological orientation of medieval scholasticism.

## II

There is some truth in most of these views, but it is difficult to derive from them a clear and coherent picture of Renaissance humanism that would do justice to the movement as a whole. It is thus more useful perhaps to go back to the Renaissance meanings of the terms *humanist* and *humanities,* from which the modern term *humanism* is clearly derived. It seems that "humanist," probably coined in the slang of university students, designated a professional teacher of the humanities, and that "humanities," or *Studia humanitatis,* was understood to include such subjects as grammar, rhetoric, poetry, history, and moral philosophy. This well-defined cycle of studies consisted, in other words, of the subjects that would train a student to speak and write well, both in prose and in verse and primarily in Latin (which was still the accepted language of the schools and of the Church, of law, and of international diplomacy); it included the study and writing of history, and finally one of the philosophical disciplines—moral philosophy. Since the humanists were firmly convinced that it was necessary for each genre of writing to follow the models of ancient literature, the study of the Greek and Latin classics became a central and inseparable part of humanistic education: to study poetry meant to study the ancient poets as well as to learn how to write verse. In this way we can understand why Renaissance humanism was both literary and scholarly in its central concern, that classicism was at its heart, and why it spread through the influence of the humanists into all of Renaissance civilization. When the Renaissance scholars took over the classical term "humanities" for the studies in which they were interested, they meant to emphasize the human values inherent in these subjects, and the teaching of moral philosophy was an essential part of their program. In this way they were humanists also in the twentieth-century sense of the word.

Yet Renaissance humanism, unlike its twentieth-century namesake, was strongly committed to a cultural program and ideal, and it is this ideal that all Renaissance humanists have in common. The particular philosophical, religious, or political ideas by which modern historians have tried to define Renaissance humanism are actually found in the writings of some humanists, and many of them are intrinsically quite significant. Yet since these ideas were not shared by all humanists, and since such a large part of the work of the humanists was not concerned with ideas at all, but was literary or scholarly in character, a proper definition or understanding of the movement as a whole cannot be based on them. On the other hand, since the main, and, as it were, professional concern of the humanists was limited to the humanities, we should not assume, as many scholars do, that humanism was identical with Renaissance civilization or Renaissance learning as a whole. Theology and law, medicine and mathematics, astronomy, astrology and alchemy, logic, natural philosophy and metaphysics, the vernacular literatures, the visual arts and music were all vigorously cultivated during the Renaissance but not primarily by the humanists. Each discipline had its own traditions and development, and was pursued by its own specialists. If all were strongly influenced by Renaissance humanism, this influence was largely external to the discipline itself and limited in its nature. It was owing to those humanists who had a personal interest or competence in one or more of these other disciplines, or to those specialists in the other disciplines who had enjoyed a humanist education in their youth, as became more and more the rule after the middle of the fifteenth century. The nature of this humanist influence is also characteristic: it consists primarily in the introduction of fresh classical sources and in the restatement of their ideas, in the vogue of classical quotations and allusions, in the use of the newly refined methods of historical and philological scholarship, and in an attempt to replace the specialized terminology of the medieval schools, their tight methods of arguing, their elaborate commentaries and disputed questions, by treatises, dialogues, and essays written in a smooth and elegant style.

Since moral philosophy, unlike the other philosophical disciplines, was considered a part of the humanities, we can easily understand that the moral thought of the Renaissance was closely associated with the humanist movement. A considerable part of the moral literature of the Renaissance was written by humanists, or by laymen with a humanist training, and practically all writers on moral subjects were influenced by humanism. The connection of this literature with humanism accounts for several of its peculiar features.

Many, if not all, of the humanists were teachers, so that their moral thought was strongly centered on the education of the young. The humanists considered classical antiquity their major guide and model in thought and literature and their moral writings are accordingly studded with quotations from Greek and Roman authors, with episodes from classical history and mythology, with ideas and theories derived from ancient philosophers and writers. Finally, the humanists were professional rhetoricians, that is, writers and critics, who wished not only to say the truth, but to say it well, according to their literary taste and standards. They believed in the ancient rhetorical doctrine that a professional speaker and writer must acquire and show skill in making any idea that is related to his chosen topic plausible to his public. Consequently, a given idea is often expressed in phrases that aim at elegance rather than at precision, and many times, especially in a dialogue or in a speech, opinions may be defended with vigor and eloquence that are appropriate for the occasion, but do not express the author's final or considered view.

## III

Moral teaching is often contained in literary genres cultivated by the humanists where a modern reader might not expect to find it. The humanists inherited from the ancient and medieval grammarians and literary critics the view that moral instruction is one of the main tasks of the poet. Hence there is a moral or even moralistic note in some of the poetry they wrote, and in the interpretation they gave of the ancient poets in the classroom and in their published commentaries. The humanists also followed ancient and medieval theory and practice in their belief that the orator and prose writer is a moral teacher and ought to adorn his compositions with pithy sentences quoted from the poets or coined by himself. To facilitate his task, a humanist would gather quotations and sentences in a commonplace book, and some writers would publish collections of sentences, proverbs, or historical anecdotes from which an author could freely quote on the appropriate occasion. Plutarch's *Apophthegmata,* in humanist translations, enjoyed great popularity for this reason, and Erasmus's *Adagia,* collected from many ancient sources and revised and enlarged several times by the author, was printed and used, though not always quoted, for several centuries.

Finally, another branch of study cultivated by the humanists, history, had moral significance for them. The humanists shared the view of many ancient and medieval authors that one of the tasks of historiography is to teach a moral lesson. Much Renaissance historiography is sustained by this belief. In the same way, the extensive biographical literature produced during the period is often animated by the desire to supply the reader with models worthy of imitation. The medieval lives of saints provided a precedent, since they too were written to provide the reader with models of pious conduct. But it makes a difference whether the persons whose lives are described as models of human conduct are Christian saints or ancient statesmen and generals, philosophers and poets, contemporary princes, citizens, or artists. The Renaissance continued to produce biographies of the saints, but it left a much larger number of secular biographies. The lives of famous ancients as written by Petrarch and other humanists were clearly intended to provide models for imitation, since classical antiquity was for the humanists the admired model in all fields of human endeavor. No wonder that in a famous humanist controversy the relative superiority of the Romans Scipio and Caesar served as a basis for discussing the merits of republican and monarchical government. When Machiavelli in his *Discourses on Livy* holds out the institutions and actions of the Roman republic as a model to his contemporaries, he follows the practice of his humanist predecessors, and he states his underlying assumption more clearly than any of them had done: human beings are fundamentally the same at all times, and therefore it is possible to study the conduct of the ancients, to learn from their mistakes and from their achievements, and to follow their example where they were successful.

If we turn from these writings of the humanists in which a moral or moralistic interest appeared to those works which deal explicitly with moral philosophy, we may notice the favorite genres used for this kind of literature. Most important are the treatise and the dialogue, and later on, the essay. More marginal forms are the oration and the letter, the most widespread forms of humanist literature, which at times, serve to express moral ideas. The letter was especially popular with the humanists, as it allowed them to express their views in a personal and subjective fashion, although they considered letter-writing a branch of literature, and gave the same polished elegance to their letters as to their other literary compositions. To these we might add the collections of sentences, proverbs, and commonplaces.

The language of these writings was usually Latin, but the use of the vernacular appears especially in Tuscany during the fifteenth century, and becomes more widespread in the rest of Italy and of Europe during the sixteenth. The choice of language indicated the reading public to which an author wished to address a given work. Latin writings were intended for an international audience of scholars and of educated alumni of humanist schools, while within a particular country or region works in the vernacular were read chiefly by a middle class of ladies, businessmen, and artisans who were able to read and eager to be entertained and instructed, but who usually knew no Latin and lacked a humanist school education or a university training.

## IV

The existence of this large body of moral literature written by humanists and popularizers, and of the still larger body of humanist learning and literature, is in itself a significant historical phenomenon. We are confronted with a vast body of secular learning, nourished from ancient sources and contemporary experience, and basically independent of, though not entirely unrelated to, the medieval traditions of scholastic philosophy and science, theology and law. As a part of this learning, or derived from it, we find a body of moral thought that is never opposed to religious doctrine—often explicitly harmonized with it—existing side by side with religious doctrine and claiming for its domain wider and wider areas of human life and experience. There are several medieval precedents for such secular moral thought, but these were different and more limited in scope. Certain moralists like Cicero, Seneca, and Boethius had enjoyed a continuous popularity throughout the Middle Ages, and medieval grammarians had tried to provide moral interpretations of ancient poets such as Ovid and Virgil. This tradition was apparently absorbed by Renaissance humanism in its beginnings in the fourteenth century. When Aristotle's writings were all translated into Latin and adopted as textbooks of philosophy at Paris and other universities during the thirteenth century, his *Ethics,* along with his *Politics,* his *Rhetoric,* and the *Economics* attributed to him, was expounded in the classroom, and a number of commentaries on these works owe their origin to this teaching tradition, although the course on ethics was an elective rather than a required course, and considered less important than logic or natural philosophy. Thus Aristotle's doctrines of the virtues and of the supreme good, and also his theory of the passions as presented in the *Rhetoric,* were well known to students of philosophy and to many others. When the humanists took over much of the teaching of ethics in the fifteenth century and wrote general treatises on moral subjects, they continued to use the Aristotelian writings, which recommended themselves by their topical completeness and the wealth of their detail, and the humanists often tended to follow his views though they might interpret them in a different way or combine them with theories derived from other sources. Finally, in the later Middle Ages there had developed a code of moral conduct for knights, that is, for a privileged class of laymen, and this code found its literary expression in lyrical poetry, in romances in verse and prose, and in a few theoretical treatises. The moral literature of the Renaissance was similarly intended for laymen rather than for clerics. Yet aside from its heavy classical equipment which had been lacking in the medieval literature of the knights, it was written by and for a different class of people: it had a different political, economic, and social foundation.

Renaissance humanism, which began in Italy toward the very end of the thirteenth century, at the earliest, cannot be explained as a delayed but direct result of the economic and political development of the city communities that began in the eleventh century. For even a theory of a "cultural lag," whatever that may mean, does not seem to supply the missing link, as there was, after all, a distinctive tradition of learning and literature in twelfth- and early thirteenth-century Italy that was not humanistic. On the other hand, an urban, not a feudal society provided at least the background of Renaissance civilization. The Renaissance humanists wrote their moral works for their fellow scholars, for their students, and for an elite of businessmen and of urbanized noblemen who were willing to adopt their cultural and moral ideals. During the sixteenth century, ever wider circles of the middle class seem to have taken interest in this literature.

Political theory was traditionally a part of ethics or a supplement to it, and the Renaissance moralists took a strong and sometimes primary interest in political theory. The nature of their political ideas varied a good deal according to circumstances. There was a tradition of civic and republican humanism, especially in Florence, and to a lesser degree in Venice, whose historical significance has been recently emphasized by Hans Baron and other scholars. Yet much Renaissance political thinking developed also along monarchical lines, especially during the sixteenth century. Both Machiavelli and Thomas More were also linked to the humanist movement.

Aside from the political treatises, the moral literature of the Renaissance addressed itself mainly to the private individual. The political and economic realities of the day are taken more or less for granted, and the purpose of the moral treatise is to give theoretical or practical instruction to the individual, especially to the young. The lines between decency and success are not always as clearly drawn as we might wish, and as a result, the word virtue came to have a curious ambiguity. It meant moral virtue, to be sure, but Machiavelli's *virtù* stood more for the strong character that assured political success, and the "virtuoso" was distinguished by intellectual and social skill rather than by moral excellence.

At this point, we might very well stop to consider the variety of meanings of the term "moral thought," both for the Renaissance and in its wider applications. When we speak of the morals of a person or a period, we think primarily of actual behavior, and assume that this behavior expresses some conscious or unconscious convictions, although it may be quite contrary to the professed ideals of the person and of the time. In this respect, the Renaissance, and especially the Italian Renaissance, enjoys a dubious reputation. In the popular view, which seems to find support in Symonds and other historians, the Italian Renaissance was a period of political ruthlessness, of crimes of violence and of passion; and the glittering melodrama of dagger and poison seems to provide an appropriate foil for the admired beauty of Renaissance poetry and painting. Examples of crime and cruelty were numerous in the Renaissance, in Italy and elsewhere, as they are in other periods of history, including the Middle Ages and our century. However, not all the stories and anecdotes that found their way from the Renaissance chroniclers and gossip-writers into modern textbooks of history are well documented, and those that we can accept were probably disapproved of in their own time as much as in ours. Moreover, it would be quite wrong to assume that such misdeeds dominated the picture of public or private life during the Renaissance. There were a great many decent people whose conduct agreed with the highest moral standards.

Yet, ignoring the actual conduct of people during the Renaissance or whatever secret or unexpressed thought may have guided them, and examining those moral ideas that we find more or less explicitly stated in the literature of the period we find that moral subjects were discussed in a variety of ways. An author may describe the actual moral customs and manners of his time, either through examples, as is often done in narrative literature, or through a discussion of their general traits, without explicitly setting forth any standards of how people should behave. He may also, however, try to guide the conduct of people, especially of his younger readers, by prescribing how they should behave. Description and prescription are often confused in our contemporary discussions of moral and social problems, and they cannot always be kept apart in Renaissance literature, but it would help proper understanding of such discussions if the distinction is clearly kept in mind. In the literature which emphasizes the prescriptive aspect and tends to set standards for the young, we must distinguish between those authors who are mainly concerned with rules of prudence and expediency, and teach their readers how to behave in order to get along with other people and to have a successful career, and those who emphasize honesty and moral decency regardless of their practical consequences. In works of the latter kind there is often a mixture of ethical theory, which properly belongs to philosophy, and of moral exhortation and persuasion, which belongs to oratory and tends toward edification. Finally, there is the literature of strictly philosophical ethics, which intends to set forth general principles of moral thought and which is prescriptive only in an implicit way or by deducing rules of conduct from those general principles. This literature may take the form of systematic handbooks of ethics or of monographic treatises dealing with specific topics in ethics.

All these types are present in the moral literature of the Renaissance, and it would be wrong to say that any of them is limited to a particular phase of the period. However, the literature of the fifteenth and early sixteenth century is more frequently concerned with moralistic prescription and edification. As the sixteenth century progresses, rules of expediency and descriptions of manners and customs tend to prevail. One gets the impression of a more settled society in which standards of conduct and manners are well established and the main task of the young man is not to acquire valid ethical principles through independent critical thinking but rather to assure his success by learning how to adjust to life—that is, to the accepted modes of moral thought and conduct. This literature gains in historical and psychological interest what it loses in ethical solidity, and it leads the way towards such famous examples of seventeenth-century literature as Gracian, La Bruyère, or La Rochefoucauld.

## V

In contrast to the books of manners stand the philosophical treatises on ethics that supply whatever theoretical structure and systematic thinking on moral problems there was during the Renaissance. Because of the general direction of Renaissance humanism, most, though not all, of their subject matter is derived from classical sources. The authors known during the

Middle Ages, especially Aristotle, Cicero, and Seneca, continue to be important and in some ways become even more important, as there is a greater effort to interpret and to utilize them in great detail. Equally important are some other sources of ancient moral philosophy made available for the first time by humanist scholarship. These new sources include most of the writings of Plato and of the Neoplatonists, Stoic authors such as Epictetus and Marcus Aurelius, Sceptics like Sextus Empiricus, and Epicureans like Lucretius. Diogenes Laertius supplied new information on several schools of ancient thought, especially on Epicurus. Of equal, if not even greater, importance were a number of popular ancient moralists not identified with any particular school of philosophy, such as Xenophon and Isocrates, Plutarch and Lucian. The number both of their translations and of the quotations taken from them shows that they were among the favorite sources of Renaissance humanists.

The impact of these various sources and schools on the moral thought of the Renaissance was varied and complex. Moreover, the history of moral thought during the Renaissance is related to, but not identical with, the history of philosophy. Only a part of the moral literature of the period came from philosophers in the technical sense of the word, or was systematic in content. On the other hand, some of the most important philosophers of the Renaissance, and even entire groups and schools of Renaissance philosophy, such as the Aristotelians, the Platonists, and the philosophers of nature, were not interested primarily in ethics but made their major contributions to other parts of philosophy, especially logic, metaphysics, and natural philosophy. With these qualifications, we may say that there was a solid body of Aristotelian ethics throughout the Renaissance period. Its most obvious expressions are the numerous editions, translations, commentaries, and summaries of the ethical writings of Aristotle, among which the *Eudemian Ethics* now takes its proper place for the first time, and of their ancient and medieval interpreters. This literature has not been sufficiently explored until recent times, and we are just beginning to learn more about it. However, we may safely say of the Aristotelian ethics what has become apparent about Renaissance Aristotelianism in general. It continues in many ways the traditions of medieval Aristotelianism, which were very much alive at the universities, in Italy as elsewhere. On the other hand, there was among the humanists a strong tendency to recapture the genuine thought of Aristotle apart from its supposed distortions by medieval translators and commentators. Finally, there were all kinds of combinations on the part of Aristotelian philosophers, who tried to reconcile and to synthesize what seemed to be valuable in the scholastic and humanistic interpretations of Aristotle. In the study of ethics, as in other disciplines, the main contribution of the humanists to Aristotelian studies was to supply new translations based on a better philological understanding of the Greek text. This is more important than one might suspect. For in an author as difficult and elusive as Aristotle, whose every word was (and still is) considered by many thinkers as the ultimate source and authority of philosophical truth, a different translation may be equivalent to a different philosophy. Moreover, whereas the medieval scholastics treated Aristotle pretty much in isolation, the humanist Aristotelians read and interpreted Aristotle in close conjunction with the other Greek philosophers and writers. On the whole, the humanist Aristotelians were primarily interested in Aristotle's ethical writings. Leonardo Bruni translated and summarized only Aristotle's *Ethics, Politics* and *Economics,* while Francesco Filelfo wrote a summary of ethics based on Aristotle. Ermolao Barbaro, though not limited to Aristotle's ethical writings, favored them in his lectures and in a summary of ethics. Philip Melanchthon, Luther's colleague, wrote several treatises on ethics, in which Aristotle's doctrine is preferred to that of other ancient philosophers, and it was due to Melanchthon's influence that the Reformed universities of Protestant Germany continued to base their teaching of philosophy on the works of Aristotle.

As a result of this widespread study of Aristotle, practically every writer of the period was acquainted with the main doctrines of Aristotelian ethics and was inclined to adopt them or to discuss them. Aristotle's views that the supreme good of man must include a minimum of external advantages and that the contemplative life is the highest goal of human existence are as familiar in the moral literature of the Renaissance as are his distinction between moral and intellectual virtues, his definition of the moral virtues as habits and as means between two opposite vices, and his detailed descriptions of individual virtues and vices.

Plato's influence on the moral thought of the Renaissance is much more limited than Aristotle's, in spite of the well-known role played generally by Platonism in Renaissance philosophy. Plato's early dialogues, to be sure, deal with moral topics, and were widely read in school, mainly in courses of Greek. Yet we do not find any system of ethics based primarily on Plato, as so many were on Aristotle. This is due partly to the unsystematic character of Plato's writings. More important, the leading Platonists of the Renaissance, like their late ancient and medieval predecessors, were interested in questions of metaphysics and cosmology rather than of ethics. They were not so much concerned with specific moral problems or theories but tended to reduce all ethical questions to the single task of attaining the contemplative life. Some of their specific theories that are relevant to moral thought we shall encounter later. The most important and widespread contribution of Platonism to the subject is the theory of love, based on the *Symposium* and *Phaedrus,* which was to constitute the subject matter of poems and lectures and of a special branch of prose literature. Among the moralists not committed to any special school of philosophy, quotations and borrowings from Plato were frequent, and became increasingly so after the rise of Florentine Platonism during the second half of the fifteenth century.

Stoic ethics as expressed in the writings of Seneca, and discussed in Cicero's philosophical works, had been a familiar ingredient of medieval moral thought, and continued to exercise a widespread influence during the Renaissance, when the writings of these Roman authors became even more popular than they had been before. The Stoic view that the supreme good of man consisted of virtue alone and that to secure virtue all passions must be thoroughly eradicated was generally known and often approved. Some Stoic theories appealed even to thinkers, such as Pomponazzi, who cannot be labeled as Stoic philosophers in their general orientation. Yet in contrast with this popular and eclectic Stoicism based on Cicero and Seneca, which permeated the moral thought of the fifteenth and early sixteenth century, it was only during the latter part of the sixteenth century that the Greek sources of ancient Stoicism became better known and that systematic attempts were made to restate Stoic philosophy (and especially Stoic ethics) in its original purity. The distinguished humanist, Justus Lipsius, compiled from the ancient sources a valuable handbook of Stoic ethics that was to enjoy great popularity during the seventeenth century, and the French writer, Guillaume Du Vair, gave a more literary expression to the same doctrine. Most Renaissance humanists found Stoic ethics uncongenial on account of its rigidity. The great vogue of pure Stoicism came only in the seventeenth century. In order to understand this later appeal, we must remember that the Stoics are rigorous only in their emphasis on the difference between virtue and vice, but reserve a very large area of human life to the things they call morally indifferent. Where questions of virtue and vice are not involved the Stoic sage is allowed and even encouraged to follow expediency. With virtue and vice often limited to a few ultimate decisions, the sway of expediency becomes very large indeed, and the Stoic moralist, while continuing to be rigorous in theory, may turn out to be lax, if not selfish, on most practical questions. The same may happen to the Platonist (and to the mystic), as soon as he has to act on matters unrelated to the life of contemplation.

The ethics of Epicurus, which proposed intellectual pleasure as the chief end of human life, was widely known in the Renaissance, and frequently discussed. Most humanists rejected Epicurean ethics and were more or less influenced by Cicero's unsympathetic account of that doctrine. Yet gradually the more favorable presentation of Epicurus in the works of Lucretius and Diogenes Laertius became better known, and Epicurus's emphasis on intellectual pleasure was more fully appreciated. Thus Epicurean ethics was endorsed by a few humanists, such as Lorenzo Valla and Cosimo Raimondi, and some of its tenets made an impression on thinkers whose general outlook was very different—for example, Marsilio Ficino.

Finally, ancient scepticism had a number of followers in the Renaissance, especially in the sixteenth century, when the writings of Sextus became more widely known. The main appeal of scepticism was in its claim that by abandoning all rigid doctrines and opinions we free ourselves from unnecessary worries and are left to face only the unavoidable necessities of life. If we wish to have a standard for our conduct, we should follow the customs of our country, at least in all matters that concern other people. In this way the boundaries between moral standards and established manners tend to be blurred, although there may remain a realm of personal and individual life in which we may think and do as we please. Scepticism in matters of reason is by no means incompatible with religious faith, as the example of Augustine may show; consequently this position had many more followers during the sixteenth century than is usually realized. The chief expression of this sceptical ethics is found in some of the essays of Montaigne, and in the writings of his pupil, Pierre Charron.

## VI

The influence of ancient ethics on the Renaissance is not limited to an acceptance of the main systematic theories of antiquity by some Renaissance thinkers. The constant use of specific ancient ideas or sentences or examples in the discussion of moral topics is more widespread. This eclectic use of ancient material, for which some favorite author such as Cicero could serve as a classical model, is especially characteristic of the humanists and their popular followers. In this way, particular ideas or sentences taken from a given philosopher, such as Plato or Aristotle, were indiscriminately combined with those of other philosophers who held a very different position on major questions or with those of ancient moralists like Isocrates, Lucian, or Plutarch, who cannot even be credited with a coherent systematic position in philosophy. Thus the sharp boundaries between philosophical concepts or theories derived from different sources tend to vanish. Furthermore, Renaissance humanists were not so much interested as modern scholars are in emphasizing the distinctive traits of various periods, schools, and writers of antiquity or in playing up one against the other. They tended to admire ancient literature in all its periods and representatives (although some authors were more admired than others), and to be syncretistic as well as eclectic; that is, they liked to harmonize the views of various classical authors, and to extract from their writings a kind of common wisdom that could be learned, imitated, and utilized.

The numerous classical quotations that characterize most humanist treatises and even the essays of Montaigne, and which are apt to bore and annoy the modern reader, were not vain displays of empty erudition, although they might often serve this purpose. The quotations served as authorities—as confirmations of the validity of what the author was trying to say. Quotations from recognized authors were counted by ancient theorists of rhetoric among the forms of proof that an orator was supposed to produce. Augustine had emphasized the authority of Scripture as a chief source of theological discourse, and during the Middle Ages not only theology but each discipline of knowledge employed its standard authorities, along with rational arguments, in support of its theories. For a Renaissance humanist, a sentence from a classical writer served as such an authority, and if he added to his quotation what seems to us an arbitrary interpretation, he merely did what his predecessors and contemporaries also had done. In a period in which the emphasis is on authority and tradition, originality will assert itself in the adaptation and interpretation of the tradition. Moreover, there may be some originality even in the choice of one's quotations. It makes a difference whether an author keeps quoting the same passages that had been quoted by his predecessors or for the first time introduces new quotations, singling them out from their context and, as it were, discovering their significance.

The frequency of quotations and of commonplaces repeated in the moral literature of the Renaissance gives to all but its very best products an air of triviality that is often very boring to the modern critical reader, especially when he is acquainted with the ancient sources from which the quotations are drawn and in which they seem to have a much more subtle and precise meaning. If we want to do justice to these Renaissance writers we must try to understand the circumstances under which they wrote, and the purposes which they had in mind. Whenever many books of the same type are written, most of them are bound to be dull and mediocre, and only a few will stand out by reason of their authors' intellectual or literary merits. Human inventiveness seems limited, and repetition is the rule rather than the exception, even where no direct copying or plagiarism is involved. After all, no single reader was expected to read all the treatises on the same topic, just as a modern student will not read more than one or two textbooks on the same subject. Each treatise is addressed to its own readers, and must supply to them the same amount of general information that other readers may derive from other works on the same topic. This is even more the case with orations, which were delivered on only a single occasion and were published only incidentally when they happened to be very successful. An oration is composed to entertain and edify its audience by adapting general ideas to the occasion. While it was the custom in Florence to have each incoming group of magistrates treated to a speech in praise of justice, it was not so important that the orator should produce new or profound ideas about the meaning of justice—it was his job to impress his listeners with their duty to follow justice in the administration of their office. This was surely of great practical importance for the city as a whole. Since the oration was a principal form of humanist literature, the example might be applied to its other branches. Each moral treatise had to exhort and edify its readers by instructing them in matters of great practical and human importance, and this was in most instances more valuable than the presentation of novel or original thoughts. In other words, we should not approach the average moral literature of the Renaissance with excessive expectations as to its depth or originality, but with an awareness of its limited purposes, and a recognition that it was well suited to these objectives.

## VII

The frequency of ancient ideas and quotations in the moral writings of the Renaissance humanists, and of humanist literature in general, raises another question that has been the subject of much debate: what was the attitude of the Renaissance humanists toward Christianity, and in what sense and to what extent were they inclined toward paganism? The charge of paganism was made against the humanists by some theologians of their own time, and it has been repeated by a number of modern historians, some of whom have turned the charge into praise. There were, however, very few attempts to revive the pagan religions of classical antiquity, although this has been charged by contemporaries and by modern scholars in a few instances. Although much was made of pagan mythology in the poetry and also in the prose treatises of the period, it was not intended to replace the use of Christian religious thought and imagery but to supplement it. In most instances it was no more than a literary ornament sanctioned by ancient precedent. Where it served a more serious intention, its use was justified by allegory—by attributing to the pagan stories a hidden meaning that was in accordance with Christian truth. This attitude culminates in Pico della Mirandola's notion of a poetic theology, that is, of a philosophical and theological truth that could be discovered through the allegorical interpretation of pagan poetry and mythology. Yet the main impact of "paganism" on the moral thought of the Renaissance consists in its heavy indebtedness to ancient philosophical ideas, which we have already noted. The task of assimilating the moral and philosophical thought of the ancients to Christianity presented itself to the Church Fathers and again to many medieval thinkers. From these earlier attempts, the Renaissance differed at least in degree, if not in kind. The Church Fathers tended to fit Christianity into the ancient modes of thought that had been previously familiar to them and to their contemporaries. The humanists wanted to adapt classical ideas to a previously accepted Christian view of the world. Nevertheless, the affinity between the humanists and the Church Fathers has been stressed with some justification by modern historians like Toffanin, and the humanists themselves were to some extent aware of this affinity. For when they defended "poetry," that is, humanist learning and the reading of the pagan authors, against the theological critics of their own time, they cited the precedent of the Church Fathers. No doubt Bruni's translation of the letter in which Basil, one of the Fathers, defended the reading of pagan poets by a Christian youth owed its tremendous popularity to this issue. There were many humanists who were not concerned with religious or theological problems, and did not touch on them in their writings. Those who did, and they were important, never undertook a general critique of the religious tradition such as appeared in the eighteenth century. They usually praised the Bible and the Church Fathers as the Christian classics, and attacked scholastic theology as a barren distortion of original Christian doctrine and piety. A few of them attacked the weaknesses they observed in the Church of their time, and especially in monasticism. When the humanists wrote about moral subjects, either they tried to combine and to harmonize ancient and Christian ideas in the manner of Erasmus, or they discussed moral topics on a purely classical and secular basis—without however indicating any hostility toward Christianity, but rather taking for granted the compatibility between the two, as was done by Alberti and many other Italian humanists. In the sixteenth century, after the Protestant and Catholic reformations, we find humanist scholars and moralists among the followers of both major camps, as well as among those who favored some of the smaller heretical movements, or who tried hard to keep aloof from the religious struggle. This shows once more, that Renaissance humanism as a whole cannot be identified with a particular set of opinions or convictions, but is rather characterized by a cultural ideal and a range of scholarly, literary, and intellectual interests that the individual humanist was able to combine with a variety of professional, philosophical, or theological convictions.

## VIII

If we try to survey in more concrete detail the moral thought of the Renaissance period, it seems best to focus on the chief genres and themes of this literature, rather than on the ideas of individual writers and thinkers. The character of this literature, with its uncertain position between philosophical and popular thought, its dependence on classical sources, and its widespread eclecticism and triviality, seems to call for such an approach.

The most technical type of Renaissance literature on moral topics is the general treatise on ethics that was usually written for the use of students. Since Aristotle was and remained the chief basis of university instruction in the philosophical disciplines, many general treatises on ethics take the form of commentaries on Aristotle's *Nicomachean Ethics* and *Politics,* or of introductions, paraphrases, and summaries of those works. In the fifteenth century, the commentary of Donato Acciaiuoli and the *Compendium* of Ermolao Barbaro deserve mention; and in the sixteenth century there was Francesco Piccolomini, a Paduan, and a few other scholars such as Alessandro Piccolomini, who composed a handbook of Aristotelian ethics in Italian, indicating by this very fact that he was addressing himself to a broader educated public. Outside of Italy, the introductions of Jacques Lefèvre d'Etaples' to Aristotle's writings on moral philosophy and Melanchthon's ethical writings represent the most influential attempts to restate Aristotle's ethics—

especially his belief that the natural goods contribute to the supreme good of happiness and that the moral virtues are means between two opposite extremes—and to harmonize this natural ethics with the teachings of Scripture. John Case's moral questions on Aristotle, which originated in Oxford, are important as a rare example of a type of literature that must have flourished also at the English universities to a greater degree than is usually realized. More eclectic but still largely Aristotelian are the handbooks of Francesco Filelfo and of Sebastian Fox Morcillo. An early and very popular introduction to ethics, Leonardo Bruni's *Isagogicon Moralis Disciplinae,* follows Aristotle in the discussion of the moral and intellectual virtues, but advances a somewhat ecelectic view on the supreme good. He bases the ultimate end of human life mainly on virtue but also grants some importance to external advantages and thus stays close enough to Aristotle's position, but at the same time he claims that this view is essentially identical with those of the Stoics and Epicureans. The most consistent attempt to present Stoic ethics in a systematic handbook was made by Justus Lipsius toward the end of the sixteenth century. Its major effects were to be felt only during the following century.

Aside from such handbooks of ethics, there are a number of more informal humanist treatises and dialogues in which the central topic of ancient ethics, that is, happiness or the supreme good, is discussed. Whereas Petrarch had blamed Aristotle for his belief that man may attain his ultimate end during the present life, an attitude echoed by Bartolommeo Fazio and others, many writers identified the goal of life with the knowledge and enjoyment of God but thought that this goal could be attained during the present life, at least by some people and for some time. This view was held especially by the leading Platonist, Marsilio Ficino, who wrote several short treatises on it. Bartolommeo Platina stresses endurance and wisdom in a Stoic sense, and Pietro Pomponazzi approaches Stoicism rather than the view of Aristotle when in his treatise on immortality he defines moral virtue as the task peculiar to human beings, and emphasizes that this virtue is its own reward, just as wickedness is its own punishment. Also the Epicurean view that pleasure is the supreme good found its defenders. The most famous of them, Lorenzo Valla, considers Epicureanism as the best among the pagan philosophies but endorses as his own view a kind of Christian Epicureanism in which the pleasures of the present life are abandoned for the sake of the pleasures, both physical and spiritual, which are promised in a future life to the faithful Christian.

A number of humanistic treatises deal with individual virtues, a subject that occupies a large part of Aristotle's *Ethics* and now is singled out for monographic treatment. Several of the virtues are discussed in the moral treatises of the Neapolitan humanist, Giovanni Pontano, such as courage, magnanimity, or prudence. Attempts to define the respective virtues are accompanied by a variety of moral rules and examples, and the concern is as much with stylistic elegance and moral edification, as with precise philosophical definitions or distinctions. Similar treatises were written by several Italian and other humanist writers.

A whole literature was dedicated to the highest virtue, wisdom, which was identified either with the attainment of pure knowledge, or with moral and practical ability in the affairs of life. The latter tendency culminated in Pierre Charron, theologian and sceptical philosopher of the early seventeenth century. Analogous treatises were written on some specific vices such as ingratitude or avarice. There is a famous treatise on avarice by Poggio Bracciolini, in which some of the beneficial effects of this vice also are mentioned, in a way which some historians have tended to link with the spirit of modern capitalism.

## IX

The humanist movement was closely identified with a reform of the program and curriculum of the secondary schools. Many of the humanists were professional tutors or school teachers, and it was through the training offered in the schools that most of the educated persons of the Renaissance period were influenced by humanist ideas, which they then carried into the larger spheres of public and professional life. Hence it was natural that the humanists would be very much concerned with the tasks and problems of education. The treatises on the education of the young form a large and important genre of humanist prose, and thanks to these treatises Renaissance humanism occupies as prominent a place in the history of educational theory as in that of educational practice.

The most influential early treatises were by Pier Paolo Vergerio the Elder and by Leonardo Bruni, to which we may add the treatise on education attributed to Plutarch that was translated by Guarino of Verona, who along with Vittorino da Feltre was the most famous and successful humanist teacher in fifteenth-century Italy. Other influential educational treatises were written by Maffeo Vegio and by Enea Silvio Piccolomini, a prominent humanist who entered the ecclesiastic career and finally became pope under the name of Pius II. Outside of Italy, educational treatises were written by many humanists such as Erasmus and Vives, by Wimpfeling and Camerarius in Germany, and by Ascham in England. These treatises were written either for the young students themselves or for the parents of prospective students to convince them of the value of a humanist education. A good deal of attention is paid to the praise of Greek and Latin literature, whose study formed the core of humanist instruction, and to the value of such an education for the future citizen or statesman. Often the author would offer actual reading lists, discussing the merits and educational value of specific classical authors and their different works. Aside from the genuine concern for a ruling class thoroughly imbued with a cultural heritage of unquestioned intellectual importance, the humanist educators laid much stress on the moral value inherent in the study of ancient literature, history, and philosophy. Through the reading of the classical authors, the student was to acquire a fund of moral ideas, sentences, and examples that would give him the necessary preparation to face the tasks of his own life. In stressing the moral value of a classical education, the humanists effectively countered the charge made by some theologians that the reading of the pagan poets and writers would corrupt the morals of the young. The humanists knew, of course, that there was much in ancient literature that could not stand muster before a strict Christian censor, and many of them did not hesitate to emulate it in prose and verse, pleading with Catullus that their life was pure though their verse might be licentious. Yet they knew how to distinguish between a literature written by and for adults and the requirements of the education of the young. In their treatises on education they would usually omit from their reading list those ancient writings that gave rise to moral criticism, and Erasmus added the pointed remark that we should be careful not to imbibe the manners of the ancients along with their literature. In this way, the humanists managed to link their cultural ideals very closely with the moral aspirations of their time, and to make their educational program acceptable to all but the most narrow-minded theologians.

The actual human ideal of the Renaissance has often been characterized as that of the *uomo universale,* the universal man, or to use a modern phrase, the well-rounded personality. We rarely encounter this slogan in the literature of the period, but the actual life of persons like Leon Battista Alberti or Leonardo da Vinci seems to illustrate a quest for excellence in a great variety of pursuits, and the educational treatises of the time envisage a person who would achieve reasonable distinction in physical and artistic, intellectual and practical activities. This is also apparent in another large branch of literature that is concerned, not with education in general, but with the training of particular groups or classes of society.

A large number of treatises is dedicated to the education or the description of the good prince, and this literature has attracted a great deal of attention among historians of literature and of political thought. The "mirror of princes" was an important branch of literature during the later medieval centuries, and it has been shown that the ideal of the Christian king, based on Germanic customs and theological theories, was gradually transformed under the impact of the study of Roman law and of Aristotle's *Politics*. In fifteenth-century Italy, monarchical states were firmly established in Naples and Milan, and on a smaller scale, in Piedmont, Ferrara, and Mantua, not to speak of the numerous tiny and ephemeral principalities. It is against this background that the treatises on the best prince by humanists like Platina or Pontano and others must be understood. Important new sources for these treatises were several works of Isocrates and Plutarch that were widely diffused in a number of different translations. These humanist treatises were largely theoretical and gave much space to a list of the virtues that the prince should possess and to ancient examples of good conduct. It is characteristic that the tone of these treatises is secular rather than religious and that the reward promised to the good prince is everlasting fame rather than blessedness in a future life. The quest for fame was a central concern of the humanists and of their contemporaries, and the power of its appeal may be discovered in many episodes and writings of the period.

Another topic discussed in these treatises was the relation between virtue and expediency, and the authors of these usually concluded with Cicero that the most virtuous course of action is also in the long run the most advantageous. It has been pointed out by Allan Gilbert, Felix Gilbert, and other scholars that Machiavelli's *Prince,* though original in its extreme realism and its exclusive stress on expediency, is linked in its themes and problems with the late medieval and early humanist literature on the best prince. In the sixteenth century, the establishment of strong national monarchies outside of Italy forms the background for an important series of humanist treatises by Budé, Sepulveda, and others. The most famous is Erasmus's *Education of a Christian Prince,* which is explicitly introduced as a counterpart of Isocrates' treatise *Ad Nicoclem,* which Erasmus had translated. The prince is expected to read a number of ancient writers, in addition to the Bible. Among his suggestions for the administration of the state, Erasmus reminds the ruler that he is merely a member of the state, that his rule rests basically on the consent of the people, and that the public welfare is the only standard of the laws. Erasmus wants to limit the death penalty to extreme cases and urges the rulers to submit their quarrels to arbitration, advocating on religious grounds the ideal of universal peace, a subject which he also treated elsewhere.

## X

In fifteenth-century Italy, the ideal of republican liberty was as much alive as that of the monarchical state, as many humanist writings show. The Roman republic was as much a model for imitation as the Roman Empire, and it was no coincidence that the superiority of Scipio interpreted as a symbol of republican virtue was defended by Poggio, a Florentine citizen, against the claims of Caesar that were supported by Guarino, a subject of the Marquess of Ferrara. The comparison between different constitutions in the works of Plato, Aristotle, and Polybius found parallels in the writings of Francesco Patrizi, Aurelio Brandolini, and Machiavelli—who in his actual political career and in his *Discourses on Livy* attested his preference for the republican form of government. When Florentine political liberty was being undermined by the Medici regime, Alamanno Rinuccini wrote, but probably did not publish, his *De libertate*. Historians often exaggerate the significance of the fact that many of the city republics of the twelfth and thirteenth century succumbed to various forms of despotism during the fourteenth and fifteenth. The Venetian republic, ruled by its tightly restricted but responsible and educated nobility, became more powerful than ever, and was considered, on account of its wealth and stability, as a model by many political writers. The Florentine republic, which showed much less stability and underwent a variety of changes and revolutions, maintained its power and independence against several attacks from the outside and acquired, especially in the fifteenth century, a cultural and artistic predominance that was recognized throughout Italy and Europe. When Florence was threatened during the late fourteenth and early fifteenth century by the repeated attacks of the Visconti princes of Milan, who were expanding their rule over large areas of northern and central Italy, Florence mobilized against them her intellectual as well as her material resources. In this political crisis, many Florentine humanists emphasized the ideals of the republican state and of the responsible citizen called to govern that state. Hans Baron in a series of studies has forcefully described this civic humanism which flourished in Florence during the first half of the fifteenth century, and it certainly deserves attention as one of the most impressive phases of Renaissance humanism, even though it would be quite mistaken to identify Renaissance humanism as a whole with this Florentine civic humanism. There was a good deal of "despotic humanism" even in fifteenth-century Italy, and it would be quite impossible to comprise under the heading of "civic humanism" the entire political literature of the Renaissance period, let alone the large body of humanist literature that was not concerned with political problems at all. Florentine civic humanism found its best expression in the writings of Leonardo Bruni, Leon Battista Alberti, and Matteo Palmieri. Humanist learning is presented by them as serving the active life of the citizen involved in the affairs of his business and of his republic. He will not only occupy his leisure with the reading of the best authors, but will follow in his own life and activities the examples and precepts offered in their writings. It was not always mentioned but evidently understood that the prominent citizen was often called upon to deliver speeches, or to compose letters, of public importance, and that his humanist training would give him the necessary literary ability to accomplish these tasks with sufficient distinction to earn a good reputation for himself and for his city. Florentine history between 1434 and 1537 was characterized by a gradual transition from a republican form of government to the monarchy of the Medici—a development which was slowed and sometimes interrupted by a strong resistance on the part of the followers of the republican tradition. The political strife between the various parties was accompanied by literary controversy, as often happens, and the decline and fall of the Florentine republic thus produced a long series of political treatises defending the republican form of government and expounding the best ways to give it stability and perfection.

All Italian cities, whether their government was republican or monarchical, had a class of noble families of feudal or commercial antecedents. Its political influence varies greatly from place to place. In Venice, the nobles were the ruling class which monopolized all public office. In Naples, the feudal nobility possessed large landed property and traditional privileges, but the kings tended to reduce these privileges and to build a modern monarchy and a bureaucracy of trained persons directly responsible to them, just as the kings of England, France, and Spain were to do in the sixteenth century. In Florence, the older families were divided into bitterly opposed factions, and depending upon the regime prevailing at a given time, some of them were excluded from office or even exiled, while others shared the administration of the republic with able persons of more modest origins. Everywhere, regardless of their political position, the families of the nobility managed to maintain a good deal of wealth and social prestige, and their style of life served as model for the newcomers who established themselves through business enterprises or political careers or even through professional success. However, with the exception of Naples and possibly Rome, this nobility was no longer feudal in character but thoroughly urbanized and hence may be called more appropriately a patriciate. The humanists succeeded in gaining this important class for their cause, educated their children, and impressed upon them the conviction that they needed a good education by humanist standards to be worthy of their social status. On the other hand, the humanists cherished the ambition of attaining for themselves a comparable social position, and at least some of them succeeded. For the trained humanist could have a career as chancellor or secretary of princes and republics, and thus was able to contribute his share, along with the much larger body of lawyers, to what was to be called in later centuries the *noblesse de robe*. Against this background, it is quite understandable why the humanists of the fifteenth century were interested in the problem of nobility and why they should focus on the question whether nobility is or should be based on birth or on personal merit. The question had been discussed by a few late medieval authors, and some of them had already emphasized the role of personal merit as a basis of nobility. In the fifteenth century, there was a whole series of treatises, *De Nobilitate,* in which this problem is investigated further. In the treatises by Poggio Bracciolini, Buonaccorso da Montemagno, Bartolomeo Platina, and the still unpublished but interesting dialogue of Cristoforo Landino, the thesis that nobility rests on virtue is strongly defended. The problem is treated in typically humanist fashion in the work of Buonaccorso da Montemagno, which enjoyed tremendous popularity. Two Romans compete for the hand of a noble woman, and support their claims in elaborate speeches, one of them praising his illustrious ancestry, the other his personal achievements. The author does not tell us which of the two married the girl, but the greater force seems to be in the second speech which defends the claims of merit. The tendency apparent in these treatises has led many scholars to consider the preference for personal merit as against inherited nobility as typical of Renaissance humanism. This is to some extent justified, but not entirely so. The authors of the treatises we have mentioned were for the most part Tuscans. We should not overlook the fact that the claims of the Neapolitan nobility were defended by one of its members who was himself a humanist, Tristano Caracciolo, and those of the Venetian nobility by Lauro Querini, another well-known humanist who happened to be a Venetian nobleman himself. It is apparent once more how difficult it is to identify humanism as a whole with any given set of opinions, although these opinions may be held by some of its representatives. The common denominator is always, not a set of opinions, but a cultural and educational ideal.

## XI

Another group of significant Renaissance moral treatises tries to describe, and to propose for imitation, the human ideal of the perfect citizen, magistrate, courtier, or gentleman. It is the ideal of a member of the ruling class, apart from its political connotations, held out as a model for young and old people alike. This genre, represented in the fifteenth century by some treatises of Alberti, Platina, and others, became especially important in the sixteenth. The most famous work of the group, Baldassarre Castiglione's *Book of the Courtier,* was translated into several languages and found imitators all over Europe. This work, which has great stylistic merit and occupies an important place in the history of Italian prose literature, clearly envisages a member of the aristocracy, and reflects many personal traits of its author who was active as a diplomat for many years in the service of the princes of Mantua and of the papal Curia. Castiglione's *Courtier* represents a human ideal of great breadth; it might be said to reflect the concept of the *uomo universale,* and it clearly exercised a civilizing influence upon the ruling classes of Renaissance Europe. Aside from the traditional knightly virtues of courage and physical prowess, the courtier is expected to have polished manners, to be an able participant in elegant conversation, to have a good literary education, and to be moderately accomplished in the arts of painting, music, and dance. An English counterpart is Sir Thomas Elyot's *Boke of the Governour,* in which moral and religious considerations play a somewhat larger role. Later in the century, the emphasis shifts more and more to a description of manners practiced in good society and to the requirements of polite conversation. Giovanni della Casa's *Galateo,* and Stefano Guazzo's book *On Civil Conversation* were widely read, translated, and imitated, and form the core of a large literature in all languages, usually described as books of courtesy, of conduct, or of manners. Louis Wright has shown that for England this literature more and more addressed itself not only to the members of the aristocracy, but also to the middle class of merchants and professionals who were eager to strengthen their social position by imitating the manners of the older ruling class. This literature prepares the way for the treatises on the perfect gentleman that were to be composed in the seventeenth century. Yet it also contains a good many prudential rules and seems to be intended partly for the young man of talent and modest means who is trying to get ahead in life and make a career. The straight preaching of moral virtues, so prominent in the early humanist treatises, now occupies less and less space, although the possession of these virtues is taken more or less for granted.

## XII

Aside from the generalized ideal of the courtier or gentleman, many treatises were written on the duties of persons who occupied a particular status, or practiced a particular profession. There were books on the duties of a magistrate or ambassador, or even on the duties of a bishop, in which moral prescriptions were combined with advice concerning the practical conduct of affairs. In the extensive literature of treatises on art that was written during the Renaissance period, the technical rules of the craft were embellished with moral advice for the artist. What Cicero and Quintilian had required of the orator, namely that he should combine moral stature and a general education with the technical competence appropriate for his profession, was now applied to all other professions, and especially to that of the artist. The painter, the sculptor, and the architect not only acquired a higher social status and prestige than they ever possessed before or afterwards, they also tended to combine artistic skill with literary, scholarly, and scientific interests and competence—as we may see in the writings of Alberti, Piero della Francesca, Leonardo, Dürer, Michelangelo, and Rubens—and hence to appropriate for their profession the moral claims advanced originally by the humanist scholars.

One of the chief innovations brought about by the Protestant Reformation was the abolition of the monastic orders, which had played such an important role during the Middle Ages and which retained and even increased their importance in the modern Catholic world. The radical move of the Reformers was preceded, as is well known, by centuries of medieval attacks on the vices and shortcomings of the monks and friars, charges that were at least in part justified and that the Catholic Reformation of the sixteenth century tended to obviate. The humanists contributed their share to the critique of monasticism. Valla and others wrote against the monks, and Erasmus in his *Praise of Folly* poured a good deal of ridicule upon them. Yet it should be noted that Erasmus in this work did not spare any class of contemporary society, not even his own, the grammarians and rhetoricians; elsewhere he insists that the pious life was not a monopoly of the monastic orders, asserting an ideal of lay piety which he inherited from the "Modern Devotion," the Dutch mystic movement in whose schools he had received his first education. Yet he nowhere advocates the abolition of the orders. Among the earlier Italian humanists, we find several writers and scholars of distinction, such as Petrarch, Salutati, and Ermolao Barbaro, who actually came out in praise of the monastic life, and there were many learned monks, such as Ambrogio Traversari, who took a significant part in the humanist movement. Again it would be wrong to identify humanism as a whole with one or the other opinion on this important question.

A good deal has been written by Burckhardt and others about the place of women in Renaissance society. Women had not yet acquired an important place in professional life, and their activities were still largely confined to the house and the family. Yet within this limited range they were respected, and at least a few of them, especially the daughters of princes, noblemen, and scholars, received a literary and scholarly education and distinguished themselves as patrons of learning, or even as scholars and writers in their own right. Thus it is significant that one of the most important humanist treatises on education, Leonardo Bruni's *De studiis et litteris,* was dedicated to a woman. A series of treatises by fifteenth-century humanists deal with the family and with marriage, and hence have a good deal to say about the moral and practical duties of the housewife and mother. Famous and influential specimens of this literature are Francesco Barbaro's *De re uxoria,* and Alberti's treatise *Della famiglia.* The former emphasizes moral advice, and the latter contains charming pages on the way the wife of a wealthy citizen is supposed to assist her husband and to govern the household, servants, and children. In the sixteenth century, Castiglione in his *Courtier* devotes a special section of his work to the court lady, the female counterpart of his male subject, and Vives composed a significant treatise *On the Education of a Christian Woman.* Later in the century, in Italy as elsewhere, a whole series of treatises was written on the conduct of women, in which prudential rules played a large part and some advice was even offered on how to dress and how to use cosmetics.

## XIII

A large segment of literature extending from the end of the fifteenth to the end of the sixteenth century deals with the subject of love. A famous medieval example had been Andreas Capellanus's book on courtly love, in which the customs of French chivalry received a more theoretical, though not a more philosophical, expression than in the lyric and epic poetry of the period. More philosophical was the lyric poetry of Cavalcanti, Dante, and their contemporaries in Italy, and the prose speculation on love began with Dante's *Vita Nuova* and *Convivio* as well as with the commentaries on Cavalcanti's obscure poem. This whole literature was given a new impulse and direction by Marsilio Ficino, the head of the Platonic Academy of Florence, and one of the leading Platonists of the Renaissance. He supplied to Western readers the first complete translations of Plato's *Symposium* and *Phaedrus* (parts of which had already been translated by Leonardo Bruni), and also published important commentaries on these two dialogues. In particular, the commentary on the *Symposium* became very famous. Basing himself primarily on Plato but transforming his doctrine under the influence of other philosophical, theological, and literary traditions, Ficino understood the love for another human being as a preliminary form and disguise of the basic love that each human being has for God and that finds its fulfillment only in the direct enjoyment and knowledge of God—a goal that is reached during the present life by only a few persons and for a short time, but will be attained forever in the future life by those who have aspired to it while on earth. Without rejecting sexual and earthly love, Ficino praises above all the pure and celestial love, that is, the mutual affection and friendship between two persons who are dedicated to the contemplative life and hence recognize that their mutual relationship is founded upon the love each of them has for God. This divine love Ficino claimed to define according to the teachings of Plato, and hence coining a term that was to become famous as well as ridiculous, he called it "Platonic" or "Socratic love." The doctrine of Platonic love constitutes only a small, though important, part of Ficino's philosophical system, but it enjoyed a wide popularity apart from the rest of his work, especially among poets and moralists. The notion of Platonic love was taken over and adapted by many poets, including Lorenzo de' Medici and Michelangelo. Moreover, Ficino's commentary on Plato's *Symposium* became the fountainhead of a whole literature of love treatises, in Italy and elsewhere, in which the philosophical notion of Platonic love was repeated, developed, and sometimes distorted. The authors of these treatises include distinguished philosophers, such as Pico della Mirandola, Leone Ebreo (from whom Spinoza seems to have borrowed his notion of the intellectual love of God), Francesco Patrizi, and Giordano Bruno, as well as famous writers like Bembo and Castiglione. For the last book of Castiglione's *Courtier* deals precisely with Platonic love along the lines defined by Ficino, and through this work the theory attained a very wide diffusion indeed. In the later treatises, the original link between Platonic love and the contemplative life was gradually lost, and the cult of Platonic love came to be a hypocritical disguise for refined sexual passion, or an empty game fashionable in good society. However, we should try to understand that originally it had a serious philosophical meaning, and that a good deal of serious talk and writing on love in the sixteenth century was shaped by the Platonist "philosophy of love."

## XIV

Another typically humanist fashion in which the various forms of human life were discussed during the fifteenth and sixteenth century was the so-called comparison (*paragone*). Ancient rhetoric had insisted that it was the task of the orator to praise and to blame, and the praise of some virtue or quality was often combined with the blame of its contrary. To show their skill, orators even composed mock praises of bad or ridiculous things such as tyranny or baldness, and it was against this literary background and upon such models that Erasmus wrote his admirable *Praise of Folly*. Rhetorical contests left their traces in medieval Latin and vernacular poetry where the contrast between winter and spring, youth and old age are common themes. In humanistic literature, the rhetorical contest between two contrasts or rivals was a favorite sport, and we have encountered several examples already: the comparison between Scipio and Caesar, between republic and monarchy, and Buonaccorso's comparison between nobility by birth and by merit. In the same way, the merits and relative superiority of various arts, professions, or ways of life were frequently discussed. There are treatises on "arms and letters," debating the advantages of the military and the literary life. Leonardo da Vinci seriously argued that painting was superior to the other arts and sciences, and Michelangelo was consulted on the question of whether painting or sculpture was superior. The humanist defense of poetry, of which we have spoken before, took the form of attacking other learned disciplines, as in Petrarch's invectives against a physician. There was a whole literature on the relative merits of medicine and of law that had its roots in the rivalry of the university faculties and in which distinguished humanists such as Salutati and Poggio took an active part. Salutati sided with the jurists because the law had a greater significance for the life of the citizen and of the state. Several historians would like to consider this as the typically humanist position, but it happens that Poggio, no less a humanist than Salutati, voted in this contest in favor of medicine.

The argument used by Salutati in this discussion and on other occasions touches upon another more serious issue, the relative merits of the contemplative and of the active life. The distinction occurs already in Aristotle, who tends, along with most ancient philosophers, to consider the life of contemplation, rather than that of action, to be most perfect and desirable. A notable exception was Cicero, the Roman statesman, who insisted upon the political duties of the responsible citizen. During the Middle Ages, the life of contemplation was usually associated with the monastic ideal and was more or less persistently praised. In the Renaissance, we hear again several voices in praise of the active life, such as those of Salutati, Bruni, Alberti, and Palmieri, and these views have been emphasized by Hans Baron and other scholars as an important aspect of their civic humanism. Eugene Rice goes even further and treats the emphasis on the active life in these humanists, in some sixteenth-century writers and in Pierre Charron, as an important development leading away from the monastic ideal of the Middle Ages to the this-worldly and practical orientation of the modern age. Although it is significant that, from the fifteenth century on, the active life was finding more partisans among the writers of the age, the monastic life also had its defenders among the humanists, as we have seen, and even Salutati, one of the chief protagonists of the active life, wrote a whole treatise in praise of the monastic life, a fact that has puzzled several of his interpreters. Moreover, the ideal of the theoretical or contemplative life became dissociated during the Renaissance from the specific ideal of monasticism, and rather identified with the private existence of the scholar, writer, and scientist, no doubt under the influence of ancient philosophy, and this secularization of the contemplative life seems to me no less characteristic of the Renaissance (and of modern times) than the simultaneous emphasis on the claims of the active life. This tendency appears already in Petrarch's praise of solitude, and it is in this sense that the Platonists of the Florentine Academy praised the life of contemplation which occupied a central place in their philosophy. The most famous document in which the question is debated is Cristoforo Landino's *Camaldulensian Disputations,* a dialogue in which the active life is defended by Lorenzo de' Medici and the contemplative life by Leon Battista Alberti—and the victory seems to go to the latter. In the sixteenth century, Pomponazzi considers the theoretical life as superior but uses the practical life to define the end of man, as this life is peculiar to man and all human beings are able to have a part in it. In Montaigne there is a strong, though by no means exclusive, emphasis on the solitary life of contemplation, and most other philosophers take its superiority for granted, whereas the popular moralists insist on the needs and claims of the active life. Far from being resolved in the sixteenth century, the question is still with us. Whereas many writers decry the "ivory tower" of the intellectual, others would still insist on the right of the scholar, artist, or scientist to concentrate on his peculiar task. The rival claims of the active and contemplative life seem to illustrate a perennial human problem, and there seems to be no permanent answer to it, but each time, each profession, and each person will have to find a viable compromise.

Another similar question that was widely debated in Renaissance thought was the relation between the intellect and the will, or between knowledge and love. This question overlaps that of the contemplative and active life, but is not entirely identical with it. For some partisans of the contemplative life, for example, Petrarch, would still place will and love above intellect and knowledge, since they consider the willing of the good and the love of God as a part, and even as the most important part, of the contemplative life. The problem occupies a very important place in the history of Western thought. It has been rightly asserted that the concept of will is absent from ancient Greek philosophy. Plato, Aristotle, and other Greek thinkers know a conflict between reason and desire, but they inherited from Socrates the conviction that reason is capable by its own power to know the good, to put it into practice, and to overcome the resistance of any contrary desire. In the Christian view, this Greek belief in the independent power of reason was far too optimistic. In order to overcome his native propensity to evil brought about by Adam's fall, man needed the grace of God. On the basis of this Christian conception, Augustine formulated his notion of the will. Aside from his faculty of knowing, man has an independent faculty of willing. It is the will that was corrupted by Adam's fall, and that must be purified by divine grace if we are to attain the good. Medieval thought inherited from Augustine this distinction between will and intellect, and the relative merits of these two faculties became the subject of important discussions, with Thomas Aquinas, among others, emphasizing the superiority of the intellect, whereas Duns Scotus and other "voluntarists" insisted, in accordance with Augustine, on the superiority of the will. This question, in spite of its scholastic origin, continued to occupy the humanists. Both Petrarch and Salutati favored the superiority of the will. In the Platonic Academy of Florence, the problem was evidently a favorite topic of debate, as we may learn from Ficino's correspondence, and from the treatise of one of his pupils, Alamanno Donati. Ficino himself apparently changed his view on the matter in the course of his life, favoring at first the superiority of the intellect but insisting in his later writings on the importance of the will and of love for the ascent of the soul to God. His arguments show that the concept of will could be associated with the life of contemplation no less than with that of action.

## XV

Renaissance thought was interested not merely in moral rules of conduct or in the specific ways of life that an individual might choose according to his status or profession, but also in the general situation in which human beings find themselves on earth, in the chief forces determining this situation, and in the place man and his world occupy within the larger universe. There has been a widespread belief that Renaissance humanists held an optimistic view of life and were prone to enjoy this earth without caring as much for the future life after death as their medieval predecessors had. It is true that the concern with earthly life and its problems tended to increase from medieval to modern times. Nevertheless we must try to avoid exaggerated opinions. Even in Lorenzo de' Medici's famous lines, "Let him be happy who so desires, for we are not sure of the next day," which used to be quoted as the quintessence of the Renaissance view of life as frivolous and superficial, we have learned to hear melancholy undertones. Historians like Walser and Trinkaus have shown that the writers of the period were keenly aware of the miseries and ills of our earthly existence. Sickness and poverty, exile and imprisonment, the loss of friends and relatives were a common experience, and when Poggio and other humanists wrote about the misery of the human condition, they had no difficulty collecting ancient and modern examples to illustrate the frail and transitory state of earthly happiness. Lest we think that some classes of men are untouched by the miseries that befall the common lot, the humanists wrote special treatises about the unhappiness of scholars and of courtiers, and especially of princes. These treatises were full of examples from history, and they were intended to warn their readers not to trust their happiness and to comfort the unhappy with the record of the ills suffered by others that were worse than their own. This chorus of lament may seem to be out of tune with many real and imagined traits of the period, but it is nearly universal. The Platonic philosopher Ficino invokes the shade of Heraclitus to weep at the misery of men, as he would laugh with Democritus at their folly.

This feeling that man has to suffer many vicissitudes and that the events of his life, whether good or bad, are largely beyond his control was interpreted by the writers and thinkers of the period in a variety of ways that were not always consistent with each other, but that lend a common note to the literature of the Renaissance. Divine providence was stressed by the theologians and never denied by any other thinkers, but popular and philosophical writers frequently played with the notions of fortune and fate.

The concept of chance was repeatedly discussed by ancient philosophers and played a role in the thought of Aristotle, and especially in that of Epicurus. In the moral thought of late antiquity, chance was given an important part in human affairs, and its power was even personified and worshiped as the goddess Tyche or Fortuna. During the Christian Middle Ages, Fortuna remained pretty much alive, not as a goddess, to be sure, but as an allegory and as an instrument of God. In the Renaissance the power of Fortuna is again very often mentioned. She appears in emblems and allegorical pictures as well as in the writings of the period. Statesmen and businessmen hoped that this blind and arbitrary power would bring them success, and Machiavelli devoted some striking pages to the description of its role in history and politics.

Many thoughtful persons were not satisfied with this whimsical rule of Fortuna over human affairs, but believed instead, or additionally, in the power of an inexorable fate. The view that all earthly events were rigidly determined by an unbroken chain of antecedent causes had been held by the ancient Stoics, and it was revived in a more or less modified form by Pomponazzi and other thinkers. Still more widespread was the belief in astrology, an elaborate system that presented itself as a science and tried to tie all earthly events, with the help of detailed but flexible rules, to the influence of the stars. This system, which had passed from the Babylonians into late antiquity and was transmitted through the Arabs to medieval Europe, was usually opposed by the theologians but was supported by the philosophers and scientists. During the Renaissance, astrology had a few opponents, such as Petrarch and Pico, but on the whole its prestige rose higher than ever before, both among scholars and laymen. The belief that all human affairs were governed by the motions of the stars was satisfactory to many people because it seemed to give some significance and regularity to the vicissitudes of life. The astrologers claimed to be able to predict the future of persons and countries, and in their passionate desire to know and to control their future, people were as little disturbed as in other times by the inherent contradiction in prophecy (for how can I change the future to my advantage if it is dependent on unchangeable laws, and how can I predict the future if I or others can do anything about it?) and as willing to forget the numerous predictions that were not confirmed by the outcome.

Different from the belief in fate is the theological doctrine of predestination, which also played an important part in the discussions of the period. Augustine had emphasized against the Pelagians that not only all earthly events but even our own moral choices and actions were foreordained by divine forethought and will, and the problem of how predestination can be reconciled with human free will gave rise to many difficulties in medieval theology and philosophy. The problem came to the fore with the Protestant Reformers, Luther and Calvin, who completely denied free will, something neither Augustine nor his medieval successors had clearly done. The question was of importance also to secular thinkers before the Reformation, as the example of Valla and Pomponazzi shows. Valla argued that it was easy to reconcile divine foreknowledge with human free will but considered the relationship between God's will and human freedom as a mystery of faith. Pomponazzi gave an intricate defense of predestination as well as of fate, but his attempt to make free will appear compatible with both of them seems neither clear nor convincing.

The concepts of fortune, of fate, and of predestination express in different ways and on different levels the feeling that human life is governed by divine and natural powers over which we have no control and to which we must submit more or less helplessly. Yet most Renaissance thinkers did not stop with the assertion of these superhuman powers, but tried in some way to uphold and defend the power of man over his own destiny, in the face of fortune and fate. The attempt is in itself significant even where it seems to be inconsistent or unsuccessful. Already the ancient Stoics, the most outspoken proponents of rigid fate, had struggled to assert the role of human freedom within a system of complete determinism. The later Stoics found their solution in the view that the wise man, while enduring patiently the external circumstances of his life which he is unable to change, is entirely free in his thought and in his moral attitude. In a more popular fashion, they opposed the power of reason and virtue to that of fortune and claimed for the wise man an inner victory even when he may seem to be outwardly defeated. This is the keynote also of much humanist thinking and writing on the subject. In his extremely influential treatise on the remedies of good and bad fortune Petrarch opposes reason to the passions in good Stoic manner and exhorts his readers to overcome through virtue the hold that good and bad fortune alike have on our minds. Salutati also opposes virtue and wisdom to fate and fortune. The recurrent theme in Alberti's moral writings is the victory of virtue over fortune, and Ficino restates the same view, adding a Neoplatonic note by basing moral virtue on the life of contemplation. After having described the power of fortune, Machiavelli also insists that the prudent statesman is able to overcome, or at least to modify, the power of fortune. Guillaume Budé teaches his readers to despise the external circumstances of life, which fortune may give or take away. Just as these thinkers wish to oppose the power of fortune, Pico della Mirandola made a strenuous effort to oppose the power of fate. His elaborate attack against astrology was actually a defense of human freedom, and the arguments that he uses show very clearly that his attitude was prompted by moral and religious as well as by scientific considerations. This same concern for man's moral autonomy was to prompt such humanist thinkers as Erasmus and Sepulveda to defend free will against Luther's exclusive doctrine of predestination.

## XVI

The themes and ideas that we have briefly discussed may illustrate the way in which Renaissance thinkers were preoccupied with moral and human problems. It has often been asserted that Renaissance thought, in contrast with medieval thought, was man-centered, not God-centered, or—to quote a rather unfriendly remark of Gilson—that the Renaissance was the Middle Ages minus God. Such statements are obviously exaggerated, since Renaissance thought as a whole was anything but indifferent to God, and since hardly any thinker of the period denied the existence of God, however his conception of God may have differed from various forms of religious orthodoxy. Yet the humanists who have attracted most of the attention of

Renaissance historians were interested primarily in moral problems, frequently to the exclusion of theology and metaphysics, of natural philosophy and other learned disciplines. The very name "humanities," which they adopted for their studies, emphasized their concern with man in a programmatic fashion. No wonder that they were inclined to stress the importance of human problems and to extol the place of man in the universe. Already Petrarch argues in his treatise *On His Own and Other People's Ignorance* that it does not help us to know the nature of animals unless we also know the nature of man, and in his famous letter describing his ascent of Mont Ventoux he opposes his admiration for the human soul to the impression made upon him by mountains and the sea. It is significant that the latter passage is woven out of quotations from Seneca and Augustine, for the Renaissance doctrine of the dignity of man was nourished in many ways by classical and Christian sources. In the fifteenth century, the excellence of man was the theme of special treatises by Giannozzo Manetti and others. Especially in Manetti's treatise, the dignity of man is based not only on his biblical similarity to God, but above all on his varied achievements in the arts and sciences, which are described at great length. This favorite humanist theme then received a more metaphysical treatment at the hands of the Platonic philosophers. Marsilio Ficino dedicated several books of his chief work, the *Platonic Theology,* to man's achievements in the sciences and in government, emphasizing the universality of his knowledge and of his aspirations. When he restates the Neoplatonic conception that the universe is made of several degrees of being that extend from God at the summit to the corporeal world at the bottom, he intentionally revises the scheme in order to assign a privileged place in its center to the rational soul of man, thus making it the bond and knot of the universe, second in dignity only to God Himself. Pico della Mirandola went even further. In the famous *Oration,* which deals only in its first half with the dignity of man, and in other writings, he states that man does not occupy any fixed place in the universal hierarchy, but can freely choose his place in it. For he has no fixed nature but possesses all the gifts that had been distributed singly among the other creatures. Thus man is capable of leading many forms of life from the lowest to the highest. Pico's view is echoed in Vives's *Fable on Man;* man is introduced here as an actor capable of playing the roles of all other creatures. The central position of man in the universe, half way between animals and angels, is accepted also by Pomponazzi as a sign of man's excellence. Thus we may say that under the impact of a humanist tradition, systematic philosophers as different from each other as the Florentine Platonists and Pomponazzi assigned to man a privileged position in their conception of the universe. The emphasis on man's universal skill in the arts and sciences will recur in Francis Bacon's notion of the reign of man over nature, and thus there is an echo of the Renaissance glorification of man in the ideology that still underlies the technological aspect of modern natural science.

However, even on this issue that seems to be so close to the heart of Renaissance humanism, the period does not speak to us with a single voice. Even in the fifteenth century, Pope Innocent III's treatise *On Contempt for the World,* which constituted the foil and starting point of Manetti's work, was widely read and had its imitators. In the sixteenth century, a strong reaction against the excessive glorification of man may be noted. In the Protestant Reformers there was a tremendous emphasis on the depraved nature of man, and this view was probably expressed in conscious protest against the current stress on his dignity. Also Montaigne, otherwise so far removed from the theology of the Reformers and so close to humanist thought, goes a long way in his *Apology of Raymond de Sebond* to criticize the unfounded opinions on man's privileged place in the universe, and to insist on his humble position and on the vanity of his aspirations.

This Renaissance concern for man and his place in the universe may also account for the great prominence given during that period to the question of the immortality of the soul. The notion that the individual human soul is immortal had been strongly defended by Plato and the Neoplatonists, whereas Aristotle and other ancient philosophers held ambiguous or contrary opinions. Augustine had adopted the Neoplatonic view, and he was followed by all medieval Christian thinkers. With Renaissance Platonism, the question assumed a central importance that it had never had before. Ficino actually designed his *Platonic Theology* around this problem and tried to demonstrate the immortality of the soul against the Aristotelians by a variety of arguments. This emphasis on immortality appealed to a large number of poets, philosophers, and theologians, and it is tempting to assume that it was under Platonist influence that the immortality of the soul was adopted at the Lateran Council of 1512 as an official dogma of the Catholic Church. When the leading Aristotelian philosopher, Pietro Pomponazzi, set out to show that personal immortality cannot be demonstrated by reason, he not only accepted it as an article of faith, but also stressed that the human soul, even according to reason, is immortal at least in some respect (*secundum quid*), on account of its high place among the material forms. Moreover, by returning to the problem many times in published treatises and unpublished questions and lectures, Pomponazzi showed how much he was puzzled by the question and how great an importance he attributed to it. On the other hand, his treatise of 1516 gave rise to a large number of written attacks upon his position by philosophers and theologians, and the question continued to be debated beyond the end of the sixteenth century. The statement that Renaissance students were interested in problems of the soul rather than of nature, often repeated after the nineteenth century French scholar Renan, is based upon the misinterpretation of an episode in which a group of students wanted to hear a course on Aristotle's *On the Soul* rather than on his *Meteorology,* but it contains a grain of truth that may well be based on better evidence.

It might be in order to indicate very briefly at this point in what ways the moral thought of the humanists, even though it was primarily concerned with individual conduct, also led to broader social, political, and humanitarian ideals. The theory of friendship occupied an important place in the ethics of Aristotle, Epicurus and Cicero, and its value is very often stressed in the letters and other writings of the humanists. In the Florentine Academy, the concept of friendship is closely associated with those of Christian and Platonic love, and Ficino liked to think that the members of his Academy were bound to one another and to himself, their common master, by a tie of Platonic friendship, thus forming a close community after the model of the ancient schools of philosophy.

In political thought, not only were the humanists concerned with the education of princes and magistrates, or with the relative merits of republican and monarchical government, but some of the Renaissance thinkers began to reflect on ideal commonwealths more perfect than the ones in existence. Thomas More's *Utopia,* a highly original work in spite of its obvious indebtedness to Plato's *Republic,* was the first of an important genre that was to flourish down to the eighteenth century. Its example was followed by Campanella, Bacon, and many lesser writers. The influence of this utopian literature on social and political reforms in modern times has been generally recognized. Another contribution to social reform was Vives' treatise on assistance to the poor, written at a time when the responsibility for public relief was taken over by the cities in the Low Countries.

No less important was the contribution of Renaissance thought to the development of the ideal of religious toleration. This ideal arose first in the fifteenth century against the background of medieval controversy with Judaism and Islam and of the echoes of the polemics of the Church Fathers against ancient paganism. In the sixteenth century, the problem acquired a new poignancy in the face of religious dissent, persecution, and war within Western Christendom. Without abandoning a belief in the superiority of his own religion, Nicolaus Cusanus advocated perpetual peace and toleration between the different creeds dividing mankind. Ficino praised the solidarity and fellowship of all human beings, and insisted that religion was natural to man, and that all religions, though different in their practices and in the degree of their perfection, contained a common core of truth and expressed in some way the worship of the one true God. Moreover, Ficino maintained that there was a basic harmony between the true, Christian religion and the true, Platonic philosophy; and he accepted the apocryphal writings attributed to Zoroaster, Hermes Trismegistus, Orpheus, and Pythagoras as witnesses of an early pagan theology and philosophy that prepared the way for Plato and his followers, similarly as the Old Testament foreshadowed the New. These notions added a new and explicit force to the general humanist belief in the wisdom of the ancients and its compatibility with Christian religious teaching, and they exercised an enormous influence during the sixteenth century. Equally important were the ideas of Pico della Mirandola, who went even further. According to him, all known philosophies and religions contained some elements of truth, and he proposed to defend in a public disputation nine hundred theses taken principally from ancient and medieval, Arabic and Jewish, philosophers and theologians. In particular, he maintained that the writings of the Jewish Cabalists represented an ancient oral tradition, and were in agreement with the teachings of Christianity. In the second part of his famous oration, which was actually composed as an introductory speech for his projected disputation, Pico eloquently expresses his belief in the universality of truth in which every philosopher and theologian participates to a greater or lesser degree. A hundred years later, in his famous *Sevenfold Conversation,* which was widely circulated in manuscript but not printed until recent times, Jean Bodin defends the claims of all the different religions. In the seventeenth century, Herbert of Cherbury laid the ground for deism by describing a natural religion consisting of the common core of all the various human creeds.

## XVII

In spite of these broad and interesting ramifications, the moral thought of the Renaissance was fundamentally individualistic in its outlook. Of course, the term individualism has several meanings, and its applications to the Renaissance have aroused a good deal of controversy among historians. It cannot be denied that outstanding human individuals are found in other periods of history, including the Middle Ages, or that medieval nominalism emphasized the reality of the individual physical thing. When we speak of Renaissance individualism, the term should be understood in a different way. Above all, Renaissance thought and literature are extremely individualistic in that they aim, to a degree unknown to the Middle Ages and to most of ancient and modern times, at the expression of individual, subjective opinions, feelings, and experiences. Every humanist takes himself very seriously and thinks that everything he has heard and seen is eminently worth recording. Treatises on highly abstract subjects are intermixed with personal stories, gossip, flattery, and invective to a degree and in a manner of which a modern scholar, like his ancient or medieval predecessors, would be thoroughly ashamed. Hence the widespread Renaissance preference for the letter as a form of literary expression in which the author may speak in the first person, for the biography in which another person is vividly delineated in all his concrete qualities, and for the diary and autobiography in which both these traits are in a way combined. The rise of portrait painting in the visual arts seems to indicate the same general tendency. In a curious way, this individualism is blended in both art and literature with a strong classicism and formalism that might seem to be incompatible with it, but actually contributes to it a special color and physiognomy. Where moral precepts are involved, the literature is of course full of the most general rules, but these rules are addressed to the effort of the individual person, just as they are based on individual historical examples. This subjective and personal trait pervades most humanist literature, and it is apparent already in its first great representative, Petrarch. He vents his opinions, his likes and dislikes, his scruples and preoccupations, whereas objective statements on general problems are rather rare and incidental even in his philosophical writings. When we come to the end of the Renaissance, this subjective and personal character of humanist thought finds its most conscious and consummate philosophical expression in the *Essais* of Michel de Montaigne. Montaigne had received a humanist education, he knew Latin before he knew French, and his quotations from ancient authors, especially Plutarch and Seneca, fill many pages of his writings. The essay, in the form which he created and bequeathed to later centuries, is written in the first person, like the humanist letter, and is equally free in its style and structure: we might call the essay a letter written by the author to himself. Montaigne shares with the humanist his exclusive preoccupation with moral questions, his lack of interest in logic and metaphysics and the other learned disciplines, as well as his dislike for the scholastic type of learning. His philosophical position, though flexible, shows the impact of ancient skepticism, and to a lesser extent, of Stoicism. He writes on a variety of moral topics, often starting from classical examples or sentences. He would always refer to his personal experience, and draw the lesson for himself. His skepticism, from which he excepts only his religious faith, is prompted by observation and experience. He knows how complex and changeable all human affairs are. Circumstances alter all the time, and so do our moods. Most of his thoughts are prompted by introspection. What all humanists actually felt but did not express in so many words, he states most bluntly and clearly, namely, that he intends to talk primarily about himself and that his own individual self is the chief subject matter of his philosophizing. "Authors communicate themselves to the public by some peculiar and strange quality; I, for the first time, through my entire self, as Michel de Montaigne, not as grammarian or poet or lawyer. If the world complains that I speak too much of myself, I complain that the world does not think only of itself." (*Essais,* III, 2) Yet by making of his personal way of talking a philosophical program, by elevating introspection and the observation of actual human conduct to the rank of a conscious method, Montaigne already passes beyond the boundaries of humanist thought and literature, and leads the way toward the psychological study of moods and manners that was to characterize the moral literature of the seventeenth century.

## XVIII

While a scholar may be concerned with the complexities of a historical period which he is trying to understand, the layman and the student look for a broad synthesis that selects and emphasizes those aspects of the past that are significant for them and for their time, and constitute, as it were, a contribution to contemporary civilization. Such a view seemed easy when there was an unquestioned faith in the present and future status of our civilization, and in its steady and almost inevitable progress. In our own time, this faith has been shattered in many ways. There is no doubt notable progress in technology and in the natural sciences, and there is a good deal of hope for social and political progress, as there should be, since such progress depends at least in part on our efforts, and hence is our own responsibility. Yet the future is not completely under our control and is, at least to that extent, uncertain. There is constant change but no steady progress in a variety of fields, and a growing awareness that every gain, though necessary and desirable, may have to be paid for by some loss. The present—shifting, complex, and inconsistent—ceases to be a firm measure for selecting what is significant in the past. Concentration on the present and rejection of the past are actually widespread at this moment, but such attitudes are lacking in wisdom and are not likely to last very long. Philosophers, linguists, critics of the arts and of literature, and practitioners of the social sciences often treat present realities as if they were absolutes, valid for all times and places, and as if there were no alternatives. This outlook is narrow and provincial, and one of the tasks of historical scholarship, so widely ignored, is to broaden our outlook, to open our eyes to the achievements of the past, even where they differ from our own. In historical recollection, we may vicariously relive what is gone because it is intrinsically significant, and hence we can understand it. And by thus preserving it, we keep it available for the future that may still make a use of it which we cannot now foresee. The study of history is highly important in any living tradition, and we like to think of ourselves as heirs of such a tradition, which we call Western civilization. If the future belongs to a broader world culture, which will contain many strands other than those of the Western tradition, we still think and hope that it will include what we consider to be the best in the heritage of Western civilization.

If we look back upon the moral thought of Renaissance humanism for part of this heritage some of its most general traits will become apparent. Many of them are related to the social and professional situation in which most of the humanist writers found themselves. As scholars and writers professionally concerned with the study of history and of the classics, as well as with moral problems, they were thoroughly influenced by the form and ideas of ancient literature and philosophy, but at the same time eager to give expression to their personal feelings and experiences. As a result of their work and efforts through several centuries, the subject matter of the humanities was established as a branch of secular learning that included moral philosophy as distinct from, but not necessarily opposed to, theology and the natural sciences. It represented a peculiar combination of literature and scholarship that tended to disintegrate in the following centuries, but it left a double heritage that has more or less survived to the present day and that seems very much worth preserving. On the one hand, there are the historical and philological branches of knowledge that have greatly extended the range of their subject matter and refined the instruments of their research (as an echo of their origin in Renaissance humanism they are still called, in old-fashioned French and Italian, the moral sciences). On the other hand, there is a Renaissance tradition of literary culture that is not limited to formal techniques but is concerned with broad human and philosophical problems, without accepting the limitations (and/or responsibilities) of professional philosophy. This latter tradition was revived by nineteenth-century Romanticism and has recently found an influential representative in George Santayana, the American philosopher. After having surveyed the contributions made by Renaissance humanism to moral thought, some of them modest and trivial, we cannot help concluding with the hope that its double heritage, scholarly and literary, though now threatened by the onslaught of several competing forces may survive in the future.

## *FOR ADDITIONAL READING*

H. Baron. *The Crisis of the Early Italian Renaissance.* 2 vols. Princeton, 1955.

———. *Humanistic and Political Literature in Florence and Venice at the Beginning of the Quattrocento.* Cambridge, Mass., 1955.

W. Bouwsma. *The Interpretation of Renaissance Humanism.* Washington, 1959.

J. Burckhardt. *The Civilization of the Renaissance in Italy.*

D. Bush. *The Renaissance and English Humanism.* Toronto, 1939.

A. Campana. "The Origin of the Word 'Humanist,'" *Journal of the Warburg and Courtauld Institutes,* IX (1946), 60–73.

E. Cassirer, P. O. Kristeller, J. H. Randall, Jr., eds. *The Renaissance Philosophy of Man.* Chicago, 1948.

F. Chabod. *Machiavelli and the Renaissance.* Cambridge, Mass., 1958.

A. C. Crombie. *Augustine to Galileo: The History of Science A.D. 400–1650.* London, 1952.

Desiderius Erasmus. *The Education of a Christian Prince.* Translated with an introduction by Lester K. Born. New York, 1936.

W. K. Ferguson. *The Renaissance in Historical Thought.* Boston, 1948.

D. M. Frame. *Montaigne's Discovery of Man.* New York, 1955.

A. H. Gilbert. *Machiavelli's Prince and Its Forerunners.* Durham, N.C., 1938.

F. Gilbert. "The Humanist Concept of the Prince and *The Prince* of Machiavelli," *Journal of Modern History,* XI (1939), 449–83.

E. H. Harbison. *The Christian Scholar in the Age of the Reformation.* New York, 1956.

H. Haydn. *The Counter-Renaissance.* New York, 1950.

J. Huizinga. *The Waning of the Middle Ages.* London, 1924.

P. O. Kristeller. *The Classics and Renaissance Thought.* Cambridge, Mass., 1955.

———. *Studies in Renaissance Thought and Letters.* Rome, 1956.

Michel de Montaigne. *Complete Essays.* Translated by D. M. Frame. Stanford, 1958.

J. C. Nelson. *Renaissance Theory of Love.* New York, 1958.

H. R. Patch. *The Goddess Fortuna in Mediaeval Literature.* Cambridge, Mass., 1927.

J. H. Randall, Jr. *The Making of the Modern Mind.* Boston, 1940.

*The Renaissance: A Symposium.* New York, Metropolitan Museum of Art, 1952.

E. F. Rice, Jr. *The Renaissance Idea of Wisdom.* Cambridge, Mass., 1958.

J. E. Sandys. *A History of Classical Scholarship.* 3 vols. Cambridge, 1908–21.

J. L. Saunders. *Justus Lipsius: The Philosophy of Renaissance Stoicism.* New York, 1955.

F. Seebohm. *The Oxford Reformers.* London, 1867.

J. A. Symonds. *Renaissance in Italy.* 7 vols. London, 1875–86.

H. O. Taylor. *Thought and Expression in the Sixteenth Century.* 2 vols. 2d ed. New York, 1930.

C. Trinkaus. *Adversity's Noblemen: The Italian Humanists on Happiness.* New York, 1940.

R. Weiss. *The Dawn of Humanism in Italy.* London, 1947.

W. H. Werkmeister, ed. *Facets of the Renaissance.* Los Angeles, 1959.

E. Wind. *Pagan Mysteries in the Renaissance.* New Haven, 1958.

W. H. Woodward. *Studies in Education during the Age of the Renaissance.* Cambridge, 1906.

———. *Vittorino da Feltre and Other Humanist Educators.* Cambridge, 1905.

L. B. Wright. *Middle-Class Culture in Elizabethan England.* Chapel Hill, 1935.

# X

# THE REFORMATION

*Roland H. Bainton*

The Reformation disrupted the religious unity of Europe in the sixteenth century and established over and against the Roman Catholic church a group of churches known as Protestant. At the same time the spirit of reform within the Catholic church led to an improvement in morals and a more precise clarification of doctrine. These statements seem sufficiently objective, but there are some Catholic historians who use the term Reformation for the Catholic reform and refer to the Protestant as the pseudo-reformation, while the Protestants call their movement the Reformation and characterize the Catholic response as the counter-reformation. Others again avoid the issue by talking of the *Zeitalter der Glaubensspaltung,* the age of the confessional split. Whatever the terminology, the Church of Rome was confronted in the sixteenth century for the first time since the barbarian invasions with a sizable and continuing Christian rival.

Apparently then, the sixteenth century marked a great discontinuity with the Middle Ages. Some would date from this period the beginning of modern times. But others would narrow the gap, some by claiming that the Reformation merely brought to completion a disintegration already long under way —the vessel was already cracked and the Reformation merely gave the tap which caused the pieces to fall apart—and others by saying that the vessel did not fall apart and the Reformation was, after all, not so distinct from the Middle Ages.

## I

We may begin by inquiring into the state of Christendom at the end of the medieval period. The thirteenth century is commonly regarded as the peak of power, prestige, and inner cohesion of the medieval church. This was the century of Pope Innocent III, of Francis and Dominic, of Bonaventure and Aquinas, and, at the close, of Dante. The Gothic style flourished, the Crusades continued, commerce grew ever brisker. The papacy, though not a temporal power, save in the lands of the Church and to a degree over feudatories, such as Sicily, Portugal, and England, nevertheless exercised more authority throughout the whole of Europe than any single monarch. The friars renewed the monastic ideals of poverty and humility while abandoning permanent residence in monasteries in order to minister to the centers of urban culture. The great scholastics integrated faith and knowledge, revelation and reason, the supernatural and the natural in an architectonic structure to which corresponded the terrestrial hierarchies of church and state.

But these unities began to be disrupted in the very moment of their greatest achievement. The anomaly of the history of the Church in the West is that there should have been a plethora of schisms during the first four hundred years, then none at all from the barbarian invasions to the end of the twelfth century. One cannot but wonder why. The reason may have been that, with the earlier low intellectual level, churchmen did not quarrel over doctrine—there was scarcely one outstanding heretic to a century—but this will not explain why they did not quarrel over something else. Perhaps their energies were consumed in the battle with paganism and only after Europe was converted did the church come to have sufficient security and vitality for internal dissension. Again, sheer indifference may explain the lack of contention. Certainly there were periods in the Middle Ages when the church was not distinguished for zeal. But whatever the explanation, we must recognize the fact of Christian unity.

In the late twelfth century, however, southern France and northern Italy began to pullulate with sects and heresies. Some historians find the explanation in the importation of anti-Christian ideas from the East by returning Crusaders. Some think that the revival of cities and the formation of trade guilds were conducive to the spread of subversive ideas. But some see the seeds of schism in the same bag with the seeds of the church's great efflorescence: Both power and disintegration resulted from the urge to reform. The Cluniac and Hildebrandian reforms sought to impose Christian peace on lay society, to make the monasteries ascetic and the church pure and powerful. There resulted the Peace of God and the Truce of God, the Cistercian monastic revival and the papal theocracy. But none of these achievements satisfied the ardent. The peace movement issued in the Crusades, Cistercian poverty turned into industry and thrift, and the papal theocracy maintained itself for a relatively short time and then only by adroit political manipulation and rueful frequent acceptance of unpalatable *faits accomplis* like the Fourth Crusade. The disillusioned but still ardent were for "a reformation without tarrying for any," to use a later puritan slogan. The Albigensian heretics in southern France shamed the loose-living clergy by their austerity. The Waldenses refused to discontinue lay preaching. Then came Arnoldolisti, Petrobusiani, Humiliati, Patarini, Fraticelli, so that much of the sectarianism of Protestantism was anticipated over a span of three hundred years. The rising force of national states sometimes coalesced with sectarianism as, for example, in England, in the case of Wycliffe (1320?–84) who had a strong resentment against a French papacy; and in Bohemia where the revolt started by John Hus (1369–1415) was tinctured by resentment against the inroads of German Catholicism.

These sectarian movements developed, if they did not spring, from a number of subversive ideas. The Albigenses revived the ancient Gnostic dualism of spirit and flesh, condemned marriage altogether, and denied that Christ could be present in the physical elements of bread and wine. Such anti-sacramentalism struck at the very core of Catholicism, whose piety is focused on the altar and whose sacerdotalism rests on the exclusive prerogative of the priest to perform the sacraments which convey salvation. The ideal of Christian perfection and the imitation of Christ might strengthen orthodoxy and obedience, as among the Dominicans and several branches of the Franciscans, but again, might issue in rebellion, if the church impeded a realization of the ideals. This happened in the case of the Fraticelli. Even more subversive were ideas which cut the anchorage in history of the church as a great continuing institution. Predestination cut from behind, and eschatology from the front. If the true church is the church of the predestined, chosen by God from before the foundation of the world, and if this church does not necessarily correspond to the church on earth and its hierarchy, then the church of the elect may be only a handful of saints, and the pope himself may be, as Wycliffe said, "a damned limb of Lucifer." Hus in Bohemia shared with Wycliffe the predestinarian view.

Eschatology was a danger because if, as it suggested, the present age would shortly terminate, and if the great church on earth would be dissolved into the church of the spirit, then the aura of the church terrestrial was dimmed by the radiance of the "eternal Gospel" about to dawn. These ideas and terms were set forth in the late twelfth century by the Calabrian Abbot, Joachim of Fiore, who periodized history into three ages: of the Father, of the Son, and of the Spirit. The advent of the third was expected in the year 1260. The figure was derived from the number of days spent in the wilderness by the woman in the book of Revelation. When the third age did not begin in 1260, the device of the eschatologists was to take a date in early church history which when added to 1260 would throw the great advent into the near future. Such apocalyptic dreams were cherished by the Fraticelli and the Hussites to be picked up later by the radical sects of the Protestant Reformation.

Thus, among these early sects we find moral zeal, national feeling, a predestinarian view of the church, and often millenarianism, which occasionally caused violent revolution, as in the case of the Hussites. And in one group or another, and for one reason or another, we find a rejection of the sacramentalism of the Church.

At the same time, without schism or heresy, a change was taking place in the thinking of the Church. The greatest revolution may have been implicit in the attacks on the scholastic synthesis. The high scholastics were moderate realists in philosophy who held that all of reality is bound together by intrinsic ties of law and logic. Church, state, and matrimony are therefore not simply convenient or pragmatic associations on a contractual basis, but each is a "universal" whose parts are held together by rationally demonstrable laws in the order of being. Against this view arose the variegated philosophy known generally as nominalism which maintained that all of the categories of the mind are constructs for classifying objects which seem in some respects to be alike. But reality actually consists of unrelated particulars, or rather particulars related only by contiguity in place and time. Extreme nominalism may make for contractualism in the state, covenantism in the church, and casual partnership in marriage. Some of the great doctrines of the Church were also affected, notably that of the Trinity, for if there be no universal substance to hold the three persons in unity, then they will become three gods and the end will be tritheism. The conclusion of the nominalists was not to reject the doctrine of the Church, but only to say that according to reason it is demonstrably false, though nevertheless to be accepted on faith. Philosophy and theology were thus split apart, and the teaching of the Church had to be derived by deduction from revelation without the support of natural reason. There resulted, if not two kinds of truth, at any rate two kinds of logic. And where reason failed, the authority of the Church was exalted. The basis of ethics likewise changed, for instead of the universal principles of natural law, ethics came to depend increasingly on the arbitrary will of God who, as natural law theorists had already sensed, by sheer fiat might decree the polygamy of the patriarchs or the unprovoked conquest of Canaan. And if the Church were the representative of such a God on earth, she might be equally arbitrary.

In administrative and political power the Church of the late Middle Ages fell from the unsteady pinnacle of the thirteenth century. In the fourteenth century she was driven into exile at Avignon, in what is now southern France, for a period close to seventy years, called, appropriately, the Babylonian captivity. In 1378 came the great papal schism, when Pope Urban VI returned to Rome without the cardinals, who then chose a new pope, while the pope at Rome in turn created new cardinals. The schism was not completely healed until 1449 when the last counter-pope resigned. During the interim valiant efforts were made to end the schism by summoning church councils. The supporters of this movement were called Conciliarists, many of whom planned to de-centralize the Church, fixing authority not in popes but in councils of churchmen. By the fourteenth century, however, the growing strong national monarchs made any return to full papal power in Europe virtually impossible. If the papacy hoped to check conciliarism, it would have to recognize, as it eventually did, the new claims of lay rulers.

The end of the schism came during the Renaissance in Italy. The papacy recovered its unity and struggled vigorously to suppress conciliarism. Julius II (ruled 1503–13) declared it to be heresy to summon a council without the consent of the pope, but despite the brilliance of the Renaissance popes, the former prestige was never recovered. The papacy had become something between an Italian city-state and a universal power. The struggle for supremacy in Italy involved principally five city-states, Venice, Milan, Florence, Naples, and Rome. But Rome was different from the others in that as the seat of the Church she had special involvements with the great European states, England, France, Spain, and the Empire. The Italian struggle was aggravated when Charles VIII of France invaded the peninsula with gunpowder in 1498 and European politics were further complicated when Charles V, King of Spain, became the Holy Roman Emperor early in the sixteenth century. For all of his orthodoxy, he entered into conflict with the pope and his imperial troops even sacked Rome in 1527. During the entire previous half century, there was no pope distinguished for spirituality save at the very end. The aged Dutchman, Hadrian VI, lasted for only a year, just long enough to give a foretaste of the asceticism of the counter-reformation.

But piety was not universally moribund in the late Middle Ages. There were several religious movements of vitality and each of them fed into the

Reformation. The Brethren of the Common Life in the Netherlands, from whom emanated the devotional classic, *The Imitation of Christ,* cultivated a practical piety focused on love for the suffering Lord. They eschewed the refinements of scholasticism and of philosophy in general because they believed that the Trinity is better pleased by adoration than by speculation. Little theology seemed needed for salvation since, it was pointed out, the penitent thief believed only that Christ could get him into paradise and this little sufficed for his salvation. The Brethren relied on education for disseminating their ideal and had members in various schools throughout Europe.

The German mystics, represented by Eckhart and Tauler and the anonymous *Theologia Germanica,* were not opposed to theology, but the core of their piety consisted in the struggle to ascend through purification and illumination to unification with the ultimate being of God. Eckhart spoke of absorption into the great abyss of being, so much so that his orthodoxy was suspect. And Tauler emphasized love, saying that God rewards only out of love; He rewards only love; and love is the only reward. This type of piety seemed in danger of rendering superfluous the historic incarnation of God in Christ because the mystical experience of union with God is independent of time.

The Neoplatonic revival at Florence, another aspect of religious life during the Renaissance and before the Reformation, was mystical and had a tendency to dispense with the Christ of history. To the Florentine humanist, man stood at the center of the great chain of being with power to descend to the level of the beasts or to ascend into union with the Ineffable One; no mediator is needed. The ascent of man is in part away from the corporeal toward the spiritual. Hence Neoplatonic piety tends also to disparage the body so that physical media were deemed inappropriate for the expression of the divine. The eucharist may thus be retained only if the physical elements of bread and wine are deemed to be purely symbolic.

Another aspect of the Renaissance, humanism, refers in one sense to the study of humanities, literature, *belles lettres* which the humanists introduced into the curricula of the universities. Among the literature to be studied they included the writings of the early Christian fathers and the New Testament itself. Their comparative and linguistic studies raised critical problems as to the authenticity of texts and the authority of interpreters. In all such investigations the humanists desired freedom from ecclesiastical control.

The man who epitomized three of these movements was Erasmus of Rotterdam. He was educated by the Brethren of the Common Life and espoused their undogmatic piety. He was influenced by Florentine Neoplatonism to disparage the external manifestations of religion; and was committed to the humanist program of the unrestricted critical study of Christian sources.

These various movements made for tolerance. The Brethren of the Common Life decried theological speculation, the source of so much intolerance. The Mystics stressed union with God, rather than dogmatic rectitude. The Neoplatonists perceived that Christianity was not the only religion which could be accommodated to their scheme and looked with a charitable eye on Judaism and Islam.

In contrast with this scholarly piety, popular piety was often very crude and took on extravagant forms. Because of the obsession with the cult of death which developed after the Black Death in 1348, tombstones were ghastly in their realism, portraying worms in the entrails. Among the most popular books were those entitled *Ars Moriendi* (*The Art of Dying*). But death as such was not so much the object of terror as that which followed, namely the Judgment Day when the fiends would take the lids off the tombs, seize the dead by their not yet disintegrated locks, and bolt them into hell. To reassure tortured spirits, the Church offered various expedients. Appeal was directed not so much to Christ, as to his gracious Mother and the saints; and their favor was to be won by pilgrimages to their shrines, veneration of their relics, and appropriation of their merits.

The saints were esteemed to have been better than they needed to be for their own salvation. Their lives had terminated with an unexpended balance of good works and this residue had been accumulated in a treasury of the merits of the saints, *thesaurus meritorum sanctorum,* from which the pope could make a transfer to those whose accounts were in arrears. Such a transfer was called an indulgence. The practice of granting indulgences went back centuries to the Crusades. At first those who took the cross were accorded the same remission of penalties for sins which would have accrued had they stayed at home and gone on a pilgrimage. This was really only a substitution of one penance for another and did not yet involve a transfer of credit. Then the same benefits were conferred upon those who could not join the Crusade but could make a financial contribution. In this way indulgences first came to be used as a device for raising money, but they were granted only to remit penalties for sin imposed on earth. Eventually, some indulgences went further and granted remission of sin as well as penalty, not only on earth but in purgatory. Strictly speaking, indulgences were not sold but were given away and in return the grateful recipients made contributions. The handling of the indulgence was, however, strictly timed to coincide with the contribution. By this means Gothic cathedrals, hospitals, universities and even bridges were financed throughout Europe.

## II

Such, in brief, is the background of the Reformation of the sixteenth century. The revolt originated with one man, Martin Luther. What impelled him? Some have seen in his critique of Rome another instance of moral indignation against the corruption rampant in the Church in the beginning of the sixteenth century. No one denies that there was corruption, least of all Catholic historians who have sometimes even magnified it in order to exalt the work of the Catholic Reformation. Clerical concubinage was in some quarters a recognized institution with taxes paid for mistresses and bastards. Financial abuses, the sale of ecclesiastical offices, pluralism—that is, the holding of several offices at once—and therefore absenteeism from most of them—these scandals loomed large in all proposals for reform.

The Catholic historians of fifty years ago were disposed to explain the Protestant Reformation in terms of this decadence of the Church. Denifle held that the Reformation was simply the perpetuation of the Catholic abuses minus a bad conscience. Instead of abolishing clerical concubinage by restoring clerical celibacy, Luther instead instituted clerical marriage and pronounced it holy in the eyes of God. But Grisar, the Jesuit historian, has interpreted Luther as a passionate reformer whose intemperate zeal led to clashes with ecclesiastical authority. This interpretation puts Luther in the succession of the medieval sects. But Luther himself said: "What differentiates me from previous reformers is that they attacked the life whereas I attack the doctrine." His objection was to the teaching of the Catholic church.

The fault with the teaching of the Church was that it obscured the biblical picture of man's plight and the way of salvation. Luther agonized over man's plight and even more over his own plight in recurrent periods of depression. Luther's disturbance was rooted in religion. Given the intense piety in which he had been reared, he was obsessed by the imminence of death and the judgment to come and he could find no security in the intercession of the saints and the Virgin because these were contingent on some effort on the part of man, and Luther could not bring himself to feel that anything whatever on the part of man could effect any reconciliation with God.

Luther's initial conflict with Catholic doctrine centered on the picture of man and his capacities. The Church taught that man without God can do nothing. By virtue of the grace which comes before performance of a good act, called "prevenient grace," he can do something worthwhile for his soul or for other men. What he then does is accounted to his credit; he may even accumulate superabundant credit. Here is the theological basis for the doctrine of indulgences.

Luther's conclusion was that man alone can do absolutely nothing for his peace or salvation, although he himself endeavored to do everything which the Church prescribed. Nothing seemed more efficacious than to take the cowl and this he did. Once in the monastery he scorned the easy way and sought to take the kingdom of heaven by storm through ascetic practices and the torture of the flesh. But Luther could never persuade himself that he was poor enough or hungry enough, let alone pure enough, to satisfy the exacting requirements of God, who demands perfection whereas perfection is impossible. And even should one today fulfill one of God's demands, the very success would open up new possibilities for perfection which if not realized would constitute failure on the morrow. Having exhausted self-help Luther then explored all of the solace which the Church offers the sinner rather than the saint. The sacrament of penance is designed to issue in the absolution of sins. The sacrament involves four parts: contrition, confession, absolution, and satisfaction. Luther was convinced that no one can be sure of adequate, that is, absolutely disinterested contrition; and no one can ever make any satisfaction. But there remains confession, and here he sought to clear the slate by remembering and confessing all the wrongs he had ever done. He was disconcerted to discover that even after confessing for six hours, he would come out and recall something else with which he would run back. His confessor grew petulant and told him that if he wished to confess so much he should do something worth confessing, like killing his father and his mother instead of bringing in these "dollies' sins." But Luther's problem was not whether sins were big or little but whether all had been expunged. And he soon came to realize that he could not remember everything and what was more serious, he could not recognize everything, because man does not perceive that he has done wrong until confronted by the accusation of God. Therefore, confession can never clean the slate. From the German mystics Luther learned that man can cease to strive and simply yield himself, sinking into the abyss of the godhead. But for Luther sinfulness could not be overcome by absorption because sinfulness impedes union with the All Holy. Man is too unclean to be taken up into God.

By such reflections, Luther was driven to near madness. Then his confessor drew him away from too constant preoccupation with himself by making him a lecturer on the Bible in the University of Wittenberg. From 1513–16 Luther lectured on the Psalms, Romans, and Galatians. In the course of these lectures he came into the clear with a new picture of God, of man, of Christ, and of salvation.

## III

Luther rediscovered the historical character of the Christian religion. Christianity is a religion rooted not in nature, though God may be discerned in his handiwork; not in contemplation, because God must be rightly understood before He can be adored; but rather in history. God is a God whose power and majesty, love and mercy, are disclosed in His mighty deeds. The feasts of Christianity are commemorative. Christianity rests on a deed of God in time, when the Word became flesh, when God was uniquely manifest in Christ Jesus. The incarnation of God in man, the death and resurrection, reveal a God whose essence is not wrath but mercy, who despite man's rebellion, humbled Himself, taking the form of a servant to expunge man's sin, Himself endured the pangs of the cross, and by His resurrection displayed His victory over sin, death, and all the hosts of darkness. That God should do all this is perfectly incredible. Luther agreed with the nominalists, by whom he had been trained, that this picture of God is contrary to philosophy, but for him the discrepancy was not so much logical as moral. Man can understand the words which tell him that God created man in His own image and when man defied his maker, instead of wiping him out, stooped to become a man and to die an ignominious death. The words are plain but who can understand the meaning, for what man would ever do so much for another, and how, then, can he fathom the condescension of God? But this is what scripture tells us God did. This we must believe. We must believe that God did it. But merely to believe is not enough. We must surrender our wills, all our pretense of goodness and, confessing simply that we are unclean, throw ourselves upon God's mercy, accept His grace. We can then rejoice in the abundance of His love, and in gratitude spontaneously fulfill His will. This is justification by faith.

For Luther, the ways in which the Catholic Church had obscured this simple message were not at first apparent. Luther initially envisaged no reform of the Church other than in education, for he would give to the Bible a larger place in the theological curriculum. He was to become a Reformer *malgré lui*.

This happened because he was made a pastor as well as a professor and as a pastor he was responsible for the cure of souls. His parishioners were securing indulgences. The particular indulgence which they obtained exceeded all that had gone before in its pretensions. It would insure the remission of sins, although it did not indeed permit future sins; nevertheless, he who sinned in the future would receive preferential treatment. Those who obtained indulgences for others already in purgatory need not themselves be contrite for their own sins. The preacher who hawked these indulgences promised immediate release from purgatory, "As soon as the coin in the coffer rings, the soul from purgatory springs." The money from the expected contributions was to go, all of it ostensibly, to build the basilica of St. Peter's in Rome. Actually, half of the sum was to reimburse the new Archbishop of Mainz, Albert of Hohenzollern, for fees already paid to the pope for pluralism in the holding of three sees at once. The third of these, at Mainz, had given Albert the primacy of the Church in Germany and to secure it he had already borrowed 10,000 ducats from the great bankers, the Fuggers.

On the eve of All Saints Day, October 30, 1517, Luther posted on the door of the Castle Church at Wittenberg his famous ninety-five theses, a document in Latin designed in accord with ancient custom to serve as a basis for a disputation. There were ninety-five propositions but not so many points. The basic contentions were three. First, that the pope should not strip the fleece from his German sheep to build a basilica at Rome. The second was that the pope had no jurisdiction over purgatory and if he did he should empty the place gratis. The third was the most radical, a denial of the treasury of good works. No one has any superfluous credit. The treasury of the church is the gospel, and he who is truly contrite will seek rather than flee penalties—"He is damned who flees damnation."

The theses within two weeks were translated into German and acquired a popularity which Luther had never expected. Why did they meet with so great a response? The denunciation of the financial exploitation of Germany would of course invoke enthusiasm on the part of all Germans. But the Germans of the imperial Diets had been saying this sort of thing for a hundred years and nothing drastic had happened. The claim that the pope had no control over purgatory would be endorsed by the more moderate theologians. But the complete denial of the whole theory of the extra-abundant merits of the saints went counter to the greatest and best theologians and flatly contradicted the Catholic doctrine of man.

Did those who rallied to Luther at this time grasp all this? The question does not permit an answer, but this is clear—that Luther's colleagues on the faculty at the University of Wittenberg backed him to a man because they believed that he had correctly expounded the views of the Apostle Paul. Luther was considered by his colleagues to be a true exponent of the Sacred Word.

The pope was compelled to deal with the case and commissioned Prierias, a Dominican, the Master of the Sacred Palace, to respond to Luther. In so doing, Prierias asserted that "whoever does not rest on the doctrine of the Roman Church and of the Roman Pontiff as the infallible rule of faith from which even Sacred Scripture draws its strength and authority, is a heretic." This statement posed the problem of authority. Prierias was an extreme papalist and part of the tragedy of the Reformation is that those in the Roman church who dealt with Luther were extremists. The indulgence which Luther had attacked was the most extravagant of all and the condemnation by Prierias was no less extreme because he declared scripture itself to depend for its authority upon the Catholic church. Luther retorted, "If this be so, what need or use is there for Holy Scripture? Why not burn it all and content ourselves with these unlearned lords at Rome?"

A long, maturing controversy came to a head at this point. In the early centuries the Church had not sensed any conflict between scripture, tradition, and the institution. One further aspect of the disintegration of the religious unity the late Middle Ages was the emergence of this split. When in the early fourteenth century Pope John XXII declared that Christ had property, the Franciscans branded the pope as a heretic and William of Occam, their spokesman, appealed to scripture against the pope. Wycliffe and Hus declared that the Church and scripture could never be at variance because the only true church is that church which adheres to scripture, though it be only a remnant. This was to define the church as a sect. The Conciliarists sought to divert authority from the popes to councils as the interpreters of scripture. But they did not allow individual judgment, and, when John Hus exercised it, they burned him at the stake. In the meantime, throughout the fifteenth century, extreme papalists made the Church, epitomized in the pope, to be the organ of revelation to such a degree as to render scripture and tradition superfluous. This was the point reached by Prierias. His argument was elaborated by others who claimed that the church is lord of scripture because the church made the scripture, inasmuch as the church selected those books which should constitute the scripture. Luther went beyond the sects in his rejoinder. He answered that the church did not make the scripture. The Word of God made the church. The Word is God's redemptive deed in Christ. The Word made the church. The church then decided what books contained the Word. The scripture is not the Word; it is the manger which holds the baby Jesus who is the Word. The Word is the norm by which to judge the church and also by which to judge the scripture. For within scripture there is a hierarchy of values depending upon which books best proclaim the Word. In the New Testament Luther preferred John's Gospel and the Pauline epistles. In the Old Testament he liked Genesis which relates that Abraham was saved by faith, the Psalms because they were so penitential, Habakkuk which contains the verse "The just shall live by faith," and Jonah because by faith the prophet composed a Psalm "in the unventilated belly of the whale." In his reply, then, to Prierias, Luther flatly denied the infallibility of the pope and the infallibility of councils. He was left with the Bible, to be interpreted by those trained in humanist philological methods and guided by the Holy Spirit.

## IV

The pope summoned Luther to Rome. Unsolicited, Luther's prince, Frederick the Wise of Saxony, then intervened to insist that his subject should be tried only on German soil. Frederick was the senior elector of the Holy Roman Empire, and was therefore an extremely important political figure, even though he ruled over only a small territory. He was a fascinating character: a medieval prince loyal to the Empire and loyal to the Catholic church; a staunch German not to be manipulated by the Italian Renaissance papacy; a devout Christian, aware that often enough the civil arm had reformed the spiritual and that state as well as the Church had a responsibility for Christendom; a man of reverence for learning who had therefore founded the University of Wittenberg, that its faculty should be his mentors as to the law of man and the will of God. He did not propose now that his professor, supported by all of his colleagues, should be snuffed out by some committee of papal sycophants at Rome. The pope, who could not afford lightly to alienate the senior elector of the Holy Roman Empire, acceded to the request and arranged that Luther should be heard by one of the noblest and most distinguished theologians of the day, Cardinal Cajetan, who was attending the Diet meeting at Augsburg in Germany.

The intervention of Frederick raises the question whether the Lutheran Reformation could have succeeded anywhere else than in Germany. Some say that the political decentralization was essential to its success. Had Luther appeared in a strongly consolidated monarchy like France, Spain, or England, he would have been suppressed at once. But in the little principality where the prince was well disposed he could succeed. This statement does not exhaust the possibilities. To be sure, if the Holy Roman Empire had been so tightly knit that the emperor could do as he pleased, Luther would not have gone on for long. His books were first burned in the Netherlands where the emperor Charles was an hereditary prince and did not need to consult the estates. But the Reformation was later introduced into England under the most despotic of the Tudors. A more accurate statement would be that no religious reform could have succeeded without at least the benevolent neutrality of the civil authorities. Luther would have fared no better in his German state than in Spain if Frederick had been ill disposed. The real question is why Frederick was well disposed.

Some would answer that he lusted after the goods of the Church. The usual economic explanation of the Reformation is that the princes broke with Rome in order to expropriate ecclesiastical goods. But they did not need to break with Rome for that. The goods of the Church had been constantly expropriated from the days of Charles Martel to Cardinal Wolsey, who suppressed monasteries in favor of colleges. The losses of the Church were made up by new donations and the process continued. Frederick gave Luther his support because he suspected that Luther might be right. At any rate, he would not suppress him until convinced that he was wrong.

Luther then was tried by Cardinal Cajetan at Augsburg in 1518. The cardinal confronted him with the bull *Unigenitus* which set forth the theory of the *thesaurus meritorum sanctorum*. After some sparring, Luther repudiated the bull, thereby impugning not only the authority of the pope, its author, but also of the canon law in which it had been incorporated. The cardinal told Luther to leave and not to return unless he were ready to recant.

Luther had reason to think that this was the end, and it might have been save for one of those fortuitous or predestined coincidences of history. The emperor Maximillian died, and the election to the Holy Roman Empire was pending. The heads of the great national states were eligible: Henry of England, Francis of France, Charles of Spain. But Pope Leo was loathe to see the power of any of the three augmented by that of the imperial dignity. He preferred a less formidable prince and his choice fell on Frederick the Wise who might indeed have been elected had he voted for himself. During 1518–19, the year when the election was pending, Frederick's vote was, in any case, of supreme importance, and the pope was willing to relax the pressures on Luther in order not to alienate his prince. That was how it came to pass that Luther, already judged by the cardinal to be a heretic, was permitted to debate publicly at the great University of Leipzig with the renowned disputant John Eck. The debate centered on the antiquity of the papacy, the point being that, if it went back to the time of the apostles, it might be regarded as a divine institution. But if it arose more recently then it was of human origin. Luther argued that the papacy as it existed in his day was not over four hundred years old and rested only on human authority. Eck rejoined that this sounded like John Hus. Luther at first vehemently repudiated the imputation, but after having examined the Acts of the Council of Constance, which condemned Hus, reported that some of his articles were most right and evangelical. Eck had scored, for to identify an opponent with a heretic already condemned and burned was sufficient to clinch the case.

One would have supposed that surely now Luther would have gone to the stake. Instead he became the hero of Germany. One reason may well have been the publication of his collected works. But their dissemination may have been due to popularity rather than the reverse. Was, then, his following won because men misunderstood his doctrines? How many understood what he was trying to say? One must concede that some of his early allies had not fathomed his theology. Those nationalistic Germans led by Ulrich von Hutten saw in Luther the German prophet inveighing against the treatment of the Fatherland as if it were the pope's milk cow. Hutten was quite willing to start a war against the papists; yet any use of the temporal sword in the name of the gospel was utterly anathema to Luther. Erasmus and the humanists likewise rallied because they saw in him a new Reuchlin, an earlier great champion of unimpeded Hebrew studies in the universities. Now Luther seemed to be the champion of biblical scholarship against ecclesiastical intimidation.

But Luther also had a large popular following. Lortz, a recent Catholic historian, is prepared to think that Catholic piety in that period had so far degenerated as to consist largely in externalities, trafficking in grace, pilgrimages, the cult of relics, and the securing of indulgences, and Luther's success is itself to be taken as the proof that his critique appeared accurate and right to the people, who still had a sufficient sense of the essentials of Christianity to perceive a discrepancy between current corruption and ancient truth. In other words, Luther's central message was understood, even by the masses.

The pope could not dally indefinitely. The king of Spain was elected Holy Roman Emperor as Charles V in 1519. He was deeply orthodox and of no mind to tolerate heresy in his domains. But at the same time he was astute enough politically to understand that he could not rule a people without its consent and he was ready therefore either to push the case or to temporize. The pope at length ceased to temporize and from his hunting lodge in the month of June, 1520, issued the bull, *Exsurge,* which gave Luther sixty days in which to make his submission. The clock did not start to tick until the bull was actually delivered to the person named, and even the German bishops so obstructed its publication, that John Eck, to whom the delivery was entrusted, took four months to place the document in Luther's hands on the 10th of October, 1520.

## V

During the interim in which the bull was seeking him, Luther issued a series of tracts, even more devastating in their onslaught on Rome. *The Address to the Christian Nobility of the German Nation* was issued in August, 1520. It was a manifesto of reform essentially medieval in character. The nobility to whom it spoke was the ruling class in Germany, including the emperor. Luther appealed to them to reform the Church, partly because they were baptized members in a Christian community. Here was the old idea of a Christian society in which church and state were correlative arms, each with a responsibility to reform the other. At the same time Luther called upon the nobility as "fellow priests," in accord with his doctrine that all Christians are priests in the spiritual sense, though they are otherwise assigned to particular offices, whether of the ministry or government or what not. His point was that the magistrate was not spiritually inferior to the cleric and that the state should operate in its own right without ecclesiastical interference. This, too, was good medieval theory in the imperialist tradition. One finds it already in Dante. Yet the state might invade the province of the church if the church were recreant in its morals and temporal administration. In this sense, Luther proceeded to outline a reform of the Church in externals. He would pare the pomp, curtail the wealth, and restrict the power of the papacy, which should become a purely spiritual institution virtually on a Franciscan pattern. The temporal affairs of the Church should be administered by national churches.

The tract displayed a crescendo of invective, combining the themes of the century-old "complaints of the German nation," the virulence of Ulrich von Hutten, and the sectarian theme of the contrast of Christ and Antichrist. Luther inveighed that the pope takes with him on a pleasure ride three thousand mule drivers whereas Christ and Peter went on foot. Christ washed the disciples' feet, but the pope requires kings and emperors to kiss his toe. The pope is Antichrist, the man of sin, the son of perdition. May Christ "destroy the devil's nest at Rome."

Yet despite the virulent invective, this tract was not so radical as its successor, a theological treatise entitled *The Babylonian Captivity,* which argued that the sacraments of the church had been captured by the Church of Rome. In this tract published in October, 1520, Luther reduced the seven sacraments almost to two. Extreme unction was to be abandoned entirely. Confirmation, ordination, and marriage were to be retained as rites of the church but not as sacraments, because a sacrament must have a visible sign of an invisible grace and must have been specifically instituted by Christ. Marriage could not be a sacrament, although approved by Christ, because it was not instituted by him but by God in paradise. It belongs therefore to the order of creation and is valid for all peoples, the Turks and the Jews included. It cannot, then, be a Christian sacrament because a Christian sacrament must obviously be uniquely Christian. Marriage may be solemnized by the church but it is essentially a civil relationship. The door was thus opened to the secularization of marriage.

This left three sacraments: penance, baptism, and the mass. Luther did not deal drastically with penance; neither did he leave it intact. Penance, as we have noted, consisted of four parts, contrition, confession, absolution, and satisfaction. During his own travail Luther had denied the possibility of perfect contrition and of any satisfaction. Confession he still deemed wholesome, though it should be voluntary and might be made to any fellow Christian and not necessarily to an ordained minister. Baptism and the mass alone thus remained as sacraments in the proper sense and both were altered.

Baptism was a problem for Luther because he said that a sacrament is of no value apart from the faith of the recipient. Yet he was ready to administer baptism to babies and justified this procedure on the ground that their faith is dormant or that they are sustained by the faith of their sponsors. The retention of infant baptism provided a social basis for the church, because if every baptized child may be accounted in some sense a Christian and if every child in the community is baptized, then the church and the community may be considered coterminous and the entire society may be regarded as Christian.

The mass offered the greatest ground for revision. Luther preferred to call it the Lord's Supper, though the word mass was not entirely abandoned. In the Catholic mass Luther objected, as had Hus, to the withdrawal of the wine from the laity. He excluded masses for the dead said by the priest without a congregation because the mass must be a fellowship and communion of believers with each other and with their Lord. Luther roundly rejected the doctrine of the mass as a repetition on the altar of the crucifixion because Christ was sacrified once and for all upon the cross. Here is another example of the way in which Luther anchored Christianity in a deed of God in history. Finally, he rejected the Catholic doctrine of transubstantiation, the claim that when the priest pronounces over the elements the words "This is my body," a change takes place and although the accidents remain, the substance of bread and wine is altered into the substance of the body of Christ. Luther denied that any change takes place; the words of the priest do nothing to the elements. That being so, the prerogative of the priest is largely eliminated. His authority in Catholicism depends upon this, that by virtue of the power conferred on him in ordination he is able to perform on the altar the very miracle of making God present in bodily form. Luther asserted that there is no miracle. Nevertheless Christ is bodily present because he said, "This is my body." How he is present we do not know. We can only say that Christ's body is "with, in, and under" the elements. The priest's words do not make it so, because Christ's body is everywhere present. Christ as God pervades all reality. What, then, is special with regard to his presence on the altar? Only this, that here He is peculiarly discerned. On account of the weakness of man, God has ordained special modes of self-disclosure. One is the preaching of the Word, and the other is the administration of the sacraments. The minister does no more in the one case than in the other, and for neither does he require a tactual apostolic succession. He should be trained, approved and set aside for his office by the clergy, though in an emergency, he might be commissioned by a local congregation.

*The Babylonian Captivity* among all Luther's writings was the most disruptive of medieval Catholicism. When Erasmus saw it, he declared the breach with Rome to be irreparable. Condemnation could not be long deferred after this. The papal bull reached Luther on October 10. The sixty days expired on December 10. On that day he burned the papal bull. In January the pope signed another bull announcing that Luther's time limit had expired and that he was now under excommunication, but, curiously, this bull was not actually promulgated until the following October and a bull to take effect had to be publicly announced. For technical and political reasons the bull had to be returned to Rome for redrafting. This delay was responsible for Luther's appearance at the Diet of Worms.

This was the Diet of the German emperor at which the young Charles V was for the first time to meet with the estates. Frederick the Wise, who had long insisted that Luther should not be condemned without a fair hearing, now proposed to the emperor that Luther be brought before the Diet. The emperor agreed, but then rescinded his consent at the insistence of the papal nuncio who wanted the Diet simply to condemn Luther without a hearing. It must be borne in mind that for the burning of a heretic two condemnations were necessary; he must be pronounced a heretic by the Church, which then turned him over for punishment to the secular arm; the state had then to confirm the judgment of the Church, place the rotten member under the civil ban, and commit him to the stake for the salvation of his soul. But the first step in this sequence was lacking, so long as the bull was withheld. When the papal nuncio called upon the Diet to place Luther under the ban, some asked why the Diet should take action when the Church had not condemned him. The nuncio then found himself driven to argue before the assembly, largely lay in character, that Luther was a heretic. But they were not inclined to pass judgment unless Luther himself were heard. And the emperor therefore had to revert to his original plan and summon the accused.

Luther had two hearings; the first was at the close of the day when the Diet was poorly attended. He was shown his books and asked whether they were his. Had he been willing to disown the *Babylonian Captivity,* the other matters, including even papal infallibility, might have been discussed. But Luther acknowledged all as his writings. Would he then stand by everything which he had said? The door to reconciliation with Rome was thus re-opened. Luther was suddenly overwhelmed by the sense of responsibility and asked time for consideration. As an act of exceeding grace, he was permitted to wait until the following day and as a result was to make his address before a packed session.

When Luther was asked again whether he would stand by all that he had written, he proceeded to classify his works into three groups. But the examiner drew him up sharply with a demand for a candid answer without qualification. "Do you or do you not repudiate your books and the errors which they contain?" Luther replied:

> Since then Your Majesty and your lordships desire a simple reply, I will answer without horns and without teeth. Unless I am convicted by Scripture and plain reason—I do not accept the authority of popes and councils, for they have contradicted each other—my conscience is captive to the Word of God. I cannot and I will not recant anything, for to go against my conscience is neither right nor safe. God help me. Amen.

The emperor would trifle no longer. He waited for some of Luther's more staunch supporters to go home and then issued the Edict of Worms which placed Luther under the ban of the Empire. Luther had already left the city and was "captured" by the connivance of Frederick the Wise who had him hidden for a year at the Castle of the Wartburg. At first shatteringly depressed, Luther quickly regained his composure and set himself at work to translate the New Testament into German. In an incredible three months the task was completed though he was to spend the rest of his life in revision. The second edition of Erasmus' New Testament served as the basis. Luther's language was chaste, choice, rich, varied, rhythmic, sonorous, and profound. Luther knew Greek and he knew German but also his spirit had waited upon the Lord.

The exile at the Wartburg was not a retreat for long. Reports kept coming from Wittenberg, some of them heartening. The mass was being given, both the bread and the wine, to the laity. But some reports were disquieting. Luther had already endorsed clerical marriage in one of his earlier tracts, but what about monastic vows? Could monks as well as priests marry? Melanchthon, Luther's colleague at Wittenberg, argued that monastic vows were not binding because they could not be kept. But Luther replied that the question was not whether they were attainable but whether they had been commanded by God. He searched the scriptures and came to the conclusion that monastic vows had never been enjoined and were not binding.

Then came rumors of violence in Wittenberg against the mass. Luther made a swift reconnaissance incognito and concluded that he could not long remain in hiding. An invitation came soon from the town council at Wittenberg to come home and re-establish order. Frederick the Wise warned Luther that no protection could be afforded a man under the ban of the Church and the Empire. Luther replied that he was not asking for protection. In fact, he could better protect the elector by his prayers than the elector could protect him by his sword. And with no safe conduct, condemned alike by the Church and state, Luther forsook his asylum and came back to build a church. This was a turning point in his career. Thus far he had been the great rebel. He had attacked indulgences, papal infallibility, conciliar infallibility, the pomp and power of the papacy, the system of the seven sacraments, the theory of the mass as a sacrifice and a miracle, clerical celibacy, and monastic vows. Now he must build a church.

## VI

He began by preaching moderation. Let there be no violence. To be sure, there are abuses in the church "so also men have gone wrong with women and wine, but should we therefore abolish women and prohibit wine?" This is not to say, as some have said, that Luther went back on his own program of reform. As a matter of fact, in a few years his earlier recommendations were realized. But the pace was slower and extremes were avoided. Luther was driven more and more to moderation by the extravagances of his followers and was soon to find himself in the middle of the way between the Catholic and Protestant sectaries.

Two figures in his own camp distressed him greatly. The first was his older colleague, Carlstadt, who was a proto-Puritan. Influenced by the Neoplatonic disparagement of the corporeal, which he may have received from Erasmus, Carlstadt objected to the use of the pictorial in religion. There should be no images of the saints or the Virgin nor even a crucifix in the churches. There also should be no church music, no diverting tintinabulation, and he affirmed that there is no physical presence of Christ at all in the sacrament. The bread and wine are merely symbols. He asserted that we feed on Christ only by faith in our hearts in the Spirit. One wonders why Carlstadt retained the eucharist at all. But Luther was as materialistic as Catholics in the sense that he believed that the material is fit for divine communication. Since God in Christ became flesh, the flesh may be portrayed and religion may be conveyed through the eye, through the ear, and through the mouth. But this very approach to religion was what Carlstadt challenged.

Furthermore Carlstadt was an egalitarian. Luther, it is true, had proclaimed the priesthood of all believers. All are priests, he said, but he went on to add that all are not ministers. He wanted a trained ministry and saw no reason why the minister should not be distinguished by a special dress and appellation, but Carlstadt wanted to be called only *Bruder,* not *Doktor*. He would wear not a robe but a peasant's smock, and thought it wrong that a minister should receive financial remuneration. To support himself and his family, Carlstadt became a farmer on the side. "Good God!" ejaculated Luther, "what would I not give to look into the eyes of friendly animals instead of having to put up with a cantankerous congregation!" Many of the features of Carlstadt's reform were to recur in English Puritanism among the Congregationalists, the Baptists, and the Quakers.

Even more disquieting for Luther, was Thomas Müntzer, whose religion was rooted in German mysticism. The only true Christian, said Müntzer, is the Christian who has died to self and been united with the source of all being. He must experience a new birth in the Spirit. Those who have had this experience are the elect and by virtue of the experience can recognize each other and form a community, a *Bund*. This possibility Luther flatly denied. There are no signs, he declared, whereby the elect can be distinguished from the non-elect. But, obviously, if they can be identified then the way is open for the establishment of a holy commonwealth. Müntzer sired the idea if not the actuality, of the Protestant theocracy resting on election and to be distinguished from the Catholic theocracy which rests on sacramentalism and sacerdotalism. Those chosen by God and identified by the new birth are able to form a holy commonwealth. To these, his saints, God has given the kingdom. He will speedily inaugurate it with great power and wonder in the second coming of the Lord. At this point Müntzer revived the eschatology of the late Middle Ages. Luther also believed that the Lord's coming was not remote, but he was of no mind to set dates and centered his piety on redemption rather than release. Müntzer's program might have been quietism, simply to wait for the Lord, but, disdainful of logic, Müntzer leaped from eschatology to revolution, declaring that now was the time of the harvest. The elect were the angels who should put the sickle to the tares. He found a following only among the peasants and perished by execution in the ensuing debacle of the Peasants' War (1525–26).

Luther was horrified by the programs of the peasants and of Müntzer. The peasants seemed terribly wrong in seeking to redress both economic and ecclesiastical grievances by the sword which may be wielded only by the magistrate. In the hands of the common man the sword could lead only to anarchy, not to justice. Least of all should the minister embrace the sword, because the gospel demands suffering. When, then, Müntzer, an ordained evangelical minister, unfurled the banner of the peasants' revolt in the church itself, Luther cried "Smite him down."

Müntzer raised even deeper issues as to the seat of religious authority. Here even more than anywhere else, Luther found himself battered from both sides. Erasmus, the humanist Catholic, asked Luther by what authority he interpreted the scriptures. Luther answered, "By the Spirit." Erasmus asked how he knew he had the Spirit. Luther answered, "Through the scriptures." Erasmus pronounced this circular reasoning. Then came Müntzer, saying that indeed the Bible can be understood only through the Spirit. The Apostles were in the Spirit when they wrote the Bible. We must be in the same Spirit as the Apostles if we are to understand the Bible, but if we are in the same Spirit as the Apostles we do not need the Bible. The written book may indeed become an impediment. "Away with the book. It is Bible, Babel, Bubble." Luther answered (using the image of the Holy Spirit as a dove), "Unless you cite scripture I do not care if you have swallowed the Holy Ghost feathers and all."

Luther insisted on the Word and on the Spirit. He could not accept any attenuation of the unique self-disclosure of God in Christ. Authority resides in God's deed; the witness to that deed is the scripture. This must be interpreted by humanist philological techniques, but also by spiritual insight. But how then does one get this insight? Can one do nothing but wait? Luther's only answer was that one must steep oneself in scripture until the Spirit descends and the heart leaps into flame.

In the midst of these controversies, Luther was giving shape to a church. He revised the liturgy, first in Latin, then in German. He prepared two catechisms, one for adults and one for children. He issued a hymn book with a number of hymns of his own composition; for some he wrote both words and music. He published a body of sermons which served as models for his preachers and throughout his life until his death in 1546 he produced a prodigious body of biblical commentaries.

But he ceased to be the public figure he had been in earlier years. Since he was under the ban of the Church and the Empire, he could not attend any of the Diets. Melanchthon took over the role of spokesman on such occasions and to the German princes fell the role of witnesses for the evangelical cause. At the Diet of Augsburg in 1530 the prospect that the Protestant rulers might have to "let goods and kindred go, this mortal life also" was very real. And in the 1540s when the emperor was at last free to come to Germany with Spanish troops to suppress the reform, the common people and the princes alike stood in danger. But theirs was the spirit of George of Brandenburg who, at the Diet of Augsburg, refused to participate in the Corpus Christi procession and when summoned to answer before the emperor said that rather than renounce his faith, he would suffer the emperor to cut off his head. Whatever may have been the conglomeration of motives which gave an initial impetus to the Reformation, within a decade it had become a cause for which to die.

No longer a public figure, Luther made one more great contribution to reorganizing the Christian community when he founded a Protestant parsonage. He had said earlier that none would give him a wife, but when a convent of nuns under the impact of his teaching left the cloister and arrived at Wittenberg—"vestal virgins more eager for marriage than for life," facetiously remarked a contemporary—Luther was confronted with the responsibility of finding suitable homes for the escapees. He succeeded with all save Catherine von Bora. The candidate selected to marry her was not acceptable and she suggested, not too subtly, that Dr. Luther himself would do. He discerned here the hand of God and the course of duty. He did not pretend to be violently enamored but became very devoted to his wife and family. The combination of patriarchalism and tenderness together with non-sentimental devotion did much to set a style for the German home and made possible the ministerial family.

## VII

In the meantime reform movements sprang up independently not only of Rome but also of Luther—Zwinglianism and Anabaptism, Calvinism and Anglicanism. This phenomenon has led some Catholic historians to point out that schism begets schism and the end of the process is atomization of the church. The generalization is not without truth because sectarianism is by definition divisive. But several qualifications are in order. A single fission does not necessarily end in complete disintegration because the process often arrests itself and even reverses. Protestantism continued the sectarian process of the late Middle Ages until the peak of divisiveness was reached in the

Puritan movements. Thereafter Protestant sectarianism receded to be replaced by the ecumenical movement of modern times.

The Protestant movements of the sixteenth century were not, however, examples of a series of secessions from secessions, since they were largely independent of each other and arose because of the manifest need for reform which produced also the parallel movements within the Church of Rome. Again, the seemingly endless proliferation of sects in Protestantism is partly an illusion created by the lack in most instances of a centralized religious authority within the groups. The Lutheran churches did not make a pope out of Luther or a Rome out of Wittenberg. Geneva was a cradle and asylum, but not a Jerusalem or a Mecca for the Reformed churches. Only the Anglican church had a centralized structure. But lack of ecclesiastical unity did not preclude intercommunion. Finally, despite all seeming atomization, the varieties of Protestantism scarcely exceeded three. There was a Lutheran-Anglican type, which might be called Catholic-Protestantism, because it retained the union of church and state, viewed the church as coterminous with the community, and was ready to employ the material and sensuous in the form of art, music, and the sacraments as a device for communicating the divine. The second type of reformed faith brought consociation of church and state together with an aversion to material aids to religion. The third is the Anabaptist type, which likewise disparaged the physical, but went further than all in the rejection of the affiliation of church and state and even of the state itself in its coercive aspect. The differences are obvious but are not to be exaggerated, for all agreed with Luther on those points on which he differed from Rome.

The movement of Zwingli arose independently of Luther in the German Swiss town of Zurich in the year 1519. Zwingli averred that he had learned from Luther not a single idea but only the courage to do and say what he had already believed. Yet his agreement with Luther was broad. When they met at the Colloquy of Marburg in 1529 they found themselves in wide accord. The point of difference was on the presence of Christ in the sacrament. There were, however, other differences, in particular three, for Zwingli was a biblicist, a Neoplatonist, and a Swiss patriot.

He was a biblicist in the sense that his start was not a spiritual ordeal, as for Luther, but a book, the source book of Christianity. Zwingli had been nurtured in the school of Erasmus and the humanists with their passion for a return to the sources of the classical and Christian tradition. When the Greek New Testament of Erasmus appeared, Zwingli memorized the

Pauline epistles in the original tongue. No one who did this could miss the doctrine of justification by faith. When, then, Luther declared its full implications Zwingli perceived that he had correctly interpreted the sacred text. Luther had arrived at his understanding by way of an ordeal which would almost surely have made him a Paulinist even though he had never known Paul. Zwingli read the book and saw that Luther had rightly grasped its meaning.

Because the Bible is the source book of Christianity, Zwingli argued that all of it is important. The novelty of Zwingli's preaching when he began his ministry at Zurich in 1519 was that he discarded the traditional selection of particular portions of scripture for each Sunday of the year and instead preached on the entire Gospel of Matthew with no omissions and translated directly from the Greek text lying on the pulpit before him. There was, consequently, not the same hierarchy of values in the scripture for Zwingli as for Luther and the Bible became the pattern for the structure of the church. The offices of the church should be only those named in the New Testament.

The linking of the Old Testament and the New Testament was tighter for Zwingli than for Luther, who united the two by Christology rather than by ecclesiology. For Luther the Old Testament foreshadowed the New because the pre-existent Christ, speaking and acting through the patriarchs, Moses, and prophets, was developing in symphonic fashion the drama of redemption. Through the Old Testament ran certain themes and motifs—as for example the theme of sacrifice exemplified in the murder of Abel, the near sacrifice of Isaac, the suffering of the Lord's servant in the Prophet Isaiah. The theme recurs in varied forms always similar, never the same, combining reminiscence and anticipation until resolved in Christ. But for Zwingli the union was ecclesiological. The Christian Church was the new Israel of God, the successor of God's people, a chosen race, an elect nation. Like Müntzer, he held that the elect can be approximately identified. The test for Zwingli was faith. This whole notion was utterly alien to Luther. For him the true Church of God was invisible and could not be made actual on earth, for the visible Church must include side-by-side the elect and the non-elect. For Zwingli those who professed the faith were elect according to all reasonable charity, and the inhabitants of Zurich adhering to the Reformed faith might be considered God's chosen people. And this meant practically everybody in the town, for only a few Catholics remained after the introduction of the reform.

For Zwingli the sacraments were signs of belonging to this community, corresponding to similar signs in the Old Testament. Baptism was the successor to circumcision. It might be given to infants because it meant so little. It was the token that they were under the aegis of the holy community. And the Lord's Supper was significant as a public confession of faith. He who stood up and in the presence of the congregation went to the altar thereby gave testimony and in so doing conferred a greater benefit upon the witnesses than he himself received from the bread and wine.

This reduction of the sacraments to signs had back of it the Neoplatonic disparagement of the physical which Zwingli derived from Erasmus and Pico, the leader of the Florentine Neoplatonic academy. Like Carlstadt, Zwingli rejected music in worship and this is all the more remarkable because Zwingli was proficient on six instruments and was himself a composer. But the purpose of music, he said, is to put children to sleep, not to worship God. The organ was removed from the church at Zurich. All of the images likewise disappeared and the walls were whitewashed. The sacraments of the Lord's Supper remained because of the command of the Lord, "Do this in remembrance of me." But nothing more was involved than a rite of remembrance and a witness to the faith.

Zwingli's position was thus anomalous. He opposed material expressions of religion but made the people of God visible in history. For Luther, worship was of the eye, ear, and the mouth, but the people of God remained invisible. For Zwingli, the externals of worship were the "letter that killeth" but the people of God were a tangible community. Perhaps there is here a seed of activism, the use of religion as a basis for reforming society, because if the zealous people of God must be so restrained while worshiping, how are they able to manifest their piety save in action outside the church?

Zwingli himself was very much of an activist in politics. As with other Protestant sects, local problems of a non-religious nature helped make more intense certain sectarian religious tendencies. Zwingli was a Swiss patriot who at first combined Erasmian pacifism with opposition to the hiring of the Swiss as mercenaries to the European powers. His first tract was a warning to the Swiss ox not to be lured from his pastures. Zwingli himself for a time had served as a chaplain to the Swiss troops in the papal armies and as a chaplain had the duty of reporting hundreds of casualties to broken homes. Revolted by the mercenary system, Zwingli persuaded Zurich to renounce it altogether. This policy isolated Zurich from other cantons and exacerbated the friction over the religious issue with the Catholic cantons Uri, Schwyz, and Unterwalden. Zwingli perceived that a religious war would be the outcome and at this point forsook his pacifism. The concept of an actual people of God in history had in the past helped support or inspire the idea of a crusade, a holy war on the behalf of a religious community. The welfare of Switzerland had counseled the abandonment of enlisting in foreign armies but fighting for the honor of God transcended even the welfare of Switzerland. Two religious wars ensued called the wars of Kappell. In the second, Zwingli fell on the field of battle, with helmet and sword. Luther saw in his death, as in the execution of Müntzer, a divine judgment upon a minister who desecrated the gospel by defending it with any weapon save the sword of the Spirit.

In Zwingli's circle arose the Anabaptists, meaning those who repeat baptism. In this instance we come closest to a schism arising from a schism. The definition of Anabaptism is, however, difficult because it was part of an amorphous movement of dissent against not only Rome but against all the varieties of Protestantism. To describe the welter of the Protestant fringe some have used the term "the left wing of the Reformation." The objection to this terminology is that the left wing calls not only for a right wing but also for a middle. There must then be three divisions. The case is supposedly simplified by using the term "the radical reformation," but this does not greatly help. There are still three: the Catholic, the conservative Protestants, and the radical Protestants. The real difficulty is that whatever the term, the lines can be drawn only after determining a point of reference. If the union of Church and state is the criterion then Catholics, Lutherans, Zwinglians, Calvinists, and Anglicans are on one side and the Anabaptists on the other. But if the attitudes to art and music and the sacraments are the standard, then Zwinglians and to a large degree the Calvinists belong with the radicals. If the readiness to engage in armed revolution is the test, then Zwingli and Calvin are clearly on one side. Luther's position on revolution was somewhat ambiguous and will be discussed later. The Anglican church was never revolutionary, but the Puritans were; the Anabaptists were divided. If belief in the Trinity is the standard then the Anabaptists belong with the established churches and only the Socinians are to the left; but if the rejection of infant baptism is the point of reference the Socinians belong with the Anabaptists. Obviously, whatever the terminology the categories cannot be neat.

Anabaptism arose in the circle of Zwingli, and its first difference with him was as to the speed of the proposed religious reforms. Zwingli, imbued with his idea of the holy community, believed that he, as a priest of that community, should act only with the concurrence of the community. Therefore the celebration of the mass should not cease until the people were persuaded to accept the purified faith. Zwingli fully expected that after a public disputation the town council would render a favorable verdict. The town council, though strictly a civil body, was the organ of the religious society. Until the council spoke, Zwingli would continue to say mass in a form accommodated to the mind of the congregation and the will of the magistrate. The mood of the Anabaptists might well have been couched in terms of the later Puritan slogan of "a reformation without tarrying for any." Zwingli was soon delivered from his dilemma because the council did abolish the mass.

During this dispute, however, the Anabaptists had raised more serious issues. They claimed that the true church can never be identified with an entire community even though its members subscribe to the faith. The mark of election is the rebirth, as Müntzer had said, but no one could pretend that all of the inhabitants of Zurich were twice born. The community does not constitute the church. Therefore, the magistrate cannot act for the church as well as for the community. At least the magistrate should not invade with his sword the territory of the church, for the new birth must always be entirely unconstrained. Force has no place in creating belief. The church must therefore be a voluntary society. This does not mean that it is simply a fraternity based on pure human choice. The church is rather a community in which the twice-born acknowledge each other and band together in accord with God's choice. This is possible only for adults. Therefore, only adults should be baptized. Infant baptism is no baptism but only "a dipping in the Roman bath."

In the little town of Zollikon, near Zurich, laymen in peasant garb came to the public fountain from which the horses drank and, with no robes or ritual, baptized each other in the name of the Father and the Son and of the Holy Ghost. When this was reported to the magistrates of Zurich, one of them remarked, "There's more to this than appears." He was right. The Anabaptists held that the church should be financially supported from voluntary contributions of its members and not from tithes levied and collected by the government. The Anabaptist program included three propositions: the church is a voluntary association, the church and the state should be separate, and religious liberty should prevail.

In that age, these were most radical affirmations. The separation of church and state meant the abandonment of the tradition which went back for two thousand years to Rome, Greece, and Israel. That the state could prosper without an official religion had been inconceivable, and if the separation disrupted the hierarchic structure of medieval society, it was even more alien to Zwingli's idea of a holy commonwealth. The clash with the Anabaptists could not have occurred on a more sensitive issue.

The magistrates at Zurich invoked against the Anabaptists the ancient Roman law, the Code of Justinian, which visited the death penality on those who repeated baptism. The law had been directed against the Donatists, schismatics, and heretics of the early church, who rebaptized any Catholics who came over to them. The Anabaptists, according to their definition, did not come under this law for they claimed that since infant baptism is no baptism, they were not baptizing over again. But their opponents fastened on them the term Ana-baptist, which means over-again-baptizer, in order to bring them under the provision of the Code of Justinian. In accord with Roman law, an Anabaptist leader was drowned in the lake of Zurich in 1526.

Anabaptism nevertheless spread because every member might be called upon to engage in missionary journeys. The movement traveled down the Rhine into the Netherlands; Germany also was affected. Anabaptism threatened to supplant the established churches and the arm of the state was invoked to arrest the spread. The Diet of Speyer in 1529 (the Diet at which the Protestants acquired the name of Protestants because they protested against an invidious rule which allowed Catholic minorities in Protestant lands but refused Protestant minorities in Catholic lands) inflicted the penalty of death upon the Anabaptists throughout the whole of the Holy Roman Empire, and these "Protestants" concurred. The Catholics burned and the Protestants drowned all of the outstanding leaders among the early Anabaptists.

Martin Luther himself was very slow to endorse any penalty for them beyond banishment. But by 1531 he came to condone capital punishment, not for heresy but for blasphemy and sedition. In his eyes, the Anabaptists were seditious, not because, as he feared, they might emulate the revolution of Thomas Müntzer, but rather because by their pacifism they would destroy the state whose very essence for him consisted in the use of the sword. By their refusal to be soldiers and magistrates the Anabaptists would disintegrate the state and were, therefore, seditious. A few Anabaptists were also violent revolutionists, and there was a brief outburst at the town of Münster in Westphalia when they took over the city and commenced their reign. It was brief because the Catholics and Protestants combined to sack the city. After the debacle, much of Anabaptism was gathered up by two groups, the Mennonites and the Hutterites, but Menno discarded all extravagances: revolution, reliance on dreams and visions, the appeal to the Spirit divorced from the scripture, and polygamy, which had been practiced at Münster. He inculcated instead a simple, undogmatic biblical piety and a disciplined deportment. There are affinities between his Christianity and that of the earlier Brethren of the Common Life, and both movements flourished in Holland. The Hutterites took refuge on the eastern fringes of Europe where feudal noblemen were sufficiently independent to grant an asylum to Hutterite colonies of a hundred persons, multinational in population and established for communal living. The program sought to exemplify Franciscan poverty while diverging from the Franciscan pattern in that the Hutterian colonies rested on a family basis. Mennonite and Hutterite groups survive until our own day in considerable numbers.

## VIII

The most active, expansive, and widespread form of Protestantism was Calvinism. Originating independently in Geneva, then itself an independent city, Calvinism combined many of the features of the other varieties of Protestantism. Calvin was a Frenchman who fled from persecution in Paris to Basel, where he published his great *Institutes of the Christian Religion* (1536), a codification of Protestant doctrine. Calvin's point of departure is not justification by faith but the knowledge of God, and the emphasis throughout is on man's duty to glorify his Creator rather than to worry about his own personal destiny. His fate has been settled by God and is to be accepted whatever it may be. If anxiety, then, ceases as to one's destiny, energy may be released to labor in the church and in society for the exemplification of God's glory.

Inadvertently and against his will Calvin came to head the Reformation at Geneva. The city prior to his coming had just thrown off the authority of its Catholic bishop and the Duke of Savoy, with the aid of troops from Protestant Berne who introduced the Reformation by putting images of the saints down the wells. The city was in turmoil which the fiery Protestant evangelist, Farel, was not able to control. When the young scholar, John Calvin, passed through the city, Farel invited him to stay and take the lead. Calvin demurred but Farel threatened him with hell and damnation if he declined God's call. Such a plea Calvin could not resist. He and Farel labored together until both were exiled by the restless Genevans, who had not shaken off the yoke of the bishop to put their necks into the more galling yoke of the ardent gospelers. But Geneva without the reformers was in such confusion that they were invited to return. Calvin came alone and after further friction gained the control he enjoyed for the decade of the 1550s until his death in 1564. During this period he was able to realize his program.

For Calvin the sect was the church. Like the Catholics, the Lutherans, and the Zwinglians he desired that the church should be coterminous with the community. Like the Anabaptists he believed that the church should be a community of holy Christians or saints. Zwingli also had this ideal but was less rigorous about the marks of the saints. Calvin had three tests for the approximate recognition of the elect. The first, as with Zwingli, was the depth and sincerity of the individual's faith. The second, as with the Anabaptists, was a godly deportment. The third was not the test so crucial for Müntzer, the Anabaptists, and later the New England Puritans, of a profound emotional experience of the new birth without which one could not be admitted to the Lord's table. Rather he who chose and loved to come to the Lord's table was presumably of the elect. The faith, the life, and the sacrament were thus the marks. Those who exhibited these signs were in reasonable charity to be deemed God's chosen people.

But if the church should consist only of the saints and if the church should be coterminous with the community, the only way to realize this combination would be to exclude the non-saints from the community, and this was the trend in Geneva. The excommunicated, who remained unreconciled with the church after half a year, could not expect to remain in the town. The expulsion of the non-elect was compensated by the reception of the elect from without. At Calvin's instance, Geneva received into her citizenship six thousand refugees for religion who were added to an original population of thirteen thousand.

The exclusion of the dissenters and the inclusion of the consenters made of Geneva a select community, almost as select as a monastery or an Anabaptist colony. Geneva has been called a *ville église,* a city that was a church. The form of the government was not theocratic in the strict sense. The church did not rule the state. There was parallelism of church and state and a division of functions. The theory of harmony between church and state was never more perfectly realized. Excommunication was in the hands of the church but matters spiritual were not excluded from the jurisdiction of the magistrate and the town council banished and invited ministers. It was the town council which sat in judgment on the heretic Michael Servetus and condemned him in 1553 to be burned at the stake. Calvin, to be sure, denounced him, but Calvin did not decide his fate. Indeed, Calvin interceded with the request that he be executed with the sword, but the council insisted on the flames. A community so organized and so imbued with a common ideal could act in unison. This of itself may explain why Geneva was so activist, but there were also other reasons, both ideological and circumstantial, for Calvin, as we have noted, believed like Müntzer and Zwingli, in making actual the holy commonwealth. He prescribed attainable tests for membership, directed man to the glory of God, and assumed a time span for the unfolding of God's plan in history, since the return of Christ was projected indefinitely into the future, making possible the erection of God's kingdom through the instrumentality of the saints on earth. "The church restored," said Calvin, "is the kingdom of God." And the Calvinists, exploiting unique local political and economic conditions, strove in France, Holland, the British Isles, and notably in the New World to establish holy commonwealths.

## IX

The boundless zeal of the Calvinists was accentuated by the opposition which they encountered. Only after a decade of struggle did Calvin obtain control in Geneva. In France, Holland, England, and Scotland, Calvinism was to be involved in civil wars. The right of armed resistance to tyranny in lands where they were minorities came to be agitated for in Calvin's circle. On this issue Luther had been extremely hesitant. He had frequently declared that the sword must never be taken to defend the Gospel. The German jurists, toward the end of his life, persuaded Luther that if the emperor undertook to suppress Protestantism by force of arms he would be violating his coronation oath and could then be resisted by the German princes. A lower magistrate could thus resist a higher magistrate in the name of the constitution. This doctrine speedily subsided in Lutheranism after the achievement of legal toleration in the Peace of Augsburg in 1555. But Calvinism was not included in this peace. Calvin had said that inferior magistrates might resist tyrants. Specifically, in France a Protestant uprising could be justified if headed by a prince of the blood. Calvin had in mind Condé of the House of Bourbon but Calvin's associate Beza went on to justify also popular revolution and this became the political doctrine of the *Monarchomachi* (opponents of the monarchy) in France.

The problem for France was acute. The ancient tradition was that of *"un roi, une loi, une foi,"* one king, one law, one faith. Switzerland was the first example of one country with two religions, but Switzerland was only a small country and at the outset was a confederation and did not have a king. But France was the first of the modern national states to achieve consolidation. Should her unity, already challenged by dissident nobles, now be further rent by diversity of religion? The ruling house in France, the House of Valois, set itself firmly to maintain the religious and political integrity of France. Persecutions followed. The nobility who were resisting the consolidation of the monarchy were at first so passionately addicted to either Protestantism or Catholicism as to be willing to wreck political unity. Some supported Protestantism, namely part of the House of Bourbon and notably the House of Chatillon to which belonged the Protestant leader Gaspard de Coligny, who was murdered with his followers on St. Bartholomew's Day, 1572. The House of Guise was fervently Catholic and ready to overturn the monarchy if it should embrace the Protestant faith. The problem became acute when the House of Valois ended without male issue. The heir to the throne was Henry of Navarre, a Bourbon and a Protestant, who was to reign as Henry IV from 1589–1610. The Guise and their party would not recognize him unless he abjured his faith. At last he did so, while at the same time granting a large measure of toleration to the Huguenots, as the Protestants were called. They might practice their faith in specified localities and were eligible to all public offices. The Edict of Nantes, which enshrined this policy in 1598, was possible only because of the growth during the course of the struggle of the party, the *Politiques,* who put the political above the religious interest of France. They argued that it was better, like Germany and Switzerland, to recognize two religions in one land than to split the country politically along confessional lines. In other words, they supported religious toleration as politically expedient. They could do so, however, only through diminution of their own religious interest. They would scarcely have been able to take this position had they believed that there can exist only one true religion and that upon the profession of this religion depends not only the salvation of souls but the temporal welfare of the state. A certain scepticism had in fact invaded their thinking, the view that perhaps there is more than one way to salvation, and that perhaps bliss in heaven, being uncertain, is not to be preferred to tranquillity on earth.

In Holland the struggle was complicated by the effort of the Low Countries to throw off the suzerainty of Spain, whose king, Philip II, was ardently Catholic. This monarch imposed on the Netherlands Spanish troops and the Spanish Inquisition. All branches of Protestantism were opposed to this regime, moderate Catholics of the Erasmian type were alienated by Philip's rampant orthodoxy, and no one relished the quartering of Spanish troops. The spirit of the opposition was epitomized by William of Orange, himself a moderate, who was successively a Catholic, a Lutheran, and a Calvinist. The intrinsic differences among religious groups did not matter greatly to him and his own changes of faith were dictated by matrimonial alliances. He was a Lutheran when he married the granddaughter of Philip of Hesse and a Calvinist when married to the daughter of Coligny. This does not mean that he was insensitive to religion, only that he was not confessionally rigid. In him, too, one discerns something of the spirit of Erasmus. He had also an eye to trade and observed that wars of religion would ruin the Netherlands as a market of the world. The independence of the Dutch Republic was practically achieved in 1609 but only at the expense of a division between Belgium and Holland. The south remained Catholic; the north became Calvinist of a rigid type. Nevertheless "liberal" movements in the succession of Erasmus also flourished in Holland and eventually took shape with the Arminians and the Remonstrants. Holland, in temper, if not by express edict, was ahead of other countries in religious liberty, and in the seventeenth century was to be a refuge for English dissenters. Here the Anabaptists first obtained toleration.

The Reformation in England differed from that in other lands because it was so largely the work of the crown. The initial split was medieval in character, a quarrel between a king and the pope over the matter of marriage. In such cases, in an earlier time, the king would do what he pleased. The pope would excommunicate him. After a time the king would capitulate on terms which gave him most of what he wanted. Henry may have supposed that by cutting off the pope's income from England and marrying to satisfy himself, he would incur a temporary penalty and then relations would be resumed. What he really expected we do not know, but a century earlier this could easily have been the outcome.

Henry's particular problem was to obtain an heir to the throne. His wife, Catherine of Aragon, had given him a number of children, of whom only one survived birth, and she was a girl—the Princess Mary. Henry's proposal was that the pope annul his marriage, and this could readily have been arranged because Henry had married Catherine contrary to the law of Leviticus, which forbids marriage with a deceased brother's wife. At the time of the marriage a dispensation had been granted by Pope Julius II. This dispensation could now be declared faulty and the union could be annulled. Then Henry would be free to marry. The pope was confronted by an acute dilemma. If Henry were refused he might secede (as indeed he did), but if obliged in his wish then Charles, Holy Roman Emperor, King of Spain, and nephew of Catherine of Aragon, would be affronted, and to affront Charles would be highly indiscreet, since his troops had lately sacked Rome and brought the papacy under Spanish domination. But Henry was no more willing to submit to a papacy controlled by Spain than Wycliffe had been more than a century earlier in the case of a papacy controlled by France. The immediate cause of the break in England was thus that the papacy had ceased to be international. Henry grew impatient with the delay, cut off the pope's annates, renounced papal authority, and established an English national church, the *Ecclesia Anglicana* with the king as its head. This was in 1534.

The theory which justified his procedure is called Erastianism. It is the doctrine that the state may determine the form of religion, but this doctrine was never meant to cover any other than the Christian religion. It was the extreme antithesis to the papal doctrine that the pope held the two keys, both the spiritual and the temporal. Under Erastianism, the king was said to hold the two keys. The changes in religious practice otherwise were slight. Henry introduced the Bible in the English tongue into all of the churches. Coverdale, who received the commission to supply the copies, utilized the translation of Tyndale (d. 1536) which, until then, Henry had been buying up to burn. Its author had been captured on the continent and sent to the stake. The incompleted portions of the translation were supplied by Coverdale. The great innovation of Henry's reign was the suppression of the monasteries. Doctrine, especially at the end of his reign, remained intact. Catholics who refused to accept the royal supremacy gave their lives, among them Cardinal Fisher and Thomas More.

Henry had a succession of wives, one of whom bore a son who succeeded as Edward VI in 1547. His brief reign lasted only six years. During this period England was less involved in foreign alliances and more influenced in religious affairs by foreign refugees than in any other period. The refugees from the attempt of Charles V to exterminate Lutheranism in Germany came largely to England. The Reformation in England was thereby influenced increasingly to become Protestant in doctrine. The great monument of the reign was the Book of Common Prayer (1549–52), the work of Archbishop Cranmer, a magnificent achievement of religious devotion couched in stately and sonorous prose.

Edward was followed in 1553 by his half-sister Mary, the daughter of

Catherine of Aragon. England, after all, did have a queen and England cared more for the House of Tudor than for the Protestant faith. Mary, who had always remained a Catholic, even during the reign of her brother, restored the jurisdiction of the pope and sent more than two hundred of the Protestant clergy to the stake, among them Archbishop Cranmer. He was confronted by a frightful ordeal of conscience because he was an Erastian who held that the government might determine the form of religion. But could the government restore obedience to a church which denied that the government could determine the form of religion? After many recantations Cranmer was nevertheless condemned to be burned and required first to read his final recantation. Instead he reaffirmed his faith and went smiling to the stake.

Then in 1559 Elizabeth, a daughter of Henry VIII by Anne Boleyn, came to the throne. Elizabeth mingled religious conviction with political astuteness. What was politic for England in that year is difficult to determine. The Lutherans had attained recognition on the continent in the Peace of Augsburg of 1555. In 1559 France and Spain had made peace with the mutual agreement to extirpate heresy. In Scotland the Queen Regent Mary of the French House of Guise died and was succeeded by her daughter, Mary Stuart, to be known as the Queen of Scots. One could not be sure in that year that she might not restore Catholicism in her lands. And Elizabeth, her cousin in England, could not in the year of her accession foresee the rise of the Dutch Republic, the Edict of Nantes, the defeat of the Armada, and the triumph of John Knox, the leader of the Scottish Calvinists. She may have decided for Protestantism out of conviction, but she certainly was of no mind to alienate any more of her subjects than necessary, and desired a settlement acceptable to the greatest number. Of course, this settlement could not satisfy Rome, so long as it did not recognize Rome, but it might accommodate the varieties of Protestantism and not unduly irritate those of Catholic persuasion. The Elizabethan settlement proposed to solve the religious problem by comprehension. There should be no territorial division within the land, as in Germany or Switzerland. England should have only one religion. But the requirements of that religion should be so latitudinarian or ambiguous that only a handful of extremists would be unable to conform. The latitude should apply rather to doctrine than to liturgy. In the Elizabethan national church people need not think alike, but they must worship alike if they were to worship together. Therefore, the Book of Common Prayer must be uniform for all England. But the doctrinal phrases for the celebration of the Lord's Supper could be taken either in a Zwinglian or a Lutheran sense. Thirty-Nine Articles (1562) demanded subscription on the part of all, but allowed breadth of interpretation. Much of the Elizabethan settlement has endured to this day, but it was to be severely challenged in the next century by the Puritans, and the ideal of one church for the whole of England has had to be abandoned. There is indeed only one established church, but the dissenters are numerous and recognized.

In Scotland the religious question was partly one of national existence. Scotland was then independent of England and in her quarrels with England often looked to France. But if France encroached unduly, then the Scots turned to England. France was Catholic; England vacillated in settling her religious problems. Geographical considerations seemed to some to point to the wisdom of a union with England, but political union in that day was unthinkable on the basis of religious diversity. If Scotland had been united with England under Edward VI, the religion would have had to be Protestant; under Mary, Catholic; and under Elizabeth, Protestant. Such was the situation in 1560. Distrust of the French and vigorous Protestant preaching against the Catholics had led in that year to the expulsion of all French troops and to the abolition of the mass on pain of death. Then came John Knox and Mary Queen of Scots to Scotland. A less congenial pair could not have been contrived. Mary was a princess from the House of Guise, the widow of the most Catholic king of France, and, for all her follies, not to say her crimes, an unflinching believer in her church. John Knox was a Calvinist, steeled by a year as a galley slave on a French ship. He emerged when chance for reconciliation had passed. Luther was dead; Servetus had been burned; the Roman Inquisition had been established; Erasmianism was crushed. Knox confronted an aroused and militant Catholicism with his claim that one celebration of the mass is worse than a cup of poison. When Mary insisted on having mass in her private chapel, he was convinced that if she had her way, Catholicism would be restored in Scotland. To her face he defended the view that subjects might rebel against sovereigns who violated the true faith. The eventual outcome was the flight of Mary to England where she was held in protective custody until plots to assassinate Elizabeth and enthrone Mary in England led to her execution. In the meantime Knox had triumphed in Scotland and Presbyterianism with its system of church government through assemblies became the established religion. Under Mary's son, James VI of Scotland, the two countries were eventually united, for on Elizabeth's death in 1603, James VI also became James I of England. The union was possible only because both countries were Protestant. Yet the fact that the one was Presbyterian and the other Anglican contributed to the outbreak of the civil war of the Puritan period at mid-century.

## X

The Reformation in Spain and Italy is largely the story of Catholic reform. Protestantism in these lands gained only a slight footing. Spain's situation was peculiar because she had only so recently achieved her religious and political unity. In the early Middle Ages three religions had existed side by side in the Iberian peninsula: Islam, Judaism, and Christianity, with a measure of cultural interchange. Toledo had been a great seat of translations from the Arabic. The spirit of the Crusades enflamed a vast effort to unify the peninsula on the side of Christendom. Under intense pressure many Jews became Christian around 1300. To root out any remnant of Judaism among them the Inquisition was established in 1482, and unconverted Jews were expelled in 1492. The same year Granada fell and similar pressures were applied to the Moors. By the 1520s repression had so far succeeded that Spain felt sufficiently secure to allow for a decade of tolerance in the spirit of Erasmus, but when Lutheranism posed a new threat to the unity so lately won the machinery of the Inquisition was revived. The last great auto-da-fé (literally act of faith, meaning the burning of heretics) occurred in 1559.

Spain was to be the driving force of the Catholic, often called the counter-reformation, but it was not "counter" in Spain to begin with because it began prior to the emergence of Luther. The reform movement in Spain at the end of the fifteenth century exhibited an amazing blend of fanatical attachment to medieval Christianity and an openness to Renaissance tendencies.

Cardinal Ximenes is in this respect a revealing figure. A Franciscan friar, he walked barefoot and wore a hair shirt. Made confessor to Queen Isabella, primate of Spain, and chancellor of Castile, he expended the wealth of the Church and of the state to expel the Moors and himself incited the troops in the attack on Oran. At the same time, he was a humanist scholar, a founder of the University of Alcala, which included chairs in Hebrew and medicine, and was responsible for the great Complutensian Polyglot, which first offered the entire Bible in the original tongues, not only the New Testament in Greek but also the Old Testament in Hebrew.

More typical of Catholic reform in Spain was Ignatius Loyola, the founder of the Jesuits, because by his time Protestantism had arisen to affect the course of Catholic reform. Loyola was a knight devoted to the Queen of Spain. Because of a wound received in a tournament he dedicated himself instead to the Queen of Heaven. He went through a period of agonized spiritual searching comparable to that of Luther, and emerged with an assurance and undeviating devotion comparable to that of Calvin. The cause for Loyola, as for Calvin, was indeed the glory of God, but also the authority of the pope. One should obey, said he, like a cadaver. But, although the Jesuit—the order founded by Loyola was called Jesuit from Jesus—should be unrelenting in disciplining himself, he should be tender in dealing with sinners, placing no unnecessary obstacle to their availing themselves of the Church's means of grace. Since the enormity of the sin depends on the intention of the sinner, if there be any doubt as to his motives, let him be given the benefit. This was the doctrine called *probabilism*. The great work of the Jesuits was in education and in missions. It was the Catholics in the sixteenth century, the Jesuits and the Franciscans, who engaged in missions in the New World. The Protestants in that century were too busy trying to convert the "heathen Christians" to undertake expeditions to the pagan heathens.

In Italy Protestantism was to gain more of a hold than in Spain, but not enough for survival. Two explanations are offered for the failure in this land. The first is economic, that the gold came over the Alps at the behest of the Church, but this did not affect the whole of Italy, and there were Italian states with grievances against Roman exploitation. Another explanation is that the Latin character is irresistibly drawn by the lure of Catholicism, whereas the northern peoples find Protestantism more congenial. To this it may be said that the most vigorous among the Protestant movements, namely Calvinism, had its initial strength in Latin France. Conversely in the Germanic lands, the Rhine country, Bavaria and Austria remained largely Catholic. As for southern France and Italy, these were the two regions most infested with sectarian movements in the late Middle Ages. With greater plausibility one may suggest that in Italy sectarianism was spent. Another consideration is the adroitness of the Renaissance popes in channeling rampant zeal into the service of the Church. The Capuchins in the age of the reform were a new branch of the Franciscans, imbued with ideals which might have made them rebels like some earlier Franciscans, had they been suppressed.

Again one may note that Italy did not have the same doctrinal preparation for Lutheranism as did Germany. The preaching of the friars of the fifteenth century in the peninsula was highly moralistic, directed against specific sins: prostitution, usury, luxury, extortion, sodomy, the wearing of vanities, feuding, etc. The cry was for penitence, with the implication that contrition would assuage the divine anger. The spirit was remote from Luther's justification by faith, with which the teaching of the German mystics was much more in accord.

Nevertheless, the reform movement did gain a hold in Italy. The circle of the devout Spaniard at Naples, Juan Valdes, stimulated a type of mystical piety which fed into both the Protestant and the Catholic reforms. One of his disciples, the general of the Capuchins, Ochino, became a Protestant. Something of a Protestant mass movement may be inferred by the number converted back by the end of the century, but our information is meager and histories of the Reformation in Italy resolve themselves into biographies of the few leaders who came to public notice.

The rationalist movements of the Reformation were led chiefly by refugees from Latin lands. For the most part they operated as individuals, but one organized movement resulted, that of the Socinians in Poland and later in Holland. The name is derived from that of the Italian Fausto Sozzini.

The spirit of reform in Italy found expression rather in the renovation of the Church of Rome. There developed two principal groups among the Catholic reformers; both desired an improvement in morals, but one was latitudinarian and Erasmian about doctrine and the other was rigidly orthodox. The leader of the "liberals" was Contarini, who at the Council of Ratisbonne in 1541, attended by Melanchthon and Calvin, was ready to accept justification by faith. He was repudiated by the church on his return to Italy and died almost immediately. The Roman Inquisition was established the next year in 1542. The leader of the intransigents was Caraffa who became Pope Paul IV, in 1555 and committed some of the "liberals," even exalted churchmen such as Cardinal Morone, to the chambers of the Inquisition. The Council of Trent began its long work in 1545 and lasted, with lapses, until 1563. It was to assert eventually that tradition and scripture stand on an equal footing, and it was to repudiate the doctrine of justification by faith.

By 1560, however, the lines were drawn. The Protestants had gained such a measure of political recognition and such strength among the populace that either to conquer or convert them was not feasible. The Church of Rome undertook instead to define her position over against the challenge. Most of what the reformers rejected was reaffirmed, after having first been clarified, and the ambiguity and latitude of earlier days were at an end.

## XI

The social consequences of the Reformation have been variously assessed. The other two great movements of the sixteenth century were the expansion of capitalism and the growth of nationalism, both already well under way. Protestantism certainly accommodated itself to the new developments. Some historians hold that it gave to both a definite stimulus.

With regard to capitalism a distinction must be made between its structure and the spirit. The structure increasingly involved banking and credit with the taking of interest on loans. All of these practices were entrenched before the emergence of Protestantism. The Italian and the German banking houses, such as the Fuggers, financed the emperors and the popes, and charged for it. The demand for interest, or usury, as it was called, made difficulty for the church because of the prohibitions in the Old Testament (Lev. 25:36 and Deut. 32:19). The religious condemnation was fortified by the argument of Aristotle that money is sterile. But in practice the prohibition was evaded by various devices, and if the church forbade lending at interest she herself borrowed at interest until by the end of the sixteenth century 60 percent of her current income went to pay the interest on debts.

Luther and Calvin are credited with having broken down the medieval restrictions, because Luther said that the Old Testament provisions applied only to the Jews and Calvin refuted Aristotle. Nevertheless, both Luther and Calvin adhered to the ethic of Aquinas who allowed a contract of mutual risk, but forbade a contract of fixed return whereby a certain percent must be paid at a given time whether or not the borrower had prospered. Similarly Luther and Calvin allowed interest at only 5 percent in the case of those unable to work and only in case the enterprise for which the loan was made had succeeded. With regard to the devices of the capitalist system Protestantism rather retarded than stimulated.

But the "spirit of capitalism" differs from the structure. It has been defined as that spirit which enlists a fury of work alike from the laborer and from the entrepreneur and discourages luxury spending as incompatible with what has been called "inner worldly asceticism," that is, asceticism in the midst of society rather than in a monastery. Those imbued with this ideal could do only one of two things with their money: give it away, that is philanthropy, or put it back into the business, that is, build up capital. Calvinism even more than Lutheranism is credited with instilling this spirit on the ground that work was a psychological necessity to convince oneself of one's election. Now certainly for Calvin this does not apply, because he considered concern for one's salvation to be unworthy. But he did teach furious effort for God's glory. This has meant that Calvinists have displayed unwonted vigor in anything to which they have put their hands. Such activity may make money. But the phenomenon is not new in the sixteenth century nor in Protestantism. Monastic orders in the Middle Ages like the Cistercians were plagued by the wealth which accrued through their industry and frugality and wrecked their poverty.

As for nationalism, the term covers two aspects. The first is the welding of the inhabitants of a given area into a homogeneous culture. Presbyterianism certainly helped to unite the Scots, as Catholicism did in the case of the Irish. The other aspect is the consolidation of power within a cultural area, and in the sixteenth century this meant the strengthening of the monarchy. Both aspects collided in a measure with the universalism of the Catholic church and the control of the popes over monarchs. But both developed in some instances within and in others outside the framework of Catholicism. There was certainly no need to become Protestant in order to develop an integrated and centralized national state, nor can it be demonstrated that the adoption of Protestantism hastened the process. England indeed became Protestant, but Spain and France were also national states. Spain was ardently Catholic and France at the height of her monarchical development banished the Huguenots. The national state could perfectly well attain independence of Rome in finances and appointments to ecclesiastical livings without rejecting the spiritual authority of the pope. In England Henry VIII did not become a Protestant in order to be a strong monarch, but because he was a strong monarch he was able to become Protestant. The experience of his daughter Mary in returning to Rome without a revolution shows that in the sixteenth century England preferred the Tudors to the faith. One may seriously doubt whether the development of nationalism was either a cause or an effect of the Protestant movement.

In one respect the spirit of intransigence which the religious conflict fanned in both camps militated against political absolutism, because if the government sought to suppress either Protestantism or Catholicism there was armed resistance. We have noticed the lengths to which the Protestants were prepared to go. The Jesuits were no less intransigent, and the wars of religion were punctuated by the assassinations of rulers. Of course, if a monarch espoused the faith deemed to be true, his rule might then be defended as of divine right, but in general the religious struggles tended to entrench the doctrine of lawful rebellion.

As for the forms of government, both confessions made alliances with whatever form would at the moment grant the greatest favor. Protestantism was allied in Germany with the princes, in England with the monarchs, in Poland with the feudal nobility, and in Hungary the Protestants preferred the rule of the Turks to the Hapsburgs. Catholicism for centuries had been pragmatic in its negotiations and did not change in this regard after attaining greater doctrinal rigidity.

One of the greatest problems accentuated by the religious cleavages of the century was that of religious liberty for minority groups and dissenting individuals. When the formal unity of the church was rent and heretics came to be too numerous to burn individually, the Catholic church itself had to choose between civil wars or toleration. In principle most Protestants at first were no more tolerant than the Catholics. They, too, believed that the truth of God is of supreme importance and that to deny it imperils souls, as well as temporal tranquillity. But the Protestants, too, had either to exterminate or to tolerate. We have already seen that in France, England, and the Netherlands political and economic necessities eventually weighed in favor of tolerance. There were, however, religious arguments for toleration derived mainly from two tendencies in the late Middle Ages, namely mysticism, which considered religion too inward to be reached by the sword of the magistrate; and humanism, which demanded freedom in pursuit of the truth. These tendencies worked more potently for liberty when freed from the centralized religious authority of the Church. In breaking that authority Protestantism, however, at first addicted to belief in a single saving truth, nevertheless unwittingly contributed to liberty. Some Protestants, however, even in the sixteenth century were committed to liberty on principle, and gathered up in their pleas many divergent lines of approach. None did so more eloquently than Sebastian Castellio. In his protest against the execution of Michael Servetus in 1553, Castellio argued that we are not sure enough of dogma to apply the faggot to those who reject it. Controversy itself proves uncertainty. We are not good enough to persecute. Moreover, constraint is ineffective because it destroys true religion which depends upon sincerity. Constraint cannot engender faith and, above all, burning dissenters at the stake is a violation of the spirit of the gentle Christ. Castellio's influence persisted especially in Holland and England. John Locke was steeped in his ideas.

But above all the contribution of the Reformation lay in a restoration of the waning Christian consciousness of Europe. A resurgence of intolerance was for a time its unhappy concomitant. But can there be profound conviction without some measure of intolerance? Those who will die for an idea are all too ready to kill for it. This is a dilemma which the Reformation has bequeathed to our age.

### *FOR ADDITIONAL READING*

R. H. Bainton. *The Age of the Reformation*. Princeton, 1956.
———. *Here I Stand, A Life of Martin Luther*. New York, 1950.
———. *Hunted Heretic, The Life and Death of Michael Servetus*. Boston, 1953.
———. *The Reformation of the Sixteenth Century*. Boston, 1952.
H. Boehmer. *Road to Reformation*. New York, 1946.
O. Farner. *Zwingli the Reformer*. New York, 1952.
H. Grimm. *The Reformation Era*. New York, 1954.
E. H. Harbison. *The Age of Reformation*. Ithaca, 1955.
H. Holborn. *A History of Modern Germany, The Reformation*. New York, 1959.
P. Hughes. *A History of the Church*. 3 vols. New York, 1947–49.
T. M. Lindsay. *A History of the Reformation*. 2 vols. New York, 1916.
F. Littell. *The Anabaptist View of the Church*. Boston, 1958.
C. L. Manschreck. *Melanchthon the Quiet Reformer*. New York, 1958.
J. T. McNeill. *The History and Character of Calvinism*. New York, 1954.
F. M. Powicke. *The Reformation in England*. Oxford, 1941.
E. G. Rupp. *The Righteousness of God*. London, 1953.
P. Smith. *The Age of the Reformation*. New York, 1920.
W. Walker. *John Calvin*. New York and London, 1906.

# XI

# THE EMERGENCE OF THE EUROPEAN STATES-SYSTEM

*John B. Wolf*

The seventeenth century has been given many names: The Age of Absolutism, The Century of French Hegemony, The Age of Power, The Age of the Baroque, A Century of Crisis. None of these formulas actually encompasses all the vital forces of the century; indeed, it is probably unwise to attempt to bring all the irrational and unruly forces unleashed by war, religious conflict, political and dynastic ambitions, new technologies, and new conceptions of man, nature, and the universe, under a single formula. One thing, however, is certain: this seventeenth century was responsible for the creation of new and the extension of old institutions that have subsequently become the political framework for the lives of modern men. In both internal and international politics the differences between the institutions of Europe at the death of Philip II (1598) and those at the death of his great grandson, Louis XIV (1715) indicate that a revolutionary change had taken place in the interval.

In 1600 every government in Europe had to regard contingent anarchy in the form of civil rebellion as a constant in political life; a century later such rebellion was out of the question unless the rebels could gain control of the king's army. In 1600 the rulers of Europe talked much about their absolute power, but in actual fact they lacked both money and personnel to make that power effective; by 1715 the military and police powers, directed and administered by officials of the treasury and the war ministry, had taken on the contours of a modern state.

Unquestionably the most important factor in the process that created the new states-system was the rise of standing armies and navies. It was the desperate requirements made by the military that forced men to develop new sources of taxes and to find new personnel to collect and administer royal revenues; at the same time the rise of standing military establishments required the development of new bureaus for the superintendence and surveillance of the army and navy. As one might expect, there was an enormous difference between the armies and navies of 1600 and those of 1715. At the time of the death of Henry IV (1610), wars and the threats of war implied the use of relatively few men: a few thousand soldiers made up an army while ten to thirty thousand soldiers constituted a very large force for any of the powers. By the time of the death of Louis XIV, a single commander could manage sixty thousand and more men, while France had an army of over four hundred thousand. But a closer glance reveals even more important changes. In 1600 the soldier was commanded, supplied, and totally cared for by his captain; indeed he was loyal to his captain rather than to the king who happened to be employing him. By 1715 the soldier wore the king's coat, carried the king's weapon, and was cared for by the king's officials. In France, there was even an old soldiers' home for him when he became infirm. The differences in the navies of the two periods is equally striking. A naval vessel of 1600 was like the little ships in the battle with the Spanish Armada, a warship of the line of 1715 could have held its own with almost any ship built up to the era of steam power. In 1600 the navy was something assembled for a particular action; in 1715 the navy was a standing institution employing thousands of men. The bureaucratic state emerged to supply, control, and direct these military institutions; the states-system of Europe grew out of the balance of military power that subsequently developed on the European continent. In both cases it was the wars of the century that acted as the dynamic force in the creation of new institutions.

Twentieth-century men who have seen wars upset traditional political forms, reorganize economic and political institutions, and drastically control men's lives, will have no difficulty in understanding how important warfare can be in human affairs. For good or for evil warfare is a creative force in society. Not only do decisions reached on the battlefield very often have tremendous implications for the direction of political evolution, but also the very existence of military institutions with their demands for money, men, and material, with the necessity for organizing and controlling the activities of soldiers and sailors, acts as an imperious force in society. An earlier generation, seeking to end wars by ignoring or distorting their importance, tried to believe that "wars never settle anything." They argued this because wars do not necessarily "settle things" to the satisfaction of interested parties, but the student of history cannot miss the fact that a great many things have been "settled," and a great many institutions have been either created or transformed by war. As we shall see in this chapter, wars in the seventeenth century were important in the development of the political institutions that emerged as the European states-system, that is to say, the bureaucratic police state and the government of Europe as a community through the organization of the balance of power.

## I

The seventeenth century opened with an inheritance of unsettled questions from its predecessor. The reformations of the Christian church and the efforts of princes to impose their authority more firmly upon their subjects had inspired a half-century or more of civil wars in which religious flags often provided cloaks for political rebellion, and the confusion of the two issues made difficult any resolution of the problems. Nor did the confusion end there. The fact that Philip II of Spain, the most powerful prince in western Christendom, was deeply involved in almost all of these civil wars either as contender against rebellion in his own lands, or as an interested party supporting the Catholic factions in civil wars elsewhere, gave an international character to the problems confronting the individual states and thereby reduced the possibility of a clear-cut decision either on the battlefield or in the council chamber. At the opening of the seventeenth century the deaths of Philip II, of Elizabeth I, and of a number of other principals only seemed to mark an end to the conflicts associated with their names; another half-century and more had to pass before civil rebellions could be controlled to the point that they would not spill over into international wars.

A most important source of civil rebellions had roots that antedated the Reformation era. Throughout the later Middle Ages the interplay between the ever-increasing authority of the great territorial princes and the traditional rights and pretensions of their great vassals emerging from the feudal past was a persistent European political problem. Europe was a pluralistic political society in which hierarchies of power from the simple authority of the country nobleman on his lands up through baron and duke to the pretensions of the king in his palace, were often in opposition, but the most important source of conflict emerged from the apparent encroachments of royal officials upon what passed for traditional rights of the great noblemen. The petty squires usually did not count in these contests; it was the king and his great vassals who found themselves in competition for the right to decide political issues, and curiously when conflicts flared up both sides contended that the other was attempting to create revolutionary institutions incompatible with the traditional patterns of society. In a sense both were correct, for what seems to be involved is that the dynamic forces of economic, political, and intellectual life opened new vistas for action, new problems for statesmen, and both the king and his vassals strove to interpose their authority in the new area. In the conflicts that resulted, the princes had the advantage much of the time, but even in the sixteenth century their advantages were not overwhelming enough to discourage their opponents, and at the opening of the seventeenth century, the issue was nowhere finally resolved.

Among the reasons for the rise of princely power from the thirteenth to the eighteenth centuries were: the development of a money economy that allowed princes to substitute mercenary soldiers for the feudal levies, the acceptance of Roman law with its conception of the authority of the emperor, the emergence of a new kind of official, often bourgeois in origin and dependent upon the prince for wealth and position, and perhaps above all, the historical evolution of Europe from the fourteenth century onward with ever-widening opportunities beckoning princes to fill political voids that had appeared. Machiavelli did not create "the prince" of the sixteenth century, he only described him. At the end of the sixteenth century princes all over Europe assumed that they had the right to govern by their royal prerogative. Prelates and philosophers had been assuring them for more than a century that their power was directly from God and that God would sustain their action. Elizabeth of England reflected their faith when she said that He who had made her queen would give her the wisdom to govern; her successor James I was even more emphatic in that he wrote a whole book to prove the divine right of kings. Rulers elsewhere were equally sure of their power. The Valois kings of France ended their decrees with the formula: "for this is my good pleasure." Henry IV, who had to face the realities of a kingdom torn by civil war, cynically remarked that he could not talk about his absolutism the way James of England did because he was too busy trying to make people obey his commands. Nonetheless Henry, too, believed in his right to rule. However neither proclamations about the divine right of princes nor their pretensions to absolutism could still the voices, nor paralyze the arms, of men who regarded princely action as an encroachment upon their traditional rights and privileges, in short, on their "liberties." Only superior military force could compel them to accept the fact that the pluralism of medieval society was greatly modified by the emerging political structure of Europe.

The problem of princely power inevitably varied with the ancient feudal constitutions of Europe. In Germany, for example, the feudal order had seen the development of a federation of great fiefs, and the constitution for the Holy Roman Empire of the German nation that had emerged in the fourteenth century was a confederation of lay and clerical princes and townsmen. As a result the German problem had two aspects: the tensions between the rights of the princes and the authority of the emperor on the one side, and on the other the conflict between the claims of the princes and the rights of their own vassals within the principalities. The former was fought out in the Diet of the Empire and on battlefields of civil war; the latter in the *Landtäge* of the principalities and rebellions in the towns and countryside. The princes talked much about "German liberties" and the constitution of the Empire; their vassals spoke of "provincial liberties" (Bavarian, Saxon, Hanoverian, and other) and tried to curb the tax-gathering activities of their rulers.

This question of "liberties" and princely power was different where the ancient feudal constitution had been less decentralized, or where time had undermined the decentralized character of the constitution. In France for example, the feudal kingdom had been a federation in which the great barons (dukes and counts) were actually the peers, indeed even often the military superiors, of the king. But the history of the kingdom had brought the titles of all these feudal duchies into the hands of the king with the result that France remained a federal state in that each province had different laws, privileges, and local governments, but all were directly under the king's rule since the great vassals had ceased to exist. However there were great noblemen in France with enormous wealth and tremendous appetite for power; some were native French families, others were related to sovereign princely houses in Germany and Italy; in either case they were related by marriage with each other and with the cadet lines of the royal family. Traditionally these great families had furnished the king with soldiers and councillors; they had taken the place of the ancient quasi-sovereign feudal dukes as the men who helped the king to manage the kingdom. In the sixteenth and seventeenth centuries they were royal governors in the provinces. They commanded the king's troops as constables, lieutenant generals of the infantry, admirals of the fleet, and marshals and generals of the king's army. Occupying such positions they were able to dispose power that could be used either for the king or for the service of rebellion. The king's brother or the cadet lines of the royal family usually supplied these rebellions with leadership. The presence of the king's brother, uncle, or cousin at the head of a rebel army made rebellion a relatively safe and often profitable enterprise; this was the pattern of the "religious" wars of the sixteenth century. One can see how profitable these rebellions were by the concessions that Henry IV had to make to secure the support of the "great ones" for his throne. By these settlements the great nobles made their governorships into hereditary offices, secured grants of money or the rights to collect tariffs or tolls, and in general pillaged the rights of the crown. These privileges and grants then became French "liberties" to be protected against further encroachments from the king. Henry was able to keep a balance between the royal power and that of the nobles, but after Henry's death, first Marie de Medici as regent and then the young king Louis XIII had to face armed revolts that often crippled the power of their government.

Elsewhere in Europe the same pattern of tensions between the "liberties" of great noblemen and the centralizing efforts of princes created similar situations. In Hungary, the magnates, confronted with German Hapsburg rulers who were necessary to them as defenders against the Turks, tried to limit the authority that these rulers could exert by forming leagues and by identifying themselves with the Calvinist party. A similar situation between king and magnates emerged in Bohemia and in Poland, though of course, each community had its particular differences rooted in its history. In England the Tudor monarchs had quenched rebellion by great lords, but the emergence of a numerous, wealthy, and ambitious class of country gentlemen, who could easily make alliances with city men, created a situation dangerous to the Stuart kings of the seventeenth century.

The argument about the justice, as well as about the wisdom, of the extension of royal power into the areas formerly filled by the authority of great lords, municipal corporations, and other ancient institutions has continued down to modern times. Both sides had strong arguments. As so often in human affairs, they depend upon the assumptions that one makes about the world.

## II

If the pretensions, ambitions, and real or fancied rights of the great nobles constituted one of the important problems inherited from the sixteenth century, the reformations of the Christian church and the attendant problem of the co-existence of different confessions was another. There had actually been four "reformations" of the Christian church rather than one: the Protestant

(Lutheran), the Reformed (Calvinist), the "radical" or "withdrawn" (Anabaptist and Brethren), and the Counter Reformation (Roman Catholic). Of these only two were still aggressively active by 1600: the Calvinists and the Roman Catholics. The Lutherans, after winning the right of the prince to determine the religion of his subjects at the Diet of Augsburg, 1555 (*cujus regio eius religio*) tended to lose their revolutionary fervor; Lutheran clergymen seemed interested only in preserving the *status quo*. The Anabaptists and Brethren violently attacked by Catholic, Lutheran, and Reformed princes, were almost annihilated before the middle of the sixteenth century; they continued to exist in isolated islands in central and eastern Europe, without a leadership that knew how, or wished, to extend their community. Both the Catholics and the Calvinists presented a very different picture: they were both aggressively ambitious to extend their empires and willing to try to enlist military force to serve their ends. Also, curiously enough, of the voices raised in favor of religious toleration at the turn of the seventeenth century, the Calvinists and the Catholics were the most eloquent, for both were anxious to have their co-religionists tolerated by princes of other faiths. On the other hand, whenever either of these groups had the power, they found that toleration was an anathema to both man and God. The Calvinist and the Roman Catholic churches were unquestionably dynamic forces in the organization of politics at the opening of the seventeenth century.

The reform movement in the Roman Catholic church was well under way before Luther's death; in the second half of the sixteenth century it gathered force by the Council of Trent, the action of the Vatican, and above all, the zeal of religious orders like the Jesuits, Capuchins, the Oratory, and others. Dedicated men with the same sort of religious fervor that had inspired Luther pressed reform in all directions, so that today the Roman Catholic church counts as saints a host of men who dedicated their lives to the success of the counter-reformation. This movement operated politically in many different ways. The reformers attempted to convert the brothers who had fallen away from the faith by preaching, by teaching, or by force. This meant that they established schools and colleges, sent out missionaries, and finally urged princes to use political power to force conversion. In countries like France, where the religious wars of the sixteenth century had demonstrated the impossibility of suppressing the Calvinist church (in French official documents "Pretended Reformed Church"), a compromise emerged granting toleration to the dissident minority. The reader of sermons, of "harangues" before the king and his ministers, and of memoirs of clergymen knows what eloquence and what arguments were used to persuade the French king to reverse the edict of toleration. Indeed the counter-reformation leaders accepted "toleration" only as a step in the direction of the extinction of the tolerated heresy. The political leaders of the reformed community in Bohemia, fearful of the action of Ferdinand von Hapsburg who rightfully was identified with Jesuit advisors, risked their lives and fortunes in their fear that the Diploma of Toleration would be withdrawn.

Papal policy might vary from time to time due to the exigencies of the situation, but in general the European policy of the counter-reformation can be described as an effort to combine the Catholic crowns of Europe, under the leadership of the Spanish Hapsburgs, in a grand alliance against the "protestant" and "reformed" princes. Spain was not always willing to assume this leadership, and the other Catholic princes often excused themselves from such a policy, but in every court in Europe there was a Catholic, or "devout," party urging it. After the death of Henry IV this line of thought resulted in the double marriage of Spanish Hapsburg and French Bourbon princes and princesses; by sending a Bourbon princess to Madrid and a Hapsburg infanta to Paris, men hoped to heal the Franco-Spanish hostility and to unite the two crowns against the "enemies of God." The Counter Reformation "devout" party was usually, however, only one of several factions in every court, and it was not always successful in urging its line of action. Indeed, even in Rome there was a strong faction that feared Spanish hegemony, that dreaded the possibility that the pope might become a puppet or a tool of the Spanish king.

However, in 1600 the work of Catholic princes, soldiers, educators, missionaries, and preachers was a powerful current in European life. Jesuit schools were educating the elite of the Catholic world to believe that God placed the obligation upon them to heal His community of Christendom; these Jesuit academies, colleges, and universities provided the best education available to a young Catholic, and the number of the leaders of Catholic Europe trained in them is formidable proof of their influence. Where the Jesuits left off, the Capuchins, or the members of the Oratory, or the followers of Francis de Sales or Vincent de Paul, or one of the other reformers, took over as protagonists in the drama played out for the soul, the mind, and the body of Europe. Some of these men were gentle, some were ruthless, but all of them strove, with wide effects, to bring Europe back to the communion of the Roman Catholic church by one means or another.

Although the reformed Calvinist community lacked the appearance of a central direction comparable to that provided by the papacy, nonetheless it also presented a militant front to the world. The Roman Catholic reformation was not actually "directed" from Rome; it was a pluralistic effort dependent upon hundreds of dedicated men. The Reformed or Calvinist community was much the same. Although the little cliques of theologians, statesmen, and preachers at Geneva, Leiden, Heidelberg, and one or two other centers provided a leadership not unlike that given the Roman church from Rome, Paris and Madrid, it was the hundreds of dedicated ministers, teachers, and politicians all over northern and central Europe who gave force to the Reformed or Calvinist bid for power. These men, whether they were found in the Huguenot assemblies permitted by the French king, the council chambers of the governments of the United Netherlands or of the Count Palatine of the Rhine, or in the academies where the elite of the Calvinist youth was educated, or the pulpits of the Reformed churches, were fighting for "the cause," and by that they understood a movement supported by God Himself. The hard core of leadership of the Reformed community was made up of men who knew each other personally, who accepted the principle tenets of the Reformed faith, and who believed fervently in the righteousness of their cause. They may have lacked the unity of command of the Jesuit order, but they were as sure of their position and as dedicated to their program as any of the Catholics were to theirs.

If one looks beyond the dedicated leaders of the Reformed church, it becomes apparent that, like the Catholics, the Calvinist community also was not completely united on the program of action of the church leadership. In each country local conditions and local interests modified the action of the militants. The very nature of the problem confronting the several Reformed churches perhaps acted to prevent complete unity. The political philosophy of the Calvinists rejected the passive surrender to the prince and the doctrine of divine right accepted by the Lutherans; thus Calvinist missionaries proselytized in countries where the prince not only disapproved of them but also persecuted their church. In such cases, the Calvinist doctrine allowed subjects to rebel against princes who were obviously unsympathetic with God's work. This political philosophy made Calvinism attractive to many men who wished justification for rebellion, and provided religious flags for their political revolts. In such cases the problem at hand, rather than the welfare of the Reformed cause in Europe, naturally took precedence.

Nonetheless there was enough of a constant problem facing the Reformed community to create a "Calvinist" program in Europe. In general it could be said that at the very center of this program was a determined opposition to the house of Hapsburg. In the Netherlands this was the inevitable result of the fact that the revolt of the northern provinces (which had become the United Netherlands) had been a revolt against the Hapsburg house, and that even though there was a twelve-year truce signed in 1609 between the king of Spain and his erstwhile subjects recognizing the *de facto* independence of the northern provinces, it was clear that the Hapsburgs really did not give up the hope of recovering their control over them. In Germany it also was the house of Hapsburg, the cadet or German line, that was the principle opponent of Calvinist ambitions. The German religious peace of 1555 had not provided for toleration of the Calvinists; only the Lutheran and Catholic princes had the right to determine the religion of their subjects. Thus the Calvinists had no legal position, and they were always subject to pressure from the emperor. It should cause no surprise that the German Calvinist politicians regarded the Hapsburg house as the target of their hostility particularly when Ferdinand, an ardent Catholic, became its head. In the kingdoms of Bohemia, Hungary, and Transylvania, and on the frontiers of the German empire, the Calvinist cause and the claims of the great noblemen were often synonymous. Like so many noblemen in France a half-century earlier, these great princes found it convenient to express their political hostility to their Hapsburg kings by joining the Reformed religion. They needed the house of Hapsburg to protect them from the Ottoman threat, but they were unwilling to see this German dynasty exercise any considerable power in the kingdom. Thus from the Netherlands, through Germany, Bohemia, Hungary, and Transylvania, hostility to the house of Hapsburg helped cement the political structure of the Reformed community.

In France and in Scotland, the other two kingdoms with large congregations of the Reformed church, the issue was not so clear. Both feared the Hapsburgs as protagonists of the Catholic counter-reformation, but the political position was seriously modified by internal problems of the kingdom unrelated to the Hapsburgs. Thus in France about 1624 the Huguenots revolted against their king at the time when the French royal government was allied with and actively assisting the German Protestant and Reformed princes; the Huguenot city of La Rochelle not only rebelled but also brought in English aid at the time when Richelieu and Louis XIII were most anxious to check the rising star of the Hapsburgs in Germany. Yet in spite of this apparent break in the interests of the Reformed community, when the Calvinists weighed their chances or when their opponents drew up balance sheets, the Huguenots of France with their walled towns, their military forces, and their traditions of rebellion had to be counted.

## III

The history of the seventeenth century was influenced by many things other than the tensions between central governments and great noblemen and the conflicts between competing religious groups. The idea of divine right of princes, which was so widely accepted, entailed a series of influential ideas about the nature of the political process and the relations between princes. Seventeenth-century statesmen would never have understood arguments about rights to territory based upon nationalism or popular sovereignty; they believed that God had created and was sustaining the world, and that He had created political society by granting to princes the power to govern but retaining to himself the authority (right) to govern. Subjects, some argued, had the right to appeal to heaven (rebel) against a bad prince; others protested that it was God alone who had the right to act thus, that the subject had only his tears and his prayers against a tyrannical ruler. Such arguments would not, of course, prevent the great lords, led perhaps by a member of the royal family or by a peer whose title was as ancient as the king's, from raising the standard of revolt against the king. In either case these noble rebels pretended to act on the traditional conception of royal sovereignty; they were not overthrowing the king—they sought only to force him to change his policy.

Even more important was the implication of this doctrine when the territories of several princes were involved. God alone gave sovereign rights by His decisions about births and deaths of claimants to hereditary thrones or by his intervention in earthly elections of elective ones. In any case, princes were constrained to recognize each other's sovereignty, and political theorists with the prestige of a Grotius or a Puffendorff argued that territory taken by force had to be restored to its "rightful" owner. Before the seventeenth century was over this obligation had been cynically violated, but this fact does not argue away its importance.

Indeed the whole picture of dynastic politics is fundamentally related to this basic assumption about legitimate claims in the political world. There were but few important treaties in this era in which the marriage of young princes was not an important consideration, and few wars in which the legitimate or assumed rights of heirs were not involved in the contest. The combinations that inheritance might create were so important in the relations of princes that even the thought of a fortuitous series of events recreating the Empire of Charles V made princes everywhere as fearful for the "liberties" of Europe as their own leading barons were solicitous of the "liberties" of the great ones of the kingdom.

Although it was generally assumed that a prince could not extend his holdings by the use of naked force, it was also assumed that the king, any king, was a soldier and would lead his armies in war. The office of "king" was at once a military and a judicial office; the judicial role was usually left to men trained in the law while the king himself was expected to lead his armies. Every young prince was trained to be a soldier, indoctrinated by tales of the gallant deeds performed by his predecessors, and taught that his fame would ultimately depend upon his military actions. Nor was the prince the only one so educated. The important noblemen of the realm as well as the petty country knights also brought up their children with the assumption that they were members of a warrior class and therefore would become soldiers. Furthermore they were taught that royal preferment, wealth, honor, and power were all to be had from the role of the soldier. It may be that younger sons of the nobility, often called the vulture class of feudal society, held more firmly to the idea that the sword would open the route to fortune, but it was a common belief held by men from the lowest to the highest nobility of the land. Thus the soldier king could depend upon soldier vassals, and the king who was slow to go to war would soon hear harsh words from the men in his court who regarded war as the route to power and wealth.

## IV

In 1619 a war broke out in Bohemia over the succession to the crown; four decades later men who had been children when the war started wrote a treaty on an island of territory between the French and Spanish frontiers ending the epoch of warfare that began when members of the Diet of Bohemia threw Archduke Ferdinand's representatives out of the window of the palace at Prague. This war that began much as had any of the civil rebellions of the sixteenth century ended with the emergence of political institutions and ideas that were to provide a foundation for the modern secular state: results quite unforeseen and surely undesired by the men who began it. The war is a valuable study of how conflicting religious and political tendencies brought new political and military techniques of the states-system to birth.

The religious wars of the preceding century by 1619 had left the Holy

Roman Empire of the German nation a near-ruin. The imperial power had lost much of its effectiveness and the princely power was yet to be developed. An uneasy peace existed between the Catholic and the Protestant factions; there were two leagues, one Catholic, the other the Protestant Union; they were undoubtedly illegal if the imperial constitution had any meaning, but in that unstable political climate they had become necessary. The German problem was further aggravated by the fact that the peace of 1609 between Spain and the United Netherlands was only a twelve-year truce which both sides fully expected to end in reopened warfare. As a result there was a Spanish Hapsburg army in the Netherlands facing the Dutch army across the frontier, and that Spanish army depended upon transportation routes through Germany for replacements, supplies, and money. The problems of Germany were further complicated by the fact that the German Hapsburg holdings in Austria, Styria, Tyrol, Bohemia, Hungary, and several smaller countries which had been divided among several princes in 1600, were being reunited in the person of Ferdinand of Styria, a vigorous prince devoted to absolutism, Catholicism, and the house of Hapsburg. The peace of Germany was in a delicate balance: it obviously could be upset by any issue that threatened the interests of either party in the religious controversy. This was a situation that would allow ambitious men to fish in troubled waters; it was one that led cautious men to seek compromise.

In 1618 at the court of the Electoral Prince Frederick of the Rhine Palatinate there were men willing to try to gain advantages from the situation. Count Frederick was a young man with possibilities. His uncles were those important men, the Prince of Orange, Stadtholder of the Netherlands, and the Duc de Bouillon, military leader of the Huguenot faction in France; his father-in-law was James I of England. His wife was a vastly ambitious young woman. Frederick himself was too young to develop a master plan for action, but his principal advisor, the prince of Anhalt, was a politician with both skill and imagination. He was important in the international Calvinist circles; with friends from Geneva, to Transylvania, to Edinburgh, he dreamed of a Calvinist alliance that would include England, the Netherlands, the German princes, and the Hungarian, Bohemian, and Transylvanian Calvinist magnates and perhaps even France, to be directed against the house of Hapsburg. Anhalt succeeded in getting his master elected head of the Protestant Union in Germany, and had begun the spinning of the web of alliances when the situation in Bohemia offered the opportunity to strike a blow at his opponent.

The other protagonist in this early stage of the drama was Archduke

Ferdinand von Hapsburg. Ferdinand had been born to the crown of Styria, but a fortuitous series of deaths also made him heir to all the family holdings in central Europe. His childless uncle Matthias, who held both the thrones of the Empire and of Bohemia, persuaded, bribed, and perhaps bullied the powerful Diet of the latter kingdom (composed mostly of nobles) to elect Ferdinand as his successor. By this time Ferdinand was already known as a disciple of the Jesuits, as a counter-reformation prince with definite ideas about the role that God had placed upon his shoulders. In Styria he had given non-Catholic subjects the choice of migration or conversion, and there was little reason to believe that he would be more tolerant on the throne in Bohemia. Ferdinand was also known as a prince with strong opinions about royal prerogatives. In his German provinces he had steadily undermined the privileges and powers of the *Landtäge* (provincial assemblies), and with the aid of university-trained jurists, he was in the act of creating a bureaucracy, independent of the nobility, to administer the land. Here was a prince that threatened both the religious and the political "liberties" cherished by many of the important people in Bohemia.

The religious picture of Bohemia was confused by the coexistence in uneasy peace of Catholics, Lutherans, Brethren, Calvinists, and even a few Hussites. When it became apparent what Ferdinand's election might mean to them, a clique in the Bohemian Diet, led by Calvinist politicians, decided to reverse the election by declaring it null and void because it had been obtained by undue pressure. These were the men who threw Ferdinand's representatives from the window, in the famous "defenestration of Prague"; they also decided to offer the throne of Bohemia to Frederick of the Palatinate, the Calvinist champion who, they believed, could rally Calvinist Europe to defend their action. On the very day in 1619 that the Diet of the Empire elected Ferdinand Holy Roman Emperor, news arrived in Frankfort of Frederick's acceptance of the crown of Bohemia.

The problem presented by this election becomes intelligible in light of the action of the other German princes. On the frontiers of Bohemia lay the lands of Bavaria and Saxony. The electoral duke of Saxony, John Georg, was a Lutheran, a constitutionalist, a man desiring peace, and, unfortunately, a drunkard. John Georg finally allowed himself to be persuaded that Frederick's action was illegal and joined the Catholic Ferdinand with his military power in the attack on Bohemia. He rationalized his action by the belief that he might guarantee the religious liberty of Bohemia. The fact that Ferdinand had ceded a small province to him for his aid also encouraged him. The other important neighbor of Bohemia was Maximilian of Bavaria. He was the leader of the Catholic League and controlled the Catholic army commanded by Tilly. Maximilian joined Ferdinand in the attack on Bohemia, but only after Ferdinand had promised to give him Frederick's electoral seat in the Diet of the Empire.

The representatives of Ferdinand and Frederick enlarged their conflict when both appealed to the young Louis XIII for French aid. France had traditionally supported the German princes against the Hapsburg emperor, but this time the French king, himself at war with his Huguenot subjects, regarded Frederick's acceptance of the Bohemian throne as part of a widespread Calvinist plot, and urged the Lutheran German princes to stand aside in this conflict. The French attitude seems to have determined the attitude of the Protestant Union in Germany.

The allies that Anhalt had hoped to rally either failed to materialize, or were unable to act decisively; on the other side, the forces that Ferdinand finally mustered won a victory at White Mountain (1621) that resulted in the expulsion of Frederick from Bohemia. Frederick escaped and Ferdinand ruthlessly suppressed the revolutionary forces, revised the Bohemian constitution to make the formerly elective throne hereditary in his house, and distributed the lands of the rebels among his faithful followers. The battle of White Mountain gave the Hapsburgs wealth and power at the expense of the "liberties" of Bohemia, that is to say at the expense of the Protestant nobles who had attempted to exclude Ferdinand from the throne.

After the defeat at White Mountain, Frederick's army retreated across Germany toward the Palatinate closely followed now by the Bavarians, for Maximilian of Bavaria had been promised Frederick's electoral hat. At the same time Spain, ready to reopen the war against the Dutch, brought her army into the Palatinate from the Netherlands to guarantee control over communications on the Rhine. What had begun as a Bohemian civil war was to become a German war for control over the Rhineland.

This second period of the war is usually called the Danish phase because Christian of Denmark, supported by several German princes and subsidized by the kings of France and England, entered the war in defense of "German liberties" and the Protestant religion. At the same time, the French government, aroused over the prospect of the extension of Ferdinand's imperial power, and anxious to aid their Dutch allies against Spain, cut the Spanish line of communication through the Alps. The tide of war, however, ran heavily in favor of Emperor Ferdinand. The army of the Catholic League was joined by a new imperial army brought into being by a Bohemian nobleman named Wallenstein, who rapidly proved his genius as an organizer by creating the largest and the best army in Germany. From the first it weighed the scales heavily in Ferdinand's favor, but since it was organized on the principle that the costs of the army should be borne by the territories that it occupied, this instrument of imperial power soon became unpopular with all the princes of Germany. This made no difference; Wallenstein knew how to supply his army, he paid his men better than any other commander, asked them few questions about their past or their religion, and allowed them great license in their treatment of civilians. Soldiers from all Europe flocked to his banners; even Tilly, co-commander of the imperial forces, complained that Wallenstein seduced his men.

Warfare moved slowly in the seventeenth century, but by 1629 Frederick's army had been driven into eastern Europe where it broke up and its commander, Mansfeld, was killed. Christian of Denmark and his German allies were decisively beaten, and the king was forced to sign a peace. The French intervention also came to nothing when rebellions at home forced the French to withdraw from Switzerland and effectively prevented any further interference.

Thus, by 1629, Ferdinand's power in Germany was greater than that of any emperor since the reformation, and with Wallenstein's armies continuing to grow even though the Danes were no longer a threat, there was good reason to believe that the emperor might well clip the "German liberties," that is to say the rights of the princes, and establish an imperial despotism. The first "flight" of the imperial eagle was a measure close to Ferdinand's heart, for he was a devout Roman Catholic perhaps even before he was an imperialist; his Edict of Restitution ordered, without the consultation of the Diet, that all lands and foundations taken from the Roman church since 1555 must be restored. The religious implications of the Edict were important, but the political ones were even more imposing. There was scarcely a non-Catholic prince who would not be forced to restore property; a number of important princes would be reduced to the rank of mere noblemen; the fate of a number of great towns, including Augsburg, was involved, and all this had been brought about by an edict issued by the emperor on his own authority. The Edict of Restitution, added to the grievances that the princes had against Wallenstein for his exactions in their lands, was enough to create a crisis in the Empire.

Thus at the moment of victory, the emperor suddenly was confronted with his enemies both at home and abroad. Unfortunately for him, he was vulnerable in two ways: first he wanted his son Ferdinand to succeed him in the imperial title; secondly, he, too, was fearful of his general, for Wallenstein was trying to give him a revolutionary conception of the role of emperor, trying to cut him loose from his connections with the Spanish Hapsburg interests, and finally, trying to build for himself (Wallenstein) a position of princely power in Germany unsuited to his past and his birth.

However, the political situation of the years 1629–30 was very different from that of a decade earlier. In the first place, John Georg, the elector of Saxony, and his more timorous colleague, the elector of Brandenburg, after the Edict of Restitution tried to establish a constitutional party to curb Ferdinand's authority, and John Georg began the collection of an army commanded by one of Wallenstein's best generals. The Catholic Maximilian of Bavaria was also a "constitutionalist"; he now turned on the emperor and objected to Ferdinand's acting without consulting the Diet. Catholic and Protestant electors thus joined hands to "persuade" Ferdinand to dismiss his general, but they could not force the emperor to give up the Edict of Restitution.

The great danger in the crisis, however, was not the problems between Ferdinand and the electors, but rather the threat of foreign military intervention. In France Cardinal Richelieu and Louis XIII were shocked at the rise of Hapsburg power in Germany and the Low Countries, but as long as they had to fight the Huguenots and noble factions in France, they could not risk open entry into the conflict. There was another European prince whose career as king and soldier made him seem to be a proper tool for the French to use against this Hapsburg danger. Without fully realizing what he was doing, Richelieu secured a peace between Gustavus Adolphus and the king of Poland, and then subsidized the Swedish king for an invasion of Germany from the north. Ferdinand was scornful of the "petty northern invader," and Gustavus Adolphus' brother-in-law, the elector of Brandenburg, and John Georg of Saxony were appalled at the idea that they might become involved in his venture. No one knew what the Swedish king would do.

When he landed in Germany Gustavus Adolphus was in his middle thirties and already had two full decades of warfare behind him. He was a brilliant administrator, an able leader, and a man with expanding ambitions; he regarded warfare as the natural and normal condition of life. He was unquestionably sincere when he announced that he came to Germany to defend "German liberties" and the Protestant religion against a tyrannical emperor, but he perhaps should have added that he also hoped to gain control of the German Baltic coast. As soon as his veteran armies tasted victory, he began to see himself as ruler of a north German-Swedish empire. There were many people in Germany and in Europe who recognized Gustavus Adolphus as the Protestant hero, but there were others who understood that his ambitions in Germany were a threat to the Protestant princes and also ended all hopes for settling the war. With Swedish intervention the war ceased to be a German civil conflict and became a European war.

When the Swedish army met Tilly's Catholic imperial forces at Breitenfeld, the new Swedish tactical use of infantry and artillery carried the day; the imperial army was defeated, and Gustavus Adolphus marched across middle Germany imposing huge contributions on the clerical states in his way while his allies, John Georg's Saxon army, invaded Bohemia and captured Prague. With the Swedish "Lion" on the Rhine Richelieu suddenly understood that he had not employed a mercenary general whom he could control; instead he had released a new force in Germany that might be as dangerous to France as the Hapsburgs, and in addition would be disastrous to the Catholic church. Fortunately for Richelieu's peace of mind, the Swedish Lion had only a year to live. Gustavus launched his army south into Bavaria; Tilly was killed, and the whole countryside desperately ravaged. The Swede then turned northward to meet the new imperial army in Saxony. At Lützen in 1632 Gustavus Adolphus was killed. So many of his allies were relieved to hear the news that many people wondered whether the bullet had come from the front or the rear.

The imperial army at Lützen was commanded by Wallenstein. Even Maximilian of Bavaria, who had fought so hard for his dismissal, had urged Ferdinand to reappoint this general to command. For his part Wallenstein had reassembled his army only after imposing conditions upon the emperor: like other generals before and after him, Wallenstein tried to use his army to make himself into a ruling prince; he may even have dreamed of making himself emperor of a great state in eastern and central Europe. His career was a perfect example of the power that a mercenary army gave to its commander, and of the danger to the prince who employed him. Wallenstein's own fate was decided when Ferdinand became convinced that he was dabbling in treason; at the emperor's orders Wallenstein was assassinated in 1634 by mercenary officers who had sworn fidelity to him. Both his life and his death were the stuff for drama (see Schiller's trilogy) and evidence of the need for more dependable military institutions.

The death of Gustavus Adolphus did not end the war, for the Swedes were determined to keep the foothold that their master had won on the south coast of the Baltic sea. The Spanish and imperial forces jointly met the Swedish army at Nördlingen (1634), and the Swedes suffered a catastrophic defeat. The Spaniards pushed on into the Spanish Netherlands; the imperial troops went to Prague where a peace treaty was negotiated that might have ended the war in Germany if there had been only German interests at stake.

While the war was being fought in Germany, the conflict between Bourbon France and Hapsburg Spain threatened at any moment to boil over into open warfare. Indeed the warfare in the Netherlands and Italy, the revolts in France, the battles in Germany, were all related to the moves made in Paris and Madrid. Richelieu had thought that he was employing Gustavus Adolphus to fight against his Hapsburg enemies; at the same time the Spanish minister had paid money to the French Huguenots in revolt against Louis XIII. The party of the devout Catholics everywhere sided with Spain, but there were other men who regarded the conflict as political and not religious, as a contest between Bourbon and Hapsburg for the hegemony of Europe. That it was only chance that religion was introduced as an issue became more and more clear after the battle of Nördlingen and the Peace of Prague of 1635 left Lutheran princes like John Georg of Saxony allied with the Catholic emperor, and Catholic France allied with the Protestant Dutch and the Swedes. In 1635 the French monarchy declared war against the Spanish Hapsburg complex to prevent the collapse of the anti-Hapsburg coalition.

By the time that Louis XIII declared war against his Hapsburg cousins three military patterns were becoming firmly established in Europe. There existed, in effect, three different kinds of armies. The oldest type was the result of the feudal levy; that is, the king called up his noblemen to serve in his army against his enemies. The first French armies that Louis and Richelieu collected were largely made up of these brightly clad, carefree noblemen; they practically melted in the face of the ragged veterans of the imperial army. The second type of military institution was the mercenary army under the command, pay, and supply of a soldier of fortune. Wallenstein and a dozen other men of lesser fame led these armies. The men in the ranks, as well as their officers, fought for money and the chance of personal gain rather than for loyalty to a prince; at the end of a battle, the victorious army simply enlisted its prisoners and attempted also to enlist the stragglers from the defeated army. Its officers changed sides as easily as the men.

These mercenary armies, forcing tribute from occupied lands, fought the Thirty Years' War in Germany and were responsible for much of the havoc that the war left in its path. The third type of army, under the king's direct control, had a more national character, but only just developing. Although comprising the core of the Spanish and Swedish forces it does not loom large on the military scene in 1640 for there were several important obstacles to its development. In the first place princes still regarded an army as something that one assembled for a specific task and disbanded as soon as that task was finished. The idea of a proper standing army had disappeared with the break-up of the Roman legions, and it was difficult to recover. Secondly, a standing army requires two important things that barely existed in Europe before the mid-seventeenth century: the first is a large and constant stream of revenue flowing into the king's treasury and with it treasury officials who could administer the uses of this money; the second is a war office capable of assembling supplies, recruiting and paying men, and, perhaps most difficult of all, controlling the officers who command the army. By 1600 the weakening Spanish monarchy organized by Philip II had the rudiments of such an organization, but none of his successors was able to make the machine function smoothly. Richelieu and Louis XIII tried to organize the bureaucratic machinery to superintend an army of this type for France, but only a part of the armies that fought for France in the Thirty Years' War was actually controlled by the king's officials. Richelieu, just like Emperor Ferdinand, had to hire mercenaries; his general, Bernard of Saxe-Weimar, was almost as dangerous to his interests as Wallenstein had been to those of the emperor.

One of the reasons that Richelieu and Louis XIII had delayed entering the war was their fear of the traditional type of soldiers. They did not want to use the feudal device of arming French noblemen who might lead a revolt in France, and they did not like the other prospect of hiring a self-interested, ambitious foreign mercenary. In the first years of intervention in the war, France suffered because it had not solved this problem: France was invaded, Paris threatened, and the French war effort seemed meager indeed. However Richelieu concentrated much of his own efforts and those of his "creatures" on the building of a professional army, commanded and superintended by the king's own officers and officials, and emphasizing discipline and technical improvement. This effort paid dividends after the deaths of both the king and the cardinal when France won a brilliant victory over the Spanish at Rocroi in 1643. In the years that followed, this national professional army, subject to the king's war minister, became the standard for all the armies of Europe. The war had thus speeded the development of an instrument essential to the power of the monarch both in domestic affairs and international relations.

Following the French active intervention in 1635, the war in Germany continued to be indecisive; the emperor could not muster enough force to drive out the foreigners. The Swedes were incapable of more than raids from their Baltic bases into the middle of Germany. The French operated successfully in the Rhineland, and after the battle of Rocroi they seemed to have the better of the fight in the Netherlands, but this rise of French military power also aroused fear of France in the hearts of their Dutch ally, the United Netherlands. The Dutch Protestant burghers were afraid that the prince of Orange, with French aid, might make himself king, and at the same time they decided that a weak and decadent Spanish power in Brussels, even if Catholic, would be better than the vigorous French monarchy as a neighbor. The result was that from 1643 onward, Dutch policy more and more protected the interests of their old Catholic enemy in the Spanish Netherlands. The war continued, and Germany was cruelly devastated while the contestants tried to find a formula that might allow it to end.

A break in the deadlock came when the vigorous and inventive Prince Frederick William of Brandenburg-Prussia mounted the electoral throne in 1640. His first act was to accuse the emperor of delaying the progress toward a peace in an effort to rebuild the imperial power, and then, on his own, he made a treaty of peace with Sweden. The next important move was the separation of the Franco-Spanish war from the war in Germany; this allowed the Hapsburg-Bourbon duel to go on to its bitter end, unencumbered by the problems of Germany, and without the German emperor's aid to his Spanish relatives. Finally Emperor Ferdinand had to recognize that the old constitution of the Holy Roman Empire was dead and that the German princes must henceforth control their own destiny. Ferdinand could do this because he already recognized that not northern Germany but his dynastic holdings in south Germany, Bohemia, and Hungary were the pivots of his power, and the principal concern of his policy.

The story of the writing of the treaties of Westphalia is long and complex; there were endless delays and endless arguments. A wit remarked that the child that the wife of the French ambassador was carrying at the moment would be born, grow up, and finally die before the congress could complete its work. But when one considers the mass of territorial readjustments, the thorny problems of precedence and protocol, to say nothing about those of religion and politics, that had to be ironed out while the negotiators were following the news of the war and constantly readjusting their peace demands to it, it is not surprising that it took a long time to write the treaties.

The Peace of Westphalia (1648) provided Germany with a new constitution superimposed upon the morbid Holy Roman Empire of the German nation. In this new Germany the princes gained the right to make treaties with foreign states and thus to behave as independent powers. Moreover, the larger princes of Saxony, Brandenburg, Bavaria, as well as a number of those in the next rank, emerged with considerably enlarged territories, thereby giving the principalities the opportunity to inherit the future of central Europe. The Hapsburg power in central Europe was fundamentally changed by this fact; henceforth the emperor at Vienna was also a prince, ruling a complex of principalities and kingdoms in the German, Bohemian, and Hungarian territories on the Danube. The same treaties gave France a foothold in Alsace and Sweden one in Pomerania, and both of these states were left in a position to interfere with the political situation in Germany. The Swiss Confederation and the United Netherlands were both recognized as independent and outside of the Holy Roman Empire.

The treaties also confirmed the century-old formula of the Diet of Augsburg that left the princes in control of the religious life of their people and at the same time recognized Calvinism as well as Lutheranism and Catholicism. But the most important religious aspect of the Peace was the fact that religion, however important when the war began, now played so small a role. The Thirty Years' War was the last great European conflict in which religious issues were significant, and the peace of Westphalia properly can be said to mark the triumph of secular concerns over religious interests in politics.

## V

The treaties of Westphalia ended the German phase of the Thirty Years' War, but not the Franco-Spanish conflict. Mazarin, Richelieu's successor, cleverly separated the Austrian and Spanish Hapsburgs, reserving for a later treaty the settlement of Franco-Spanish problems and frontiers. But his program for ending the war with Spain was rudely interrupted by a domestic rebellion in France, the *Fronde,* that threatened for a while not only to undo the work of Richelieu, Louis XIII, and Mazarin, but even to bring into jeopardy the crown of France itself. We now see the *Fronde* as a sort of "birth pains" of the French monarchy in its rise to hegemony in Europe, but at the time no such outcome could have been predicted.

The problems of the seventeenth-century French monarchy were rooted in the religious wars of the sixteenth century. At the end of those wars Henry IV was forced to barter away much of the real power of his crown to secure recognition of his right to rule. The Huguenot party emerged almost as a republic within the kingdom, controlling walled towns, soldiers, and tax revenues, holding periodic assemblies, and electing "a protector." At the same time the great noble families (*les Grands:* Guise, Épernon, Montmorency, and others) also emerged from the wars heavy with spoils taken from the crown: they had obtained hereditary governorships and other offices, the rights to collect tolls, enormous grants of money often in the form of "rentes" payable annually from the king's revenue. Perhaps more important they had learned the lesson of the civil wars, namely, that rebellion—indeed, even the threat of rebellion—was profitable and relatively safe for the rebels as long as they had a prince of the blood as their leader. With *les Grands* and the Huguenots in possession of so much power, it is not surprising that Richelieu explained to the young king Louis XIII that his policy would be to ruin the Huguenot party, to humble the great nobles, and finally to raise the prestige of France in Europe.

This statement of policy may have been made after the fact, but it was truly the program of the great cardinal. With Richelieu at the helm (after 1624), rebellions ceased to be profitable: the rebel chieftains formerly had been bought off; now they were executed by a royal commission especially selected to find them guilty. The king's brother Gaston and his mother Marie were forced into exile for their share in these plots; Marie never returned to France and Gaston came back only after submitting to the king. Richelieu's war on the power of the great nobles led him to destroy their fortifications, take action against them when they fought duels, and most important, perhaps, to dilute their ranks by the creation of many new peers, thus placing greater social distance between them and the royal family.

The Huguenots, too, were to lose their political and military independence. Richelieu and Louis XIII carefully disentangled the valid religious interests of the Reformed church from the political and military guarantees that it had extorted from Henry IV. La Rochelle provided the first great test of their policy. The city revolted against the king and allied itself with the English to protect its military and economic independence. In the subsequent struggle, the city was besieged for over a year; the ill-planned English expeditions were beaten off; and in the end La Rochelle surrendered unconditionally (1629). Without interfering with the religious privileges of the *Rochellais,* the king's government destroyed their military power: the walls of the city were leveled so that a plow could pass through the foundations and a royal garrison occupied the only fortifications permitted to remain for the defense of the harbor. Within two years (1631) the other great Huguenot towns of the south suffered approximately the same fate: by the peace of Alais the political and military privileges that set the "party" apart from the rest of France were taken away, but the rights of the Huguenots to practice their religion, and to serve the king's government and army were fully respected. Louis XIII and Richelieu were not happy to be tolerant of the "so-called reformed religion," but they recognized that toleration was wise.

In the process of recouping the authority of the crown, Louis XIII and Richelieu aroused other antagonisms. By the early seventeenth century the traditional officers of the kingdom had ceased to be responsive to the crown: most of the important governorships had become hereditary, the tax officials, judges, and officers of the Parlements and other sovereign courts and many other officials "owned" their positions and had the right to sell or will them without consulting the crown as long as they paid an annual tax. Thus the crown's power to remove or punish unfaithful servants was drastically reduced. To circumvent this situation Louis and Richelieu developed the policy of sending representatives of the royal council into the provinces with the power to act in the name of the king; these "circuit riders" could quash a writ of Parlement, give summary justice, supervise collection and distribution of tax revenue, and exercise the police power of the crown. By the time Louis and Richelieu were on their death beds, near mid-century, these officials of the council were all well on their way to becoming the famous intendants of the French monarchy; their powers cut across those of the governors of provinces, the Parlements and other courts, the tax officials, the urban magistrates; they and their subdelegates could act effectively and directly in the name of the king. Inevitably, they became the most hated men in France, at least in those quarters that suffered loss of power from their activities. As might be expected, there were influential men who wished to force the king to give up these powerful aids to his authority.

Richelieu and Louis XIII came into conflict with the Parlement of Paris on several other counts. The Parlements were, in fact, off-shoots of the king's council that had long since settled down to regular domiciles while the king's council continued its traditional peripatetic habit of following the king in his travels. In the course of their development, these Parlements (the one in Paris was the most important of several) obtained the right to refuse, at least temporarily, to register any edict of the king that, in the opinion of the judges, was contrary to the traditional laws and customs of the kingdom. Since, however, the Parlement was merely an extension of the king's council, the king could force registration of his edicts by a personal appearance (*lit de justice*) in Parlement. Even so, this parlementary remonstrance did have some of the attributes of judicial review. As Richelieu and Louis became deeply involved in the Thirty Years' War, first by providing subsidies and later by direct intervention, they found themselves in conflict with the Parlement because of their tax measures. Louis was impatient of the black-frocked judges who talked about the misery of the kingdom and failed to understand the importance of his war policy. Finally he brusquely warned them that he wanted "my Parlement" to dispense justice among subjects and "not to interfere with *my* state." Louis XIII, rather than his famous son, was the man capable of saying *l'état, c'est moi*. There was nothing that the judges could do; they stored up this grievance along with those that they had against the king's "circuit riders." Like the great nobles who had suffered from the "fury" of the morose king and the all-powerful cardinal, they waited anxiously for death to remove their enemies.

Richelieu and Louis XIII died within a few months of each other in 1642–43 ending one of the most remarkable stories of collaboration between king and minister in all history. The Parlement gladly set aside the dead king's testament and installed Anne of Austria, the queen-mother, as regent for the five-year-old Louis XIV; the judges were now confident that their advice would be listened to more attentively than it had been under Louis XIII. With the regency, the prisons opened, freeing the nobles who had been prisoners of the late ruler, and the decrees of exile were lifted, allowing enemies of Richelieu to return. All these people fully expected Anne to reverse the policies of her husband, for she too had suffered humiliation from the late king and cardinal. Anne, however, was the daughter of the king of Spain, the granddaughter of Philip II; she took seriously her role as regent for her son and had no trouble at all in recognizing that her program must be identical with that of her late husband. Not only did she not dismiss Richelieu's "creatures" from office, she also took as her first minister, and perhaps also as her secret husband, Mazarin, the very man that Louis XIII and Richelieu had designated as Richelieu's successor. Mazarin, a cardinal but not a priest, was one of the most subtle diplomats of the era; as a naturalized Frenchman, this Italian-born minister piloted France safely through problems of international war and civil rebellion.

The storm that was to blow up so violently in 1648 had already begun as soon as Louis XIII closed his eyes, but Anne and Mazarin managed to stave it off by a nice mixture of diplomacy and force. Less cruel than Louis XIII, Anne merely imprisoned noblemen who plotted to murder her minister, while she tried to manage Parlement by diplomacy when possible, using the *lit de justice* as a last resort. Each year, however, the problems of the regency became more and more difficult as the war became more costly. One French army was operating in the Netherlands, another in the Pyrenees, and there was a German army in the pay of France in the Rhineland. In addition French money supported the Swedish army, the Portuguese rebellion, and was used freely to buy the support of petty German princes. For France all this meant new taxes, sale of new offices, loans, and other expedients. The really serious conflict with the Parlements came when Mazarin imposed taxes that cut deeply into the pockets of the justices of Parlement, and other sovereign courts; it did not take long for their officers to see a parallel between their conflicts with the crown and those of the English Parliament with Charles I, which were about to end with the latter's losing his head. In their own propaganda, the Parlementarians became "fathers of the country," "senators," and "heroes" fighting tyranny. They won the support of the Parisian crowds. It was easy to blame everything upon Mazarin: he was an Italian; he was becoming very rich; he was destroying the French traditional customs.

The conflict with the Parlement moved from the erection of barricades in Paris to the flight of the king and queen, and open war between Paris and the crown. This was the first *Fronde,* the Parlementary *Fronde.* It was not completely settled before the second *Fronde* broke out; the *Fronde* of the still ambitious nobles. Actually the situation in France was so complex in this period from 1648 to about 1652 that any generalization has to be both wrong and inadequate. The great nobles, led by Condé, the victor of Rocroi, raised the standard of revolt and called in the Spanish to help them fight their own king's government. Louis XIV later wrote to his son in his *Mémoires,* that, had Condé been victorious, the kingdom probably would have been partitioned between the house of Condé and of Bourbon; brought up during the civil wars of the *Fronde,* it is not surprising that Louis XIV later did all in his power to prevent the recurrence of such events.

The two *Frondes* were both broken, but not without much fighting and long and tortuous negotiations. The queen was forced twice to send Mazarin into exile, but she wisely continued to profit from his advice even when he was in Germany. Instructive in understanding the role of the king in seventeenth-century society was the effect of the declaration of Louis XIV's majority and his consecration at Rheims. With one stroke the whole status of the government changed; a major king had the right to call whomsoever he wished to be his advisors, and the will of a major king could not be challenged by Parlement since legally the Parlement itself was no more than an expression of that will. Louis XIV recalled Mazarin who came back to France leading an army recruited in Germany; along with Turenne, Mazarin broke the back of the noble *Fronde* and forced Condé into exile in 1652.

Once the civil war was liquidated, Mazarin turned his attention to the war with Spain. It was difficult in the mid-seventeenth century to obtain a military decision because no army was ever mobile or flexible enough to reach the heart of the enemies' territory; furthermore fighting Spain was like hammering at a pillow: a French victory in the Netherlands in no way deprived the Spanish king of his lands in Italy or Spain. Final victory could only be had by attrition. It might well have taken much longer to win if Mazarin had not been willing to ally France with Cromwell's England. The audacity of this move can be appreciated only if one recalls that Cromwell's England had beheaded Louis XIV's uncle and had long been an object lesson of the noxious fury of popular or representative government for the boy king.

Even with Condé to lead their armies, the Spanish were no match for the combined forces of England and France. Cromwell's model army and the new army that Le Tellier, as minister of war, and Turenne, as commander-in-chief, were building for France won smashing victories. Condé's own victory over the Spanish at Rocroi in 1643 has been called the end of Spanish hegemony; the later defeats that he suffered, while commanding Spanish forces on the Netherland coasts, clearly underlined the fact that Spain had become a hollow giant.

The Spanish king was ready to recognize the defeat of his kingdoms when Mazarin and Anne threatened to marry the young Louis XIV to a Savoyard princess. It had always been understood in Spain that Marie Thérèse, Philip IV's daughter, was to become queen of France; the war had to end to accomplish this marriage. Thus dynastic ambitions rather than interests of state brought Spain and France to the conference table to end the war that had been started forty years before when Frederick of the Palatinate accepted the throne of Bohemia.

The Treaty of the Pyrenees (1659) marked the end of the Spanish, and the opening of the epoch of French hegemony in Europe. Spain surrendered two provinces and gave Marie Thérèse as bride for Louis XIV. There was a long series of provisions prohibiting France from aiding the rebelling Portuguese, restoring Condé to his honors and property in France, and regulation of all manner of things between the two kingdoms. But the important things about the treaty were: first, that it made perfectly clear the declining status of Spain and the rise of France; and secondly, that it provided the basis for a French Bourbon claim to the Spanish crowns. It was the intention of the Spanish negotiators to exclude Marie Thérèse and her heirs from the Spanish throne; they hoped to reserve this honor for the Hapsburg family. To this end the treaty elaborately provided for renunciations on the part of the new queen of France. However the contract also called for the payment of a large dowry; and the French insisted upon making the renunciations dependent upon its payment. When the Spanish objected to such a provision, they were asked if Spain did not intend to honor the dowry debt! In fact the dowry was larger than Spain could pay. But there was another difficulty involved in forcing a princess to renounce her throne; she could renounce for herself, but she could not bind her unborn descendants. Their rights to the throne were in the hands of God.

The marriage of Louis XIV and Marie Thérèse was destined to provide an axis for European politics for the next half century. Charles II, the dull-witted and sickly son of Philip IV of Spain, could not produce an heir, and therefore the succession to his throne, contested by his relatives in Vienna and Paris, remained a disturbing element in European politics until its settlement in 1713 in the treaties following the War of the Spanish Succession.

## VI

In western Europe the Treaty of the Pyrenees marked the end of the civil and international wars of the first half of the century; there followed a short period of calm in which men could take stock of the preceding years. One thing that everyone could agree upon was that the civil and international wars had created great disorder. A distinguished historian, summing up the effects of the period, has described it as nothing less than a grand *mêlée* of conflicting forces almost completely lacking in structure or form. Statesmen and princes of the era were aware that this *mêlée* made it very difficult to follow any constructive program. The spectacles of Richelieu and Louis XIII frustrated in their European policy by the rebellions of Huguenots and nobles; of Anne and Mazarin deflected from their efforts to bring Spain to terms by the *Fronde* and the treasons of a prince of the blood (Condé); the problem of princes in Germany whose states were willy-nilly drawn into conflicts not of their making: all these could be reproduced to a greater or lesser degree everywhere in Europe. In any count of the problems facing princes and statesmen of the mid-seventeenth century, disorder must have stood first on the list since they had all seen or experienced for themselves the fortunes of civil rebellion or of interstate conflict. Not all of them had been driven from their capitals as had the boy Louis XIV, but nearly all of them understood that their political future, indeed perhaps their lives, were dependent upon their ability to cope with the forces of violence and disorder. Men with this background might spend money building a palace or even a church, they might toy with mistresses or follow dogs in the hunt, but they could never dismiss the haunting fear aroused by the chaos that seemed to cry out for some organization to tame its wild force.

The generation that came to power in the second half of the century had grown up under the sign of war. As children they had listened to stories of the heroic deeds of soldiers; as youths they played "war" in the castle yards (Louis XIV, for example, had a fort for his "playhouse" in the garden of the Palais Royal); and as young men they followed the armies as apprentices learning the art of war. Should anyone be surprised to learn that they regarded military conflict as natural, or that they relied upon soldiers as a principal source of power? Louis XIV explained to Turenne that he must have an army capable of intimidating the forces of evil in the kingdom. The young Frederick William of Brandenburg-Prussia insisted that a prince had the alternative of paying subsidies to a stronger neighbor to secure military protection or of building for himself a military force strong enough to protect his lands. While these two men may have been the most striking examples of this attitude, they were by no means the only ones, for they were not the only princes who had eaten the bread of exile in their own land and faced armed foes in the guise of foreigners or of their own rebellious subjects. For men, brought up in such an era of conflict, there was one answer to their problem: military power was needed to give peace and tranquillity to the land, and to assure obedience to their rule.

Nor were the princes and their ministers the only ones who learned this lesson from the forty-odd years of war and disorder. The ill-paid, poorly disciplined soldiery, commanded by mercenary captains, subject to little or no authority, carried the miseries of war to all Europe and brought home the fact that uncontrolled military forces create only disorder. Today historians are in the process of rewriting the story of the Thirty Years' War, rejecting some of the atrocity stories and some of the devastation that nineteenth-century historians accepted at face value, and yet anyone who has seen Jacques Callot's prints depicting the horrors of war will not miss the fact that these conflicts created great misery for the whole population. No better illustration can be found than the French experience. The *Fronde* introduced into the French civil war troops trained in the Thirty Years' War in Germany; the derangement accompanying their passage through the countryside caused Frenchmen to lose their enthusiasm for the "liberties" demanded by the *Frondeurs*. Royal authority and the concomitant discipline of royal absolutism was a relief from mid-seventeenth century civil war, so that the people in the country as well as in the towns grew ready to welcome the emergence of effective royal police power. The "liberties" of the great nobles and local powers as well as those of religious parties no longer seemed to be worth the chaos that their defense created.

This was not the first time that Europeans had been faced with the question: "What is the greatest good of the community?" In the sixteenth century when it proved impossible to extirpate heresy by fire and the sword without destroying the social and economic life of the community, men like Bodin had explained to their fellow subjects that religious unity is a desirable "good," but that the greatest "good" in the community is the maintenance of peace and tranquillity that allows an orderly life. By 1660, after a half-century of warfare in which German, French, Bohemian, and other "liberties" provided flags for rebellion, a great many people began to wonder if these "liberties" were worth the cost. It was one thing to defend these "liberties" in a feudal society; it became quite another in a society in which the art of war had changed so drastically. The *mêlée* convinced men that some authority was needed, an authority that would have the police power necessary to back its orders.

Was it this that accounts for the influence of Hobbes upon his contemporaries? Many men objected vigorously to Hobbes' explanation of the basic psychological problem for they did not like to see themselves as Hobbes saw them when without law: mean, suspicious, wicked, and brutal.

They also were shocked by Hobbes' materialism and refusal to accept the intrinsic truth of religion in politics. Yet there was no difficulty in finding a host of men who were willing to place the sword in the hands of a great central power, what Hobbes called the *Leviathan,* in order to guarantee public tranquillity. When cliques and parties "shared" the sword and introduced ill-paid and undisciplined mercenary soldiers into the community, life too often resembled Hobbes' famous description of life in the state of nature: "short, mean, nasty, solitary and brutish." Bishop Bossuet, court preacher to Louis XIV and preceptor of his son, developed a Christian defense of absolute rule by providing biblical evidence to justify the royal exercise of power. But by the time Bossuet wrote, the people in France were already willing to accept and to pay for the royal power necessary to suppress disorder. The *Fronde* had given the French monarchy the "secret weapon" needed to destroy the *Frondeurs* and to prevent the recurrence of such a movement; the nation became convinced that internal tranquillity and public peace were more important than the "liberties" of nobles, of parlementarians, or even of Huguenots. Thus Bossuet echoed the attitudes of his contemporaries when he called upon the king to exercise the power that God placed in his hands. Often the political philosopher is a mirror in which one finds most clearly reflected the aspirations and the hopes of the men of his day. The civil disorder in Bossuet's time called for the creation of a state capable of exercising police power that would assure tranquillity.

## VII

The central institution necessary for the creation of police power in the seventeenth century was the new army. If we look forward to the end of the century it becomes clear that the new military institutions were, in effect, a re-introduction of the principle of the Roman legions. The new army was a standing army, maintained in peace as well as in war; it was an army clothed, armed, and cared for by the king's war office. After seeing how dangerous a Wallenstein, or a Condé, or a Bernard could be when they commanded soldiers loyal only to themselves, it was clear that some other form of military organization was imperative. As one might expect, rather than create entirely new military institutions, what was done was to take the armies of the mercenary captains and place them under the king's war ministry. The army still remained mercenary; it was largely commanded by adventurers and its ranks were filled by rabble, social misfits, and others wishing for one reason or another to avoid civilian life. But one striking difference was that both the officers and the men now looked to the king's treasury for their pay and to the king's favor for their advancement; and both could be subjected to the king's discipline.

This raises an interesting question. Since the new army presupposes that the king's financial resources will be equal to the task of supporting it, does this not mean that the new army did not appear until the economy of Europe could provide the taxation necessary for this task? No simple answer will be satisfactory for while it is clear that Europe's economy had to be equal to the task, it is also clear that the people who supplied the money had to be willing to see their money used for military purposes. Furthermore, as Sombart, the economic historian, has pointed out cogently, the very existence of the standing army itself helped create the wealth needed to support it; the army became the first "mass market" and as such acted as a dynamic force in the economy of Europe.

What stands out incontestably is that the new standing armies were a creative force in the development of the bureaucratic institutions of the modern state. The armies and navies required the raising of theretofore unheard of sums of money and the administration of large enterprises: thus the number of officers needed for the treasury and war ministry grew enormously. Like the armies that they served these new bureaucratic machines were not created *de novo,* but developed out of the previous governmental machinery. In the Germanies the men who formerly administered the prince's household affairs and his agricultural enterprises, the officers of the *Kammer,* emerged as the officials in charge of revenues used by the army; in France the secretaries of state grew into ministers of the king in charge of the bureaus that administered war, finance, foreign affairs, and the household. The rapid increase of business in each of these areas resulted in an increase of personnel and a rise in the prestige of the functions of government.

The importance of these emerging institutions can be measured by the changes that they wrought in the role of the king. At the opening of the seventeenth century, the king was still a relatively free agent, supervising with the aid of a few councillors, the business of his state, and holding in his own hands most of the information needed to manage his affairs. By the end of the century the king had become the head of a bureaucratic machine that was absolutely necessary because of the magnitude of the task of government; he had to rely upon his subordinates both for suggestions about policy and for the execution of his program. In effect he had become the first servant of the state machinery which now guided his actions along with those of the rest of his government. Louis XIV found this development completed in his own lifetime. When he took over the government of his kingdom in 1661, the whole administration of the country had to pass through his hands; by the time he died in 1715 the bureaucracy governed the kingdom, leaving to him the task of reviewing key aspects of policy that the ministers felt should be referred to him.

The interests of royal policy were also modified by the fiscal demands of the new military institutions; if the king were to collect the money necessary to support his army and navy, his subjects must be rich enough to supply him with that money. Even in the Middle Ages princes had made regulations concerning commerce and manufacturing, but in retrospect their action seems haphazard or at least inconclusive. By the seventeenth century, however, the situation was ripe for government to act effectively upon the economy. It is no accident that this is the period when that body of politico-economic thought that we variously call "Mercantilism," "Kammeralism," "Colbertism" appeared on the European scene. These economic doctrines were not innovations but rather elaborations of economic practices that were rooted in medieval legislation. In their simplest forms they proposed to regulate commerce in such a way that there would always be a balance of payments due the kingdom which would be made in gold or silver. These metals were universally valuable, they were necessary for the payment of soldiers, they were important for the king's treasury. This simple "bullion" theory was very popular in the sixteenth century when men were trying to understand what was really happening to the treasure that came to Europe from the Spanish New World. One thing was evident: those countries that could sell more than they bought in the markets of the world were able to import treasure, and this became an article of faith for some of the "economists." This sort of thinking could be duplicated in the medieval town's legislation as well as in the measures taken by medieval kings.

By the mid-seventeenth century, however, the "bullion" theory of political economy was undergoing radical revision or at least elaboration. It was becoming more and more clear that wealth was connected with the internal prosperity of the kingdom ("creation of plenty" as the men of the day expressed it), and therefore that the political-economic policy must concern itself with such things as roads, the establishment of new industries, and the organization of old industries, the attraction of skilled workers to the kingdom, and other such projects. The men who urged these policies were either officials or advisors of princes, and practically all of them were of bourgeois origin. They proposed measures intended to make the kingdom rich by encouraging the growth of industry, the expansion of argriculture, and the extension of commercial activity. Their programs were not intended primarily to increase the comfort and wealth of the king's subjects; what was wanted was an increase in wealth so that the king could secure more revenue from his taxes! These royal advisors were first of all state builders; they wished to control and channel the development of economic life to make their prince's government strong, that is to increase his military establishments. Their programs sometimes resulted in considerable economic advancement for the community, sometimes in meddlesome interference with the affairs of businessmen, but always they caused an increase in the number of officials in the employ of the government, and a complication of the problems of domestic and international politics.

The growth of the bureaus concerned with the collection of money and the administration of the military installations was paralleled by the development of ministries concerned with foreign affairs. At the opening of the seventeenth century it was uncommon for a prince to maintain a permanent ambassador at the court of another monarch. When there was business to conduct, a special emissary was delegated for the mission, and he returned as soon as the task was completed. The organization of foreign affairs, too, was simple to the extreme; there were no specialized foreign offices with archives and personnel since the work was largely done by the king's council and a secretary. In the course of the century, however, the practice of establishing permanent embassies in the important courts of Europe became common, and bureaus of foreign affairs presided over by a minister became the rule. Even by the end of the century not all foreign correspondence was channeled through one minister alone; nonetheless, the fact that the foreign minister ruled a bureau commanding the services of translators, code officials, and other men with special information about the problems of foreign countries tended toward that goal. The fuller development of the diplomatic corps and the ministries of foreign affairs was to be the work of the eighteenth century, but by 1700 the characteristic forms for the diplomacy of the European states-system had already clearly appeared.

It would be folly to insist that the bureaucratic institutions for the administration of the treasury, the military, and the conduct of foreign affairs were solely the result of the attempt of princes to cure the disorder resultant from the *mêlée* of civil rebellion and international war. No one will deny that the forms of European political organization have very deep roots in the ancient constitutions of European society, some of them reaching beyond the times of Charlemagne. And yet the observer cannot fail to see that the precise forms of the bureaucratic police states of Europe were importantly influenced by the disorders of the first half of the seventeenth century.

## VIII

As we have seen, in the first two-thirds of the seventeenth century civil rebellions and international conflict created a *mêlée* in which statesmen could develop a program of action only with great difficulty. In the latter part of the century, when civil rebellion was discouraged by the disparity between the forces available to rebels and those at the disposal of the king, programs based on dynastic and states' interests were able to become the creative forces in international affairs. France under Louis XIV compelled political change and improvisation by attempting to assume the hegemony of the European world that had fallen from the hands of the Spanish Hapsburgs. Out of the effort to prevent the French king from becoming master of Europe, there emerged the institution of the balance of power, or, as it was later to be called, the Concert of Europe, by which the European community adjusted its interests. This new institution was not to become an orderly way of managing the affairs of the continent, but it was the only system that the political and cultural pluralism of Western society would tolerate, and since that pluralism, with its concomitant tensions, may well be of great importance in the subsequent civilization of the West, the system of balance of power by which it expressed itself assumes considerable importance.

Louis XIV never intended to impose the balance of power upon Europe, and he never understood his historic role in the formation of the European community. He had been brought up to believe that he must achieve his *gloire,* that is to say, that he must fulfill his destiny; Mazarin had often impressed upon him that he had both the possibility of greatness and the responsibility to achieve it. It is therefore not surprising that, when Mazarin died leaving Louis to manage his own affairs, the young king inaugurated a period of intense activity. Cooperating with the advisors that he had inherited from the cardinal, Louis struck out in all directions to make his government strong and his reign notable; reforms in the army, in the administration of justice, in the organization of economic life followed one another with rapid succession. This was the period when the basic ordinances for the organization of the bureaucracies in France were promulgated; during the rest of the reign there were to be many edicts concerning governmental organization, but they were usually merely modifications of the earlier ordinances. Since France was the most populous and perhaps the richest of the kingdoms of Europe, this burst of energy was quickly transformed into real power. The army that Richelieu had started became, under Louvois, the foremost military instrument in Europe and at the same time, with Colbert attending to commerce, colonies, and finance, the king's treasury became the most prosperous on the continent. Louis did not need to build the great colonnade of the Louvre to prove to Europe that his reign was starting auspiciously; perceptive men understood that money and soldiers augured an era of French hegemony.

Since Louis and his whole generation were brought up during wars and taught that they in turn would wage wars, it was to be expected that the young French king would use these military resources, and since his government was now in full command of the kingdom, their use would unquestionably be applied beyond the frontiers. As he explained to his son in his *Mémoires,* he was confronted with the choice of making war on England as an ally of the Dutch or upon Spain to secure his wife's inheritance; as he tells it the problem was just that simple! In another place he adds that as soon as there was talk of war, his "court was flooded with gentlemen demanding employment." In other words the moral and political climate not only implied that the king would use the force that he had, but also encouraged him to do so.

Actually, of course, Louis' decisions to make war were not as haphazard as they seem in his *Mémoires;* Louis' foreign policy continued the traditional aims of establishing the hegemony of the French Bourbon family and humbling the Hapsburgs in Spain and Austria. The marriage policies of the preceding half century had brought two Spanish princesses to France, one to be the mother, the other the wife of Louis XIV, and the provisions of the marriage contracts were such that the Bourbons might expect to inherit the thrones of Spain in default of the Hapsburg male line. The death of Louis' father-in-law, Philip IV, produced a situation in Spain that made this prospect more than a mere hope, for the sickly child king, Charles II, was the last Spanish Hapsburg male heir. For the last thirty-five years of the seventeenth century this poor creature, unable to produce an heir, occupied the throne while Europe plotted or feared the division of his crowns. While the throne in Madrid was obviously the prize sought by French diplomacy, there was also a more limited traditional goal, namely the annexation of the Spanish Netherlands. These territories were of great strategic and economic importance to France. The acquisition of the throne in Madrid with its overseas lands upon which the sun never set, and the annexation of the Netherlands on the northeastern frontier were constant territorial goals of French policy throughout the reign of Louis XIV. Naturally these ambitions aroused the fears and hostility of other powers in Europe.

The Spanish empire was not the only moribund empire in 1660; the Holy Roman Empire of the German nation was in an even more dilapidated state. French ambitions in the Empire were less well defined than those directed toward the throne of Spain, and yet from the time of Mazarin until the sensational rise in power of the Danubian monarchy under Leopold I in the late 1680s, French statesmen toyed with the idea of placing a Bourbon prince upon the throne of the Empire. And throughout the reign of Louis XIV, French policy was directed toward a division of central and eastern Europe so that the Bourbons rather than the Austrian Hapsburgs could control the development of political affairs.

Although the drive of France to the hegemony of Europe was unquestionably of paramount importance in affecting high politics in the latter seventeenth century, there were other important forces at work. In the southeast of Europe, in the Ottoman Empire, the reforming viziers of the mid-seventeenth century understood that the Turkish state had either to expand militarily or collapse, for its political life was predicated upon continuing conquest. The long naval war with Venice, the war with Persia, and the drive up the Danube, were all part of an effort to give vitality to an empire that was largely no more than an army of occupation in a conquered country. Actually, as the century was to prove, the Ottoman Empire was as moribund as the Spanish, but when Kara Mustapha appeared before Vienna with 200,000 men in 1683, this was not easy to see.

Also of great significance in the politics of the latter seventeenth century were the economic monopolies of the United Netherlands. The Dutch managed to make their market the center for much of the international trade of the day. In Amsterdam one bought French wine, Swedish iron and copper, English tin, German linen and wheat, Spanish cork; indeed almost all the products of international commerce. Traders from all Europe brought or sent their goods to the United Netherlands and exchanged them there for the goods of other nations. The Dutch grew rich as merchant middlemen, as shippers, as bankers and insurance brokers, and as finishers and graders of the raw materials that came into their hands. They also drew upon themselves the envy and dislike of merchants elsewhere, and of statesmen who regarded the Dutch market as a legitimate prey for their own predatory economic policies. The Dutch and the English fought two short wars over problems connected with trade; the English Navigation Acts attempted to supplant the Dutch multilateral trade with unilateral trade between England and the other commercial states. Both Colbert and Louis XIV regarded the Dutch market with jealous eyes; the Dutch war of 1672 may not have been primarily caused by economic rivalry, but the hostility that grew out of commercial competition created an atmosphere of Franco-Dutch antagonism.

In general we can say of the sources of conflict that in the late seventeenth century dynastic and states' interests combined to take the place that religion, feudal liberties, and the problems of the crumbling Spanish hegemony of Philip II had played in the first part of the century. Fortifications, tariffs, alliances and subsidies, and the hopes and fears of French Bourbon and Austrian Hapsburg princes about the many territories of the Spanish crown all combined to provide stuff for war.

However, these wars created something beyond and outside any of these things. The primary fact that emerged from the epoch of war was that Europe learned to check the overpowering force of the French monarchy by developing coalitions. These coalitions, in turn, became the basis of the political mechanism, "the balance of power." When in the opening years of the eighteenth century, Peter I brought Russia into the orbit of the West under circumstances that drew the Slavic state into the system of military balances, the "constitution" with which Europe governed itself from about 1700 to 1914 was already launched upon its career. The emergence of this states-system was to provide one of the most significant themes in the history of European civilization for the next two centuries.

## IX

In the early years of his reign, Louis XIV started on his quest for greatness. He sent an expedition against the Algerian pirates, another against the Turks who were invading the Danube basin, and also gave halfhearted aid to the Dutch in their trade war with England. None of these adventures could bring notable advantages to his house. With the death of Philip IV in 1665, however, the French found a suitable pretext for action. There was no question about the rights of the sickly child, Charles II, to the throne in Madrid, but

French lawyers insisted that provincial legal codes in the Spanish Netherlands justified the French king's demand that his wife and son, as heirs of Philip IV, should receive those territories. The lawyer's brief that was presented to the Spanish, as well as the other courts of Europe, to establish this claim was a formidable document, but no one was deceived: the argument was useless unless backed by arms. The French invasion of the Spanish Netherlands in 1667 to establish Marie Thérèse's rights has been called the War of the Devolution: the legal rights that Louis pretended to defend were the "rights of devolution."

While the Spanish government at Madrid and at Brussels rejected completely the French claims, they were in no position to stop the French armies. However there were other people in Europe who had reason to object to the French annexation of the Spanish Netherlands: the Dutch politicians in the United Netherlands were the first of these for they had long since reached the conclusion that a weak Spain would be a safer neighbor than a strong France. From the time of the battle of Rocroi (1643), this conviction had been an important aspect of Dutch policy. The English, too, were easily persuaded that they would greatly prefer to have the Scheldt River in the hands of a weak Spanish government; military opinion held that an attack on England from the continent could be best launched from this point, and Englishmen not only believed this but acted upon it for the next three hundred years. Thus, in face of the French menace to their real or imagined interests, the Dutch and the English composed their own differences with the Peace of Breda (1667), and formed an alliance to check French aggression. They were able to associate Sweden with this alliance, and then offered, with thinly veiled threats, to arbitrate the Franco-Spanish conflict.

Somehow this intervention had not been foreseen in Paris; in any case Louis was unready to engage in a war both with Spain and with the newly formed triple alliance, and so the offer was accepted. The treaty that was written at Aix-la-Chapelle (1668), however, was in no way a solution of any problem; France, in effect, was left in possession of the territories that her armies had taken. This meant that the French king was given cities like Audenarde as enclaves in the Spanish Netherlands which were an obvious invitation to soldiers and bureaucrats to try to join these islands to the rest of France by securing the territory that separated them. Nor were Marie Thérèse's rights clearly settled; the peace simply ended the war leaving the bulk of the Spanish Netherlands still in the hands of Spain. The only thing that men did learn was that a coalition of military powers could indeed check the aggressive action of one power, even if that power were France. The shortness of the conflict did not raise the second question, namely: how does a coalition of powers hold together in the face of their divergent interests?

The importance of this second question was not lost on France. It was obvious that the Dutch were the heart of the opposition to French control of the Spanish Netherlands, and that their power would have to be broken before Louis could realize his ambitions in these provinces. This was most irritating to the young French king. It seemed to him that the Dutch were ingrates who had forgotten that without France they probably could never have won their independence; but what could be expected from men with bourgeois origins and revolutionary and republican traditions? He did not forget that his own ancestors (Charles V and Philip II) had once ruled these lands by divine right. Would it be possible to break up the alliance that these Dutchmen had called into being, and then remove Dutch opposition to Bourbon "legitimate" ambitions by force? This was the big question. Louis tried to answer it by creating his own coalition against the Dutch. This effort provoked the same question: How was France to maintain a coalition in face of the divergent interests of her allies?

On paper Louis' coalition against the Dutch was a formidable one. He detached Sweden from the hostile alliance by a mixture of bribery of the members of the regency government and a guarantee of a subsidy for the Swedish crown. The German princes whom Mazarin had combined in an alliance to assure the treaties of Westphalia and French influence in Germany were mobilized by subsidies to support a French war against the Dutch; even the elector of Brandenburg accepted French money and presumably French advice. Emperor Leopold of Austria was isolated from his Spanish relatives and the United Netherlands by a treaty that agreed upon a division of the Spanish empire between his family and the French Bourbons; the first of the many "partition treaties" that attempted to solve the thorny problem of the Spanish territories. Finally, the English king, Charles II, made a secret alliance, negotiated in part by his sister, who was also Louis' sister-in-law; by this treaty Charles agreed to join his naval forces in the war that was to destroy once and for all Dutch military and commercial power. If one merely looks at the treaties, the coalition was a work of art designed for the destruction of the Dutch by neighbors who had suffered from Dutch military, and even more, from Dutch commercial power: all of Louis' "friends" had good reason to hate the Dutch for their republicanism, their commercial monopolies, their egoistic economic regulations, and their political and naval arrogance. However if one looks below the surface of the treaties it becomes clear that the coalition was unstable; it overlooked the fact that with the removal of the United Netherlands from its military-commercial prominence, Europe would have to face a tremendously increased Bourbon power, and even French subsidies could not sweeten this fact.

While his diplomacy forged the coalition, Louis' soldiers and bureaucrats prepared the military forces for the destruction of the United Netherlands. Europe had not seen an army of this kind since the days of the Caesars; the French had organized a military establishment that seemed to be a crushing force, and Louis gave the command of this army (since he did not really command it himself) into the hands of two of the finest generals of the era: Turenne and Condé. Here was an interesting juxtaposition of the new and the old: the army was organized and controlled by royal bureaucrats from the king's war ministry; it was commanded, however, by a prince of the blood and by a descendant of one of the oldest and most powerful feudal families of France. Before the war was over there was considerable friction between the king's bureaucrats and his soldiers, but at the opening of the campaign, inspired by the vigorous leadership of the young king, this war machine was a formidable force. Like the coalition, it seemed to be a complete answer to Dutch objections to French ambitions in the Netherlands.

The war that followed in 1672 has been called "the Dutch War." Louis' armies marched up a corridor in northwest Germany provided by his Rhineland allies and attacked the Dutch from the rear. At the same time the Anglo-French naval forces swept through the Channel in an effort to clear the seas of Dutch ships. With such force thrown in the fray, the campaign of 1672 should have been a *blitzkrieg* crushing all opposition. But seventeenth-century transportation was difficult; armies had to march to their destination and their supplies and equipment had to follow them over bad roads and slow river transport. Furthermore, soldiers, attuned to siege warfare, were unwilling to press past a hostile fortification that might menace their rear. Thus the summer campaign was slowed by dozens of sieges and difficult transportation. This gave the Dutch time to cut the dykes and inundate a large part of the land over which the French army had to pass if it were to strike the heart of the United Netherlands. In ordering *Te Deums* to be sung in the churches of France to celebrate the capture of city after city, Louis and his advisors seemed to miss the fact that their war could not succeed if the French army failed to overrun the entire Netherlands; they thought that the Dutch, as "reasonable men," would recognize the futility of further resistance and accept their terms. Exactly the opposite happened. The French terms were so crushing that the Dutch decided to fight to the last rather than accept them. A revolution in Amsterdam placed Prince William of Orange and his faction in control, and he immediately set out to defend what was left of his land and to try to find allies. This task was lightened by the impression that Louis' army and his conditions for peace made upon Europe. Men who a few years before had heard so much about German, French, or Bohemian "liberties" now could well wonder what was to happen to European "liberties" after a French victory. The Spanish government in Brussels rightly understood that once France ruled the United Provinces, the Spanish Netherlands would soon thereafter also be governed from Paris. Frederick William of Brandenburg, seeing his Rhineland holdings overrun by French troops, also concluded that French subsidies might not be worth their cost, and Emperor Leopold came to understand that his house and the Empire were both endangered by the rising French threat. Finally even Charles II was forced by the English Parliament to withdraw from the French alliance. In 1673 the French position in the Rhine valley was "exposed"; by 1675 Louis was forced to give up all the conquests of the first year of the war and to confine his military operations to territory closer to the frontiers of France in the Spanish Netherlands, Alsace, and Franche-Comté. In the place of a French coalition against the Dutch there had emerged a coalition against France; only the regency government in Sweden held firm to its French alliance, an act for which it was to suffer cruelly at the hands of the Brandenburg-Prussian armies.

The new anti-French coalition, however, was not organized so that a unified war effort could be achieved; each of the allies was primarily interested in problems close to home, and no leader emerged with enough prestige to make them work closely together. The Dutch worried away at the French fortresses in the lower Rhineland; Frederick William attacked the Swedish positions in Pomerania; Emperor Leopold's armies operated in Alsace; and the Spanish were unable to do more than weakly defend themselves in the Netherlands and on their own frontiers. Thus while the coalition gave Louis considerable trouble, it was unable to bring effective force to bear upon him. Indeed, even though he was obliged to withdraw his forces from their exposed position in the lower Rhine, every year Louis won "victories" in the Netherlands, in Alsace, and in Franche-Comté that could be celebrated by more *Te Deums* in Paris. Nonetheless, the coalition was obviously giving France considerable trouble; indeed by 1676 it was clear that French arms probably would not be able to impose peace upon their enemies; the coalition, even without centralized direction, seemed about to force a stalemate.

The military thinking of the period was in part responsible for the fact that neither side could win a decision. Armies were too difficult to raise to be risked in a battle unless the outcome were almost certain; both soldiers and statesmen preferred the slower and safer war of sieges, of position, of maneuver. Field armies might operate within a few miles of each other all summer, occasionally exchanging blows when small reconnaissance parties ran into each other, but never risking a field battle. Strong places were besieged and stormed in violent, bloody actions; but these were limited conflicts both in the objectives and in the number of men committed. Louis liked to conduct a siege, but he, like the majority of his contemporaries, was afraid of an infantry battle by which the war could be won—or lost—in an afternoon. Thus this "Dutch War," which had become a general war, drew itself out monotonously, costing ever larger and larger sums of money, and disturbing the peace and commerce of a large part of western Europe. The French fiscal machine seemed better able to sustain the expense, but by 1677 both France and her enemies were strained by the effort to a point where all wanted peace.

The war ended in 1678. Louis' armies made a surprise raid into the Spanish Netherlands and captured Ghent; this was too close to the heart of the United Netherlands for comfort. At the same time Charles II, pressed by the English Parliament to join the coalition against France, offered a "mediation" that was at the same time a threat that the English navy would reenter the war, this time on the side of the Dutch. And in Spain the war was creating both political and fiscal chaos to the point where peace was imperative. A Dutch embassy visited Louis' camp in the Spanish Netherlands. They were perfectly willing to see France annex the Spanish province of Franche-Comté, far from their own frontiers, providing that their own territory remained inviolate and that the French would agree to a commercial treaty. Spain could not object, the emperor and the Brandenburgers were unable to carry on without the Dutch, and Charles II in England was anxious to avoid military involvement. In 1679, by the treaties of Nymwegen, western Europe again was at peace, or so it seemed.

Although Louis had not achieved the objectives he had in mind when the war began, nonetheless, the war and the treaty of Nymwegen were imposing evidence of French power. None knew this better than the elector of

Brandenburg: he was forced to return his conquests to the Swedish monarchy, even though his armies had been victorious, simply because the French king demanded it. Europe was quick to understand the basis of Louis' power: it was his army, the bureaucratic machine that supported and directed that army, and finally the French economy, organized and directed by the government. Four years after the treaty of Nymwegen, when the opportunity opened for the reconquest of Hungary, a pamphlet written by one of Leopold's councillors, appeared in Vienna explaining that the Danubian Hapsburg state could become a power like France by the conquest and organization of Hungary provided that a bureaucratic machine emerged to govern the Hapsburg lands. This was the pattern of Europe after the Dutch war: European political society was committed to establishing and maintaining standing armies and navies on a scale undreamed of a generation earlier.

## X

France again took the lead. The Dutch war convinced Louis that he needed a powerful navy as well as an army; under Colbert's guidance the small French naval establishment expanded into a force equal to the combined navies of England and the United Netherlands. New "ships of the line" mounting 120 guns set new standards for naval construction, just as the new equipment that Louvois was developing for the French army was setting new standards for land armaments. The France that could find the money for these military expenditures was also building the great palace of Versailles as a proper setting for her great king and his effective government; the challenge to Europe could only be met by imitating the governmental machinery that made it possible. The bureaucratic, military, police state that was emerging in France was thus the "wave of the future."

Nor was this French challenge merely a gesture that could be accepted or ignored, for French policy following the treaties of Nymwegen proved that the peace was only a truce. On the advice of his foreign minister, Louis set up courts in the borderlands between France and the German states to which he gave the task of "discovering" exactly what territory had been ceded by the treaties of Westphalia and Nymwegen. Seventeenth-century treaties, rather than drawing frontier lines, spoke of "provinces and their dependencies." Such phrasing was an opportunity for exploitation, for "dependencies" could be interpreted to include all sorts of things. Of course the French "Courts of Reunion" quickly found that much of the territory adjacent to lands already occupied by virtue of the treaties of Westphalia and Nymwegen also belonged to the French king, whereupon the French army immediately carried out the decision of the court by invading the disputed territory. The emperor of Austria, several German princes, and the kings of both Sweden and Spain lost lands by "court order" in which the French king acted as plaintiff, judge, and executor. Anti-French pamphleteers could not determine where this forward march would stop: France was annexing more territory in time of peace than she had gained by war. Leagues, or at least plans for leagues against France began to preoccupy the courts of Europe.

But one did not attack the king of France without preparation. His army was the finest in Europe, his navy was the largest on the seas. His bombardment of the Barbary coastal towns of North Africa and of Genoa as punishment for displeasing him was evidence of the terror that he could create; his magnificence in the new palace at Versailles was a picture of imposing grandeur that could not be overlooked. Before making war on France, the rest of Europe had to look to its resources.

At this juncture, central Europe was forced to meet attack from the east as well as French encroachment in the west. The French annexed the imperial city of Strasbourg and the city of Casale in Italy in 1681; the next year military preparations in the Ottoman Empire and agreements between the sultan and the Hungarian and Transylvanian enemies of the Hapsburgs clearly indicated that it would be folly to make war on France until the back door of the Hapsburg Danubian monarchy were closed. Negotiations attempted in Constantinople demonstrated that the grand vizier, Kara Mustapha, had no intention of being put off from his project to invade and subjugate central Europe. The Turks, with the assurance of the French ambassador that no French troops would assist the emperor, were sure that Leopold of Austria would be helpless before a determined assault. In the summer of 1683 an Ottoman army of some 200,000 men marched up the Danube valley, brushed aside the imperial forces that tried to stem the advance, and laid siege to the city of Vienna. In 1683 Leopold thus could not check the French encroachments in the Rhineland; he had too much to attend to in his own capital.

Louis XIV then earned for himself the title "the most Christian Turk in Versailles" for he saw this turn of events as an opportunity to force the emperor and the king of Spain to recognize the annexations of his Courts of Reunion. While the Turks ringed Vienna, French armies invaded the Spanish Netherlands, subjected some of the cities to systematic bombardments, and formally laid siege to Luxemburg. Peace, Louis insisted, could be had between the emperor and France, if the emperor would only agree to recognize France's "legitimate" territorial claims; according to Louis, the emperor, not France, was preventing Germany from defending itself against the Turks. Fortunately for Leopold, a combined German-Polish army broke the Turkish siege of Vienna, and sent Kara Mustapha's armies down the Danube in precipitous flight, leaving the Germans with the problem of deciding whether it would be more profitable to make war against France or against the Turks; obviously there could be no question of war against both at the same time. Under pressure from his German allies, and the urging of his own soldiers and bureaucrats, Leopold decided to make a truce with France. Louis was willing to sign a truce that would guarantee his Rhineland acquisitions for twenty years.

The war in Hungary became the center of European attention. Pope Innocent XI made it into a Christian crusade, attracting money and volunteers from all Catholic Europe. The emperor, the Republic of Venice, the king of Poland and the tsar of Russia joined in a "holy" alliance against the enemies of the cross. This was Russia's first intervention in European politics, but her war efforts amounted to practically nothing. However, both the emperor's armies and those of Venice won striking victories. The Turkish forces were driven out of Hungary, out of Transylvania, and by 1688 the imperial armies were hammering at Belgrade. At the same time the Venetians landed in the Morea (the Peloponnesus), swept the tip of Greece free of Turkish soldiers, and captured Athens. The French ambassador at Constantinople wrote alarming letters to his king telling of the disorder in the Turkish armies and finances, of the disasters that overtook their every effort, and of the expectation that Leopold would soon be in Constantinople dictating terms. Nor was it merely that the Turks were being defeated. In Hungary a new imperial army was emerging with new military techniques: the pikemen, who had been so necessary to protect the musketmen from cavalry, were replaced by musketmen with bayonets, and the volley firing that Gustavus Adolphus had first introduced on the battlefield more than a half century earlier began to come into its own. To cap it all, a revolution in the kingdom of Hungary made its crown hereditary in the house of Hapsburg, suppressed the right of rebellion theretofore enjoyed by the Hungarian nobles, created a Hungarian chancellory manned by bureaucrats at Vienna, and crowned Archduke Joseph, Leopold's son, as king. The Danubian monarchy of the Hungarian, Bohemian, and German lands was emerging as a formidable military force.

While these events were changing the political face of eastern and central Europe, another series of events in England also unleashed a revolution that was to create a new military power in the west. Upon the death of Charles II (1685) his brother James II mounted the English throne. The Test Act that had forced James to give up control of the English navy because he was a Roman Catholic did not keep him from the throne. Anglican advocates of the divine right of kings reasoned that since James' heirs, Princess Mary and Princess Anne, were both Protestants and married to Protestants there was no real danger to religion if this Catholic prince became king. James, however, felt the urgency of his position: he began systematically to staff the army and the administration with Catholics for whom he waived the disabilities of the Test Act; he introduced Catholic teachers into Oxford University; he tried to force the Anglican clergy to accept his actions; and finally his wife gave birth to a son. Protestants might call the baby an impostor, Catholics might regard him as a miracle, but everyone understood that with a Catholic heir, James might rig elections to Parliament, legalize all his actions, and bring England back into the fold of the Roman Church. These events came to a climax in 1688 about the same time that the imperial siege of Belgrade, the pleas by the Ottoman government for peace, and the election of Archduke Joseph to both the crown of Hungary and the dignity king of the Romans (successor to his father as Holy Roman Emperor) all indicated that central Europe had a new political order.

These movements in the east and the west were closely followed by all of Europe. In the Netherlands, Prince William of Orange, who was both Stadtholder of the United Netherlands and husband of King James' daughter Mary, kept in close touch with the Whig politicians in England. These men were staunch Protestants, and more important, they had developed a political theory that insisted upon the primacy of the law over the king and were quite willing to invite William to bring an army to England to force James II to do their bidding. However, as long as French armies were within reach of the Netherlands, William could not move to support James' enemies in England. Louis, on the other hand, concentrated most of his attention upon central Europe. If the Turks should be forced out of the war, if Leopold actually could mobilize the resources of Hungary and Bohemia and his German lands, then the hegemony of France and with it his newly won "rights" in the Rhineland as well as his claims to the Spanish inheritance might well be in jeopardy. As for the prospects of a civil war in England, Louis reasoned that such a conflict might actually help his cause for he believed that the

Protestant and Catholic factions were about equal in strength and therefore a civil war would be a long drawn out action that would remove England from the political arena for some time.

France's decision set all Europe in motion. With an army and a navy second to none, Louis believed that he could check the onward imperial march, keep the Turks in the war, and guarantee his own position in the Rhineland; he invaded Germany in 1688. This invasion in the West heartened the Turks in the East to stay in the war and allowed William of Orange to transfer part of his army to England since the Netherlands were no longer in danger of a French attack. Within a few months of the French declaration of war, James II was deposed, William and Mary crowned king and queen in England, and a coalition composed of the Holy Roman Emperor, all of the German princes, the United Netherlands, England, and Spain emerged to challenge France. The "holy war" in the East thus merged into a war, fought all over Europe as well as in the new European dependencies beyond the seas. In the traditional histories of Europe, this war is variously called: the War of the League of Augsburg, the War of the Palatinate, the Anglo-Dutch Trade War against France, and, of course, in its central European phase, the Holy War. This confusion of titles further warrants the use of a more exact title: the First World War, 1683–1699.

## XI

This war produced revolutionary changes in the European political and military order. The conflict itself was familiar: sieges, maneuvers, an occasional field battle that failed to force a decision. But behind this façade of war of position, a new military structure was under construction. The pikemen disappeared entirely; in their place were infantry armed with flintlock muskets that could fire more rapidly than the cumbersome weapons of earlier periods. These were also elongated by a "ring" bayonet so that cavalry could not win an easy decision by shock action. The infantry were supported by the artillery and engineers who were assuming the status of soldiers rather than working men. The number of field pieces as well as their increasing effectiveness were to redeem the promise that Gustavus Adolphus' guns had made a half century or more earlier. The cavalry too were changing. Gone was most of the personal armor for the cavalry were now mounted on lighter horses and armed with horse pistols and heavy sabers for shock attack.

These soldiers were clothed, fed, and supplied by the king's commissaries and commanded by men who obeyed the king's war minister. This latter fact was not always a happy circumstance for daring generals sometimes found themselves held in leash by conservative civilian commissars and officials. Indeed, the full significance of this infantry that could learn to keep up a continuous volley of fire, artillery that could dominate a section of the battlefield, and cavalry that could be massed for rapid assault did not become apparent for a generation, until Eugene of Savoy, Marlborough, and Villars demonstrated in the War of the Spanish Succession what could be done by a decisive field battle. Nonetheless, the seed time for the new military order was this first world war that began in 1683.

With the rise of professional armies under royal control numbering hundreds of thousands of men, the problem of providing money for their maintenance grew apace. Louis once remarked that victory would be assured to the side that had a gold coin after its opponent had used his last one, and indeed this was almost what happened. All the protagonists in this new war attempted to find financial expedients that would fill the treasury. On the continent the age old methods of sale of offices, forced loans, borrowing against future taxes, and utmost expansion of existing taxes were used, but there was still a gap between income and expenses. One thing always accompanied the rise in income; an increase in the bureaucratic personnel needed to collect and administer the revenues; the armies and the machinery of government expanded together.

Only in England did a good policy emerge that provided the money needed to fight the war. The English revolution of 1688 that placed William and Mary on the throne established the principle that Parliament was supreme in the land. Parliament accepted the responsibility for finding the money needed to support England's war efforts and to subsidize England's allies. The important thing was that Parliament could and did tax for the war effort on a scale that no monarch had ever been able to achieve. Under the new political order of the revolution of 1688 the king's treasury officials explained their financial needs to the members of Parliament, who in turn provided funds that were required. This relationship between the representatives of the people who would pay the tax and the government officials who collected and spent it was England's secret weapon in the war. The other English institution that emerged with help to fight the war was the Bank of England. While Parliament might vote the money, the Bank, by developing credit facilities, provided the cash needed to pay soldiers and allies. Ultimately England's great contribution to the developing structure of the European states was this mechanism by which revenue could be raised and organized to mobilize the military potential of the society.

This first world war, like the so-called "Dutch war," was a coalition effort against France, but this time the fact that William of Orange was both king of England and Stadtholder in the United Netherlands, and that the majority of the German princes were paid subsidies by either England or the United Netherlands, gave a measure of unity to the effort unknown in the earlier wars. The emperor, the duke of Savoy, and the king of Spain did not coordinate their actions completely with the powers under William's direction, but the coalition did operate together more or less as a unit. The greatest difficulty with the coalition was its lack of a first class military leader until it found one in Eugene of Savoy at the very end of the war in the operations in the Danube basin. Louis XIV was unable to take advantage of this weakness of the coalition largely because the French also lacked imaginative leaders: only Marshal Luxembourg was willing to risk a serious field battle; the rest of Louis' general officers, like himself, preferred the "safe" warfare of sieges and maneuvers. This war of attrition accentuated the problems of finance and military administration. The war drew itself out year after year with neither side able to win, and both sides mired in economic disorder.

By 1695 the economic situation in France, aggravated by several years of bad harvest, reached a point where peace was necessary. Peace could only be achieved by surrendering some of the French conquests and recognizing limits to French ambitions, and, above all, only if the coalition could be broken. Savoy was the weak link in the chain of Louis' enemies: by offering her duke the whole of French gains in Italy since the days of Richelieu, Louis persuaded him to sign a treaty of peace (Peace of Turin, 1696) that would allow the French army in Italy to be moved to the Netherlands or to Germany. This started an avalanche of negotiation resulting in the treaties of Ryswick (1697). Louis' letters to his ambassador in Constantinople reveal his embarrassment in these negotiations. He had used every stratagem to keep the Turks from making peace only himself to desert the common cause when he received terms that he could accept. At Ryswick France was able to keep most of the annexations of the Courts of Reunion, but the treaties not only established the limits of French expansion but also imposed upon Louis recognition of the results of the revolution of 1688 in England. Two years later at Karlowitz (1699), the Ottoman Empire made peace with the emperor, Venice, Russia, and Poland. The Turks paid the big price of defeat:

they ceded Hungary and Transylvania to the emperor, the Morea to Venice, and frontier territories to both Poland and Russia.

The peace treaties of 1696–99 were not important merely because of the territorial changes or even because the French king was forced to recognize limits to his ambitions; much more significant was the implicit recognition that two new great military powers had come into existence: England and the Danubian monarchy. Three decades earlier neither of these states alone or jointly could measure up to France, but by the end of the seventeenth century they had become effective counterweights to French power. By learning something of the art of organizing a coalition through the experience of war, they were on the way to the creation of a new European system.

## XII

Indeed, in the years immediately following the treaty of Ryswick a series of treaties were written that gave clear indication that Europe was groping toward some government for the continent as a whole. The unresolved problem was the succession to the Spanish thrones. Charles II somehow had managed to stay alive, but he had been unable to produce an heir. Every year that passed made it more and more evident that the imminent contest for the possession of his throne was a most dangerous threat to the peace of Europe. In an effort to provide for this eventuality without recourse to arms, the English, Dutch, and French governments negotiated the so-called "partition treaties." The first (1698) would have placed a Bavarian prince on the throne in Madrid and partitioned part of the Spanish European possessions between France and Austria. When the young Bavarian died untimely, a second treaty (1700) divided the lands between the heirs of Louis XIV and of Leopold I. Unfortunately for the peace of Europe, neither Leopold in Vienna nor the Spanish government in Madrid wanted to accept this solution. Leopold believed that his son Karl could inherit the whole of the Spanish Hapsburg empire; in Madrid the grandees and politicians, appalled at the idea that their empire might be partitioned, were determined to have Charles II will it to a single heir, and to one that could defend the inheritance. This could only be a French prince, for France alone was near enough and powerful enough to undertake such an assignment. Thus, although the diplomats of Europe were groping for a peaceful solution of the question, the stubbornness of the emperor and the ambitions at the Spanish court nullified the efforts of saner councils.

Charles II died in 1700 before any European solution could be agreed upon. He left a testament by which he willed his entire empire to Philip, the second grandson of Louis XIV. In the event that Philip should refuse this gift, the entire inheritance was to go to Karl, the second son of Leopold I. The vital decision obviously was up to the king of France. Louis' secret information told him that neither England nor the United Netherlands would fight unless the crowns of France and Spain were united; he also understood that Leopold would fight rather than accept a partition of the Spanish empire. Thus if Louis were to turn down the handsome gift of the king of Spain with the hope of obtaining his share of the Spanish inheritance provided by the partition treaties, he undoubtedly would have had to fight Leopold to secure it, for the court at Vienna was in no mood for compromise. It was questionable if England and the United Netherlands would have helped France in this venture. On the other hand if he accepted the testament of the Spanish king, he would have to fight Leopold, but in this case Spain would be on his side and he could hope that the Dutch and English would be neutral. Since war seemed inevitable, Louis decided to fight it under the most favorable conditions, and for the complete prize: he announced that his grandson had become Philip V of Spain. As his secret information had indicated, both England and the United Netherlands more or less ungraciously recognized the new king, while the Danubian Monarchy prepared for war.

What would have happened had Louis acted wisely after this decision will never be known; he did not, and his lack of wisdom antagonized England and the United Netherlands. Louis first persuaded his grandson Philip to grant special privileges to French merchants in the markets of the Spanish colonies; then he expelled the Dutch soldiers from the fortifications in the Spanish Netherlands where they had been placed by the treaties of Ryswick as a guarantee against France. By replacing them with French soldiers, Louis affronted both England and the United Netherlands, and gave the anti-French factions in both countries reason to call for an alliance against French aggression. When England, the Danubian monarchy, and the United Netherlands were signing a treaty that would create a new coalition against France, James II, in exile, died at St. Germain outside of Paris, and Louis recognized his son as the legitimate king of England. This act did not precipitate the war that followed, but it justified it in the eyes of Englishmen who might have otherwise wished for peace.

The French position at the opening of the war in 1701 was very strong. Spain and its empire was an ally, and the electorates of Bavaria and Cologne came into the conflict on the side of France. In other words the Franco-Spanish forces not only occupied all the disputed territory, but also held a strong outpost in the very heart of Germany. Furthermore, the coalition of France's enemies received what might have been a dangerous reversal at the outset of the war. William III, who as king in England, Stadtholder in the United Netherlands, and an implacable foe of Louis XIV, had been very important in the organization of the coalition, died before the first blow could be struck. His successor on the throne was James II's daughter Anne, a woman of limited intelligence, who, fortunately for the coalition, gave her favor and trust to John Churchill, Duke of Marlborough. Marlborough had been trained as a cadet in the new French professional army. He became a great soldier and an able administrator; with his relative, Godolphin, he took over the direction of the war in the west. Leopold, too, found a soldier: Eugene of Savoy, a French born prince, related both to Mazarin and to the house of Savoy, who had failed to get recognition in France but who had won his first brilliant victories as a soldier for the empire. In the War of the Spanish Succession he quickly proved himself to be both a general and an administrator of the first order. Eugene and Marlborough directed the coalition and led its armies to victory.

In the War of the Spanish Succession the political and military forms that had been hammered out in the preceding conflicts clearly demonstrated the extent of the revolution in arms and administration that had taken place. Everything was different from the makeshift of the first part of the seventeenth century. Of course under the pounding of war the tinsel and braid of these proud new military organizations wore off, but the essential parts remained as characteristic of the new order.

This war over the Spanish succession started as if it were merely a continuation of the earlier conflicts, but with soldiers like Marlborough and Eugene in command it soon developed different patterns. Eugene's first Italian campaign in 1701 showed what a brilliant general could do; with forces considerably inferior in number, he tied down the whole French army and defeated it thoroughly, even capturing its general. In 1704, Eugene and Marlborough combined their forces against the Franco-Bavarians in south Germany, and at Blenheim completely routed their enemies, capturing all Bavaria and clearing the French out of Germany. Timid politicians in England and the Netherlands were frightened by the cost in blood and the possibility that the battle might have been lost rather than won; thus the next year the generals were "chained" by the civilian officials. The following year, however, the soldiers got loose again and by the battle of Ramillies (1706) swept the French out of the Spanish Netherlands. There were to be several other crushing battles. At Turin (1706) Eugene cleared the French out of Savoy; in the battle of Audenarde (1708) Marlborough rewon the Netherland fortifications that timid and greedy politicians had lost the year before. At the battle of Malplaquet (1709), in which the French also were led by a general who was aware of the possibilities of the new army, the Allies won a technical victory, but one that they could not afford to repeat because their losses were so great. This "qualified defeat" heartened the French, but did not alter the fact that French hegemony in Europe had been destroyed by the armies of Marlborough and Eugene, and there was no alternative to a peace that would recognize the new politico-military structure of Europe.

But the War of the Spanish Succession was more than just a war against France; it was also a war for the crown of Spain, and the two contenders, Archduke Karl of Austria, as Charles III, and Philip of France, as Philip V, were both in Spain with armies to argue their respective claims. The Archduke, however, although himself a Roman Catholic, had armies composed of Dutch, English, and German Protestant troops, while Philip's forces were Roman Catholic French, Italian, and Spanish soldiers. At one time Philip's armies were commanded by the English-born bastard son of James II whose mother was Marlborough's sister, and Archduke Karl's forces were commanded by a French-born Huguenot who had been driven from his home by the revocation of the Edict of Nantes. The conflict raged back and forth in Spain, but by 1709, when the French had been roundly defeated in Flanders, Germany, and Italy, Philip's soldiers were definitely winning the war in Spain, and Philip and his Savoy-born princess (whose brother was a leader of the anti-French coalition) had won the loyalty of the leading Spanish politicians.

The coalition against France was able to maintain united action as long as Marlborough retained the confidence of the queen of England and that of the Estates General in the United Netherlands. He was willing, indeed, anxious to work with Eugene and the politicians in the Danubian monarchy. Nothing demonstrates more clearly the connections between internal and foreign policy than the events that wrecked the coalition. The Tory party in England, representing conservative and isolationist interests in the country, succeeded in replacing Marlborough's wife, Sarah, by a woman of their own party as the favorite and confidante of the Queen. When Marlborough's friends lost Anne's support, they could no longer govern England, and in a short time Marlborough himself was removed from command of the army and direction of affairs (1710). Then the isolationist Tory ministers made peace overtures to Louis XIV. From the point of view of the Tory ministers there was no other reasonable course of action. The death of Leopold's successor, Emperor Joseph I of Austria in 1711, left Karl as Holy Roman Emperor and ruler of the Danubian monarchy; there seemed little reason to fight so that he could also be king of Spain. Furthermore, Louis was ready to give favorable terms that would make it folly to fight merely to support Dutch or German interests. On the other hand England's allies regarded this action a treachery: perfidious Albion! When England withdrew from the coalition against France there was no alternative to a general peace; Emperor Karl tried to hold out to save his throne in Spain, but without English support it was a hopeless claim.

We lump together the treaties ending this war as the treaties of Utrecht and Rastatt (1713–14). They might be called the last of the "partition treaties" for, in fact, they disposed of the lands of the Spanish crowns by dividing them between the several contenders. Louis' grandson, Philip V, retained Spain and the Spanish overseas empire and part of Italy. The Austrian Hapsburgs received the Netherlands and part of Italy. England secured Gibraltar, slave trade concessions, and colonies in America. The United Netherlands gained the right to control the strategic frontier fortifications. Since the settlement also included a guarantee that the thrones of France and Spain, although both now held by the Bourbons, would never be united, it might be said that these treaties not only provided the basis of public law for Europe, but also proclaimed that secular considerations, rather than divine right had become the underlying principle of European political life.

## XIII

From the point of view of the developments throughout the century that we have been following, however, the peace of 1713–14 was also important as evidence of the emergence of a new political order in Europe. The wars had brought into existence three great military powers, France, England, and the Danubian monarchy, and these powers, cooperating with their smaller neighbors, gave Europe its government. It is no accident that following the peace of Utrecht, l'abbé de Saint-Pierre came forward with the first serious proposal for the establishment of a league of nations to maintain the peace; he, and his contemporaries understood that the emergence of great military powers, capable of maintaining military installations in time of peace as well as of war, had created a new order of politics for the continent. The long epoch of haphazard disorder, when religious and political rebellions made the politics of Europe into a *mêlée* of divergent interests, was now replaced by a more orderly and rational pattern. The mechanism of the balance of power and international diplomacy could not assure peace to the continent, but henceforth the peace of Europe was not to be disturbed by civil rebellions unless the rebels could secure the support of the military forces of the kingdom. Even though it could not always prevent the outbreak of war, the balance of power and diplomacy were able to regulate many problems that heretofore could only be settled by a contest of force. L'abbé de Saint-Pierre was unable to convert the princes of Europe with his plan for "perpetual peace," but the vision that he proposed, based upon the new states-system of Europe, was to continue to haunt European politics for the next two and a half centuries.

While the War of the Spanish Succession was finishing the outlines of this new system of politics in the West, on the eastern borderlands of Europe another war was creating another great military power that would eventually become part of this European system. Peter the Great's Europeanization of Russia was in a way a repetition of the seventeenth-century experience of the western states. One must not miss the fact that his important reform was the creation of a Russian army of one hundred thousand men and the building of a Russian navy that became mistress of the Baltic Sea. The war with Sweden's Charles XII (1700–21) forced Peter to accomplish this task; otherwise, he faced defeat and, with it, subordination of his empire. To build this military installation, Peter had to turn his ancient Slavic state upside down, for Russian institutions were in no way prepared to support such armed forces. Just as the West created bureaus for the management of taxes, soldiers, and diplomacy, and developed new officials to administer the state, so Peter's reforms did the same thing. Sometimes Peter's revolution is lost behind the colorful tales of the shaving of beards, the smoking of pipes, the westernization of dress, the reform of the calendar: these were only the froth of a revolution born, nurtured, and matured by the imperious demands of war. From 1695, when Peter discovered at Azov that he needed a new army if he were to have any success in war, until the treaty of Nystad in 1721, the mainspring of the Petrine revolution was the necessity of organizing a state that could muster soldiers and sailors capable of facing European military forces. When Russia accomplished this task, Russia was ready to become influential in the European balance of power and in the concert of European diplomacy. Thus Peter's saga in the East is both a recapitulation and an epilogue of the principal political drama of the West in the seventeenth century.

### *FOR ADDITIONAL READING*

J. R. Boulenger. *The Seventeenth Century.* New York, 1920.

G. N. Clark. *The Dutch Alliance and the War Against French Trade, 1688–1697.* London, 1923.

———. *The Seventeenth Century.* Oxford, 1929.

———. *War and Society in the Seventeenth Century.* Cambridge, 1958.

C. J. Friedrich. *The Age of the Baroque, 1610–1660.* New York, 1952.

E. Heckscher. *Mercantilism.* 2 vols. London, 1935.

F. L. Nussbaum. *The Triumph of Science and Reason, 1660–1685.* New York, 1953.

D. Ogg. *Europe in the Seventeenth Century.* London, 1943.

G. Schmoller. *The Mercantile System and Its Historical Significance.* London, 1884.

C. V. Wedgwood. *The Thirty Years War.* New Haven, 1949.

J. B. Wolf. *The Emergence of the Great Powers, 1685–1715.* New York, 1951.

R. Mousnier. *Les XVI et XVII Siècles.* Paris, 1956.

P. Sagnac and A. de Saint-Léger. *La prépondérance française, Louis XIV (1661–1715).* Paris, 1935.

G. Zeller. *Histoire des relations internationales: Les Temps modernes.* 2 vols. Paris, 1953, 1955.

W. Goetz. *Propyläen Weltgeschichte, Das Zeitalter des Absolutismus.* Berlin, 1931.

# XII

# CONSTITUTIONALISM AND THE SOVEREIGN STATE IN THE SEVENTEENTH CENTURY

*Maurice Ashley*

The concept of indivisible sovereignty, as it was to be expounded by Jeremy Bentham and John Austin in the Victorian Age, was not known to early Europe. In theory, this was because secular rulers were regarded as subject to many limitations imposed by a Christian view of human society; men were required to render unto Caesar the things that were Caesar's, but to God the things that were God's. Kings were expected to obey God's laws, the moral law, or the "natural" law. In practice, rulers were not only at times actually in vassalage to the pope as God's representative on earth, as was King John of England to Pope Innocent III, but they might hold at least some of their possessions of an earthly overlord, as the kings of Scotland did for centuries from the kings of England or as the kings of England held Gascony from the king of France. Early kings promised by their coronation oaths or by charters to accept the immemorial customs of the land; and decisions made both locally and nationally could, and sometimes were, overruled as being contrary to baronial, manorial, or other ancient customs. A whole complicated network of legal relationships permeated English society, and only the strongest of kings could assert authority over all his subjects. Even then he was compelled to recognize practical and traditional limitations upon his rights. Bracton, writing in the thirteenth century, said that the king was subject to the law. Even statute laws, made by the king in parliaments, were known to have been held by judges to conflict with the immemorial customs of the realm and therefore to be invalid.

Above all, however, the difficulty in evolving a theory of absolute sovereignty in the so-called Middle Ages was the doctrine of dual obedience to

God and to man. Only very slowly was this doctrine called in question: indeed it was still accepted by Roman Catholics in England and Protestants in France in the sixteenth and seventeenth centuries. In 1552 the English Protestant bishop Hugh Latimer declared that obedience was due to the king or to men in authority except when their commands conflicted with the laws of God. But with the decline of the papacy after its golden age a purely secular theory of the State began to arise. John Wycliffe and William of Occam, writing in the fourteenth century, had both propounded it. Wycliffe had maintained that the powers of the secular sovereign were circumscribed only by the "natural law"; Occam had written that "those who have not one king are not one kingdom." Niccolo Machiavelli, writing in the early sixteenth century, though not a systematic political thinker was among the first Europeans to emphasize clearly the secular character of the State, to separate politics from morals, to minimize the importance of that greater Christian society which had dominated the thinking of earlier times, and to discuss matters of power and security in concrete and realistic terms. Whether he envisaged a doctrine of "sovereignty" in the later Victorian sense is still disputed. By sovereign most men meant, and long continued to mean, nothing more than the head of the State.

Machiavelli sought to strengthen the Italian state of Florence, in which he was born, and perhaps to secure Italian independence. And afterwards throughout the sixteenth century there was a general movement in Europe toward the formation of stronger and more closely administrated nation states. This movement had been largely the product of the Protestant Reformation, from which emerged, as the smoke of battle subsided, the doctrine *"cujus regio illius religio."* In England the nation state had been immeasurably fortified in the reign of King Henry VIII. The late A. F. Pollard stressed how the concentration of a great deal of both secular and ecclesiastical authority in the hands of King Henry VIII's Lord Chancellor and leading minister, Cardinal Thomas Wolsey, had offered a pattern for the autocratic power or "sovereignty" of the second Tudor king. Certainly in England, once the authority of the pope had been finally repudiated in the reign of Queen Elizabeth I and the title of Supreme Head or Governor of the Church of England had been annexed to the titles of the monarchy, something approaching what was later called sovereign power was perceived actually to exist. Christopher St. Germain, a lawyer writing during the reign of Henry VIII, had attributed to the King in Parliament an almost unlimited authority both in Church and State; and once the royal supremacy over the Church was established there evolved a "novel theory of an omnicompetent Crown in Parliament."

Thus political theories followed the political facts; and it was not surprising that the first reasonably clear theory of political sovereignty was expounded toward the end of the sixteenth century by a Frenchman, Jean Bodin. Bodin was much read in England and had a profound influence on political arguments in the first half of the seventeenth century. Bodin conceived the possession of a "puissance souveraine" to be the essential characteristic of a fully formed state. This sovereign power, he said, consisted in an absolute and unlimited authority to make laws. Yet Bodin was not prepared to admit, as Thomas Hobbes was later, that the sovereign power was above the law and need not itself obey the law. He did not break away from the older view that princes were subject to divine and to natural laws, and within his idea of natural law was comprehended the notion that the sovereign must respect the sanctity of both private property and the family unit. It was also still his view that a subject could disobey the command of a king or magistrate if it was inconsistent with the law of God, though, like some other political thinkers of his time, he did not confer any overt approval on the right of rebellion. Men might be martyrs, if they wished, as Thomas Cranmer, Archbishop of Canterbury, had been in the reign of Queen Mary I, but basically man's duty was (as Cranmer thought) to obey his prince in all worldly things.

## I

Such was the background to political thought when King James I ascended the throne of England in 1603. As King of Scotland since he was just over a year old, James could claim to be an old and experienced king. He had come to a land where the authority of the crown was far higher than it had ever been in Scotland. Even the English Puritans—opposite numbers of his own Presbyterian subjects across the border—had thus far generally accepted the view that constituted political power was ordained by God and that there was no natural right of rebellion. While in Scotland the Presbyterian Kirk had, from the days of John Knox, asserted claims to rule the state in matters ecclesiastical, in England the essential identity of Church and State was widely asserted and approved. Richard Hooker, the most brilliant prose writer in the reign of Queen Elizabeth I, had set himself to establish this. Like the rest, Hooker believed that once laws had been made by constituted authority they must be obeyed; otherwise the whole fabric of society was undermined. But equally he assumed that the laws promulgated by the sovereign power would be consonant with the laws of God and the laws of nature. These, then, were the two fundamental thoughts accepted at the beginning of the seventeenth century when James became king of England: first, that while secular rulers were extremely powerful, they were expected to govern within the framework of natural and divine laws; and, secondly, that while in the last resort subjects might disobey laws that affronted their consciences, they had no divine right to rebel against properly constituted authority.

Whatever the theories of the age might be, the rulers of England, as distinct from the "absolute" kings of France or Spain, were not in fact free to decide policy without consulting representative bodies. They had inherited a parliamentary tradition, stretching far back into history, which had been admitted even by such potent personalities as King Henry VIII and Queen Elizabeth I. The king ruled as a King in Parliament, and it was parliament that had acquired the right to make statute laws and to vote taxes. In practice therefore the king could not rule for long without parliaments; for his hereditary revenues only allowed him to manage without taxation in times of complete peace, which were comparatively rare, while new laws were needed whenever social conditions changed. At the same time parliament—and in particular the elective House of Commons—had begun to take on a character and sense of duty of its own. The Tudors had used the House of Commons to achieve and to press through the Reformation settlement; Queen Elizabeth I had invoked the assistance of the House in warding off the threat of the Counter Reformation. During her reign much of the procedure of the lower house was formulated, though its members had not yet fully established their right either to freedom of speech or freedom from arrest. The queen had refused to recognize the right of parliament to concern itself with matters of foreign policy or religion. But she had, in effect, often been obliged to take account of the opinions and attitudes of her "faithful Commons." From time to time she had gracefully, if reluctantly, yielded to their wishes. She had never been able completely to crush the critics who formed a rudimentary opposition to her ministry from the very earliest years of her reign. Thus, in the words of Sir John Neale, parliament had been "schooled as the hostile critic of the prince," and before she died Queen Elizabeth had become "the splendid though involuntary betrayer of the cause of [absolute] monarchy."

Such was King James I's inheritance. Seeing, as he had from a distance, the formidable powers of the Tudors at work, it is doubtful if he had at first recognized the growing strength of the House of Commons. In a book, which he incautiously wrote and published before he came to the throne, entitled *The Trew Law of Free Monarchies Or the Reciprock and Mutuall Dutie Betwixt a Free King and his Naturall Subjects* (1598) he put forward his view of the origin and authority of kingship and the duty of a people. He believed that the power of kings was derived from an ancient right of conquest and was sanctioned directly by God. He urged a number of impressive, if somewhat vague, doctrines about the authority of kings. He asserted that in Scotland the kings had always been the makers of the law, while kings themselves were bound by existing laws of their own volition. But the people must obey their king, because he had been appointed by God and only God could unmake him, for He alone was his judge. Thus they must suffer evil kings as well as good ones. King David, he remarked, had called kings themselves gods. Later he repeated this doctrine before the judges in 1616 and went on to observe that it was "atheism and blasphemy to dispute what God can do," adding that "so it is presumption and high contempt in a subject to dispute what a King can do."

Such was King James's somewhat rhetorical conception of what came to be called "the divine right of kings." But of course in the early seventeenth century everyone held a providential view of political society, as men had done in the previous century and much earlier: no one would have denied that the king's powers were derived from God—but then so was all power, right down to that of fathers of families and masters of servants. Thus the new king's doctrines could be said to be no more than provocative platitudes; they did not imply any claim to the complete and absolute sovereign power of Hobbes or Austin.

Moreover, King James, with all his faults, was a highly intelligent man. He realized the practicalities of the situation and after sampling the temper of the English parliament, he did not press unpalatable theories too far. When in 1610 the Houses of Parliament prepared to deliver a protest against a book written by Dr. John Cowell, Regius Professor of Civil Law at Cambridge University, entitled *The Interpreter* (1607), in which he wrote that the king was "above the law by his absolute power" and added that the three estates only took part in legislation by reason of the monarch's good will, the king repudiated those doctrines (though he had preached something much like them himself) and ordered the suppression of the book. And whatever King

James may have argued in theory, in fact he based his authority on the same historical precedents as Queen Elizabeth had. His case, and that of his son, King Charles I, was that there must be residuary or discretionary powers in the Crown to take action in an emergency, if necessary overriding the ordinary law of the land, for reasons of state. It is worth noting that two distinguished authors of King James I's reign, his Lord Chancellor Francis Bacon, who was disgraced, and Sir Walter Raleigh, whom he sent to his death on the scaffold for treason, both accepted that view of the powers of the monarchy.

## II

This constitutional interpretation of the residuary or prerogative powers of the monarch was upheld in three historic cases in the courts. The first case was that of a merchant, John Bate, who refused to pay an "imposition" or extra import duty on currants on the ground that the king had levied this duty illegally. The Chief Baron of the Court of Exchequer drew a distinction between the king's "ordinary" and "absolute" power and maintained that since foreign affairs (including foreign commerce) were controlled by the "absolute" power, the king was within his rights in levying an imposition on foreign commerce by his prerogative. The second case, known (inaccurately) as the Five Knights' case, related to the imprisonment by the king's order of a number of persons who had refused to subscribe to a loan to the government. The prisoners demanded to be released on bail on the ground that no cause had been shown for their imprisonment. Their counsel in the Court of King's Bench appealed to Magna Carta, while the Attorney General invoked the king's "absolute power" deriving from his position as the "fountain of justice." Lord Chief Justice Hyde ruled that if the warden of the prison certified that the men were committed by special command of the king for "matter of state" then there were ample precedents against their being bailed except at the king's pleasure. The third case was the celebrated one of John Hampden, Member of Parliament for Wendover, who in 1638 refused to pay ship money, that is to say a general contribution toward the upkeep of the navy demanded by royal writ. Here the Court of King's Bench was divided in its opinions, but nine out of the twelve judges confirmed the legality of the writ to Hampden on the ground that the king had the right to charge his subjects for the defence of the realm in times of danger and that he alone was the judge of the imminence and gravity of that danger. Sir

Robert Berkeley made it clear that the king could not "at all times and on all occasions impose charges on his subjects in general without the consent in Parliament."

These three cases established that the essence of the king's "absolute power," as distinct from his "ordinary" power, was in his right to take action overriding the ordinary law in an emergency and that he himself was the sole judge of the emergency. This had little or nothing to do with the divine right of kingship or the nature of the ultimate law-making authority. It merely was an affirmation that English common law recognized that in a time of crisis the executive could take emergency action, even if it conflicted with ordinary legal procedures. Both Queen Elizabeth I and King James I had been careful not to make excessive use of this extraordinary right. But when in the reign of King Charles I it came to his ordering the imprisonment of members of parliament who criticized the conduct of the government or to levying a general tax, as in the case of ship money, when there was no immediate war in sight, then it appeared both to parliamentarians, to common lawyers, and to publicists as if the royal prerogative was being stretched too far and was deliberately exploited to undermine the "fundamental laws" of the kingdom.

Although the judges in the reigns of the two early Stuarts upheld the conception of absolute prerogative powers on the basis of precedents, other lawyers of the time emphasized that the authority of the monarch was, and always had been, subject to the common law of the land, which stretched back to immemorial ages. This point has well been brought out recently in an extremely stimulating book by J. G. A. Pocock. Mr. Pocock quotes from Sir John Davies, who was attorney general in Ireland in 1612:

> This *Customary Law* is the most perfect and most excellent, and without comparison the best, to make and preserve a Commonwealth. For the *written laws* which are made either by the Edicts of Princes, or by the Councils of Estates, are imposed upon the Subject before any Trial or Probation made, whether the same be fit and agreeable to the nature and disposition of the people, or whether they will breed any inconvenience or no. But a *Custom* doth never become a Law to bind the people, until it hath been tried and approved time out of mind, during all which time there did thereby arise no inconvenience; for if it had been found inconvenient at any time, it had been used no longer, but had been interrupted, and consequently it had lost the virtue and the force of a Law.

This view of the dominant virtues of the customary or common law was developed and underlined by Sir Edward Coke, who himself had been Chief

Justice of the King's Bench. Out of it was built up a concept of a "fundamental law" of the land going back beyond the Norman conquest into Anglo-Saxon times and establishing rights and privileges in subjects, both in their property and in their persons, which no monarch might infringe. This belief in the antiquity of the common law, whose value was "tried and approved time out of mind" and whose principles were passed down from generation to generation, also gave birth to the idea of there having been an ancient English constitution which prerogative action by the king could not touch. Coke himself died in 1634, but this teaching of his embodied in his *Institutes* and *Reports* had a vast influence on men's thinking in the 1630s, when King Charles I was ruling without a parliament and exerting his prerogative powers to the full, and in the 1640s, when the "Long Parliament" met and the great civil war began.

## III

Historians will not be found to agree upon the causes of the civil war. In the Victorian age those historians who accepted Coke's interpretation that there existed "fundamental laws" of the constitution approved the contention of the parliamentarian side, led by John Pym, that King Charles I by his "absolutist" government had broken those laws. Other historians have stressed the religious factors in bringing about the civil war, pointing out that for various reasons the Long Parliament, which the king was compelled to summon in 1640 because of his failure in the wars against his Scottish subjects, was largely Puritan in its complexion and was opposed to the anti-Puritan attitude of the ecclesiastical authorities, led by Archbishop Laud and supported by the king. Certainly what had been established beyond question is that many of the members of the Long Parliament who, when the civil war came, declared themselves royalists were originally in favor of a reform of the Church, in particular of the reduction in the powers of the bishops, as well as the abolition of some prerogative powers that had been exercised by the king and of the courts that had been set up by the Tudors. Thus these divisions were not basic, and it was only when the argument was pushed to extremes that a breach came. Social historians have argued that since the Protestant Reformation there had been a change in the English class structure and that the classes represented in the House of Commons, being now wealthier and more conscious of their position, were naturally demanding a larger share than before in the making of political decisions. Finally, and most recently, there has been a return, notably among American historians who have made a special study of the parliaments in the reign of King James I, to a more refined "Whig interpretation of history." A movement in opposition to the Crown has been traced back as far as the earliest parliaments in the reign of Queen Elizabeth I, and "opposition" to the Court is a word commonly found once more in up-to-date constitutional histories. Yet there is little doubt that the idea of an organized parliamentary opposition to the Crown was a new one. The older idea that parliament was an expansion of the king's Great Council, meeting to give him advice and support rather than to air grievances, died hard. As late as 1640 the Reverend William Chillingworth was imprisoned by order of the House of Commons because he said "we had sides and parties in the House, which was but one body, so to set a division amongst us."

Broadly it may be said that civil war came because King Charles I was a stubborn and incompetent monarch whose foreign and domestic policies had proved failures, whose methods of government were thought by many to be arbitrary, and whom a majority in the House of Commons refused to trust. The final breach came over what may perhaps be called a constitutional issue, namely the failure of parliament to extract from the king the right to control the army or militia. It was then, in the first half of the 1640s, that political theorists came forward to justify the act of rebellion and to reconsider the whole problem of sovereignty in the state.

Some of the theorists looked back for their arguments to Coke's concept of fundamentals. Neither John Pym, the political leader, nor Oliver Cromwell, one of the military leaders of the parliamentary side, were theorists. As early as 1628 Pym had declared that there was no such thing as "sovereign power"—and he stuck to that view—while Cromwell was later to recognize that an executive needed to possess discretionary powers to maintain order in the state in a time of national emergency. The real argument of the time boiled down to two questions: who was to judge when a national emergency existed (for nobody really thought that there had been any emergency during the years after 1629 when King Charles I was pressing his prerogative powers hard so as to obtain money to govern without a parliament); and, secondly, granted that the monarch had exceeded his powers by attacking the fundamental laws of private property and individual freedom, was there a right of rebellion?

One of the ablest political thinkers of this age was Henry Parker, son of a leading Sussex landowner. He was born in 1604 and educated at Oxford and

Lincoln's Inn. He began to expound his political theories in seven pamphlets published during 1642, the year when the civil war began. Parker believed that parliament, being the representative of the responsible classes in England, was sovereign, and he taught that this was true in law because it was true in fact. The Stuarts, he claimed, had forfeited their right to sovereignty because of their bad government, and he saw the civil war as a struggle whose aim was permanently to transfer the essence of sovereignty from the king to parliament, which was capable of exercising it in the general interest. He denied that royalty was sacrosanct or that its authority was based upon the Holy Scriptures or past history. The king had wielded his power in trust for his people, and when he violated their trust he gave up his power. He argued somewhat vaguely that the royal prerogatives were limited by the law and that King Charles I had not merely overridden the law, but even threatened to become an Asiatic despot.

Parker's originality lay in fact in his bold opinion that "sovereignty," which must be "supreme and complete" and clearly vested, should now be taken away from the king in parliament, where previously it had rested, and placed fully in the hands of parliament. He asserted that King Charles I by his incompetence and violation of his duties had indeed voluntarily surrendered his sovereignty to parliament, which henceforward should become omnicompetent and omnipotent. Parker would not have admitted that this conception meant that a tyrannical parliament was now to be substituted for a tyrannical king. He believed that the freedom of the citizen would be protected by the law and of course by a sense of responsibility in parliament. But he noted that "the liberty of every member must be subordinate to the liberty of the whole body." Thus he failed to grapple with one of the most difficult problems in the theory of sovereignty: how it could be made compatible with political liberty.

Philip Hunton, the author of a *Treatise of Monarchy,* published in 1643, did not go as far as Parker. His work was an academic discussion of the different kinds of monarchy, but he maintained emphatically that England was a "mixed monarchy" and that the king's power was limited by the original constitution or contract and by agreements to which his ancestors had been a party. If the king violated those limitations, he might be actively resisted. As to the question of what determined whether the king had exceeded his rights, that was left to the "conscience of mankind." King Charles I had attempted to convert a mixed monarchy into an absolute monarchy and was therefore rightly resisted.

Other parliamentarian authors of this period included William Prynne and Henry Robinson. Prynne argued that parliament is a high court and could therefore properly bring the king to judgment if he disobeyed the law, while in his *Sovereign Power of Parliaments and Kingdoms* (1643) he virtually committed himself to parliamentary sovereignty. Robinson maintained that a king ruling by his own will was an irresponsible tyrant, while a king who ruled by counsel of parliament could be superfluous. Recent events had shown that the monarchy had become inconvenient and unbearable, while parliament, now matured in responsibility, might claim to have full sovereignty transferred to itself.

On the royalist side much of the argument of those who pleaded the virtues of a "mixed monarchy" was accepted. This acceptance, it has recently been suggested, was brought about by the tone of King Charles I's reply to the Nineteen Propositions submitted to him on the eve of the civil war. In that reply the king himself adumbrated a concept of mixed monarchy that would have been distasteful to his father. The royalists, however, emphasized that a mixed monarchy could not exist without a king. The country had customarily been governed by the King in Parliament; for parliament to turn against the king was to destroy the ancient constitution. The Reverend Doctor Henry Ferne, one of the most capable of these royalist writers, stressed that they had no intention of defending absolute power or raising the monarchy to "an arbitrary way of government." It was, however, he observed, the parliamentarians who were seeking absolute powers and undermining the constitution by appealing to nonexistent fundamental laws.

Such were the political arguments that were bandied about on the eve of and during the civil wars. Both sides asserted that they were fighting for the king, the Church, and the constitution. The king, his enemies said, had broken his coronation oath and the "fundamental laws"; it was for a breach of the fundamental laws that the king's greatest servant, the Earl of Strafford, was sent to his death by the Long Parliament. The Puritans—and some who were not Puritans in the fullest sense of the word, like Pym and Sir John Eliot—yet claimed that the Church had been corrupted and that the bishops were exercising secular powers in their courts; and the constitution was conceived to stretch back beyond the memory of man and to guarantee property rights of subjects which had been menaced by the claims of royal prerogative to ship money or forced loans. Thus, before the battle began, the king was persuaded to renounce the prerogative courts of the Tudors and even to agree to the right of the Long Parliament to sit as long as it wished. Then in the early peace proposals sent to the king, as, for example, the Nineteen Propositions of June, 1642, parliament sought the right to approve the appointments of ministers of state and members of the Privy Council, to control the education and marriage of the king's children, to advise on the government of the Church, as well as to command the militia. In the Propositions of Oxford (February, 1643), parliament demanded also that the king should consent to the abolition of the bishops. The propositions of Uxbridge and Newcastle, presented after the king was defeated, went so far that Charles I recognized that if he agreed to them, he would cease to be more than a purely ornamental figure in the state. But the earlier propositions in fact embodied revolutionary demands that had scarcely been made before even in the days when King Henry III or King Edward II were humiliated by their barons and were not to be realized for generations—and then only in practice rather than in constitutional theory.

Some modern historians have attempted to argue that Pym and his friends were not really revolutionaries; but if they were not, it is hard to say who is a revolutionary. The theory of "mixed monarchy"—much older, it has been suggested, than the theories of Sir Edward Coke—was invigorated and pressed to its uttermost extremes. And later when the New Model Army, led by Oliver Cromwell and Henry Ireton, his son-in-law, quarreled with the majority in the Long Parliament, it became clear to them too that an absolutist parliament might be as dangerous to the liberty of the individual as an absolutist king. It was only then that men began to recognize the perils of the all-embracing "sovereignty" sought for parliament by Henry Parker or William Prynne and to revive the concept of a mixed monarchy or a balanced constitution with a new and different emphasis.

## IV

It was during this period, when the army and parliament were quarreling, that there emerged those who were virtually the first advocates of political democracy in Britain, who came to be known as "the Levelers." Even their greatest admirers would hardly claim for them that they were clear or profound political thinkers. Their leader, John Lilburne, was one of nature's self-appointed martyrs, quarrelsome, noisy, enthusiastic, emotional, deeply religious, brave, and stubborn. He had been imprisoned and maltreated by the government of King Charles I for distributing pamphlets attacking the bishops and consequently was at first a keen advocate of the parliamentarian side, for which he fought as an officer in the first civil war. His propensity for picking personal quarrels, however, brought him into conflict both with the House of Lords and with the House of Commons; and although he at first wrote in praise of the House of Commons, he and his followers came to lose faith in parliament as it was traditionally constituted. Indeed, William Walwyn, the best educated of the Levelers, specifically pointed to the dangers of parliamentary sovereignty.

Lilburne derived a number of his ideas from Coke, but, as has recently been pointed out, he differed from this apologist for the fundamental laws and the ancient constitution in one very important respect: whereas Coke had claimed that King William the Conqueror had confirmed and upheld the immemorial Anglo-Saxon laws, which embodied the wisdom of the ages, Lilburne emphasized that there had been a Conquest and that the law, as it existed in the seventeenth century, derived from the tyranny of the Conqueror. In theory, the Levelers looked back to a golden age before the Conquest when Englishmen were free and equal; but now, they asserted, they had lost all their liberties and must appeal for their restoration in the light of "natural right" or "reason." While, therefore, they believed that the House of Commons must exercise the supreme power, what they envisaged was a very different House from the "Rump" of the Long Parliament which was ruling after the civil war. What they had in mind was a House of Commons whose members should be elected in equalized constituencies on the basis of manhood suffrage and that the House should be dissolved and replaced by a new one every year on the second Thursday in March. Thus parliament would be made genuinely to represent the electorate and should be under its control.

> I look upon the House of Commons [wrote Lilburne] as the supreme power of England, who have residing in them the power that is inherent in the people, who yet are not to act according to their own wills and pleasures, but according to the fundamental constitutions and customs of the land, which I conceive provides for the safety and preservation of the people. . . .

In the first "Agreement of the People," a draft constitution that was drawn up by the Levelers in 1647, it was stated that the power of parliaments was "inferior only to theirs who choose them," and it added that parliament must not interfere with "matters of religion" because those were questions of conscience, that it must not conscript men to join the armed forces, that it must not punish those who had expressed political opinions about the civil wars, and that all the laws it made must be good and equal and "not evidently destructive to the safety and well-being of the people."

Thus what the Levelers were concerned to ensure was less the sovereignty of parliament than the sovereignty of the people as a whole. They believed in government by consent and they attempted to limit "sovereignty" or political power by providing for frequent general elections and specifying certain general rights—above all, freedom of conscience—which might not be infringed either by the legislature or by the executive. Parliament was to be firmly under popular control and was to be "the absolute supreme derivative power from all the Commons of England." The civil wars, they argued, had destroyed the old constitutional edifice; the king and House of Lords must be abolished. The nation had clearly reverted to a "state of nature" in which by an agreement of the people as a whole a democratic constitution could be established, based on "the principles of safety, flowing from nature, reason, and justice."

Undoubtedly Lilburne and his followers and the "agitators" in the New Model Army—agents elected by the common soldiers to represent their point of view in the general army debates—spoke instinctively out of a sense of being underdogs, whose rights had long been denied to them. Reading the Bible had given them a concept of the equality of men in the eyes of God. Moreover during the civil war they had seen the aristocracy and their natural rulers overthrown and humiliated. This radical approach is well represented in a pamphlet entitled *A General Charge or Impeachment of High-Treason* written in 1647 by a sectarian preacher named Clarkson (quoted by Mr. P. Zagorin):

> Who are the oppressors but the nobility and gentry; and who are the oppressed, if not the yeoman, the farmer, the tradesman, and the labourer? . . . When you the communalty calleth a parliament, they are confident such must be chosen that are the noblest and richest . . . but . . . your slavery is their liberty, your poverty is their prosperity.

When, after the first civil war ended, the question began to be discussed what form the future government of England should take, the Leveler point of view, though perhaps the most interesting in the light of future history, was only one of many, and certainly not the most influential. The majority of the Rump Parliament were Presbyterians and lawyers, who were more or less conservative in their outlook. These men had no wish to abolish either the monarchy or the House of Lords, but merely to restrict the authority of the king and enhance the power of parliament. They believed that King Charles had broken the fundamental laws of the constitution and that once his usurped powers had been done away with and his rights defined and restricted, the old system, as they saw it, could be safely restored. This party wanted to have a national Presbyterian Church controlled by the State and, having shorn the monarchy of most of its former powers, were prepared to leave Charles I as the ceremonial head of government, while conferring effective sovereignty upon a parliament of landowners. Such was what has been called "the Party of the Right" on the Puritan side.

Next came the leading officers of the army, nicknamed "the Grandees," and headed by Oliver Cromwell's able son-in-law, Henry Ireton. Ireton favored a written constitution in which the relative powers of the king, the House of Lords and Commons, and of a Council of State should be plainly set out and defined. Like the Levelers, Ireton was in favor of a biennial parliament and a more equal distribution of members among the constituencies, but he did not believe in manhood suffrage. Equally, he accepted the principle of liberty of conscience, which meant the abolition of the Church of England, but not necessarily its replacement by a rigid Presbyterian system. On the other hand, he argued that in order that law and order might be maintained it was essential for magistrates to be able to punish fanatical religious enthusiasts for breaches of the peace. Ireton and Cromwell were, above all, pragmatical in their outlook on politics. They were, in a phrase once used by Cromwell, "not wedded or glued to forms of government." They wanted to retain the monarchy because it was a convenient and necessary institution, not because it was ordained of God; they were willing to meet the point of view of the Levelers by specifying certain reforms that should be carried out after a settlement had been achieved. But, beyond everything, they were anxious to work out a constitutional scheme which would be accepted by the majority of men of standing, would ensure order, and would safeguard the rights of property and freedom of worship by all Christians.

In the autumn of 1647 a famous debate took place, held under the auspices of the General Council of the Army at Putney near London, where the advocates of the Levelers' point of view and of Ireton and the Grandees clashed with each other. These debates have been preserved to us in part and throw a flood of light on the Puritan approach to constitutional questions. In his introduction to his edition of these debates Professor A. S. P. Woodhouse has written:

From the vantage ground of a later century no one will doubt that the most important political doctrine to emerge from the revolution [of 1642] was one temporarily defeated, but destined to ultimate triumph, the sovereignty of Parliament. . . . The direct debt of this doctrine to Puritanism does not appear to be great. Its indirect debt is, on the other hand, immense; for Parliament allied itself with the forces of Puritanism and asserted its own sovereignty by claiming its right to undertake reform of religion. The doctrine of Parliamentary sovereignty is not necessarily a doctrine of liberty or of democracy. It is significant that we find arrayed against it, in the Debates, the most extreme forms of Puritanism, both democratic and anti-democratic.

That indeed is the central interest in these debates. The initial discussion on whether covenants made must be kept, though theoretically exciting, led nowhere, but at a later stage when the question of manhood suffrage came up the conflict was clear: it ranged over the nature of sovereignty and whether government must be based on consent. Colonel Thomas Rainborough said:

I think the poorest he that is in England hath a life to live, as the greatest he; and therefore . . . I think it's clear that every man that is to live under a government ought first by his own consent to put himself under that government; and I do not think that the poorest man in England is not at all bound in a strict sense to that government that he hath not had a voice to put himself under; and I am confident that when I have heard the reasons against it, something will be said to answer those reasons, insomuch that I should doubt whether he was an Englishman or no, that should doubt of these things.

The Levelers therefore required that a democratic constitution should be founded on agreement by the whole people and that henceforward parliament should be elected by all men over twenty-one who were not in receipt of assistance from the poor rates. To that concept Henry Ireton was unalterably opposed. He promptly answered Rainborough in these terms:

I think that no person hath a right to an interest or share in the disposing of the affairs of the kingdom and in determining or choosing those that shall determine what laws we shall be ruled by here—no person hath a right to this that hath not a permanent fixed interest in the kingdom [i.e., property-owners].

Ireton went on to argue that this was not inegalitarian, for the forty-shilling freeholder had as great a voice in the election of a knight of the shire as a man that had an income of £10,000 a year; but he thought that if votes ceased to be based upon property then a "fundamental part of the civil constitution" would be taken away. The Levelers claimed that the right to elect was part of every Englishman's birthright and was a "natural law." Ireton vehemently denied this. He said that "by that same right of nature, whatever it be" that gives every man an equal right to choose him that shall govern him, "he hath the same right in any goods he sees—meat, drink, clothes to take and use them for his sustenance. In other words, Ireton argued that the democratic principle undermined the very fabric of the state.

To Ireton's arguments Rainborough retorted that the analogy which was drawn between the right of the propertyless man to vote and his right to steal was completely false. If it was the law of nature that men should consent to government, so too it was the law of nature—or the law of God—that "Thou shalt not steal." "I wish," he answered, "you would not make the world believe that we are for anarchy." For that was the second or derivative argument of both Ireton and Cromwell: that democracy "tends to anarchy, must end in anarchy." The Levelers did not accept it and indeed did not believe it. "I hope," said another of their representatives in these debates, "that we may live to see the power of the King and the Lords thrown down, that yet we may live to see property preserved." But Ireton refused to separate the two arguments. If the propertyless were given the vote, he insisted, "why may not those men vote against all property?" The laws of nature, he asserted, had nothing to do with the matter. Property was "of human constitution."

So that fascinating argument swung to and fro more than three centuries ago. Neither side in the army had any wish to confer absolute power on elected parliaments. Both sides wanted to keep parliament under the control of the people and to prevent religious liberties from being infringed. But whereas the Levelers and their friends maintained that the parliamentary soldiers had been fighting to recover their birthrights and privileges as Englishmen, which was to have a share in the government of their country, Ireton and the Grandees of the army said that both safety and prudence demanded that the control of government should stay in the hands only of the "fixed and settled people of this nation."

In the end, a compromise was patched up, and toward the end of 1648 a revised version of the "Agreement of the People" proposed that the franchise should be granted to householders assessed for poor relief. The same "Agreement" listed eight reservations on the powers of parliament including a prohibition against any interference with the free exercise of religion. But this compromise was never put into effect. The execution of King Charles I in January, 1649, the final "purge" of parliament by the army that preceded it, the threats from abroad—all precluded the introduction of any novel constitution or freely elected House of Commons, if the new English Commonwealth hoped to survive. The Levelers then threatened subversion and tried to stir up mutiny in the army. When they failed to do so, Lilburne, who had once condemned the Stuart monarchy, turned in his volatile way to offering his alliance to the exiled royalists, if they would promise to introduce a democratic constitutional system of which he approved. This was a mirage. Within ten years the Leveler movement and its leader were dead, and they do not enter again at all seriously into the constitutional history of the seventeenth century. One of the Levelers, Edward Sexby, who, like Lilburne, entered into negotiations with the royalists, managed to propagate their opinions in France; but they took no roots.

## V

Meanwhile during the middle of the seventeenth century four authors were writing on the subject of political theory, whose work contributed in various ways to the evolution of ideas: these were Sir Robert Filmer, Dr. Thomas Hobbes, James Harrington, and John Milton. Although the earliest to write in point of time was Filmer, his principal book was published much later and posthumously and therefore will be discussed last.

Hobbes was born in 1588, was a student at Oxford at the time of the Gunpowder Plot against King James I, and published his first book on political theory, *De Cive* in Latin in 1642. The book by which he became best known, his *Leviathan or The Matter, Form, and Power of a Commonwealth Ecclesiastical and Civil* was first published in 1651. In it Hobbes' aim was to discuss the nature of the State and the basis of sovereignty. Living in a world where states were constantly threatened with disruption by rebellions and civil wars and where religious fanaticism still promoted assassination and revolt, he sought the secret of stability. He refined and strengthened Bodin's doctrine of sovereignty, and he was powerfully influenced by the Cartesian approach to philosophy, although he did not accept dualism. To him the body was all; thought was caused by the pressure of external objects on the senses. Though he has sometimes been linked with Francis Bacon, the father of inductive reasoning, Hobbes was no scientist in a modern sense. Essentially he was a deductive reasoner who stressed the importance of definitions and "significant speech": "The light of human minds," he wrote, "is perspicuous words, by exact definitions first snuffed and purged from ambiguity." No author of his time was more ingenious then he was in taking up traditional words and phrases and redefining them to give them an entirely new meaning suitable to his own theories.

That ingenuity he applied, in particular, to two phrases commonly used by political writers of the sixteenth century and earlier—the "social contract" and "the state of nature." A distinction has been drawn between this "social contract," in which men are supposed to have agreed together to give up their "natural rights" in order to set up a government and the "contract of government" whereby an organized community comes to terms with its future ruler. Whether these two terms were always clearly separated may be doubted, but in any case Hobbes' "original contract" was one in which men were imagined to have voluntarily agreed together to have given up all their natural rights to a sovereign power, which was "the Leviathan" or "artificial man." The reason they did so was that the "state of nature" was in reality a state of war of all against all. Since all men are roughly equal in their capacities and are motivated by an unending struggle for power "that ceaseth only in death," this is inevitable; they live within a government in a condition of common fear and enmity without any security or hope of peace. Therefore they must have "a common power to keep them in awe and to direct their actions to the common benefit."

The sovereign power that is thus created is indivisible, inalienable, and unlimited; furthermore it cannot be revoked. There is no right of rebellion in a subject, for that would imply the destruction of the state. The sovereign makes no contract with the subject; what he commands is the law, what he says is right, for "the law is all the right reason we have." For how can there be any other logical basis for what is right? I think one thing is right, you another; so we must leave it to the government to define and determine the punishment for what is wrong. "Such authority," wrote Hobbes, "is to trump in card-playing, save that in the matter of government, when nothing else is turned up, clubs are trumps." Sovereignty, to Hobbes, was an all powerful unity above the law. To it belonged not merely the rights of the executive, but of the legislature and judicature as well. To admit that there can be a possible conflict of authorities is again to undermine the whole basis of the state. In the same way to allow that a subject possesses inalienable rights would be to destroy all authority. Therefore Hobbes was careful to say that a man's "natural rights" consisted only of the right to self-preservation and not to kill or accuse himself, while his "laws of nature," "command men to seek peace, to keep their covenants, to show gratitude, and to avoid cruelty or provocation." It is interesting to reflect that, judging by his speeches in the debates at Putney, Henry Ireton would have accepted Hobbes' view of the "laws of nature." Other elements in Ireton's political outlook have affinities with Hobbes' way of thinking, though unfortunately we have no proof that Ireton read his books. (*The Leviathan* was not published until the year Ireton died, though his *Behemoth* was published in 1642.)

Some critics have attempted to convict Hobbes of inconsistencies; others, more astute, have simply written that "it is idle to qualify or defend such a political philosophy: it is rotten to the core." Men, it is said, are not motivated by a mere desire for power; that is psychologically unsound. All government must ultimately be based on consent, for men will not be ruled by fear; men do possess natural rights, and one of these is to rebel against a corrupt or wicked administration; and so on. Even that staunch royalist the first Earl of Clarendon wrote a book criticizing Hobbes on the ground that the sovereign "tacitly" agrees to obey rules of justice. But granted Hobbes' premiss that without a powerful and effective government men will always revert to a state of war or anarchy, his arguments for an all-embracing sovereign who determines what is right and wrong are logical, if frightening; and they have been widely accepted and enforced throughout the history of mankind right down to the times in which we live.

Yet it is possibly an exaggeration to say that Hobbes' political philosophy is emptied of all moral content and is rotten to the core. Hobbes was thinking in terms of the troubles of his own lifetime and was convinced that he had found a solution for them in his taut definition of sovereignty. His concept of an original state of nature in which all men had agreed to give up all —or nearly all—of their natural rights in order to secure peace and safeguard property was of course merely a fiction. He was considering how to ensure that peace and order might be permanently and securely established. And as Howard Warrender has recently persuasively argued, Hobbes also believed that "political society can be established and sustained only if there are a certain number of men who are generally prepared to do their duty, quite apart from the coercion of human sanctions."

James Harrington was born in 1611 and had spent much of his youth abroad, notably in the Dutch Netherlands and in Venice, where republican governments existed. "In the Netherlands he had seen what a people can do. In Venice what institutions can achieve. The former turned his interests in the direction of politics; the latter made him believe in political science." He was a realist and a sceptic. Rumor had it that he refused to kiss the pope's toe or to believe in Italian miracles. In 1647 he attempted to help in the negotiation of a settlement between parliament and the king, and for a time he served Charles I as a Groom of the Bedchamber. John Aubrey wrote that "the King loved his company; only he could not endure to hear of a Commonwealth; and Mr. Harrington passionately loved his Majesty."

Thus Harrington was a gentler figure than Hobbes. Moreover, unlike Hobbes, he believed in inductive reasoning. He appreciated the realistic arguments about the practical problems of government put forward by Machiavelli; he drew on the experiences of the Dutch and Italian states; he regarded the Bible not as a treatise of moral instruction but as a source book of Jewish history. He thought that the history of mankind showed that governments rose and fell because the seat of power in states had not been made dependent upon the preponderance of property, and by that he meant the ownership of land. According to him, that "principle" had been recognized by Joseph, by Solon, by Caesar, and many others. Therefore Harrington's two leading concepts were that there must be a balance of property in a state, and that there must be rotation in its government. By such means security might be attained and political power not abused.

First and foremost, then, Harrington accepted an economic interpretation of history and thought that the classes that possessed economic power necessarily exerted political power in a state. Unlike Henry Ireton, who claimed that power ought to depend upon property, Harrington argued that it already did so. Harrington said that an army was "a beast that had a big belly and must be fed"; provided it was fed, it would obey the government. (Incidentally, if the Long Parliament had been true to this teaching, it might never have been overthrown by the army.) In his *Oceana* (1656), written about an imaginary state or Utopia, Harrington proposed that to achieve stability individuals should be limited to the possession of land with a rentable value of £2,000 a year in England and Ireland and £500 in Scotland, while marriage portions should be limited to £1,500. This meant (since he estimated that the total rents were worth £10,000 a year) that about 5,000 families would be the real rulers of the state, not therefore a "pure democracy" but a "natural aristocracy." "By his socialist division of property," wrote H. Russel Smith, "he hoped to make republican institutions possible. By keeping power in the hands of the steadier section of the community, which is engaged in agriculture, he hoped to avoid the extreme form of democracy."

Harrington proposed to divide the country into 50 "tribes," based upon 10,000 parishes, to have a senate of 300 and an assembly of 1,050, whose members were to be paid. The senate was to draft the laws, the assembly to vote upon them: "a popular assembly without a senate cannot be wise," he wrote; "a senate without a popular assembly cannot be honest." He favored a number of ingenious devices, such as voting by ballot, indirect elections, a rotation of the members of the senate (one third to change every year) and a separation of the functions of debating and voting between the two houses. He approved of a state church, but thought that liberty of conscience should be upheld. In his view, liberty of conscience depended upon the existence of "civil liberty," which he thought would be guaranteed by his balance of power. "Without liberty of conscience," he observed, "civil liberty cannot be perfect; and without civil liberty, liberty of conscience cannot be perfect." He proposed that both the judiciary and the army should be elective; he wanted compulsory free schools; and he was uncomfortable about colonies. Though he was antidemocratic, basically his mind was intent on individual freedom.

The political theories of Harrington exerted a profound influence upon his time, upon thinkers as different as John Milton and Lilburne's successor as Leveler leader, John Wildman. One supposes that they did so because they grappled both with the question of security that had so much concerned Hobbes and the problem of liberty; while, on the one hand, they provided against the dangers of democracy, which worried men like Ireton and Milton, who sought an aristocratic republic—the aristocracy of virtue rather than of social position—they could be adapted to meet at least some of the democratic claims put forward by the Levelers. To Hobbes of course such fanciful theories had no appeal whatsoever; to his mind Harrington was offering not stability but anarchy, for Hobbes could see no virtue in "mixed monarchy" or the division of functions between different organs in the state. Other later criticisms of Harrington were to the effect that he laid too much importance upon the ownership of land, that other factors, such as tradition and the rule of law, are the proper foundations upon which government must be based; and that the division between the right to propose laws and vote upon them is not practical. His belief in the virtues of a republican system made him unpopular at the Restoration, when he was accused of conspiracy, was imprisoned, and died, apparently of melancholia, in 1677. Hobbes, though suspected (rightly) of being an atheist, kept out of trouble and lived to the age of ninety-one.

Both Hobbes and Harrington had to wrap their arguments in elusive language, and for this reason their contribution to political science—by Hobbes of a deductive and psychological character, by Harrington of an analytical and economic kind—have been misunderstood until fairly recent times. But their thought was more profound—although, to liberals, more dangerous—than the crop of often ill-digested ideas produced by John Lilburne and the Levelers, by Gerrard Winstanley and "the Diggers," who advocated a primitive form of agrarian communism, or by Walwyn and others who preached various sorts of millenarianism. In calling for manhood suffrage the Levelers were, it is true, the heralds of democracy; but modern Communist or authoritarian states, basking under such names as social democracy, owe more to Harrington's concept of the economic interpretation of history and Hobbes' plea for the all-powerful and unbreakable state than they do to Lilburne or Winstanley.

Although some of his admirers have made more far-reaching claims for him, John Milton, the great poet, was a muddled and eclectic political thinker. He had begun, like other Puritans of his generation, by trying to separate the material world from the world of the spirit, while at the same time insisting that the king must govern in accordance with God's Testaments and the natural law. The state, he thought, should confine itself to men's actions, leaving to the Church the duty of concerning itself with the mind of man. One of the "natural rights" of the people was freedom from tyranny. But Milton never was a democrat. He would have assented to the dilemma put by the Puritan writers, Henry Ainsworth and John Cotton: "If the people be governors, who shall be governed?" In the 1640s Milton was engaged in writing his divorce tracts and his appeal for the freedom of the press from prepublication censorship—the *Areopagitica*. When the second civil war broke out, after the failure of the parliamentarians to reach a political agreement with the king, Milton suffered some disillusionment and commented upon the loss of divine guidance and the need for the reestablishment of faith and peace. It was not until after the death of the king that Milton began his political pamphleteering.

Milton defended the execution of King Charles I in the light of the traditional Puritan faith: men were "free by nature" to depose a tyrant, since a magistrate ought to rule by the laws of justice. In his *Tenure of Kings and Magistrates* (1649) he spoke in terms of "right reason," "the very principles of nature," and "the unwritten law of common right" as justifications for the king's execution. In practical terms, he claimed that this was the deed of the people, acting through their parliament. The difficulty was of course that parliament had been "purged" and represented only a minority of the population. Milton was required in fact, as he knew, to defend not "the people" but the Independent party, led by Oliver Cromwell, who had pushed through the execution and set up the Commonwealth. Where now did the supreme authority lie and how could it be justified? "Milton," writes Arthur E. Barker, "sought with others for sovereignty; and his simultaneous assertions of the right and authority of the people, Parliament, the Rump, the Army, and finally of Cromwell, are less satisfactorily explained by the fallaciously simple charge of insincerity than by the manifest confusion of affairs and opinions which surrounded him and destroyed the party he defended."

The fact would appear to be that Milton soon realized that sovereignty could in no way be assigned to the people as a whole. The success of the pamphlet entitled *Eikon Basilike,* condemning the king's death as a martyr, which he was required to answer in his *Eikonklastes* caused him to doubt the virtue of the nation as such, for he spoke of the "besotted and degenerate baseness" of an "ungrateful generation." He came therefore to draw a distinction between "the people" and "the multitude." The tangle of arguments that he employed to justify first the Rump and then the Cromwellian Protectorate on the basis of "natural law," "the people's good," justice, and necessity, were properly condemned by Hobbes, who thought that the poverty of his arguments was not redeemed by his magnificent Latin periods. Broadly, it would appear that Milton was influenced by the point of view of the Fifth Monarchists who believed that the second coming of Christ was not far off and that in the meantime the nation ought to be governed by God's chosen people. The millenarianism which colored the writing of other Puritans like Winstanley and Lilburne was refined by Milton and influenced by his admiration for Oliver Cromwell, whom he served. In Cromwell himself there was a streak of this millenarianism: that was why, after the overthrow of the Rump, he first tried the experiment of government by a "nominated assembly" of Saints, chosen by the Independent churches. Milton, like Cromwell, had high hopes of this gathering of the Puritan elect. For he had now reached the conclusion that the will of the majority was as likely to be tyrannous as that of the king. He thought therefore that sovereignty should be conferred on the "natural aristocracy" of the nation.

This view was widely held in the later half of the seventeenth century and for a variety of reasons. Monarchy had failed; "the multitude" was untrustworthy; democracy would lead to anarchy and communism. Therefore an oligarchy or government by the few was the remaining solution. Harrington's senate (like the guardians of Plato) offered that kind of government, which was based in turn on the Venetian senate, then widely admired. Henry Vane the Younger advocated such a solution, as Algernon Sidney was to do later. And the republican critics of Cromwell, led by Arthur Haselrig and Thomas Scot, were also no democrats: they too would have been content to place both the executive and the legislative power in the hands of a chosen few, led by themselves, as it had been in the years immediately succeeding the execution of King Charles I. But, apart from historical parallels —as, for example, the Sanhedrin of the Old Testament—it was hard to find any convincing argument for the much boasted virtues of oligarchy. Sir Robert Filmer asked: "If the sounder, the better and the upright part have the power of the people, how shall we know or who shall judge who they be?" Hobbes was equally caustic about deciding who had the eminence in virtue above all others that entitled them to have sovereignty bestowed upon themselves.

Sir Robert Filmer's own solution of the problem of sovereignty was very different. For many years this seventeenth-century thinker was only remembered as a political writer whom John Locke had wasted time in criticizing, but his importance is now recognized as one of the ablest apologists for Stuart royalism. He was born in Kent in the same year as Hobbes, 1588; he was the eldest son of a family of eighteen. Educated at Trinity College, Cambridge, and Lincoln's Inn, he became a justice of the peace at Maidstone and lived the life of a country gentleman. He was a man of genuine culture. His best known work *Patriarcha, a Defence of the Natural Power of Kings Against the Unnatural Liberty of the People* was written in the years 1638–40 and was inspired possibly by the argument about the legality of ship money levied by Charles I; he was imprisoned for two years after the civil war began, wrote several other books, and died in 1653. His *Patriarcha* was not published until 1680.

The essence of his political philosophy was summed up in six propositions that he wrote just before he died:

1. That there is no form of government, but monarchy alone.
2. That there is no monarchy, but paternal.
3. That there is no paternal monarchy, but absolute, or arbitrary.
4. That there is no such thing as aristocracy or democracy.
5. That there is no such form of government as a tyranny.
6. That the people are not free by nature.

From these propositions it will be seen that he was critical of most other writers on politics in his time. He adopted his principle of sovereignty unaltered from Bodin, and he would have agreed with Hobbes that rebellion against a sovereign has no other result but a reversion to sheer anarchy. He would also have agreed with Hobbes that a state of nature is a state of war. But he disagreed with Hobbes in his view that men are naturally equal or with Milton that they are born free. On the other hand, he accepted Hobbes' view that "mixed monarchy" is an impossibility and is indeed another name for anarchy. On that basis he wrote a book attacking Philip Hunton's work on monarchy.

Filmer took the essence of his argument from a close study of the Holy Scriptures. What did they say and show? Did they not demonstrate that "mankind is naturally endowed and born with freedom from all subjection and at liberty to choose what form of government it please." On the contrary, what they said was precise and clear. Adam had been created by God as the sole sovereign of the world with power to rule over Eve and over their children. "The desire for liberty was the cause of the fall of Adam." The subordination of Adam's children was "the fountain of all regal authority" by the ordination of God Himself, and was handed down through Noah from generation to generation. The scriptures give no examples of the people choosing their king; and parliaments are quite a modern invention. Each political state therefore is simply a rightfully constituted human family and subjects are expected to obey their kings, as children obey their father and a wife obeys her husband. All law is the expression of one indivisible human will. The commands of a patriarchal monarch must never be resisted. Nor does the possession of landed property enter into the question of government, as Harrington argued; for all the land ultimately belongs to the king and he arranges the laws of property as he thinks fit.

Thus Filmer stuck fast by the lessons of history as expounded in the Holy Scriptures. There never had been a social contract, any more than there had been a state of nature or a state of war; for all men in the world cannot possibly at any time have agreed to establish a commonwealth. Nor did history show that kings became tyrants. "We have enjoyed a succession of kings from the Conquest now near about 600 years. . . . We reckon to the number of twenty-five of these Princes of the Norman race, and yet not one of these is taxed by our histories for tyrannical government." Monarchical government was therefore natural, native, and benevolent; it was neither voluntary nor contractual, but ordained. To destroy the monarchy, as the English parliamentarians did in 1649, was to destroy the state.

Peter Laslett has written that Filmer's "great advantage as a thinker was the ability to combine the subtleties of the doctrine of sovereignty with the crude assumptions of patriarchalism." This made him an extremely effective critic of the crudities on the other side as exemplified in the "state of nature," the "law of nature" and the principles of "fundamental law" with which the parliamentarians bolstered up their case for constitutional government or "mixed monarchy." Nor was the argument for patriarchy as absurd as it sounded at first, for in the seventeenth century most communities were patriarchies. The family was the root of society and most industry, as well as farming, was carried out on a family basis. The "master" ruled not merely over his wife and children, but over his servants and apprentices; what he said was right; what he ordered was the law. Marriage in the upper classes was institutional and rarely based on love; divorce was almost unobtainable; only a wealthy widow could hope to be a ruler—and she usually was not a widow for long. Thus the case for patriarchy in politics appealed very forcibly to the royalists and was much more to their taste than the dangerous ingenuities of the materialist Hobbes, whose arguments were logically as applicable to the Cromwellian Protectorate as to the Stuart monarchy. It was because Filmer's arguments were so persuasive and so appropriate to the society in which he lived that Locke and others considered it essential to refute them.

Some modern critics have at last done justice to Filmer. Of course the overwhelming importance that he attached to the Old Testament as a source of political precept and history is no longer accepted. On the other hand, historians, notably Sir Henry Maine, have agreed that mankind has proceeded from status to contract and not from contract to status. J. W. Allen showed that Filmer was an original and destructive critic, who really grappled with the problem of political obligation; he exposed both Hobbes's state of nature and Milton's rule of law. But his historical argument—that a "pure absolute monarchy" is the best government of all, has never been a tyranny, and therefore never likely to be a tyranny—flew in the face of common sense and common experience. Though ordered society and the human family may be the most natural institutions, government itself is artificial and may be changed, sometimes for the better. That at least is what the parliamentarians and most later generations have believed. On the whole, English history shows that they were right.

## VI

While these political theorists were engaged in discussing the fundamentals of sovereignty, England was actually experimenting with a variety of constitutions. After the Nominated Assembly of "Saints," an ill-considered and hastily constructed method of government, had failed, Oliver Cromwell was appointed Lord Protector of the Commonwealth of England, Scotland, and Ireland under a written constitution known as the "Instrument of Government." It is believed that this constitution was drawn up largely by Major-General John Lambert and derived some of its principles from the "Heads of the Proposals" (which he also helped to draft) and the Levelers' "Agreement of the People." The "Instrument" provided that the "supreme legislative authority" should reside in the people assembled in parliament and in one person, the Lord Protector, while the chief magistracy or executive should belong to the Lord Protector "assisted by a council." The Council of State was named in the "Instrument," but future councillors were to be chosen by the Protector out of a list of names submitted by parliament. Parliament, which had to meet at least once every three years, was elected by voters who possessed property valued at £200 in the counties; seats were redistributed, and the number of borough or urban constituencies reduced. If bills passed by parliament did not receive the consent of the Protector in twenty days, they automatically became law. The chief officers of state had to be chosen with the approval of parliament. The Council was required to advise the Protector on matters of war and peace and to choose his successor when he died. Liberty of worship was guaranteed, but not extended to "popery or prelacy."

If the Protector be considered to have taken the place of the monarch in the old constitution, the "Instrument of Government" was an excellent blueprint for "mixed monarchy." For legislation was left to parliament (ordinances passed when it was not sitting required its confirmation) and the Protector had no "negative voice," while in administration he was required to carry his Council with him and to receive the confirmation of his principal ministerial appointments from parliament. These were precisely the kind of constitutional checks that the Long Parliament had tried to impose on King Charles I at the time of the outbreak of the civil war, although, since the framers of the "Instrument" trusted Oliver Cromwell, they were less severe than the conditions offered to King Charles when the first civil war ended.

The terms of the "Instrument of Government" when examined lend full confirmation to the argument of such modern historians as Margaret Judson and J. W. Gough: practical politicians in the first half of the seventeenth century, from Pym onwards, did not regard the constitutional struggle that culminated in the execution of King Charles I as being a struggle over "sovereignty," but over the different organs in the state. The king's rights were limited; the people's rights were established by the "fundamental laws." Parker, Hobbes, and Filmer might have written in terms of an indivisible sovereignty and laughed at the notion of "mixed monarchy," but the majority of politicians did not see it that way, especially the students and admirers of the ancient common law of the land. Lambert himself had been educated in the Inns of Court, and so had been many of the country gentry in the Long Parliament. The common law, they believed, was intended, above all and from the earliest times, to protect both private property and the rights of the individual. The king himself was bound by the laws of his realm, which he promised in his coronation oath to uphold. The "Instrument of Government" was in tune with this line of thought and in fact provided not for a sovereign power centered in Cromwell but a balanced constitution or "mixed monarchy."

It is true that when the first Protectorate Parliament met a number of its members, led by Sir Arthur Haselrig, refused to accept the binding force of a constitution drawn up by the army and even claimed that government ought to be in the parliament alone. In the end, however, all but ninety of the members agreed to accept what Cromwell called the "four fundamentals" of this constitution—that the government should be carried on by a single person and parliament, that parliaments should not make themselves perpetual, that there should be "liberty of conscience," and that neither the Protector nor parliament should have exclusive control over the power of the sword. But if the extreme oligarchic republicans like Haselrig were still afraid that the Protector might acquire something approaching absolute powers, the leaders of the army were equally determined that parliament itself should not become absolute.

Because of these mutual fears the "Instrument" did not work; it was considered by many, especially by the lawyers, to violate the legal traditions of the country. The proposal was therefore put forward early in 1657 that Oliver Cromwell should be offered the Crown and thus become a constitutional monarch in name as well as in fact. This move, sponsored by lawyers and exroyalists, represented to some extent a conservative reaction against political experiments, for their scheme also included the revival of a Second

Chamber, the existence of which would necessarily reduce the powers of the Council of State and diminish the danger of the House of Commons becoming too powerful. One of the gaps that had been left in the "Instrument of Government" and was in fact exploited by the Protector and his Council was that parliament did not exercise full control over the choice of its own members. The returning officer had been required to obtain a written acknowledgement from the electors that the members whom they chose should not have authority to alter the government as settled in one single person and parliament, while clause XVII of the "Instrument," which said that members elected should be "persons of known integrity, fearing God, and of good conversation," had been used as an excuse to exclude a large number of members from the second Protectorate Parliament who were known to be hostile to the government.

Cromwell clearly recognized that these new proposals embodying the revival of kingship, which were known as "the Petition and Advice," were aimed at reducing both his own powers and those of his Council (which was to be renamed the Privy Council in accordance with monarchical practice) and that the title of king was being dangled in front of him as a mere "feather in his cap." Yet he appreciated the argument that monarchy accorded with the ancient laws and traditions of the land. In the end he refused the title, but instead was given the right to nominate his own successor as Protector. The extreme republicans disliked this constitution even more than the "Instrument." Sir Henry Vane argued that because it was a virtual revival of monarchy it would lead straight to the restoration of the Stuarts. Though its conservatism was agreeable to some, the excluded members, led by Haselrig, who were now allowed to flock back into the House of Commons, were determined to sabotage it, and by picking a quarrel with the new upper house rapidly succeeded in doing so.

The short period of five years during which Cromwell was the chief executive is often thought of by those who have not studied its history carefully as being a military dictatorship. Nothing is further from reality. In each of the three constitutional experiments made in the years 1653–58—the Nominated Assembly, the "Instrument of Government," and the "Petition and Advice,"—Cromwell attempted to be (and very largely was) a constitutional ruler, laying down the military in favor of the civil sword, and trying to clothe his government in written and constitutional forms. He failed to do so completely, partly because of the inflexible claims to full authority of the oligarchical republicans like Haselrig and Vane. After he died and they had helped to destroy the Protectorate of his son Richard, they found that their own absolutist rule through a single chamber consisting of members, many of whom had been elected some nineteen years earlier, was ineffective and unpopular. For eighteen months anarchy prevailed and the republican oligarchy disintegrated so that in the end there was no practical alternative but the unconditional restoration of the Stuarts.

## VII

"Though this is an Absolute Monarchy," declared one of the judges, Sir Orlando Bridgeman, at the trial of the regicides in 1660, "yet this is so far from infringing the people's rights, that the people, as to their properties, liberties, and lives, have as great a privilege as the king." In other words, the new King Charles II was still bound by the common law of the land and by what the disciples of Coke thought of as the fundamental laws and the ancient constitution. The king might be absolute, but he was not arbitrary. Moreover in practice many of the prerogative rights exercised by Queen Elizabeth I and the two early Stuarts, notably their prerogative courts, were now abolished, along with feudal tenures. And acts to which King Charles I gave his consent before he left London retained their validity. These acts included not only legislation to which King Charles I had agreed abolishing the prerogative courts and the criminal jurisdiction of the Privy Council but also those aimed at preventing the monarch from levying taxation in any form, direct or indirect—such as ship money and customs duties—without the consent of parliament. It was, however, still possible after 1660 for the King to suspend the enforcement of acts of parliament or to dispense with them in particular cases. Moreover the executive might order the arrest of individuals and send them to prison in outlying islands where a writ of habeas corpus could not touch them: such for example, was the fate of James Harrington and the former Leveler leader, John Wildman. In his Declaration of Breda, made before he returned home, King Charles II promised to leave to parliament the decision upon many of the tricky questions of policy that had to be settled after the Interregnum; thus he recognized that he was a parliamentary king. Indeed the great historian Gardiner spoke of the Restoration as being a restoration of parliament, even more than a restoration of the monarchy; and a more recent historian has described King Charles II as having been a constitutional king.

Nevertheless conflicts arose between king and parliament. At the beginning Charles II's first parliament, known as the "pensionary" or "long" parliament, which sat intermittently for eighteen years, was more royalist than the king. But before it was dissolved in 1679 two hundred new members had come in and it was even described by contemporaries as having become "republican" in outlook. Charles II's pro-French policy came under criticism from members, and royalist pamphleteers found it necessary to defend the king's prerogatives of making war and peace. The later parliaments of King Charles II's reign were strongly opposed to the king's determination to prevent the exclusion from the succession of his brother, James, Duke of York, who had declared himself openly to be a Roman Catholic; and the division between the exclusionists and the nonexclusionists gave rise to the nicknames of "Whigs" and "Tories," which were used to describe British parties for many generations to come. The exclusionists argued that the king in parliament could upset the succession if he chose to do so, but the Tories claimed that the monarchy was established by divine right and no law could alter what God had settled.

This breach between the king and the majority in the lower house engendered a new spate of argumentative political theories, such as those of Nevile and Sidney, Halifax and Locke.

Henry Nevile was a disciple of James Harrington and indeed is said to have had a share in the writing of *Oceana*. He was a member of the House of Commons during the Protectorate of Richard Cromwell and advocated the use of the ballot there. In 1680, the same year in which Filmer's *Patriarcha* was published, Nevile produced a book called *Plato Redivivus*. It was cast in the form of a conversation between a noble Venetian, who was supposed to be visiting England, and two Englishmen, and its intention was to apply Harringtonian principles to the political circumstances of the reign of King Charles II. Nevile thought, like Hobbes, that the state of nature was a state of war, but argued that in setting up a government the individual retained wide rights. The people, he wrote, have entire freedom in their lives, properties, and their persons, which can only be touched by existing laws or laws made in parliament, not by the will of the king. The sovereign power, Nevile asserted, resided in the three estates of King, Lords, and Commons, and he thought that in terms of property, the king's share of political authority had become excessive. In earlier times, when the king lived on his own revenues, he might have been entitled to exert wider powers, but now that feudalism had disappeared and the Commons owned an increasingly large share of the landed property of the country, the monarchical powers ought to be reduced: indeed, he said that they were "usurped." In accordance with Harrington's teaching, Nevile urged that the making of war and peace, the control of the army, the nomination of officers of state, and the control of the public revenue ought all to be taken away from the king and placed in the hands of councils, whose membership should be annually rotated. Parliaments should meet every year, peers should be chosen by parliament, not by the king, and the two houses of Parliament should approve of ministers, who ought to be appointed by a Privy Council, to which members of the governing councils did not belong. In other words, Nevile advocated an extremely complicated system of checks and balances, but left hardly any powers to the king.

Algernon Sidney's book on politics, though written at the same time as Nevile's, was not published until 1698. Sidney himself, who had been a critic both of Oliver Cromwell and King Charles II, was executed because of his alleged complicity in the so-called Rye House plot against Charles II. The manuscript of his book, which was called *Discourses Concerning Government,* was used in evidence against him at his trial on the ground that it was republican. The book was in fact an attempt to refute Filmer's *Patriarcha* on historical grounds. Sidney's argument was that instead of governments having been ordained by God to be patriarchal, they had always been based on the consent of peoples, whether they were Jews, Greeks, Romans, or Englishmen. People resolved freely to unite and obey laws; but liberty, he claimed, was one of men's natural rights and it was the people who set up kings. When kingship was established the ruler entered into a treaty promising to maintain the rights of his subjects. If kings became tyrants, then their subjects had the right to overthrow them for their failure to respect the people's liberties. No form of government was divine and no government could be entrusted with absolute power. Sidney thought a monarchy was dangerous and that democracy was impractical. He therefore believed aristocracy the best form of government, but recognized that it tended to become exclusive; and therefore he allowed for the existence of a monarch with very limited authority who should be advised by a council of the virtuous and administer laws promulgated by the people. Thus Sidney, like Nevile, favored a balanced government, but permitted only an extremely circumscribed authority to the monarchy.

There was a degree of practicality about the proposals both of Nevile and Sidney, though their arguments were carefully wrapped up in phraseology suited to the needs of their day. Neither of them accepted Hobbes' or

Filmer's views about absolute sovereignty. To them, indeed, these presented the supreme danger of threatening the liberties of the subject. James Tyrell, a lesser known political writer who attacked both Filmer and Hobbes, also urged that the laws of nature and right reason were unalterable and acted as a restraint upon a sovereign. George Savile, Marquis of Halifax, who served as a minister to King Charles II, was even more practical in his approach. Dr. G. P. Gooch has described him as the most subtle and original thinker of the Restoration era and as the first utilitarian. Like Harrington and Sidney, he was anxious to avoid the extremes of monarchy on the one side and of democracy on the other. In his *Character of a Trimmer,* written in 1684, but not published until later, he wrote as follows:

This innocent term Trimmer signifieth no more than this, that if men are together in a boat and one part of the company would weigh it down on one side, and another would make it lean as much to the contrary, it happeneth there is a third opinion of those who conceive it would do as well if the boat went even, without endangering the passengers.

Halifax had a great veneration for the rule of law, but thought that the laws could be and had been at times abused by the monarchy. He was opposed to absolute monarchy, "a thing that leaveth men no liberty," but considered that democracy or republicanism led to anarchy. As a statesman, he had actively opposed the Exclusion Bill, which would have destroyed hereditary monarchy; on the other hand, like Sidney and Nevile, he was in favor of limitations on the monarchy should a Roman Catholic like James II become king, limitations by statute that might have made it into a largely ceremonial institution. Monarchy should, in his opinion, be "a cherishing and protecting power," and the laws should provide alike against "devouring prerogatives and licentious freedom." Neither kings nor parliaments should be arbitrary. Both rights of property and the liberty of Christian worship (including liberty for both noncomformists and Roman Catholics) should be guaranteed. He sought "a wise mean" between two "barbarous extremes." Just as the secular government should "trim" between monarchy and parliamentarianism, so the Church should "trim" between Puritan fanaticism and popish "dreams."

Halifax therefore offered a guide to practical politics, based upon a golden mean. He was not concerned with appealing for the preservation of liberty either to a "state of nature" or to a "social contract." He was concerned, as his biographer pointed out, with "the broad facts of human nature and actual experience." He did not even advocate a right of rebellion against a government that exceeded its just bounds. He was content to observe that "the people can seldom agree to move together against a government but they can, to sit still and let it be undone." And that was more or less what happened in 1688. Halifax himself then stood on one side, and having been a minister of both the later Stuarts, found himself, agreeably enough, also a minister and adviser of Prince William of Orange, who overthrew his father-in-law, King James II, in the "glorious revolution." Thus Halifax demonstrated the advantages of the golden mean in his own political life.

## VIII

It used to be thought that John Locke was the later apologist for the revolution of 1688; but it is now known that his celebrated work *Treatises of Government* was largely written well before the revolution took place and only amended and brought up to date afterwards. Locke was born in 1632, the son of a Somerset attorney, who fought on the parliamentarian side during the civil wars. He was educated at Westminster school and Christ Church, Oxford, where a fellow political theorist, James Tyrell, described him as having been "one of the most learned and ingenious young men in the college he was of." He took a medical as well as an arts degree and in 1667 became personal physician to Lord Ashley, afterwards first Earl of Shaftesbury. Shaftesbury was the leader of the Whig or exclusionist party and Locke was more than his medical adviser. The two *Treatises of Government,* which established Locke's reputation as a political philosopher, were written about 1681 as a reply to Filmer's *Patriarcha* and were connected with Shaftesbury's movement to ensure a Protestant succession to the English throne.

Like Sidney and his friend Tyrell, Locke thought it first of all necessary to refute Filmer. He argued that because children are required to obey their parents, they are not necessarily born into political subjection. In any case, he argued that the Holy Scriptures did not prove conclusively that a father had absolute power over his children, and neither had a king such power over his subjects. Not only kings but all people on earth were descended from Adam; therefore the king's descent from Adam was no certain proof that God had endowed him with absolute patriarchal power. Having dealt with Filmer, Locke explained in his second treatise his own constructive ideas about government. It has sometimes been said that Locke was, above all, a utilitarian and the father of empiricism. Maurice Cranston, however, has argued that Locke was profoundly influenced by Descartes and that his rationalism should not be underestimated. His approach to political theory was certainly much closer to the abstract deductive reasoning of Hobbes than those writers who claimed to found their theories upon history or Scripture.

Locke, like Hobbes, conjures up an imaginary picture of a "state of nature," which really afforded a way of presenting the premises for his political arguments. Men, he wrote, are born in "the state of nature" with a title to perfect freedom. The natural liberty of man is to have only "the law of nature" for his rule. According to this law of nature, every man has a right to punish an offender because in "the state of nature" there is no common judge with authority. The law of nature teaches all mankind that "no one ought to harm another in his life, health, liberty, or possessions." But the power of punishment that every man has in "the state of nature" to enforce "the law of nature" may lead to disorder. Hence the need to set up a government. Thus Locke's "state of nature" does have, as has recently been pointed out, some striking similarities with Hobbes' "state of nature." But the basic difference between the two thinkers is that Locke aims to prove that before a government is set up men already possess a number of important natural rights; and when they establish a government they do not forfeit those rights.

Locke also agrees with Hobbes that men are naturally equal (though children are subjected to their parents until they reach a rational age). They are also, as Aristotle said, political animals. They find it necessary to conclude a social contract in order to establish a common judge and prevent the dangers of disorder. In the state of nature men were free, equal, and independent and could not be subjected to another without their own consents. In the original contract or compact, men agree together to surrender only so much of their natural liberty as they regard necessary for the assurance of an ordered society. Locke's social contract is a general agreement to set up a government, but to the establishment of government men give only a "tacit consent." Government is simply a fiduciary trust, and if the government betrays its trust, then another government can be put in its place.

The duty of a government is to protect life and property and to guarantee men's "natural rights." The right of property is natural. Men "mix their labour" into property and so make their possessions their own. (Hence, it has been argued that Locke was the originator of the "labor theory of value.") The liberty of men in society is "to be under no other legislative power but that established by consent in the commonwealth." And the freedom of men under government is to have a standing rule to live by, common to every man of that society and made by the legislative power erected in it. Since men cannot forfeit their power over their own lives, since they possess a property in their own persons, and since through their own labors, they acquire private property, these constitute fundamental rights which, by the "moral" or "natural" law, cannot be infringed by any sovereign. Thus Locke's sovereign, unlike Hobbes', Filmer's, or Parker's, is closely circumscribed. Men do not give up all their rights to it. The "law of nature" or the "law of reason" is supreme, and the essence of political liberty is that men are subjected only to known laws. If a ruler attempts to step outside those bounds, he may be overthrown. For the body politic is an artificial body, created for limited purposes. A government may be dissolved without society itself being dissolved. So Locke's argument leads clearly to a right of rebellion, and justified both Shaftesbury's revolutionary movement against King Charles II and later, as amended, justified the Glorious Revolution against King James II.

Locke's four important contributions to political theory were therefore that he maintained that the powers of a government are limited and not absolute (to employ later phraseology, that it was an association for particular purposes), that the "consent" of the people is the sole basis of a government's authority, that the government works within the framework of a rule of law, and finally that it is lawful to resist an unjust and unlawful sovereign. Hobbes of course would have argued—and no doubt Filmer too, and perhaps Henry Ireton—that the distinction that Locke drew between political "society" and political "government" was a false one; that his "natural rights" were purely imaginary, because it is government itself that secures the rights of property. What Locke was preaching therefore was not an ordered society, but anarchy. How could a sovereign function if he were limited by all sorts of natural and moral laws? How could he command obedience if what he said could be construed as being unlawful? How could a government be maintained if there was always a latent right of rebellion? Was this practical politics? Sir William Blackstone wrote later in his *Commentaries on the Law of England* (1769) that "Mr. Locke and other theoretical writers . . . thought that the people always retained a supreme power to remove or alter the legislative." He added, "However just this conclusion may be in theory, we cannot adopt it nor argue from it, under any dispensation of government actually existing." Moreover, it has been pointed out in modern times that Locke was no democrat: he, like Ireton, was the apologist for the property-owner; his was a "freeholder theory of the state." Like Harrington, he wanted to make the world safe from democracy. For the mass of the people were propertyless: they owned nothing but their labor. His system of "natural rights" might even be used to make them into slaves.

But there was a great deal of common sense in what Locke wrote, as there was too in Tyrell, in Sidney, in Nevile, and even in Clarendon—in fact, in all those writers who in the reign of King Charles II contended against the extreme claims of Hobbes or Filmer to an all-embracing and indivisible sovereignty. Locke insisted that the government was responsible to the community and not the community to the government; that it was the duty of the government to serve the public good. He believed too in religious toleration and the value of education. Whatever the logical and intellectual defects of his arguments were (and the present-day linguistic philosophers can make mincemeat of most seventeenth-century philosophers), however much he may have overstressed the virtues of private property, he is justly considered to have been a protagonist of the liberal approach in politics, and for those who believe in that liberal approach, he wielded his pen on the side of the angels.

## IX

To turn from theory to the actual political situation, King Charles II had triumphantly fought off the movement to exclude his Roman Catholic brother, James, from the succession to the throne—with the help of Tories who thought it was not lawful to resist an anointed king—and had also preserved intact his prerogative of making war and peace. He had yielded some concessions to the Whigs, bided his time, and then achieved his revenge. But when his brother James became king, he proved far less clever. King James II made no attempt to conceal his intention of obtaining equality of rights, if not predominance of power, for his fellow Roman Catholics, either by invoking the aid of loyal Anglicans or by appealing for the support of nonconformists. But the memories of the "Popish Plot" were too recent and those of the fires of Smithfield in the reign of Queen Mary I too intense for him to enlist these means; and when his friend, King Louis XIV of France, in October, 1685, revoked the Edict of Nantes and thereby began—or rather continued more fiercely—the persecution of his French Protestant subjects, the news aroused strong emotions on the other side of the Channel which militated against King James' aims. He was therefore obliged to make use of his prerogative powers—even though he must have remembered that the civil wars were partly fought against the excessive use of those very powers forty-five years earlier.

The unsuccessful rebellion of the Protestant Duke of Monmouth at the outset of the reign gave King James II an excuse to triple the size of his army and he proceeded to appoint to it Roman Catholic officers, although that was clearly contrary to the Test Acts against Catholics passed in his brother's reign to exclude Catholics from holding office under the Crown. Sir Edward Hales, colonel of a foot regiment, who was a member of the Roman Catholic Church, was given a "dispensation" by letters patent under the Great Seal to hold his commission. Hales's coachman then brought a collusive action against him at Rochester Assizes for breach of the Test Acts, and he was indicted and convicted. Hales produced the royal dispensation and appealed to the Court of King's Bench. Here the chief justice and ten out of the eleven other judges found that the royal dispensation was valid. The chief justice said that the kings of England were sovereign princes, that the laws of England were the king's laws, and that therefore it was "an inseparable prerogative in the kings of England to dispense with penal laws in particular cases, and upon particular necessary reasons."

The king now applied the dispensing power not merely to appoint Roman Catholic officers (Hales himself was appointed Master of the Ordnance) but to appoint Roman Catholics as county and local officials, to appoint Catholic members to the Privy Council, to appoint Catholic heads of university colleges, and even to allow converts to Catholicism to retain their benefices in the Church of England. On April 4, 1687, James II published a declaration of indulgence suspending all penal laws against Roman Catholics and nonconformists alike and permitting them freedom of public worship. A year later he published a second declaration of indulgence and ordered that it should be read in the churches. When the Archbishop of Canterbury and six bishops presented a petition to the king remonstrating against this order, the bishops were accused of seditious libel on the ground that they had allowed their petition to be published. "This is the standard of rebellion," the king exclaimed, an ironical remark in view of the fact that most of the bishops were staunch supporters of the doctrine of "nonresistance." The Court of King's Bench left the verdict to a jury and the bishops were acquitted. In the same month of June, 1688, when the trial took place, an heir was born to the king's Roman Catholic wife. The knowledge that a Roman Catholic dynasty might now be fastened upon the country was a signal for organized rebellion. On the very day that the bishops were acquitted an invitation, signed by seven leading men, both Whigs and Tories, was sent to the king's Dutch son-in-law, Prince William of Orange, asking him to bring an armed force to defend English liberties and to uphold the Protestant religion.

The revolution of 1688 was bloodless, and King James II fled to France. A "Convention" parliament, modeled upon that which had recalled King Charles II to the throne in 1660, met in January, 1689, and passed two famous resolutions. The first was that

> King James II, having endeavoured to subvert the constitution of his kingdom by breaking the original contract between king and people; and, by the advice of Jesuits and other wicked persons, having violated the fundamental laws; and having withdrawn himself out of the kingdom; has abdicated the Government and that the throne is thereby vacant.

The second was

> That it hath been found by experience to be inconsistent with the safety and welfare of this Protestant kingdom to be governed by a Popish Prince.

These were Whig resolutions. The Tories criticized the idea of an "original contract." The second Earl of Clarendon said "this breaking of the original contract is language that hath not long been used in this place; nor known in any of our law books or public records." Furthermore the Tories were not happy about the use of the word "abdication." Other solutions suggested were that James II should be restored upon conditions, that he should be considered insane and a regency established, or that the king having broken his "contract," a new king might be elected in his place. In the end the Whigs won the argument. James II was declared to have broken his contract, he was deemed to have abdicated or "deserted," and the throne was therefore said to be vacant. After this the Prince and Princess of Orange were declared to be King and Queen of England.

Parliament, however, took the opportunity to restrict the powers of the monarchy by a declaration of rights which later took the form of a bill. This bill declared that it was henceforward illegal for a king to suspend statute laws without the consent of parliament or to use the "dispensing power as it hath been used to late." It was subsequently made clear that the dispensing power could be used only if the right to do so was specifically given to the Crown in a statute. It was also declared illegal to erect a court of ecclesiastical commission (as King James II had done), to levy money without the consent of parliament for longer time or in other manner than it had been granted, or to raise a standing army in time of peace without the consent of parliament. Furthermore the bill laid down that the election of members of parliament was sacrosanct, that excessive bail should not be demanded by the courts, that jurors in trials for high treason should be freeholders, that it was the right of the subject to petition, and that parliaments should be summoned frequently.

The Bill of Rights has been described as the greatest English constitutional document since Magna Carta. Like Magna Carta it dealt with a number of specific grievances. It did not concern itself with broad theoretical principles of sovereignty and contained no reference to the social contract. It was buttressed, however, by a coronation oath to which the new rulers subscribed. They swore to observe the statutes of parliament and to uphold the Protestant Reformed religion. Finally, when toward the end of the new king's reign it became clear that neither King William III nor his sister Princess Anne, the heiress presumptive to the throne, would themselves have heirs, an Act of Settlement was passed in parliament and the opportunity was taken to impose further limitations on the powers of the monarch. Henceforward it was laid down that the holder of the Crown "should join in communion with the Church of England as by law established" (King William had been a Calvinist), that a monarch might not engage in war in defence of any dominions or territories that did not belong to the Crown of England without the consent of parliament, that the monarch might not leave the country without the consent of parliament (this clause was later repealed), and that only Englishmen, Scots, or Irish might become members of the Privy Council (King William had appointed Dutchmen to it). Two other important clauses were to the effect that "no person who has an office or place of profit under the king or receives a pension from the Crown" might become a member of the House of Commons. Though this clause was later modified, it laid down the principle that government officials might not be members of parliament; this principle was ultimately to serve as the basis for an independent British civil service. The other clauses were to the effect that judges should hold office during good behavior and only be removable on an address from both Houses of Parliament; this secured the independence of the judiciary.

Thus at the end of the seventeenth century very substantial limitations had been imposed on the rights and powers of the English monarchy. The position of parliament had been immeasurably strengthened. For it had finally been established that members of parliament had complete freedom of speech and could not be charged in the courts of law for anything they did or said within the walls of parliament. England now became involved in a long war against France that lasted intermittently until the end of the reign of Queen Anne: this meant that the executive was dependent upon parliament for taxation, and, quite apart from the Triennial Act, which was passed in 1694, and required a new parliament to be called every three years, the monarchy became increasingly dependent upon parliament for money. The Mutiny Act of 1689 which, like the Triennial Act, was passed to fulfil principles laid down in the Declaration of Rights, also tended to make regular parliaments necessary, since the act was valid only for a year or two, and without its renewal discipline could not be maintained in the army. But the act did not have the far-reaching constitutional importance that was once assigned to it by historians: in the first place, it only concerned soldiers within the kingdom in time of peace; the Crown could still by prerogative prescribe a military code for troops outside the kingdom in time of war. In fact the Crown had not abandoned its right to raise troops on its own authority and in the years 1698–1701 actually managed to carry on without a Mutiny Act at all.

King William III was no Whig and was anxious to cling to all his prerogatives. He retained the right to make peace and war, and was in full control of foreign policy. He retained the right (of which Nevile had disapproved) to nominate all high officers of state, regardless of their party affiliations, to dismiss judges (until the Act of Settlement), to veto bills, though he did not do so after 1696, and so on. He inclined to think of the extreme Whigs as republicans and the only reason why he was doubtful about the Tories was that he knew some of them still believed that they owed their allegiance not to him but to "the King over the water": but he liked their attitude to monarchy. The idea that a two-party system of parliamentary government was introduced into England in 1688 is no longer accepted by historians. For one thing, parties remained extemely fluid, kaleidoscopic, and for many years a group of King's Servants or Queen's Servants (usually about a hundred in number) acted as an influential force inside the House of Commons. Secondly, the modern cabinet system had not yet come into being and there was no such thing as joint ministerial responsibility to a dominant party in the Commons. The king could therefore dismiss a minister or ministers without breaking up his government or requiring a general election. Sir Lewis Namier tells us that when King George III introduced a personal form of government under his friend Lord Bute, he was merely exercising the same sort of constitutional rights as had been exercised by King William III.

## X

The doctrines of the political theorists seem to have had very little impact upon the constitutional settlement of 1689. It is true that the phrase "social contract" was employed by the Whigs and was introduced into the famous resolutions of that year. But the contract to which reference was made was not in fact the original social contract described either by Hobbes or Locke, who had both talked about men agreeing together that a government should be set up. What the Whigs of 1689 were thinking of was what Mr. Gough has called the "contract of government," that is to say a contract between the executive or "sovereign power" and "the people" whereby the king agreed that certain laws—natural, fundamental, or historic—should never be infringed by him. But the "original contract" was in any case recognized by most politicians to be a figment of the philosophic imagination, not a historic reality. If it had ever existed, why, it was asked, was it not referred to in Magna Carta or in the Treason Statute of 1352? A study of early history would have shown that when appeals were made to restrain the authority of the Crown on constitutional grounds they were made to the kings' coronation oaths or, in other words, to their "contracts of government."

Even the doctrine of John Locke that government was, or must be, based on the consent of the people was hard to relate to the actual political situation. For where were "the people" who gave their consent? In some constituencies known as "boroughs," the franchises had been tampered with again and again, by Cromwell, by Charles II, and by James II and were often in the hands of small oligarchies. The county franchise was, it is true, based still on the forty-shilling freeholders, but no attempt had been made since the Interregnum to revise the representation of the counties so that there should be some fair relationship between the number of members of the House of Commons and the population in the constituencies. Since the Levelers disappeared about 1659, when the last Leveler leader accepted the theories of James Harrington, there had been no cogent pleas for a democratic system. In theory at least neither Catholics nor nonconformists had the right to take part in government. Thus to say that the new revolutionary settlement was founded on the consent of the people as a whole was a mockery. It was left to Edmund Burke years later to invent an argument about virtual representation.

Another doctrine to which some lip service was paid at the Revolution and which had been beloved by parliamentarians in the first half of the seventeenth century lost ground by the end of it—namely the doctrine that the government was bound by fundamental laws. The phrase again was used in the resolutions of 1689. But the fundamental law, Lord Halifax pointed out, gave no flexibility to government and was "in general an unintelligible notion." "To deny a subsequent parliament the right of repealing any law," he wrote, "doth by consequence deny the preceding parliament the right of making it." It was now recognized that the king in parliament was supreme, for the king could neither make laws nor impose taxes nor in fact manage without parliament. To deprive parliament, whether it was regarded as a supreme court or a supreme legislature, of the power to make decisions or alter existing laws because it was bound by some obscure ancient fundamental laws stretching back to time immemorial offended the common sense both of many English lawyers and all practical politicians: it was an insult to the wisdom of parliament.

In fact the British constitutional outlook was essentially eclectic. It is noticeable in studying the history of Britain in the seventeenth century that whereas such written constitutions as the Levelers' "Agreement of the People," Ireton's "Heads of the Proposals," or Lambert's "Instrument of Government" were never generally acceptable to the ruling powers nor had worked in practice, documents like the Petition of Right, the Grand Remonstrance of 1641, the Bill of Rights, and the Act of Settlement, which outlined specific and actual grievances against the Crown were extremely effective. In fact, here lies the basic difference between the British and the later French and American approaches to constitutional problems. Harrington, Locke, and Sidney had more influence upon the shaping of the constitution of the United States of America than they had on the revolutionary settlement in the seventeenth century.

Only in one respect may it be plausibly argued that John Locke and his fellow political theorists had any considerable impact on the course of contemporary history, and that was in advocating a right of rebellion. As we have seen, at the beginning of the century and long before, the right of rebellion was anathema to the majority of political writers. There were only a few exceptions among Jesuit and Presbyterian extremists who were prepared to defend political assassination for religious reasons. But most Puritans as well as Royalists had been inclined to say that authority was divine and so too was obedience: even an evil ruler must be obeyed until better days came and God intervened to punish him. The right of rebellion, Hobbes and Filmer insisted, meant the dissolution of the state, the end of government, and the coming of anarchy. But Locke, whose father had fought in the civil wars, as had the fathers and brothers of most of the later Whig writers, had understood that a time might come when an autocratic or tyrannical government could no longer be tolerated. They had seen their fellow Protestants overwhelmed in Germany and in France; but they had also seen the Dutch republicans win their freedom from the tyranny of Spain by fighting; they remembered too how the Scots had defended their religion in the two Bishops' Wars. Thus again, to some extent, the right of rebellion was a common-sense doctrine, and no doubt it was practice as much as theory that lent conviction to it. On the whole, the impartial historian may feel that the theorists had only a very limited influence on the development of the stirring events of the seventeenth century.

It used to be said that the history of England in the seventeenth century was that of a struggle between king and parliament for "sovereignty." Few historians today would regard that as other than an oversimplification. What emerged at the end of the century was roughly what the theorists called "a mixed monarchy." The king still possessed prerogatives that he might exercise, including the right to take action to defend the state in a crisis. Such discretionary powers must exist—and have always existed—in every executive. On the other hand, the legislative supremacy of parliament—its "sovereignty," if one cares to use that word—had been achieved, although the executive still retained practical means (as it does yet in Britain today) of influencing the structure of parliament. Finally, and perhaps most important of all, the independence of the judiciary was affirmed by the Act of Settlement; this, in terms of later history, was the greatest safeguard established during the century for the liberty of the individual citizen. But the idea of the sovereign state, as conceived by Bodin, Parker, Hobbes, or Filmer, with complete and inalienable powers resting in the hands of either a monarchy or an aristocracy, was not achieved then and never has been in the history of Britain. Men have talked about the sovereignty of parliament; yet some discretionary powers always rest with the executive. Men have talked too about the sovereignty of the people, but that has never been a convincing constitutional conception, even when decorated by the ingenuities of a Rousseau or a Hegel. In Britain the idea that parliamentary government is in essence an association for very wide purposes has been more generally accepted in our own times than the idea that it is an organ of "sovereignty" in Hobbes' sense, since it is clear that other associations, so long as they can maintain their influence, whether they be trade unions, employers' federations, churches, or a free press, or pressure groups of one kind or another, will always be a limiting factor on the supremacy of parliaments. And in the United States of America and in other English-speaking nations federal systems have been designed precisely with the purpose of militating against autocratic sovereignty. In the seventeenth century it was the kings who learned that they could not exercise a full political supremacy, but that they must acquiesce in parliamentary controls and recognize a rule of law. And that in itself was a valuable contribution in the evolution of modern constitutional ideas.

## *FOR ADDITIONAL READING*

J. W. Allen. *A History of Political Thought in the Sixteenth Century*. London, 1928.

———. *English Political Thought, 1603–1660*. London, 1938.

M. Ashley. *John Wildman: Plotter and Postmaster*. London, 1949.

A. Barker. *Milton and the Puritan Dilemma*. Toronto, 1942.

G. N. Clark. *The Later Stuarts*. Oxford, 1955.

M. Cranston. *John Locke*. New York, 1957.

G. Davies. *The Early Stuarts, 1603–1660*. Oxford, 1959.

R. Filmer. *Patriarcha*. Ed. by P. Laslett. Oxford, 1949.

H. C. Foxcroft. *A Character of the Trimmer*. Cambridge, 1946.

J. Frank. *The Levellers*. Cambridge, Mass., 1955.

S. R. Gardiner. *The Constitutional Documents of the Puritan Revolution, 1625–1660*. Oxford, 1906.

G. P. Gooch. *Political Thought in England from Bacon to Halifax*. London, 1937.

G. P. Gooch and H. Laski. *English Democratic Ideas in the Seventeenth Century*. Cambridge, 1927.

J. W. Gough. *The Social Contract*. Oxford, 1936.

———. *Fundamental Law in English Constitutional History*. Oxford, 1955.

T. Hobbes. *Leviathan*. Ed. by M. Oakeshott. Oxford, 1946.

W. S. Holdsworth. *The History of English Law*. London, 1938.

W. K. Jordan. *Men of Substance*. Chicago, 1942.

B. Kemp. *King and Commons, 1660–1832*. New York, 1957.

J. Locke. *The Second Treatise of Civil Government*. Ed. by J. W. Gough, Oxford, 1946.

J. Locke. *Two Treatises of Government.* Ed. by P. Laslett. Cambridge, 1960.

C. H. McIlwain, ed. *The Political Works of James I.* Cambridge, Mass., 1918.

W. M. Mitchell. *The Rise of the Revolutionary Party in the English House of Commons, 1603–1629.* New York, 1957.

D. Ogg. *England in the Reign of Charles II.* Oxford, 1956.

———. *England in the Reigns of James II and William III.* Oxford, 1955.

J. G. A. Pocock. *The Ancient Constitution and the Feudal Law.* Cambridge, 1957.

F. Pollock. *An Introduction to the History of the Science of Politics.* London, 1920.

C. Robertson. *Selected Statutes, Cases, and Documents to Illustrate English Constitutional History, 1660–1832.* London, 1949.

W. Schenk. *The Concern for Social Justice in the Puritan Revolution.* London and New York, 1948.

H. F. R. Smith. *Harrington and his Oceana.* Cambridge, 1914.

J. R. Tanner. *English Constitutional Conflicts in the Seventeenth Century.* Cambridge, 1928.

H. Warrender. *The Political Philosophy of Hobbes.* Oxford, 1957.

A. S. P. Woodhouse. *Puritanism and Liberty.* London, 1938.

F. D. Wormuth. *The Royal Prerogative, 1603–1649.* Ithaca, 1939.

P. Zagorin. *A History of Political Thought in the English Revolution.* London, 1954.

# XIII

# THE DEVELOPMENT OF MODERN SCIENCE

*Ernest Nagel*

The intellectual revolution produced by the rise of modern science during the sixteenth and seventeenth centuries consisted not only in altering radically men's conceptions of the universe and their place in it. It also involved the erection of a fresh ideal of knowledge and ultimately the construction of new instruments, both physical and intellectual, for transforming the physical and social environment. The rise of modern science was no less potent as an agent helping to discredit medieval philosophy than was the commercial civilization that replaced the medieval agricultural economy.

We will appreciate the revolutionary significance of modern science more fully, however, if we first note some of the distinctive assumptions of medieval science—assumptions against which an experimentally based mathematical science had to contend. Medieval science was in the main ancillary to a theology that placed greater value on the salvation of man's soul than on man's ability to discover the physical conditions for the order of events. The primary concern of medieval thinkers was to understand the order of existence as illustrating the divine goodness and to see how that order ministered to man's spiritual needs. On the other hand, how man's salvation was to be achieved and in what way the facts of the universe testified to the possibility of that salvation were questions regarded as definitely settled by a fixed and complete doctrine.

The fundamental premises of this doctrine were believed to be supplied either by divine revelation or by a number of selected authorities—the Bible and its interpretation by the Church Fathers, and eventually also Aristotle, after his writings were absorbed into the fabric of Christian thought. The physical and cosmological ideas of the medievals thus consisted of a fusion of Christian theology and Greek science. Although the medievals frequently

This chapter appeared in previous editions of *Chapters in Western Civilization.*

exhibited a genuine interest in the observable facts of nature, such facts served them in the main as illustrations and confirmations of principles held antecedently on other grounds. The materials of observation were therefore not used systematically for making new discoveries or for putting old beliefs to a crucial test; and in consequence the modern conception of experimental inquiry was almost entirely lacking.

The intellectual method of the medievals was controlled by a characteristic way of analyzing the objects of their experience. If we should ask a contemporary student trained in modern science what it is that makes a given object, a hen's egg for example, behave the way it does, and why it exhibits certain traits, his answer would undoubtedly be formulated in terms of measurable physical and chemical interactions. A medieval scientist, on the other hand, would reply differently. He would in all likelihood invoke certain "powers" resident in the object, such as the power of developing into a chick; and these powers would be conceived as consequences of the inherent "nature" or "form" of the object. Just as all the properties of a circle follow from its definition, or "essence," so all the distinctive traits of things were regarded as the necessary implications of the "forms" that permeate their matter. This distinction between the "form" and "matter" of things played a central role in medieval thought.

Every object in nature was interpreted as having a "matter" and a "form." Matter, considered by itself, was taken to be something incomplete and intellectually opaque, and only the "forms" of things were regarded as knowable and as capable of being formulated in language. Knowing adequately what a thing is, meant knowing what its distinctive "form" is; and knowing what the "form" of a thing is, meant knowing what are the natural realizations of that thing's inherent powers. Thus, to know what a hen's egg is, was equivalent to knowing its natural eventuation or proper end. Accordingly, medieval science was concerned with ascertaining the objectives toward which things could be viewed as striving, and not with discovering the physical conditions or causes of their behavior. "Final causes," "ends," or "purposes," were the primary principles of its explanations; and an approach to the study of nature which substituted mathematical principles of invariable sequence for final causes was thus at intellectual antipodes to the science of the Middle Ages.

This fundamental distinction between the "matter" and the "form" of things was coupled with a moral interpretation of the universe derived in part from neo-Platonic sources. According to this interpretation, the perfection of a thing consists in its being intelligible and luminous to the intellect, so that the rank of an object in the scale of perfection depends on the thoroughness with which its "matter" is permeated by intelligible "form." This interpretation was in turn based on the view that the world was created by a perfect God as a manifestation of His goodness. However, all created things possess some "matter" which is recalcitrant to the entrance of intelligible "form," and in general a thing is less perfect according as it is more removed from the divine perfection.

The world was therefore conceived as a hierarchical order of beings differing radically in their degree of perfection, each endowed with a "form" or "essence" determining its place in the hierarchical series. One such series is illustrated by the sequence: God, the angels, man, animals, plants, minerals; and analogous hierarchical orders were believed to be exhibited in the rankings of ecclesiastical, political, and economic dignitaries. It was consistent with these assumptions to believe that things were not to be analyzed in quantitative terms, since the reasons for the behavior of things were to be sought in the kind and the perfection of the "form" they embodied and not in their material organization. Accordingly, the heavens and the earth were regarded as qualitatively different and as made of a different stuff. Celestial bodies, it was supposed, are incorruptible and their motions are inherently circular and uniform, while terrestrial objects are subject to change and their natural motions are rectilinear and variable. In brief, the conception of a universal law to which both celestial and terrestrial bodies conform was foreign to the medieval outlook.

If we bear these cosmological assumptions in mind, it will not be surprising to find that the intellectual tool of medieval science was primarily the logic of hierarchical classification. For, in the light of these assumptions, the central problem of inquiry was to determine for a given object what essential "form" it possessed and under what type or genus of being that "form" was to be subsumed. Thus, one systematic classification of the various types of being was formulated with the help of a simple logical device. The analysis began with Substance, the most inclusive type of being. It then distinguished two kinds of substances, the Corporeal (that is, those which have a body) and the Incorporeal. It next divides bodies into two distinctive kinds, the Animate (or Living things) and the Inanimate. Living things were then further distinguished into those which were Sensitive (the Animals) and the Insensitive. Animals were next divided into those which were Rational (Man) and those which were Irrational. And finally men were distinguished by the individual traits of Socrates, Plato, and so on.

The following arrangement of these distinctions, known as the Tree of Porphyry, makes evident at once the relations of various types of being. It shows, for example, that Socrates is a man, that man is a rational animal, that an animal is a sensitive living thing, and that a living thing is a corporeal substance.

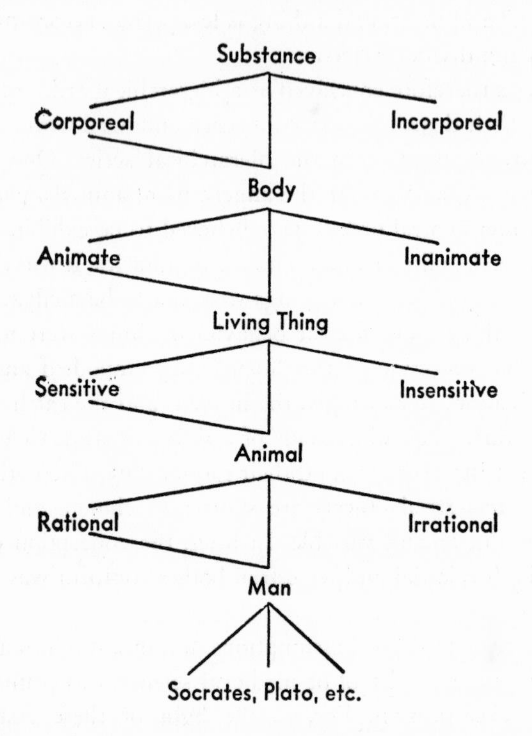


Let us consider Porphyry's Tree a bit further. It shows that man is a rational animal, and that Socrates is a man. What then is Socrates? The answer is obvious, and is perhaps even more obvious if we arrange these propositions in the following order:

Man is a rational animal.
Socrates is a man.

For we can directly conclude from them the consequence:

Socrates is a rational animal.

This analysis illustrates the logical structure known as the syllogism. The syllogism then is a series of three propositions, two of which are the premises, the third being the conclusion necessarily implied by them. It is evident that if the premises of a syllogism are once granted, the conclusion can be obtained logically (or dialectically) from them, without making any use of experiment or observation. Consequently, if we recall that for the medieval thinkers the ultimate premises of their beliefs were accepted as final and complete, the central task of their science could only be that of making explicit by syllogistic reasoning the various consequences entailed by them.

Their writings were in fact replete with syllogistic deductions, which effected a remarkably impressive unification of their beliefs. They succeeded in exhibiting the implied meanings of their convictions, they showed upon what authoritative premises various individual items of belief depended, and by ingenious interpretations and distinctions they brought order and a large measure of consistency into their authorities. Nevertheless, the logical integrations which they effected were in the end primarily systems of classification, in which various distinctions were subsumed under appropriate headings. Their procedure, while irreproachable as formal logic, tended to assume that the causes of things could be ascertained by logical analysis alone. And in this procedure the quantitative determination of the interactions of things was largely irrelevant. It is with the victorious emergence of just such a quantitative, relational approach to the study of nature that we shall be concerned in what follows.

The rise of an experimentally based mathematical science of nature helped to destroy the medieval cultural pattern. But it also became a factor of paramount importance in the subsequent institutional reorganization of Europe. In the first place, once the ancient certainties had been discredited, an authoritative method of inquiry was needed with which to discover as well as defend against traditional critics the mathematical interpretation of nature. The new science, fortified by its brilliant successes in physics and astronomy, gradually perfected its principles of logic; and the methods of the mathematical sciences of nature came to be looked upon as norms for conducting inquiries into all matters pertaining to politics, economics, and morals. In this way the authority over men's beliefs concerning nature and society, heretofore exercised by institutionalized religion, was gradually transferred to the methods of the new sciences.

In the second place, while the disinterested pursuit of truth for its own sake was a highly prized way of life, the new experimentally controlled study of nature had practical fruits as well. Men learned how to do familiar things more efficiently than before and how to achieve a control over natural forces where previously blind routine and chance had been the order of the day.

New inventions and new technologies were the most obvious and easily understood benefits of the developing sciences; and navigation, mining, medicine, and the military and industrial arts were gradually transformed. Thus, the new sciences provided the knowledge required for organizing an expanding economy, while at the same time the needs of society served as stimuli for scientific research. In this way modern science became an institution integral to modern society: it became an honored profession, sustained and encouraged by men and communities who would have at best exhibited only a mild interest in the more speculative aspects of disinterested research. In a word, therefore, many of the characteristic features of our own society are the products of the modes of thinking instituted during the sixteenth and seventeenth centuries.

The labors of the pioneers of modern science had as their direct fruits the establishment of mathematics, astronomy, physics, chemistry, and biology, in something like their present form. The achievements of these men did not always receive immediate public recognition and had little effect upon the minds of the great mass of their contemporaries. In a limited space it would not be possible to do more than catalogue the principal contributions to knowledge made in this period. Nevertheless, the student should bear in mind the tremendous expansion of the intellectual and physical horizon which was produced by an impressive series of great and minor students of nature. Thus, the circulation of the blood was discovered by William Harvey (1578–1657); William Gilbert (1540–1603) conducted researches in magnetism; experiments in chemistry and gaseous pressures were made by Robert Boyle (1627–91) and others; Marcello Malpighi (1628–94) and Antony Leeuwenhoek (1632–1723) made microscopic analyses of living organisms and so opened up new fields of research; and Thomas Sydenham (1624–89) reconstructed medical theory and practice. Some of these achievements were spectacular and impressed their contemporaries as having revolutionary significance. Others had to pass through a period of incubation and development before their full import was perceived. In any event, however, the sheer mass of new information which became accessible, the bold challenges which were repeatedly given to views sanctified by tradition, acted as an exciting stimulus for the radical revaluation of men's attitudes toward nature and society.

In what follows we shall concentrate exclusively upon the dramatic development of modern astronomy and mechanics. We shall restrict ourselves to understanding the innovations of Copernicus, Kepler, Galileo, and Newton, and their significance in changing the medieval world-outlook. We shall attempt to understand the essential features of the method of mathematical natural science. And finally, we shall indicate what promise the new science held for its contemporaries, and what steps were taken to realize it by institutionalizing scientific research.

## I

The causes which produced the rise of modern science are complex, and cannot here be discussed in detail. It will be well to dismiss at once two rather widely held misconceptions concerning its origins. Medieval science was overthrown, it is sometimes stated, when Galileo simultaneously dropped a one-pound and a hundred-pound cannon ball from the top of the Tower of Pisa. For in showing that the balls did not acquire speeds proportional to their weights, but struck the ground together, he refuted the Aristotelian scholastics and inaugurated experimental science. Again, it is often held that it was the enthusiasm for classical learning by the literary humanists of the Renaissance which shook off the dead hand of uncritical tradition and encouraged the independent exploration of nature.

The actual history, however, is quite different. There is in fact no evidence that Galileo ever performed the experiment so frequently attributed to him; and, as we shall see, the conception of an experimentally controlled inquiry into nature was a slow growth, not a bolt out of the blue, which owed much to ancient and medieval scholars. Furthermore, literary humanists such as Petrarch had only disdain for the patient experimentation and the use of quantitative methods which characterize modern physics. Indeed, the fashion of holding in contempt the study of nature, which the humanists fostered, even when they ridiculed the aridity of scholastic philosophy, is perhaps one reason why the high tide of scientific discovery did not set in until the seventeenth century. The following points concerning the origins of modern science should be noted.

A fairly continuous tradition of an experimentally controlled mathematical science of nature can be traced from ancient times up to the sixteenth century, a tradition with firm roots in the medieval culture of the twelfth, thirteenth, and fourteenth centuries. This tradition was conveyed to Western Europe by Mohammedan scholars, after a high type of civilization was established in Spain by the Moors in the tenth century. The Arabic followers of Mohammed, though no profound scientific innovators, had the gift of absorbing and applying the intellectual achievements of the Greek and Hindu cultures with which they came into contact; and they knew the great mathematical, physical, and biological treatises of these peoples in Arabic version.

These writings were gradually translated into Latin, and by the end of the twelfth century Christian Europe had available in this form the medical and anatomical works of Hippocrates and Galen, Euclid's *Elements of Geometry,* Ptolemy's *Almagest* (the great astronomical classic of antiquity), and various Hindu writings on algebra. Under the inspiration of Graeco-Arabic conceptions, medical schools were established in southern Italy in that century; and the next century saw the founding of similarly inspired schools in other parts of Europe—at Oxford, Paris, Padua, and elsewhere—which specialized in the study of mathematical physics and medicine.

It is true that many of the investigators at these places, such as Roger Bacon (1214-94), had no clear conceptions concerning experimental-mathematical methods; and their physics was often only a mixture of the number-mysticism they acquired from Neoplatonism and an uncritical acceptance of unverified common beliefs. Nevertheless, they were often remarkable prophets of the coming experimental sciences, and they encouraged the view that mathematics is the language in which the book of nature is written. By the end of the fifteenth century, however, a notable series of students at various centers of learning—Robert Grosseteste, William Occam, John Buridan, Nicolas Oresme, Nicolas Cusanus, and many others—had anticipated ideas in mathematics, astronomy, mechanics, and optics which were not successfully exploited until one or two hundred years later.

When Galileo's scientific career began, the revival of Alexandrian mathematical science was in full swing; the writings of Archimedes, Apollonius, and other Alexandrian Greeks inspired a critical reconsideration and reconstruction of Aristotelian physics, and a number of scientists in Italy were busy with the theory of projectiles and the principles of dynamics.

The urban civilization which began to develop by the twelfth century provided incentives for travel and exploration, as well as the wealth and leisure for the theoretical study of nature. Contact with new peoples and new continents inevitably loosened the binding force of medieval ideas. And however devoutly the traders and merchants might profess their Christianity, the restricting habits engendered by parochial religious practices could not long withstand the requirements of success in commerce.

Moreover, the expanding commercial economy made increasingly large demands upon crafts and techniques, and offered substantial rewards for practical innovations. Thus, commerce required better methods of navigation, and successful navigation depended on improved astronomical knowledge; the latter in turn required more careful observations of the celestial bodies and more reliable tables of stellar positions. Again, new instruments of warfare set new problems in military fortifications and gunnery—problems which could ultimately be solved only by a comprehensive theory of mechanics. Moreover, men and communities, enriched by the expanding economy, patronized or encouraged the creation of paintings, sculptures, works of architecture and of civil engineering; and the force of competition led practitioners of these various arts to improve their skills by a study of human anatomy, perspective, and mechanics. Nor must we overlook the stimuli to anatomical and physiological research when an increasing population made the problems of health and medicine loom larger than ever before.

The study of nature was therefore almost from the outset more than a purely theoretical enterprise. And it is noteworthy that efforts to establish a science of dynamics, which in the fourteenth and fifteenth centuries had received little recognition from the general community and which lapsed with the death of talented amateurs, by the end of the sixteenth and seventeenth centuries were publicly encouraged because of the economic, military, medical, and artistic needs of society.

The social demands upon the natural sciences placed a premium upon results which were practically applicable and which provided reliable control over the physical environment. Vague speculations and unverified conclusions could not resolve pressing technological issues; and it is not unlikely, therefore, that a partial reason why modern science became increasingly quantitative and precise is that it was expected to satisfy concrete, practical needs. A recent historian of the period, G. N. Clark, has stated his findings as follows:

Experimentation was taken over into science . . . not once and for all but by long-continued contact, from art, from mining, and from the skilled handicrafts in general. . . . Science took over from economic production more than its procedure; it caught also something of its spirit or temper. The scientists and the men of thought generally, who had been prone to elaboration for its own sake, to impressive mystifications, became, as we say, business-like. In their language and habits of thought they became precise, economical of effort. They fitted their means to their ends, and always kept a purpose in sight. In all this they resembled the men who were making or selling things for money; and this was due, at least partly, to the influence of such men. . . . If the search for perpetual motion and the philosopher's stone . . . was relinquished by the end of Newton's time for something better, it was partly due to the positive practical spirit of the business man. Indeed, this spirit even helped science to hold fast that part of its method which seems at first sight most high and abstract—the mathematical part. It has long been recognized that the introduction of rational accounting in business in the later Middle Ages was another result of the habit of quantitative thinking which was married to experimentation in the work of Galileo and Newton. Science was applied in business; we must not forget that business was applied in science.

We must not, however, confuse the satisfactory solution of specific technological problems with the creation of a theoretical science of nature, even if the former may set the stage for the latter. The invention of new machines and the resolution of specific problems of practical life often occur without recognition of the general principles involved in either. Certainly for the men of the seventeenth century the construction of a genuine science of nature required the formulation of universal and systematically interconnected laws. Thus, for example, simply knowing how to bisect a given line with compass and ruler does not make a man a geometer. He is a geometer only when he recognizes the principles which control his construction and sees why, in terms of them, the two segments he obtains must be equal. Accordingly, the artisans and craftsmen of the sixteenth and seventeenth centuries were not theoretical physicists, however much their problems and techniques may have contributed toward Galileo's theoretical discussions. We must constantly bear in mind that the great achievement of these centuries was the discovery of fundamental modes of analysis and general principles of natural order, in terms of which the solutions to different special problems were systematically connected.

Nor must we make the mistake of supposing that the practical motive for scientific research is the exclusive or even the primary one. We have already noted the sustaining example of the Graeco-Alexandrian tradition of science as a factor in the emergence of a mathematical science of nature. We must also note that the medieval conception of a divinely ordered universe, and the medieval aspiration to know God, were no less powerful influences to that end. There can in fact be no question that the disinterested desire to know, the desire to find an intelligible order in nature simply for the delight of knowing it, was a motive in the lives of the investigators in this as in other periods. In this respect the pursuit of theoretical knowledge yields values akin to the values of religion and art. And we must not overlook the fact that the Aristotelian conception of the blessed life as the contemplation of nature's unalterable laws was an essential ingredient in the tradition absorbed by such men as Copernicus, Kepler, Galileo, Descartes, and Newton. The search for a fixed and necessary order of nature, though formulated with quantitative precision and elaborated with the techniques of mathematics, was understood by them as a search for the divine plan of the world, and in some cases at least the contemplation of that order was taken to be the contemplation of God Himself.

## II

The Ptolemaic theory of the heavens was almost universally accepted for fourteen centuries. Copernicus's proposal in 1543 to abandon it in favor of an alternative theory, which seemed to run counter both to common sense and Scripture, was a revolutionary event. However, for about seventy years after the publication of his *De Revolutionibus Orbium Caelestium* (*Concerning the Revolutions of the Celestial Spheres*), the heliocentric interpretation of celestial motions met with no significant opposition from the Church; and only a few mathematicians and philosophers of the day understood its far-reaching significance.

A proper appreciation of Copernicus's scientific merits requires some familiarity with the geocentric theory of Ptolemy. We shall therefore first outline the essentials of the latter, and so place ourselves in the position to grasp the fundamentals of the mathematical interpretation of nature. We must begin by asking just what the problem of the astronomer is. Let us recall some familiar facts, most of which were well known to the ancient Chaldeans and Babylonians. The various bodies visible in the sky, such as the sun and the stars, seem to revolve regularly around the earth, and to rise in the east and set in the west. However, this gross regularity is complicated by a number of apparently irregular special motions. In the first place, the sun rises later and sets earlier in winter than in summer, and appears higher and farther north in the skies during the latter season than it does in the former. Also, the moon is sometimes invisible even in fair weather; it exhibits characteristic phases; and it rises at different hours of the day as it waxes and wanes. In the second place, the stars seem to be embedded in a vast sphere which, in addition to its daily rotation, completes another rotation once a year; for as the seasons change different stars are displayed at the same hour of the night. And in the third place, some of the stars, called the planets, seem to wander in the firmament and to occupy different positions with respect to the other stars which seem to be relatively fixed. Moreover, the planetary motions have a curious aspect. They appear to move rapidly forward at some times, at other times to be motionless, at still other times to have a retrograde motion, and finally to move forward again. Figure 1 represents this phenomenon for the planet Mars.

These facts will suffice to state the astronomer's problem. As his very name suggests, the astronomer's task is to exhibit the complicated and seemingly irregular motions of the celestial bodies as illustrations of a fixed and simple law. He will therefore inquire, for example, whether the motions of Mars as they appear to the observer are its *real* motions. He will thus attempt "to save the appearances," to use a Platonic phrase, by discovering a simple pattern of uniform behavior, capable of being formulated mathematically, which will account for the apparently random wanderings of the planet.

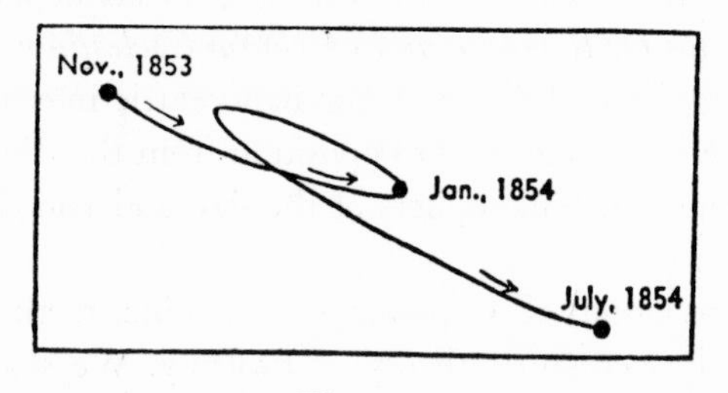


*Figure 1*

APPARENT PATH OF THE PLANET MARS AMONG THE FIXED STARS

Now the ancient Greeks succeeded in constructing a theory which introduced order and simplicity into their conception of the heavens. For various reasons they held that uniform circular motion is the most perfect and noble, and that the dignity of the heavens required celestial motions to be of this kind. According to Aristotle, moreover, consistent with his distinction between celestial and terrestrial "matter," the heavenly bodies are embedded in a series of incorruptible crystalline spheres having different radii, with the earth at their center and the stars in the outermost sphere. In the third century B.C., Aristarchus proposed a heliocentric theory of the heavens, but this idea was not developed until Copernicus exploited its possibilities. Meanwhile, it was the Alexandrian geometers who worked out the details of the geocentric theory, and it was Ptolemy's codification of it in the second century A.D. which became the standard astronomical treatise of Europe for the next fourteen hundred years.

Let us consider how the Ptolemaic theory was able "to save the appearances." Ptolemy assumed a fixed earth situated at the center of the universe, with the celestial bodies moving uniformly on circular orbits. However, he did not assume, as did Aristotle, that these bodies were carried along by *physical* spheres. And we must keep in mind that he offered his theory as the simplest geometrical representation of the celestial motions and not as a picture of the actual physical constitution of the world. He accounted for the curious shuttling motion of the planets, such as Mars, by an ingenious mathematical device. He assumed that although Mars moves uniformly upon a circle, the center of this circle moves uniformly upon the circumference of another circle, the earth being near the center of the latter.

This is shown in Figure 2. The primary circle with the earth at or near its center is called the *deferent;* the circle upon which Mars moves and whose center moves on the circumference of the deferent is called an *epicycle.* A little reflection will show that by properly adjusting the radii of the deferent and epicycle and by assigning appropriate speeds to Mars and the center of the epicycle, the apparent motion of the planet can be obtained and calculated as the combined effect of the assumed real motions.

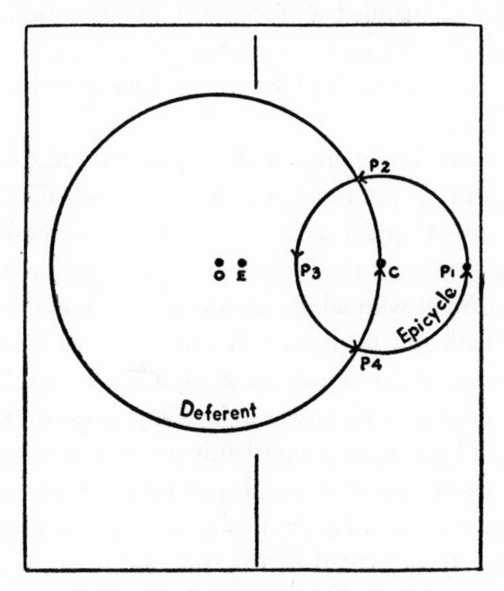


*Figure 2*

EPICYCLIC MOTION OF A PLANET

*O* is the center of the deferent, *E* the earth, *C* the center of the epicycle. Arrows indicate direction of motion along the circumference. When the planet is at $P_1$ its forward speed, as observed from *E,* is large, because it then has the combined speeds of *C* upon the deferent and of the planet itself upon the epicycle. When the planet is at $P_3$, and if we suppose that its speed along the circumference of the epicycle is greater than the speed of *C* on the deferent, it will appear to be moving backward. When the planet is near $P_2$ and $P_4$ it will appear to be motionless.

Ptolemy thus succeeded in "saving the appearances" on the supposition of fixed uniform circular motions for all the celestial bodies. However, in order to bring his calculations into agreement with the observed motions of these bodies, he frequently had to postulate supplementary epicycles: that is, circles with centers moving on other epicycles, and so on. As a more detailed account of Ptolemy's system would show even more clearly, in spite of its initial simplicity its final form was quite complicated, and the mathematical computations required for working it were wearisome. By the time of Copernicus, seventy-nine epicycles were needed to account for the motions of the heavens.

Nevertheless, the Ptolemaic astronomy was a genuine scientific theory, which brought a variety of different phenomena under a common set of principles. It was a theory worked out with mathematical precision, adequate to the facts as then known. It is well to note, also, that Ptolemy was not a slave to unanalyzed observation or to the dictates of uncritical common sense. The explanation of planetary behavior, which his theory offered, required the assumption of epicyclic motions that were obviously not capable of direct observation and that demanded a disciplined mathematical imagination for their discovery. And whatever its weaknesses may have been, its great merit was that it exhibited the motions of the heavens as subject to a relatively simple and precise law.

We are now prepared to appreciate the significance of Copernicus's revolutionary proposal to base the theory of the heavens on the idea of a moving earth and a fixed sun. Copernicus had no fresh astronomical facts with which to dispute the correctness of the Ptolemaic system; and he himself noted that the latter was consistent with all the known observational data. He was, however, displeased with the mathematical complexity of that theory; and he was dissatisfied with the fact that so many unrelated epicycles had to be arbitrarily introduced into it if it was to be adequate to the data. A system of this sort seemed to him "neither sufficiently absolute nor sufficiently pleasing to the mind." Copernicus was thoroughly convinced that the order embodied in the heavens must be a simple and coherent order; and he believed therefore that only that theory could be the true one which organized the facts with the maximum of logical coherence. In his judgment the heliocentric theory met this condition while the geocentric theory did not. In the Dedication of the *De Revolutionibus* to Pope Paul III, he explained the grounds of his dissatisfaction with the astronomers who followed Ptolemy:

In determining the motions of the sun, moon, and of the other five planets, they fail to employ consistently one set of principles and hypotheses, but use methods of proof based only upon the apparent revolutions and motions. . . . Nor have they been able to discover or calculate from these various hypotheses which is the shape of the world and the fixed symmetry of its parts; but their procedure has been as if someone were to collect hands, feet, a head, and other members from various places, all very fine in themselves, but not proportionate to one body, and no single one corresponding in its turn to the others, so that a monster rather than a man would be formed from them. Thus in their process of demonstration which they term a "method," they are found to have omitted something essential, or to have included something foreign and not pertaining to the matter in hand. This certainly would never have happened to them if they had followed fixed principles. . . .

Therefore, having turned over in my mind for a long time this uncertainty of the traditional mathematical methods of calculating the motions of the celestial bodies, I began to grow disgusted that no more consistent scheme of the movements of the mechanism of the universe, set up for our benefit by that best and most law-abiding Architect of all things, was agreed upon by philosophers who otherwise investigate so carefully the most minute details of this world. Wherefore I undertook the task of re-reading the books of all the philosophers I could get access to, to see whether anyone ever was of the opinion that the motions of the celestial bodies were other than those postulated by the men who taught mathematics in the schools. And I found first, indeed, in Cicero, that Hicetas perceived that the Earth moved; and afterward in Plutarch I found that some others were of this opinion. . . .

Taking this as a starting point, I began to consider the mobility of the Earth; and although the idea seemed absurd, yet because I knew that the liberty had been granted to others before me to postulate all sorts of little circles for explaining the phenomena of the stars, I thought I also might easily be permitted to try whether by postulating some motion of the Earth, more reliable conclusions could be reached regarding the revolution of the heavenly bodies, than those of my predecessors.

And so, after postulating movements, which, farther on in the book, I ascribe to the Earth, I have found by many and long observations that if the movements of the other planets are assumed for the circular motion of the Earth and are substituted for the revolution of each star, not only do their phenomena follow logically therefrom, but the relative positions and magnitudes both of the stars and all their orbits, and of the heavens themselves, become so closely related that in none of its parts can anything be changed without causing confusion in the other parts and in the whole universe. . . .

The chief technical innovation of Copernicus arose from his insight that the Ptolemaic device of distinct epicyclic motions for the several planets merely transferred to each of the planets separately the yearly revolution of the earth around the sun. Figure 3 will make clear in what way the apparent oscillatory motion of a planet can be explained on the hypothesis that both the earth and the planet revolve around the sun with unequal periods. Copernicus was thus able to effect an essential simplification of the theory of the heavens; and while he could not altogether dispense with epicycles, he

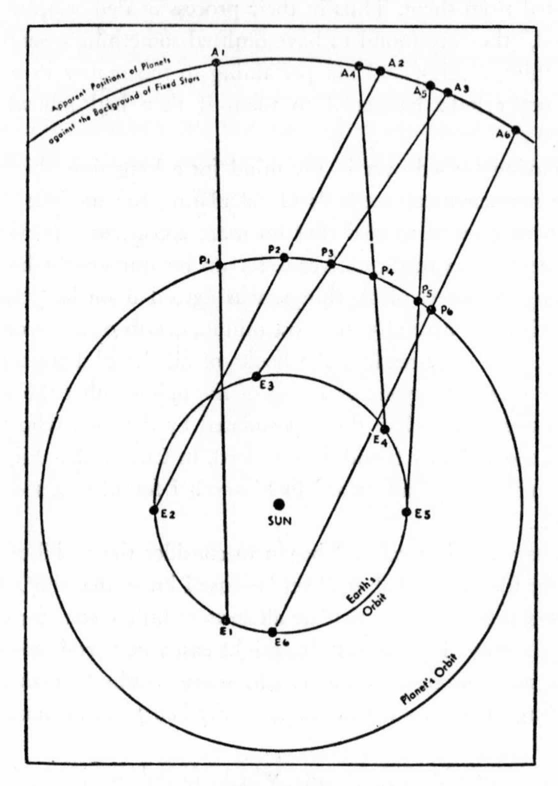


*Figure 3*

THE ORBITS OF THE EARTH AND AN EXTERIOR PLANET, AND THE APPARENT MOTION OF THE PLANET AS VIEWED FROM THE EARTH

$E_1$, $E_2$, $E_3$, $E_4$, $E_5$, $E_6$ represent successive positions of the earth on its orbit around the sun, while $P_1$, $P_2$, $P_3$, $P_4$, $P_5$, $P_6$ are the corresponding positions of the planet on its own orbit. The straight lines represent the lines of sight from the earth to the planet. At $E_1$ the planet will appear to the observer on the earth as situated at $A_1$ with respect to the fixed stars, and so on for the other positions of the earth. As the earth moves through the positions $E_1$, $E_2$, $E_3$, the planet will appear to advance rapidly from $A_1$ to $A_3$; as the earth moves from $E_3$ to $E_4$, the planet will appear to slacken its speed, then become almost stationary, and finally reverse the direction of its previous motion: as the earth moves from $E_4$ to $E_5$, the planet will again appear to slacken its retrograde motion, become stationary, and then once more acquire its former forward speed.

reduced the number to thirty-four. (It is well to remember, however, that even on our present astronomical theory, the moon and the satellites of the other planets all take part in a type of epicyclic motion.)

But however much Copernicus differed from Ptolemy in the way he proposed to "save the appearances," his reconstruction of astronomy was controlled by a number of assumptions which he shared with the latter.

Like Ptolemy he supposed the universe to be finite and enclosed in the sphere of the fixed stars, though he did believe the celestial distances to be much greater than the ancients had imagined. He accepted as axiomatic that the motions of the heavenly bodies are circular and uniform; and he maintained that any deviation from such motions "must arise either from irregularity in the moving power, whether this be within the body or foreign to it, or from some inequality of the body in revolution. . . . Both of which things the intellect shrinks from in horror, it being unworthy to hold such a view about bodies which are constituted in the most perfect order."

Above all, Copernicus had a sturdy faith in the simplicity and rationality of the natural order. It was this faith that made it possible for him to advance a theory which not only went counter to ingrained tradition and the apparent reports of the senses, but even seemed to be in disagreement with critical observations. Thus, the phases which Venus must exhibit on the heliocentric theory were not observed until Galileo's telescope made them evident years later; and it was not until 1838 that Bessel was able to detect apparent shifts in the relative positions of the fixed stars as a consequence of the earth's annual circling of the sun.

As already noted, the publication of Copernicus's work produced no immediate changes in the general climate of opinion. Few of his contemporaries saw in it a threat to the dominant religious outlook. And most of these seemed to have been persuaded by a fraudulent preface supplied by Copernicus's editor that the book proposed, not a new theory concerning the physical constitution of the world, but merely a convenient device for simplifying astronomical computations. In the end, however, it became clear that Copernicus had made a serious breach in the medieval outlook. He successfully challenged the traditional dogma of a fixed earth; and by assigning to the latter a type of motion which had been reserved exclusively to the heavens, he contributed to breaking down the Aristotelian distinction between the terrestrial and the celestial. Copernicus made no commitments as to the character of the bodies which, together with the earth, circulated around the sun. But presently others, such as Giordano Bruno (1548–1600), used the heliocentric theory as a basis for preaching the doctrine of a plurality of worlds: of the planets inhabited by living creatures like man, and of other suns or stars accompanied by similarly inhabited planets. And so the Christian epic, which seemed to depend on the earth with its unique human inhabitants being at the center of the universe, appeared to many to have lost its universal meaning and validity. Bruno was burned at the stake for his heretical opinions. But the realization that human history is not the only drama in the cosmos, and that our parochial point of view is not the only possible one, was not so easily destroyed once it had achieved publicity.

The next important advance in theoretical astronomy was the direct outcome of improved observations on the celestial bodies. Tycho Brahe (1546–1601), a Danish noble, constructed instruments which enabled him to record the positions of the planets with a precision hitherto unknown. Although his observations were carried out before the invention of the telescope, his practice of repeating his readings of the stellar positions and of continuing the study of a planet over many years enabled him to reduce his errors to not more than 1 to 2 minutes of an arc. (A minute is a unit of angular measure. One minute is the sixtieth part of a degree, and one degree is 1/360th part of the circumference of a circle.)

These data fortunately fell into the hands of Johannes Kepler (1571–1630), a one-time assistant of Brahe. Kepler was an enthusiastic Copernican, in part because the sun was assigned the central position in the universe by that theory. For as the following quotation from one of his early writings will show, he had a mystic reverence for the sun and endowed it with divine qualities.

Of all the bodies in the universe the most excellent is the sun, whose whole essence is nothing else than the purest light, than which there is no greater star; which singly and alone is the producer, conserver, and warmer of all things; it is a fountain of light, rich in fruitful heat, most fair, limpid, and pure to the sight, the source of vision, portrayer of all colours, though himself empty of colour, called king of the planets for his motion which alone we should judge worthy of the Most High God, should He be pleased with a material domicile and choose a place in which to dwell with the blessed angels. . . . Since it does not benefit the first mover to be diffused throughout an orbit, but rather to proceed from one certain principle, and as it were, point, no part of the world, and no star, accounts itself worthy of such a great honour; hence by the highest right we return to the sun, who alone appears, by virtue of his dignity and power, suited for this motive duty and worthy to become the home of God Himself, not to say the first mover.

On the other hand, Kepler was also a painstaking astronomer, and he discovered that the positions of the planets as determined by Brahe's observations did not conform with their positions as calculated from the Copernican theory. He was an excellent mathematician, and he shared the Neoplatonic faith in nature as the embodiment of a simple mathematical order. He was to spend twenty-five years of indefatigable labor in determining the true orbits of the planets.

We may appreciate the curious mixture in Kepler of a superstitious number-mysticism, a high order of mathematical competence, and a scrupulous regard for the facts of observation, if we recite two incidents in his researches. One of his early discoveries, the glory of which he said he would not renounce "for the whole Electorate of Saxony," was an approximate but chimerical correspondence between the planetary orbits and the five regular solids. (In Kepler's day only five planets were known: Mercury, Venus, Mars, Jupiter, and Saturn. A regular solid is one in which all the angles and sides are equal. There is a proof in Euclid, which goes back to Plato's pupils, that only five such solids are possible.) He explained it as follows:

> The Earth is the circle, the measure of all. Round it describe a dodecahedron [a twelve-sided regular solid], the circle including this will be Mars. Round Mars describe a tetrahedron [a four-sided regular solid], the circle including this will be Jupiter. Describe a cube around Jupiter, the circle including this will be Saturn. Then inscribe in the Earth an icosahedron [a twenty-sided regular solid], the circle inscribed in it will be Venus. Inscribe an octahedron in Venus, the circle inscribed in it will be Mercury.

He was overjoyed at his discovery. "The intense pleasure I have received from this discovery," he wrote at the time, "can never be told in words. I regretted no more the time wasted; I tired of no labor; I shunned no toil of reckoning, days and nights spent in calculation, until I could see whether my hypothesis would agree with the orbits of Copernicus or whether my joy was to vanish into air." However, that Kepler's construction was really quite fantastic is at once evident if we recall that it loses its entire point with the discovery of additional planets (for example, Uranus in 1781).

On the other hand, in his attempt to find a combination of circular motions which would yield the observed paths of the planets, Kepler at one time found a difference of only eight minutes of an arc between his calculations and Brahe's numerical data. But even this small discrepancy did not satisfy his standards of precision, for he declared:

> Since the divine goodness has given to us in Tycho Brahe a most careful observer, from whose observations the error of 8′ is shown in this calculation . . . it is right that we should with gratitude recognize and make use of this gift of God.

. . . For if I could have treated 8′ of longitude as negligible I should have already corrected sufficiently the hypothesis. But as they could not be neglected, these 8′ alone have led the way toward the complete reformation of astronomy, and have made the subject-matter of a great part of this work.

Kepler worked for years on the assumption that the celestial motions are circular and uniform, without succeeding in finding orbits for the planets adequate to the facts. It finally occurred to him that perhaps these orbits are ovals and not circles; and since he was familiar with the theory of conic sections as worked out by Apollonius in the third century B.C., he decided to use the ellipse as the simplest type of oval curve for plotting the positions of the planet Mars. In 1609 he discovered what is known as Kepler's First Law: the planets move on elliptic orbits with the sun at one focus. He thus succeeded in "saving the appearances," but only at the price of surrendering the axiom that celestial motions are circular, as well as the axiom that their speeds are uniform. However, in the same year he discovered his Second Law of planetary motion, which compensated him for the loss of the latter axiom. For he found that the line joining the sun and a planet sweeps out equal areas in equal times. This is illustrated in Figure 4.

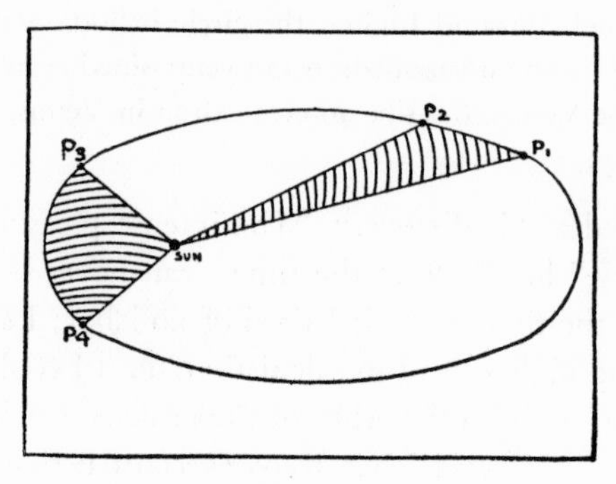


*Figure 4*

KEPLER'S FIRST TWO LAWS OF PLANETARY MOTION

The sun is at the focus of the ellipse. The planet covers the distance from $P_1$ to $P_2$, and from $P_3$ to $P_4$, in equal times. These *distances* are not equal, for the planet moves more rapidly when it is nearer the sun than when it is farther away from it. But the *areas* swept out in equal times (indicated by the shadings) are equal. This is the meaning of Kepler's Second Law.

Ten years later, Kepler discovered his Third Law, which connects the period of one complete revolution of a planet with its average distance from the sun. One essential preliminary task for the subsequent Newtonian synthesis was now completed. Kepler's ecstasy knew no bounds:

What I prophesied two-and-twenty years ago, as soon as I discovered the five solids among the heavenly orbits—what I firmly believed long before I had seen Ptolemy's Harmonies—what I had promised my friends in the title of this book, which I named before I was sure of my discovery—what sixteen years ago I urged as a thing to be sought—that for which I joined Tycho Brahe, for which I settled in Prague, for which I have devoted the best part of my life to astronomical contemplations, at length I have brought to light, and recognized its truth beyond my most sanguine expectations. It is not eighteen months since I got the first glimpse of light, three months since the dawn, very few days since the unveiled sun, most admirable to gaze upon, burst upon me. Nothing holds me; I will indulge my sacred fury; I will triumph over mankind by the honest confession that I have stolen the golden vases of the Egyptians to build up a tabernacle for my God far away from the confines of Egypt. If you forgive me, I rejoice; if you are angry, I can bear it; the die is cast, the book is written, to be read either now or by posterity, I care not which; it may well wait a century for a reader, as God has waited six thousand years for an observer!

Kepler's technical contributions to natural science were far more original and profound than those made by Copernicus. He showed more clearly than the latter the power of daring mathematical analysis to exhibit the invariable order of the heavens. In spite of his mystical vagaries and his superstitious belief in the causal power of mathematical relations, he established the fruitfulness of scientific method—conceived as the use of carefully formulated hypotheses whose logically deduced consequences are to be verified by painstaking observation. His work made evident that the order of nature is not to be understood in terms of the place of things in a hierarchy of perfect beings; on the contrary, nature is to be understood as the embodiment of principles quantitatively expressed and mathematically elaborated. Indeed, Kepler firmly believed that only those properties and qualities of the world are real which can be determined quantitatively and whose mutual relations can be grasped with the certainty of mathematical truths.

The *coup de grâce* to the medieval cosmology was supplied by Galileo Galilei's (1564–1642) telescopic demonstration of the validity of the heliocentric theory. A report reached him that a Dutch lens-maker had made distant objects more visible by combining two lenses; and he promptly constructed a telescope for himself which he turned upon the heavens. His observations, published in 1610 in his *Sidereal Messenger,* were startling. He established the fact that the moon had mountains whose heights he was able to calculate from the shadows they cast. He discovered Jupiter to have four satellites revolving around it, so that a small-scale model of the solar system was actually observable. He showed that Venus had phases as was to be expected on the Copernican theory, and that therefore the planet did not shine by its own light. He was able to establish that a new star which had suddenly appeared at the turn of the century must be situated in the region of the fixed stars. And he discovered dark spots or "blemishes" on the face of the sun, from whose motions he was able to conclude that the sun itself makes a monthly rotation on its axis.

The Copernican theory thus received a crucial observational confirmation, and it was no longer easy to regard it simply as a convenient mathematical device for facilitating computations. But above all, Galileo had removed almost the last ground from under the age-old belief that the heavens were perfect, immutable, and essentially different from earthly things. No wonder that dogmatic defenders of the Aristotelian physics were dismayed and resentful, and used every fantastic argument they could devise to disprove or minimize Galileo's findings. A prominent professor of philosophy presented his case against Galileo's discoveries as follows:

> There are seven windows given to animals in the domicile of the head, through which the air is admitted to the tabernacle of the body, to enlighten, to warm, and to nourish it. What are these parts of the microcosmos? Two nostrils, two eyes, two ears, and a mouth. So in the heavens, as in a microcosmos, there are two favorable stars, two unpropitious, two luminaries, and Mercury undecided and indifferent. From this and many other similarities in nature, such as the seven metals, etc., which it were tedious to enumerate, we gather that the number of planets is necessarily seven. Moreover, these satellites of Jupiter are invisible to the naked eye, and therefore can exercise no influence on the earth, and therefore would be useless, and therefore do not exist. Besides, the Jews and other ancient nations, as well as modern Europeans, have adopted the division of the week into seven days, and have named them after the seven planets. Now, if we increase the number of the planets, this whole and beautiful system falls to the ground.

The founders of modern science clearly did not have a monopoly on number-mysticism! Galileo wrote Kepler:

> What would you say of the leading philosophers here to whom I have offered a thousand times of my own accord to show my studies, but who, with the lazy obstinacy of a serpent who has eaten his fill, have neither consented to look at the planets, or moon, or telescope? Verily, just as serpents close their ears, so do men close their eyes to the light of truth. To such people philosophy is a kind of book, like the Aeneid or the Odyssey, where the truth is to be sought, not in the universe or in nature, but (I use their own words) by comparing texts! . . .

Oh, my dear Kepler, how I wish that we could have one hearty laugh together! Here, at Padua, is the principal professor of philosophy whom I have repeatedly and urgently requested to look at the moon and planets through my glass, which he pertinaciously refuses to do. Why are you not here? What shouts of laughter we should have at this glorious folly! And to hear the professor of philosophy at Pisa labouring before the grand duke with logical arguments, as if with magical incantations, to charm the new planets out of the sky.

But the Church also took a hand in the controversy. The toleration it had shown for the new learning in the preceding centuries was being slowly dissipated by the threat to its authority which the Protestant Reformation represented. Copernicus's *De Revolutionibus* was placed on the Index in 1616, until it should be corrected so as to make the heliocentric theory appear simply as a convenient mathematical hypothesis; and Galileo was warned to teach the Copernican ideas only in this manner. In 1632 Galileo published his most important astronomical work, the *Dialogue on the Two Chief Systems of the World, the Ptolemaic and the Copernican.* Although he complied formally with the Church's instructions, his incomparable marshaling of the arguments for the new view and his devastating ridicule of the Aristotelian scholastics deceived no one as to his genuine convictions. Personal resentments against Galileo by the reigning Pope Urban and other highly placed individuals doubtless played a role in the denouement. He was summoned to appear before the Inquisition in Rome, and after a long drawn-out hearing he was compelled to "abjure, curse, and detest" the Copernican doctrines as a heresy. The *Dialogue* and astronomical writings of Copernicus and Kepler were placed on the Index, from which they were not withdrawn until 1835.

## III

Further advances in the mathematical interpretation of nature required the development of the theory of mechanics, and especially that portion of it (called dynamics) which treats of the motions of bodies. If the foregoing account of the establishment of the heliocentric theory has made no mention of the conditions or causes which maintain the planets, in their orbits, the reason for the omission is simple. Neither Copernicus nor Kepler had ideas on this subject which were in advance of the traditional ones or which were other than crude and primitive. The foundations of dynamics were laid by Galileo, and his investigations in this domain constitute the chief ground for his fame; but the principles he discovered were not successfully applied to the motions of the heavens until Newton generalized and improved upon them.

Let us review the general outlook in science at the time Kepler finished his work. There was overwhelming evidence that astronomical phenomena embodied invariant laws, mathematical in character, but different from those regarded as valid by ancients and their medieval followers. A serious blow had been given to the Aristotelian view that celestial bodies are incorruptible and perfect, and to this extent at least the dogma of a qualitative difference between the heavens and the earth had been successfully challenged. Finally, a beginning had been made in establishing a method of inquiry which, dispensing with final causes as explanatory principles, combined the use of mathematical hypotheses with careful observation and experimentation.

On the other hand, terrestrial motions were in the main still not seen as embodiments of a mathematical necessity as rigorous as that which obtained in the heavens. In spite of Archimedes and his development of the science of statics (the theory of bodies in equilibrium), in spite of the practical achievements of artisans and engineers, and in spite of various familiar if superficial bits of knowledge concerning terrestrial motions, a quantitatively determinate science of such phenomena was at best still only a daring hope. Again, while the authority of medieval physics was becoming discredited, there was still no clear, generalized, and authoritative formulation of the method and objective of the new approach to the study of nature. Until these things were accomplished—until the scope of mathematical, experimental techniques was enlarged to include terrestrial phenomena within the framework of a comprehensive philosophy of nature—the scientific revolution was not complete. We must now briefly outline the final steps in achieving this new philosophy.

Although Galileo's *Dialogue* was placed on the Index and he was banished to a small country estate, he continued his scientific studies. In 1638 he published (at Leyden) the epoch-making *Dialogues and Mathematical Demonstrations Concerning Two New Sciences,* which contained the basis for all future work in dynamics. Its opening passage, with a reference to the famous Arsenal of Venice, recognizes Galileo's intellectual debt to the instrument-makers and practical mechanics of the Italian cities. But the central section of the book begins with a succinct summary of Galileo's achievements:

My purpose is to set forth a very new science dealing with a very ancient subject. There is, in nature, perhaps nothing older than motion, concerning which the books written by philosophers are neither few nor small; nevertheless I have discovered by experiment some properties of it which have not hitherto been either observed or demonstrated. Some superficial observations have been made, as for instance, that the free motion of a heavy falling body is continuously accelerated; but to just what extent this acceleration occurs has not yet been announced; for so far as I know, no one has yet pointed out that the distances traversed, during equal intervals of time, by a body falling from rest, stand to one another in the same ratio as the odd numbers beginning with unity.

It has been observed that missiles and projectiles describe a curved path of some sort; however, no one has pointed out the fact that this path is a parabola. But this and other facts, not few in number or less worth knowing, I have succeeded in proving; and what I consider more important, there have been opened up to this vast and most excellent science . . . ways and means by which other minds . . . will explore its remote corners.

With the details of Galileo's investigations we cannot concern ourselves; but one fundamental difference between his approach to the study of motion and that of Aristotle should be noted. According to the latter, a body in motion, whether it is moving uniformly or not, requires a continuously acting force if it is to remain in motion. Galileo rejected this mode of analysis. He maintained, on the contrary, that a body moving with constant speed along a straight line (that is, with a constant *velocity*) requires *no* force to sustain its motion; on the other hand, a force is required to produce any change in the velocity of a body, that is, any change in direction or rectilinear speed.

Galileo thus made the capital distinction between velocity and acceleration (as a change in velocity is called). He thereby became the discoverer of the principle of inertia, subsequently formulated by Newton as the first law of motion: a body at rest or moving with a constant velocity will remain at rest or persevere in its state of motion unless acted upon by an external force. On Galileo's view, therefore, it was no longer "natural" for a moving body to seek a resting place; for a body once in motion along a straight line will "naturally" continue to move indefinitely in the same direction if no force comes to act on it. An immediate consequence of the principle of inertia is that a body moving along a circular orbit is undergoing acceleration, and must therefore be moving under the influence of some force. But the full import of this proposition for the theory of the heavens was not understood until Newton's work made it evident.

Galileo's dynamical researches thus showed that terrestrial motions were as amenable to quantitative study and mathematical analysis as were the celestial ones. They proved that a part of the cosmos, hitherto regarded as inferior and imperfect because it did not exhibit an invariable order, was in fact just as much subject to simple regularities and constant laws as were the heavens. To Galileo this was no surprising conclusion. For he shared with Kepler and his other scientific contemporaries the unquestioning faith in a thoroughly rational universe, capable of exploration in all its parts with the tools of mathematical analysis. He once formulated this faith in unmistakable words:

True philosophy expounds nature to us; but she can be understood only by him who has learned the speech and symbols in which she speaks to us. This speech is mathematics, and its symbols are mathematical figures. Philosophy is written in this greatest book, which continually stands open here to the eyes of all, but cannot be understood unless one first learns the language and characters in which it is written. This language is mathematics and the characters are triangles, circles and other mathematical figures.

And elsewhere he wrote:

Nature being inexorable and immutable, and never passing the bounds of the Laws assigned her, as one that nothing careth whether her abstruse reasons and methods of operating be, or be not exposed to the Capacity of Men; I conceive that that, concerning Natural Effects, which either Sensible Experience sets before our eyes, or Necessary Demonstrations do prove unto us, ought not, upon any account, to be called into question, much less condemned upon the testimony of Texts of Scripture, which may, under their words, couch Senses seemingly contrary thereto; In regard that every Expression of Scripture is not tied to so strict conditions, as every Effect of Nature: Nor doth God less admirably discover himself unto us in Nature's Sacred Dictions.

For Galileo, no less than for Kepler, the fundamental properties of the world were precisely those which can be explored mathematically.

It would therefore be a serious misunderstanding of Galileo's temper of mind to see him, as some have done, as an enthusiastic gatherer of indiscriminate facts and a contemner of rational, deductive methods. He once remarked that "ignorance had been the best teacher he ever had, since in order to be able to demonstrate to his opponents the truth of his conclusions, he had been forced to prove them by a variety of experiments, though to satisfy his own mind alone he had never felt it necessary to make any." And he prefaced his demonstration of the paths of projectiles with the statement:

The knowledge of a single fact acquired through a discovery of its causes prepares the mind to understand and ascertain other facts without need of recourse to experiment, precisely as in the present case, where by argumentation alone the author proves with certainty that the maximum range occurs when the elevation is 45°. He thus demonstrates what has perhaps never been observed in experience, namely, that of other shots those which exceed or fall short of 45° by equal amounts have equal ranges.

On the other hand, as has already been seen, he did not neglect the role of observation in inquiry, and he did not believe that a purely logical argument, unsupported by experiment, could establish a truth of nature. Indeed, the cogency of Galileo's procedure resided both in the demonstrative force of his arguments and in the confirmation of his conclusions by experimentally determined facts. For Galileo the true method of science consisted in the proper marriage of mathematics and experiment. As he saw it, the order of nature is to be discovered not by blind reliance on unanalyzed experience nor by exclusive devotion to mathematical demonstration, but by interpreting sensible experience in terms of mathematical principles. He made his protagonist in the *Dialogue on the Two Chief Systems of the World* declare:

I cannot sufficiently admire the eminencie of those men's wits that have received and held it to be true, and with the sprightlinesse of their judgments offered such violence to their own senses, as that they have been able to prefer that which their reason dictated to them, to that which sensible experiments represented most manifestly on the contrary. . . . I cannot find any bounds for my admiration, how that reason was able in Aristarchus and Copernicus, to commit such a rape upon their Senses, as in despight thereof, to make her self mistress of their credulity.

Galileo never formulated in detail the method which he believed yields authoritative knowledge of nature's order; but his accounts of the steps taken by him in arriving at his various conclusions illustrate clearly enough what he thought were its essentials. It has become customary to distinguish three such steps, labeled with his own names for them. 1. The *resolution* or *analysis* of the phenomenon studied must first be performed, in order to discover in it the mathematical principle connecting its basic relevant features. Thus, the resolution of freely falling bodies finds in them the law of accelerated motion. 2. The consequences of the principle must be *demonstrated*. 3. These consequences must be tested by an appropriate *experiment*. These steps are clearly exemplified in the following crucial account by Galileo of the law of freely falling bodies:

A piece of wooden moulding or scantling, about 12 cubits long, half a cubit wide, and three finger-breadths thick, was taken; on its edge was cut a channel a little more than one finger in breadth; having made this groove thus straight, smooth, and polished, and having lined it with parchment, also as smooth and polished as possible, we rolled along it a hard, smooth, and very round bronze ball. Having placed this board in a sloping position, by lifting one end some one or two cubits above the other, we rolled the ball, as I was saying, along the channel, noting in a manner presently to be described, the time required to make the descent. We repeated this experiment more than once in order to measure the time with an accuracy such that the deviation between two observations never exceeded one-tenth of a pulse beat. Having performed this operation and having assured ourselves of its reliability, we now rolled the ball only one-quarter the length of the channel; and having measured the time of its descent we found it precisely one-half of the former. Next we tried other distances, comparing the time for the whole length with that for the half, or with that for two-thirds, or three-fourths, or indeed for any fraction; in such experiments, repeated a full hundred times, we always found that the spaces traversed were to each other as the squares of the times, and this was true for all inclinations of the plane, *i.e.,* of the channel, along which we rolled the ball. We also observed that the times of the descent, for various inclinations of the plane, bore to one another precisely that ratio which, as we shall see later, the author had predicted and demonstrated for them.

It must not be supposed that Galileo understood his method to be a blueprint for successful invention and discovery, as rules for infallibly hitting upon the truth. The conception of scientific method as a set of practical maxims which would achieve this latter end, was brought into prominence by Francis Bacon (1561–1626). Bacon was a lawyer, for a time Lord Chancellor of England, and a brilliant man of letters. He was filled with the vision of the power over nature which the new science could win for mankind, and he was an enthusiastic propagandist for systematic, cooperative research. We shall discuss this phase of his influence in greater detail presently. But he was no scientist in his own right; he rejected the Copernican theory as folly, and he made sport of the work of Galileo. Unlike the founders of modern natural science, he did not appreciate the role of mathematics in scientific research; and unlike them, also, he believed that simply by a patient gathering of facts the cause or principle involved in them could be sifted out automatically. Accordingly, he had no sound understanding of the actual procedure of the new science, and, in spite of the popularity of his views on scientific method, the actual practice of scientists profited little from them. William Harvey, the discoverer of the circulation of the blood, said of him: "He writes of science like a Lord Chancellor." It must nevertheless be added that through Bacon's great admirer, Robert Boyle, Bacon's ceaseless emphasis upon the need for basing the study of nature upon experiment became an essential part of the intellectual heritage of future investigators, and in particular of no less a man than Newton.

However that may be, Galileo's mechanical researches and his conception of the requirements of natural science gave additional impetus to the final victorious emergence of the new world-view. There remained the task of stating in its full generality the hypothesis of a universal mechanics—applicable to all domains of existence, terrestrial and celestial, organic as well as inorganic—and of carrying through in detail the program of research which it entailed. Such a comprehensive philosophy for the mathematical interpretation of nature was supplied by René Descartes (1596–1650), while its detailed application to physics was successfully worked out by Isaac Newton (1642–1727).

Descartes was admirably equipped to be the grand philosopher of the new outlook. He was not only trained in the scholastic philosophy, and thus knew its limitations as well as its strength; he was also a distinguished contributor to mathematics and physics, and understood at first hand the implicit requirements and potential scope of the mathematical interpretation of nature. He developed and established, if he did not actually discover, the principles of analytical geometry—that is, of the systematic application of algebraic methods to the study of space. He made significant additions to optics. And he outlined a general theory of motions and sketched a system of the world, according to which all changes are the result of impacts between contiguous bodies. The planets were supposed to be carried around the sun, like straws in a whirlpool, by the vortex motions of the all-pervading matter in which they are imbedded.

The strength of Descartes's contemporary influence, however, was derived from his writings on the new method of science. They commanded a widespread respect, both from practicing scientists and educated laymen, in part because they seemed to be confirmed and supported by his concrete scientific contributions. Indeed, in his personal development, Descartes's conception of the true method of science arose directly out of his preoccupation with specific technical problems. He experienced an ecstatic vision in his twenty-fourth year, in which the outlines of a universal mathematics appeared to him and which led him on to study the general problems of method. His first published work, the *Discourse on the Method of Rightly Conducting the Reason and Seeking for Truth in the Sciences* (1637), contained the essentials of his philosophy, and was supplemented by appendices aiming to show its application to physics and geometry.

Descartes's philosophy may be viewed as a passionate search for scientific certainty, a certainty which he found adequately realized only in arithmetic and geometry. According to him, these sciences alone "deal with an object so pure and uncomplicated that they need make no assumptions at all which experience renders uncertain, but wholly consist in the rational deduction of consequences." But if we ask why these sciences possess this excellence, Descartes's answer is that, in pursuing them, we begin with the intuition of things that are so simple and clear that no error can arise. Accordingly, the true method of the sciences must imitate mathematics. We must accept only that which is clear and distinct and evident; we must resolve every problem and every object into its simple components; and we must finally proceed deductively to build up a system of necessary truth. As Descartes himself put the matter:

It is possible to say that those propositions which are immediately deducted from first principles are known now by intuition, now by deduction, *i.e.,* in a way that differs according to our point of view. But the first principles themselves are given by intuition alone, while, on the contrary, the remote conclusions are furnished only by deduction.

These two methods are the most certain routes to knowledge, and the mind should admit no others. All the rest should be rejected as suspect of error and dangerous.

As a consequence, Descartes believed that the extensive or spatial qualities of objects are their fundamental ones; and he was confident that all other qualities can be reduced to combinations of these extensive traits. Thus he declared:

The Nature of body consists not in weight, nor in hardness, nor color and so on, but in extension alone.

Whatever you suppose color to be, you cannot deny that it is extended and in consequence possessed of figure. Is there then any disadvantage, if, while taking care not to admit any new entity uselessly, or rashly to imagine that it exists, and not denying indeed the beliefs of others concerning color, but merely abstracting from every other feature except that it possesses the nature of figure, we conceive the diversity existing between white, blue, and red, etc., as being like the difference between . . . similar figures? The same argument applies to all cases; for it is certain that the infinitude of figures suffices to express all the differences in sensible things.

Since, therefore, all objects may be resolved into complexes of simple natures (such as figure, extension, and motion), and since these simples can be grasped by the intellect with complete clarity and certainty, a universal mathematics or mechanics, which would be applicable to everything without exception, is an obvious possibility. So at least Descartes believed:

As I considered the matter carefully it gradually came to light that all those matters only were referred to Mathematics in which order and measurement are investigated, and that it makes no difference whether it be in numbers, figures, stars, sounds, or any other object that the question of measurement arises. I saw consequently that there must be some general science to explain that element as a whole which gives rise to problems about order and measurement, restricted as these are to no special subject matter. This, I perceived, was called "Universal Mathematics" . . . because in this science is contained everything on account of which the others are called parts of Mathematics. We can see how much it excels in utility and simplicity the sciences subordinate to it, by the fact that it can deal with all the objects of which they have cognizance and many more besides. . . .

I do not accept or desire any other principle in Physics than in Geometry or abstract Mathematics, because all the phenomena of nature may be explained by their means, and sure demonstration can be given of them.

Descartes thus supplied the theoretical basis for extending the scope of the mathematical interpretation of nature. He viewed the world as a machine whose structure is knowable in mathematical terms; and he regarded even living bodies, including the human, as simply physical automata, capable of being exhaustively studied in terms of the methods of the new science. Descartes did indeed except God and the human soul from the dominion of a universal mechanism—exceptions, gratefully accepted by many of his contemporaries, which permitted the pursuit of natural science without fear of its encroachment upon matters of religion and morals. But followers of Descartes, such as Baruch Spinoza (1632–77), did not hesitate to apply the geometric method to the study of human passions. In his *Ethics,* in which the contemplation of nature's eternal order was identified with the love of God, Spinoza prefaced his demonstration of the nature of human emotions with the following observations:

Most writers on the emotions and on human conduct seem to be treating rather of matters outside nature than of natural phenomena following nature's general laws. They appear to conceive man to be situated in nature as a kingdom within a kingdom: for they believe that he disturbs rather than follows nature's order, that he has absolute control over his actions, and that he is determined solely by himself. They attribute human infirmities and fickleness, not to the power of nature in general, but to some mysterious flaw in the nature of man, which accordingly they bemoan, deride, despise, or as usually happens, abuse: he, who succeeds in hitting off the weakness of the human mind more eloquently or more acutely than his fellows is looked upon as a seer. Still there has been no lack of very excellent men . . . , who have written many noteworthy things concerning the right way of life, and have given much sage advice to mankind. But no one, so far as I know, has defined the nature and strength of the emotions, and the power of the mind against them for their restraint.

I do not forget, that the illustrious Descartes, though he believed, that the mind has absolute power over its actions, strove to explain human emotions by their primary causes, and, at the same time, to point out a way, by which the mind might attain to absolute dominion over them. However, in my opinion, he accomplished nothing beyond a display of the acuteness of his own great intellect, as I will show in the proper place. For the present I wish to revert to those, who would rather abuse or deride human emotions than understand them. Such persons will doubtless think it strange that I should attempt to treat of human vice and folly geometrically, and should wish to set forth with rigid reasoning those matters which they cry out against as repugnant to reason, frivolous, absurd, and dreadful. However, such is my plan. Nothing comes to pass in nature, which can be set down to a flaw therein; for nature is always the same, and everywhere one and the same in her efficacy and power of action; that is, nature's laws and ordinances, whereby all things come to pass and change from one form to another, are everywhere and always the same; so that there should be one and the same method of understanding the nature of all things whatsoever, namely, through nature's universal laws and rules. Thus the passions of hatred, anger, envy, and so on, considered in themselves, follow from this same necessity and efficacy of nature; they answer to certain definite causes, through which they are understood, and possess certain properties as worthy of being known as the properties of anything else, whereof the contemplation in itself affords us delight. I shall, therefore, treat of the nature and strength of the emotions according to the same method as I employed heretofore in my investigations concerning God and the mind. I shall consider human actions and desires in exactly the same manner, as though I were concerned with lines, planes, and solids.

Descartes's philosophy did not create a revolution in science, since it was in the main only an authoritative expression of the assumptions and implicit goals of many of its leaders. And although some of Descartes's specific scientific contributions acquired a permanent value, many of his physical speculations, such as the theory of vortex motions, were not developed rigorously by him, and were in fact soon found to be in serious disagreement with more careful investigations. Nevertheless, his writings had a profound influence upon his contemporaries and successors, and contributed enormously to the formation of the modern climate of opinion. They made popular the view, in a manner that was difficult to ignore or refute, that nature is to be understood as a mechanical order and not in terms of final causes or criteria of perfection. And they standardized the notion—with profound consequences for the slowly emerging sciences dealing with biology, politics, and economics—that every adequate explanation must be framed in terms of simple, elementary properties, connected by self-evident laws.

The actual realization of Descartes's ideal of a universal mechanics, at least for the phenomena of physical motions, was the achievement of Isaac Newton (1642–1727). Newton's procedure was dominated by the Cartesian conception of the mathematical method as the rational way for studying nature, and it was also profoundly influenced by the Galileo-Bacon-Boyle view on the indispensable role of experiment in science. Building on the foundations laid by Galileo in dynamics, Newton constructed a cosmology, worked out with superb mathematical detail and verified in an abundance of empirical data, which established authoritatively the identity of the laws regulating both terrestrial and celestial motions. His *Philosophiae Naturalis Principia Mathematica* (*The Mathematical Principles of Natural Philosophy*), published in 1687, was genuinely epoch-making: it brought together into a unified system the labors of all preceding investigators in physics and astronomy; it wrecked beyond repair whatever intellectual props still remained for the medieval world-view; and it established the norms and directions of scientific inquiry for the next two centuries. The book went through three editions in Newton's lifetime, and found a host of popularizers not only in England, but also in France (where Voltaire made the Newtonian philosophy fashionable), Central Europe, and even in America. Pope's famous couplet expressed the sentiments of Newton's contemporaries:

> Nature and Nature's laws lay hid in Night,
> God said, Let Newton be, and all was light.

And a hundred years after the appearance of the *Principia,* Lagrange, himself a mathematician and physicist of the first rank, could still declare: "Newton was the greatest genius that ever existed, and the most fortunate, for we cannot find more than once a system of the world to establish."

A brief summary of some of Newton's achievements will give the measure of his intellectual stature. He formulated explicitly the principles of dynamics, and devised a general formula from which the law of accelerated motion, as discovered by Galileo, as well as Kepler's three laws of planetary motion were all necessary consequences. He showed, for example, that the moon's motion conforms to the same law of freely falling bodies, if the moon's distance from the earth is taken into consideration, which holds for bodies at the earth's surface. He thus advanced the conception of a universal gravitational force acting between all material particles with an intensity inversely proportional to the square of their mutual distances. He concluded that such a force, emanating from the sun, is sufficient to keep the planets in their courses and to explain the motions of the comets, while such a force with its origin in a planet will account for the orbits of its satellites.

Moreover, in order to carry through his mathematical deductions, Newton invented the method of "fluxions" (his name for what is now called the differential calculus), perhaps the most remarkable tool ever devised for analyzing mathematically continuous changes of any conceivable type. He showed how to calculate the masses of the sun, planets, and satellites. He demonstrated the oblate shape of the earth before this shape was determined by geodetic measurements. He explained the precession of the equinoxes (that is, the slow conical motion of the earth's axis, illustrated by the circular path traced out by the earth's north pole among the fixed stars). And he accounted for the main features of the tides as consequences of the attractive force of the sun and moon exerted upon the waters of the earth. In brief, therefore, familiar as well as novel phenomena of the heavens and the earth fell into place within a unified system, whose various propositions were rigorously derived from a few physical principles taken as axioms. Newton's grand synthesis of physical knowledge proved concretely that the mechanism of the universe is thoroughly knowable, even if only experiments conducted on the surface of a minor planet were available for eliciting its mathematical principles.

Newton impressed his age not only by his specific additions to physical knowledge; his work was also construed as the model which sound investigation in every field ought to follow. He himself was conscious of the importance of a sound method of inquiry, and his technical writings are interspersed with many comments on its nature. "We offer this work as mathematical principles of philosophy," he said in the Preface to his *Principia,* "for all the difficulty of philosophy seems to consist in this—from the phenomena of motions to investigate the forces of nature, and then from these forces demonstrate the other phenomena." Indeed, this brief statement contains the essentials of his method as he understood it: to find by analysis the fundamental principles embodied in phenomena; to generalize these principles and mathematically to elaborate their consequences; and finally to exhibit the physical validity of these latter by an appeal to observation and experiment. In his own procedure and by his own account, Newton thus fused into an indissoluble unity both the mathematical and the experimental traditions of the new science.

That Newton saw clearly the necessity for an experimental foundation for his work, without minimizing the claims of mathematical formulation and rigor, is evident from the *Rules of Reasoning in Philosophy* with which he began the third book of the *Principia,* as well as from other writings. Thus, in a retort to an attack by Robert Hooke on his theory of colors, Newton declared:

I said, indeed, that the science of colours was mathematical, and as certain as any other part of optics; but who knows not that optics, and many other mathematical sciences, depend as well on physical sciences, as on mathematical demonstration? And the absolute certainty of a science cannot exceed the certainty of its principles. Now the evidence, by which I asserted the propositions of colour, is in the next words expressed to be from experiments, and so but physical: whence the propositions themselves can be esteemed no more than physical principles of a science. And if those principles be such, that on them a mathematician may determine all the phaenomena of colours, that can be caused by refractions, and that by disputing or demonstrating after what manner, and how much, those refractions do separate or mingle the rays, in which several colours are originally inherent; I suppose the science of colours will be granted mathematical, and as certain as any part of optics. And that this may be done, I have good reason to believe, because ever since I became first acquainted with these principles, I have, with constant success in the events, made use of them for this purpose.

He was constantly warning his reader against the introduction into science of occult qualities and "hypotheses"—that is, of conjectural causes for phenomena, such as Descartes's vortices, which are not adequately based on observation. By hypotheses Newton meant propositions "assumed or supposed without any experimental proof." Thus in a letter to Cotes he wrote that

. . . [just] as in geometry, the word "hypothesis" is not taken in so large a sense as to include the axioms and postulates; so, in experimental philosophy, it is not to be taken in so large a sense as to include the first principles or axioms, which I call the laws of motion. These principles are deduced from phenomena and made general by induction, which is the highest evidence that a proposition can have in this philosophy. And the word "hypothesis" is here used by me to signify only such a proposition as is not a phenomenon nor deduced from any phenomena, but assumed or supposed—without any experimental proof.

Conceiving of hypotheses in this sense, Newton wrote in the General Scholium to the third book:

Hitherto we have explained the phaenomena of the heavens and of our sea by the power of gravity, but have not yet assigned the cause of this power. This is certain, that it must proceed from a cause that penetrates to the very centres of the sun and the planets, without suffering the least diminution of its force; that operates not according to the quantity of the surfaces of the particles upon which it acts (as mechanical causes use to do), but according to the quantity of the solid matter which they contain, and propagates its virtue on all sides to immense distances, decreasing always in the duplicate proportion of the distances. . . . But hitherto I have not been able to discover the cause of those properties of gravity from phaenomena, and I frame no hypotheses; for whatever is not deduced from the phaenomena, is to be called an hypothesis; and hypotheses, whether metaphysical or physical, whether of occult qualities or mechanical, have no place in experimental philosophy. In this philosophy particular propositions are inferred from phaenomena, and afterwards rendered general by induction. Thus it was that the impenetrability, the mobility, and the impulsive force of bodies, and the laws of motion and of gravitation, were discovered. And to us it is enough that gravity does really exist, and act according to the laws which we have explained, and abundantly serves to account for all the motions of the celestial bodies, and of our sea.

But perhaps the clearest expression of Newton's standpoint on questions of method is contained in the following quotations from his *Opticks:*

The Principles [such as gravity and cohesion] I consider not as Occult qualities, supposed to result from the specifick forms of Things, but as general Laws of Nature, by which the Things themselves are formd; their Truth appearing to us by Phaenomena, though their Causes be not yet discovered. For these are manifest Qualities, and their Causes only are occult. And the Aristotelians gave the Name of occult Qualities not to manifest Qualities, but to such Qualities only as they supposed to lie hid in Bodies, and to be the unknown Causes of manifest Effects: Such as would be the Causes of Gravity, and of magnetick and electrick Attractions, and of Fermentations, if we should suppose that these Forces or Actions arose from Qualities unknown to us, and incapable of being discovered and made manifest. Such occult Qualities put a stop to the Improvement of natural Philosophy, and therefore of late Years have been rejected. To tell us that every Species of Things is endowed with an occult specifick Quality by which it acts and produces manifest Effects, is to tell us nothing: But to derive two or three general Principles of Motion from Phaenomena, and afterward to tell us how the Properties and Actions of all corporeal Things follow from those manifest Principles, would be a very great step in Philosophy, though the Causes of those Principles were not yet discovered: And therefore, I scruple not to propose the Principles of Motion above mentioned, they being of very general Extent, and leave their Causes to be found out. . . .

As in Mathematics, so in Natural Philosophy, the Investigation of difficult Things by the Method of Analysis consists in making Experiments and Observations, and in drawing general Conclusions from them by Induction, and admitting of no

Objections against the Conclusions, but such as are taken from Experiments or other certain Truths. For Hypotheses are not to be regarded in experimental Philosophy. And although the arguing from Experiments and Observations by Induction be no Demonstration of general Conclusions: yet it is the best way of arguing which the Nature of Things admits of, and may be looked upon so much the stronger, by how much the Induction is more general. But if at any time afterwards any Exception shall occur from Experiments, it may then begin to be pronounced with such Exceptions as occur. By this way of Analysis we may proceed from Compounds to Ingredients, and from Motions to the Forces producing them; and in general, from Effects to their Causes, and from particular Causes to more general ones, till the Argument end in the most general. This is the Method of Analysis: And the Synthesis consists in assuming the Causes discovered, and established as Principles, and by them explaining the Phaenomena proceeding from them, and proving the Explanations.

Newton was more confident than succeeding generations of scientists have become that the analysis of phenomena can uncover indubitably and once for all the fundamental principles of a science, and that experiment can establish with unfailing certainty the universal physical validity of their mathematical consequences. Newton's confidence was indeed contagious, and the eighteenth-century workers in the social as well as the natural sciences shared with him this fundamental rationalistic assumption. Much critical spade work still remained to be done before this rationalistic heritage in Newton's philosophy could be undermined. But when the critical reconstruction finally came, it was itself a product of the powerful impulse which the Newtonian synthesis gave to experimental-mathematical inquiry.

## IV

The steps in the establishment of the mathematical interpretation of nature, which have been outlined above, do not cover the entire ground of events in the development of modern science. The parallel transformations, and the great names associated with them, in the physics of liquids and gases, in optics, chemistry, medicine, physiology, zoology, botany, and geology, have been neglected in this account. But enough has been said to make clear the essentials of the experimental-mathematical method as the founders of modern science conceived it, and to indicate what elements in it were taken over by the increasingly numerous inquirers into the nature of man and society.

It should be noted, however, that the intellectual achievements which have been described did not immediately affect the thinking of the great masses of men. For the understanding of these achievements a special training is required, and this training was not supplied to its students by most universities of the period. A petition for university reform, submitted in 1649 to the British Parliament, is symptomatic of the fact that the new learning was still far removed from the minds and bosoms of university students. The petitioner declared:

I have ever expected from an university, that though all men cannot learne all things, yet they should be able to teach all things to all men; and be able either to attract knowing men from abroad out of their owne wealth, or at least be able to make an exchange. But how far short come we of this, though I acknowledge some differences between our universities? We have hardly professours for the three principall faculties, and these but lazily read,—and carelessly followed. Where have we anything to do with Chimistry, which hath snatcht the Keyes of Nature from the other sects of philosophy by her multiplied experiences? Where have we constant reading upon either quick or dead anatomies, or occular demonstrations of herbes? Where any manual demonstrations of Mathematicall theorems or instruments? Where a promotion of their experiences which if right carried on, would multiply even to astonishment?

Many of the leading investigators of nature were in fact not associated with the established seats of learning; this was true, for example, of Kepler, Descartes, Boyle, and Huygens. It was only much later, and in part as a consequence of much agitation, that the universities became, as they are today, centers of research and of the propagation of scientific knowledge.

Nevertheless, the new science was slowly taking firm root in the institutions of seventeenth-century society. As has already been noted, many of the new experimental and theoretical discoveries had a clear-cut relevance for the arts and crafts of the day. And in consequence, the continued growth of science was sustained by, because it in turn helped to sustain, the development of commerce, manufacture, mining, and the arts of war. Indeed, many of the most enthusiastic and vocal devotees of science saw its greatest significance in the practical contributions it made to human welfare and in the increased power it gave over nature. Even Descartes, who cannot be accused of myopic practicality, emphasized this aspect of the new knowledge:

[The principles of Physics] caused me to see that it is possible to attain knowledge which is very useful in life, and that, instead of that speculative philosophy which is taught in the Schools, we may find a practical philosophy by means of which, knowing the force and the action of fire, water, air, the stars, heavens and all other bodies that environ us, as distinctly as we know the different crafts of our artisans, we can in the same way employ them in all those uses to which they are adapted, and thus render ourselves the masters and possessors of nature. This is not merely to be desired with a view to the invention of an infinity of arts and crafts which enable us to enjoy without any trouble the fruits of the earth and all the good things which are to be found there, but also principally because it brings about the preservation of health. . . .

The most eloquent voice raised in behalf of knowledge as an instrument of control was that of Francis Bacon. He saw the reason for the small progress of science during the past, not only in the circumstance that it had been wedded to scholastic methods, but also in the fact that its "goal itself has not been rightly placed. Now the true and lawful goal of the sciences is this: that human life be endowed with new discoveries and powers." His proposed reform of the sciences was directed toward achieving just this objective: "Although the roads to human power and to human knowledge lie close together, and are nearly the same, nevertheless on account of the pernicious and inveterate habit of dwelling on abstraction, it is safer to begin and raise the sciences from those foundations which have relation to practice, and to let the active part itself be as the seal which prints and determines the contemplative counterpart." Bacon's conception of the nature of scientific method was inadequate. But his enthusiasm for planned experimentation, and his sketch for a cooperative research institute (the House of Solomon, described in his *New Atlantis*), had an enormous influence on the establishment of scientific research as a recognized profession and a valued social institution.

Scientific societies, meant for the experimental study of nature, were in fact slowly coming into being, first as informal gatherings and later as formally constituted bodies having the approval and support of the state. Probably the earliest of these private gatherings began to meet in 1560, in Naples, but it had only a brief existence. In Rome, the *Accademia dei Lincei* (*Lincei,* lynx, symbolized the battle with error and falsehood.) to which Galileo belonged, was established in 1603. It had plans to found branches in all parts of the world for the gathering of factual data, and it thus anticipated some of the ideas of Bacon's House of Solomon. It had a distinguished career; but with the Church's condemnation of the work of Galileo and the death of its founder and patron, the Duke Fredrigo Cesi, its activities steadily declined and ceased to exist altogether by 1657. In that year the Medici organized at Florence the *Accademia del Cimento* (Academy of Experiment), which endured for ten years. Its membership was composed chiefly of Galileo's disciples and their students, and its organization was quite informal.

During its short but brilliant life it conducted experimental investigations in most branches of natural knowledge, and contributed substantially to the improvement of such fundamental instruments as the thermometer, the barometer, and the microscope.

The London Royal Society also arose out of informal meetings of scholars and amateurs of science. Their weekly meetings were begun in 1645, and were held in London, frequently at Gresham College; during the Civil War the meetings were continued at Oxford, but were again resumed in London in 1660. The group included some of the leading mathematicians and other outstanding scientists of the day, as well as a somewhat miscellaneous collection of merchants and members of the nobility and the clergy. Its deliberations and experiments slowly acquired a certain notoriety, and Robert Boyle, an early member, referred to it as the "Invisible College." A memorandum on a meeting in 1660 states that "amongst other matters that were discoursed of, something was offered about a designe of founding a Colledge for the promoting of Physico-Mathematicall Experimental Learning." And some verses written at the time, *In praise of the choice company of Philosophers and Witts who meet Wednesdays weekly at Gresham College,* help to state the aims of the society and its contempt for the established universities:

At Gresham College a learned knot
Unparalleled designs have layed
To make themselves a corporation
And know all things by demonstration.

These are not men of common mould,
They covet fame but condemn gold.
The College Gresham shall hereafter
Be the whole world's University.

Oxford and Cambridge are our laughter;
Their learning is but pedantry.
These new Collegiates do assure us
Aristotle's an ass to Epicurus.

In 1661 the Invisible College was formally incorporated by royal charter as the *Royal Society of London for Promoting Natural Knowledge;* but although royal approval was thus given to the pursuit of experimental study, largely because of its potential contributions to the arts of trade and navigation, financial assistance was not forthcoming from the royal treasury.

In its early days the Society patterned its activities largely on the Baconian ideal of knowledge. Bishop Sprat, an early member and its first historian, in describing its beginnings declared: "I shall only mention one great man who had the true imagination of the whole Extent of this Enterprise as it is now on foot, and that is the Lord Bacon in whose books there are everywhere scattered the best arguments that can be produced for the Defence of experimental philosophy, and the best Directions that are needful to promote it." And Boyle expressed unambiguously the hopes he expected to see realized by its activities:

I must ingeniously confesse to You, *Pyrophilus,* That I should not have neer so high a value as I now cherish for Physiology, if I thought it could onely teach a Man to discourse of Nature, but not at all to Master Her; and served onely, with pleasing Speculations to entertain his Understanding without at all increasing his Power. And though I presume not to judge of other Mens Knowledge: yet, for my own particular, I shall not dare to think my selfe a true Naturalist, till my skill can make my Garden yeeld better Herbs and Flowers, or my Orchard better Fruit, or my Field better Corn, or my Dairy better Cheese than theirs that are strangers to Physiology . . . Methinks it should be a Disparagement to a Philosopher, when he descends to consider Husbandry, not to be able, with all his Science, to improve the precepts of an Art, resulting from the lame and unlearned Observations and Practice of such illiterate persons as Gardenners, Plowmen, and Milkmaids. And indeed, *Pyrophilus,* though it be but too evident, that the barren Philosophie, wont to be taught in the Schooles, hath hitherto been found of very little Use in Humane life; yet if the true principles of that fertill Science were thoroughly known, considered and applied, tis scarce imaginable, how universal and advantageous a change they would make in the World. For in Man's knowledge of the Nature of the Creatures, doth principally consist his Empire over them (his Knowledge and his power having generally the same Limits).

Boyle also argues "that the Goods of Mankind may be much increased by the Naturalist's Insight into Trades"; and he proceeded to establish two things: "The One; That an Insight into Trades may Improve the Naturalist's Knowledge. And the Other; That the Naturalist, as well by the skill thus obtain'd, as by the other parts of his knowledge, may be enabled to Improve Trades." And in fact the Society did concern itself with the construction of instruments and techniques relevant to the commercial, manufacturing, and agricultural problems of the day. It collected curious objects and various bits of information from the four quarters of the earth, intending to compile a comprehensive natural history of the world in the approved Baconian manner. And through its permanent secretary, it conducted an extensive correspondence with foreign learned bodies, which culminated in the publication in 1664 of the *Philosophical Transactions,* one of the first regular periodicals devoted to scientific subjects.

Much of this early work of the Society was highly uncritical, and is now only of antiquarian interest. For example, one of the queries, typical of the others, which was submitted to the resident-general of Batavia as part of the project for a natural history of the world was "What river is there in Java that turns wood into stone?" The miscellaneous material so carefully gathered by the Society shows clearly that a sound method in science was not an easy conquest and that fruitful research cannot be achieved on the strength of good intentions alone. Nevertheless, the formation and the growth of the Royal Society also illustrate the gradual institutionalization of science and its incorporation into the warp and woof of modern social policy.

Similar scientific societies were established on the Continent of Europe. At the strong urging of Colbert, Louis XIV established the *Académie des Sciences* in 1666, and supported it with the resources of his treasury. Colbert was aware of the economic values of scientific research, and encouraged the *Académie* to direct its inquiries along lines which would strengthen his mercantilist policy. The organization of the French academy became a model for many of the research institutes which soon dotted the map of Europe: of these latter, the Berlin Academy, organized in 1700, deserves special mention. Before long, most of these learned bodies issued regular scientific publications, and the business of professional research was well under way.

Thus, formally organized institutes of research came into being partly because of the efforts of disinterested scholars, partly because of the pressure exerted by the problems of a commercial civilization, and partly because of the encouragement of public officials. For each of these the need for such institutes became progressively greater: for the pure scientist, because the expense involved in constructing suitable instruments and in conducting experiments required a large community to bear the financial burden; for the merchants and manufacturers, because only a permanent group of trained scientists could solve the technological problems perpetually arising from their occupations; and for the statesmen, because they recognized that prosperity in times of peace and success in times of war both depend on the cultivation of knowledge that yields power over man and nature. The love of truth, the desire for honor and fame, the hope for material gain and political power, were all factors in the furtherance of research; severally and jointly they have helped to make "Mathematicall-Experimentall Learning" an integral part of modern society.

The need for making the results and the spirit of this learning accessible to a wider audience was partly met by encyclopedic expositions of the significant achievements of science. The most notable of these was the French *Encyclopédie,* whose contributors were the outstanding intellectual figures of the eighteenth century, and whose influence was felt not only in France but throughout Europe and America for the next two hundred years. The *Encyclopédie* made evident the conviction that the institutionalization of science is both a factor in social change and a model for social organization.

One further, though less obvious, feature of the institutionalization of science must be briefly noted: the social nature of scientific activity. The complexity of modern research, like the complexity of a modern industry, both invites and requires a cooperative division of labor. Analogous to the way in which an industrial product is the outcome of an interrelated economic system, the intellectual products of science are the achievements of a professional community. Accordingly, what is sometimes called "scientific truth" is not simply a personal or individual product, even though the activities of gifted individuals count heavily in its genesis. For if by "scientific truth" is understood a conclusion warranted by scientific inquiry, scientific truth is the product of a community of habitually cooperative workers, which evaluates the adequacy of every specific investigation.

The following points will make evident the extent to which scientific activity, including the evaluation of its findings, is thoroughly social in character:

(1) No research institution, and even more obviously no individual student of nature, has all the instruments and opportunities for thorough-going research. The sheer cost of some instruments makes their indefinite duplication wasteful, if not prohibitive. And such factors as a favorable physical environment (for example, a large percentage of clear days in the case of astronomical observation), the availability of certain source materials, or the existence of special human talent, place further restrictions upon research projects. In consequence, specialization inevitably sets in.

(2) However, specialization is compatible with a flourishing state of scientific development only if cooperation between various centers of specialized research becomes a habitual matter. Thus, Kepler, though not himself gifted as an observational astronomer, used the observational data of Tycho Brahe;

while Newton relied on the data supplied by the Greenwich Observatory in developing the details of his theories. Different specialized researches are frequently highly relevant to one another, so that one condition for the effective investigation of nature is the free communication of ideas between various centers of study.

(3) But the communication of ideas is feasible only if a common language exists for effecting their transfer. There must be agreement on terminology and notation, and there must be conventions as to metrical units. The requirements of communication thus lead to bureaus of standards for setting up and enforcing norms of measurement, and to international committees for establishing a uniform technical vocabulary and a standard symbolism.

(4) Moreover, the communication of ideas is fruitful only to the extent that a common standard of workmanship is recognized at the various centers of research. For if one group of workers has no confidence in the findings of another group, a division of labor with respect to scientific research is futile. Accordingly, research is required to be conducted by recognized methods, whose operations are in principle always open to inspection and control. And the findings of an inquiry will in general be regarded as well established only if they have been obtained by standard methods or if they are repeatedly confirmed by other investigators. Thus, Galileo's report that he observed Venus to exhibit phases would report nothing more than an item in his biography, if his claim were not capable of repeated verification by any competently trained student of the heavens.

It is a commonplace of modern scientific method that isolated, nonrepeatable observations carry little if any weight, and that on the contrary observations become significant only if they are obtained in accordance with the warranted methods of the scientific community. Analogous remarks are pertinent, *mutatis mutandis,* in considering the adequacy of a theory to some subject matter, or the validity of some bit of mathematical reasoning.

The institutionalization of science thus involves not merely the construction of certain obvious material structures (such as laboratories and schools), however important these may be. It also involves the establishment of a cooperating community of professional workers, within which a division of labor is effected and standards of competence are developed. It is a fundamental characteristic of modern science that its conclusions are not evaluated by an appeal to some ineffable intuition or to some selected authority. The warrant for these conclusions comes from the type of method used in reaching them, and thus ultimately from the funded experience of a community of professional students.

## *FOR ADDITIONAL READING*

E. A. Burtt. *The Metaphysical Foundations of Modern Physical Science.* London, 1925.

H. Butterfield. *The Origins of Modern Science, 1300–1800.* London, 1949.

G. N. Clark. *Science and Social Welfare in the Age of Newton.* Oxford, 1937.

R. G. Collingwood. *The Idea of Nature.* Oxford, 1945.

*Discoveries and Opinions of Galileo.* Ed. by Stillman Drake. New York, 1957.

A. Einstein and L. Infeld. *The Evolution of Physics.* New York, 1938.

J. Jeans. *The Growth of Physical Science.* New York, 1948.

A. Koyré. *From the Closed World to the Infinite Universe.* Baltimore, 1957.

H. Lyons. *The Royal Society, 1660–1940.* Cambridge, 1944.

M. Ornstein. *The Role of Scientific Societies in the 17th Century.* Chicago, 1928.

G. de Santillana. *The Crime of Galileo.* Chicago, 1955.

G. Sarton. *Introduction to the History of Science.* 3 vols. Baltimore, 1927–48.

———. *The Life of Science.* New York, 1948.

K. Seligmann. *The Mirror of Magic.* New York, 1948.

R. H. Shryock. *The Development of Modern Medicine.* New York, 1947.

J. W. N. Sullivan. *Isaac Newton, 1642–1727.* New York, 1938.

A. N. Whitehead. *Science and the Modern World.* New York, 1925.

E. Whittaker. *From Euclid to Eddington.* Cambridge, 1949.

XIV

# THE WORLD OF THE ENLIGHTENMENT

*Franklin L. Ford*

"Enlightenment," wrote Immanuel Kant in 1784, "is man's release from his self-incurred tutelage. Tutelage is man's inability to make use of his understanding without direction from another. . . . *Sapere aude!* 'Have courage to use your own reason!'—that is the motto of enlightenment." Kant's definition has the ring of an intellectual manifesto, a call to battle. One might better say a call to continue the battle, for its author was looking back over a century of European thought, as well as appealing to the future.

In the German original of the above quotation, the key work is *Aufklärung*. "Enlightenment," its literal equivalent in English, did not come into general use to denote a movement in intellectual history until the nineteenth century, after the term had been popularized by Kant and his compatriots. However, as a common noun referring both to knowledge and to the mental capacity to put such knowledge to good use, "enlightenment" had been familiar in English since the seventeenth century. Unlike its Latinate cousin, "illumination," enlightenment carries no suggestion of the mystical or the supernatural. You may feel that your mind has received illumination through sudden insight, a vision, or a flash of heavenly intuition sent directly from God. But with respect to a given problem you may say to a fellow mortal: "Enlighten me," with the full expectation that he can give you the relevant facts and suggest a conclusion on which you can both agree.

Such an expectation seems at first glance to be prosaic, even humble. It lacks the awesome grandeur of divine radiance bursting upon the soul. Yet enlightenment too has had its own kind of radiance for all who esteem the human mind. Notice the pride that informs Kant's definition. He is speaking of a great liberation. Enlightenment was not just a quality of mind or a happy state of society. To its devotees it seemed an active, almost tangible thing, a wave of information and critical analysis that could sweep away the walls of prejudice, superstition, and senseless tradition, leaving men free.

There is no denying that problems arise as soon as this evocative word is capitalized and given an article to escort it. "The Enlightenment" is one of those historical labels—others include "the Renaissance," "the Reformation," "the Industrial Revolution"—that are too imprecise to be used with complete ease and confidence, but too convenient (and by now too popular) not to be used at all. Thus, anyone who employs such a term is obligated to make it clear to his readers just how he conceives its meaning.

The Enlightenment will be portrayed and discussed in this chapter as the dominant, though never the only, movement in European thought from roughly the mid-1680s to the mid-1790s. The last two decades of the seventeenth century witnessed epoch-making developments within the greatest nations of Europe—developments matched by startling strides in scientific and critical thought. Both in events and ideas, new challenges and new conditions merged into what a modern writer has called "the crisis of the European conscience." Conversely, at the end of our proposed period the French Revolution dramatized the smashing of hallowed institutional forms in a struggle from which no European state emerged wholly unchanged. Simultaneously, this international upheaval involved another crisis of conscience that gave new meanings to the most cherished words and values of the preceding era.

We shall be dealing not precisely with the eighteenth century but with a period of just over one hundred years—the *siècle des lumières,* as the French call it, or sometimes the "century of the *philosophes*." It is worth pausing to ask what a *philosophe* was in the age he called peculiarly his own. To his enemies he was an irreverent scribbler, an impudent critic, an enemy of the hallowed traditions. To his friends, he was what Denis Diderot in 1743 obviously described as his highest personification of himself: "The *philosophe* . . . is an honest man who acts in all things according to reason, and who combines good morals and sociable qualities with a mind disposed toward reflection and precision."

It is this ideal of rational, benevolent, and socially responsible intelligence which has led some historians to challenge the very notion of the Enlightenment as a historical epoch. Haven't most thinkers since the ancient Greeks esteemed reason, by one definition or another? Wouldn't Kant's and Diderot's specifications make *philosophes* of Descartes in the seventeenth century, Erasmus in the sixteenth or, for that matter, Hegel, Comte, Marx, and Mill in the nineteenth? Was the so-called Enlightenment anything more than a poorly defined phase of a much longer intellectual era, stretching from the early Renaissance to the antirationalist reaction of fifty to seventy-five years ago?

The Enlightenment *was* distinctive, because of its spirit, its vocabulary, and its particular views of reason's role in human affairs. We must not, however, overlook the fact that during the late seventeenth century and throughout the eighteenth there were numerous European thinkers who by no means shared this spirit, this vocabulary, or this view of reason. Nor should we pass over the sharp disagreements among the *philosophes* themselves or exaggerate the degree to which the *siècle des lumières* should be isolated from the rest of modern history—here the doubters are right to hoist warning flags. In short, we shall discuss points of view that characterized numerous "opinion leaders" of the period from the 1680s to the 1790s, but there will be no effort to indicate a blanket unanimity, which simply did not exist.

No less important than proposed boundaries in time are the outlines of geography. We shall be concerned here only with the European peoples, although at this time Europe was nearing the peak of its power to project its ideas around the world. Indeed, it is not uncommon to find the Enlightenment treated even more narrowly, as though it had been essentially a French phenomenon, with the rest of Europe partaking by radiation, so to speak, from the source of energy, which was Paris. British and German contributions, however, were much too significant to warrant any such approach. Italy —and to a lesser extent the Low Countries, Switzerland, Scandinavia, and the English colonies on the North American coast—would also have to be included in any complete survey of the period's intellectual productivity. Other nations generated much less on their own, but the new ideas were at least received and discussed by literate groups from Lisbon to St. Petersburg.

## I

At first glance our designated period was not one in which diplomacy and war had much to do with cultural history. Diderot, for instance, man of countless interests though he was, scarcely mentioned French foreign relations in his voluminous writings. Goethe mocked the Holy Roman Empire, of which he was a citizen. David Hume and Horace Walpole maintained their amiable intercourse with French friends throughout the 1750s and 1760s, when Britain and France were at war for huge imperial stakes. Nevertheless, in the relations among states lay some important characteristics of the age, and hence some major determinants of its intellectual range and temper.

For one thing, the very waning of popular involvement in such relations marked a change from the zealous fury of the wars of religion and a difference from the nationalistic frenzy of nineteenth- and twentieth-century conflicts. After the Peace of Westphalia in 1648, few men still deluded themselves that the true faith, no matter how one conceived it, could be imposed by battle. At the same time, men had not yet learned to fight for an image of nationhood that made every citizen of the opposing state an enemy to the death.

Not that the Enlightenment flourished in an era of peace and understanding. The period was studded with bitter clashes. In the 1680s the Turks besieged Vienna and then began their long retreat down the Danube before the resurgent Austrians. Meanwhile, Louis XIV prepared to launch the War of the League of Augsburg (1689–97) against a set of enemies destined at last to check further French expansion in his reign. Louis' last war, over the Spanish Succession (1701–14), was one of the costliest, and battles such as Blenheim and Malplaquet were among the bloodiest, Europe had yet experienced. The pivotal struggle of the eighteenth century (1756–63) revealed its scope and complexity by the variety of names given to it. To Viennese and Berliners it was the "Third Silesian War"; to Parisians and Londoners, the "Seven Years' War"; to New Yorkers and Bostonians, the "French and Indian War." Meanwhile, in the east, Poles, Swedes, Russians, and Turks periodically slaughtered each other.

Yet, these conflicts, for all their viciousness, were far less distracting for civilians in general and for men of letters in particular than the great battles over religion had been. Who cared any longer if one's king sent his hired soldiers off to some more or less prearranged battleground to fight other hired soldiers over the title to a border fortress of a remote sugar island in the Indies? The professionalism and relatively limited aims of early modern warfare left the cultured elite of Europe remarkably free to reflect, to correspond and to travel, even across hostile frontiers. A *philosophe* was apt to see in international relations as then conducted only one aspect worthy of comment: their apparent idiocy. In this he was perhaps a trifle unappreciative. The cynical cannibalism of dynastic states was doubtless an affront to his reason; but in his freedom to decide for himself whether or not to worry about war, the *philosophe* was luckier than he knew.

The age of the Enlightenment could be characterized as a period during which criticism of existing institutions was mounting in an ever louder and bolder crescendo—the period before those institutions were modified to any significant extent in response to such criticism. Despite the fact that the era witnessed at its outset a rational and nonviolent revolution in England (1688), and despite eighteenth-century instances of specific changes—for example in Prussia—the general impression of "lag" is inescapable. If the changes made after 1789 were ultimately to go far beyond the demands of most pre-Revolutionary reformers, political conditions before that date kept such demands coming in a steady stream.

Few *philosophes,* be it noted, lived under conditions of ruthless tyranny. The kingdom of Prussia, for example, apparently Spartan in its civil and military discipline, was actually renowned for its toleration of ideological dissent long before Frederick the Great's accession in 1740 (though it was unquestionably he who clinched this reputation by saying: "My subjects may think and say what they like, as long as they do what I like."). Other formal despotisms, such as the Hapsburg and Russian empires, generally relaxed their repressive regulations for the literate, Frenchified, and reassuringly conservative upper classes. Even in the lands of the Inquisition—Spain, Portugal, Naples, Rome, Venice, Savoy—freedom to read had gradually become much greater than freedom to speak or to publish. Still, under all these regimes, whether Catholic, Protestant or Orthodox, political repression remained in some degree outrageous to many intellectuals. At the other end of the scale stood Holland and Great Britain. The native *philosophes* of these two maritime nations were almost the only European thinkers of the age who were, on the one hand, free to debate political reforms and, on the other, little impelled to do so—at least until about the final third of the century. There were always exceptions, of course; but by the standards of the day, British and Dutch men of letters suffered neither terror nor galling indignities.

It is to men who lived under "inefficient tyranny" that one must look for sustained political agitation. Thus it was the British North American colonies, where official acts were exasperating but official repression ill-sustained, that produced at first vehement protests and, finally, rebellion. As noted above, both England and Holland knew increasing unrest in the 1770s and 1780s, as did the Austrian Netherlands in the latter decade. Similarly, in certain Swiss cantons, notably Geneva, and in the local principalities and free cities of Germany a combination of political abuses and a general inability to smother political objections produced its predictable crop of criticism.

(Goethe once remarked that even at their worst the small German states were good places for a writer, since the border was never very far away.)

Undeniably central, however, was the situation in France. Under Louis XIV (1643–1715) French writers had been able to publish more satire and protest than was allowed them by the letter of the law. Under his successors, Louis XV (1715–74) and Louis XVI (1774–92), French life seemed at times to prove that man lives freest under a decaying despotism. Still, both the decay and the vestiges of despotism continued to oppress French intellectuals, whether *philosophes* or not. Until the mid-1700s, writers were frequently imprisoned for their works, and down to the very end of the Old Regime the Council of State, the Parlements or the University of Paris might condemn a book to be burned by the common hangman. Even after 1750, when more and more friends of the Enlightenment held high governmental positions, the Bourbon monarchy remained cluttered with administrative relics and inequities calculated to outrage abstract reason, narrow self-interest, generous humanity—or all three combined.

The Westphalia settlement of 1648, without mentioning numerous smaller denominations, officially sealed the division of western Christendom into Catholic, Lutheran, and Calvinist components. During the next century-and-a-half, ecclesiastical problems confronting thoughtful Europeans were by no means uniform or simple. The Pietists of Germany and the Wesleyans (Methodists), whose influence radiated far beyond England from the 1730s onward, were highly successful in spreading differing but related gospels of intense personal faith. On the other hand, the clergies of the official churches —whether Catholic as in France, Spain, Austria, and Italy; Lutheran as in Denmark, Sweden, and many German states; Anglican in England; Calvinist as in Scotland, the Netherlands, and parts of Switzerland—enjoyed their social privileges and avoided spiritual excitement. The influence and prestige of the papacy, despite the unquestioned respectability of such pontiffs as Clement XI (1700–21), Benedict XIV (1740–58), and Pius VI (1775–99), had greatly diminished. Many worthy priests and ministers still strove to demonstrate in action the meaning of Christian love; and we shall see that the period was not devoid of theological disputes. Even among clergymen, however, after the death of the French Bishop Bossuet (1627–1704), there was not—on the Continent at any rate—a single major figure who combined intellectual eminence with steady attention to the tasks of organized religion.

Closely related to the period's relative lack of ecclesiastical interest was the stagnation of many institutions of higher learning; for the universities, with only a few exceptions, were most emphatically not the intellectual centers of the Enlightenment. The exceptions included Cambridge in England (for a period around 1700, at least), Leyden in the Netherlands, and certain German universities: Halle, Göttingen, Basel, Strasbourg (the latter two still actually German in spirit and organization though under the flags of Switzerland and France, respectively). In all these places there were significant groups of scholars who tried to keep up with the new ideas, whether they shared them or not. However, most of the great bastions of past (and future) learning—Oxford, Paris, Louvain, Heidelberg, Bologna, Alcalá in Spain—were either ignored by the intellectually adventuresome or, as in the case of Paris, looked upon as veritable strongholds of obscurantist reaction. Formal religion, at one of its historic low points, had laid a dead hand on the very universities which had once shared its glories.

The economic conditions in the century before Europe's first great industrial expansion had a direct bearing on the progress of the Enlightenment. In most western and central European countries (Spain was perhaps the only notable exception), the period after the peace settlements of 1648–60 saw a moderate improvement, and the period after Louis XIV's wars a much greater one, in the general level of well-being.

This judgment, needless to say, must be understood in relative terms. Poverty still oppressed broad areas of European society. By later standards, not more than one out of a hundred Englishmen, Frenchmen, or Dutchmen lived in a warm, well-lit and well-furnished home, ate appetizing and healthful food, wore comfortable clothes, and enjoyed much leisure. If one speaks of Italians, Prussians, or Poles, he should probably say: "not one in a thousand." Nevertheless, actual famine struck less and less frequently, epidemic disease had begun its stubborn retreat, and the obsessive terror of destitution had receded. As the European death rate slowly declined, the population of nearly every nation increased significantly. Improving roads and ships, faster communications, cheaper and more efficient publishing methods encouraged cultural activity and insured the distribution of its products.

For even the least affluent man of letters, all this meant a securer physical existence than many of his predecessors had enjoyed. As in all ages, of course, there were in the eighteenth century numerous thinkers who began life with independent means: Shaftesbury, Montesquieu, Walpole, Beccaria, Goethe,

Holbach, Condorcet, to mention only a few. At least one, Voltaire, had no such beginning but became rich by virtue of his writings. Many others shared the fortune of Diderot, Rousseau, and Herder, surviving early hard times to enjoy at least a comfortable degree of prosperity once fame was achieved.

Of greater historical importance than the economic status of authors, however, was the rapid expansion of their audience. Though wealthy patrons continued to play a part in the support of culture, it was a role that declined throughout the period. Becoming steadily more numerous were people who could not have subsidized art or literature by their individual donations but who nevertheless had enough education to appreciate, enough money to buy, and enough leisure to read the century's swelling mass of publications. There is no wholly reliable way to compare the number of readers reached within, let us say, ten years of publication by Pascal's very "popular" *Provincial Letters* in the 1650s and by Voltaire's *Candide* a century later, but a not unreasonable guess would be that Voltaire's immediate reading public outnumbered Pascal's by at least four to one.

Was there ever another such age of conversation? People talked in the antechambers of palaces, in fashionable salons and at the dinner tables, in academies and coffee houses, cafés and theater lobbies. They talked with a sense of participating in a major cultural activity. The pious editor and critic, Fréron, wrote scornfully that the "bright lights" of his day (mid-eighteenth century) were hostile to the Church only because they could not bear to keep quiet during the Mass. Yet as Fréron himself well knew, something more was involved than just idle chatter. Conversation was the negotiable currency of a tremendous boom in ideas. If some of the ideas were unoriginal and some of the remarks merely snide, there remained beneath the foam a rich brew of curiosity, inventiveness, and critical intelligence. Even thinkers we tend to picture as relatively isolated by eighteenth century standards were in fact heavily dependent on companionship. Rousseau, for example, withdrew dramatically in 1756 to a cottage some ten miles from Paris—then became furious at Diderot and other friends for not visiting him more often!

The age of the Enlightenment was also a golden age of letter writing. So popular was the personal epistolary style that it served as a conventional form of publication. Friedrich Grimm, for example, became famous as an essayist and commentator through news letters he wrote to various German princes over the whole second half of the eighteenth century. *Letter to* —— was a favorite kind of title for even the most impersonal pamphlet. Literate people wrote many letters, long letters, letters composed with transparent pride of authorship and dealing with subjects from the cosmic to the embarrassingly intimate. Such people also valued the letters they received from others, as witness the huge collections which were carefully saved and passed on to posterity.

The literary salons are among the features of the Enlightenment most familiar to any modern reader. But the salons were not really very substantial institutions. They depended on the wealth and whims of a few hosts, or more often hostesses; and aside from a tendency to be faddish and intolerant, they suffered from the fact that personal gossip is almost always more amusing than serious discourse. Two other settings for exercising the mind came much closer than did the salons to filling the gap left by the decadence of universities. One was the learned academy; the other the public reading room.

At the pinnacle of the hierarchy of academies stood certain august bodies dating from the seventeenth century: the *Académie Française* (1635), the Royal Society of London (1660), the French Academy of Sciences (1666). Others of at least comparable stature appeared in the eighteenth century: the Prussian Society of Sciences at Berlin (1700, reorganized as the Royal Academy after 1740), Czar Peter the Great's Academy of Sciences at St. Petersburg (1724), the Swedish Academy of Science at Stockholm (1739), and so on. In 1742, even the British colonies across the Atlantic (which by 1769 were to produce eighteen fellows of the Royal Society) established as close to a "national academy" as their circumstances would permit: the American Philosophical Society at Philadelphia.

The part played by all these foundations in lending form and prestige to higher learning can scarcely be exaggerated. The major figures of the Enlightenment—Newton in England, Leibniz in Germany, Fontenelle in France, Benjamin Franklin in America—lavished on their respective academies the pride and attention that in earlier times such men would have reserved to religious establishments. Below the level of royal or national foundations, but no less characteristic of the age, were countless smaller bodies organized under municipal or private auspices to consider intellectual problems. Here, for example, is the roll of provincial academies established in the cities of France during roughly the first half of the eighteenth century: Lyon (1700), Montpellier (1706), Bordeaux (1712), Pau (1720), Béziers (1723), Marseilles (1726), Toulouse (1729), Montauban (1730), La Rochelle (1723), Dijon (1740), Rouen (1744), Clermont-Ferrand (1747), Auxerre (1749), Besançon (1752).

A good example of the private academy, organized by a circle of friends, was the Parisian club, the *Entresol,* which for a number of years after 1724 held a three-hour meeting each Saturday evening on the Place Vendôme in the Abbé d'Alary's mezzanine apartment (whence the name of the society). It contained some two dozen nobles, clergymen, judges, and royal administrators; and its weekly program was carefully regulated to provide one hour for discussing newspaper or magazine articles, one hour for criticizing newly published books, and one hour for hearing reports by members on their own research in progress. Not the least interesting characteristic of the *Entresol* was the variety of backgrounds of its members: nobles and bourgeois, professional men and priests. It is a reminder of the relatively broad social base that the Enlightenment enjoyed through most of its duration.

Academies provided forums for specialists. The other institution mentioned above, the public reading room, provided the means by which a wider audience could appreciate the fruits of specialization. Lending libraries increased both in number and in size; for while books became cheaper as they became more numerous, only the wealthy could yet afford to own everything they read. Still more characteristic of the period were the mushrooming collections of current periodicals, often housed in a single parlor or at the back of a café and accessible to anyone willing to pay a nominal subscription fee. They provided a most varied diet of reading matter, as witness the offering of Treitlinger's "newspaper room" in the Swedish Coffee House at Strasbourg in the 1780s: twenty-nine periodicals in French, fifty-four in German, two in Italian and one (the London *Evening Post*) in English. In an age without television, radio, movies, phonographs, baseball parks, or papers delivered at one's door, many a literate townsman each week spent at his reading club a prodigious number of hours.

## II

Every period has its share of fascination with the timeless problems of human existence: the purpose of life, the meaning of death, the workings of the physical world, the possibility of a Creator and Judge outside the perceivable limits of that world, the enigmas of human relations, the nature of knowledge, truth, beauty. Up to a point, this continuity of interests makes the record of man's thought an indivisible whole and seems to defy all efforts at singling out "periods" or specific "movements."

Nevertheless, the ways in which these fundamental questions are raised, the particular degree of emphasis accorded each of them, the widely shared (and often unstated) assumptions underlying proposed answers—such elements do differ from age to age, lending to each its intellectual climate, helping to determine its intellectual contributions. Just here, in fact, is where we may hope to find the common ground on which the *philosophes* stood even while they disagreed sharply in their individual answers to the perennial riddles of existence.

It is an inadequate view of the Enlightenment to say merely that "it believed in reason." More specifically, it placed confidence in a particular application of rational intelligence, namely, analytical method. In this respect, René Descartes (1596–1650) remained the guide and master of the *philosophes*. In his *Discourse on Method* (1635), the great French systematizer had laid down four rules, deceptively simple and marvelously concise, by which he had decided to conduct all of his own investigations:

> The first was, never to accept anything as true when I did not recognize it clearly to be so, that is to say, to carefully avoid [sic] precipitation and prejudice, and to include in my opinions nothing beyond that which should present itself so clearly and so distinctly to my mind that I might have no occasion to doubt it.
>
> The second was, to divide each of the difficulties which I should examine into as many portions as were possible, and as should be required for its better solution.
>
> The third was, to conduct my thoughts in order, by beginning with the simplest objects, and those most easy to know, so as to mount little by little, as if by steps, to the most complex knowledge, and even assuming an order among those which do not naturally precede one another.
>
> And the last was, to make everywhere enumerations so complete, and surveys so wide, that I should be sure of omitting nothing.

These then had been the demands of Descartes and of the "Cartesian" method he had bequeathed to the Enlightenment: insistence on clear and distinct ideas, the subdivision of each issue into its final, irreducible elements, the ordering of all such elements (if necessary, by imposing artificial order), and finally, meticulous completeness in detecting the relevant items. They were demands which testified to a boundless faith in the human mind's capacity for clear, dispassionate, consecutive, and comprehensive thought.

The route which Cartesianism prescribed for arriving at the truth was by no means the only imaginable one. A mystic, for instance, might urge that the mind prepare itself for sudden and complete comprehension by refusing to commit itself to any specific, cramping line of thought. Another approach, that of medieval scholasticism, would be to move forward, alertly to be sure, but along a road already marked out by the signposts of faith and tradition. (Fundamentally, Descartes differed from the scholastics only in his rejection of traditional inhibitions against original doubt and in his relentless insistence on examining first premises.) Or again, facts might be accumulated, aimlessly at first, and allowed to organize themselves, as it were, into their own patterns.

The analytical method, however, had no use for such guides. "Analysis" means literally the process of breaking material down, resolving it into its components, whether the material in question be a chemical compound or a body of received beliefs. To this breaking down, Cartesianism had added the further step of an orderly rearrangement of the elements into a coherent argument. It asserted with a confidence bordering on arrogance that critical intelligence must question, must pick things apart, before it can move ahead toward answers.

Important as it is to recognize the continuing influence of Descartes on the Enlightenment, it is just as important not to conjure up an idea of Cartesianism triumphant in all respects. For while the *philosophes* honored Descartes's tenacious, geometrical mind, most of them rejected his belief that clear and precise ideas are "innate," that is, implanted in the mind before birth. As a busy scientist, Descartes himself had had to recognize other possible sources of ideas. It was none the less obvious, by the end of the seventeenth century, that his greatest contributions had been made in the abstract fields of mathematics and theoretical physics, while his notions about the sciences of observation, notably astronomy and physiology, had not stood up in the face of accumulating information.

"Empiricism" is the doctrine that all knowledge is based on experience, whether in its ordinary ebb and flow or prearranged for experimental purposes. To the extent that Descartes had rejected this view, his and the empirical methods cried for reconciliation. By the end of the seventeenth century, discontent with Cartesian deduction centered not on how it disciplined human thoughts, but rather on how it explained the origin of the thoughts themselves.

The empirical argument that permitted thinkers to abandon Descartes's theory of knowledge while retaining his logical method was set forth in *An*

*Essay Concerning Human Understanding,* published in 1690 by the English physician and philosopher, John Locke (1632–1704). Denying the existence of innate ideas, asserting that man's mind at birth is merely a *tabula rasa,* "white paper, void of all characters," Locke proceeded to inquire: "Whence comes it by that vast store, which the busy and boundless fancy of man has painted on it with almost endless variety?" His answer was twofold. First, our senses bring to our minds data ranging from yellowness, sweetness, roughness, melodious sound, or acrid odor to more complicated images and impressions. Second, experience "furnisheth the understanding with ideas" by letting the mind perceive its own operations. Thus to the first source, *sensation,* is added a second, *reflection.* Locke tried to explain in modestly reasonable terms just how it is that we have both ideas about things and ideas about ideas.

The *Essay Concerning Human Understanding* was basic to an amazing range of Enlightenment thinking. What Locke had done was to bridge a gap still troublesome for the seventeenth century but no longer, for the eighteenth, a problem of even comparable magnitude. Hereafter, one might draw on both Cartesianism and on empiricism. Actually, aside from the matter of the origin of ideas, the conflict between Cartesianism and empiricism, between deduction from innate ideas and induction from observed facts, has often been exaggerated. A demonstration such as Sir William Harvey's classic of scientific methodology, *Essay on the Motions of the Heart and the Blood* (1628), had summarized a brilliant series of experimental observations, interpreting them by no less brilliant strokes of both deductive and inductive logic. Nevertheless, there is no denying that Descartes's "innate ideas" had embarrassed critical thought, and by getting around that obstacle, Lockian empiricism cleared the way for analysis, armed with the doctrines of sensation and reflection, to move ahead.

Locke strengthened the demand for full honor to experimentation and observation, but their possibilities had been sketched long before Descartes and Locke by Sir Francis Bacon in his *Novum Organum* of 1621. It had been vindicated in a crescendo of triumph by the physical scientists.

There is no need here to repeat the familiar catalogue of great names and achievements, which had earned for the seventeenth century the eloquent title, the "century of genius." We need, however, to try to imagine what it meant to live at the end, or just after, that century. From the comfortable distance of nearly three centuries we can describe with cool appreciation the contributions of a Pascal, a Huygens, or a Leibniz. We cannot, however, easily recover the staggering power with which the achievements of early modern science struck the minds and imaginations of the men of the Enlightenment.

The issue was not just one of being duly impressed by the results of Galileo's experimental methods or grateful for the usefulness of Torricelli's barometer. It was equally, and more significantly, a matter of spiritual excitement. A universe supposedly ordered but, in its actual operations, still shrouded in mystery, even for the greatest minds of antiquity and the Middle Ages, had suddenly begun to yield up its secrets. And they made sense! The blood in a human body did not just rush aimlessly about; Harvey had been able to demonstrate that it circulated in a marvelously purposeful and efficient way. Kepler's proof that the cube of the time required for each planet's rotation around the sun was directly proportional to the square of the same planet's distance from the sun gave assurance that the heavens themselves could be encompassed in a pattern of rationality. Above all others, for his own and immediately following generations, it was Sir Isaac Newton who seemed to fulfill that assurance. Every aspect of mechanics, from the celestial down to the most minute, seemed to fall into place on the basis of Newton's universal law of attraction and the rules of force and motion he was able to derive from it. No less important, the orderly "clock universe" suggested by Newton's writings offered a basis for eighteenth-century discussions not only of science but also of religion, ethics, and even art. The year 1687, when his great work, *Mathematical Principles of Natural Philosophy,* was published, has probably been used more than any other to mark the beginning of the Enlightenment.

Contrary to an all too common misconception, the soaring geniuses of the seventeenth century had not bequeathed to succeeding generations a bland, smug certainty about the structure and prospects of the natural world. They had, however, launched on its momentous career the conviction that a question rightly posed could lead to an answer comprehensible in terms of human reason and consistent with human experience. Their dignified invitation to inquire, to observe, to experiment, to record, and to ponder was at once challenging and flattering to the intelligence of man.

With critical inquiry now allied to empirical knowledge, the Enlightenment's characteristic definition of rational thought was essentially complete. Thus we may seek to define what reason itself meant to the *philosophes,* as distinguished from ancient Greek sages, medieval scholars, or twentieth-century symbolic logicians.

Characteristic of the age was a tendency to see reason at least partly in contradistinction to its extreme, sometimes even caricatured, opposites: lust, emotional enthusiasm, superstition, blind obedience to traditional authority. Of these enemies, the last loomed as by far the most formidable, for passion, enthusiasm, and superstition could all be contemptuously decried as living on ignorance. Wisdom alone, it seemed, should place a check on the witless emotions and the fear-laden prejudices of the savage mind. On all these fronts, education would ensure reason's triumph. The authority of tradition, on the other hand, also claimed to base itself on education—false education, by the *philosophes'* lights, but education decked out in solemn robes, brandishing ancient records, sacred books, and hoary dogmas. Thus the newer apostles of reason engaged in a frontal assault on dogmatic tradition, viewed as the central enemy. In as much as the passions, fears, and superstitions of ignorant minds seemed to them the main reinforcements of dogma, the *philosophes* could conceive of all the enemy forces as defending the same set of walls.

No single writer of the seventeenth century did more than Pierre Bayle (1647–1706) to focus the empirical-analytical attack on tradition. Bayle, a southern French scholar and critic who spent the bulk of his adult life as an exile in Holland, was proud to call himself a Cartesian. His special contribution, however, was the marshaling of historical erudition in the service of criticism, something Descartes would never have done. Quite naturally, since he was a Protestant, he devoted much time and effort to castigating Louis XIV's persecution of the Huguenots. So strong was Bayle's hatred of orthodoxy, however, that he often clashed with Protestant zealots as well; and he succeeded in making himself anathema to the exiled Huguenot leaders in the Dutch provinces.

In countless pamphlets, in his periodical *News of the Republic of Letters* (1684 ff.), above all in his huge *Historical and Critical Dictionary* (1697), Bayle poured scorn on religious prejudice and, by implication, on tradition-based political authority as well. It was not only, perhaps not even primarily, because of his theoretical views that Bayle joined Newton and Locke as one of the early idols of the Enlightenment. At least equally important was his fearless insistence that every belief must justify itself in terms of both history and logic. Since his *Dictionary* also taught the eighteenth century the artful use of footnotes and cross-references to purvey unorthodox ideas without openly defying the censor, Bayle was an important precursor of the Encyclopedists' technique, as well as their spirit.

To the *philosophes,* however, reason's task did not end with the smashing of ignorant beliefs and smug intolerance, however essential that work appeared. Reason had a further, constructive purpose; in their eyes it alone could ensure reliable communication and final agreement among the men who must build the future. Careful observation, clear memory, dispassionate analysis—surely, if these could expose cant and bigotry, they could also provide the lucid realm where decisions for improving man's lot could be taken by informed and unselfish minds.

Obviously, such minds stood in need of a standard of judgment that would be free of special pleading and the accidents of human error. That need was filled, triumphantly at first, somewhat less perfectly after the middle of the eighteenth century, by a source that at the outset seemed both infallible and friendly to mankind: nature. In its earliest formulation, the new faith in nature was almost childishly unrestrained and trusting. Nature represented the antithesis of all that was ugly, unjust, and capricious in traditional authority. Nature played no favorites. Nature had the predictable symmetry of celestial orbits, the power of growth, the beauty of color and light. Above all, harmonious nature seemed to confirm, in the relations of tangible things, the promise that "right reason" could supply a basis for agreement among diverse ideas.

As we shall see, especially when discussing ethics and aesthetics, the *philosophes'* surrender to natural values was neither total nor abject. They did not commit themselves to honor cruelty or lust, or to admire physical monstrosities simply because these things appeared in nature. Instead, they were inclined to regard evil and ugliness either as accidental lapses from an essentially perfect order, or as instances of man's difficulty in understanding that order. In Pope's soothing words of 1733: "All Nature is but Art unknown to thee; all chance, direction, which thou canst not see." Man must strive to understand natural elements—but in so doing he was free to select and arrange those elements as guides to his behavior and his art.

"True nature" and "right reason" were thus enthroned as the twin deities of the Enlightenment. As in many other cases of shared thrones, there was to be a mighty falling out. Furthermore, nature itself would appear in different guises to rationalists, sentimentalists, and utilitarians. It would have been asking too much, however, in those first enthusiastic decades, to expect men to foresee the full range of future disagreements. It was enough, for the time being, to seek a more rational way of life for man, by nature's standards. "Unnatural" took its place beside "uncivilized" as a term of crushing opprobrium, for civilization itself was to obey the highest laws of nature.

The humanistic ideal is the insistence on man as the final measure of all things. We tend to identify this standard first with classical antiquity, especially as interpreted for the modern world by those artists and thinkers of the fifteenth and sixteenth centuries who gave special emphasis to the humanistic features of classicism, as they sought to recover its intellectual and artistic treasures. In this as in many other respects, the Enlightenment was a direct heir of the Renaissance. So far as humanism was concerned, however, the *philosophes* spent less and less time thanking the ancients and more time projecting man's interests into the future. Humanism was set against "unnatural" other-worldliness. If nature was both rational and benign, how could life be bad? If life was good, then why talk only of the future after death? Why treat man's sojourn in this world as nothing but a short and inevitably grim interlude of preparation for the hereafter? And why treat man, if he lives naturally, as having been mired in sin since the Fall of Adam and Eve?

In posing such questions, the *philosophes* practically dictated to themselves a series of answers that made humanism seem hostile to Christian doctrine as it had come down from the Middle Ages. Actually, of course, a man need not cease to be a Christian simply because he becomes a humanist in his interests and his outlook. Alexander Pope's Catholicism did not prevent his writing:

> The bliss of man (could pride that blessing find)
> Is not to act or think beyond mankind.

It is nevertheless true that "Christian humanism" was less strongly represented in the eighteenth century than it had been in the sixteenth, or would be again in the nineteenth and twentieth. So impressed have some historians been by this observation that they have ended by blaming the Enlightenment's form of humanism for the decline of formal religion.

Let us grant that much antireligious, or better, anticlerical literature of the period proceeded from humanistic biases. It still seems clear that Enlightenment humanism was not so much a cause as an effect of Christianity's troubles. The lifelessness of the formal churches did little to kindle interest or to promise success in absorbing the new scientific findings, however staunchly some divines—Anglican, Lutheran, and Catholic—strove to make such absorption possible. Into the partial vacuum left by disappointment with the older churches rushed humanism, offering excitement, hope, and a persuasive ethical message of its own. Man on earth *was* becoming the measure of at least very many things.

The principle of utility offered humanists the chance to convert their preoccupation with mankind into a series of political, social, and moral precepts. The question at hand was a direct one. Having rejected the authority of scholastic theology, a *philosophe* could no longer say: "I must do thus and so because it accords with my place in God the Father's plan for the universe, as explained to me by the Church." Equally unmoved by Calvinist orthodoxy, he was just as unable to say: "In my sin and helpless ignorance, I must act thus in the fearful hope of doing honor to the Almighty." What guide, at once rational, natural, and humane, should determine his choice among varying lines of action?

The answer, before the eighteenth century began its debates about ethics, sounded simple enough: "My guide must be usefulness to mankind." Utility may be defined in different ways and measured by many competing standards; but, like nature, it seemed to speak with a clearer voice to the early *philosophes* than to even their own immediate successors. Clergymen, teachers, soldiers, diplomats, landed gentlemen, even kings themselves would, at the outset, simply be asked to justify their acts and sometimes their very existence before the bar of utility. How wondrously useful, cried that first generation, had been the scientific discoveries of the seventeenth century! How useful to Englishmen the Glorious Revolution of 1688! But how useless to Frenchmen had been Louis XIV's religious intolerance and his vainglorious wars of conquest! And how utterly useless the cloistered life of monks and nuns, and the pedantic nonsense of theological metaphysics!

In all fairness, it must be said that Enlightenment thinkers soon came to recognize the difficulties inherent in seeking to define social utility. What, after all, *is* most useful to society—political stability, increasing creature comforts (i.e., a balance of pleasure over pain), physical power, cultural brilliance, rising population? And don't these various aspirations frequently come into conflict? Is an act that immensely benefits a few people preferable to one that slightly improves the lot of a huge majority? Yet every one of a *philosophe's* other assumptions impelled him to override all objections and to insist that no act or idea shall be called good unless it be socially useful. Of all the premises of Enlightenment thought, at its broadest level of agreement, none required less frequent restatement, because none was more confidently accepted.

One final assumption merits attention, before we turn to some specific disciplines of philosophy. This was the awareness of living in the midst of fundamental, historical change. At the end of the seventeenth century, surely, change was amply evident to anyone willing to see it. Changes could be either seen or predicted in the political, religious, and economic life of almost every major European nation. In the long quarrel between the "Ancients" and the "Moderns," the latter seemed by 1700 to have convinced the majority of critics that art and literature *were* on the move, building creatively on the stately foundations of antiquity.

Two characteristics of the ensuing century help to define, but also to qualify, the period's complex response to change. First, it would not be accurate to say that all thinkers acknowledged, let alone welcomed, the need to adjust to any fundamental movement going on around them. Many clergymen denied that theology should be reexamined critically. Many professional scholars in the universities insisted that learning was essentially changeless, and that the aims of formal instruction must be changeless, too. Thus, for the dawning eighteenth century, the awareness of change was *not* shared by all thoughtful men. Instead, it was one of the distinctive traits of the *philosophes,* a badge of "enlightenment."

The second characteristic to be noted cuts across even this virtual unanimity of the *philosophes* about the existence and importance of change. Men may agree that things are on the move, yet remain sharply divided as to where they are going. If I say to you: "The world is very different from what it was fifty years ago," you may reply: "Yes, it's much better, and it will be better still fifty years from now." In short, you believe in *progress.* However, while still agreeing with me, you may answer instead: "Yes, and it's going to keep right on getting worse." You will then have typed yourself as a pessimistic believer in *decline.* Or again, you may respond: "It is different now, but in fifty (or a thousand) years more I suspect it will again be pretty much as it was then." That is, you posit recurrence in *cycles*. Or yet again, you may observe wearily: "It is different, and more changes are coming; but they don't mean anything—the world isn't headed anywhere in particular." You will thus have chosen the philosophy that all is *flux* or aimless motion.

The doctrines of decline, cycles, and flux are worth keeping in mind as one approaches any Enlightenment thinker, for the *philosophes'* strong awareness of change and movement has often been mistakenly described as a flat, uncritical faith in progress. Actually, the "enlightened" argued endlessly among themselves as to the direction, the consistency, and the meaning of the changes they saw about them. While almost none of them, except possibly Rousseau in his gloomiest strictures, preached a theory of decline, it was a rare spokesman of the age who did not at some stage of his career entertain a cyclical theory, at another a doctrine of flux, thus asserting only part of the time a belief in comforting, unilinear progress.

It is evident that we have had to use considerable caution in sketching even a few base lines of Enlightenment thought. For example, we have been unable to accept a total separation between deductive and inductive reasoning. We have admitted that an esteem for reason was by no means peculiar to the period, whatever its preoccupation with certain of reason's uses. And we have insisted on the difference between an often bewildered recognition of change and any unanimous belief in progress.

Nevertheless, it has seemed worthwhile to identify certain underlying premises. Hence we have emphasized the faith in analysis, the appeal to experience, the demand that reason destroy untenable dogmas and build better foundations for authority, the view of nature as both benign and comprehensible, the acceptance of humanity and utility as standards of value, the awareness of movement in man's affairs. All these tenets underlay the *philosophes'* more specific contentions and gave to these men their shared place—as distinct from their widely varied individual roles—in the background of contemporary civilization.

## III

It would obviously be impossible, in a single essay, to catalogue all the problems that absorbed even a selected list of Enlightenment thinkers. We have, however, already noted that a major intellectual movement takes its personality from the characteristic way in which its apostles attack questions. Thus, if we are to understand both the areas of agreement and the divergencies of opinion among the *philosophes,* we must consider how they brought to bear on a series of such questions the widely shared assumptions we have just been reviewing. It is in its specific contributions to various intellectual disciplines, that the Enlightenment reveals itself most clearly to any reader prepared to look at those disciplines through the eyes of other men, in a departed but still peculiarly vivid age.

For centuries the unchallenged queen of Western thought had been religion. Even when, with the medieval proliferation of philosophy, fields such as science and political theory had recovered some of their ancient prestige, the "queen" had still exacted tribute, demanding that all worldly doctrines submit to judgment by her standards. Generation after generation of Europe's most powerful minds had gone on pondering theological questions as their main business, whatever other interests they might follow. The seventeenth century—the century of Milton, Pascal, Descartes, and Spinoza, not to mention the deeply pious Leibniz and Newton—had seen no turning away from religion as the central object of contemplation.

Against this background, the eighteenth century's contributions to theology appear remarkably thin. It is not enough to say merely that the wonders of physical science had diverted most of Europe's intellectuals away from the traditional questions of religion. Nor can we posit some catastrophic deterioration in the human leadership of churches, for nothing so abrupt can be documented. Last but not least, we should avoid the flat assertion that "reason" in general was crowding out "faith." Why should not reason remain in the service of faith, as it had for a Thomas Aquinas, or a Descartes?

Far from being able to rely on any simple, exclusive interpretation, we shall have to bear in mind a number of factors which, in combination, sapped the energy of systematic theology. No doubt scientific inquiry did beckon to many men who might in another age have been church scholars. Doubtless too, the complacency and rigidity of established hierarchies repelled some adventurous intellects. And reason, if conceived as primarily dedicated to analysis and criticism, could scarcely accept all the claims of religious orthodoxy. Notice, however, that it is only by putting together all these elements, while at the same time keeping in view all the other premises of the *philosophes,* that we can approach a full understanding of the decline of theology.

Since the appropriate word is "decline" and not "extinction," we have still to ask what kinds of religious debate did remain active. On the Catholic side, the authority of the papacy went on being hotly debated by proponents of national autonomy. Gallicanism remained an active force in France, resisting, as it had for hundreds of years, all "ultramontane" appeals to the Vatican over the head of the king or those of French bishops. In the Holy Roman Empire, the later decades of the century witnessed sufficient acclaim for the antipapal doctrines of the suffragan bishop of Trier, J. M. von Hontheim, (whose pen name was "Febronius") to make *Febronianism* seem a German and Austrian version of Gallicanism.

Such conflicts over church government, however, belonged more properly to "ecclesiology" than to theology, strictly defined. So far as theology itself was concerned, the only serious battle within the Catholic Church pitted the Jansenists of France and Italy against opponents of their neo-Augustinian creed. At the heart of that creed lay the doctrine of predestination, assuring salvation to some mortals and damnation to others on the basis of an immutable decree passed in advance by a God of inscrutable justice. Against so austere a conception, Jesuit thinkers in particular mounted the argument that a far kinder God than that of Augustine or Jansenius (or, they pointed out, Calvin) left man a margin of free will by which to determine his own fate. When the Society of Jesus was expelled from one European nation after another, beginning with Portugal in 1759, and especially after the pope himself dissolved the order in 1773 (it was not revived until 1814), Jansenist theology appeared victorious. Even contemporaries recognized, however, that the Jesuits had been struck down less because of their views on such issues as free will and the need to take a permissive view of pre-Christian rituals among converted peoples than because of partisan opposition to the Society's political activities and its traditional devotion to papal authority. In the meantime, Jansenism had deteriorated markedly since the heroic age of Pascal and Racine in the mid-seventeenth century, until its most prominent features seemed to be animosity toward all other Christians and the hysterical worship of daily miracles among the "convulsionaries" of Paris.

The Protestant clergies of England, Holland, Switzerland, Germany, and Scandinavia were engaged in disputes between fundamentalists, who wished to yield nothing with respect to the Bible's literal inspiration, and modernists like the University of Halle's liberal theologian, Christian Wolff (1679–1754), who believed that traditional faith could and should come to terms with the rational tenets of science. In other quarters, as mentioned earlier, Methodists, Pietists, and such older sects as the Quakers pressed the claims of personal religion. Setting essentially intuitive conceptions of the believer's direct experience of God against what they denounced as the hollowness of formal liturgy, they rebelled against the regular Anglican and Lutheran churches. But these Protestant debates, like those of Jansenists and Jesuits in Catholic countries, often seemed far removed from theology in its purest, most formal expositions.

More "philosophizing," in this abstract sense, went into treatises on religion by men who would acknowledge no ties with any sect or denomination. Deism, for example, represented a serious, if never widely popular, attempt to develop a faith which could meet on their own terms the scientific discoveries and the critical standards of the Enlightenment. Up to a point, this coincided with what men like Wolff were attempting to do within the Christian churches; but to achieve the same end, most Deists felt impelled to take theology out of the churches and away from the Bible.

The hallmark of Deism was the belief in a reasonable God, discernible through the natural order. As a modern historian has put it, on the *philosophes'* behalf:

> The God of the Middle Ages and of the Reformation had been not only a tyrant but a magician, exhibiting his power chiefly by suspending and violating the usual order of nature. The God of the Enlightenment became a mathematician and a mechanic, revealing his perfection by the formulation and application of inviolable laws.

Newton and other great scientists had presented educated men with a "clock universe," and it is scarcely surprising that some of those men proceeded to conjure up a God who would have been content to construct the clock and set it going, thereafter letting it run without any miraculous tampering. In positing such a God, they felt they had arrived at a new and rational, or as they preferred to call it, "natural religion." From John Toland's *Christianity Not Mysterious* (1696) through the pamphlets of Viscount Bolingbroke (1678–1751), Deism had a particularly strong representation in England. On the continent, too, varying formulations of natural religion came from Voltaire, Rousseau, and Diderot in France, Reimarus and Lessing in Germany. Even in America, Franklin had been writing Deist tracts since his youth in the 1720s.

A comfortable resting place for men disinclined to push their religious inquiries too relentlessly, Deism served only as a way station for other men who finally could not feel that they knew enough about God to visualize him even as an expert clockmaker, the "Author of the Universe." Such men had nowhere to stop short of the denial of all religious certitude. This chilly, skeptical view, called agnosticism by the nineteenth century, "Pyrrhonism" by the seventeenth and eighteenth, included a denial that we can be any more certain that there is *not* a God. Thus a Diderot or a Lessing, after substantial Deist periods, ended in a state of doubt suspended between faith in God's existence and certainty of His nonexistence.

Most famous of all the skeptics, and most devastating in his logical attack, was David Hume (1711–76). In the *Dialogues Concerning Natural Religion,* which he kept hidden during his lifetime, Hume has the Deist and the spokesman for orthodox, revealed religion destroy each other's logical positions. This leaves the field clear for the third disputant, Philo, the author's own protagonist, who outlines with pitiless clarity the dilemma of all religious belief, however "natural." How, he asks, can one set up a God by definition outside the realm of human comprehension, and then pretend to know anything about Him through either reason *or* revelation?

The most positive contribution that Deists and Pyrrhonists alike made to the Enlightenment lay in their case for toleration. If all religious principles were, in Hume's words, "sick men's dreams," then how could reasonable men ever persecute anyone on the basis of a particular set of such principles? If Jews, Christians, and Mohammedans had different but equally imperfect inklings of the single divine truth, as in Lessing's *Nathan the Wise* (published in 1779, coincidentally the same year as Hume's *Dialogues*), why should they feel justified in slaughtering each other over doctrinal differences? For eighteenth-century skeptics, as for Montaigne two hundred years earlier, no faith had a sufficiently firm basis to warrant forceful propagation. For Deists, all of religion consisted in nonsectarian reverence for a distant, undemanding God who could scarcely be served by wrangling over liturgy or the Gospels. How far European thinking had moved from the view that intensity of dogmatic faith was the mark of civilization is revealed in Voltaire's words from the *Treatise on Tolerance* (1763):

> The supposed right of intolerance is absurd and barbaric. It is the right of the tiger; nay, it is far worse, for tigers do but rend in order to have food, while we rend each other for paragraphs.

The steady decline of religious persecution throughout most of Europe in the eighteenth century suggests that this was an area of public policy that philosophy invaded with more than ordinary success.

Atheism, the explicit belief that there is no God, was not nearly so widespread during the era of the Enlightenment as was either Deism or Pyrrhonism. The difficulty of determining just how widespread it was arises partly from the fact that, like other highly charged labels in other times, "atheist" was a handy word for a religious conservative to use on any thinker who expressed serious doubts about the authority of any traditional dogma. Thus, the Huguenot divine, Jurieu, and the Catholic bishop, Bossuet, agreed for once in applying it to Pierre Bayle, who was assuredly no atheist. Similarly, in England Bishop Warburton hurled it at Deists such as Toland and Matthew Tindal (1653–1733), the latter for having in 1730 published *Christianity as Old as Creation,* a treatise viewed by its author as decidedly pious. Hume, whose scorn of all certitude definitely extended to the affirmations of real atheists, knew that he could not publish his *Dialogues Concerning Natural Religion* without being promptly branded as one of their hated number.

Uncompromising atheism found expression primarily among French *philosophes* of the second rank. The heavy materialism of La Mettrie's *Man a Machine* (1748) left no place for either God or the soul. Claude Helvétius did introduce a kind of God into his *On Man* (1773), but this God only denied His own existence and sent mankind off on its own. Baron d'Holbach, in several avowed works of the 1770s, and probably in many others whose authorship has not been finally established, made belief in God a sign of both ignorance and cowardice.

Atheism was most unusual in the religious thought of the Enlightenment. While the vast majority of Europeans went right on believing as they had for centuries, the *philosophes* did, it is true, sometimes strike off into unknown country. Yet almost all of them took along the belief that religion, if it were simplified, scraped clean of encrusting superstitions, brought into accord with nature and reason, could still lend stability to society and direction to individual lives. If the Enlightenment's religion seems pale and tentative, in comparison with the awesome thunders of the Church Fathers, this was not because the original questions had lost all interest for cultured men. Rather, it was because theology had now to make compromises with an unprecedented number of critical theories.

The Enlightenment's standard view of its own scientific achievements is likely to impress a twentieth-century student as unduly self-satisfied. Granted that, especially in the "life sciences," considerable advances were made in the eighteenth century, we are apt to feel that contemporaries exaggerated the scientific accomplishments of their age. Here is Jean le Rond d'Alembert (1717–83), one of the chief editors of the great French *Encyclopédie,* writing in his *Elements of Philosophy* (1759):

Natural science from day to day accumulates new riches. . . . The true system of the world has been recognized. . . . The discovery and application of a new method of philosophizing, the kind of enthusiasm which accompanies discoveries, a certain exaltation of ideas which the spectacle of the universe produces in us; all these causes have brought about a lively fermentation of minds.

Five years earlier Diderot, greatest of all the Encyclopedists and in general highly sensitive to contemporary currents and future possibilities, had gone much further in praise of his own times:

I dare almost assert that in less than a century we shall not have three great geometers left in Europe. This science will very soon come to a standstill where the Bernoullis, Eulers, Maupertuis, Clairauts, Fontaines, d'Alemberts, and La Granges will have left it. They will have erected the columns of Hercules. We shall not go beyond that point.

Yet neither in mathematics, in physics, nor in astronomy did the Enlightenment come close to matching the epochal discoveries of the preceding age. Important as were the probability formulas of the Basler, Nicklaus Bernoulli (1687–1759), or James Bradley's study of astronomical light rays in the 1720s and 1730s, or Benjamin Franklin's confirmatory electrical experiments at mid-century, they hardly rivaled the huge strides taken by Kepler or Boyle, Huygens or Newton in the 1600s. As for chemistry, despite the work of Lavoisier in France, Boerhaave in Holland, and Priestley in England, a present-day viewer cannot avoid the impression that this science was only beginning its period of expansion at the end of the eighteenth century.

Biology, botany, zoology, and medicine all seemed to forge ahead more swiftly, perhaps because in these fields the seventeenth century had left more to be done. This period witnessed, for example, the first small victories in the counterattack against epidemic disease and some very substantial advances in surgery. In the biological sciences as a group, the most significant figure was the Comte de Buffon (1707–88), whose *Natural History* of 1767 inspired loud and eventually rewarding arguments over the classification of species, as well as "nature watching" essays by countless devoted amateurs.

All in all, however, the Enlightenment seems less important for its scientific discoveries as such than for three other developments. One was the massive *diffusion* of scientific knowledge through academies, periodicals, and the books of successful popularizers such as Bernard le Bovier Fontenelle (1657–1757). The second was the spreading *invasion of other disciplines,* from politics and economics to musical theory, by scientific terms and methods. The third was an enthusiastic *application* of science to tools and machines of all kinds, to industrial dyes and agricultural techniques, to road building and shipbuilding, and to countless other uses. It is worth paging through the volumes of prints appended to the *Encyclopédie* if only to see the elaborate care with which the practical techniques of crafts and industries were illustrated, especially if they embodied innovations.

It should be reemphasized that to stress the popularization of science, its expansion into other fields, and its application to productive enterprises is by no means to suggest that it was declining in absolute importance. On the contrary, d'Alembert was quite right about the "lively fermentation of minds," and if Diderot was wrong about the "end of mathematics," he was right when he went on, in the same passage, to sketch the bright prospects of the biological sciences. In terms of the acceptance and propagation of its gospels, this *was* an age of science. Furthermore, if an interval of intense concentration on technology, on applied theory, had to lie between the Scientific Revolution of the sixteenth and seventeenth centuries on the one hand and, on the other, the Industrial Revolution of the nineteenth, the Enlightenment supplied just such an interval.

## IV

To an extent belied by the self-assumed title, "age of science," a veritable obsession with the philosophical problems of both personal and social morality gave the Enlightenment its most popular debating ground. The reason is not far to seek. By the late seventeenth century, many European thinkers had come to repudiate the traditional claim of organized religion that ethics must be viewed as a subdivision of theology. Pierre Bayle, in his *Thoughts on the Comet* (1682), flatly denied that to be moral a man must be religious. After examining the cruel cynicism that outward piety too often masks, he developed the view that an atheist might perfectly well be honest, tolerant, and kindly. Many men of the time, while they might not share Bayle's vehemence (and even he did not actually espouse disbelief as a guarantee of goodness), nevertheless accepted the spreading conviction that morality and religious faith constituted quite separate realms of discourse.

In rejecting theological claims, however, the *philosophes* in no sense repudiated the need to define good and evil. Their humanistic concerns alone sufficed to give a special urgency to their discussions in this field. Throughout the period of the Enlightenment, as earlier portions of this chapter might lead one to expect, there were two criteria which were advanced over and over again as the bases of ethical judgment. One was natural morality. The other was social utility. These two themes could be made to support each other, and few *philosophes* missed a chance to claim that their ethical systems were at once natural and socially useful. Nevertheless, natural morality has certain implications which ultimately set it apart from a rational calculus of simply what is good for society.

At its simplest, the naturalism of the Enlightenment rejected the doctrine of original sin and insisted that man is by nature benevolent and sociable. Why, then, are men ever cruel or perfidious? The Earl of Shaftesbury, writing in 1699, both suggested the reasons and warned of the results:

> Since in the common and known sense of vice and illness, no one can be vicious or ill except either—
>
> 1. By the deficiency or weakness of natural affections;
>
> Or, 2. By the violence of the selfish;
>
> Or, 3. By such as are plainly unnatural; it must follow that, if each of these are pernicious and destructive to the creature, insomuch that his completest state of misery is made from hence, to be wicked or vicious is to be miserable and unhappy.

Jean Jacques Rousseau, in his two *Discourses* of the early 1750s and in his treatise on education, *Émile* (1762), was more inclined than Shaftesbury had been to blame artificial constraints, perverse refinements, faulty social institutions, even calculating rationality itself for the evils of the human condition. Like the wise and benign South Sea Islanders of Diderot's *Supplement to the Voyage of Bougainville,* Rousseau's natural man was generous and compassionate until society made him otherwise.

Against this inspiring, though scarcely documented, vision should be set the utilitarian view, which was also, be it noted, present in the above quotation from Shaftesbury. Occasionally in the eighteenth century, utility was reduced to the self-centered estimate of pleasure or pain that a given action seemed likely to entail for the doer himself. In general, however, the whole social ethic was supported by the claim that what is best for society will also be best for its individual members. In other words, it *pays* a man to avoid crime, to be friendly and helpful to others. Paradox appeared only as individual self-seeking came to be identified as a source of social progress. Mandeville, in his *Fable of the Bees* (1714), argued that a prosperous society thrives on the personal vices of its members; this seemed unduly sardonic to most readers. Yet it eventually supplied the basis, in the works of Adam Smith, Jeremy Bentham, and others, for the conversion of some of those apparent vices into "economic virtues," because they served to enrich society.

Two of the most important moral philosophers of the Enlightenment—David Hume and Immanuel Kant (1724–1804)—defy easy classification as either naturalists or utilitarians. Hume *was* a utilitarian in insisting that social habit was a wise, well-tested basis for morality; the best line of action for the general good was suggested by what, historically, had been most useful to men. Yet in defining why, individually, we choose to act one way or another Hume seemed to rely heavily on innate psychological qualities. Both in his *Treatise of Human Nature* (1740) and in his *Enquiry Concerning the Principles of Morals* (1751), he developed a theory that human motivation involves a "moral sense," "propensities," and a "customary association." In short, he conceived of these inner forces as the basic sources of man's behavior; and he set the habits that these helped form in place of sharply rational estimates of pleasure versus pain or, for that matter, of abstract social needs.

Kant, like Hume, posited a suprarational moral sense, the "categorical imperative" as he develops it in his *Critique of Pure Reason* (1781). Unlike Hume, however, the German thinker also asserted that human reason can grasp an abstract "practical imperative" quite apart from what is emotionally desirable or socially useful. Declaring that "rational nature exists as an end in itself," he demanded that man "so act as to treat humanity, whether in thine own person or in that of any other, in any case as an end withal, never as a means only." In Kant, the humanism of the Enlightenment merged with the moral individualism of his Protestant Christianity. The result was a stern demand that man take full personal responsibility for respecting the dignity and rights of other men. Sense of duty!

Considering the variety of their views on the sources or *sanctions* of morality, the amount of agreement among Enlightenment thinkers as to the *content* of morality is truly remarkable. Their "ideal type," as an ethical image, was someone sympathetic toward mankind, intolerant only of fraud and superstition, broadly receptive to new ideas even if they threatened him personally. He respected life, freedom, property. He might be sexually promiscuous, by the standards of formal monogamy, but he must not let his passions overpower his reason or turn him ruthless and irresponsible. If no *philosophe* quite lived up to this image, that is the normal fate of ethical ideals. At the very least it marshaled humanism, utilitarianism, and rationalism behind moral demands which were far from ungenerous.

As noted earlier, the Enlightenment's generally accepted theory of knowledge or cognition was based on empiricism. The view that experience inscribes all knowledge on the mind, whatever subsequent combinations and refinements the mind itself might then achieve through reflection, remained unchallenged for an overwhelming majority of the *philosophes*.

The most persuasive popular development of this Lockian theory of knowledge was the *Treatise of Sensations* (1754) by a learned French clergyman, the Abbé de Condillac. Although relatively late among the basic works of the Enlightenment, Condillac's essay was important as the first fully elaborated attempt to solve a problem that had been left over from the seventeenth century. Descartes had sought to demonstrate the objective reality of the mind or spirit, and he had done the same for the physical world. But how do these quite different orders of reality act upon one another? Locke had discussed the importance of experience but not, so to speak, its machinery. He had examined the mind's uses of sensation, but he had not explained fully how sensation bridges the gap between objects or events and incorporeal ideas.

Various efforts, many of them lacking in consistency and conviction, had been made to treat this problem. Père Malebranche, in his *Metaphysical Conversations* of 1688, described a divinely ordained coincidence of *events* and *ideas,* by which each event supplied the "occasion" for an idea in keeping with God's plan for the universe. The Irish Anglican prelate, Bishop Berkeley (1685–1753), decided that only ideas have reality, that the "real world" is a projection of our minds. At the other extreme, La Mettrie, whose atheism we have already noted, set forth an unqualified doctrine of materialism. His *Man a Machine* described the mind as simply one part of a predictable, helpless, and irresponsible human organism, reacting blindly to physical stimuli.

Condillac's reassuring treatise seemed to take up where Locke left off, while avoiding all these extremes. Man is influenced by the real world, acting on him through his five senses; but each sensation increases his powers of retention, combination, *and volition*. Hence, man in turn reacts upon the world, shaping its details to suit the dictates of his calculations of self-interest and social good. Some of Condillac's demonstrations are still very interesting to read. (He deals, for example, with problems of synesthesia, e.g., "seeing" music as color; and like Diderot before him he examines cases of recovered or newly acquired senses, trying inconclusively to determine whether a man blind from birth, if he suddenly gained eyesight, would be able to recognize geometric shapes he had previously known only by touch.) On the other hand, much of his confidence in the clarity and reliability of rational choices based on sensory perception appears superficial to anyone acquainted with today's more complex, and often less optimistic, theories of motivation. Even at his most "dated," however, Condillac was important for having put man's mind into touch with physical phenomena, while saving his human dignity.

Several problems of knowledge remained unsolved for eighteenth-century philosophers, as they still remain today. How do we know, for example, that cause and effect, as discerned in the instances we have been able to observe, have held true in all the countless ones we have not observed, or will hold true throughout the future? The best the Dutch scholar 's Gravesande could do, writing early in the 1700s, was to declare that God assures us of natural consistency and recurrence: "The Author of Nature has made it necessary for us to reason by analogy, which consequently can be a legitimate basis for our reasoning." If 's Gravesande was too complacent, David Hume was too rigorously skeptical, at least for his contemporaries. Asserting that all we actually observe is a customary sequence of events we know about, he concluded that on this basis of mere association in time, we impose an artificial notion of cause and effect. As Hume put it in his *Treatise of Human Nature:*

> This removes all pretext, if there yet remains any, for asserting that the mind is convinced by reasoning of that principle *that instances of which we have no experience must necessarily resemble those of which we have.* (Hume's italics)

Like much that Hume wrote, the essay in question disturbed, without convincing, most thinkers of his day. Far more popular was the debate over the extent to which reason can give order to our impulses and the data of our senses, converting them into true wisdom. Claude Adrien Helvétius, in his *Treatise of Man* (1773), announced that men are essentially reasonable, adding optimistically that

> if words were precisely defined, and their definitions ranged in a dictionary, all the propositions of morality, politics, and metaphysics would become as susceptible of demonstration as the truths of geometry.

Helvétius' bland assurance that the mind is potentially a pure, uniform tool of judgment excited ironical replies from many writers, including Diderot, but it was characteristic of the age that on both sides of the argument were men who believed in a substantial degree of rational control.

It should by now be almost unnecessary to observe that for the *philosophes* epistemology was not under divine law, nor subject to revelation from heaven. Here, as in the case of ethics, theology had lost its hold. Instead, any theory of knowledge was called upon to explain how human beings, aided only by their physical senses and the physical organs called brains, understand their environment. A few thinkers throughout the period (principally the Germans Leibniz, Wolff, and Kant) held a more "idealistic" doctrine, in the technical sense of the term; but in general, as one modern analyst has put it, "For the Enlightenment, epistemology *was* psychology." It was a psychology of avowed conflict between reason and passion, and in this respect was less naïve than sometimes portrayed. The world it predicated, however, was with few exceptions orderly and understandable. Man had only to make proper use of his natural tools of comprehension.

One of the most striking features of the Enlightenment was the attention accorded to questions of taste and beauty. No period of high intellectual vitality is indifferent to the more specifically artistic aspects of culture. Seldom in history, however, have so many of the scientists, moralists, and social philosophers of an epoch taken time—which they would have emphatically refused to consider "time out"—for the purpose of debating theories and standards of beauty.

The acceptance of sensation as the source of knowledge doubtless made inevitable a high degree of fascination with all that is pleasing to the senses. Equally important was the faith that reason can everywhere establish norms of judgment that must finally be acknowledged by all rational minds. Also, a frankly humanistic range of interests can scarcely fail to honor activities and creations which other-worldly creeds must condemn, at worst, as sinful or, at best, as vain and wasteful. Despite all these obvious explanations, however, a modern student cannot fail to be struck by a roll of writers on aesthetic theory that includes Newton, Locke, Leibniz, Shaftesbury, Condillac, Hume, Diderot, Kant, Edmund Burke, and countless other famous names.

It would be a massive over-simplification to call the aesthetics of the Enlightenment simply a cold array of rational canons. Even Goethe, who while a young man in the 1770s joined the German revolt against "French formalism," admitted in later life that he and his comrades of the *Sturm und Drang* had done less than justice to their opponents. Throughout the entire period we have been examining, emotion and sentiment were fully represented.

What seems to have given the Enlightenment its reputation for artistic aridity—including the hostile charge that it was an "age without poetry"—is not its actual record of production but rather the programmatic statements composed by some of its aesthetic theorists. Even the lively minds of Montesquieu and Diderot were so committed to the ideal, if not the unlimited possibility, of rational control that they gave birth to treatises on taste as a conception of beauty achieved through obedience to changeless laws of harmony and fixed proportions. Diderot's eventual conversion to the view that a painting's greatness lies in its power to evoke varied responses in the spectator hardly canceled the formalism of his *Philosophical Inquiry into the Origin and Nature of the Beautiful* (1751). Much earlier, in his *Treatise on Harmony* (1722), the French composer Jean Philippe Rameau had tried to give logical form to the beauty of sounds. Dryden in England, Boileau in France, Gottsched in Germany—all sought to ensure dignity and precision in literature, often at the expense of emotional richness.

Nevertheless, subsequent criticism of the Enlightenment, especially by nineteenth-century Romantics, can now be seen to have been as unfair as it was self-adulatory. The struggle to bring beauty under the dominion of reason was itself "natural" for the *philosophes.* One may charge them with total failure or, if one perceives beauty in form and clarity as well as in intensity of feeling, credit them with uneven success. One cannot, however, without missing a key chapter in the history of aesthetics, ignore their earnest demand that the human mind accept its responsibility for analyzing and disciplining color, line, and sound according to explicit laws of taste.

## V

Surely one of the most overworked, and least substantiated, generalizations about Enlightenment thinkers is that with practically a single voice they espoused the social demands of the commercial middle class. When middle class men and aristocrats, priests, and princes considered laws, as opposed to the customs of their time, as theorists they felt themselves to be on common ground. For one thing, in natural law (perceived sometimes in history, sometimes in human aspirations to justice observable all around them) they had what seemed to them a universally valid standard of judgment—i.e., the rules of justice were applicable to all men, simply as men, everywhere and always. At the same time, men lived under particular "positive" laws, which needed to be subjected to pitiless scrutiny and denounced whenever they failed to accord with the laws of nature. Bearing in mind the all but universal fascination with law on the part of the *philosophes,* we can here illustrate their range of responses by brief references to just three among them: Charles de Secondat, Baron de la Brède et de Montesquieu (1689–1755); Jean Jacques Rousseau (1712–78); and Cesare Bonesana, Marchese di Beccaria (1735–94).

If any of the major theorists of the age represented an exception to the eighteenth century's lack of emphasis on what we should now call sociology, it was Montesquieu. For in his great work, *The Spirit of the Laws* (1748), he tried above all to relate the rules of political life to the social mores, historical traditions, and even the differing climates of various nations. In his awareness of diversity, he was a precursor of modern social science. Montesquieu, despite his recurrent appeal to "natural relations" and to common sense, did not propose to elaborate a universal set of laws. On the contrary, he sought to provide an analytical system for identifying the *spirit* that permeated the laws of *any* given society. He argued that while virtue was the prime quality to be nurtured by the laws of a republic—their proper spirit, in other words—a monarchy's constitution was essentially dependent on honor, while an aristocracy's had moderation as its central principle. Far more conservative than most of his French friends and critics, he valued stability, a realistic awareness of "things as they are," and a balanced recognition of varying interests, including traditional privileges. Hence, he was the French aristocracy's most eloquent defender against encroachments by the royal administration. Hence too, he indulged in misinformed admiration, further exaggerated by later commentators, for what he took to be the British political system of separation of powers.

Rousseau, the French-Swiss genius, who differed from Montesquieu in practically everything save independence of mind, approached law not so much in relation to stable government as in terms of its bearing on individual development. By an irony of intellectual history, his profuse and contradictory excursions into political theory have led some twentieth-century scholars to brand him as the spiritual father of totalitarian dictatorship. Such a charge seems unfounded, but it is important to try to understand how the clashing themes of liberty and authority come together in Rousseau's writings, especially in *The Social Contract* (1762).

We should have clearly before us the figure of this tormented exile from Calvinist Geneva, caught between his unruly passions and his sense of guilt, convinced that society had corrupted him, along with all other civilized men. What we know of Rousseau's biography in itself neither validates nor invalidates his ideas, but it helps to explain his approach to even the ponderous topic of law as a highly personal problem, a problem of ethics. Throughout his writings runs an anguished concern with two closely related contradictions in human life. First, man at birth can be inclined toward moral good, but in maturing tends ever more strongly toward vice and hypocrisy. Second, in Rousseau's own words concerning the political order, "man is born free, and is everywhere in chains."

Sadly accepting the almost complete inescapability, under modern conditions, of large political units, Rousseau defined the social contract as one under which "each person gives himself to *all,* but not to any *individual.*" Each member of society contributes to society's sovereign voice—the "general will"—which must, by definition, be the highest expression of both reason and self-interest. There is no denying that Rousseau is inconsistent about the actual mechanics of legislation. On the one hand, he says that "it would take a god to give laws to men." On the other hand, admitting that even the general will needs to be formulated and directed toward specific issues, he visualizes first a legislator (an original drafter of fundamental laws) and then the people, enacting laws for its own governance.

In the final analysis, however, Rousseau remains a moralist, asserting that no free man can be given a law by anyone but himself. The element in his doctrine that becomes almost mystical—and easy for dictators to pervert—is the idea that each citizen's rational "will to do right" must necessarily accord with the general will, even if the citizen is momentarily unable to see the correlation. Hence, coercion to which men have agreed beforehand is justified in the name of the general will and for the common good.

It would be foolish to try to reconcile all of Rousseau's strictures, even on this limited, if central, point. However, through the smoke and clouds of his rhetoric came flashes of powerful insight, which made him perhaps the only major *critical* political theorist of the Enlightenment. He acknowledged that power and freedom are forever in a state of tension. He asserted that "good laws" are those which make the good man a good citizen. In fact, he ended with a set of demands, which Kant was to adopt with enthusiasm—demands for ethical self-discipline on the part of individuals and ethical regard for individuals on the part of the state.

Far humbler in his aims than Rousseau and more limited in his range of interests than Montesquieu was Beccaria. His book, *On Crimes and Punishments,* published at Milan in 1764, was in many respects only an intelligent summary of views on law, judicature, and penology already expressed piecemeal by various other writers. Yet few others among the *philosophes,* possibly only Voltaire and Adam Smith, were destined to have such a prompt and powerful effect on the conditions of European life as this shrewd and level-headed Italian nobleman.

Beccaria demanded a series of major shifts in the conduct of trials and the treatment of criminals. Penalties should be well advertised and uniform for each crime, regardless of the social position of the felon. The aim of punishment should not be vengeance but the deterrence of further crime, for which latter purpose good police work, i.e., increased likelihood of arrest, would serve better still. The severity of each penalty should be clearly adjusted to the hurt incurred by society as a result of a given crime. (Beccaria was one of the first to note the senselessness of considering practically everything from murder to petty theft a capital crime, as most countries still did in the eighteenth century.) Torture, he argued, was unreliable for getting evidence and degrading to society if simply added to a sentence of death.

Although Beccaria had a good deal to say about the brutalizing effects of cruelty and the pity due innocent wretches confronted with torture, he relied more heavily on reason than on sentiment to make his massive case for reform. If society should concentrate on preventing crime, not just on punishing it, this was primarily because a preventive emphasis would yield better results for the inevitably limited effort which could be expended. Keeping the death penalty for minor crimes would mean that sneak thieves, if surprised in the act, would go on murdering witnesses, as in the past, since this helped their chances of escape without increasing the punishment that awaited them for theft alone. Torture was irrational because it tested not a suspect's veracity, but his coarseness or sensitivity of nerve fiber. Yet for all the coolness of his intellectual approach, Beccaria remains one of the most appealing figures of the Enlightenment, a persuasive voice in the campaign to achieve what Kant would later call "man's release from his self-incurred tutelage."

## VI

Although social and legal theories must inevitably suggest questions about types of government, most of the *philosophes* tended to be less interested in trying to define the formal structure of a civil polity than in setting its ethical and utilitarian goals. As we have seen, Montesquieu, though a nobleman, tried to balance the needs of monarchies, aristocracies, and democracies. He explicitly condemned only the classic perversions of those forms, that is, despotism, selfish oligarchy, and mob rule; but, not surprisingly, he preferred for France a constitutional monarchy guaranteeing full respect for the nobility and other privileged "intermediate bodies." Rousseau, for all his contributions to later democratic sentiment, takes up no cudgel against crowned heads in *The Social Contract:*

> I . . . give the name "Republic" to every State that is governed by laws, no matter what the form of its administration may be: for only in such a case does the public interest govern. . . . Every legitimate government is republican.

Notice, he does not claim the reverse, that only republican government, as we now conceive of it, could be called legitimate. More explicit was Immanuel Kant, who wrote in 1795 that in his scheme of perpetual peace "the civil constitution of each state shall be republican," then hastily warned against "the common error of confusing the republican with the democratic constitution."

The only antimonarchical republicanism to come out of the Enlightenment, aside from a few radical English tracts and some highly conservative glosses on the existing constitutions of the Dutch United Provinces, the Swiss cantons, and a few German city-states, was produced by the British colonists in North America. Jefferson, Franklin, Madison, and Adams were steeped in the political theories of limited resistance, the separation of powers, and the ultimate force of popular sovereignty. Certain French *philosophes* hovered in spirit over the American Revolution, but far more important were Locke and the earlier seventeenth-century English opponents of Divine Right monarchy.

It should be noted, however, that even the Declaration of Independence, while in essence a bill of particulars directed against a monarch, George III, is not a general denunciation of monarchy as such. It begins with an assertion of human rights which could reasonably be respected by a wise and benevolent king. And despite the circumstances of rebellion, the Declaration ends without pledging "our Lives, our Fortunes, and our sacred Honor" to anything further than freedom and independence for the several colonies, with their eventual form of government left unspecified. The American leaders, though deeply apprehensive of the mob and of "faction," did renounce the possible advantages of constitutional monarchy; and their decision was a momentous one. Unlike the case for independence, however, it had not been dictated by the ideals of the Enlightenment.

Some historians, impressed by the *philosophes'* willingness to use the power and legitimacy of anointed princes in order to achieve reforms, have denied that the age ever got beyond an obsequious belief in "enlightened despots." It is true that Frederick II of Prussia, Catherine II of Russia, Joseph II of Austria, and several lesser monarchs both flattered and were flattered by some of the most renowned theorists of the eighteenth century. As a recent biographer of Voltaire has pointed out, however, even that most celebrated spokesman for enlightened despotism was anything but uncritical of princes. In general, the *philosophes* preached the need for using available political means. That generally meant monarchy, for after all, even the seventeenth-century English had ended by restoring their kings. To admit, however, that the *philosophes* almost all accepted monarchy as the appropriate institution for administering rational innovations is quite different from saying that their writings have no relevance to a world in which monarchies have practically disappeared.

## VII

With respect to the relations *among* states, at the beginning of the eighteenth century, the Abbé Charles Irénée Castel de Saint-Pierre adapted certain seventeenth-century pacifist doctrines to the tragic scene at the end of Louis XIV's wars. His treatise on *Perpetual Peace in Europe* (1712) demanded a continuing "congress system" or league of nations, pledged to unite at once against any aggressor. And again, at the end of the century, as the great conflicts of the Revolutionary era spread over Europe, Immanuel Kant in turn wrote his *Perpetual Peace*. Kant was more precise than Saint-Pierre, setting forth in great detail the rules of nonaggression and nonintervention. He was also more insistent that a rule of law among states could be achieved only if the states themselves were internally constructed on the basis of legal safeguards for their citizens. He was not, however, much more realistic than the good Abbé had been about the chances of obtaining this happy state of affairs.

Despite their willingness to sympathize with pacifist ideas, most of the other *philosophes* viewed war as one of the last of mankind's irrational exercises that seemed likely to be eradicated. Yet the intellectual labors of the Enlightenment ultimately contributed to civilized criticism of "jungle diplomacy" in two ways that were at once less direct and more effective than explicit projects for peace. One of these ways involved the ceaseless ridicule that the century poured upon martial glory. War takes such grandeur as it can claim to possess from its extreme seriousness, its appearance of tense drama, even its horror. But expose war as a game of aimless, vainglorious nincompoops in command of bewildered regiments of buffoons—show it, in other words, as Voltaire does in *Candide*—and you rob it of all claim to human reverence. Such a portrayal applied, for the time being, only to the shallow duels of eighteenth-century princes using mercenary armies. The "people's wars" of the 1790s and ensuing decades seemed to take on a new dignity. Still, the derisive image was there for Tolstoy to revive, at Napoleon's expense, in *War and Peace*.

As long as nations were thought of as closed commercial units, each one prospering only at the expense of others, the line between peace and war was a hazy one. In fact, war might be thought of as nothing more than a risky, but potentially lucrative, extension of economic competition. But what happened to the notion of profitable conflict when the nature of competition itself was reexamined? At this point we pass from the diplomatic-military field to the fields of commerce, finance, and industry, for the other way in which certain of the *philosophes* undermined what Holbach ironically termed "the sanctity of slaughter" lay in economic theory.

Mercantilism was a legacy of medieval town economies to the national economies of the early modern period. Mercantilist ideas were never elaborated (even by Louis XIV's great minister, Jean Baptiste Colbert, whose name we associate so closely with them) to a degree justifying the use of the word "system." As a set of governmental assumptions and policies, however, they unquestionably constituted a major feature of the "old world" that confronted the *philosophes*.

The first of the mercantilist tenets was that national power demands the careful husbanding, even the hoarding, of economic resources: raw materials, skilled labor, shipping, and—above all—hard cash. The mercantilist's ideal envisaged an industrious population, wasting little on the purchase of imported luxuries, adding value to goods by labor, selling them abroad at a profit, and thus ensuring the steady inward flow of precious metals in the form of specie or bullion. This ideal of a favorable trade balance further included close governmental supervision to maintain standards of workmanship, to prevent the smuggling in of foreign products, and to ensure maximum use of native ships and land transport so that the nation should not lose money by having to pay carrying charges to outsiders. Finally, the ideal national economy of the mercantilist was ready for war, by virtue of its self-sufficiency, and able to profit from war by crippling the industries, seizing the ships, and invading the markets of a foreign competitor.

The Enlightenment did not eradicate all these premises and goals. Indeed, it did not even assail some of them, including the desirability of home-owned shipping and the need to have some thought of military preparedness at all times. Numerous thinkers did, however, strike at the mercantilist dogmas at two major points with enough success to expand and complicate the very definition of national economic well-being.

The first target was the mercantilist view that coinable metals were the critical gauge of a society's wealth. As early as 1741, the versatile David Hume published an essay, *On Money*. Hume admitted that increased specie might confer some short-term benefits on the national treasury, but he insisted that in itself it betokened no necessary increase in the prosperity of individual subjects or citizens. The only dependable result, as more money flowed into the economy, was a rise in prices. This in turn might for a time have the effect of enriching certain producers; but in the long run, given the liquid tendency of prices to even out at a new level, it brought no benefit to anyone in the country. By driving up the face value of exports, it would actually hamper foreign trade unless exchange rates were promptly adjusted. He further warned that an accumulation of bullion should not be thought of as a guarantee of military power. Here, money and prices could be profoundly misleading:

> Our small [British] army of 20,000 men is maintained at as great expense as a French army twice as numerous. The English fleet, during the late war, required as much money to support it as all the Roman legions, which kept the whole world in subjection, during the time of the emperors.

Well, if bullion was not the true measure of wealth, what was? The answer of the French *Physiocrates,* as they came to be called, was loud and clear: agricultural production. François Quesnay (1694–1774), Mercier de la Rivière (1720–97), the great royal minister Anne Robert Jacques Turgot (1727–81), and other apostles of physiocracy conceded that skilled labor could increase the value of agricultural (or mineral) products, while commerce could exchange them for other commodities needed by society. Let the government never forget, however, that the underlying wealth had to come from nature. In addition, let it never forget that a country's natural productivity was greatest when regulated and interfered with least. The state should encourage and favor the agricultural classes, but for the rest it should allow human needs to determine the "natural" movement and use of nature's wealth. Hume's warnings about money were thus assimilated into a doctrine that stressed real productivity. It was, we should also note, a productivity that gained nothing from the impoverishment of neighboring states and was actually hurt by war's diversion of manpower to sterile pursuits.

A second line of attack on mercantilism was also adumbrated in Hume's essay, while at the same time it sharpened the Physiocrats' demand for minimal state interference. Instead of stressing the natural sources of wealth, however, it paid more heed to the possible increase in prosperity through the division of labor. It found its classic expression in a work with a sweeping title: *An Inquiry into the Nature and Causes of the Wealth of Nations* (1776). The author was a Scot, Adam Smith (1723–90). Already known for a book on moral sentiments, Smith had yoked his ethical concerns to the study of political economy, as had his teacher, the famous Edinburgh professor of moral philosophy, Francis Hutcheson (1694–1746). Like many other *philosophes,* including their fellow-Scot, David Hume, both men attacked a technical problem on the basis of specific views about human life and motives.

Smith's "economic man" is at once acquisitive and rational. His appetites drive him to productive effort and to the thrifty investment of his profits, but his reason restrains him from criminal rapacity and convinces him that he prospers best in the midst of general prosperity. Reason also dictates that each man concentrate his labor on the form of production for which he is best suited. The same applies, on a giant scale, to whole nations. Thus, although a primitive, solitary family may have to provide for all its own needs, the first rise in the standard of living must be dated from the beginnings of exchange. As soon as a tribe knew division of labor, argued Smith, as soon as an expert bow and arrow maker could devote himself to his craft, bartering his excess weapons for the products of a builder of huts, a tanner of skins, a shoemaker, then and only then could the entire tribe begin to be better armed, housed, clothed, and shod. So now in the eighteenth century, he continued, it was foolish to pay dear for inferior products manufactured within one's country, when comparable goods of better quality might be more cheaply obtained from outside sources and paid for by exporting the best and most plentiful products of native industry.

Smith's doctrine of noninterference, or *laisser faire,* the free play of forces including commodities, money, and labor, is familiar as the gospel of private capitalism in its triumphant era. However, there are three observations to be made concerning his persuasive treatise, if only to relate it to other currents of Enlightenment thought. First, Smith accepted the Physiocrats' claim that close attention be paid to natural resources; but he applied a broader definition of such resources, refusing to emphasize agriculture at the expense of other sources of value, especially industrial labor. (It would be tempting to call him typically British in this regard, were it not for the fact that his famous discussion of fruitful specialization, using the example of a pin factory, seems to have derived all its technical details from Diderot's article on pin-making in the *Encyclopédie!*)

The second point to be emphasized is that while *The Wealth of Nations* made peace appear attractive in economic terms, Smith conceded that *laisser faire* itself must often yield to prudent considerations of military and public policy. Free trade, for him, did not require that a nation enrich a potential enemy by buying its products, however excellent and inexpensive they might be, nor by shipping to it strategically critical supplies. Neither did division of labor demand that a nation abandon all efforts to produce within its own borders the minimum needs of war.

Third and last, while Smith's "free play of forces" was supposed to enrich all citizens as the economy generally expanded, there was an undeniable coldness about the implications of this freedom, especially as applied to labor. Economic man was lauded for his self-seeking; and presumably he must be allowed to exploit all resources, including the toil of his fellow men. For the swelling industrial and commercial middle class, such exploitation held the promise of a prosperity which might eventually filter down to other citizens (and Smith saw himself as a friend of the working man). In the meantime, however, society was presumed to have no right to intervene in the often heartless process of buying cheap and selling dear, whether the buying referred to wool or child labor. Without Smith's intending any such thing, classical economics, born under the humane sun of the Enlightenment, was on its way to becoming the "dismal science."

## VIII

It is common, even today, to encounter the nineteenth century's often reiterated charge that the *philosophes* were antihistorical. "How could they," we are asked, "have had any real interest in the past?" Must not the Cartesian elements in Enlightenment philosophy have been hostile to "cluttering the mind" with historical facts? Would not a critical approach to traditional authority necessarily have made history appear the source of countless errors, misrepresentations, and fraudulent claims? Did not an acute awareness of change necessarily lead men to scorn the past, glorify the present, and peer eagerly ahead toward the future?

These questions, actually a priori assertions in thin disguise, have one fatal weakness. In running after all the apparent reasons why the Enlightenment *should* have been antihistorical by its very nature, they collide with unblinkable evidence that, taken as a whole, it *was not* anything of the sort. Instead, its craze for learned correspondence, its flood of scholarly publications, and its call to question everything contributed to a set of major advances in historiography. Not only were the raw materials for historical research produced and disseminated on a scale never before approached, but, even more important, there was created a general atmosphere friendly to the investigative mind. It is no doubt true that most *philosophes* (at least outside Germany, a special case to be examined later) approached history in a particular way which distinguished them from us, trained as we are in terms of nineteenth-century "historicism." In going to the past for lessons and warnings, they seem to have felt a liberation or separation from that past, a critical remoteness, which clashes with modern ideas of the present as an integral development of history. Even among French and English writers of the eighteenth century, however, historical interest produced strides in both conception and technique that were highly significant for the study of history.

Voltaire's *Century of Louis XIV* (1751), for example, was a pioneering effort to portray many more aspects of a departed age than just its wars and treaties. In calling back to life the social and artistic features of the preceding reign, Voltaire also demonstrated greater fairness and objectivity than one finds in many of his other writings. David Hume and the Abbé de Condillac are less important for their excursions into this field than for other philosophical ventures; but the former's *History of England* (1754–61) and the latter's *General History* (1755) both contain arresting passages. More truly a precursor of modern historical canons of scholarship than either of these two was a Scot, William Robertson, who wrote *The History of Scotland* (1759) and *The History of the Reign of Charles V* (1769).

Both Hume and Condillac must be counted among the many eighteenth-century writers who shared in the effort to reconstruct conditions of pre-civilized life through ancient documents (notably including the Bible), as well as through descriptions of primitive tribes still being encountered in America and Oceania. The origin of language, for instance, was a dependable source of fascination. Another was the birth of religious sentiment. Were the first gods deified natural objects and forces—stars, mountains, the wind, the rain? Or were they initially human heroes, accorded divinity and more abstract significance through legends that arose after they had lived? Or did the beginning of religion belong to the darker areas of psychopathology, to the "trauma of the Flood," as a recent scholar has termed it, to fetishism, to brutal panic spreading by what Holbach called "sacred contagion"? None of these questions could be answered by strictly historical methods, and all of them bore on other disciplines, such as theology, psychology, and aesthetics. Yet the very fact that such questions did engage men's minds so strongly testifies to the constant presence of interest in times past.

Faced with this brief set of references to inquiries into the past by leading figures of the Enlightenment, we should return for a moment to the questions at the beginning of this section. What were the counterforces that prevented (1) Cartesianism, (2) antitraditionalism, and (3) progressionism from completely blighting historical inquiry? With respect to the first point, let us not forget the all-important step that we have seen even Descartes's most devoted followers taking by the end of the seventeenth century: the adaptation of his critical method to ideas empirically acquired. Only the master's faith in innate ideas had been hostile to historical research. Once Pierre Bayle, for example, abandoned that specific point of faith, he was able to make his *Dictionary* of 1697 a clear demonstration of what history and Cartesian analysis could do when allied against the forces of orthodoxy.

The mention of Bayle suggests the answer to our second question, namely, how enmity toward traditional authority could be reconciled with a historical approach. It could be so reconciled, we now realize, if history itself were used to combat superstition, expose old claims to privilege, upset ill-founded rights of exploitation. The *philosophes,* after all, counted among their spiritual ancestors Lorenzo Valla, the fifteenth-century scholar whose archival researches had uncovered the fraudulence of the *historical* argument for the papacy's temporal power in Italy, i.e., that it stemmed from the (forged) "Donation of Constantine."

In two senses, anticlerical and liberal, the crowning work of Enlightenment historiography was Edward Gibbon's *Decline and Fall of the Roman Empire,* published in successive volumes from 1776 to 1787. Repudiating St. Augustine's mighty defense of the Christian Church, written almost fourteen centuries earlier, Gibbon set out to show that it *had* been Christianity that had undermined the confidence and sapped the strength of Imperial Rome. Simultaneously, Gibbon was seeking to write the tragedy of classical freedom. He tells us that for a time he considered writing instead of the triumph of liberty in the modern Swiss Confederation, but finally chose ancient Rome's decline because he could not face having to do extensive research in German!

Turning finally to the third ostensible enemy of historical thinking, namely, the idea of progress, we should recall our earlier observation that a widely shared awareness of current change is by no means identical with a unanimous faith in progress. A recent monograph, dealing exclusively with French historical thought during the Enlightenment, shows clearly the prominence of pessimism or sometimes merely indifference in the writings of, among others, Montesquieu, Voltaire, Diderot, and Rousseau. It must be admitted that all these writers had more optimistic moments, when they showed greater confidence in future progress than one might guess from reading only their remarks about historical decline or flux. The fact remains that much of the eighteenth century's thinking was at once gloomier and more subtle than we sometimes assume.

Equally important is the fact that the most consistent apostles of progression were themselves not indifferent to history. However much better one expected the future to be, its very superiority had to be projected on the basis of some knowledge of the past. Turgot, for example, in his *Discourses on Universal History* (1750), portrayed human wisdom and beneficence as constantly increasing in the midst of an otherwise changeless natural world.

And notice the title of the century's most famous progressionist tract, the Marquis de Condorcet's *Sketch for a Historical Picture of the Human Mind.* This work, which has been called the "testament of the Enlightenment," was written during 1793–94, when its author was hiding in Paris, vainly attempting to escape the Robespierrian Terror. Despite his own predicament, Condorcet could still visualize man's progress through ten stages, from barbarism to complete peace and rationality. More striking still, given the circumstances, he asserted that the tenth and climactic phase was about to begin.

In fairness to those who persist in considering the Enlightenment either inimical or indifferent to history, we must not claim for it every forward step taken by historical research during the period from the 1680s to the 1790s. Archival labors on documentary sources were dominated by such pious scholars as Ludovico Muratori (1672–1750) in Italy and his French predecessor in this field, the Benedictine monk Jean Mabillon (1632–1707). Another type of antiquary was outraged by the cosmopolitanism of the *philosophes.* Just such a one was Justus Möser, whose *History of Osnabrück* (1768) was one long paean to local patriotism. Nevertheless, the center of gravity, so far as historical contributions are concerned, clearly lies within the area of the Enlightenment, unless—and this is a highly important qualification—one places wholly outside that area two men as difficult to characterize as they are essential to any summary of historical thought in the eighteenth century. One was an Italian, Giambattista Vico (1668–1744); the other a German, Johann Gottlieb Herder (1744–1803). Together, they illustrate the importance of retaining wide geographical boundaries for one's conception of the Enlightenment.

Vico's *Principles of a New Science* (1725) unquestionably contains a number of propositions not encountered in the works of the other *philosophes.* He repudiated Cartesian analysis, demanding instead that one seek to comprehend each culture of the past in terms of its "sense of the world," its "group mind," in short, in terms of mystical totality. He saw in human history the recurrence of cycles comprising barbarism, primitive organization, and higher organization, each cycle revealing an ever repeated progression from superstition through poetry to knowledge and another progression from a theocratic to an aristocratic to a republican form of government.

Despite Vico's obvious importance for twentieth-century prophets such as Spengler and Toynbee, it would be wrong to think of him as a wholly isolated figure in his own time, a lonely enemy of the Enlightenment laboring in a Neapolitan garret. For one thing, his obscurity was nowhere near so complete during the eighteenth century as was believed until quite recently. (His work was praised by Italian scholars and reviewed by French learned journals before his death, while in 1787 it captured the imagination of Goethe during the latter's famous journey to Italy.) For another thing, his doctrine itself allowed for possible progress, since recurring stages of culture always appear under different external circumstances, suggesting not so much a circular track as a spiral. Even his piety, while unacceptable to northern Deists and skeptics, at least forced him to accord the Judaeo-Christian development a place outside his general scheme of cycles. Only if the Enlightenment's historical philosophies are all caricatured as a single system of shallow, materialistic optimism, can Vico be seen as other than a brilliantly eccentric man of his own times.

The problem with respect to Herder is quite different. Unlike Vico, he did not live in the first half of the chronological period we have been investigating. Instead, he published his chief contributions, notably including *Ideas on the Philosophy of Human History* (1784–91), after all the major Enlightenment historians had written their main works. There is thus a temptation to picture Herder as turning his back on a set of outworn ideas, while heralding a new age. In many ways, his message did appear original, even rebellious. Opposed to the view of primitive man as terrified and ignorant, which was far more popular among the *philosophes* than was the "noble savage" (except for certain debating purposes), Herder wrote of the dignified *Urvolk*. This was the culture-nation in its pristine form, experiencing the thrill of its own new-found religion, shaping the language that would forevermore express the nation's unique personality. Scorning the neoclassical search for timeless, universal values, he elevated Moses, Homer, and Shakespeare to the rank of "culture-heroes" precisely because each had epitomized the particular genius of his own people.

Admirers of Herder have emphasized his strong feeling for language, his awareness of nonrational forces in history, his insistence on seeking to grasp all the richness of each culture, accepting each on its own terms. His critics, on the other hand, condemn the violence of his early attacks on French standards in particular and cite him as the first great spokesman for truculent nationalism of the sort that would one day deliver his own German *Volk* into Nazi hands. Only a few scholars, however, have faced directly the question of Herder's residual ties with the Enlightenment.

There would be no point in trying to make of this complicated figure just one more *philosophe,* in the old-fashioned, particularly French sense of the word. We should, however, recognize that his central notion of organic historical development was rooted in over a century of previous German philosophy. It ran back in lineal succession to the "monads" of Leibniz, the individual, dynamic units on which he had built his universal system. If such units could be conceived at every level from the atom through the single human personality to the planet, Herder seemed to be asking, then why not the cultural and social organism as well? Furthermore, Herder was deeply involved in characteristic Enlightenment disputes over religion, beauty, and language. However unorthodox some of his answers may have been, he accepted the questions and, in important respects, the ways of argument of his own century. Even his cultural nationalism eventually had room for more cosmopolitan generosity than one might expect from the first formulations of his youth. The longer he lived, in fact, the more Herder, like Goethe, seemed a *philosophe;* but even the young Herder, if Germany is included in the Enlightenment, cannot be left out of it.

## IX

Whatever their caustic disagreements with regard to specific answers, the *philosophes* did ask certain questions in certain ways; and by doing so, they constituted a cultural movement whose varied legacies may still be seen in the twentieth-century world. And not only the European world—"contemporary civilization," girdling the globe, has absorbed and adapted to its own varying conditions the intellectual heritage of late seventeenth- and eighteenth-century Europe. Hence we should ask ourselves what value and what relevance are to be found in that heritage.

The judgments on the Enlightenment, as seen from our times, have been diverse and often hostile. We have already noted the charge that its social criticism and its political liberality opened the sluice gates for a democratic flood, which in the twentieth century has swept away all restraints upon totalitarianism, be it Communist or Fascist. More moderate and hence more telling was the criticism of the brilliant historian whose *Heavenly City of the Eighteenth-Century Philosophers* attempted to stand the Enlightenment on its head. In that famous work, published in 1932, Carl Becker portrays the *philosophes* as latter-day scholastics, substituting for immortality the esteem of posterity, revering Nature instead of the Trinity, but seeming in their fears and faith more like Thomas Aquinas than like present-day philosophers. That skillful but irresponsible argument passed over the immense changes from what might be called the "intellectual mood" of the Middle Ages wrought by early modern thinkers. It did, however, underscore the differences between Enlightenment ideals and the findings of psychology after Freud, physics after Einstein, and sociology after Weber and Pareto. There is no doubt that the world around 1900 saw a revolt against the direct heritage of Descartes and Locke, Bayle and Leibniz and Newton, unmatched by anything that had occurred in the intervening two hundred years.

Another line of attack upon the Enlightenment, more particularly religious in tone, is to denounce its lack of respect for "system"—indeed, its explicit rejection of the great, over-arching philosophical structures we recognize in the works of Plato, Augustine, Aquinas, Calvin, and Descartes. Seen from this point of view, the *philosophes* appear irreverent toward philosophical order, each preferring to go his own way into ethics, aesthetics, epistemology, or whatever other subject attracted him, without seeking to fit his particular conclusions into a disciplined system of ideas about the World, God, and Man.

It is easy, in retrospect, to identify various troubles that beset the Enlightenment theorists. Nature, for example, proved harder to reconcile with Reason than had seemed likely in the first enthusiasm for the benign, comprehensible "clock universe." Instead, Nature struck down good men and innocent children, tore beautiful Lisbon to pieces with a "senseless" earthquake in 1755, and presided leering over an apparently endless series of triumphs of greed and passion at the expense of reasonableness and good will. Taking this position, the French historian Paul Hazard has painted the entire eighteenth century in somber colors. For him, Nature "betrayed" a rationalism which never was her equal; and from Rousseau onward, sentiment (even sentimentality) reasserted itself in a rising curve toward the high point of early nineteenth-century Romanticism.

There are other charges frequently leveled against the Enlightenment by its highly rebellious descendants in our own day and age. Perhaps most characteristic, because it appears in so many connections and in so many forms, is the complaint that the *philosophes'* ideas were principally negative, stressing the errors of the past, the delusions of myth, the idea of liberty as freedom *from* artificial restraints instead of freedom *to* achieve certain positive tasks and services. No matter if this negativism is frequently overstated and the view of countless theorists misrepresented to sustain the impression. The view of the Enlightenment as witty, corrosive, and shallow—true of certain of its figures, but scarcely true of a century of stubborn, often deeply serious argumentation—survives as a stereotype.

Some of the Enlightenment's admirers appear all too ready to accept the stereotype, and to defend it as though wit, impudence, and aggressive reformist zeal are self-evident virtues. Yet we have seen in passing how inadequate those terms are when applied to Diderot, Hume, or Kant, and to Rousseau, Beccaria, or Lessing. We have also seen how much deeper some of the period's intellectual streams become if one breaks away from total concentration on France. Notice, for instance, how many additional strands of development we take in when we expand our definition of the Enlightenment to include what a German means by *Aufklärung*.

Historians in the late nineteenth century or in the early 1930s, deeply dissatisfied with a seemingly inert liberalism and with their own place in a society it dominated, were correspondingly skeptical about the Enlightenment heritage of Western man. Historians in the later 1930s and the 1940s, face to face with Hitler's Germany and the strident denunciation of both rationality and humanity, rediscovered the dignity of an age that had at least insisted that a man think with his mind, not "with his blood," and that he accept individual moral responsibility for the way he treated other men. The future may bring still stronger reasons for honoring the not so shallow and not so chilly legacy of the *philosophes*. Their questions were often badly posed, and their answers sometimes smacked of ill-founded confidence in quick response. Yet there remains something impressive in the very persistence and imagination that went into the asking of the questions. What was written of the great *Encyclopédie* on the occasion of a bicentennial celebration at Paris in 1950 might fairly be said of the Enlightenment as a whole: "Almost everything in it is superannuated except its spirit—nothing of that is out of date."

## *FOR ADDITIONAL READING*

C. Becker. *The Heavenly City of the Eighteenth-Century Philosophers*. New Haven, 1932.

C. Brinton, ed. *Age of Reason Reader* in the Viking Portable Library. New York, 1956.

W. H. Bruford. *Germany in the XVIII Century*. Cambridge, 1952.

H. Butterfield. *The Origins of Modern Science, 1300–1800*. New edition. New York, 1959.

E. Cassirer. *The Philosophy of the Enlightenment.* Translated by F. C. A. Koelln and J. P. Pettegrove. Boston, 1955.

A. Cobban. *In Search of Humanity: The Role of the Enlightenment in Modern History.* New York, 1960.

P. Gay. *Voltaire's Politics.* Princeton, 1959.

P. Hazard. *The European Mind: The Critical Years (1680–1715).* Translated by J. L. May. New Haven, 1953.

———. *European Thought in the Eighteenth Century.* Translated by J. L. May. New Haven, 1954.

F. E. Manuel. *The Eighteenth Century Confronts the Gods.* Cambridge, Mass., 1959.

R. R. Palmer. *Catholics and Unbelievers in Eighteenth-Century France.* Princeton, 1939.

P. Smith. *The Enlightenment, 1687–1776.* Vol. II of *A History of Modern Culture.* New York, 1934.

A. Vartanian. *Diderot and Descartes: A Study of Scientific Naturalism in the Enlightenment.* Princeton, 1953.

H. Vyverberg. *Historical Pessimism in the French Enlightenment.* Cambridge, Mass., 1958.

A. M. Wilson. *Diderot: The Testing Years, 1713–1759.* New York, 1957.

H. Woolf. *The Transits of Venus: A Study of Eighteenth-Century Science.* Princeton, 1959.

# INDEX